Monographs of the Hebrew Union College Number 23

In the Service of the King: Officialdom in Ancient Israel and Judah

Monographs of the Hebrew Union College

1. Lewis M. Barth, *An Analysis of Vatican 30*
2 Samson H. Levey, *The Messiah: An Aramaic Interpretation*
3 Ben Zion Wacholder, *Eupolemus: A Study of Judaeo-Greek Literature*
4 Richard Victor Bergren, *The Prophets and the Law*
5 Benny Kraut, *From Reform Judaism to Ethical Culture: The Religious Evolution of Felix Adler*
6 David B. Ruderman, *The World of a Renaissance Jew: The Life and Thought of Abraham ben Mordecai Farrisol*
7 Alan Mendelson, *Secular Education in Philo of Alexandria*
8 Ben Zion Wacholder, *The Dawn of Qumran: The Sectarian Torah and the Teacher of Righteousness*
9 Stephen M. Passamaneck, *The Traditional Jewish Law of Sale: Shulḥan Arukh, Hoshen Mishpat, Chapters 189-240*
10 Yael S. Feldman, *Modernism and Cultural Transfer: Gabriel Preil and the Tradition of Jewish Literary Bilingualism*
11 Raphael Jospe, *Torah and Sophia: The Life and Thought of Shem Tov ibn Falaquera*
12 Richard Kalmin, *The Redaction of the Babylonian Talmud: Amoraic or Saboraic?*
13 Shuly Rubin Schwartz, *The Emergence of Jewish Scholarship in America: The Publication of the Jewish Encyclopedia*
14 John C. Reeves, *Jewish Lore in Manichaean Cosmogony: Studies in the Book of Giants Traditions*
15 Robert Kirschner, *Baraita De-Melekhet Ha-Mishkan: A Critical Edition with Introduction and Translation*
16 Philip E. Miller, *Karaite Separatism in Nineteenth-Century Russia: Joseph Solomon Lutski's Epistle of Israel's Deliverance*
17 Warren Bargad, "*To Write the Lips of Sleepers*": *The Poetry of Amir Gilboa*
18 Marc Saperstein, "*Your Voice Like a Ram's Horn*": *Themes and Texts in Traditional Jewish Preaching*
19 Emanuel Melzer, *No Way Out: The Politics of Polish Jewry, 1935-1939*
20 Eric L. Friedland, "*Were Our Mouths Filled with Song*": *Studies in Liberal Jewish Liturgy*
21 Edward Fram, *Ideals Face Reality: Jewish Law and Life in Poland 1550-1655*
22 Ruth Langer, *To Worship God Properly: Tensions Between Liturgical Custom and Halakhah in Judaism*
23 Nili Sacher Fox, *In the Service of the King: Officialdom in Ancient Israel and Judah*

In the Service of the King

Officialdom in Ancient Israel and Judah

Nili Sacher Fox

HEBREW UNION COLLEGE PRESS
CINCINNATI

Library of Congress Cataloging-in-Publication Data

Fox, Nili Sacher.
In the service of the king : officialdom in ancient Israel and Judah / Nili Sacher Fox.
p. cm. – (Monographs of the Hebrew Union College; no. 23)
Includes bibliographical references and index.
ISBN 0-87820-422-9 (cloth : alk. paper)
1. Jews–Politics and government. 2. Palestine–Court and courtiers–Titles.
3. Palestine–Social life and customs–To 70 A.D. 4. Jews–History–1200–953 B.C.
5. Jews–History–953–586 B.C. 6. Bureaucracy–Palestine–History. I. Title. II. Series.

DS111.2 .F69 2000
933–dc21

99-058266

Printed on acid-free paper in the United States of America
Typeset by Posner and Sons Ltd., Jerusalem, Israel
Distributed by Wayne State University Press
4809 Woodward Avenue, Detroit, MI 48201

In loving memory of my grandparents
Israel and Grete Sacher
Max and Betty Raab

and my great-grandmother
Mina Nadel
ז״ל

Contents

Preface ix
Abbreviations xii

1. INTRODUCTION
Thesis and Scope 1
Political Setting at the End of Iron Age I 4

2. QUESTIONS OF METHODOLOGY
The Comparative Method in Biblical Studies 9
Historicity of the Deuteronomistic and Chronistic Sources 14
Epigraphic Sources 23
Unprovenienced Material 23
Paleographic Dating 32
Prosopography 36

3. STATUS-RELATED TITLES
A. Son of the King – בן המלך 43
B. Servant of the King – עבד המלך 53
C. Elders, Senior Officials – זקנים 63
D. "Children," Junior Officials Raised at Court – ילדים 72

4. FUNCTION-RELATED TITLES
A. Minister over the Royal House – אשר על הבית 81
B. Scribe – ספר 96
Excursus: Scribes as Judicial Officers 108
C. Herald – מזכיר 110
D. "Companion," Confidant of the King – רע(ה) המלך 121
E. "Second" to the King, Personal Escort – משנה 128
F. Advisor to the King – יועץ למלך 132
G. Minister over the Corvée – אשר על המס 136
H. Prefect(s), Overseer of Prefects – נצב/נצבים 141
I. Governor of the City – שר העיר 150
Excursus: The Term שר 158
J. Judge – שפט 164
K. Gatekeeper – שער 172

5. MISCELLANEOUS DESIGNATIONS
A. Household or Personal Steward – סכן/סכנת 178
B. Estate Steward, Squire, Handmaid – נער/נערה 182
C. "Officer" – שטר 192
D. "Eunuch," Palace Attendant – סריס 196

6. ASPECTS OF ADMINISTRATION REVEALED IN INSCRIPTIONS
Land Grants, Supply Networks and Regional Administration 204
A. Samaria Ostraca 204
B. *LMLK* Impressions 216
C. Rosette Impressions 235
D. Arad and Other Judean Inscriptions 242
Systems of Accounting: Hieratic Numerals and Other Symbols 250

7. CONCLUSIONS
Royal Functionaries and the State-Organization 269
Foreign Influence on the Israelite Bureaucracy 276

Tables
A. 1. A Chronological Index of Titles and Personal Names of Functionaries in the Bible and in Epigraphic Records 281
2. An Inventory of Personal Names with Titles Appearing on Published Unprovenienced Epigraphic Material 302
B. Hebrew Titles in the Biblical and Epigraphic Records and Their Foreign Analogues 306
C. 1–10. Genealogies of Court Families 308

Map
Distribution Map of *LMLK* and Rosette Impressed Handles 312

Bibliography 313

Index of Biblical Sources Cited 344
General Index 352
Index of Foreign Terms 363

Preface

The modern historian who attempts a reconstruction of aspects of ancient Israelite society faces a tall task. Extant sources outside the biblical corpus are few and fragmentary. The Bible, the most substantial and comprehensive account, is a composite of authentic documents and interpretations colored by the ideologies of later writers who interwove various strands of tradition. As such, the reliability of the biblical material is inconsistent and the perspective not necessarily representative of Israelite culture as a whole. In spite of these obstacles, scholars have a deep-seated need to penetrate the world of ancient Israel and to understand its inner workings. Reasons vary, not the least of which stem from the desire to resurrect the voices of distant ancestors so that a bridge spanning from the past to the present can be built. In my own endeavor to construct portions of that bridge, it became clear early on in my writing that any honorable intentions I may have had to produce a truly objective study would be hampered by numerous assumptions and preconceived notions, even on a topic relatively unencumbered by theological issues. Still, I persisted at the attempt, for objectivity cannot be discarded any more than an ancient, undeciphered inscription that clouds our understanding and begs to be reexamined can be ignored. It is with full awareness of the aforementioned limitations that I present this study to the reader.

In antiquity, as in modernity, titles were conferred on persons both as identifying markers of their function-related roles in society and as honorary epithets assigning specific status. Recent scholarly analyses of the many Near Eastern titles have been instrumental in illuminating various features of the administrative systems prevalent in those societies. Bureaucratic organizations were especially concerned with the proper labelling of their constituency. As is evident from the wide assortment and frequent usage of titles, the cultures of the ancient Near East underscored their significance. In Egypt, even more so than in Mesopotamia, function-related and honorary appellations were so valued that officials and functionaries of varying stations collected the titles accrued in their lifetime and preserved them in titularies resembling modern-day résumés. Admittedly, for Egyptians, the value and benefit derived from those titles extended beyond the individual's tenure on earth to an anticipated afterlife.

Israelites serving at the royal courts in Jerusalem and Samaria, or in local administrations, held titles as well, though, based on extant sources, far fewer than their neighbors. The primary focus of this study, a revised and updated version of my doctoral dissertation, is the analysis of the titles and roles of civil officials and functionaries, including key ministers of the central government, regional administrators, and palace attendants. The nineteen titles examined fall into three categories: status-related titles; function-related titles; and miscellaneous designations that can be held by a variety of functionaries.

To supplement the biblical evidence on this subject, data gleaned from non-Israelite records are utilized extensively for comparative purposes. In addition, the much expanded corpus of Hebrew epigraphic material offers alternate ancient witnesses. These recently recovered finds have allowed me to explore aspects of administration other than those deduced solely from the definition of titles and their respective roles. They include economic components of state-organization, such as royal land-grants, supply networks, and systems of accounting. My conclusions provide for a tentative, partial reconstruction of the Israelite governmental structures for different periods. A picture emerges of the major and minor positions that constituted the hierarchal organization, some of the interrelationships between the various officials, and the network that connected the central authority to the local administrators.

A secondary focus of this inquiry–a widely debated issue–is the assessment of the impact of foreign influence on the Israelite state-organizations. Contrary to previously held notions, the evidence derived from non-Hebrew sources, primarily Akkadian, Ugaritic and Egyptian documents, reveals little concrete material to substantiate theories of modeling after a foreign prototype. Instead, many features of Israelite administration are best explained as basic elements characteristic of any monarchic structure of the ancient Near East that developed to satisfy the needs of an evolving local system. Other, seemingly foreign features, have a long tradition in Canaan and probably were naturally assimilated. While my findings recognize the existence of interconnections between the cultures in this region, they emphasize the need to closely examine the Israelite system with internal evidence. It can no longer be assumed that societal development was shaped primarily by external forces.

It gives me great pleasure to express my sincere gratitude to the many people who assisted me in the completion of this study. I especially wish to acknowledge those individuals at the University of Pennsylvania and at other institutions who facilitated this research project by contributing to my graduate education. In particular, I am indebted to Professor Jeffrey Tigay, my teacher, friend, and now colleague, who as thesis advisor consistently and caringly provided his invaluable guidance. Professors Barry Eichler, David Silverman, and Eliezer Oren (Ben-Gurion University) deserve my heartfelt appreciation as well for giving graciously of their time and expertise. I also wish to thank my new colleague at the Hebrew Union College–Jewish Institute of Religion, Professor David Weisberg, who reviewed this study and amiably offered helpful comments as I finalized my revisions of the manuscript. Numerous other colleagues and friends, in the United States and in Israel, participated in this project over the years both as sources of knowledge and inspiration. Without mentioning all these individuals by name, I gratefully recognize the significance of their contributions.

Special thanks go to Professor Michael Meyer, chairman of the Publication Committee of the Hebrew Union College Press, for indicating interest in this work and then guiding me on the path to publication. I also extend my gratitude to Barbara Selya, the managing editor, for meticulously and swiftly transforming the manuscript into a book.

Financial support from several foundations was instrumental in the research and preparation of this study. I gratefully acknowledge the following organizations: the Ellis Foundation of the University of Pennsylvania; the Memorial Foundation for Jewish Culture; and the National Foundation for Jewish Culture.

Lastly, but most importantly, I wish to express my deepest appreciation for the love and emotional support of my family, especially my husband Bob and three sons: David, Jonathan and Jesse. They steadfastly held to the conviction that my undertaking would indeed come to fruition. In keeping with the tradition to honor our ancestors, I dedicate this, my first book, to the memory of my grandparents Israel and Grete Sacher, and Max and Betty Raab, and to my great-grandmother Mina Nadel, whose unfaltering spirit brought her in old age to the land of Israel.

Nili S. Fox
Cincinnati, September 1999

Abbreviations

ABD	D.N. Freedman ed. *Anchor Bible Dictionary 1–6* (New York: Doubleday, 1992)
ABL	R.F. Harper, *Assyrian and Babylonian Letters* (London and Chicago: University of Chicago Press, 1892–1914)
ABZ	R. Borger, *Assyrisch-babylonische Zeichenliste* (Neukirchen-Vluyn: Neukirchener, 1978)
ADAJ	*Annual of the Department of Antiquities of Jordan*
ADD	C.H.W. Johns, *Assyrian Deeds and Documents* (Cambridge: Deighton Bell, 1898–1923)
AfO	*Archiv für Orientforschung*
AHW	W. von Soden, *Akkadisches Handwörterbuch 1–3* (Wiesbaden: Harrassowitz, 1965–1981)
AION	*Annali dell'istituto orientale di Napoli*
AnBib	*Analecta Biblica*
AnSt	*Anatolian Studies*
AUSS	*Andrews University Seminary Studies*
ANEP	J.B. Pritchard ed., *The Ancient Near East in Pictures* (Princeton: Princeton University Press, 1969)
ANET	J.B. Pritchard ed., *Ancient Near Eastern Texts Relating to the Old Testament* (Princeton: Princeton University Press, 1969)
ARM	A. Parrot and G. Dossin eds., *Archives royales de Mari* (Paris: Geuthner, 1950–)
ArOr	*Archiv Orientalni*
BA	*Biblical Archaeologist*
BAR	*Biblical Archaeology Review*
BASOR	*Bulletin of the American Schools of Oriental Research*
BDB	F. Brown, S.R. Driver and C.A. Briggs eds., *A Hebrew and English Lexicon of the Old Testament* (Oxford: Clarendon Press, 1907)
BE	*Babylonian Expedition of the University of Pennsylvania, Series A Texts*
BIES	*Bulletin of the Israel Exploration Society*
BIFAO	*Bulletin de l'institut française d'archeologie orientale*
BibOr	*Bibliotheca Orientalis*
BJPES	*Bulletin of the Jewish Palestine Exploration Society*

BJRL	*Bulletin of the John Rylands Library*
BM	Tablets in the collection of the British Museum
BN	*Biblische Notizen*
BT	Balawat Tablets
CAD	I.J. Gelb et al eds., *The Assyrian Dictionary of the Oriental Institute of the University of Chicago* (Chicago: Oriental Institute, 1964–)
CAH	*The Cambridge Ancient History* I–III (3rd ed., Cambridge: Cambridge University Press, 1971–1982)
Camb	J.N. Strassmaier, *Inschriften von Cambyses*
CdE	*Chronique d'Egypte*
CIS	*Corpus Inscriptionum Semiticarum* 1–5 (Paris: Reipublicae Typographeo, 1881–1951)
CRAIBL	*Comptes rendus des séances de l'academie des inscriptions et belles lettres*
CT	*Cuneiform Texts from Babylonian Tablets*
CTA	A. Herdner, *Corpus des tablettes en cunéiformes alphabétiques découvertes à Ras Shamra-Ugarit* (Paris: Geuthner, 1963)
Cyr	J.N. Strassmaier, *Inschriften von Cyrus*
DN	Deity Name
EI	*Eretz Israel*
EA	El-Amarna Letters
EM	E.L. Sukenik et al eds., *'Enṣîqlôpedyâ Miqrā'ît* 1–8 (Jerusalem: Bialik Institute, 1950–1982)
GAG	W. von Soden, *Grundriss der akkadischen Grammatik* (Rome: Pontifical Biblical Institute, 1969)
GKC	E. Kautzsch, rev. A.E. Cowley, *Gesenius' Hebrew Grammar* (Oxford: Clarendon Press, 1910)
GN(s)	Geographic Name(s)
HALOT	L. Koehler and W. Baumgartner, *Hebrew and Aramaic Lexicon of the Old Testament* 1–4 (M.E.J. Richardson trans. and edit., Leiden: E.J. Brill, 1994–1999)
HDAE	J. Renz, *Handbuch der althebräischen Epigraphik* 1–3 (Darmstadt: Wissenschaftliche Buchgesellschaft, 1995)
HTR	*Harvard Theological Review*
HUCA	*Hebrew Union College Annual*
IDB	G.A. Buttrick ed., *International Dictionary of the Bible* 1–4 (New York: Abingdon Press, 1962)
IEJ	*Israel Exploration Journal*
IH	A. Lemaire, *Inscriptions hébraiques* (Paris: Les éditions du Cerf, 1977)
IOS	*Israel Oriental Studies*
JANES	*Journal of the Ancient Near Eastern Society*

JBL	*Journal of Biblical Literature*
JCS	*Journal of Cuneiform Studies*
JEA	*Journal of Egyptian Archaeology*
JNES	*Journal of Near Eastern Studies*
JPOS	*Journal of the Palestine Oriental Society*
JPS	Jewish Publication Society
JQR	*Jewish Quarterly Review*
JSOT	*Journal for the Study of the Old Testament*
JSS	*Journal of Semitic Studies*
KAI	H. Donner and W. Röllig, *Kanaanäische und aramäische Inschriften* 1–3 (Wiesbaden: Harrassowitz, 1962–1964)
KAV	*Keilschrifttexte aus Assur*
KS	A. Alt, *Kleine Schriften zur Geschichte des Volkes Israel* 1–3 (Munich: C.H. Beck, 1953–1959)
KTU	M. Dietrich, O. Loretz and J. Sanmartin, *Die keilalphabetischen Texte aus Ras-Schamra Ugarit* (Neukirchen-Vluyn: Neukirchener, 1976)
LB	Late Bronze Age
Lexikon	W. Helck ed., *Lexikon der Ägyptologie* 1–6 (Wiesbaden: Harrassowitz, 1975–1986.
LXX	Septuagint
MB	Middle Babylonian
MDP	*Mémoires de la délégation en Perse*
MT	Massoretic Text
MVAG	*Mitteilungen der vorderasiatisch-ägyptischen Gesellschaft*
NA	Neo-Assyrian
NB	Neo-Babylonian
NEAEHL	E. Stern ed., *The New Encyclopedia of Archaeological Excavations in the Holy Land* (Jerusalem: Israel Exploration Society & Carta, 1993)
NEATC	J.A. Sanders ed., *Near Eastern Archaeology in the Twentieth Century: Essays in Honor of N. Glueck* (Garden City: Doubleday, 1970)
NEB	New English Bible
ND	Nimrud Tablets
OB	Old Babylonian
OrAn	*Oriens Antiquus*
Or	*Orientalia*
OTS	*Oudtestamentische Studiën*
PEFQS	*Palestine Exploration Fund Quarterly Statement*
PEQ	*Palestine Exploration Quarterly*
PN(s)	Personal Name(s)

PRU	C.F. Schaeffer ed., *Le palais royal d'Ugarit* (Paris: Imprimerie Nationale, 1955–1970)
RA	*Revue d'assyriologie*
RAO	*Recueil d'archeologie orientale*
RB	*Revue biblique*
RdQ	*Revue de Qumran*
RLA	*Reallexikon der Assyriologie*
RN	Royal Name
RS	Ras Shamra Tablets
RSV	Revised Standard Version
SAAB	*State Archives of Assyria Bulletin*
Scripture	M.D. Coogan, J.C. Exum and L.E. Stager eds., *Scripture and Other Artifacts: Essays on the Bible and Archaeology in Honor of Philip J. King* (Louisville: Westminster John Knox Press, 1994)
SH	*Scripta Hierosolymitana*
SINSIS	B. Sass and C. Uehlinger eds., *Studies in the Iconography of Northwest Semitic Inscribed Seals* (Fribourg: Biblical Institute Fribourg University, 1993)
SJOT	*Scandinavian Journal of the Old Testament*
Solomon	L. K. Handy ed., *The Age of Solomon: Scholarship at the Turn of the Millennium* (Leiden: Brill, 1997)
TA	*Tel Aviv*
TCL	*Textes cunéiformes du Louvre*
TZ	*Theologische Zeitschrift*
UF	*Ugarit Forschungen*
Urk	G. Steindorff ed., *Urkunden des ägyptischen Altertums* (Leipzig: J.C. Hinrichs, 1906–1958)
UT	C.H. Gordon, *Ugaritic Textbook* (Rome: Pontifical Biblical Institute, 1965)
VAS	*Vorderasiatische Schriftdenkmäler*
VAT	Tablets in the collection of the Staatliche Museen, Berlin
VTS	*Vetus Testamentum Supplements*
WHJP	B. Mazar ed., *The World History of the Jewish People* 1–8 (Jerusalem: Masada, 1963–1977)
WSS	N. Avigad and B. Sass, *Corpus of West Semitic Stamp Seals* (Jerusalem: Israel Academy of Sciences and Humanities; Israel Exploration Society, 1997)
WVDOG	*Wissenschaftliche Veröffentlichungen der deutschen Orient-Gesellschaft*
YOS	*Yale Oriental Series, Babylonian Texts*
ZA	*Zeitschrift für Assyriologie*

ZÄS	*Zeitschrift für ägyptische Sprache und Altertumskunde*
ZAW	*Zeitschrift für die alttestamentlische Wissenschaft*
ZDMG	*Zeitschrift der deutschen morgenländischen Gesellschaft*
ZDPV	*Zeitschrift des deutschen Palästina-Vereins*

חסד ואמת יצרו מלך וסעד בחסד כסאו

Loyalty and constancy protect the king, by loyalty he sustains his throne (Prov 20:28)

1
Introduction

Thesis and Scope

The monarchs of antiquity, like modern heads of nations, were dependent on their circle of ministers, clerks, and attendants to carry out the affairs of state. Loyalty, as well as wisdom and efficiency, were essential for a secure throne and a smooth running government machinery. This study deals with various aspects of the administrative systems of Israel and Judah in the first Temple period. Its scope is limited to civil government, for which nineteen titles are examined, divided into three categories: status-related titles; function-related titles; and miscellaneous designations. The status-related titles are associated with rank derived from genealogy or membership in a special court group that characterizes the office-holders but is not specific to any one particular office. Function-related titles—the largest category—specify positions in the structure of the state whose status is not dependent on the personal status of office-holders. The third group encompasses miscellaneous general designations that can be held by a variety of functionaries or describe personal non-status-related traits. Titles of military and religious personnel (listed in Table A–1) are incorporated into the discussion only when those title-bearers interact with civil administrators or their offices cross into the division of civil government. Professions are not considered.

In addition to defining the various civil titles and interpreting their roles in the bureaucracy, the study evaluates other aspects of administration, discernible primarily from the epigraphic material. These include economic components of state-organization such as royal land-grants, supply networks, and systems of accounting. A key goal of the study is to create a tentative reconstruction of the Israelite governmental structure. In doing so the following socio-political issues are addressed: 1. Who were the main functionaries at the royal court? 2. What major and minor positions constituted the hierarchal structure? 3. What interrelationships are observable between the various officials? Finally, an assessment of the impact of foreign influence on Israel's state-organization is made in light of the non-Hebrew comparative material and evidence of independent development of certain Israelite institutions.

The thesis of this study is that a number of components of Israel's bureaucracy in the monarchic period can be understood best as independent developments of an evolving local system rather than features modeled on any particular foreign prototype. Those aspects that resemble the bureaucracy and state-organization of other societies in the region do so primarily because they are basic elements characteristic of any monarchic system of the ancient Near East. Likewise, linguistic affinities between a few Hebrew titles and those in Akkadian, Ugaritic or Aramaic may be the natural outcome of belonging to a common language family, Semitic. Yet, despite reservations concerning foreign models, undeniably cultural borrowing between contiguous societies is a normal ongoing process, occurring both consciously and subconsciously, and certainly Israel did not exist in a vacuum. A few seemingly foreign administrative features have a long tradition in Canaan and were naturally assimilated. Although some traces of foreign influence are apparent for periods exhibiting active interconnections between Israel and her neighbors, these do not color the entire Israelite system as an imported product.

The subject of Israelite officialdom in the monarchic period is not new to biblical scholarship. It has been addressed in various types of studies, primarily in small segments focusing on one or two titles or in the context of related topics such as state formation and kingship. Several investigations that do examine the topic on a broader scope simply present brief surveys of the material. For example, R. de Vaux's volume on the social institutions of Israel, *Ancient Israel* (1961), incorporates short discussions on civil, military, and religious officials and personnel; S. Yeivin's comprehensive Hebrew article on officialdom in the *'Enṣîqlôpedyâ Miqrā'ît* (1971) defines the titles and roles of functionaries belonging to these three divisions; E.W. Heaton's monograph entitled *Solomon's New Men* (1974) briefly examines a few offices in the Solomonic state.[1] More in-depth investigations, based on their Ph.D. dissertations, were published by T. Mettinger and U. Rüterswörden. Mettinger's study, *Solomonic State Officials* (1971), focuses on six titles of key royal ministers found in the list of Solomonic officials in 1 Kings 4.[2] Rüterswörden's work, *Die Beamten der israelitischen*

1. R. de Vaux, *Ancient Israel: Social Institutions* 1 (New York: McGraw-Hill, 1961), 119–138; S. Yeivin, "Peqidut" in *EM* 6, 540–575 (Hebrew); E.W. Heaton, *Solomon's New Men: The Emergence of Ancient Israel as a National State* (New York: Pica Press, 1974), 47–60.

2. T. Mettinger, *Solomonic State Officials: A Study of the Civil Government Officials of the Israelite Monarchy* (Lund: CWK Gleerups Forlag, 1971).

Königszeit (1985),[3] examines various civil, military and religious titles associated with the class of officials called *śrym*, as well as a few titles that seem to belong outside that class of royal functionaries. Just recently, a short study on Israelite administration focusing on the epigraphic evidence was published in Hebrew by Y. Avishur and M. Heltzer: *Studies on the Royal Administration in Ancient Israel in Light of Epigraphic Sources* (1996).[4]

As in the present study, a prominent issue in most previous treatments of this subject is the question of the origins of both the Hebrew titles and the administrative positions. It is generally assumed that because Israel as a state emerged in the region relatively late, her governmental structure was modeled after a foreign prototype(s) of a preexisting state(s). Up until and including Mettinger's study, with few exceptions, scholarly consensus held that Egypt, more than the nations of Syria–Palestine or Mesopotamia, provided that model. Mettinger's thesis, which he attempts to defend through analyses of the titles and roles of four top-ranking royal officials (house minister, royal secretary, royal herald and "friend" of the king), is that both the titles and administrative duties of Israelite bureaucrats were borrowed directly from Egypt. At the same time, he concedes that the office of superintendent of the forced levy probably belonged to a Canaanite institution and the office of chief of the district prefects was essentially Israelite. As a presupposition for his theory of direct Egyptian influence, Mettinger argues that vivid cultural interconnections existed between Egypt and Israel during the United Monarchy. Rüterswörden's investigation reevaluates those offices examined by Mettinger and includes additional ones. His conclusions systematically contradict those of Mettinger and others who hold similar views. Rüterswörden endeavors to disprove an Egyptian connection in almost every case and postulates instead that Syro-Palestinian systems directly influenced Israelite officialdom. His cursory analysis of some titles, however, necessitates a more careful evaluation of the evidence, in particular for the Egyptian material. While the works of Mettinger, Rüterswörden, and Avishur and Heltzer, as well as several other narrower studies, have made significant contributions to scholarship in the area of Israelite administration, there are unanswered questions and sufficient inconsistencies between their interpretations to warrant further study in this area. Most importantly, the underlying notion that Israelite officialdom and administrative practices were modeled af-

---

3. U. Rüterswörden, *Die Beamten der israelitischen Königszeit: Eine Studie zu śr und vergleichbaren Begriffen* (Stuttgart: Kohlhammer, 1985).

4. Y. Avishur and M. Heltzer, *Studies on the Royal Administration in Ancient Israel in Light of Epigraphic Sources* (Jerusalem: Acadamon, 1996). This study first came to my attention when I was completing the present book.

ter any particular foreign prototype, whether Egyptian, Syro-Palestinian or Mesopotamian, needs to be reexamined and evaluated on the basis of concrete evidence.

The extant archaeological remains, specifically, seals, bullae, ostraca and impressed jar handles, when used judiciously, can also contribute to our understanding of Israelite officialdom and state-administration. From that perspective, Mettinger's analysis lacks important archaeological testimony and contains some erroneous concepts due to the limited data available at the time he wrote and certain prevailing misinterpretations. Curiously, Rüterswörden, who had a much greater corpus of archaeological data at his disposal, practically ignores the epigraphic sources, mentioning certain pieces or entire archives only in passing. Avishur and Heltzer, who rely heavily on the corpus of epigraphic material for their interpretations, place equal weight on objects obtained from the antiquities market and those originating from controlled archaeological excavations.

Political Setting at the End of the Iron Age I

The beginning of the process of state formation in Israel in the latter half of the eleventh century BCE was a consequence of external and internal forces.[5] Internal developments within Israelite society played a crucial role. Factors that impacted on the pre-state political unit(s), such as demographic shifts, intensification of agriculture, and social changes, inclined the society in a less egalitarian

5. These considerations, among others, are discussed in a number of works on the subject of state formation, both for Israel specifically and in general (e.g. G. Ahlström, *The History of Ancient Palestine from the Palaeolithic Period to Alexander's Conquest* [Sheffield: JSOT Press, 1993], 421–454; W. Dever, "From Tribe to Nation: State Formation Processes in Ancient Israel," in S. Mazzoni ed. *Nuove fondazioni nel Vicino Oriente Antico: Realtà e ideologia* [Pisa: University of Pisa, 1994], 213–229; I. Finkelstein, "The Emergence of the Monarchy in Israel, the Environmental and Socio-Economic Aspects," *JSOT* 44 (1989): 43–74; J.W. Flanagan, "Chiefs in Israel," *JSOT* 20 [1981]: 47–73; F. Frick, *Formation of the State: A Survey of Models and Theories* [Sheffield: Almond, 1985]; J.S. Holladay, "The Kingdoms of Israel and Judah: Political and Economic Centralization in the Iron IIA-B (ca. 1000–750 BCE)," in T. Levy ed. *The Archaeology of Society in the Holy Land*, [New York: Facts on File, 1995], 368–398; R. Cohen and E.R. Service eds., *Origins of the State: The Anthropology of Political Evolution* [Philadelphia: Institute for the Study of Human Issues, 1978]; E.R. Service, *Origins of the State and Civilization* [New York: Norton, 1975]). The term *monarchy* in this study is inclusive of the early state during the reign of Saul and the beginning of David's kingship, an entity that some scholars consider to be more characteristic of a chiefdom (see Frick and Flanagan and Finkelstein). On the organization of pre-state Israel, Ahlström argues, contra Frick, that it represented several political units rather than one.

more stratified direction with a trend to urbanization. A lack of competent leadership, as implied by references to the unscrupulous behavior of Samuel's sons (1 Sam 8:1–5), may also have stimulated change. External pressure, especially that imposed by the Philistines (1 Sam 4–8), and to a lesser extent by the Ammonites (1 Sam 11) and Amalekites (1 Sam 15), bore heavily on the internal organization. Based on the biblical data, it is usually assumed that Philistine expansion and intrusion into Israelite territory,[6] though not necessarily the cause for the creation of a more centralized government under a monarchic system, certainly acted as a stimulus. While an analysis of the actual development of the Israelite state is beyond the purview of this study, the kind of political organization eventually adopted by the newly formed state is precisely the question at hand.

Not surprisingly, the beginnings of a bureaucracy, albeit an undeveloped one composed of family members in military positions, already existed in the reign of Saul (Table A–1 Saul). The biblical sources indicate that a more sophisticated administrative apparatus was put in place by David (Table A–1 David), who established a capital and expanded the borders of Israel. By the time Solomon inherited the throne, the enlarged national territory required a centralized complex governmental system (Table A–1 Solomon). If, as most scholars contend, David, and later Solomon, modeled Israel's bureaucracy on foreign prototypes, then conditions conducive to borrowing should be evident. Consequently, an understanding of the political circumstances of potential models in the late eleventh to early tenth centuries is essential.

Egypt's glorious empire period, the New Kingdom (ca. 1540–1070 BCE), was confined to historical records and cultural memory by the late eleventh century. A succession of mostly ineffectual Pharaohs following the death of Rameses III in 1153, accompanied by intervals of economic depression, corruption, and incursions by Libyans and Sea Peoples, had left Egypt at the end of the 20th Dynasty considerably weakened. The last Pharaoh to exploit Canaan's natural resources and maintain a measure of hegemony over the region was Rameses VI (1142–1135 BCE).[7] Subsequent Pharaohs only succeeded in maintaining trade relations with coastal cities of Syria-Palestine. The report of Wenamun, which dates to the end of the 20th Dynasty, provides insight about Egyptian

---

6. Philistine garrisons were actually installed in Israelite territory (1 Sam 10:5).

7. K.A. Kitchen, *Third Intermediate Period in Egypt (1100–650 B.C.)* (Warminster: Aris and Phillips, 1973), 243–254; D. Redford, *Egypt, Canaan, and Israel in Ancient Times* (Princeton: Princeton University Press, 1992), 283–299; D. O'Connor, "New Kingdom and Third Intermediate Period, 1552–664 BC" in B.G. Trigger, D. O'Connor and A.B. Lloyd eds. *Ancient Egypt, A Social History* (Cambridge: Cambridge University Press, 1983), 226–242.

relationships with the rulers of those now independent city-states. Noticeably, the reception accorded the Pharaonic envoy Wenamun, who was sent to Byblos to procure lumber, was cold and contemptuous. Even allowing for literary exaggerations, the narrative still clearly depicts the wane of Egyptian power and prestige in the region.[8] In Egypt itself, the Pharaoh's jurisdiction was fragmented. Smendes, the first Pharaoh of the 21st Dynasty, in reality held authority solely over Lower Egypt, while control of Middle and Upper Egypt fell to a line of army commanders.[9] Whereas some commercial and diplomatic ties seem to have continued between Egypt and Asia during the 21st Dynasty (1070–945 BCE), contact between Egypt and Israel is unattested in any source until the reign of Solomon.[10]

Further away, in the east, the Middle Assyrian Empire was engaged in a power struggle with the Arameans. Assyrian military successes in the reign of Tiglath-pileser I (1114–1076 BCE) were offset by periods of defeat during most of the eleventh and tenth centuries. With the exception of a brief revival under Assur-bel-kala (1073–1056 BCE), when Assyrian armies reached Lebanon in the west and Babylon in the south, the Arameans prevented Assyria from interfering in events in the west.[11] The Babylonians, when not involved with Assyria, were similarly occupied with Arameans. Tribes of Arameans had taken over regions along the middle Euphrates and their assaults on merchant caravans seriously affected Babylonian trade routes. They exerted considerable pressure on Babylonian cities, enough to cause food shortages and threaten the stability of the government.[12]

---

8. J. Wilson, *ANET*, 25–29; J. Černý, "Egypt from the Death of Rameses III to the End of the Twenty-First Dynasty" in *CAH* II/2: 656–657.

9. O'Connor, "New Kingdom and Third Intermediate Period," 232.

10. In his recent Ph.D. Dissertation ("The Relationship Between Egypt and Palestine During the Time of David and Solomon: A Reexamination of the Evidence," Emory University, 1998), Paul Ash examines the epigraphic, archaeological, and biblical evidence for contact between Egypt and Palestine in the Iron IIA (ca. 1000–925 BCE). A survey of Egyptian artifacts excavated in Palestine from that period indicates a relatively meager corpus of mainly small objects (i.e. scarabs), compared to the rich finds from the LB and even Iron I. Furthermore, most of the finds are confined to coastal and lowland sites, not to regions heavily populated by Israelites. It is likely that the small objects that did reach sites in Palestine did so via an indirect route, through trade with Phoenicia, rather than directly from Egypt (pp. 74–124).

11. A.K. Grayson, *Assyrian Rulers of the Early First Millennium BC I (1114–859 BC)* (Toronto: University of Toronto Press, 1991), 5–6, 85–86, 113, 117, 122, 124–126.

12. H.W.F. Saggs, *Babylonians* (Norman: British Museum, 1995), 128–133. For an up-to-date summary of circumstances in Mesopotamia, see S. Holloway, "Assyria and Babylonia in the Tenth Century BCE" in L. Handy, ed., *The Age of Solomon: Scholarship at the*

The Syro-Palestinian geo-political picture in the late eleventh century also reflected the transformation and upheaval in the region.[13] Great cities, such as Alalakh and Ugarit, as well as the Hittite kingdom, had suffered destruction at least a century and a half earlier. In Canaan itself, more than four hundred years of Egyptian domination and exploitation left the city-state princelets in a vulnerable state.[14] Invading armies of Sea Peoples from the Aegean captured coastal cities and established their own network of urban centers on Canaanite soil. The Sea Peoples' hold on Canaan had been reinforced following their failed invasion of Egypt in 1174 BCE when Rameses III settled groups of them in southern Canaan and stationed some at Egyptian garrisons. When Egypt lost control of Canaan, Philistines and other groups of Sea Peoples took the place of the Egyptian masters. By the late eleventh century, the inland Canaanite urban centers were sandwiched between an emerging Israelite polity in the Hill Country and expanding Philistine city-states from the coastal area. The power struggle that ensued, which also involved the newly formed Aramean states in the east (1 Sam 14:47; 2 Sam 8), left Israel the primary power in Canaan.[15]

Of the indigenous Canaanite peoples, it seems that only the Phoenicians maintained some status in the region during the late Iron Age I. Apparently the trade centers of Byblos, Sidon and Tyre had recovered sufficiently from the incursions of the Sea Peoples. Two kings of Byblos are known from this period: Zakarbaal, from the account of Wenamun; and Ahiram, from his sarcophagus inscription.[16] Yet notably, Wenamun's report indicates that although Byblos was involved in commercial activities, the Phoenician coast was actually controlled by one of the Sea Peoples, the Tjekker. Not until the rise of Hiram I of Tyre (ca. 969 BCE), after David weakened Philistine authority in the region, did

---

Turn of the Millennium (Leiden: Brill, 1997) 202–216. Holloway notes: "It is safe to conclude that the course of 10th century Palestinian politics was unhampered by the inhabitants of lower Mesopotamia, who could not muster the resources to sweep the blowing desert sands from the courtyard of the preeminent regional temple (the Ekur temple of Nippur) of yesteryear" (p. 216).

13. For a comprehensive picture of the region in the LB/Iron I transition period see, W. Ward and M. Joukowsky eds. *The Crisis Years: The 12th Century B.C.* (Dubuque: Kendall/Hunt, 1992); for Palestine from the 13th–11th centuries, see Ahlström, *History of Ancient Palestine*, 282–454.

14. For a detailed discussion of Egyptian policies in Canaan during the New Kingdom, see Redford, *Egypt, Canaan, and Israel in Ancient Times*, 192–237.

15. For a summary of the geo-political picture of the Philistines in Canaan between the 12th–10th centuries, see C. Ehrlich, "'How the Mighty Are Fallen': The Philistines in Their Tenth Century Context" in *The Age of Solomon*, 179–201.

16. J. Wilson; F. Rosenthal, *ANET*, 25–29, 661.

the Phoenician cities, in particular Tyre, attain full political and economic power.[17] At that time too, an active diplomatic and commercial relationship developed between Hiram and Israel's kings David and Solomon (2 Sam 5:11; 1 Kgs 5–9).[18]

These then are the political circumstances under which Israel emerged as a nation-state. The data indicate that the political vacuum created by the lack of a superpower in the region afforded the opportunity for the formation of the Israelite state, the first in Canaan, and its subsequent development into what is known as the United Kingdom.

17. M.E. Aubet, *The Phoenicians and the West: Politics, Colonies and Trade* (Cambridge: Cambridge University Press, 1993), 25–37. Possibly Hiram's father Abibaal, a contemporary of David, already benefitted from the Philistine defeat toward the end of his reign (H.J. Katzenstein, *The History of Tyre: From the Beginning of the Second Millennium B.C.E. until the Fall of the Neo-Babylonian Empire in 538 B.C.E.* [Jerusalem: Schocken Institute, 1973], 74–75. Contrast B. Peckham, who follows a higher chronology for the kings of Tyre and Sidon dating the ascension of Hiram I to ca. 980 BCE ["Phoenicia, History of," *ABD* 5:356]).

18. For a detailed discussion of the relationship between Tyre and Israel in the 10th century, see Katzenstein, *History of Tyre*, 77–115; F. Briquel-Chatonnet, *Les relations entre les cités de la côte phénicienne et les royaumes d'Israël et de Juda* (Leuven: Peeters, 1992), 25–58. Briquel-Chatonnet thinks that David associated with Abibaal more so than with Hiram, as described in the Bible (p. 32).

2
Questions of Methodology

The Comparative Method in Biblical Studies

In studies on Israelite officialdom, as in queries on a number of other biblical topics, the comparative method is commonly employed, elucidating the Hebrew sources by drawing on analogues from other ancient Near Eastern cultures. Modern comparative approaches to the study of the Hebrew Bible span nearly two centuries. The comparative method was adopted in earnest in the nineteenth century as a result of major archaeological discoveries in Egypt, Mesopotamia, and Syria-Palestine. Previously unknown epigraphic material, consisting of hieroglyphic and cuneiform texts, provided Bible scholars with literary, historical, and legal documents comparable to the biblical testimonies. The vast collection of extra-biblical data afforded the opportunity to reexamine ancient Israelite culture in the wider context of the surrounding Near East.[1]

Needless to say, the enthusiastic response to the newly acquired sources led to some hasty conclusions concerning interconnections and specific cultural affinities between Israel and her neighbors. Biblical phenomena were often reconstructed primarily on the basis of external models. Seemingly analogous laws, literary motifs, and precepts of wisdom, mostly originating from Mesopotamia and Egypt, were quickly deemed the inspiration behind the biblical material.[2] Direct borrowing was presumed for components of Israelite administration as well. Thus the majority opinion in the 1930s and 1940s held that David

---

1. For a summary of 19th century excavations and explorations in Egypt, Mesopotamia, and Syria/Palestine, as well as the history of the deciphering of hieroglyphic and cuneiform texts and their application to biblical studies, see W.F. Albright, *From Stone Age to Christianity, Monotheism and the Historical Process* (Baltimore: Johns Hopkins Press, 1957), 1–47.

2. For a detailed discussion of the uses and abuses of the comparative method in biblical scholarship, including a summary of scholarly opinions on the topic, see M. Malul, *The Comparative Method in Ancient Near Eastern and Biblical Legal Studies* (Neukirchen-Vluyn: Neukirchener, 1990), 13–78.

and Solomon had modeled Israelite officialdom, specifically the titles and roles of government ministers, after Egyptian prototypes.[3]

Criticism and challenges directed against "parallelomania," a label sometimes applied to the indiscriminate use of the comparative method, have more recently inspired caution in scholarly circles. While most scholars do not advocate discarding the basic approach, they are reconsidering the rules of comparison.[4] Scholars such as Talmon, Hallo, Tigay, and Malul, to mention just a few, have sought to establish guidelines for comparative studies in the areas of ancient Near Eastern literature, law, and history.[5] However, guidelines for understanding Israelite administration and officialdom in its greater Near Eastern context and for evaluating evidence of borrowing in that sphere have not been clearly delineated. While some criteria for discerning the latter resemble those already formulated for comparative approaches in other types of inquiries, standards applicable specifically to the subject of state-organization seem necessary.

A Method for Evaluating Evidence of Borrowing

A prerequisite to the establishment of any historical connection is the existence of avenues of transmission. To ascertain the possibility of direct borrowing, the extant evidence must indicate that interconnections between Israel and the foreign state from which a particular title or practice was allegedly borrowed actu-

3. Among others, R. de Vaux, J. Begrich and W.F. Albright ("Titres et functionnaires égyptiens à la cour de David et de Salomon," *RB* 48 [1939]: 394–405; "Sōfēr und Mazkīr. Ein Beitrag zur inneren Geschichte des davidisch-salomonischen Grossreiches und des Königsreiches Juda," *ZAW* 58 [1940–1941]: 1–29; "The Judicial Reform of Jehoshaphat" in *A. Marx Jubilee Volume* [New York: JTS, 1950], 61–82). B. Mazar's (Maisler) theory of Canaanite influence was exceptional in this period ("King David's Scribes and the High Officialdom of the United Monarchy of Israel" in S. Ahituv and B. Levine eds. *The Early Biblical Period* [Jerusalem: Israel Exploration Society, 1986], 134–135).

4. A discussion of the topic, including a response to those scholars who question the validity of the comparative method entirely, is found in W.W. Hallo, "Biblical History in its Near Eastern Setting: The Contextual Approach" in C.D. Evans, W.W. Hallo and J.B. White eds. *Scripture in Context: Essays on the Comparative Method* (Pittsburgh: Pickwick Press, 1980), 1–26.

5. S. Talmon, "The 'Comparative Method' in Biblical Interpretation – Principles and Problems," *VTS* 29 (1977): 320–356; Hallo, "Biblical History in its Near Eastern Setting," 1–26; "Compare and Contrast: The Contextual Approach to Biblical Literature" in W.W. Hallo, M. Jones and G. Mattingly eds. *The Bible in the Light of Cuneiform Literature: Scripture in Context III* (Lewiston: E. Mellen Press, 1990), 1–30; J. Tigay, "On Evaluating Claims of Literary Borrowing" in M.E. Cohen, D.C. Snell and D.B. Weisberg eds. *The Tablet and the Scroll, Near Eastern Studies in Honor of William Hallo* (Bathesda: CDL Press, 1993), 250–255; Malul, *Comparative Method.*

ally existed during the period in question.[6] Conditions for transmission can be deduced from signs of trade and/or diplomatic associations and in periods when Israel or Judah were in vassal relationships to Assyria, Babylon, or Egypt. In addition, it should be shown that a particular title or practice is indeed attested in contemporaneous records of the foreign state.[7] If the latter data cannot be secured, for example, due to a dark period in the written record, then continuity of the phenomenon at a later date should be evident.

An alternate avenue of transmission that must be considered, even if the aforementioned requirements have been satisfied, is indirect borrowing mediated through a third party. In the case of the formation of the Israelite state-organization, aspects of government bearing Egyptian or Mesopotamian characteristics could have been transmitted via local Canaanite institutions. For this theory too it must be shown that Egyptian or Mesopotamian titles and components of administration were known in LB Canaan and survived locally until the

6. Most of the data testifying to cultural transmission are pre-Israelite. Evidence of interconnections between pre-Israelite Canaan and neighboring Levantine and Mesopotamian states dates to the Middle and Late Bronze ages. For example, diplomatic and economic activities between Hazor and Mari are evident from several Mari letters dating to the 18th century (A. Malamat, "Hazor 'The Head of All Those Kingdoms,'" *JBL* 79 [1960]: 12–19). From this period there also exists a cuneiform tablet from Hazor recording a lawsuit (W.W. Hallo and H. Tadmor, "A Lawsuit from Hazor," *IEJ* 27 [1977]: 1–11). A fragment of the Gilgamesh Epic written in cuneiform script resembling that of the Phoenician Amarna letters was uncovered at Megiddo (A. Goetze and S. Levy, "Fragment of the Gilgamesh Epic from Megiddo," *'Atiqot* 2 [1959]: 121–128) and cuneiform inscribed fragments of clay liver models were found at Hazor from approximately the same period, the 15th–14th century (B. Landsberger and H. Tadmor, "Fragments of Clay Liver Models from Hazor," *IEJ* 14 [1964]: 201–218). An Akkadian letter dated to the 13th century from a governor of Ugarit to a high Egyptian official was discovered at Tel Aphek (D. Owen, "An Akkadian Letter from Ugarit at Tel Aphek," *TA* 8 [1981]: 1–17).

Pre-Israelite Canaanite connections with Egypt are attested almost continually from the earliest periods of Egyptian history through the beginning of the Iron Age I. Egyptian influence in Canaan is especially apparent during the New Kingdom, when the region was under Egyptian hegemony. For a comprehensive and up-to-date account, see Redford, *Egypt, Canaan, and Israel in Ancient Times.* Evidence of interconnections between monarchic Israel and contemporaneous Near Eastern states will be discussed in the various sections of this study.

7. D.B. Redford has demonstrated the absence of this evidence in a number of cases where scholars have posited that Israelite titles were modeled after Egyptian ones ("Studies in Relations between Palestine and Egypt during the First Millennium B.C." in J.W. Wever and D.B. Redford eds. *Studies on the Ancient Palestinian World* [Toronto: University of Toronto Press, 1972], 141–144). These arguments will be discussed in detail under the separate headings of specific official titles.

rise of the Israelite monarchy. Admittedly, this is extraordinarily difficult since Canaanite written records dating to the Iron Age I are practically nonexistent.

A different type of evidence for demonstrating borrowing relies on etymology. In the case of titularies, the ultimate proof of non-Israelite origin would be the occurrence of Hebrew transliterations of foreign official titles or epithets. Not surprisingly, these are generally absent from the Israelite corpus.[8] The next best indicators for borrowing would be calques or loan translations of the foreign terms. Those, however, imply borrowing only if no linguistic constraints limit the Hebrew designation to one possible expression. For example, if the sense of a particular title can be conveyed in biblical Hebrew solely by a single term or phrase, an inference of foreign influence cannot be made exclusively on the basis of a seemingly exact translation of a foreign term. But even these cases are rare. As will be shown, in most instances Hebrew titles are at best etymologically or semantically **related** to analogous Egyptian, Akkadian, and Ugaritic appellations. Consequently, additional criteria are required to determine the probability of foreign import.

In the process of ascertaining the origin of titles and positions of Israelite monarchic officials, a number of questions come to mind. Most of these pertain to the identification of typological similarities that are distinct from correlations stemming from historical connections. Is a particular title/office endemic in the bureaucracies of all or most of the states of the region? Is the position signified by the title a vital component of any ancient system of government, such that it would have arisen in Israel out of sheer necessity regardless of outside influence? Do semantic distinctions between the Akkadian, Ugaritic, Egyptian, and Hebrew titles for the same office imply independent development? Are other signs of independent development in the realm of administration apparent in Israel? What is the frequency of unmistakably foreign prototypes in Israelite officialdom and what conclusions can be drawn from those specific cases? Although these questions are not always easily answered, an awareness of the issues they raise is essential in attempting to define the problem at hand.

A factor normally ignored in comparative studies of royal officialdom is that evidence of cultural transmission reflected in the spheres of literature, religious practices, and artifacts does not in and of itself constitute proof or even imply influence in the area of state-organization. Governmental systems are the prod-

8. This absence is anticipated since a sovereign state with a distinct language would be expected to **translate** imported terms rather than **transliterate** them. An exceptional title that seems to be a transliteration of an Akkadian appellation is סריס (*ša rēši*), the designation for a minor court functionary (Chapter 5–D). The term סכן (*skn*) perhaps belongs to this category as well (Chapter 5–A).

ucts of multiple forces and are not traded like pots or narrated like stories. On the one hand, it is undeniable that external pressures contributed significantly to the ultimate formation of an Israelite state under David. The Philistine menace (1 Sam 4–7) followed by the elders' demand that Samuel appoint a king to govern Israel like all the nations (8:4–5) speaks to this issue. But on the other hand, anthropological analyses have demonstrated that internal forces, such as the intensification of agriculture, population growth, differentiation in wealth, and hierarchal organization, bore equally heavily on the transformation of Israel's socio-political structure.[9] Thus the creation and functioning of Israel's bureaucracy and administrative institutions, both for periods of the united and divided monarchies, must also be examined in light of internal developments independent of outside influence.

The Comparative Approach for Defining Titles

Functions associated with many Hebrew official titles are often difficult to determine due to a lack of contextual evidence from the Bible or Hebrew epigraphic sources. Etymology, while providing a partial guide for understanding the roles of title-bearers, is not a dependable measure. Usage of terms tends to evolve and branch out over time, eventually imbuing old words with new meanings. Therefore, a literal translation of an appellation may be quite misleading.[10] Thus, in instances where our understanding of a title and the duties connected to it are totally dependent on etymology due to the absence of other internal Israelite evidence, additional, external evidence should be sought. In those cases, the comparative approach can be utilized to examine the semantic range of seemingly equivalent terms in non-Israelite societies. While this method does not necessarily reveal the actual Hebrew application, it exposes an array of possibilities otherwise unknown.

A number of pitfalls inherent in comparisons of seemingly equivalent titles signal caution. First, it cannot be assumed that the jurisdictions, functions, or status of officials bearing similar titles are parallel in the various states of the ancient Near East. Just as the institution of kingship differed in Israel, Mesopotamia, and Egypt, so too the roles associated with a particular government office can vary depending on the size and complexity of the state-organization, the rank assigned to certain positions, and the number of individuals holding the same title simultaneously. In addition, the status and authority of a specific office

---

9. See Introduction n. 5, esp. Frick, *Formation of the State,* 191–204.

10. This difficulty is encountered in defining titles such as נער, שטר, and ספר, among others.

can fluctuate from one administration to another as a result of the social station or personality of title-bearers.

Conclusion

In sum, when utilizing the comparative method for defining the roles of Israelite officials and determining foreign influence, a number of variables need to be taken into account. Key considerations, which should be evaluated collectively, include internal evidence, historical connections, etymology, and the prevalence of the position or institution in the region. In reality, the limited and fragmentary data will often preclude distinguishing between cases where an office or title developed independently and those where they were borrowed. But by examining the Israelite administrative system as a whole rather than focusing on isolated bits of data, a tentative picture emerges.

Historicity of the Deuteronomistic and Chronistic Sources

Since evidence utilized in this study for the elucidation of official titles and the reconstruction of the Israelite administrative organization relies most heavily on data gleaned from the biblical texts, a discussion of the historical reliability of that material is indicated. The brief summary of pertinent issues below centers on the Deuteronomistic sources in the books of Samuel and Kings, and the Chronistic accounts of the books of Chronicles.

The Deuteronomistic Sources

Challenges concerning the historicity of biblical accounts are not a new trend in scholarship. In the last decade, however, skepticism about the historical accuracy of practically every source in the Bible has permeated the field. Literary qualities and ideological designs prevalent even in historical texts such as the Deuteronomistic sources of Samuel and Kings are often cited as markers of fictionalization. Lack of archaeological corroboration of biblical accounts is also at issue. On the whole, the current ongoing reevaluation of the material is a positive endeavor. Primarily, it has inspired caution in assessing the evidence and forced even traditionalists to rethink their constructions. Needless to say, the discussion has fostered heated debates and produced different schools of thought popularized by labels such as "minimalists" and "maximalists." Not surprisingly, the majority scholarly opinion falls into a middle ground at various points between the two extremes.[11]

11. Extreme minimalists challenge not only the historicity of the Deuteronomistic accounts, but the entire notion that a united Israel ever existed in the Iron Age. They view

While most scholars agree that the Deuteronomistic sources contain a number of historically accurate accounts of Israel and Judah from the monarchic period, disagreements focus on several key issues—namely, the authorship and dating of this material and the extent of idealization of the Davidic/Solomonic kingship. The theory that the books of Deuteronomy through 2 Kings are a composite product of a pre-exilic compiler, Dtr1, and an exilic redactor, Dtr2,[12] is more widely accepted than an alternate theory that these books represent the work of a single exilic writer.[13] But regardless of which theory one follows, it is generally acknowledged that underlying the Deuteronomistic compiling and editing are older narrative and archival sources.[14] Biblical evidence of earlier written records that allegedly were accessible to the Deuteronomistic writer(s) includes references to annal-type documents: ספר דברי הימים למלכי ישראל, "The Book of the Chronicles of the Kings of Israel" (1 Kgs 14:19 and 17 other references); and ספר דברי הימים למלכי יהודה, "The Book of the Chronicles of the Kings of Judah" (1 Kgs 14:29 and 14 other references). Although none of these documents is extant, the MT apparently contains Dtr's expansion on these sources.[15]

Another text, ספר דברי שלמה, "The Book of the Acts of Solomon" (1 Kgs 11:41)

---

biblical Israel as an artificial construct—a creation of scribes commissioned by the Persian government to invent a national identity for the newly arrived residents of Yehud. See, for example, P.R. Davies, *In Search of 'Ancient Israel'* (Sheffield: JSOT, 1992); T. Thompson, *Early History of the Israelite People from the Written and Archaeological Sources* (Leiden: Brill, 1992), esp. 353–423. The radical minimalist stance has elicited refutations from various scholars. See, for example, B. Halpern, "Erasing History: The Minimalist Assault on Ancient Israel," *Bible Review* 11/6 (1995): 26–35, 47; G. Knoppers, "The Vanishing Solomon: The Disappearance of the United Monarchy from Recent Histories of Ancient Israel," *JBL* 116 (1997): 19–44. A number of key issues are briefly debated in "Face to Face: Biblical Minimalists Meet Their Challengers," *BAR* 23/4 (1997): 26–42, 66. It should be noted that "minimalists" do recognize the existence of a state of Israel beginning in the 9th century and a state of Judah beginning in the 8th century.

12. Among others, F.M. Cross, *Canaanite Myth and Hebrew Epic: Essays in the History of the Religion of Israel* (Cambridge: Harvard, 1973), 274–289; J. Gray, *I and II Kings: A Commentary* (Philadelphia: Westminster Press, 1963), 6–9; P.K. McCarter, *The Anchor Bible, II Samuel* (Garden City: Doubleday, 1984), 6–7.

13. So M. Noth, *The Deuteronomistic History* (Sheffield: JSOT, 1981 [trans. of 1943 German]).

14. For a summary discussion of the sources, see B. Halpern, *The First Historians: The Hebrew Bible and History* (San Francisco: Harper and Row, 1988), 207–218.

15. The factual style in which a number of events are introduced in the Bible seems to reflect the annalistic style of the older court records. For example, "in the X year of king Y," "he it was who...," "in his day," "he built X...," then..." (see J. Montgomery, "Archival Data in the Book of Kings," *JBL* 53 [1934]: 49–51).

is cited as a source for Solomon's reign.[16] In addition, two lists of Davidic officials (2 Sam 8:15–18; 20:23–26) and the longer register of Solomonic officials (1 Kgs 4:1–19), seem to derive from pre-Deuteronomistic archival records of the royal court.[17] Since these lists of governmental officials are of special significance for the present investigation, scholarly concern over the veracity of the biblical portrayal of the Davidic-Solomonic age in general needs to be addressed. Clearly, the biblical portrait of the United Monarchy, in particular the vastness of the empire, the heroic feats of David and Solomon as well as their widespread fame, is an idealization of a more modest reality. In a recent comprehensive study entitled *The Age of Solomon* (1997), nearly two dozen scholars holding various stands on issues of historicity discuss the likely realities underlying the biblical narratives. Notably, for those who follow a middle position, challenging what they consider legendary accounts such as Solomon's marriage to an Egyptian princess (1 Kgs 3:1), his arbitration between the prostitutes (3:16–28), and his visit with the Queen of Sheba (10:1–13), the kernels of truth lie in the bits of data on matters pertaining to statecraft.[18] The tacit understanding is that documentation of names and positions of royal functionaries, for example, does not conceal ideological motives, especially when no genealogical significance can be attached to persons on the lists.

It is beyond the purview of this study to judiciously analyze the textual and archaeological evidence for the existence of a state of Israel in the tenth century, however large or small. Suffice it to say that the Deuteronomistic sources contain material, such as lists of monarchic officials and administrative and economic policies, that are of historical value for a tentative reconstruction of the Israelite state-organization. In support of this textual testimony, the archaeological picture of the Iron Age IIA, when viewed *in toto*, indicates the existence of a state exhibiting the characteristics of economic and political centralization.[19]

---

16. According to J. Liver this source emphasized Solomon's great wisdom ("The Book of the Acts of Solomon," *Biblica* 48 [1967]: 75–101).

17. Montgomery, "Archival Data in the Book of Kings," 47; Noth, *Deuteronomistic History*, 56, 58; Gray, *I and II Kings*, 24; J.A. Soggin (trans. J. Bowden), *Introduction to the Old Testament: From Its Origins to the Closing of the Alexandrian Canon* (Louisville: Westminster/John Knox Press, 1989), 228–229.

18. In *The Age of Solomon*, see for example, J.M. Miller, "Separating the Solomon of History From the Solomon of Legend," 1–24; H.M. Niemann, "The Socio-Political Shadow Cast by the Biblical Solomon," 252–299 esp. 279–288.

19. See most recently, Holladay, "The Kingdoms of Israel and Judah: Political and Economic Centralization in the Iron IIA–B (ca. 1000–750 BCE)," 368–398; W. Dever, "Archaeology and the 'Age of Solomon': A Case-Study in Archaeology and Historiography," in *The Age of Solomon*, 217–251.

Probably because they are closer in time and possess better documentation, the Deuteronomistic sources are more revealing for the period of the Divided Monarchy than for earlier periods. Numerous personages and accounts of events whose historicity is sustained by extra-biblical sources are scattered in the books of Kings. For example, Assyrian and Babylonian cuneiform documents preserve the names of several kings of Israel and Judah (e.g. Omri, Ahab, Jehu, Menachem, Pekah, Hoshea, Ahaz, Hezekiah, Manasseh, and Jehoiachin);[20] the Mesha stele records the successful rebellion of Moab against its overlord Israel;[21] the annals of Sargon II recount the conquest of Samaria;[22] a series of wall reliefs in Sennacherib's palace at Nineveh depicts the fall of Lachish, and his annals relate the siege of Jerusalem;[23] the Babylonian Chronicle documents the fall of Jerusalem in the reign of Jehoiachin;[24] the Siloam Tunnel inscription commemorates the completion of the underground water system attributed in the Bible to Hezekiah;[25] inscriptions on ostraca from Lachish corroborate Judah's military predicament at the end of the monarchic period;[26] and most recently, two fragments of a stele from Tell Dan seem to record an Aramean victory over Jehoram king of Israel and Ahaziahu of the House of David. The latter text contains the first nonbiblical reference to the Davidic dynasty discovered to date.[27]

Philological analyses of biblical technical terms and of phrases attested in con-

---

20. A.L. Oppenheim, *ANET*, 280–285, 287–288, 294, 308; 1 Kgs 16:23–28; 2 Kgs 9–10; 15:17–31; 16:1–17:4; 18–21:18; 24:8–15; 25:27–30.

21. W.F. Albright, *ANET*, 320–321; 2 Kgs 1:1; 3:4–5.

22. Oppenheim, *ANET*, 284–285; 2 Kgs 17–18.

23. *ANEP*, 371–373; Oppenheim, *ANET*, 287–288; 2 Kgs 18–19.

24. Oppenheim, *ANET*, 563–564; 2 Kgs 24:8–17.

25. Albright, *ANET*, 321; 2 Kgs 20:20.

26. Albright, *ANET*, 322 (Lachish Ostraca nos. 3 & 4 seem to refer to events during the Babylonian campaign in Judah, probably in 586 BCE); 2 Kgs 24–25.

27. The names of the king of Israel and the king of Judah have been partially restored. The reconstruction is based on the last two letters, רם, in the name of the king of Israel. Hazael king of Aram seems to be the author of the stele and his revolt, prior to Jehu's coup, can be dated to the mid-ninth century. The biblical account of the death of Jehoram and Ahaziah at the hands of Jehu (2 Kgs 9) may indicate that Jehu had been an agent of Hazael (A. Biran and J. Naveh, "An Aramaic Stele Fragment from Tell Dan," *IEJ* 43 [1993]: 81–98; "The Tell Dan Inscription: A New Fragment," *IEJ* 45 [1995]: 1–18).

This inscription has triggered heated discussion concerning the significance of the term ביתדוד. A number of scholars, primarily those who hold a minimalist view of the historicity of the biblical David, have argued that ביתדוד need not mean "House of David," the Davidic dynasty, but may represent a GN, a DN or the name of a temple. See among others, F.H. Cryer, "On the Recently-Discovered 'House of David' Inscription," *SJOT* 8 (1994): 1–19;

temporaneous nonbiblical sources are also instructive in isolating historical data from the greater literary composition of the Deuteronomistic books. As will be shown in this study, Akkadian and Egyptian titles (or elements of titles) mentioned in these biblical texts have analogues in native documents (e.g. *rab sārîs, rab šāqēh, śr*). Most importantly, many of the titles of Israelite officials that occur in Samuel and Kings (e.g. בן המלך, עבד המלך, אשר על הבית, נער) are duplicated on seals, seal impressions, and ostraca uncovered in archaeological excavations at Israelite sites. The philological evidence serves as additional proof that the Deuteronomistic writers incorporated older historical data into their ideological presentation of Israelite history.[28]

The Chronistic Sources

In comparison to the Deuteronomistic sources, the reliability of the books of Chronicles for the reconstruction of Israelite history has a lengthy history of scholarly debate. A number of questions are at the root of the controversy. 1. Can the Chronistic writings, which are post-exilic reports of pre-exilic Israelite history, be accurate? 2. How can we explain those accounts of the Chronicler that diverge from parallel events described in the books of Samuel and Kings, generally regarded as older and more reliable sources? 3. Are those Chronistic records that are unparalleled in the historical narratives of Samuel and Kings the inventions of the Chronicler? Summaries of discussions concerning these issues, including the history of scholarship on the topic, are detailed in a number of studies on 1 and 2 Chronicles, most recently by S. Japhet and M.P. Graham.[29] Since the present study incorporates data from Chronicles, the main arguments for their potential historical validity are briefly evaluated here.

Nineteenth-century biblical criticism was especially harsh in its appraisal of the historicity of Chronicles. Scholars such as de Wette and his follower Wellhausen maintained that Chronicles, in contrast to Samuel and Kings, was completely unreliable as a historical source.[30] With few exceptions, their view that the Chronicler presents an ideologically biased account unacceptable for

---

N.P. Lemche and T.L. Thompson, "Did Biran Kill David? The Bible in the Light of Archaeology," *JSOT* 64 (1994): 3–22.

28. Interestingly, as noted below, not all these titles are attested in the parallel accounts of the later writings of the Chronicler.

29. S. Japhet, "The Historical Reliability of Chronicles: The History of the Problem and its Place in Biblical Research," *JSOT* 33 (1985): 83–107; *I & II Chronicles: A Commentary* (Louisville: Westminster/John Knox Press, 1993), 1–49; M.P. Graham, *The Utilization of 1 and 2 Chronicles in the Reconstruction of Israelite History in the Nineteenth Century* (Atlanta: Scholars Press, 1990).

30. W.M.L. de Wette, *Beiträge zur Einleitung in das alte Testament* (Darmstadt: reprint of

the reconstruction of Israelite history was perpetuated in scholarly circles well into the first half of the twentieth century. Even champions of the Chronicler as a historian, such as Winckler in the late nineteenth century and Albright in the early twentieth, were cautious in their evaluations. Most importantly, however, they advocated a re-examination of potentially historical material peculiar to Chronicles in light of the extant cuneiform and hieroglyphic documents.[31]

By the late nineteenth century, archaeological ventures in Palestine began to play a key role in vindicating the reputation of the Chronicler. Following the discovery of the Siloam tunnel and inscription, it was realized that the report in 2 Chr 32:30 more accurately describes Hezekiah's enterprise than does its counterpart in 2 Kgs 20:20.[32] Subsequent excavations this century, revealing remains of eighth century fortresses in the Negeb, Shephelah, and Hill Country, appear to confirm a number of royal building projects mentioned in Chronicles but not in Kings (e.g. 2 Chr 26:10; 27:4).[33] A major breakthrough in Chronicles study followed the discovery of the Dead Sea Scrolls. Extant manuscripts proved that variant versions of individual books of the Bible coexisted in the

---

Halle, 1806); J. Wellhausen, *Prolegomena to the History of Israel* (1885; trans. J.S. Black and A. Menzies; New York: Meridian Books, 1957), 171–227.

31. H. Winckler, "Bemerkungen zur Chronik als Geschichtsquelle" in *Alttestamentliche Untersuchungen* (Leipzig: J.C. Hinrichs, 1892), 157–167; W.F. Albright, "The Date and Personality of the Chronicler," *JBL* 40 (1921): 104–124; "The Judicial Reform of Jehoshaphat," 61–82.

32. Robinson, in 1838, was the first modern explorer of the Siloam tunnel (E. Robinson, *Biblical Research in Palestine and Adjacent Regions: A Journal of Travels in the Years 1838 & 1852*, vol. I [London: Murray, 1867], 337–343). Later, in 1880 the Siloam tunnel inscription was discovered accidentally by a schoolboy, Jacob Eliahu, who was exploring the tunnel with his friends. His adventure is recounted by B. Spafford-Vester, daughter of the founders of the American Colony in Jerusalem (*Our Jerusalem* [Garden City: Doubleday, 1950], 90–92; cf. A.H. Sayce, "The Hebrew Inscription in the Pool of Siloam I" *PEFQS* 13 [1881]: 282-285; C.L. Conder, II-III, 285–292). The Bible contains three references to Hezekiah's tunnel: 2 Kgs 20:20; Isa 22:9–11; 2 Chr 32:3–4, 30. Only Chronicles, however, cites the specific water source, the Gihon Spring, and notes that its course was directed underground westward into the City of David. It should be realized, though, that the Chronicler's data need not have derived from any written source but would have been public knowledge among Jerusalem's residents in the days of the Second Temple. The fact that Hezekiah was responsible for this great feat was probably transmitted through oral tradition.

33. While the Chronicler's crediting of these building projects to Uzziah and Jotham cannot be confirmed, eighth-century construction and occupation are evident at a number of Negeb fortresses (e.g. Arad; Kadesh-Barnea; Tel el-Khaliefeh/ Ezion-Geber [*NEAEHL*, 82–87, 844–845, 868–870]). In addition, population growth and the expansion of towns in the Judean Hills and Shephelah in the eighth century are clearly visible from excavated sites (e.g. Tell Beit Mirsim; Gibeon; Lachish [*NEAEHL*, 179–180, 512–513, 905–907]).

Second Temple period, and the Chronicler may have had access to these. Therefore, at least a portion of his reports are traceable to earlier historical sources and need not necessarily be viewed as products of the Chronicler's own time. For example, one Samuel text, 4QSam, shows a close affinity to Chronicles and to the Septuagint's deviation from the MT.[34]

Internal biblical evidence also demonstrates that some divergent data in Chronicles may actually have originated in the *Vorlage* of Kings but for one reason or another were excluded from the MT of Kings. A particularly interesting account that exemplifies this phenomenon is the Chronicler's version of the death of Josiah on the battlefield at Megiddo (2 Chr 35:20–24). Several factors suggest that this expanded composition cannot be assigned to either the Chronicler or to a source independent of Kings. Importantly, the narrative lacks both the Chronicler's distinctive vocabulary and ideological characteristics typical of Chronicles, such as warnings delivered by prophets or Levites. On the other hand, the account seems to be patterned after a similar episode in Kings, the death of Ahab (1 Kgs 22:30, 34–37).[35] A detail not previously noted is that the expression, מה לי ולך, "what is there between me and you," spoken by Necho to Josiah to discourage him from interfering with the Egyptian army's march to Syria (2 Chr 35:21), which appears several times in earlier biblical writings, is unique to late texts here.[36] Its appearance in Chronicles is tenable if the idiom originated in a *Vorlage* of Kings.

The archaeological and biblical examples presented above are part of a growing corpus of evidence that serves to dispel scholarly notions that the Chronicler regularly fabricated his data.[37] Still, observations that events portrayed in

34. F.M. Cross, "The Contribution of the Qumran Discoveries to the Study of the Biblical Text" in F.M. Cross and S. Talmon eds. *Qumran and the History of the Biblical Text* (Cambridge: Harvard University Press, 1975), 280; S.L. McKenzie, *The Chronicler's Use of the Deuteronomistic History* (Atlanta: Scholars Press, 1984), 33–81. Some scholars, however, question the reliability of the Qumran manuscripts as First Temple period witnesses. For example, A. Rofe suggests, contra Cross, that the expanded version of Sam 11 in 4QSam[a] does not reflect an early text but shows a midrashic feature, the duplication of biblical events, known from writings of the Second Temple period ("The Acts of Nahash according to 4QSam[a]," *IEJ* 32 [1982]: 129–133).

35. For a detailed discussion, see H.G.M. Williamson, "The Death of Josiah and the Continuing Development of the Deuteronomic History," *VT* 32 (1982): 242–248.

36. The expression occurs in Judg 11:12, 2 Sam 16:10; 19:23; 1 Kgs 17:18 and 2 Kgs 3:13. My student Leah Cohen has suggested that in several cases the phrase מה לי ולך seems to function in a literary role, signaling that a major event is imminent.

37. Scholars who maintain that the Chronicler's ideology rather than additional material is consistently the source behind these accounts include, among others, P. Welten (*Geschichte und Geschichtsdarstellung in den Chronikbuchen* [Neukirchen-Vluyn: Neukirchener, 1973]), R.

Chronicles frequently bear the markings of a tendentious writer are correct. The Chronicler's ideology is clearly reflected in the material he chose to incorporate into his history and in his reinterpretation of historical circumstances. Yet those distinctions in and of themselves do not exclude his writings from the category of historiography. According to the definition of the concept of history promulgated by the noted historian J. Huizinga, "Every man renders account to himself of the past in accordance with the standards which his education and *Weltanschauung* lead him to adopt."[38] In the case of the Chronicler, phenomena of the Israelite monarchy are colored with the *Weltanschauung* of the Second Temple period. As M. Brettler aptly puts it, the Chronicler sought to "reshape" the way the earlier biblical books were viewed, perhaps as a "corrective" to those histories. When the tradition was not in conflict with his beliefs, the Chronicler retained the old version.[39]

A number of techniques evident repeatedly in Chronicles serves to alert scholars to episodes whose historical accuracy is questionable. Patterning accounts of national leaders on those of famous predecessors is common—for example, Hezekiah after Solomon and David after Moses.[40] A striking feature of the Chronicler's ideology worthy of comment is the notion of immediate retribution. It is manifest in several narratives, most prominently in the report on Manasseh's kingship (2 Chr 33:1–20). Apparently for the Chronicler, Manasseh's reign of fifty-five years represented a theological contradiction. How could an evil king who instituted foreign worship in Israel be blessed with such a lengthy reign? The writer rectifies this difficulty by asserting that, as punishment, Manasseh was imprisoned in Babylon, but while there, he atoned and returned to YHWH (33:11–12). Furthermore, the Chronicler maintains that because Manasseh's repentance was sincere, YHWH reinstated him on his throne and permitted him to secure his domain by fortifying the Ophel and the western perimeter of the City of David and by stationing troops in all the walled cities of Judah (33:13–14).

Although the Chronicler's version of Manasseh's reign is imbued with the writer's values, the account as a whole need not be dismissed as fiction. For the

North ("Does Archaeology Prove Chronicles' Sources?" in H. Bream, R. Heim, C. Moore eds. *A Light unto my Path* [Philadelphia: Temple University Press, 1974], 375–401) and R. Klein ("Abijah's Campaign Against the North (2 Chr. 13) – What Were the Chronicler's Sources?" *ZAW* 95 [1983]: 210–217).

38. J. Huizinga, "A Definition of the Concept of History" in R. Klibansky and H.J. Paton eds. *Philosophy and History: Essays Presented to Ernst Cassirer* (New York: Harper & Row, 1963), 9.

39. M. Brettler, *The Creation of History in Ancient Israel* (London: Routledge, 1995), 21–23.

40. For detailed descriptions, see Brettler, *Creation of History*, 26–41.

modern historian, it is of little consequence whether Manasseh repented for his alleged unorthodox religious practices. Rather, the real interest lies in greater historical questions: Was Manasseh actually imprisoned in Babylon, perhaps as an uncooperative vassal? Under what circumstances did he return to Jerusalem? Is he the king responsible for constructing a number of seventh-century structures uncovered in archaeological excavations in Jerusalem? While not definitive, extra-biblical sources, specifically Assyrian documents mentioning Manasseh and other vassals, contain hints that some of the Chronicler's data may be accurate.[41] Similarly, the Chronicler's assertion that Manasseh became a builder is supported from archaeological signs of national recovery.[42] Thus, by sifting the Chronistic ideology from the narrative, potential historical truths unknown from the Deuteronomistic history can be isolated.

In connection to the present study, it should be noted that official titles in Chronicles generally correspond to those in the books of Samuel and Kings, even in instances of specific officials and functionaries who are known only from Chronicles. Two exceptional cases exist. The first, the title שטר/שוטר, "officer," appears in the Pentateuch and the book of Joshua but is unattested in the Deuteronomist's accounts of the monarchic period. As such, it may reflect a resurrected pre-monarchic designation.[43] The second title, נגיד הבית, seems to be equivalent to the similar, better known title from the books of Kings, אשר על הבית, "minister over the (royal) house." Since the latter title is not found in Chronicles, it is possible that for this office the Chronicler replaced the expression אשר על, literally, "the one (who is) over," with a comparable post-exilic term נגיד, "ruler."[44] Neither of these seemingly Chronistic titles, however, implies

41. Manasseh king of Judah is mentioned in the account of Esarhaddon's campaign to Palestine, Prism B, where he appears among 22 kings ordered to transport building materials to Nineveh (Oppenheim, *ANET*, 291). In Assurbanipal's annals, Rassam Cylinder C, he is among the same group of monarchs who are obligated to accompany the Assyrian army into Egypt with heavy tribute in tow (Oppenheim, *ANET*, 294). A third fragmentary inscription from the reign of Esarhaddon refers to the 22 kings of the west in connection to reprisals taken against them for rebellious activities (R. Borger, *Die Inschriften Asarhaddons Königs von Assyrien* [*AfO* Beiheft 9; Graz, 1956] 67: 30–35). Although in the latter inscription their names are broken off, it is possible that Manasseh belonged to this group and that in this context was imprisoned (for a more detailed discussion and a summary of scholarship on this issue, see C. Evans, "Judah's Foreign Policy from Hezekiah to Josiah" in *Scripture in Context*, 166–169; Japhet, *I & II Chronicles*, 1009).

42. I. Finkelstein, "The Archaeology of the Days of Manasseh" in M.D. Coogan, J.C. Exum and L.E. Stager eds. *Scripture and Other Artifacts: Essays on the Bible and Archaeology in Honor of Philip J. King* (Louisville: Westminster John Knox Press, 1994), 169–181.

43. See Chapter 5–C.

44. See Chapter 4–A.

that the offices associated with the designations reflect the Chronicler's own time.[45]

Conclusion

A final comment is called for regarding suppositions that either the books of Samuel and Kings or Chronicles are fountains of historical truths about ancient Israel. Until recently, the Chronicler was usually targeted as the biblical source deemed to be historically untrustworthy. More current studies have questioned the reliability of the Deuteronomistic records as well, although at times to unreasonable degrees as assaults directed at anything biblical. As is apparent from extant documents, different manuscripts, exhibiting both minor and major variations in their recollections of Israelite history, circulated in antiquity. The historical accuracy of many of the events described in these reports cannot be substantiated. Therefore, individual accounts both in Chronicles and in the Deuteronomistic histories call for careful scrutiny, employing the same critical methods to both testimonies. A key consideration for the present study is that records on officialdom and state organization rarely conceal ideological motives and therefore can be utilized for their historical value.

The Epigraphic Sources

Unprovenienced Material

The corpus of Hebrew epigraphic material (e.g. seals, bullae, weights, ostraca) is composed of two categories of finds: those uncovered in controlled archaeological excavations and those acquired on the antiquities market, unprovenienced. Unprovenienced material can include chance finds, items that derive from illicit excavations, and modern creations. Utilization of these objects in scholarly inquiries presents a number of difficulties. An obvious problem is the lack of provenience, which means that the archaeological context of those items is unknown.[46] A second, more critical concern is the questionable authenticity of objects that appear on the antiquities market, since distinguishing between genuine artifacts and fakes is often difficult. A third issue involves the ethical dilemma of using material derived from illicit excavations and sold to antiquities dealers or private collectors. These obstacles devalue the

---

45. Admittedly, the existence in Chronicles of שטרים who are Levites may reflect a Second Temple practice (see Chapter 5–C).

46. In this study, the definition of unprovenienced material includes items that reached the antiquities market with claims of supposed provenience but which have not been verified.

unprovenienced corpus for purposes of archaeological and biblical studies and, as such, the topic belongs to the discussion of methodology in this study.

Anyone who has ever participated in an archaeological excavation understands the importance of context for evaluating artifacts. Painstaking care is taken in exposing objects and in recording their precise findspots. Remains of public buildings, storehouses, private dwellings, and cultic installations are used to interpret the *Sitz-im-Leben* of the objects unearthed. Information of this kind is lacking for items acquired on the antiquities market, and even the most basic fact of geographical provenience is obscure.[47] In addition, more often than not, the date of unprovenienced items can only be estimated, primarily based on paleographic criteria. Furthermore, the ethnic identity of unprovenienced material can be ambiguous because paleographic distinctions between Israelite, Phoenician, Ammonite, Moabite, and Edomite scripts are not always evident and other ethnic indicators, such as the iconography or theophoric elements in PNs may be absent.[48] Finally, it is curious that while scholars commonly bemoan the lost context of unprovenienced objects, they generally assume their genuineness.[49]

Answers to a number of key questions pertaining to authenticity and publication of unprovenienced material are instrumental in deciding how this corpus should be utilized in the present study. 1. Have any unprovenienced finds heretofore published as genuine been proven forgeries? 2. How simple or difficult is it to convincingly forge seals, bullae, and ostraca? 3. Is it possible to scientifically authenticate these types of objects? 4. What criteria are followed to determine the authenticity of unprovenienced items prior to their publication? 5. Does the publication of this material by the scholarly community serve to encourage il-

---

47. Although finds originating from excavated sites are not always found *in situ*, their geographical location is known.

48. See the list of seals whose ethnic origin is uncertain (N. Avigad and B. Sass, *Corpus of West Semitic Stamp Seals* [Jerusalem: Israel Academy of Sciences and Humanities, Israel Exploration Society, Institute of Archaeology of Hebrew University, 1997], 395–447; in future references *WSS*).

49. N. Avigad notes in the introduction to his book (*Hebrew Bullae from the Time of Jeremiah: Remnants of a Burnt Archive* [Jerusalem: Israel Exploration Society, 1986], 13), "There was no reason to suspect their authenticity, and I seriously doubt whether it would be possible to forge such burnt and damaged bullae." Similarly, in reference to seals, A. Lemaire maintains that a seal is presumed genuine unless proven a forgery (cited in B. Sass, "The Pre-Exilic Hebrew Seals: Iconism vs. Aniconism" in B. Sass and C. Uehlinger eds. *Studies in the Iconography of Northwest Semitic Inscribed Seals* [Fribourg: Biblical Institute Fribourg University Press, 1993], 245). In Avishur's and Heltzer's recent book (*Studies on the Royal Administration in Ancient Israel in the Light of Epigraphic Sources*), there is a tacit assumption that their material is genuine regardless of its mode of acquisition.

licit excavations or forgery? In the process of answering these questions a brief background on the subject of antiquities and forgeries is instructive.

Trade in unprovenienced antiquities has a long history, the effects of which served to fill museums and treasuries of private collectors. In the nineteenth century, renewed interest in the Holy Land, with the primary objective of verifying biblical data, resulted in the valuation of all types of inscribed material from Palestine. Two sensational discoveries, the Mesha Stele in 1868 and the Siloam Tunnel inscription in 1880, served to intensify searches.[50] Numerous small items, such as seals and coins that time and weather had brought to the surface, were sold to antiquities dealers and other collectors by locals who found them either accidentally or by digging at ancient sites. The field of archaeology was still in its infancy then, and few restrictions were imposed on the antiquities market. A major transformation in attitude took place when scholars began to suspect that certain objects sold as ancient relics were in fact modern forgeries. The matter came to a head with the scandal surrounding a group of inscribed Moabite statues that, among other objects, had been sold by Moses Wilhelm Shapira, an antiquities dealer in Jerusalem, to the Berlin museum.[51] An investigation by the archaeologist Clermont-Ganneau revealed that "underground" Jerusalem of the 1870s housed workshops of forgers who were manufacturing "antiquities" for an increasingly hungry market.[52]

Conditions improved in the twentieth century as more and more excavations

---

50. N.A. Silberman, *Digging for God and Country: Exploration, Archeology, and the Secret Struggle for the Holy Land 1799–1917* (New York: Knopf, 1982), 100–112; A.H. Sayce, "The Ancient Hebrew Inscription in the Pool of Siloam I" *PEFQS* 13 (1881): 282–285; C.L. Conder, II–III, 285–292; I. Taylor, IV, 292–293; S. Beswick, V, 293–296; H. Sulley, VI, 296–297.

51. Silberman, *Digging for God and Country*, 131–134.

52. C. Clermont-Ganneau, "The Shapira Collection," *PEFQS* 6 (1874): 114–118. Clermont-Ganneau became suspicious of the statues because their text was unintelligible, although the script resembled that of the Mesha Stele. Shapira was not implicated in these forgeries, but the stigma from this affair haunted him in years to come. He is best remembered for the "Shapira Deuteronomy Scroll," 15 leather strips inscribed in paleo-Hebrew with portions from Deuteronomy that were allegedly discovered near the Dead Sea by Bedouins. Shapira purchased these documents and spent several years attempting to authenticate and sell them. In 1884, having failed to convince the scholarly world of their genuineness, despondent, he committed suicide. When the Dead Sea Scrolls were discovered in 1947, efforts were made to locate Shapira's scroll so that it could be reexamined. The scroll was never found (Silberman, *Digging for God and Country*, 134–146). Circumstantial evidence suggests that it may have perished in a fire in 1899 at the home of Sir Charles Nicholson, who had purchased a number of Shapira's documents after the latter's death (A. Crown, "The Fate of the Shapira Scroll," *RdQ* 27 [1970]: 421–423). Two fragments that were sent to Germany by Shapira's widow remain unaccounted (BM ADD. 41294 no. 25).

were conducted under the auspices of university departments of archaeology or government-sponsored departments of antiquities. Archaeological methods were fine-tuned and literally hundreds of tells were excavated systematically. However, despite the advances in the field of archaeology and stricter government control over antiquities, a flood of unprovenienced material has surfaced in the region in the last twenty-five years. Numerous engraved stone seals have joined similar earlier finds. This collection of seals, together with provenienced items, now appears in N. Avigad's *Corpus of West Semitic Stamp Seals* published posthumously by Benjamin Sass, who revised and completed the volume.[53] Unprovenienced bullae, previously only known from isolated finds at excavations, began to surface in large groups in the mid 1970s.[54] Most are believed to have originated from the same archive, allegedly near Tell Beit Mirsim.[55] These comprise the hoard of 255 bullae published by N. Avigad in *Hebrew Bullae from the Time of Jeremiah: Remnants of a Burnt Archive* (see n. 49). Additional unprovenienced inscribed objects that have reached the antiquities market in the last few years or belong to private collections and were unpublished continue to appear in publications. Four volumes illustrating approximately 250 unprovenienced objects were published by R. Deutsch in 1994, 1995 and 1997 (three of these publications are co-authored by M. Heltzer).[56] Other items have

---

53. *WSS*. Many of these seals were previously published by Avigad in separate articles and books.

54. Apparently, although bullae were already known, interest was sparked by the discovery of a small archive of 17 bullae in a jug at Lachish during Aharoni's excavations in 1966 (Y. Aharoni, *Lachish V: The Sanctuary and Residency* [Tel Aviv: Tel Aviv University Institute of Archaeology, 1975], 19–22).

55. Having been informed that the bullae originated in the vicinity of Tell Beit Mirsim, Avigad, together with the director of the Department of Antiquities and the district archaeologist, visited the site where on a hill near the mound they found traces of digging (*Hebrew Bullae*, 13). It is strange indeed that no excavations ensued to verify the findspot or to uncover the potential context of the bullae. H. Shanks, in his discussion of some of these bullae, comments on this lack of follow-up. He attributes it to a "petrifying inertia" that seems to characterize the archaeological community when dealing with these problems ("Jeremiah's Scribe and Confident Speaks from a Hoard of Clay Bullae," *BAR* 13/5 [1987]: 65). It is possible, however, that no excavations followed because the evidence of digging was too widespread. Apparently, that geographic area is notorious for illicit digs.

56. The objects are comprised of ceramics, bronze arrowheads, stone and bronze weights, seals, bullae and ostraca bearing West Semitic inscriptions (R. Deutsch and M. Heltzer, *Forty New Ancient West Semitic Inscriptions* [Tel Aviv-Jaffa: Archaeological Center, 1994]; *New Epigraphic Evidence from the Biblical Period* [Tel Aviv-Jaffa: Archaeological Center, 1995]; *Windows to the Past* [Tel Aviv-Jaffa, 1997]; R. Deutsch *Messages from the Past: Hebrew Bullae from the Time of Isaiah Through the Destruction of the First Temple* [Tel Aviv-Jaffa: Archaeological Center, 1997].

been published periodically in *BAR* and other journals.[57]

Inherent in objects lacking provenience is the possibility of forgery.[58] Suspicions of forgery have been raised in reference to a number of inscribed items after their initial publication. Suspect Northwest Semitic seals are listed, among others, in the works of Diringer,[59] Naveh and Tadmor,[60] Herr,[61] Garbini,[62] and Hubner.[63] Most recently, in the preface to *Corpus of West Semitic Stamp Seals*, Naveh lists forty-nine seals and seal impressions whose authenticity has been questioned.[64] Primarily, paleographic peculiarities such as the shape and stance

---

57. Recent *BAR* publications include seals and bullae belonging to royal officials and Judean and Ammonite kings as well as several other types of inscribed objects: A. Lemaire, "Name of Israel's Last King Surfaces in a Private Collection," 21/6 (1995): 48–52; H. Shanks, "Three Shekels for the Lord," 23/9 (1997):28–32; R. Deutsch, "First Impression – What We Learn from King Ahaz's Seal," 24/3 (1998): 54–56, 62; F.M. Cross, "King Hezekiah's Seal Bears Phoenician Imagery," 25/2 (1999): 42–45, 60; R. Deutsch, "Seal of Baʿalis Surfaces," 25/2 (1999): 46–49, 66.

58. While it is not impossible for objects to be purposely planted even at excavation sites, such activity is usually detectable by professional excavators. One example of an object that seems to have been planted in the path of visitors to an excavation is the seal from Tel Qasile sketchily inscribed: עשניהו עבד המלך (*WSS*, no. 1206). It was initially considered authentic by the excavator B. Mazar ("The Excavations at Tell Qasile: Preliminary Report III," *IEJ* 1 [1950–1951]: 212). A similar accusation, but one later refuted, was leveled by Y. Yadin in reference to a broken South-Arabian stamp seal found in debris outside the city gate at Bethel. Yadin claimed that the object was actually the same broken stamp seal discovered 30 years earlier at Meshhed in southern Arabia and therefore must have been planted in the excavation site at Bethel ("An Inscribed South-Arabian Clay Stamp from Bethel?" *BASOR* 196 [1969]: 37–45). G.W. van Beek and A. Jamme, the authors of the original publication ("An Inscribed South Arabian Clay Stamp from Bethel," *BASOR* 151 [1958]: 9–16), were able to show, however, that although the two objects were strikingly similar and were probably impressed with the same seal, detectable minor differences in depth and angle of impression in the stamps suggested that indeed two distinct stamp seals existed ("The Authenticity of the Bethel Stamp Seal," *BASOR* 199 [1970]: 59–65). Also, the chief excavator of Bethel, J. Kelso, reported that when the item was found, his workers did not even request *baksheesh*, the usual reward for significant finds ("A Reply to Yadin's Article on the Finding of the Bethel Seal," *BASOR* 199 [1970]: 65).

59. D. Diringer, *Le inscrizioni antico-ebraiche palestinesi* (Florence: Felice le Monnier, 1934), 319–325.

60. J. Naveh and H. Tadmor, "Some Doubtful Aramaic Seals," *AION* 18 (1968): 448–452, pls. I–III.

61. L. Herr, *The Scripts of Ancient Northwest Semitic Seals* (Missoula: Scholars Press, 1978), 185–189.

62. G. Garbini, "I sigilli del Regno di Israele," *OrAn* 21 (1982): 175.

63. U. Hubner, "Fälschungen ammonitischer Siegel," *UF* 21 (1989): 217–226.

64. *WSS*, 12.

of letters alert scholars to the possibility that a seal is not authentic. In addition, unusual or crude iconography or a problematic PN raise questions concerning the antiquity of an item.[65] Among the suspect group are a number of Hebrew seals and bullae bearing a title as well as a PN (e.g. לברכיהו בן נריהו הספר, למעדנה בת המלך, למלכיהו בן המלך).[66] Occasionally, signs of forgery are so obvious that the inscription is rejected as a certain fake. For example, leather documents identified as Philistine by Brownlee and Mendenhall in the early 1970s[67] have been proven by Cross and Naveh to be forgeries.[68] Cross and Naveh were able to show that for one of the documents, the forger copied lines from the Siloam Tunnel inscription deviating from that text by interchanging the order of some of the letters and reversing the direction of the writing from right-to-left to left-to-right.[69]

---

65. Herr raises most of these concerns in reference to a seal inscribed למשפט. While he considers three other seals "possible forgeries," he labels that one a "probable forgery" (*Scripts of Ancient Northwest Semitic Seals*, 186–187 no. 5). Avigad had previously classified this seal as Moabite ("Ammonite and Moabite Seals" in *NEATC*, 291 pl. 30:8). Iconography that is anachronistic is also a criterion for recognizing possible forgeries. For example, Hubner argues that the winged sun disc depicted on an Ammonite seal inscribed למנחם בן מגראל belongs artistically to the Achaemenid period ("Fälschungen ammonitischer Siegel," 223–224 no. 1).

66. *WSS,* 12 (Avigad's corpus consists of 44 unprovenienced seals and bullae showing a PN plus a title. Of those, 11 [25%] are listed as being of questionable authenticity.)

67. "An announcement published by the Department of Antiquities of Jordan and the Archaeologists Dr. William Brownlee and Dr. George Mendenhall regarding the decipherment of Carian Leather Manuscripts found in 1966 in the Hebron Area, the Hashemite Kingdom of Jordan," *ADAJ* 15 (1970): 39–40; G. Mendenhall, "The 'Philistine' Documents from the Hebron Area: A Supplementary Note," *ADAJ* 16 (1971): 99–102; W. Brownlee, G. Mendenhall, Y. Oweis, "Philistine Manuscripts from Palestine?" *Kadmos* 10 (1971): 102–104; W. Brownlee, "Philistine Manuscripts from Palestine? – A Supplementary Note," 173.

68. J. Naveh, "Some Recently Forged Inscriptions," *BASOR* 247 (1982): 53–58; "Clumsy Forger Fools the Scholars – But Only for a Time," *BAR* 10/3 (1984): 66–72. F. Cross declared the inscriptions fakes at a meeting in Atlanta in 1971 (*BAR* 10/3, 69–70). Carbon 14 tests also indicated that the leather was modern.

69. Even cuneiform tablets, found by the thousands, are not immune to the forger's art and the antiquities market. An intriguing case was brought to light by the Assyriologist Erle Leichty. While studying a collection of Neo-Babylonian legal and economic tablet fragments at the University Museum, he noticed that the obverse of one tablet was a duplicate of a certain British Museum text, but the reverse of that same tablet was a duplicate of a different British Museum text. Furthermore, the tablet "turned" the wrong way. Upon subsequent investigation of similar tablets at the Oriental Institute, he discovered that these peculiarities were not the work of students practicing scribal skills. What alerted Leichty was the fact that some of the tablets were literally coming apart at the seams. Apparently

The case of one modern product, a sculpted stone disc, is especially illuminating for the present study. The story of Eliyahu Yitzhak, the creator of this item, appeared in the Israeli newspaper *Ma'riv* in 1975.[70] Apparently, as a sideline to supplement his income, Mr. Yitzhak of Afula carves stone plaques and figurines, which he sells for modest prices at local markets as mementos. One such item, a small basalt disc depicting a winged-lion and the inscription לשמע, "belonging to *šm'*," written in paleo-Hebrew, found its way to an antiquities dealer who sold it as an ancient relic to a museum for a handsome profit. Subsequently, the object was published in *Qadmoniot* by Avigad, who identified it as an Israelite 400 shekel weight of the early eighth century BCE. Avigad classified the iconography of the unusual stylized winged-lion as Neo-Hittite. He further suggested that the weight may have belonged to a government official, perhaps to the owner of the seal from Megiddo inscribed לשמע עבד ירבעם who bore the same PN and served as a high ranking minister to King Jeroboam.[71] Despite obvious peculiarities, such as the style of the lion and the elaborate decoration on a weight, Avigad never questioned the authenticity of this object in his publication.

As evident from the aforementioned accounts, it is relatively easy to produce authentic looking seals and other inscribed material. Sass notes that West Semitic seals, which are mostly cut of soft stones with simple iconography, can be a *Kinderspiel* for a talented forger.[72] Manufacturing bullae simply involves an additional process, impressing a lump of clay and then baking or burning it. One can imagine that to facilitate the process, modern seals used to produce such bullae could be cut from pliable synthetic material.[73] Ostraca and other ink inscriptions are more difficult to forge, although some attempts have gone undetected for years.[74] But one need not search out clandestine operations to show the ease of creating seals, bullae and other inscribed objects. In legitimate settings, artisans employed by museums regularly produce duplicates of authentic items for display and other purposes.

---

these tablets, purchased almost a century earlier, were forgeries. They had been cast from originals in two halves and then joined together. Time and temperature changes caused the seams to separate ("A Remarkable Forger," *Expedition* 20 [1970]: 17–21).

70. D. Mazori, "A. Yitzhak, the Sculptor from Afula, Laughs at the Experts," *Ma'ariv* July 11, 1975 (Hebrew). I thank Jeffrey Tigay for bringing this article to my attention.

71. N. Avigad, "A Sculptured Stone Weight with Hebrew Inscription," *Qadmoniot* 2/2 (1969): 60–61.

72. Sass, "The Pre-Exilic Hebrew Seals," 246.

73. One senior scholar, a paleographer who wishes to remain anonymous, maintains that forging bullae is a simpler process than forging seals (private communication, July 1995).

74. J. Naveh, "Aramaica Dubiosa," *JNES* 27 (1968): 319–325.

As noted above, the authenticity of unprovenienced inscribed items is usually judged on the basis of criteria such as material, paleography, orthography, and iconography. Thereby, if the material of the object, its script, spelling, and artistic features are comparable to those of extant items from the same region within a prescribed time frame, the object is presumed genuine. But, as demonstrated from the case of the modern winged-lion disc, almost anything is comparable to something known. In addition, scholarly analysis of ancient orthography, such as defective spelling, would be readily available to sophisticated forgers. Therefore, it seems that extra scientific detection methods are essential in establishing the genuineness of unprovenienced finds.

Scientific authentication of inscribed material, especially seals, presents a number of difficulties. Stone seals, manufactured from undatable natural elements, are nearly impossible to authenticate.[75] One technique, developed by Gorelick and Gwinnett, two physicians involved with dental research, holds promise in this area. It utilizes the scanning electron microscope (SEM) to examine tool marks on the surface of the center bores of seals. After comparing genuine and fake seals, Gorelick and Gwinnett discovered that fake seals showed similarities between the abrasion characteristics of their bores and visible differences from those on the bores of authentic seals.[76] This technique is non-destructive to the object. It is limited, however, to seals with center bores.

Authentication of bullae and pottery stamped with seal-impressions is a more feasible endeavor. Neutron activation analysis, which identifies the chemical composition of clay, can be used to determine the provenience of pottery as well as to detect the presence of any synthetic components that would indicate modern production.[77] Another testing technique used to date pottery and isolate fake pieces is Thermoluminescence (TL). By heating the pottery and measuring the glow curve emitted, its age can be ascertained.[78] In the case of ink-inscribed

---

75. C. Uehlinger, "Northwest Semitic Inscribed Seals, Iconography and Syro-Palestinian Religions of Iron Age II: Some Afterthoughts and Conclusions" in Sass, *Studies*, 270.

76. L. Gorelick and A.J. Gwinnett, "Ancient Seals and Modern Science: Using the Scanning Electron Microscope as an Aid in the Study of Ancient Seals," *Expedition* 20 (1978): 38–47.

77. This technique was used to determine the production site(s) of *lmlk* and rosette impressed handles. H. Mommsen, I. Perlman and J. Yellin, "The Provenience of the *lmlk* Jars," *IEJ* 34 (1984): 89–113.

78. P. Craddock and S. Bowman eds. "The Scientific Detection of Fakes and Forgeries" in M. Jones ed. *Fake? The Art of Deception* (London: British Museum, 1990), 288–289. This technique was used to isolate fakes from a group of 'Haçilar' type pottery figurines (ca. 5000 BCE). Of 66 objects tested, 48 turned out to be recent creations.

ostraca, however, the age of the pottery itself is not an indicator of authenticity since there is no dearth of ancient potsherds for use by modern forgers.

In reality, the testing of unprovenienced objects remains problematic even when scientific techniques are available. Frequently the objects belong to private collectors who, having paid high prices, will not allow them to be tested, a process that sometimes requires taking samples.[79] Collections in the possession of museums fare better, although unprovenienced items are not tested on a regular basis prior to publication. The need to develop reliable and safe testing techniques for inscribed material was addressed at a symposium entitled "The Iconography of Northwest Semitic Inscribed Seals," held in 1991 at the University of Fribourg in Switzerland. It was advocated that scholars publishing new material should discuss in detail on what grounds the items are presumed genuine. In addition, as much information as possible should be presented about the history of the object, from purported provenience to market.[80] More recently, in the wake of growing concern over the authenticity of dozens of newly published inscribed objects, including two significant ostraca and two unique impressions of royal Hebrew seals, לאחז יהותם מלך יהדה "belonging to *'ḥz* son of *yhwtm* king of Judah" and לחזקיהו אחז מלך יהדה "belonging to *ḥzqyhw* son of *'ḥz* king of Judah," scientific testing of ostraca and bullae were begun.[81]

A final concern is a moral one. If scholarly enthusiasm over objects derived from illicit excavations valuates them and increases their desirability, then publication can be interpreted as condoning and even encouraging illegal excavation activities. The standard arguments on this matter hold that the publication of this material is intended to salvage remnants of the past. Furthermore, even

---

79. Perhaps the fear of possibly detecting a fake is also a deterrent.

80. Sass, "The Pre-Exilic Hebrew Seals," 246; Uehlinger, "Northwest Semitic Inscribed Seals," 270–271.

81. Laboratory analysis using SEM-EDS (Energy Dispursive X-Ray) was conducted on these ostraca. Although tests showed the presence of some contaminants, the white patina that formed over the ink is indicative of the antiquity of the inscriptions (P. Bordreuil et al., "King's Command and Widow's Plea: Two New Hebrew Ostraca of the Biblical Period," *Near Eastern Archaeology* 61 [1998]: 8–9). The two royal bullae were not tested, but TL analysis was performed on two other bullae (inscribed with PNs but untitled). The laboratory reports are published in Deutsch's recent volume (*Messages from the Past*, 168–169). In an article describing the אחז royal seal impression, Deutsch details the meticulous examination of the bulla under a powerful microscope by him and several senior scholars ("First Impression," 56). F.M. Cross' publication of the חזקיהו royal bulla touches on the standard assessments for authenticity but does not mention that any scientific testing was conducted ("King Hezekiah's Seal Bears Phoenician Imagery," 42–45, 60). In light of the potential significance of these two remarkable finds, it seems advisable to commission an independent laboratory for further testing.

if the scholarly community disregarded unprovenienced finds, illicit excavations would continue because collectors who covet relics from the past always exist.[82] Be that as it may, the history of archaeological studies, beginning in the nineteenth century, clearly indicates that scholarship affects the antiquities market and the production of forgeries. Therefore, this repercussion cannot be ignored.

In light of the various problems associated with unprovenienced material, it seems that their value for studies such as the present one is rather limited. The lack of archaeological context and questionable authenticity, coupled with ethical concerns over publication, places this corpus in a category distinct from objects uncovered in controlled archaeological excavations. Consequently, the following cautious approach is adopted here: (1) Published unprovenienced items will be mentioned in discussions in this study but will constitute a separate category from the provenienced archaeological material. (2) Interpretations of official titles, administrative practices, and any other aspects of state-organization will be based exclusively on evidence from provenienced sources. (3) No conclusions will be drawn from data derived from unprovenienced material.

Paleographic Dating

Ideally, Hebrew epigraphic material is dated from information contained in the text and/or archaeologically, by the stratigraphy of the findspot. Inscriptions that lack textual evidence and are not discovered *in situ*, such as surface finds, items from mixed archaeological assemblages or fills, or material that is unprovenienced, must be dated by other means. One method commonly used is paleographic analysis. Epigraphic studies have shown that script, specifically the morphology of letters, evolves over time and certain distinguishable features characterize stages in this development. Based on datable and nationally identifiable documents, typologies have been developed for analyzing paleo-Hebrew script and differentiating it from various other West Semitic national scripts such as Phoenician, Aramaic, Moabite, Ammonite, and Edomite.[83]

82. Hershel Shanks, among others, is a staunch supporter of publishing unprovenienced objects. See his arguments in "Bringing Collectors and Their Collections Out of Hiding," *BAR* 25/3 (1999): 40–43.

83. F.M. Cross, "Epigraphic Notes on the Hebrew Documents of the Eighth–Sixth Centuries B.C.: I. A New Reading of a Place Name in the Samaria Ostraca," *BASOR* 163 (1961): 12–14; II. The Murabba'at Papyrus and the Letter Found Near Yabneh-Yam," *BASOR* 165 (1962): 34–46; III. The Inscribed Jar Handles from Gibeon," *BASOR* 168 (1962): 18–23; J. Naveh, "A Paleographic Note on the Distribution of the Hebrew Script," *HTR* 61 (1968): 68–74; *Early History of the Alphabet: An Introduction to West Semitic Epigraphy and Paleography* (Jerusalem: Magnes Press, 1982), esp. 89–112; Herr, *Scripts of Ancient Northwest Semitic Seals.*

Paleographic dating, however, does not only take into account independent national development and chronological evolution, but also considers the coexistence of distinct writing styles in the same society. One factor that affects script is the medium of the inscription. Lapidary style is associated with inscriptions incised in stone, while cursive styles are most suitable for ink inscriptions. Interestingly, in Israel, a true lapidary style is not discernable. Even inscriptions on stone show the cursive feature of shading, although the letters are still of the more formal types.[84] Cursive style characterizes the script found on other media, such as papyrus and pottery. In contrast to F.M. Cross, who classifies all variants as cursive, J. Naveh has modified the terminology slightly by dividing them into three sub-styles: extreme cursive, formal cursive, and vulgar cursive.[85] An important factor for dating purposes is that the script of lapidary inscriptions is more conservative, changing at a slower rate than the scripts of ink-inscribed ostraca or papyri. In addition, individual letters tend to evolve at different speeds, resulting in the presence of older and newer forms in the same document.[86]

While script styles are clearly related to writing material, allowances in paleographic dating must also be made for a variety of concurrent writing styles that are products of different types of scribal activity within a single culture. According to Naveh, extreme cursive is the handwriting of educated persons and, in turn, influences the two other styles. Formal cursive is characteristic of the professional scribe, and vulgar cursive reflects the writing of a less skilled person.[87] Even the more conservative script of lapidary inscriptions shows these distinctions. In his dissertation, Andrew Vaughn recently compared groups of seal impressions from the late eighth century (*lmlk* handles with PN seal-impressions) to bullae of the late seventh/early sixth century (from Lachish and the City of David) to determine if variations within the script of one period and distinctions between scripts of different periods permit paleographic dating altogether. His study reveals that seals cut in the same period show a much lower than expected degree of uniformity in the shape of individual letters. On the other hand, some distinctive characteristics in certain letters are observable when comparing the two groups of seal impressions dated approximately a century apart. Interestingly, the Siloam Tunnel inscription (ca. 701 BCE), which was

---

84. Naveh, *Early History of the Alphabet*, 66–70.

85. Cross, II. "The Murabba'at Papyrus and the Letter Found Near Yabneh-Yam," 34–42; Naveh, "A Paleographic Note on the Distribution of the Hebrew Script," 68–69.

86. F.M. Cross, "Alphabets and Pots: Reflections on Typological Method in the Dating of Human Artifacts," *Maarav* 3/2 (1982): 131.

87. Naveh, "A Paleographic Note on the Distribution of the Hebrew Script," 68–69.

heretofore a paradigm of late eighth-century script used to date unprovenienced seals, contains several innovative letter forms that are distinctive of late seventh century script.[88] Thus, Vaughn's findings, while not completely disastrous to paleographic dating based on minor diagnostic features in some letters, point to flaws inherent in the method and confirm prior views that paleographic models alone only offer a range of time within which an inscription could have been written.[89]

Obstacles to accurate paleographical dating are also apparent in studies of Attic script, archaic Greek writing. A recent analysis of Attic inscriptions on painted vases from the Archaic and Classical periods in Athens (8th–4th century BCE) is instructive for comparative purposes because the script closely resembles paleo-Hebrew and the vases are securely dated.[90] H. Immerwahr, who examined the vase-inscriptions, found a fairly regular development of writing during this time-span that corresponds to developments in the drawings of the human figures pictured alongside the inscriptions. However, he observes that it is not unusual for older and newer letter-forms to coexist, even in inscriptions of an overall advanced style.[91] His study also shows marked differences in the writing of contemporary individuals, identifiable by their signed works.[92] The inscriptions of one master, Exekias (ca. 550–535 BCE), display a clear lack of uniformity in writing style, which cannot be attributed to chronological development in his brief career of fifteen years, even if not all the inscriptions belong to his hand.[93]

88. A. Vaughn, "The Chronicler's Account of Hezekiah: The Relationship of Historical Data to a Theological Interpretation of 2 Chronicles 29–32" (Ph.D. Dissertation, Princeton Theological Seminary, 1996), 22–33.

89. Previously, L. Herr used paleographic dating to date seals to within a quarter of a century (*Scripts of Ancient Northwest Semitic Seals*). The danger of applying that method for such precise dating became evident when Herr mistook two inscriptions from one Ammonite seal (one from the front side and one from the back) as deriving from two separate seals, one of which he dated to the mid-seventh century and the other to the third quarter of the seventh century (pp. 68–69; noted by Naveh in his review of Herr's book, *BASOR* 239 [1980]: 75–76).

90. The Attic inscriptions on the vases are dated, based on the style of the corresponding figured representations, which can be identified to within a period of a decade (H. Immerwahr, *Attic Script: A Survey* [Oxford: Clarendon Press, 1990], 1). Naveh reasons on epigraphic grounds that the archaic Greek alphabet was adopted from the Phoenician in the 11th cent. after which it branched off. His arguments are based on certain letter-forms and the existence of retrograde writing in archaic Greek inscriptions (*Early History of the Alphabet*, 175–186).

91. Immerwahr, *Attic Script*, 2, 38 (e.g. the Amasis Painter).

92. Immerwahr, *Attic Script*, 42, 55.

93. Immerwahr, *Attic Script*, 34–35, fig. 6.

In dating inscriptions paleographically, Immerwahr maintains that the overall stylistic characteristics, and not the script of individual letters are revealing and decisive.[94]

An added impediment to dating Hebrew inscriptions paleographically is the slower development of Hebrew script, compared to that of other West Semitic scripts such as Phoenician or Aramaic. In a comparative study of the evolution of six letters in Phoenician, Hebrew, and Aramaic, Naveh shows that the basic forms of the letters were preserved to a greater extent in Hebrew. It seems that in 250 years of evolution, Hebrew preserved older forms and underwent less change than the Aramaic script did in 150 years. Perhaps due to political and geographical considerations, Hebrew writing was more isolated and remained traditional. Aramaic, for example, was more widespread because beginning in the eighth century it functioned as a *lingua franca*.[95] Slower development of innovative letter forms in Hebrew presents difficulties in identifying the traits of one period over another.

In conclusion, the dating of Hebrew inscribed material—especially seals and seal impressions—purely on paleographical grounds is an approximate science at best. Not only did Hebrew script evolve slowly, but other factors, unrelated to chronological development, influence the precision of this methodology. The following must be taken into account: handwriting peculiarities among contemporaries and even among the works of a single individual; the medium of the inscription and the available writing space; and the existence of intermediate forms that are not identifiable with one specific period. Opinions vary somewhat on the time-span for which paleographical dating sustains a fair degree of accuracy. For seals, generally showing a more formal, less changeable script, dating can be estimated within 100–150 years. In contrast, ostraca, which

94. Immerwahr considers the following features: sequencing of letters; horizontal and vertical spacing; the size of the letters in relationship to available space and the edge of the surface. Sequencing refers to the manner in which the letters are strung together. In the earliest period they are lined up through their middle, like strung pearls. Later, the letters with horizontal tops hang from the top as on a clothes-line. Eventually, the bottoms are lined up in a band script (*Attic Script*, 16–17). Immerwahr also points out that the writing styles should be viewed in relationship to the composition of the adjoining scenes. Stylistic characteristics of different types of Hebrew inscriptions have not been fully explored. Especially in the case of seals it remains uncertain what effect the space for engraving and the iconographic features, which were probably engraved prior to the text by another craftsman, have on the script of the text.

95. J. Naveh, "The Scripts in Palestine and Transjordan in the Iron Age" in *NEATC*, 278–279.

exhibit more cursive forms, can be dated more narrowly to perhaps 50 years.[96] But, even with these guidelines, caution must be exercised in using this method and, whenever possible, outside evidence should support the paleographic model. One particular example of the precariousness of paleographical dating is the Tel Fakhariyah bilingual inscription. Although paleographically the Aramaic script fits an eleventh century date, analyses of the cuneiform and historical data suggest a much later ninth-century date.[97]

Prosopography

Prosopography, the study of social, career, and familial connections of people,[98] is valuable in this investigation for the purposes of identifying families of royal functionaries mentioned in the Bible and connecting PNs appearing in epigraphic material with biblical personages. These types of identifications and relationships are often constructed by scholars on the basis of scant evidence, sometimes simply a common PN. Admittedly, the biblical and archaeological data rarely provide sufficient information to substantiate identity and filiation. Nonetheless, methodological criteria need to guide such associations.[99]

In reference to epigraphic sources, N. Avigad proposed guidelines for identifying persons whose names appear on seals, bullae, and ostraca with individuals of the same name known from the Bible.[100] Since the frequency of certain Israelite PNs is high in the Iron Age II and simply sharing a name does not constitute sufficient data, Avigad advanced three criteria by which to establish a sound identification. In addition to a corresponding PN, there should be (1) a matching title or epithet and (2) a genealogy of three generations and (3) chronological

96. Naveh estimates a range of 50 years for ostraca and 150 years for seals (private communication 7/95); Vaughn suggests a 100 year range for seals ("The Chronicler's Account of Hezekiah," 36–37).

97. For a discussion, see most recently, S. Kaufman, "The Pitfalls of Typology: On the Early History of the Alphabet," *HUCA* 57 (1986): 1–14.

98. For the uses of prosopography as a historical method, see S. Hornblower and A. Spawforth, "Prosopography" in *The Oxford Classical Dictionary* 3rd ed. (New York: Oxford University Press, 1996), 1262.

99. The problem is directly addressed in a recent Ph.D. Dissertation by Lawrence Mykytiuk ("Identifying Biblical Persons in Hebrew Inscriptions and Two Stelae from before the Persian Era," University of Wisconsin–Madison, 1998) in which he attempts to develop a sound methodology for identifying persons in inscriptions. As grounds for such a system, Mykytiuk discusses the reasons for previous misidentifications, such as the association of the seal of יתם with King Jotham and the name יוכן on four seal impressions inscribed לאליקם נער יוכן with King Jehoiachin (pp. 16–28).

100. N. Avigad, "On the Identification of Persons Mentioned in Hebrew Epigraphic Sources," *EI* 19 (1987): 237 (Hebrew).

synchronism. Thus, if a seal is inscribed with a PN including two generations of ancestors plus an official title and is securely dated, the seal owner can be identified with a biblical personage bearing the same PN and title who lived in the same period. Unfortunately, with one problematic exception, no example exists from the extant corpus of archaeological inscriptions where all the above criteria are present together. The exception, two bullae impressed with the inscription לברכיהו בן נריהו הספר, "belonging to *brkyhw* son of *nryhw* the scribe," identified with Baruch the scribe of Jeremiah,[101] presents difficulties because the bullae were acquired on the antiquities market and their authenticity has been called into question.[102] In all other cases for which similar identifications have been postulated, both for provenienced and unprovenienced inscriptions, Avigad's criteria are only partially satisfied. For example, the bullae of Gemariahu son of Shaphan and Azariahu son of Hilkiahu and the seal belonging to Seriahu son of Neriahu, in contrast to the biblical data (Gemariahu, a scribe [Jer 36:10]; Azariahu, a priest [1 Chr 9:11]; Seriahu, a quartermaster [Jer 51:59]), do not include titles with which to associate them, nor do they include the names of their grandfathers.[103] Another bulla, that of Jerahme'el son of the king, is unprovenienced; even if authentic, its date can only be estimated based on paleographic typology since no RN is included in the titulary (Jer 36:26).[104] Similarly, the bulla stamped with the seal of Gedaliahu the house minister cannot be connected with certainty to the biblical Gedaliah son of Ahikam (2 Kgs 25:22) because the seal lacks a patronym, while the reference to Gedaliah in the Bible lacks the title.[105] In this case the bulla could actually refer to another official by that name, perhaps Gedaliah son of Pashhur (Jer 38:1).

In his dissertation, L. Mykytiuk grapples with some of the pitfalls of Avigad's criteria. Consequently, he adds a fourth criterion, socio-political classification (i.e. nationality or ethnicity), and devises a system based on relative degrees of strength and precision. Potential identifications can fall into six grades—S (reliable), 3, 2, 1, 0, D (disqualified)—depending on answers to three categories of

101. N. Avigad, "Baruch the Scribe and Jerahme'el the King's Son," *IEJ* 28 (1978): 52–56; *Hebrew Bullae*, 28–29; Deutsch and Heltzer, *Forty*, 37–38.

102. *WSS*, 12 no. 417.

103. Y. Shiloh, "A Group of Hebrew Bullae from the City of David," *IEJ* 36 (1986): 33–34; T. Schneider, "Azaryahu Son of Ḥilkiahu (High Priest?) on a City of David Bulla," *IEJ* 38 (1988): 139–141; N. Avigad, "The Seal of Seriah, Son of Neriah," *EI* 14 (1978): 86–87. The seal of Seriah is unprovenienced and is problematic on that account as well.

104. Paleographic dating is not more exact than a 100 year range (see Paleographic Dating, above).

105. Avigad, "Baruch the Scribe and Jerahme'el the King's Son," 52–56; *Hebrew Bullae*, 27–28; R. de Vaux, "Le sceau de Godolias, maitre du palais," *RB* 45 (1936): 96–102.

questions: (1) How reliable is the inscriptional data? (2) Does the general setting of the inscription permit a match between the inscriptional person and the biblical person? (3) How strongly do specific data in the inscription count for or against an identification? The first category includes criteria such as means of acquisition, provenience, and authenticity. The second category deals with the dating, language, and socio-political classification of the inscription. The third set of criteria factors in matches between biblical and epigraphic texts affecting PNs, filiation, titles etc.[106] Unfortunately, the nature of the extant corpus of Hebrew inscriptions is such that only a handful of identifications of Israelites qualify as reliable (grade S or 3). The dependability of most other potentially reliable identifications hinges on the authentication of the objects themselves.[107]

When establishing filial relationships between individuals mentioned in the Bible, the data are sometimes less tenuous. Evidence of families of royal officials is attested from the periods of the united and divided monarchies. Certain professions, in particular those of scribe and priest, seem to have been hereditary, due to the nature of the office. Still, difficulties persist in establishing positive identifications, especially for functionaries who served during the United Monarchy in the reigns of Saul, David and Solomon. For example, Azariah and Zabud, respectively Solomon's minister over the prefects and king's "friend" (1 Kgs 4:5), carry the same patronym, Nathan, but it is unclear whether they are brothers and whether this Nathan, or one of these two Nathans, was the prophet at David's court (2 Sam 7). Several other uncertain relationships are found among Davidic functionaries.[108]

More secure data are available in connection with several prominent court families in Judah in the reigns of Josiah, Jehoiakim, and Zedekiah. Names of royal officials that predominate from the mid-seventh to early sixth centuries belong to the families of Shaphan, Neriah, Hilkiah, and Achbor. In a number of cases their patronymics include a grandfather's name (e.g. Shaphan [2 Kgs 22:3], Micaiah [Jer 36:11], Gedaliah [2 Kgs 25:22], Baruch [Jer 32:12], Seriah [51:59]), implying perhaps that they descend from a long line of dignitaries.[109] Furthermore, the fact that they appear in narrative contexts facilitates defining

106. Mykytiuk, "Identifying Biblical Persons in Hebrew Inscriptions," 34–65.

107. Mykytiuk lists only nine reliable identifications of Israelites ("Identifying Biblical Persons in Hebrew Inscriptions," 267–270, 272–273). These include two unprovenienced seals discovered in the mid-19th century (p. 268 n. 4) before any forger would have known the nuances of paleographical distinctions.

108. See Table C where uncertain relationships are marked by (F).

109. Since the status of the grandfather is often unknown, the reason for his inclusion in the patronymic is conjectural. In the case of Gedaliah, we know that his grandfather, Shaphan, was a minister of state.

their filiation and roles at the royal court. Yet even for this late material reservations exist. For example, Jehoiachin's mother, Nechushta daughter of Elnathan (2 Kgs 24:8), may be the daughter of one of Jehoiakim's prominent officials, Elnathan son of Achbor (Jer 26:22; 36:12), though the relationship is dubious.

One assumption commonly made in studies of government officials is that since the circle of Israelite royal functionaries was relatively small, a name plus a patronym is sufficient to verify a person's identity if chronological correspondence is secure. (Evidently, due to scant data, Avigad's methodology, while ideal, at present is not practical for identifying persons appearing in epigraphic sources.) However, before the above supposition is accepted as valid, it requires testing. In this connection, findings from a study of the onomasticon of Old Babylonian Sippar are interesting. R. Harris found that at Sippar no two men with the same name and patronym are attested from the same generation. Although it cannot be substantiated, she suggests that, for practical reasons, a child was not given the same name as another person in the community bearing an identical patronym. Thereby, there would only be one X, the son of Y.[110] One might suppose that a similar custom was practiced in Israel for the same pragmatic reasons. But even if this practice indeed existed in Israel, the problems encountered by scholars in their attempts to identify government officials are not necessarily solved because it cannot be assumed that such a system could encompass more than one city and its environs. Among royal functionaries, even those residing at court, probably there were natives of towns and cities outside the capital who could have borne identical names and patronyms. Nevertheless, before discarding this possibility it seems worthwhile to examine the names of officials appearing in the Bible and in epigraphic sources from approximately a single generation.

The biblical lists of officials are fragmentary, usually mentioning a small number of royal functionaries for any one reign. An exception, a corpus of close to eighty persons, is attested from the reign of David.[111] Interestingly, only three names are held by more than one individual and these are all distinguishable by their patronyms or epithets.[112] The fact that this onomasticon derived from

110. R. Harris, "Notes on the Nomenclature of Old Babylonian Sippar," *JCS* 24 (1972): 104. Based on an extant draft register containing hundreds of names, she posits that there existed in Sippar a central office in which names were registered, both for conscription purposes and as a name registry that could be consulted when naming a baby.

111. See Table A-1.

112. Jonathan son of Uzziah (1 Chr 27:25) and Jonathan, David's uncle (27:32); Benaiah son of Jehoiada (2 Sam 8:18) and Benaiah the Pirathonite (1 Chr 27:14); Jashobeam son of

the early monarchic period contains many non-Yahwistic PNs and represents a wide pool of Northwest Semitic names, could account for the rarity in duplication. Biblical data show, however, that even in later periods, when PNs are almost purely Israelite, this phenomenon is evident; those few names that do repeat are attached to distinct patronyms. One anomaly is the name of a royal official(s) in the reign of Hezekiah, Shebnah, who appears without a patronymic as scribe (2 Kgs 18:18) and house minister (Isa 22:15).[113] Thus, it seems that generally the identities of functionaries listed in the Bible are discernable, although, as shown from the case of Azariah and Zabud, who both bear the patronym Nathan, filiation is not always distinguishable.

An examination of the archaeological data for this issue can be accomplished best from the collections of names derived from two groups of seal impressions: the personal, seal-impressed *lmlk* handles and the bullae from the City of David.[114] Of the bullae from the City of David, 45 out of 49 are inscribed with PNs, of which 43 are legible. Taking duplicates into account, this collection represents a minimum of 38 and a maximum of 41 individual seal-owners.[115] There are seven recurring names: שפטיהו, אלשמע, שמעיהו, גמריהו, ברכיהו, עזריהו, טבשלום. Each name belongs to two or three persons who are differentiated by their distinct patronyms, although admittedly two patronyms are noticeably similar, זכר and בנזכר.[116] In one case an identical name plus patronym appears on two bullae

Hachmoni (11:11) and Jashobeam son of Zabdiel (27:2). The last pair may represent one person, as indicated by the context of the two lists.

113. Most scholars assume without adequate reason that the same individual held both positions (see Chapter 4–A).

114. The *lmlk* handles are mostly provenienced and have been dated to a period of one generation, the last quarter of the eighth century (Vaughn, "The Chronicler's Account of Hezekiah," 130–133, 146–147). The bullae from the City of David were discovered *in situ* and are dated to the last years of the Judean monarchy (Shiloh, "A Group of Hebrew Bullae from the City of David," 16–38; Y. Shoham, "A Group of Hebrew Bullae from Yigal Shiloh's Excavations in the City of David" in H. Geva, ed. *Ancient Jerusalem Revealed* [Jerusalem: Israel Exploration Society, 1994], 55–61). The corpus of Avigad's bullae is not considered here because it is unprovenienced.

115. For a complete list of inscribed bullae, see Shoham, "A Group of Hebrew Bullae from Yigal Shiloh's Excavations in the City of David," 57–58.

116. Five names belongs to two persons each; three persons are named שמעיהו. Three bullae belong to טבשלם and, although the same individual probably owned the three seals in question, that conclusion is uncertain. The bullae read: לטבשלם בן זכר, לטבשלם בן בנזכר and [לטבשלם] בן זכר הרפא. The patronym בנזכר could represent an error of the seal cutter, בנ occurring as the result of dittography. On the other hand, the name בנזכר may belong to a different person, the element בנ being part of the name (cf. בנגלגל, Arad ostracon no. 49). The professional title רפא, "physician," may belong to טבשלם as reconstructed or to another person.

impressed with different seals. According to Y. Shiloh, the similar script indicates that they were cut by the same artisan and therefore probably belonged to one owner.[117] Data from the onomasticon of this one Judean city, although relatively limited, imply that Harris' observation about name-giving in OB Sippar may be applicable to Jerusalem. The possible exception from the Jerusalem archive, if in fact those two seals belonged to two persons who simply employed the same seal cutter, could indicate that one seal owner was a former non-Jerusalemite or that the document sealed by the bulla was sent from another city.

In contrast to the evidence from Jerusalem, the collection of names gleaned from the personal seal impressions on the *lmlk* handles paints a somewhat different picture. This corpus of seal impressions reveals 54 distinct seals displaying the PNs of at least 36 different officials (seven of those appear only on unprovenienced handles).[118] Several individuals bear the same name or a form thereof but can be distinguished from each other by their patronyms.[119] Certain names are especially popular and repeat more than once. For example, a minimum of five officials (approx. 14%) bear the name נחם, מנחם or תנחם and at least three (approx. 8%) are named שלם or משלם. Notably, in 12 cases an identical name plus patronym appears on two or more distinct seals. Vaughn assumes that this phenomenon indicates that these 12 individuals owned multiple seals.[120] Admittedly, this possibility exists, but it is equally conceivable that these 12 PNs belonged to more than 12 individuals. That is to say, two or more persons bore the same name and patronym. It may be significant that among those names a few appear both as full forms and as hypocoristic forms.[121] Conceivably, a person could have one seal engraved with his full name and another with a shortened name or nickname. These variations, however, could actually signify marks of distinction between individuals who serve in the state-administration but bear identical PNs. As shown, the name נחם, or a form thereof, was extremely popular in the latter eighth century. The officials whose names are

117. Shiloh, "A Group of Hebrew Bullae from the City of David," 29.

118. A total of 266 handles were discovered to date, of which 184 are provenienced (Vaughn, "The Chronicler's Account of Hezekiah," 219). The seals of three persons do not include a patronym, although one includes a title: לנרא (p. 283), לעבדי (p. 284), לאליקם נער יוכן (p. 277). A fourth name without a patronym but including a title appears on an unprovenienced handle, which may belong to the *lmlk* group: לשבניהו בן המלך (p. 285).

119. For the corpus of names, see Vaughn, "The Chronicler's account of Hezekiah," Appendix III, 276–289.

120. Vaughn, "The Chronicler's Account of Hezekiah," 162.

121. For example, תנחם or נחם/מנחם, שבנא/שבניהו and צפן/צפניהו.

impressed on *lmlk* handles may have originated from different communities in Judah.[122] In that case, there is a good chance of duplication of PNs.

The above evidence indicates that in a number of instances more information than is currently available is needed to positively identify persons whose names appear in inscriptions and to establish filial connections between biblical personages. However, despite uncertainties arising from the deficient data, tentative associations can be constructed based on PNs that minimally include a patronym. In fact, due to the popularity of certain names, for the same generation a patronym is probably more revealing than a title. While this exercise has exposed obstacles inherent in interpreting the extant material, simultaneously it has raised the possibility that in antiquity a system existed for naming children within a single community that limited confusion to the extent that present-day scholars can reconstruct provisional identifications.

Reference Tables A and C contain names of government officials and functionaries gleaned from the biblical and epigraphic records. Table A–1 is a chronological index of titles and PNs from the Bible and provenienced epigraphic records grouped by reigns of Israelite monarchs; Table A–2 lists published unprovenienced material showing titles; and Table C consists of genealogies of court families. In most cases, persons attested on seals or bullae without titles and without biblical correlates cannot be safely considered government functionaries, although it is realized that many probably were.[123] An exception is the corpus of names known from the personal seal-impressions on the *lmlk* handles. In keeping with the findings presented above, tentative identifications and relationships are constructed based on PNs inclusive of patronyms for persons appearing in the Bible or in the epigraphic and biblical records. When a particular name lacks both a patronym and title but where a link is still feasible on the strength of the biblical or archaeological context, the connection is attempted with its weakness noted.

---

122. See the discussion of the *lmlk* operation, including these officials (Chapter 6–A).

123. Seals were employed for private personal uses, as well as for business purposes and as status symbols.

3

Status Related Titles

A. בן המלך – Son of the King

A title clearly associated with rank derived from genealogy is בן המלך (*bn hmlk*), "son of the king." This appellation is included in the present study for two reasons: (1) The title is borne by biblical characters who are involved in administrative roles. (2) Scholars remain divided on the definition of the title, most accepting a literal interpretation but a few still perceiving it as a functional rather than a genealogical designation.

Hebrew Corpus

In the biblical text בן המלך is attested in reference to nine men; similarly בת המלך (*bt hmlk*), "daughter of the king," alludes to two women. Often this title refers explicitly to known offspring of a monarch: Amnon son of David (2 Sam 13:4); Abshalom son of David (18:12, 20); Solomon son of David (Ps 72:1); Jezebel daughter of Ethbaal king of the Sidonians (2 Kgs 9:34); Jehosheba daughter of Joram (11:2); Joash son of Ahaziah (11:4, 12 = 2 Chr 23:3, 11); Jotham son of Azariah (2 Kgs 15:5). When mentioned as a collective, בני המלך (*bny hmlk*), "sons of the king," or בנות המלך (*bnwt hmlk*), "daughters of the king," remain unnamed: Gideon's brothers (Judg 8:18);[1] David's sons (2 Sam 13:23–36; 1 Kgs 1:9–25 [specifies Adoniah's brothers]; 1 Chr 27:32; 29:24); Ahab's family (2 Kgs 10:6–13); sons of Ahaziah (11:2); Zedekiah's daughters or other princesses (Jer 41:10; 43:6). In four instances the בן המלך named is not a known prince and his genealogy is uncertain: Joash (1 Kgs 22:26 = 2 Chr 18:25); Jerahmiel (Jer 36:26); Malchiah (38:6); Maaseiah (2 Chr 28:7). Occasionally, the expression, plural or singular, is utilized to designate princes or princesses as a special group in society without reference to their identity (2 Sam 9:11; 13:18; Zeph 1:8; Ps 45:14).

1. Gideon's brothers, although not true princes in the sense that their father was a king, were probably the sons of a local chief.

The archaeological record, counting provenienced and unprovenienced items, consists of 18 Hebrew seals and seal impressions of persons whose PN is followed by the title בן המלך. In addition, one seal and one bulla bear a PN plus the title בת המלך.[2] Unfortunately, only two of the 20 pieces derive from controlled excavations: לגאליהו בן המלך from Beth Zur and ל]שבניהו [בן] המלך from Lachish; of the two only the latter was discovered in a clear archaeological context.

Significance of the Title

The epithet בן המלך literally translates as, "son of the king," a designation that indicates either the son of the reigning monarch or of a predecessor. Since בן in Biblical Hebrew is inclusive of grandson (e.g. Gen 31:28, Ruth 4:17), the title possibly could have been conferred on princes and their offspring for several generations. This seemingly simple definition of בן המלך, however, may be complicated by several factors. (1) As mentioned above, four persons in the Bible entitled בן המלך are not associated with specific kings. (2) It seems that these four individuals hold minor administrative positions at court. (3) The בן המלך seal-owners are never connected with a RN. As a result, scholarship is divided on the true significance of this title. Clermont-Ganneau was the first to question whether the so called "son of the king" was really a member of the royal family.[3] His supposition that בן המלך can refer to royal functionaries not of royal blood was adopted and expanded by de Vaux, Yeivin, and Brin.[4] Conversely, those who regard this title solely as indicative of a descendant of a king, include, among others, Rainey, Lemaire, and, most recently, Barkay, and Avishur and Heltzer.[5] Avigad, who wavered for a time between the two opinions, also supports the latter stand.[6]

---

2. Seventeen seals and seal impressions are listed in G. Barkay, "A Bulla of Ishmael, the King's Son," *BASOR* 290–291 (1993): 109–114. His seal #8, למנשה בן המלך (Table 1, p. 111), is not included in this corpus because based on paleography and iconography it is considered Moabite. An additional seal is found in *WSS* (no. 14); recently Deutsch published another bulla in *Messages from the Past*, 65 and a seal in *Windows to the Past*, 49–51. See Table A-2.

3. C. Clermont-Ganneau, "Le sceau de Obadyahu, functionnaire royal israelite," *Recueil d'archeologie orientale* 1 (1888): 33–36.

4. De Vaux, *Ancient Israel*, 119–120; Yeivin, "Peqidut," 553; G. Brin, "The Title בן (ה)מלך and its Parallels," *AION* 29 (1969): 433–465. M. Görg reintroduced these issues in a recent article that focuses on the Egyptian evidence, but he hesitates to draw similar conclusions about the meaning of the Hebrew title ("Zum Titel *BN HMLK* ['Königssohn']," *BN* 29 [1985]: 7–11).

5. A. Rainey, "The Prince and the Pauper," *UF* 7 (1975): 427–432; A. Lemaire, "Note sur le titre *bn hmlk* dans l'ancien Israël," *Semitica* 29 (1979): 59–65; Barkay, "A Bulla of

Although the evidence overwhelmingly favors the more literal interpretation of the designation בן המלך, arguments against such an interpretation focus on the place the בן המלך occupies in lists and the lowly police-like duties ascribed to three persons so entitled: Joash, Jerahmiel and Malchiah.[7] A scrutiny of the data, however, shows that in lists of individuals, only one בן המלך, Joash, is recorded in second place, after Amon the mayor of Samaria (1 Kgs 22:26). This anomaly may be a consequence of age or other indeterminable factors.[8] In all other cases the בן המלך heads the list of officials. Notably, Maaseiah, the בן המלך killed in war, is listed first preceding even the נגיד הבית, "ruler of the house," Azrikam, indisputably one of the highest court officials (2 Chr 28:7).[9] In the group reference to ministers and princes in Zeph 1:8, the fact that the collective בני המלך is mentioned following the title שרים, may again be related to age. The prophet Zephaniah simply predicts that on the Day of YHWH, the princes as well as the rich court dignitaries will be punished.[10] If, as Brin maintains, that usage proves that the title בן המלך designates a palace office,[11] then why are these particular functionaries distinguished from the שרים, other royal officials? Only if they are indeed royal offspring, thereby belonging to a different social class, does their separate grouping serve a purpose.

One duty of a בן המלך involved the incarceration of political prisoners. Joash as בן המלך, together with Amon the mayor of Samaria, is charged with the imprisonment of the prophet Micaiah (1 Kgs 22:26–27). Likewise, Jerahmiel the בן המלך and two other officials arrest Jeremiah the prophet and his scribe Baruch (Jer 36:26). Jeremiah is confined a second time in the pit of Malchiah בן המלך in the prison compound (38:6). As Rainey aptly notes, these policing functions are not exclusive of royalty and should not be minimized.[12] According to the accounts, these prophets publicly opposed the king and thereby threatened the stability of the government, possibly qualifying their acts of rebellion as capital

---

Ishmael, the King's Son," 110–112; Avishur and Heltzer, *Studies on the Royal Administration*, 51–54. Avishur and Heltzer emphasize the view that the title בן המלך could apply to any person of royal genealogy, regardless of whether they were an actual son of a king.

6. N. Avigad, "A Seal of Manasseh Son of the King," *IEJ* 13 (1963): 133–136; "A Group of Hebrew Seals," *EI* 9 (1969): 9 (Hebrew); "Baruch the Scribe and Jerahmeel the King's Son," 54–55; "Titles and Symbols on Hebrew Seals," *EI* 15 (1981): 304; *Hebrew Bullae*, 27–28.

7. Yeivin, "Peqidut," 553; Brin, "The Title בן (ה)מלך and its Parallels," 434–435.

8. Rainey, "The Prince and the Pauper," 428.

9. Curiously, this example is not cited as indicative of status by proponents of the theory that the בן המלך was a low-ranking official. For the נגיד הבית see Chapter 4–A.

10. Lemaire, "Note sur le titre *bn hmlk* dans l'ancien Israël," 62.

11. Brin, "The Title בן (ה)מלך and its Parallels," 438–439.

12. Rainey, "The Prince and the Pauper," 428.

offenses (Exod 22:27; 1 Kgs 21:9–14). Moreover, it is conceivable that Joash, Jerahmiel, and Malchiah were not simply police guards, but held judicial roles in the central government.

Another argument put forth by proponents of the theory that the designation "son(s) of the king" can include non-royal, minor officials, is that comparable titles belonging to commoners occur in non-Israelite sources. Brin cites numerous examples from Ugaritic, Hittite and Canaanite records as evidence because in those texts the genealogy of certain persons entitled "son(s) of the king" is ambiguous.[13] The royal lineage of several of these princes, however, has been restored by Rainey[14] and, while it is true that occasionally the lack of a patronym creates confusion, not a single case exists where the genealogy of any one of these individuals proves that he/she is **not** of royal blood.

Mesopotamian and Egyptian Evidence

In Mesopotamia as well, the equivalent of בן המלך, DUMU LUGAL/*mār šarri*, explicitly signifies a son of a king or another member of the royal family. Interestingly, in the Neo-Assyrian and Neo-Babylonian periods the title *mār šarri* is used primarily to designate the "crown prince."[15] During the reigns of certain kings, *mār šarri* actually refers exclusively to the designated successor, while other princes are cited by name only. This limited usage is attested in letters and reports, and in legal and administrative texts from Nineveh dated to the seventh century.[16] These future kings, no matter how young, appear to already possess their own bodyguards, palace officials, and charioteers. Similarly, according to the Bible when two of David's sons, Absholom and Adoniah, declare themselves king-designate, each, in turn, acquires an outfitted chariot with runners (2 Sam 15:1; 1 Kgs 1:5). Apparently crown princes were distinguished from their siblings by royal pomp and, in certain periods in Assyria, by title as well.

The Egyptian equivalent of בן המלך is *s3 nswt*. Royal offspring in Egypt were involved in various aspects of the administrative organization. The chronicle of prince Osorkon, the eldest son of Takeloth II (22nd Dynasty, mid-ninth century), is especially instructive in this regard. Prince Osorkon held various civil,

13. Brin, "The Title בן (ה)מלך and its Parallels," 440–451.

14. Rainey, "The Prince and the Pauper," 429–431.

15. *CAD* Š/2, 105–112.

16. T. Kwasman and S. Parpola, *Legal Transactions of the Royal Court of Nineveh, Part I Tiglath-Pileser III through Esarhaddon* (Helsinki: Helsinki University Press, 1991), xxvii-xxix. The meaning "crown prince" for *mār šarri* is certain in a number of texts from the reign of Esarhaddon: nos. 283, 287, 288, 297–299. Even references to Assurbanipal's eldest son, who was too young to have been officially proclaimed "crown prince," seem to imply this status (p. xxviii).

military, and religious positions of authority, among them governor of Upper Egypt, army chief and first prophet of Amun. He was called to subdue a rebellion in Thebes, to subsequently restore order, to punish the rebels, and to appoint new officials.[17] Osorkon's judicial powers are emphasized in virtues attributed to him: "Foremost in judging the pleas (words) that reach his ears. Rules in the palace come into effect according to his understanding concerning them."[18]

While *s3 nswt* generally signifies a royal offspring, it is also found in titularies of persons who are not sons of a Pharaoh. A brief survey of the honorific usage of this title in Egyptian history will elucidate its unique application and show why this particular usage should not be applied to the Israelite title.[19]

In the Third Dynasty of the Old Kingdom (27th century), high officials of royal birth were distinguished from non-royal office-holders by the addition of *s3 nswt* following their official title. At that time, the office of vizier, the highest and most prestigious, was regularly held by a king's son. By the Fourth Dynasty, the titulary of every vizier included the designation *s3 nswt*, even those who were not true princes but rather more distant relations of the royal family. Eventually *s3 nswt* remained part of the titulary of certain offices regardless of the pedigree of its bearers. From the end of the Fourth Dynasty until the beginning of the 12th Dynasty (1991 BCE), administrative positions appear to have been held by commoners. In general, this practice continued through the Ramesside Period (19th and 20th Dynasties, ca. 1300–1070) with the notable exception, initiated in the 12th Dynasty, of the office of High Priest of Memphis, which was borne by true princes. In the 17th and 18th Dynasties the honorary epithet "son of the king" or "first son of the king," *s3 nswt tpy*, was conferred on certain priests of the cults of Nechbet, Amun, and others, and on some military commanders.[20] Of the latter, the most famous are the viceroys of Kush of the 18th–20th Dynasties. Their titularies always include the designation *s3 nswt n kš*, "king's son of Kush," most often followed by the title *mr ḫ3swt rsyt*, "overseer of southern lands." It is unclear whether the viceroy of Kush was ever a true prince or if the title protected bearers from the local authority. In any case, it disappears after the reign of Rameses XI with the end of the empire period.[21] Later, during the Third Intermediate Period, the Libyan chieftains of the 22nd

17. R.A. Caminos, *The Chronicle of Prince Osorkon* (*AnOr* 37; Rome: Pontifical Biblical Institute, 1958), 26–54.

18. Caminos, *Chronicle of Prince Osorkon*, 78, l. 4.

19. For a comprehensive study of the designation *s3 nswt*, see B. Schmitz, *Untersuchungen zum Titel s3 njśwt "Königssohn,"* (GMBH; Bonn: Habelt, 1976).

20. Schmitz, *Untersuchungen zum Titel s3-njśwt "Königssohn,"* 267–287, 327–333.

21. L. Habachi, "Königssohn von Kusch" in *Lexikon* 3, 630–635. An exception exists

Dynasty who governed in the Delta did adopt royal titles such as "prince." Similar phenomena took place in the south under the contemporaneous 23rd Dynasty. These title-bearers, however, were royal descendants of one line or another who functioned as semi-independent or independent rulers.[22]

The potentially confusing use of *sꜣ nswt* in the New Kingdom may be one reason why in the late 18th and 19th Dynasties the title was often qualified by other epithets. Crown princes can be distinguished by descriptives tagged on to *sꜣ nswt,* such as, *tpy,* "first," and/or *rpꜥt,* "heir," while other princes are designated *n-ẖt.f,* "of his (the king's) body" or *ḥꜣty-ꜥ,* another term for "prince."[23] There seems to be no valid reason, however, to connect the honorific title *sꜣ nswt* in the titulary of certain high Egyptian officials with the Israelite title בן המלך or to speculate that a practice similar to the Egyptian one existed in Israel.[24] As shown, the Egyptian epithet was part of a longer title that appears to have been conferred on office-holders in its entirety even when they no longer represented royalty. In addition, in Hebrew no other designations for "son(s) of the king" beside בן המלך are attested to differentiate true princes from non-royal title-bearers. Finally, the so-called low-level officials entitled בן המלך certainly cannot be compared to the Viceroy of Kush, one of the highest Pharaonic officers.

Roles of the בן המלך

In light of the discussion above, it seems safe to assume that bearers of the title בן המלך were members of Israelite royal families, many of whom took part in the state administration. As previously mentioned, the activities of three sons of kings, Joash, Jerahmiel and Malchiah, could be indicative of judicial roles. These are comparable to Egyptian princely functions gleaned from the chronicle of prince Osorkon. Traditionally, in Israel the king occupied the position of chief justice. He was entrusted with the most difficult cases and a sign of a wise king was his just decisions. Notably, when Nathan the prophet rebukes David for his affair with Bathsheba, he does so by means of a parabolic case presented to the king for judgment (2 Sam 12:1–6). Similarly, Joab the army commander reconciles David with his son Absalom by means of the case of the widow of Tekoa, who appeals her son's capital sentence for fratricide before the king (14:1–11). Toward the end of David's reign, when Absalom plots rebellion,

from the beginning of the 21st Dynasty, when Smendes' daughter carries this title to maintain her claim to revenues appropriated to this office-holder.

22. O'Connor, "New Kingdom and Third Intermediate Period," 232–242.

23. Schmitz, *Untersuchungen zum Titel sꜣ-njśwt "Königssohn,"* 315–318.

24. Contra Yeivin, "Peqidut," 553.

he succeeds in swaying a portion of the populace to his camp by promising to hear their legal disputes and to provide justice (2 Sam 15:1–6). Solomon's wisdom is epitomized in his judicious ruling in the case of the two prostitutes (1 Kgs 3:16–28). In reference to the crown prince Jotham son of Azariah, it says: ויותם בן המלך...שפט את עם הארץ, "Jotham the son of the king was judging/ruling the people of the land" (2 Kgs 15:5; cf. 2 Chr 26:21 [בנו]). Even if the verb שפט is defined in a more general sense, "to rule," judicial jurisdiction was inclusive of kingly duties and Jotham as co-regent probably assumed those responsibilities from his ailing father. It is quite possible that royal sons participated in various aspects of the judiciary, both in key and less important matters.[25]

Overall, the biblical text contains little information on the subject of offices held by the king's sons and other princes. Most of the extant data come from the more detailed accounts of the United Monarchy. Saul's son Jonathan commanded an army unit (1 Sam 14), a position probably commonly held by princes. Joab, David's nephew, served as his chief army commander (2 Sam 8:16); two other nephews, Amasa and Abishai, were army officers (2 Sam 17:25; 23:18). According to the Deuteronomist, David even appointed his sons as priests (2 Sam 8:18).[26] The Deuteronomist also mentions that Solomon appointed two of his sons-in-law, Ben-abinadab and Ahimaaz, as district prefects (1 Kgs 4:11, 15). One datum from Chronicles referring to the period of the Divided Monarchy mentions that Rehoboam assigned his sons to fortified towns throughout Judah and Benjamin (2 Chr 11:23).[27] Since the princes' responsibilities are not delineated, one can only assume that they resembled mayorships or the like.

בן המלך *Seal Owners*

As mentioned above, the relatively large collection of 12 seals, seven bullae,

---

25. In the pre-monarchic period the chief also seems to have functioned with the aid of his sons. Samuel, for example, in his old age appointed his sons to rule/judge in different areas of the country. That their duties included judicial responsibilities is evident from the writer's negative evaluation of their deeds. Apparently, two of Samuel's sons, Joel and Abijah, who served in Beer-sheba, accepted bribes and perverted justice: ויקחו שחד ויטו משפט (1 Sam 8:1–3).

26. But the Chronicler, whose ideology opposes priests not of priestly lineage, states instead that David's sons were his chief officers (1 Chr 18:17). Japhet suggests that the verse in Samuel was already corrupted by the time the Chronicler received it (*I & II Chronicles*, 352). In that case, neither source may be reliable.

27. Since this statement follows Rehoboam's announcement that he chose his son Abijah as successor (2 Chr 11:22), it is assumed that those sons who were not destined for the throne were the ones assigned to different towns in Judah and Benjamin.

and one seal-impressed jar handle showing the titles בן המלך and בת המלך (one seal and one bulla) is unfortunately composed primarily of unprovenienced finds (18 of 20). Still, certain proposals made in publications of the unprovenienced items deserve attention. Most tempting for scholars is the identification of PNs on the בן המלך seals with princes known from the Bible. Five seals and one bulla from among the unprovenienced pieces, based on PNs and paleographic dating, have been tentatively connected to biblical personages: מנשה; יהואחז; ירחמאל; אלשמע; ישמעאל; and פדיהו. Manasseh and Jehoahaz are identified as the Judean kings by those names (2 Kgs 20:21; 23:30): Manasseh the son of Hezekiah and Jehoahaz the son of Josiah.[28] The other four names are associated with princes who did not ascend the throne. Jerahmeel appears in the Bible as the official ordered by Jehoiakim to arrest Jeremiah (Jer 36:26).[29] Elishama and Ishmael are presented as grandfather and grandson (2 Kgs 25:25 = Jer 41:1);[30] Ishmael son of Nethaniah son of Elishama, a descendent of the royal family, led a rebellion against Gedaliah son of Ahikam, the governor of Judah appointed by the Babylonians after the fall of Jerusalem in 587/86 BCE. Pediah is mentioned by the Chronicler as a son of Jehoiachin (1 Chr 3:17–19).[31]

Following the methodological guidelines presented above, the aforementioned associations are problematic. Aside from the ever-present possibility of forgery,[32] the identifications are based on a single name. None of the בן המלך seals include a patronym, which, at least in cases of crown princes, would be expected to show a RN. Noticeably, several PNs repeat on two or more distinct seals dated to the seventh century, for example, נריהו (3)[33] and גאליהו (2).[34] This

28. N. Avigad, "The Contribution of Hebrew Seals to the Understanding of Israelite Religion and Society" in P.D. Miller, P.K. McCarter and P.D. Hanson eds. *Ancient Israelite Religion. Essays in Honor of F.M. Cross* (Philadelphia: Fortress Press, 1987), 202–203; "A Group of Hebrew Seals," 9. It should be noted that Avigad questions these identifications for various reasons: in the case of Manasseh, his young age, and in reference to Jehoahaz, the rooster symbol on the seal.

29. Avigad, "Baruch the Scribe and Jerahmeel the King's Son," 52–56.

30. A.H. Sayce, "Hebrew Inscriptions of the Pre-Exilic Period," *The Academy* (Aug 2, 1890): 94. Barkay, "A Bulla of Ishmael, the King's Son," 109–114. Sayce discusses the seal of אלשמע בן המלך.

31. N. Avigad, "A New Seal of a 'Son of the King'," *Michmanim* 6 (1992): 27*-31*.

32. The authenticity of seven of these unprovenienced seals has already been called into question: לגדיהו בן המלך, ליהואחז בן המלך, ליראיהו בן המלך, לנריהו בן המלך, לפדיהו בן המלך, למעדנה בת המלך, למלכיהו בן המלך (*WSS*, 12 nos. 12–15, 17, 19, 30).

33. N. Avigad, *Hebrew Bullae*, 26; "Three Ancient Seals," *BA* 49/1 (1986): 51; "The Seals of Neriahu the Prince," in A. Mirsky, A. Grossman and Y. Kaplan eds. *Exile and Diaspora. Studies in the History of the Jewish People Presented to Professor Haim Beinhart on the Occasion of His Seventieth Birthday* (Jerusalem: Ben Zvi Institute of Yad Izhak, 1988), 40–44 (Hebrew).

phenomenon is not necessarily the result of multiple seal ownership but may indicate that more than one prince bore the same name.[35] Since paleographic dating of lapidary inscriptions only provides a range of 100–150 years,[36] it is conceivable that princes of different generations owned these seals. Likewise, some of the seal-owners identified as princes from the biblical record could in fact represent other members of the royal family.

Recently, it was proposed that a jar handle bearing the seal impression לשבניהו בן המלך belongs to the group known as *lmlk* jars.[37] Thereby, the implication is that a member of the royal family participated in the *lmlk* government-authorized project. In this case, although it can be argued convincingly that an impressed pottery handle is presumably authentic, the lack of archaeological context renders the association dubious. The jar handle stamped with the seal of שבניהו is at best a *lmlk* TYPE and, as is evident from a number of complete unstamped store-jars of this type, not all were *lmlk* jars.[38] Thus, שבניהו may have impressed a container that he used for private purposes. The fact that the handle has not been tested for its clay composition presents an additional obstacle to its alleged connection with the *lmlk* operation.

Happily, two bulla from the corpus of בן המלך inscriptions derive from controlled archaeological excavations: לגאליהו בן המלך from Beth Zur and ל]שבניהו [בן] המלך from Lachish;[39] The bulla of גאליהו was not discovered clearly stratified; rather, its findspot is the fortress cistern. Consequently, it is dated roughly to the seventh century based on paleography and the inscribed weights found in the same locus. Of the two bulla, the more interesting is the one belonging to שבניהו, which is one of 17 bullae discovered *in situ* in a juglet in a store-room of Stratum II at Lachish (late 7th cent.). The fiber marks on the back of the bulla indicate that it was used to seal string tied around a papyrus document.[40] Although the nature of the correspondence is unknown, the store-room context

34. O.R. Sellers, *The Citadel of Beth-Zur* (Philadelphia: Westminster Press, 1933), 60–61; Avigad, *Hebrew Bullae*, 25–26.

35. Avigad assumes these are examples of multiple seal ownership ("The Seals of Neriahu the Prince," 42).

36. See Chapter 2 – Paleographic Dating.

37. Barkay, "A Bulla of Ishmael, the King's Son," 111 n. 4; Vaughn, "The Chronicler's Account of Hezekiah," 168–171. See Chapter 6–B.

38. D. Ussishkin, "Excavations at Tel Lachish – 1973–1977," *TA* 5 (1978): 76.

39. Sellers, *Citadel of Beth-Zur*, 59–61, fig. 52; Aharoni, *Lachish V*, 21. Both Avigad and Barkay, based on spacial considerations, restore the inscription, לשבניהו בן המלך, instead of the alternate option, לשבניהו עבד המלך ("Titles and Symbols on Hebrew Seals," *EI* 15 [1981]: 304 (Hebrew); "A Bulla of Ishmael, the King's Son," 111 n. 3).

40. Aharoni, *Lachish V*, 19–21.

suggests that commodities were involved perhaps for their distribution or for payment.

Evidence that the בן המלך title-bearers owned and used seals is significant. Seals, like titles, aside from being functional administratively, served as ornaments, protective amulets, and/or status symbols.[41] In contrast to the seals, the bullae testify to the fact that the seals from which they were made were used functionally, possibly in connection with administrative roles held by the king's kinsmen who owned them. However, because the accompanying documents are lacking, their precise functions can only be inferred in light of other sources.[42]

Conclusions

In sum, it has been shown that the titles בן המלך and בת המלך should be understood literally as designations for princes and princesses. Theories to the contrary, suggesting that bearers of these titles could have been commoners who held minor positions at court, cannot be substantiated. The Israelite material does not contain a single example of a בן המלך whose origin is clearly non-royal. On the other hand, most of those individuals designated בן/בת המלך are unquestionably members of the royal family. In addition, other ancient Near Eastern

---

41. In Egypt, for example, young princes already possessed titles and belongings imprinted with those titles. One prince who died as a child, Harnakht, the youngest son of Osorkon II (mid 9th cent.), bore the title "High Priest of Amun" when he died at the age of eight or nine. His title was found on the lid of his sarcophagus and on a bracelet buried with him (P. Montet, "La necropole des rois tanites," *Kemi* 9 [1942]: 23, 41).

On the subject of the various uses of seals in Israel, see Uehlinger, "Northwest Semitic Inscribed Seals," in *Studies*, 273–274. Of note is Uehlinger's suggestion that the seal described in Song of Songs (8:6) functions as a protective amulet (p. 274).

42. An enticing but speculative proposal by Albright deserves mention (*ANET*, 569 n. 17). Albright suggests that אלישב בן אשיהו, the commander of Arad whose name and patronym is found on three seals and an ostracon (Y. Aharoni, *Arad Inscriptions* [Jerusalem: Israel Exploration Society, 1981], 119 #s 105–107, 32 #17) was the son of King Josiah. He notes that אשיהו is an abbreviation for יאשיהו and, since the time-period fits, could refer to King Josiah. Although Albright's identification of Eliashib as the son of Josiah cannot be substantiated, his proposal is supported in part by the practice recorded in the biblical account of Rehoboam, who appointed his sons as governors or commanders of administrative centers (2 Chr 11:23). Recently the name אשיהו turned up on an ostracon from the antiquities market. In that inscription the PN is followed by the designation המלך. One of the proposed identifications is King Josiah (P. Bordreuil et al., "King's Command and Widow's Plea," 2–7). It should be noted, however, that אשיהו on the Arad inscriptions can be a name unrelated to יאשיהו, rather one that means "a man of YHWH," comparable to the name אשחר, "a man of Horus," found on a Samaria ostracon (13:3).

sources, with the exception of a special usage of the Egyptian epithet *s3 nswt*, coincide with the Hebrew evidence.

Defining the role of the בן המלך within the state-administration is a more difficult task. The existence of a בן המלך bulla supports the biblical data that members of the royal family participated in administrative roles. Presently, it is indeterminable if בן המלך seal owners bore other titles indicative of their offices. Although certain names on בן המלך seals recur on עבד המלך and other seals, the frequency of the names in the Hebrew onomasticon precludes any secure identification of owners. In reality, the proportion of royalty represented in official positions may have been much greater than the biblical data indicate. Despite these unknowns, the biblical material does confirm that princes served in various capacities in the government. Some of their duties, apparently, involved aspects of the judiciary.

B. עבד המלך – Servant of the King

A second rank-related title, one derived from membership in a special court group is the designation עבד המלך (*'bd hmlk*), "servant of the king." In the Bible and in the epigraphic material the term עבד occurs in two variant formulas: as a title following a personal name, PN עבד המלך, without specification of the royal name; and in a construct chain between two personal names, PN עבד PN, the genitive always a name attested in the corpus of Israelite kings but not identified as royal by title. The collective expression עבדי המלך (*'bdy hmlk*), "servants of the king," used in reference to unnamed persons, is frequently found in the Bible but not in Hebrew inscriptions.

Biblical Evidence

Several Israelites and non-Israelites mentioned in the Bible who function in some capacity at a royal court are identified as the עבד of a king by the expression PN עבד המלך or related phraseology. These include: Joab, David's army commander (2 Sam 18:29); Mephibosheth son of Jonathan, a pensioner at David's court (2 Sam 19:29); Naaman, an army commander of Aram (2 Kgs 5:6); Asayah, who served in the reign of Josiah (2 Kgs 22:12; 2 Chr 34:20); and Nebuzaradan, chief of the guards of Nebuchadnezzar king of Babylon (2 Kgs 25:8). In some instances this type of relationship is expressed by the phrase PN עבד RN or similarly. For example, Doeg, Saul's strongman, is called עבד Saul (1 Sam 21:8); as an officer in Saul's army, David is known as עבד Saul king of Israel (1 Sam 29:3); Jeroboam, as minister over the corvée, is identified as עבד Solomon son of David (2 Chr 13:6). The general collective עבדי המלך is attested in reference to officials and functionaries of a number of monarchs, including an unnamed Egyptian Pharaoh (Gen 50:7), Balak king of Moab (Num 22:18), Achish king of Gath (1 Sam 21:12), Hadadezer king of Zobah (2 Sam 8:7), Hiram king of Tyre (2 Chr 9:10), Saul (1 Sam 16:15), David (2 Sam 2:17), and Solomon (1 Kgs 9:27) kings of Israel and Amon (2 Kgs 21:23) king of Judah.

A definition of עבד המלך as an official title is problematic because the expression seems to be a status-related rather than function-related title descriptive of administrative duties. Therefore, additional information provided by qualifying appellations and/or a specific context is needed in order to explain the roles of individuals so entitled. The term עבד (pl. עבדים) in the biblical texts has a wide semantic range. Derived from the verbal root עבד, "to work, serve," it can carry the meaning "slave, servant, subject, courtier" or nuances thereof.[43] The rank of an עבד is usually delineated vis-à-vis that of the superior to whom he is subordinate. While an עבד in the general sense can be an ordinary slave and thus a person of very low status, more frequently the term signifies the existence of a special servant-master relationship and can involve persons of varying rank.

Servant-master relationships are attested within various groups in society, both royal and non-royal. In addition to the עבדים of the king, the עבדים of princes at court and of descendants of former dynasties (e.g. Ishbosheth, Mephibosheth and Absalom) are known from the biblical sources (2 Sam 2:12; 9:2; 14:30). Also mentioned are the עבדים of non-royal persons of means, such as the patriarchs Abraham and Isaac (Gen 24:34; 26:25). Biblical law codes (Exod 21:2–11; Deut 15:12–18) delineate regulations concerning the Hebrew manservant and maidservant עבד ואמה (*ʿbd w'mh*). Apparently, Israelites sold into servitude to fellow Israelites also bore this designation.

Another biblical usage of the term עבד is as a designation of a human relationship to God. The expression עבד יהוה (*ʿbd* of YHWH) is conferred on individuals who have a more intimate affiliation with God and/or who are chosen for a particular mission. Persons designated as the עבד of YHWH include: the patriarchs Abraham, Isaac, and Jacob (Exod 32:13); certain national leaders and officials, such as Moses (Deut 34:5), Joshua (Josh 24:29), David (2 Sam 3:18), Hezekiah (2 Chr 32:16), Eliakim (Isa 22:20), and Zerubbabel (Hag 2:23); several prophets, such as Ahijah (1 Kgs 14:18), Isaiah (Isa 20:3), Elijah (2 Kgs 9:36) and Jonah (2 Kgs 14:25); the suffering servant in Isaiah (Isa 42:1); the pious Job (Job 1:8); and Nebuchadnezzar king of Babylon (Jer 25:9).[44] The plu-

43. *BDB*, 713–714; *HALOT* 2, 773–775.

44. An unprovenienced seal, supposedly originating from a tomb in the vicinity of Jerusalem, bears this title: מקניו עבד יהוה, (*mqnyw* the *ʿbd* of YHWH). F.M. Cross suggests that this seal, which he dates paleographically to the first half of the eighth century, belonged to a priest or a chief temple musician. The reverse of the seal shows the PN prefixed by the

ral designation עבדי YHWH is found in reference to groups of people: Israel (Lev 25:55), prophets of YHWH (2 Kgs 9:7), and foreign YHWH worshippers (Isa 56:6). With a single exception, any person considered to be an עבד YHWH is one who is assessed as particularly loyal to God. The exception, Nebuchadnezzar king of Babylon, is a foreign ruler who functions as an instrument of God.

The term עבדים is also used to denote the vassal status of a nation in relationship to its overlord. Several of Israel's neighbors who were conquered by David, including Moab, Aram-Damascus, and Edom (2 Sam 8:2, 6, 14), are labeled עבדים.[45] Their vassalship is confirmed by the fact that they pay tribute and house Israelite officers, נצבים (*nṣbym*).[46] So too, in the mid-eighth century when Israel was under Assyrian dominion, its last king, Hoshea, is called the עבד of Shalmaneser (2 Kgs 17:3). At the end of the seventh century, Jehoiakim of Judah is labeled the עבד of Nebuchadnezzar of Babylon (24:1).

Based on the biblical usages of the term עבד, a few general observations can be made concerning personnel at court bearing this designation. (1) Attendants, ministers, or any functionary in the king's service can be considered an עבד המלך. (2) Comparable to the appellation עבד יהוה, עבד המלך signifies a person who has a special relationship to the king and is expected to exhibit appropriate virtues. (3) Certain prominent persons are referred to as עבדים even though they carry other titles, either explicitly stated or understood.[47]

The latter observation deserves further exploration. Initially, it is important to isolate examples of the term עבד utilized in conjunction with other titles or descriptions. As mentioned above, certain high ranking royal officials such as Joab the army commander and Jeroboam an overseer of the corvée are called עבדים. Even the crown prince can be called an עבד of the king, as is Solomon (1 Kgs 1:19). In the latter case, Solomon is distinguished from the other princes by being referred to as the עבד of David instead of simply one of "the sons of the king."

The conspirators in a number of palace intrigues are identified as עבדים of the king. Two Judahite kings, Joash and Amon, were assassinated by their עבדים (2 Kgs 12:21; 21:23). Elah king of Israel suffered the same fate at the hands of his עבד, Zimri, commander of half the chariot division (1 Kgs 16:9). In the first two

---

preposition ל, "belonging to" ("The Seal of Miqneyaw, Servant of Yaweh" in L. Gorelick and E. Williams-Forte eds. *Ancient Seals and the Bible* [Malibu: Undena, 1983], 55–63).

45. The usage of the plural עבדים in reference to a single nation may refer to the relationship of its populace to the overlord power.

46. For a discussion of נציב see Chapter 4-H.

47. Contrast Rüterswörden, *Beamten der israelitischen Königszeit*, 4–9.

cases the specific titles of the assassins are unknown.[48] Importantly, however, we can assume from the context of the scenarios that these men were trusted courtiers and officials who maintained easy access to the king's person. An instructive detail is revealed through the record of the punishment of Joash's assassins (2 Kgs 14:5). After Joash's murder, his son Amaziah did not avenge his father until his own kingship was secure. His delayed revenge implies that the killers held powerful positions at court; mere attendants most certainly would have been executed swiftly, perhaps even by the palace guards or other officers of the king.

In a different scenario, the account of Jehu's coup, several high officials who served the former king, Jehoram, refer to themselves as the עבדים of Jehu, the usurper (2 Kgs 10:5). This group includes the minister over the royal house and the city governor of Samaria. In this case, the designation עבדים clearly encompasses the attribute of loyalty. The officials of the murdered king seek to convince the new monarch that they will be his trustworthy servants.

It appears from lists of different categories of royal functionaries that members of those groups were not automatically considered to belong to the class עבד המלך. For example, in one source describing Solomon's corvée system, the designation עבד seems to be differentiated from a number of military titles. The Deuteronomist notes that corvée labor was not imposed on Israelites because they served as אנשי המלחמה ועבדיו ושריו ושלשיו ושרי רכבו ופרשיו, "soldiers, his *'bdym*, his officers, his shieldbearers, his charioteers, and his cavalry" (1 Kgs 9:22).[49] Similarly, עבדים are distinguished from another group of royal functionaries, סריסים (*srysym*), palace attendants who may have been eunuchs (1 Sam 8:15). Seemingly, while an עבד could belong to one of several classes of officials, he also needed to possess the attributes necessary to place him in a special relationship to the king.

Epigraphic Evidence

The archaeological corpus of inscriptions bearing the title עבד consists of three finds discovered in controlled archaeological excavations and a larger group derived from the antiquities market. Both the provenienced and unprovenienced collections exhibit usage of the two formulas: PN עבד המלך and PN עבד

---

48. Other assassins, with the exception of Pekah, the shieldbearer of Pekahiah (שליש – *šlyš*; 2 Kgs 15:25), are noted solely by their PNs.

49. J. Gray translates עבדיו, as "personal attaches," such as courtiers or privy counsellors (*I and II Kings: A Commentary* [Philadelphia: Westminster Press, 1963], 242). That distinction, however, is unsupported. The term is omitted by the Chronicler in his parallel account (2 Chr 8:9); other variations occur in different versions.

PN. Among the provenienced items are two seals and an ostracon. One seal is engraved לשמע עבד ירבעם, "belonging to *šm'* the servant of *yrb'm*";[50] the other reads ליאזניהו עבד המלך, "belonging to *y'znyhw* servant of the king."[51] The ostracon, Lachish no. 3, mentions טביהו עבד המלך, "*ṭbyhw* the servant of the king," in its text.[52] Another 18 published unprovenienced seals and bullae bear this title, plus a PN.[53] The title עבד המלך or עבד RN is also found on several Ammonite and Edomite seals and seal impressions.[54]

A few hints concerning the status of an עבד of the king can be gleaned from the epigraphic evidence.[55] First, it is apparent that the epithet עבד was sufficiently valued to be included on personal seals. Second, the two provenienced seals are noticeably of fine quality, indicating that their owners were persons of high status in society. The seal of שמע, probably the servant of Jeroboam II,[56] is the largest and one of the most beautiful seals known from pre-exilic Israel. Cut of jasper, it is skillfully engraved and features a detailed depiction of a roaring

---

50. S.A. Cook, "A Newly Discovered Hebrew Seal," *PEFQS* 36 (1904): 287–291.

51. This seal was found in a tomb deposit at Tell en-Nabeh together with skeletal remains and Iron Age II pottery (W.F. Bade, "The Seal of Jaazaniah," *ZAW* 51 (1933): 150–151).

52. H. Torczyner, *Lachish I: The Lachish Letters* (London: Oxford University Press, 1938), 51. Deutsch and Heltzer list another עבד seal (from Tel Qasile) as possibly belonging to the Israelite period: עשניהו עבד המלך (*Forty*, 40). However, this seal was originally dated by B. Mazar to the Persian period ("The Excavations at Tel Qasile: Preliminary Report," *IEJ* 1 [1950/51]: 212, Pl 37:F) and at present its authenticity has been questioned (see discussion in *WSS*, no. 1206). It is therefore not included in this study.

53. See Table A-2.

54. *WSS*, nos. 857–861 (859 & 860 provenienced), 1050 & 1051 (provenienced).

55. Avishur's and Heltzer's contention that owners of seals showing the formula PN עבד RN were of higher status than those with seals of the other formula, PN עבד המלך, is unconvincing. More tenable is Lemaire's observation that the formula PN עבד RN, which appears only on seals with RNs of the 8th century, reflects an earlier custom, while the formula PN עבד המלך is indicative of a later 7th–6th century practice ("Royal Signature," 50). But even Lemaire's proposal needs to be substantiated by archaeologically datable finds.

56. The date of this seal, discovered at Megiddo, is still debated because of its ambiguous stratigraphy. Most scholars date it to the reign of Jeroboam II in the mid-eighth century, based on paleographical and iconographical considerations (e.g. Cook, "A Newly Discovered Hebrew Seal," 291; Sass, "The Pre-Exilic Hebrew Seals," 221). A few others favor a tenth century date in the reign of Jeroboam I (S. Yeivin, "The Date of the Seal 'Belonging to Shema [the] Servant [of] Jeroboam'," *JNES* 19 [1960]: 205–212; G. Ahlström, "The Seal of Shema," *SJOT* 7 [1993]: 208–215; D. Ussishkin, "Gate 1567 at Megiddo and the Seal of Shema, Servant of Jeroboam" in M. Coogan and L. Stager eds. *Scripture and Other Artifacts: Essays on the Bible and Archaeology in Honor of Philip J. King* [Louisville: Westminster John Knox Press, 1994], 424). Based on a combination of paleography, iconography, and the absence of seals from tenth-ninth century material remains, I follow the eighth century date.

lion, a popular North Syrian motif.[57] The seal of יאזניהו, the servant of an undesignated king, is cut from a piece of white and black layered agate and is decorated with a rooster below the writing. It seems that the engraver attempted a fancy presentation by carving the letters into the black layer to contrast the white background of the surface.[58] It has been suggested that the seal of יאזניהו belonged to the biblical Jaazaniah son of the Maachite, a Judean officer who joined Gedaliah at Mizpah after the fall of Jerusalem (2 Kgs 25:23).[59] Notably, the seal of שמע includes the RN Jeroboam in its inscription.[60] Parallel examples of the title עבד followed by a probable RN are found on two Ammonite inscrip-

57. Sass, "The Pre-exilic Hebrew Seals," 221–223, no. 109.

58. Bade, "The Seal of Jaazaniah," 150–153. Several unprovenienced seals whose authenticity remains unproven are of fine quality as well. According to Mykytiuk's methodology, two from this group, the seals of אביו עבד עזיו and שבניו עבד עזיו, should be presumed genuine because they were purchased in the mid-19th century before forgers would have been aware of the significance of minor paleographical distinctions ("Identifying Biblical Persons in Hebrew Inscriptions," 185, 192). One seal inscribed לעבדי עבד הושע is cut of translucent orange chalcedony; the Egyptianized Phoenician iconography shows a figure holding a papyrus scepter with a winged sun-disk below (Lemaire, "Name of Israel's Last King Surfaces in a Private Collection," 48–52). Other highly decorated seals include the two ascribed to ministers of Uzziah: אביו עבד עזיו and שבניו עבד עזיו (E.O. Blau, "Bibliographische Anzeigen," *ZDMG* 12 [1858]: 726; A. de Longpérier, "Cachet de Sébénias, fils d'Osias," *CRAIBL* 6 [1863]: 288–289). Another, inscribed לאשנא עבד אחז, has been assigned to a servant of Ahaz (C.C. Torrey, "A Hebrew Seal from the Reign of Ahaz," *BASOR* 79 [1940]: 27–28). A number of aniconic seals are cut of fine stones, for example, the cream-pink ivory seal inscribed לגאליהו עבד המלך (W.J. Fulco, "A Seal from Umm el Qanafid, Jordan; *g'lyhw 'bd hmlk*," *Or* 48 [1979]: 107).

59. Bade, "The Seal of Jaazaniah," 154–156. The fact that the seal of יאזניהו was discovered in an Iron Age II context at Mizpah supports this contention. However, it should be noted that the seal's date can only be narrowed to within 100 years, from the seventh to the early sixth century, making this association uncertain.

Connections between biblical characters and seal-owners have also been attempted for three names occurring on unprovenienced inscriptions, two seals and a bulla: שבניו עבד עזיו = Shebna, minister over the royal house (Isa 22:15; S. Yeivin, "Administration" in *WHJP* 4/2, 170); אליקם עבד המלך = Eliakim, minister over the royal house (2 Kgs 18:18; P. Bordreuil and F. Israel, "À propos de la carrière d'Elyaqim: du page au majordome," *Semitica* 41–42 [1991–1992]: 87); and עשיהו עבד המלך = Asayah, an official delegate sent by Josiah to Huldah (2 Kgs 22:12; Deutsch and Heltzer, *Forty*, 49–50). However, even if the seals and the bulla could be authenticated, the identifications are conjectural because the dating is based on paleographical criteria, which can only be estimated to within 100–150 years.

60. Although the genitive personal names on עבד seals cannot be securely identified with Israelite kings, tentatively this relationship is assumed because to date all the PNs, on provenienced and unprovenienced inscriptions, are known from the corpus of biblical RNs (see Tables A-1 & A-2).

tions: a seal from the "tomb of Adoninur" in Amman inscribed לאדננר עבד עמנדב and a bulla from Tell el-'Umeiri inscribed למלכמאור עבד בעלישע.[61]

A Special Role of עבד המלך *Seal Bearers*

It can be inferred that עבד המלך seal-owners were ministers granted the privilege of royal seal-bearer. As such, they could seal documents in the name of the king, a right somewhat analogous to that of individuals bearing the title עבד יהוה, who spoke at God's behest. Stories of investiture in which a king presents a high royal official with his (the king's) ring are told of Joseph in Egypt (Gen 41:42) and Haman and Mordechai in Persia (Esth 3:10; 8:2).[62] Quite possibly, the ceremony itself was symbolic and the king did not distribute his personal signet rings to every official authorized to stamp documents.[63] Instead, royal seal-bearers carried their own seals engraved with their PNs and official titles. The appellation עבד RN or עבד המלך attests to the fact that these ministers were empowered to act in the king's name. Evidence of the practice of certifying certain officials as royal seal-bearers comes from Egypt, where scarabs of high officials often bear their PN followed by the expression *sḏ3wty bity*, "seal-bearer

61. *WSS*, nos. 859 &860.

62. J. Greenfield, following M. Streck and L. Oppenheim, suggests that an Assyrian ceremony in which Ashurbanipal presents his vassal Necho with clothes and jewelry, including *šemērū/semērū*, "bracelets, rings," reflects this type of an Egyptian style investiture ceremony ("Studies in Aramaic Lexicography I," *JAOS* 82 [1962]: 293; Rassam Cylinder col. 2 l. 11 in Streck, *Assurbanipal und die letzten assyrischen Könige bis zum Untergang*, II [Leipzig: J.C. Hinrichs, 1916], 14–15; Oppenheim in *ANET*, 295). This interpretation, however, is questionable on several counts. First, investiture in this form is foreign to Assyrian practices. Second, since the *šemērū* are designated for Necho's *rittū*, "hands," not *ubānāti*, "fingers," the term could refer to bracelets, commonly worn by Assyrian kings. Third, if Ashurbanipal had indeed given Necho a signet ring, most likely it would have been a single ring (*šemērē* is plural, as indicated by the MEŠ sign).

A number of bullae of Neo-Assyrian royal stamp seals have been found as well as references in letters to the *unqu ša šarri*, "seal of the king" (A. Sachs, "The Late Assyrian Royal Seal Type," *Iraq* 15 [1953]: 167–170; A. Millard, "The Assyrian Royal Seal Type Again," *Iraq* 27 [1965]: 12–16; "The Assyrian Royal Seal: An Addendum," *Iraq* 40 [1978]: 70; *ABL*, 469, 486 etc.). No connection is evident, however, between any specific officials at court and the privilege of using the royal seal (Greenfield, pp. 292–293).

63. To date no royal seals bearing the PNs of the kings of Israel or Judah have been unearthed in archaeological excavations. At present, the למלך impressions, which lack any RN are the primary evidence for use of a royal stamp. In addition, recent publications of unprovenienced bullae include two stamped with royal seals: לאחז יהותם מלך יהדה and לחזקיהו אחז מלך יהדה (Deutsch, *Messages from the Past*, 171; "First Impression," 54–56, 62; Cross, "King Hezekiah's Seal," 42–45, 60).

of the king," plus the title of their position at court.[64] Formulas more closely resembling those on Hebrew seals are extant on second millennium Mesopotamian cylinder seals (see below).

Mesopotamian, Canaanite and Egyptian Evidence

Semantic equivalents of the Hebrew designation עבד המלך are attested in Mesopotamian, Canaanite, and Egyptian written records. The analogous appellation in Akkadian, *(w)arad šarri*, is attested in texts from the Old Akkadian through the Neo-Babylonian periods. The term *(w)ardu*, like Hebrew עבד, can signify a simple servant or subject or it can refer to officials of the king without designating any one position in particular.[65] Persons who correspond with the king, including high level officials, regularly speak of themselves as a *(w)arad šarri*.[66] Apparently, this phrase was a standard expression of obeisance. As a collective, the king's soldiers are sometimes called the *(w)ard* of the king.[67]

In addition, analogous to the Hebrew title עבד יהוה, the worshipper of a god or goddess can be designated as his/her *(w)ardu*. This expression appears on inscribed seals, several from the Kassite period.[68] When the formula reads "servant and worshipper of DN," for example, *arad pāliḫ Sīn u Ninsīanna*, the reference is to a special devotee of the deity in question; in this case the servant of Sin and Ninsianna is a temple official.[69]

Most interesting for comparative purposes to the Hebrew עבד המלך seals are the Sargonic royal cylinder seals known as "ARAD-*zu*" seals.[70] They display the following formula: RN, PN, title, ARAD.ANI or ARAD-*zu*, that is: a king-name, the name and title of an official and the phrase "his (the king's) servant."[71] Since there are no extant seals of any kings of the Sargonic period, R. Zettler suggests

64. The title *ḫtmty bity* or *sḏ3wty bity*, "sealbearer of the king," was held by various high officials under the vizier (S. Quirke, "The Regular Titles of the Late Middle Kingdom," *RdE* 37 [1986]: 123–124). One common title among royal seal-bearers is the *imy-r pr wr*, "the one who is over the great house." For a list with references to individual private-name seals, see G.T. Martin, *Egyptian Administrative and Private-Name Seals* (Oxford: Griffith Institute, 1971), 185–186.

65. *CAD* A/2, 247–251; *AHW* 3, 1464–1466.

66. For example, the chief scribe (*ABL* 519) and chief physician (*ABL* 584).

67. *ABL* 326; 753.

68. *CAD* A/2, 250; S. Langdon, "Inscriptions on Cassite Seals," *RA* 16 (1919): 69–95 (e.g. nos. 20, 24, 53).

69. Langdon, "Inscriptions on Cassite Seals," 69, no. 2.

70. R. Zettler, "The Sargonic Royal Seal: A Consideration of Sealing in Mesopotamia" in M. Gibson and R. Biggs eds. *Seals and Sealing in the Ancient Near East* (Malibu: Undena, 1977), 33–39.

71. The possessive suffix -*zu* of ARAD-*zu* may be understood as Sumerian second

that these seals, having been presented to officials by the king upon their appointment, functioned as royal seals by bestowing on the bearer the right to seal in the king's name. Zettler observes that compared to other seals the royal seals are of uniformly high quality and their iconography is restricted to a single type of scene (combat scenes), perhaps an indication that they were cut in the same shop for a specific purpose.[72] "ARAD-*zu*" seals from the Ur III and Isin-Larsa periods are similarly inscribed. Some seals, however, read ARAD.ANI.R IN.NA.BA, "(to) his servant (the king) has presented."[73] Commonly called "presentation seals," their iconographic features include a seated figure, the king, and a figure standing facing him, the official. Sometimes an interceding deity accompanies the official.[74] The PNs on the seals belong to high royal officials (e.g. chancellor, comptroller, scribe, cupbearer) and members of the royal family.[75] I. Winter concludes that the "ARAD-*zu*" seals symbolize the seal-owner's legitimate authority to exercise power within the royal administration and his right to act in the name of the king.[76] In contrast to the "ARAD-*zu*" seals, the seals inscribed "(to) his servant (the king) has presented" may be more representative of personal gifts from the king.[77]

Akkadian tablets from Syria-Palestine also contain the term *(w)ardu*. In the Amarna letters, royal officials, whether the Pharaoh's or those of a local ruler, are commonly designated as *(w)ardu* (e.g. *EA* 40:24; 306:24), often signifying vassal status. For example, Canaanite city-state rulers bearing the title *ḫazannu*, "mayor," refer to themselves as the *(w)ardu* of the Egyptian Pharaoh (e.g. *EA* 216:17; 239:19). As these local princes frequently stress their unabiding loyalty

---

person "your" or as Akkadian -*šú*, third person "his." Zettler ("The Sargonic Royal Seal," 38 n. 1) opts for the latter, based on two examples of the feminine -*za*, "her" (Akkadian).

Occasionally these seals contain two royal names, that of the king and another member of his family. In those cases, the functionary named on the seal is believed to have served the second person, not the king (Zettler, p. 36).

72. Zettler, "The Sargonic Royal Seal," 33, 36.

73. I. Winter, "Legitimation of Authority Through Image and Legend: Seals Belonging to Officials in the Administrative Bureaucracy of the Ur III State" in M. Gibson and R. Biggs, *The Organization of Power: Aspects of Bureaucracy in the Ancient Near East* (Chicago: Oriental Institute of the University of Chicago, 1987), 72–73; J. Franke, "Presentation Seals of the Ur III/Isin-Larsa Period" in *Seals and Sealing in the Ancient Near East* (Malibu: Undena, 1977), 61.

74. Winter, "Legitimation of Authority Through Image and Legend," 70.

75. For a list of seal-owners, their positions, and the kings they served, see Winter, "Legitimation of Authority Through Image and Legend," 95–99.

76. Winter, "Legitimation of Authority Through Image and Legend," 82–83, 86.

77. Franke, "Presentation Seals of the Ur III/Isin-Larsa Period," 65.

to their Egyptian overlord, it may be presumed that the Akkadian designation *(w)ardu*, like Hebrew עבד, conveys as part of its meaning the attribute of loyalty.

The Ugaritic term *'bd* (*'abd-*) is etymologically equivalent to the Hebrew term. In a letter from Ugarit, an official of apparent high stature, perhaps a treasurer, is addressed by the king as *'bd mlk.*[78]

In Egyptian the word *bꜣk* is a semantic counterpart of *'bd* and *(w)ardu*. As in Mesopotamia and Syria-Palestine, the term *bꜣk* can refer to slaves, servants of varying rank, worshippers of a certain deity as well as high royal officials.[79] Like Hebrew עבדים, the plural term *bꜣkw* is used as a general collective classification. In the Middle Kingdom (c. 1990–1785 BCE) and New Kingdom (c. 1540–1070 BCE) the designation *bꜣk nswt*, "servant of the king," is attested often with a modifier such as *mꜣ'*, "true."[80] According to W. Ward, the title *bꜣk nswt* without other accompanying titles is purely an honorific epithet devoid of any administrative function.[81] Comparable to the Semitic examples, the *bꜣk* of a deity signifies a worshipper. Following the New Kingdom, the expression also appears as a title preceding a PN to indicate the special relationship between the deity and his devotee.[82]

Conclusions

The evidence presented above suggests that the title עבד המלך was conferred on a wide spectrum of the king's men. As a collective, the term could denote any subject of the king serving a variety of functions inside and outside the royal court. Frequently, however, the עבד was an individual of high status in close proximity to the king: a prince, an army officer, or another minister of state. It seems that in Israel עבד המלך was an honorific epithet that did not necessarily designate any one particular office, but could be held concurrently with a function-related title. Comparable usage of semantically equivalent Akkadian, Ugaritic, and Egyptian terms is widely attested. Primarily, the title appears to indicate the existence of a special relationship between the title-bearer and the king. It could denote an intimate affiliation, signify absolute loyalty and/or ex-

78. *PRU* V 18.148 r.3. The function of this royal official, Ydn, is derived from his position, "over the *ḫrdh.*" The term *ḫrd*, whose meaning is unclear, is at times associated with *ksp*, "silver." Virolleaud (p. 89) suggests defining *ḫrd* as treasure.

79. A. Erman and H. Grapow, *Wörterbuch der ägyptischen Sprache*, 1 (Leipzig: J.C. Hinrichs, 1926), 429–430.

80. For Middle Kingdom examples see D. Doxey, *Egyptian Non-Royal Epithets in the Middle Kingdom: A Social and Historical Analysis* (Leiden: Brill, 1998), 125–128.

81. W. Ward, *Index of Egyptian Administrative and Religious Titles of the Middle Kingdom* (Beirut: American University of Beirut, 1982), 1.

82. Erman and Grapow, *Wörterbuch*, 429–430.

press the special trust conferred by the monarch. In that respect the epithet עבד המלך is somewhat analogous to עבד יהוה. The עבד seals, marked either with or without a RN, probably belonged to royal ministers authorized to seal in the king's name. As such they can be classified as "royal seals." Most informative for comparative purposes are the Mesopotamian seals of variant office-holders designated "ARAD-*zu*." These seals and the Egyptian seals inscribed "royal seal-bearer" are possible typological parallels to the עבד המלך seals.

C. זקנים – Elders, Senior Officials

Biblical Evidence

A third rank-related title is זקנים (zqnym). The designation is multivocal, denoting either longevity ("old men") or status within a group ("elders"). In general, the term זקנים is applied to sub-tribal (extended families), tribal (clans) and settlement leaders.[83] Since no minimum age is stipulated and the appellation refers to social status, it may be assumed that an adult male could qualify as an elder if he belonged to a family recognized by the group as prominent.[84] Any link that may have existed between age and membership in the circle of elders is not delineated in the Bible.

As members of a group distinguished in society, the elders enjoyed a long tradition of leadership in Israelite history from the earliest period.[85] These notables were most powerful under a decentralized system of government in the pre-monarchic period, but continued to be influential during the centralized administrative system of the monarchy. The key role of the elders, which continued into the monarchic period, was in the realm of the judiciary. In several accounts they are depicted sitting in judgment or as witnesses, usually at the city gate (e.g. Deut 22:15–21; 25:7–9; 1 Kgs 21:8–11; Ruth 4:1–12). The leadership

---

83. Sometimes the term ראשים, "heads," is substituted for elders. For a detailed discussion see H. Reviv, *The Elders in Ancient Israel* (Jerusalem: Magnes Press, 1989), 15–21.

84. J. Pederson notes that זקן is a male with a full beard, thus a mature male (*Israel: Its Life and Culture* [London: Oxford University Press, 1946], 36). Often a group of elders is identified by an ethnic or geographic determinative appended to the term זקנים. This applies to Israelite and non-Israelite groups of elders: Israel (1 Kgs 8:1), Judah (Ezek 8:1), Moab and Midian (Num 22:7), Jabesh (1 Sam 11:3).

85. Comprehensive studies on the elders include: J. McKenzie, "The Elders in the Old Testament," *AnBib* 10 (1959): 388–406; Reviv, *Elders in Ancient Israel*. For a list of the distribution of the term זקנים in the Bible, see McKenzie pp. 388–389. Recently Deutsch and Heltzer published an inscribed chalkstone, allegedly originating from a burial chamber at El-Kom, which designates a particular tomb or tombs as the resting place of the זקנים, assumably the local elders: ישכב בזה זקנים (*Forty New Ancient West Semitic Inscriptions*, 27–29).

position of the elders was recognized at national cultic events such as the dedication of the Temple (1 Kgs 8:1); in the early monarchic period they took an active role in political matters such as negotiating the kingship with David and then anointing him (2 Sam 5:3).

Occasionally, however, the biblical usage of the term זקנים seems to point in another direction. Instead of signifying local leaders, it appears to carry the meaning "senior," a ranking within a specific group of functionaries attached to the central government. These cases, which are pertinent to this study, are the focus of the discussion below. In addition, attention will be given to the traditional elders in their role as judges on Jehoshaphat's Jerusalem high court, an establishment of the central government.

An account in which the definition of the designation זקנים has been widely debated is 1 Kings 12 (=2 Chr 10), the narrative describing Rehoboam's accession to the throne and the division of the Solomonic kingdom. In that scenario, Rehoboam consults two groups of advisors concerning the petition he received from the leaders of the North to reduce corvée obligations. Rehoboam is said to have conferred with a group entitled זקנים and another called ילדים (1 Kgs 12:6–11). The only information offered by the text about these advisory bodies is that the זקנים had "stood before Solomon his (Rehoboam's) father" (12:6) and the ילדים "had grown up with him (Rehoboam) and were now standing before him" (12:8). A clue pertaining to their roles is revealed by the phrases עמדים את פני, "standing before," and העמדים לפניו, "those standing before him," variations of a common biblical expression signifying service rendered by a person of lower status to one of higher status (e.g. Elijah before God, 1 Kgs 17:1; Levites before God, 2 Chr 29:11). In the context of the royal court, the person standing in service before the king most likely would be an official (cf. Gen 41:46; 1 Sam 16:21; 1 Kgs 1:2).[86] However, due to the scant data on the identity of these groups a number of variant proposals deserve attention.

The ילדים, "young men," discussed in detail in the next section, appear to be contemporaries of Rehoboam who were raised with him at court and at the time of his coronation served in some administrative capacity. In contrast, for the זקנים, two distinct possibilities exist: (1) They belonged to the traditional circle of elders who held an advisory role in the monarchic system. (2) They were courtiers who survived Solomon, the term זקנים being indicative of their seniority in contrast to the junior royal functionaries, the ילדים. The first theory is supported by scholars who maintain that a permanent royal council of clan

86. The Hebrew expression is equivalent to the Akkadian *ina pān uzuzzu/izuzzu*, which in the technical language of the court means "to do service" (e.g. *ABL* 211:13 in L. Oppenheim, "Idiomatic Accadian," *JAOS* 61 [1941]: 258).

elders functioned at the time of the monarchy.[87] They cite two additional examples where elders supposedly comprised such a council: the rebellion of Absalom, when the elders were instrumental in selecting a military strategy, at least initially (2 Sam 17:4); and during the Aramean siege of Samaria, when Ahab consulted the elders concerning Ben-Hadad's demands (1 Kgs 20:7–8). The second view is supported by scholars who understand the role of the זקנים in 1 Kings 12 as parallel to that of the ילדים. They regard both groups as representing courtiers, the זקנים the elder, senior courtiers and the ילדים the younger, junior group.[88]

A close examination of the three aforementioned cases of kings conferring with a body of זקנים yields little evidence to buttress the notion that a permanent royal council of elders existed in monarchic Israel. The first instance, the revolt of Absalom, reveals that David had lost the loyalty of the elders of Israel, who sided with the usurper. While this situation reflects the conflict between the central government and the local leadership, it does not prove in any way that the defecting elders belonged to a council installed as a component of the state administration. On the contrary, resentment probably grew because the new highly centralized government reduced the power and status of the traditional leadership.[89] Absalom apparently capitalized on that condition by promising the disillusioned Israelites the crown's ear, should he become king (2 Sam 15:2–6). Thus, it is highly likely that the elders who surrounded Absalom were the traditional heads of social units of premonarchic Israelite society.

In the second case, the narrative of Rehoboam's accession to the throne (1 Kgs 12), the זקנים appear to be a group established at the royal court. They previously served Solomon and were now ministering to his heir.[90] As mentioned above, the phrase "to stand before," which describes their relationship vis-à-vis the king, suggests that the זקנים, as well as the ילדים, included appointed royal officials, not representatives of the people. Although their individual roles

87. McKenzie, "The Elders in the Old Testament," 391; A. Malamat, "Kingship and Council in Israel and Sumer," *JNES* 22 (1963): 248.

88. M. Noth, *Könige* (Neukirchen-Vluyn: Neukirchener, 1968), 274–275; H. Tadmor, "'The People' and the Kingship in Ancient Israel" in H. Ben-Sasson and S. Ettinger eds. *Jewish Society Through the Ages: The Role of Political Institutions in the Biblical Period* (New York: Schocken Books, 1971), 57–58; Reviv, *Elders in Ancient Israel*, 100–101; T. Willis, "Yahweh's Elders (Isa 24,23): Senior Officials of the Divine Court," *ZAW* 103 (1991): 381.

89. Reviv, *Elders in Ancient Israel*, 94–95.

90. As D. Evans notes, Solomonic records mention the clan elders only in conjunction with the dedication of the Temple (1 Kgs 8:1, 3). They are never credited as royal advisors ("Rehoboam's Advisors at Shechem, and Political Institutions in Israel and Sumer," *JNES* 25 [1966]: 276).

are not discussed, as a collective they function in an advisory capacity. One question that arises is why they are entitled by the potentially confusing designation זקנים instead of a more precise title, such as זקני השרים, "senior officials."[91] The answer may lie in the nature of this pericope. While allegedly presenting an historical event, the division of the Davidic and Solomonic kingdom, the Deuteronomist seeks to justify the tragedy. He emphasizes the foolishness and shortsightedness of Rehoboam's generation, the ילדים, and the wisdom of the older, experienced generation of Solomon, the זקנים. As shown in the discussion on the ילדים, that title seems to be a technical term that served a dual purpose in the narrative, symbolizing immaturity as well as younger age. The designation זקנים can be viewed similarly. Since the status "elders" signifies mature respected leadership, it is a fitting description for the senior officials of Solomon's court. But clearly, these officials did not belong to the traditional circle of elders. In the narrative of 1 Kgs 12 the word זקנים is actually indicative of age and seniority.

In the third example, the meeting between Ahab and the זקנים on the issue of appeasing the Arameans (1 Kgs 20), the identity of the זקנים seems to be that of the traditional group of elders. They are simultaneously addressed by a slightly different title: זקני הארץ, "the elders of the land" (20:7)[92] Since Samaria was under siege, it is possible that the elders in question are those from surrounding villages who took refuge in Samaria at the onset of war. There is no evidence, however, that they comprised a permanent advisory council in Samaria or held any administrative positions. Apparently, their main function was to support the king and rally to his side. Ahab had already agreed to Ben-Hadad's demands of tribute and hostages and it was only when the Arameans demanded access to the palace that he assembled the elders to inform them that he no longer could comply: ויאמר דעו נא וראו כי רעה זה מבקש, "And he (Ahab) said, please know and understand that this one (Ben-Hadad) seeks trouble" (20:7). It is at that point that the elders in concert with the people agree with the king and advise him to refuse Ben-Hadad (20:8). Ahab's move seems to reflect a need for popular support during a crisis.[93] A comparable example is found in the account of Jehu's coup. After killing Ahab and Jezebel, Jehu places the fate of the survivors of the House of Ahab in the hands of Samaria's officials, elders and the guardians of the princes. The elders join the royal functionaries in erad-

---

91. Cf. זקני הכהנים, "elder or senior priests" (2 Kgs 19:2).

92. LXX reads "the elders." In 20:8 the populace is also involved in the discussion, וכל העם, "and all the people."

93. Reviv, *Elders in Ancient Israel*, 123.

icating the descendants of Ahab, thereby pledging their support for the usurper (2 Kgs 10:1–5).

The evidence above, while implying that the traditional circle of elders retained some influence at court, at least in the North, does not offer proof of the existence of a permanent royal advisory council of elders. This conclusion furthers the interpretation that the זקנים in 1 Kgs 12 were senior court officials. It is also applicable to another occurrence of זקנים, in 2 Sam 12. In that narrative, where a sorrowful David prays for the life of his and Bathsheba's sick infant son, persons called זקני ביתו, "elders of his (David's) house," try to comfort the king and coax him to eat with them (12:17). Later in the same episode, following the infant's death, individuals designated עבדי דוד, "David's servants," murmur to each other that they fear approaching the king because he had rejected their earlier attempts of consolation (12:18). Seemingly, the two groups, זקני ביתו and עבדי דוד, are one and the same. They are pictured in close proximity to the king, even eating at his table. As such, it is likely that they were senior royal functionaries of one type or another, known both as זקנים and עבדי המלך.[94]

A final example of "elders" who functioned in the monarchic administration deserves attention. In that account, concerning Jehoshaphat's high court (2 Chr 19), the group is not called זקנים but rather ראשי האבות לישראל, "heads of households of Israel." Undoubtedly, that usage refers to the זקנים in the sense of traditional clan leaders, not senior officials.[95] According to the Chronicler, Jehoshaphat, as part of his judicial reforms, assigned שפטים, "judges," to all the fortified settlements in Judah and also established a supreme court in Jerusalem to deal with difficult disputes in both cultic and non-cultic matters.[96] The Jerusalem

94. This connection between זקנים and עבדים was made by Willis ("Yahweh's Elders," 376–378). Similarly, he identifies the Egyptians who accompanied Jacob's bier, עבדי פרעה זקני ביתו וכל זקני ארץ מצרים, "Pharaoh's servants, the elders of his house, and all the elders of the land of Egypt" (Gen 50:7), as senior Egyptian officials (cf. Gen 24:2, עבדו זקן ביתו – the designation for Abraham's senior servant).

95. Albright, "The Judicial Reforms of Jehoshaphat," 76; Reviv, *Elders in ancient Israel*, 104.

96. The authenticity of the Chronicler's account for the period in question is always a matter of debate. For an in depth discussion of Jehoshaphat's reform, as well as a summary of scholarly opinion concerning its accuracy, see Japhet, *I & II Chronicles*, 770–779. Japhet thinks that although the narrative rhetoric is clearly Chronistic, the reform itself with its innovations is believable.

A similar judicial hierarchal system, composed of a lower and higher court, is outlined in Deut 17:6–13 (for comments on the high court, see J.H. Tigay, *The JPS Torah Commentary Deuteronomy* [Philadelphia: Jewish Publication Society, 1996], 163–165). For a comparison of the Deuteronomic and Chronistic procedures, see Japhet (pp. 773–774) and M. Weinfeld ("Judge and Officer in Ancient Israel," *IOS* 7 [1977]: 66).

bench was composed of "Levites, priests, and heads of the households of Israel" (19:8).[97] Their participation in the Jerusalem high court, a component of the central government, demonstrates the viability of traditional leadership in Israel. The precise new status of these elders, however, is unclear. Reviv maintains that this act does not herald the assimilation of elders into the state administration.[98] But, in view of the fact that these elders were "appointed" (ויעמד) by the crown,[99] it is probable that they became accountable to the king, a condition that could have undermined the independent status of their entity. Evidently Jehoshaphat understood the importance of allocating a share of authority to the זקנים while simultaneously positioning them more closely under his scrutiny.[100] The judiciary was naturally compatible with their existing role as local judges.

Elders as Administrators Outside Israel

The elders, as a local decision making body associated with legal affairs, is an institution common in Mesopotamia, Anatolia, and Syria-Palestine. In Akkadian the designation for elders, *šībūtu* (OB: LÚ.ŠU.GI.MEŠ; NB: LÚ.AB.BA.MEŠ), is derived from the term *šību*, "old man."[101] Related titles such as *amīlū ša bābišunu*, "men of their gate," and *abbū* URU *Ugarit*, "fathers of

97. Albright maintains that the significance of Jehoshaphat's judicial system lies in the fact that the courts were composed of religious personnel and lay leaders. He compares the Israelite system with the Egyptian following the judicial reform of Haremhab in the latter half of the 14th century ("The Judicial Reforms of Jehoshaphat" 78–80). Haremhab reorganized the judiciary by appointing priests and lay officials as judges (text in K. Pfluger, "The Edict of King Haremhab," *JNES* 5 [1946]: 260–276). Apparently, his aim was to eliminate corruption and assure loyalty to the crown. It must be remembered, however, that Haremhab was still in the process of mending relations between the priests of Amun and the crown after the collapse of Akhenaten's Aten cult. In the Israelite case, the participation of priests and Levites in the courts is not especially surprising since their expertise in cultic matters would be crucial. Weinfeld ("Judge and Officer," 75–76) does not view the acts of Haremhab and Jehoshaphat as extraordinary. He presents parallels from Hittite sources to show that religious personnel played a role in the judiciary in other Near Eastern cultures as well.

98. Reviv, *Elders in Ancient Israel*, 109.

99. The causative stem of the verb עמד is commonly used by the Chronicler to mean "appoint" (e.g. 1 Chr 15:17; 2 Chr 31:2) in place of פקד (2 Kgs 25:23), נתן (Deut 16:18; 1 Sam 12:13), or שים (2 Sam 17:25).

100. Jehoshaphat's concern over royal authority is evident from other acts as well. His sons were given control over certain cities (2 Chr 21:2–3) and he stationed royal troops, "officers" (נציבים), and religious personnel in all the fortified centers of his domain (17:2, 7–19).

101. *CAD* Š/2, 390–394; *AHW* 3, 1228–1229.

Ugarit," mentioned in Ugaritic texts,[102] as well as *amīlū damqūti*, "noble men," from Alalakh may also be identifiable with elders.[103] In Hittite documents the term for elders is LÚ.MEŠ ŠU.GI. as in Old Babylonian texts.[104]

Documents describing the functions of elders in the societies of the region yield similar scenes. Legal documents from Mari and Babylon from the Old Babylonian period are replete with information on the functions of the *šībūtu* and the *šībūt āli* "elders of a city."[105] The Old Babylonian elders especially, held extensive jurisdiction and influence. They not only dealt with legal issues concerning property, but were also involved in political and military matters.[106] Disputes were regularly brought for arbitration before an assembly composed of elders, *ālu* (citizenry), and a royal official, the *rabiānu*, "governor," or *ḫazannu*, "mayor."[107]

Among the Hittites, elders also constituted the local authority and ordinary judicial proceedings were under their authority. One Hittite law in particular delineates their judicial sphere. It specifies that if a stray ox is found in the countryside, it is to be delivered to the elders, but if it is found near the royal capital, it falls under the jurisdiction of the state.[108] In the case of the Hittite elders, judicial control was also exercised in concert with appointed officials, such as the town mayor. An officer of the king, the *awariyaš išḫaš* (=*bēl madgalti*), "commander of the border garrison," represented the state in legal matters on occasions when he passed through the town.[109]

Information on the authority of the elders of Syria/Palestine is found in texts from Ugarit, Alalakh, El-Amarna, and the Bible. The material from Ugarit in-

---

102. *PRU* IV, 158:18.115, 219:17.424C+397B.

103. D.J. Wiseman, *The Alalakh Tablets* (London: British Institute of Archaeology at Ankara, 1953), 31–32 no. 3:38 (see 2:27 for the term *šību*). For a detailed discussion on the Ugaritic and Alalakh material, see Reviv, *Elders in Ancient Israel*, 140, 142–143. Cf. the rabbinic expression טובי העיר (*Megilla* 27a).

104. E. von Schuler, *Hethitische Dienstanweisungen für höhere Hof- und Staatsbeamte* (*AfO* Beiheft 10; Graz, 1957), 47 III:9.

105. *CAD* Š/2, 392–393.

106. For a comprehensive description of the roles of Old Babylonian elders see Reviv, *Elders in Ancient Israel*, 155–186.

107. The precise interpretation of *ālu*, literally, "city," is uncertain. Most probably it was a council of citizens separate from the *šībūtu* (Reviv, *Elders in Ancient Israel*, 156–159).

108. A. Goetze, *ANET*, 192 no. 71; E. Neufeld, *The Hittite Laws* (London: Luzac, 1951), 160–161. Capital cases, cases against the state, and those too complicated for the local judges were tried before the royal court. The king, the supreme judge, could grant pardons for capital crimes.

109. O. Gurney, *The Hittites* (Baltimore: Penguin Books, 1964), 92–93; H.A. Hoffner, "The Laws of the Hittites" (Ph.D. Dissertation, Brandeis University, 1963), 326.

dicates that in addition to legal matters, political and financial affairs often came under the jurisdiction of the city elders.[110] They dealt with inter-state relations between Ugarit and Carchemish, specifically the protection of merchants and the apprehension of criminals. Law enforcement, both in Ugarit and Carchemish, was the joint responsibility of the elders and a state official, usually the *ḫazannu.* Royal power superseded that of the elders, but in periods when a city-state was without a king, the government fell into the hands of the elders. An example of this situation is evident from a letter written by the elders of Irqata (a city in Syria), who represented their city to the Egyptian Pharaoh.[111] Similarly, in the biblical account of the seer Balaam, the king of Moab, Balak, negotiates with the Midianite elders who seem to be in charge (Num 22:4).[112]

The administrative functions of the elders in Babylonia in Neo-Babylonian times are mentioned in sources from Sippar, Babylon, Nippur, and Uruk, among others.[113] The documents, which present a variety of cases dealing primarily with disputes over property, clearly demonstrate the elders' judicial authority. They also show, as in previous periods and among contiguous cultures, that at times decisions were made in concert with representatives from other groups in society, specifically state-officials or temple priests.[114] Notably, one letter specifies that the elders in a certain case not be office-holders, perhaps implying that some did hold official posts.[115]

In Egypt, the designation "elder" is attested in titles of royal functionaries from the Old, Middle, and New Kingdoms: *smsw h3yt,* "elder of the portal (forecourt)"; *smsw n wsḫt,* "elder of the hall"; *smsw ist,* "elder of the palace"; *sš smsw hwt-wrt,* "elder scribe of the law court"; and *ẖry-ḥbt smsw,* "elder lector priest."

110. For a detailed discussion see Reviv, *Elders in Ancient Israel,* 137–145.

111. *EA* 100:4. Read *šībūtiši* following W.F. Albright ("Cuneiform Material for Egyptian Prosopography," *JNES* 5 [1946]: 23, no. 68) instead of *šišetiši* following J. Knudtzon (*Die El-Amarna Tafeln* [Aalen: O. Zeller, 1915], 450; see most recently W. Moran, *The Amarna Letters* [Baltimore: Johns Hopkins University, 1992], 172–173).

112. According to Reviv another example of the rulership of the elders is found in the account of Gideon and the leaders of the Canaanite city of Succoth (Judg 8:5–16). Reviv maintains that Gideon negotiated with the elders rather than the officials (שרים) of Succoth, as recorded in the text. He claims that the term שרים probably reflects a later reconstruction (*Elders in Ancient Israel,* 149–150). Reviv's contention is supported by the comment at the end of the narrative that Gideon punished the city *elders* for not backing him (8:16).

113. For a list of documents with individual content summaries, see M.A. Dandamayev, "The Neo-Babylonian Elders" in *Societies and Languages of the Ancient Near East. Studies in Honour of I.M. Diakonoff* [Westminster: Aris and Phillips, 1982], 38–41.

114. For example, *Cyr.* 322 and *Camb.* 412 in Dandamayev, "The Neo-Babylonian Elders," 38.

115. *TCL* 9 137, in Dandamayev, "The Neo-Babylonian Elders," 39.

The noun *smsw*, "elder" or "eldest," which most frequently defines age, sometimes is part of the titularies of civil, judicial, and religious functionaries, as in the above examples.[116] Interestingly, when the element *smsw* is attached to a title it does not necessarily reflect the age of the titleholder but rather seems to denote the "senior" ranking of the official, comparable to occasional usages of Hebrew זקנים.[117]

Specific information is available from the Middle and early New Kingdom on the "elders of the portal." Names and titles of persons designated *smsw h3yt* appear in association with the royal family and the inner palace, where they served alongside chamberlains and overseers of the *ẖrdw n k3p*, "children of the harem (or) inner palace." Their duties are not made explicit but probably entailed guarding and ushering, in particular the area leading from the outer to the inner palace.[118] H. Goedicke suggests that they were the senior administrators of that quarter of the palace."[119]

Conclusions

The biblical evidence discussed above indicates two usages for the designation זקנים, one denoting the traditional group of elders who functioned as local leaders and the other signifying a general title for senior officials who held various positions at court. The first group, the clan elders, sometimes collaborated with state officials on administrative issues but essentially continued in the monarchic period to represent the local leadership of Israelite society. Their incorpo-

---

116. Erman and Grapow, *Wörterbuch* 4, 142–143; R.O. Faulkner, *A Concise Dictionary of Middle Egyptian* (Oxford: Griffith Institute, 1991), 229.

117. S. Quirke, *The Administration in Egypt in the Late Middle Kingdom* (Kent: New Malden, 1990), 92–93; H. Goedicke, *The Report of Wenamun* (Baltimore: Johns Hopkins University Press, 1975), 18–19. It stands to reason, however, that in many cases senior court functionaries would have been older. An interesting example is found in *EA* 59:11. In that letter, the citizens of Tunip request that the Pharaoh remember Egypt's longstanding rule over Tunip. They ask him to consult the *la-be-ru-te-šu/am-ma-ti*, "his old men" (Akkadian *labīru* = Hurrian *ammati* = "old" [*CAD* L, 29]). Presumably, "his old men" refers to veteran royal functionaries who would be cognizant of past policies.

118. Quirke, *The Administration of Egypt in the Late Middle Kingdom*, 87–93; A. Gardiner, *Ancient Egyptian Onomastica* I [Oxford: Oxford University Press, 1947], 60*; W. Helck, *Zur Verwaltung des mittleren und neuen Reichs* (Leiden: E.J. Brill, 1958), 65. Families of personnel of the inner palace seem to have resided there together with the functionaries. In his autobiography, the vizier Rekhmire mentions that upon entering the palace he was escorted to the Pharaoh by the *smsw h3yt* (A. Gardiner, "The Autobiography of Rekhmereʿ" *ZAS* 60 (1925): 64). It has also been suggested, though the evidence is slim, that the *smsw h3yt* headed small councils of judges who met in the porch area in front of the inner palace to tend to civil disputes (S. Sauneron, "La justice à la porte des temples," *BIFAO* 54 [1954]: 122).

119. Goedicke, *The Report of Wenamun*, 18–19.

ration into the high court in Jerusalem reflects their maximum involvement in the central government. Examples of elders at Samaria suggest that they were somewhat influential at court. In general, however, a cooperative working relationship between the elders and appointees of the crown seems to have been primarily a phenomenon of local administration. Similar circumstances are evident from Mesopotamia, Anatolia and Syria-Palestine from various periods.

The second usage of זקנים, as a categorization for senior royal functionaries, is evident from at least two biblical examples: Rehoboam's counsellors in 1 Kgs 12 and David's עבדים in 2 Sam 12. That sense of the designation זקנים is apparently indicative of senior ranking within the larger body of officials. In the account of 1 Kgs 12 it also implies superior insight, a contrast to the younger, foolish courtiers, the ילדים. The element *smsw* in Egyptian titularies, at least in some cases, seems to be used comparably to this second usage of the title זקנים.

D. ילדים – "Children," Junior Officials Raised at Court

Biblical Usage

The fourth status-related title, ילדים (*yldym*), designates membership in a special circle at court. Normally defined as "children," the term appears out of place as a designation for the advisors who counseled Rehoboam at Shechem (1 Kgs 12:8, 10, 14 = 2 Chr 10:8, 10, 14). Apparently though, these ילדים constitute a group attached to the royal court who participated in policy making decisions and, as such, they deserve discussion in this study.[120]

The context in which the term ילדים occurs is the account of the final events that led to the division of the United Kingdom. Following Solomon's death, an assembly of Israelites came to the cult center at Shechem to crown Rehoboam, the heir to the throne. But their loyalty was conditional on Rehoboam's compliance with their petition to lighten the heavy yoke that his father Solomon had imposed on Israel. Facing this critical decision, a shift in policy, at the beginning of his reign, Rehoboam consulted two groups, the זקנים and the ילדים. The זקנים recommended that he appease the people in order to secure their loyalty. But Rehoboam abandoned the counsel of the זקנים and took counsel with the ילדים, who are identified by the writer as אשר גדלו אתו אשר העמדים לפניו, "those who grew up with him and were standing before him" (12:8). Their advice, which the king followed, was to intensify Solomon's authoritarian demands.

One issue raised in connection with this account is the identity of the two

---

120. An article based on an earlier version of the study of ילדים appears in *BA* (N. Fox, "Royal Officials and Court Families: A New Look at the ילדים (*yĕlādîm*) in 1 Kings 12," *BA* 59 [1996]: 225–232).

groups of royal advisors, especially that of the ילדים, since they clearly are contemporaries of Rehoboam and not children. The זקנים, "elders" or "old men," have been identified by some scholars as the tribal elders, who since premonarchic times represented their tribes and took part in various decision making processes.[121] But, as shown in the previous section on זקנים, they should rather be identified as Solomon's old guard, those senior functionaries who survived him and now served his son.[122] Identifying the ילדים, however, is more difficult since the term with this particular nuance appears in the Bible only in this episode.

The closest possible analogy, which warrants some attention, is the usage of the term ילדים in the book of Daniel. In the opening chapter of Daniel, a group of royal Judean youths, exiles from Babylon, are brought before the Babylonian king Nebuchadnezzar to be trained at court to serve as royal functionaries (1:4, 17).[123] Not only is Daniel's group labeled ילדים, but the other youths residing in the palace are also identified by this title (1:10, 13, 15). Notably, once Daniel and his comrades complete their three years of instruction, they are no longer known as members of the circle of ילדים. Instead they are called by their newly acquired titles, חכימי בבל, "wise men of Babylon" (2:12).[124]

---

121. E. Lipinski, "Le récit de 1 Rois XII 1–19 à la lumière de l'ancien usage de hébreu et de nouveaux textes de Mari" *VT* 24 (1974): 431; McKenzie, "The Elders in the Old Testament," 391.

122. Noth, *Könige*, 274–275; Tadmor, "'The People' and the Kingship in Ancient Israel," 57–58; Reviv, *Elders in Ancient Israel*, 99–101.

123. Various opinions exist concerning the role of Daniel and the other foreign youths at the Babylonian court. According to the text, they were recruited for their physical and intellectual qualities (Dan 1:4). Since their training included instruction in the language and writing system of the empire, it seems they may have served as scribes, perhaps mastering the ancient cuneiform system (J. Montgomery, *A Critical and Exegetical Commentary on the Book of Daniel* [New York: Charles Scribner's Sons, 1927], 119–121). Another possibility is that they were educated in omen lore (L. Hartman and A. DiLella, *The Anchor Bible. The Book of Daniel* [Garden City: Doubleday, 1978], 129–130).

124. Generally, the description in Daniel is viewed as reflecting a Persian court setting. The education of Daniel and his comrades appears to be rooted in the Persian system (Montgomery, *Book of Daniel*, 119–121; Hartman and DiLella, *Book of Daniel*, 129–130; J. Collins, *Daniel* [Minneapolis: Fortress Press, 1993], 139–140). Other examples of this type of an institution are found in Macedonia in the fourth century. There, schools of βασιλικοί παιδες, "royal pages (literally – children)," existed for similar purposes. Members consisted of princes as well as sons of court functionaries. One goal of the "school" was to prepare future officers. Although Philip of Macedon takes credit for the development of this institution, it seems to have a longer tradition traceable to the Persian period (N. Hammond and G. Griffith, *A History of Macedonia* [Oxford: Clarendon Press, 1979], 401–402; N. Hammond, *The Macedonian State* [Oxford: Clarendon Press, 1982], 56–57).

In contrast to Daniel's group, Rehoboam's ילדים were adults of the king's generation, probably men in their thirties or forties, since the king supposedly was 41 years old when he ascended the throne (14:21). Because of their problematic designation, the identity and roles of these advisors continue to be debated. Various opinions exist: (1) the ילדים were brothers, half-brothers or other relations of Rehoboam;[125] (2) they were his "buddies";[126] (3) they were the young inexperienced officials appointed by Rehoboam;[127] Some scholars have turned to Mesopotamia in search of similar political institutions. The ילדים have been compared to the *madārū*, "district administrators," in the Mari texts. The *madārū* were regulars at the King's table and the presence of the ילדים at Rehoboam's side is explained similarly.[128] Another analogy compares the ילדים and the זקנים in Israel to a so called "bicameral" assembly in Sumer composed of men and elders, in essence two permanent councils.[129] Upon closer examination, however, no concrete historical evidence exists for such a legislature in Sumer nor is this type of a democratic institution supported by biblical data for Israel.[130]

The usage of the designation ילדים for "young men" in this narrative is generally viewed as merely a literary device to distinguish the young, arrogant, inexperienced group from the wise elders.[131] Thereby, the term does not define chronological age but rather characterizes the group's foolishness. The players in this drama are even said to be drawn as types rather than individuals.[132] If, however, the term ילדים functions solely as literary device, then a different word would be expected, the term נער, which is widely used in biblical Hebrew to signify "youth" and is commonly found in expressions contrasting "elders" with "youngsters" (e.g. Deut 28:50).[133]

---

125. Malamat, "Kingship and Council in Israel and in Sumer," 249; Evans, "Rehoboam's Advisors at Shechem, and Political Institutions in Israel and Sumer," 277.

126. Kitchen, *Third Intermediate Period*, 157 n. 307.

127. Tadmor, "'The People' and the Kingship in Ancient Israel," 57–58; S. Yeivin, "Rehoboam and Jeroboam" in B.T. Lurya ed. *Sefer Korngrin* (Tel-Aviv: Ha-Hevrah le-heker ha-Mikra be-Yisrael, 1964), 78–79 (Hebrew).

128. Lipinski, "Le récit de 1 Rois XII 1–19," 432–437.

129. Malamat, "Kingship and Council in Israel and Sumer," 247–253.

130. A. Falkenstein, "Zu 'Gilgameš und Agga'" *AfO* 21 (1966): 47.

131. Lipinski, "Le récit de 1 Rois XII 1–19," 437; Tadmor, "'The People' and the Kingship in Ancient Israel," 58; Malamat, "Kingship and Council in Israel and Sumer," 249; Gray, *I and II Kings*, 283; J. Liver, "The Book of the Acts of Solomon" *Biblica* 48 (1967): 96–100.

132. B. Long, *1 Kings, With an Introduction to Historical Literature* (Grand Rapids: W.B. Eerdmans, 1984), 135.

133. See Chapter 5-B.

Egyptian Evidence

A possibility not previously considered is that ילדים in 1 Kgs 12 is a technical term, specifically a title comparable to the Egyptian *ḫrd n k3p* (pl. *ḫrdw n k3p*), "child of Pharaoh's household."[134] This phrase first appears as a title in Egypt in the Middle Kingdom (1990–1785 BCE) but is most widely attested in the 18th Dynasty of the New Kingdom (1540–1300 BCE), after which it disappears.[135] Egyptian written records from the 18th Dynasty, primarily tomb inscriptions, indicate that the *ḫrdw n k3p* were the children of officials and palace personnel. Several generations of *ḫrdw n k3p* are attested from certain families.[136] These youngsters, often commoners from different social strata, apparently received their education and training at court together with the future Pharaoh. Some *ḫrdw n k3p* were of foreign origin, either Asiatic or Nubian.[137]

Occasionally, the *ḫrdw n k3p* functioned in the palace as a judiciary body. In one instance they signed a marriage contract.[138] In another case a master legally awarded his slave freedom in front of a council of *ḫrdw n k3p*.[139] Whereas details for these incidents are lacking, it can be inferred that under certain circumstances the group possessed judicial authority.

Apparently, the Pharaoh picked a number of his functionaries from among those who grew up with him and on whose loyalty he could count. Inscriptions belonging to officials of varying rank and palace staff reveal that several personal attendants who surrounded the Pharaoh as well as officers and adminis-

---

134. In Egyptian *ḫrd*= child, *k3p*= nursery or more generally – the royal living quarters in the inner palace where the princes were raised (Faulkner, *Middle Egyptian*, 204, 284; Erman and Grapow, *Wörterbuch*, 103–104; Quirke, *Administration of Egypt in the Late Middle Kingdom*, 117).

135. Helck, *Verwaltung*, 252–254; E. Feucht, "The *ḪRDW N K3P* Reconsidered" in S.I. Groll ed., *Pharaonic Egypt: The Bible and Christianity* (Jerusalem: Magnes Press, 1985), 38–43.

136. Feucht, "The *ḪRDW N K3P* Reconsidered," 40–41.

137. For a more detailed discussion and textual references, see W. Helck, *Der Einfluss der Militärführer in der 18. ägyptischen Dynastie* (Leipzig: J.C. Hinrichs, 1939), 34 nn. 6–8; "Palastverwaltung" in *Lexikon* 4, 650; W. Seipel, "Harimzögling," in *Lexikon* 2, 991; D. Redford, *Akhenaten Temple Project III* (Toronto: University of Toronto Press, 1988), 16–17; Feucht, "The *ḪRDW N K3P* Reconsidered," 40 n. 32, 42–43; A. Zivie, *Découverte à Saqqarah: Le vizier oublié* (Paris: Seuil, 1990), 151–175. Helck suggests that the foreign *ḫrdw n k3p* were sons of rulers, primarily Egyptian vassals, who were kept at court, partially as hostages and to be Egyptianized before they returned to their lands. Feucht questions this practice. She maintains that only one foreigner with the title *ḫrd n k3p* can be identified as the son of a ruler. However, although this title is not used, the existence of the institution associated with this title is attested in several Amarna letters (see below).

138. Feucht, "The *ḪRDW N K3P* Reconsidered," 73.

139. I. Lurje, *Studien zum altägyptischen Recht, Forschungen zum römischen Recht* 30 (Weimar: Hermann Bohlaus, 1971), 69–70.

trators retained the title *ẖrd n k3p* even as adults. Several personal seals of officials bear this title.[140] Positions held by former *ẖrd n k3p* include: butler, fanbearer, standardbearer, overseer of work projects, master shipbuilder, royal scribe, commander, and even Viceroy of Kush.[141] A recently excavated tomb at Saqqara reveals that a certain Semite by the name of 'Aper-El, whose titulary contains the title *ẖrd n k3p*, rose through the ranks to the highest office in the land, that of vizier.[142] In addition to civil positions, *ẖrdw n k3p* also attained religious offices.[143] For the common Egyptian it was undoubtedly an honor to have been a member of this elite group. Exactly how many Pharaonic officials began as *ẖrdw n k3p* is uncertain, since the title may not have been consistently recorded. More importantly, it seems to have ceased to function as a status symbol in titularies by the end of the 18th Dynasty.

Court Families in Israel

The ילדים, who grew up with Rehoboam and served him as adults, may have been childhood members of Solomon's palace-household analogous to the *ẖrdw n k3p* in Egypt. Although a list of Rehoboam's officials is not preserved in the Bible, from the reigns of other kings there exist several examples of sons of officials and religious personnel who in turn were appointed to government positions. The sons of a number of dignitaries of David's court are listed in a record of Solomonic appointees in 1 Kgs 4. For example, the sons of David's scribe Seraiah/Shisha, Elihoreph and Ahijah, succeeded as scribes (4:3); Azariah and Zabud, sons of Nathan, served as minister over the prefects and king's friend, respectively (4:5).[144] More substantial data, both biblical and epigraphic, are available from the reigns of Hezekiah, Josiah, Jehoiakim, and Zedekiah. As illustrated in Table C, evidence of two or more generations of office-holders is attested, among others, from the Shaphan (2 Kgs 22:12; 25:22; Jer 29:3; 36:10–12; Ezek 8:11), Neriah (Jer 36:4; 51:59), Hilkiah (2 Kgs 22:4; 25:18; 1 Chr 5:39–41) and Achbor (2 Kgs 22:12; Jer 26:22) families.

Notably, members of the Shaphan and Neriah families often have their

---

140. The title *ẖrd n k3p* is attested on scarabs and seal impressions of officials from the late Middle Kingdom and Second Intermediate Period (Martin, *Egyptian Administrative and Private-Name Seals*, nos. 179, 207, 1146, 1336, 1511, 1571, 1635).

141. Citations in Helck, *Militärführer*, 34 nn. 6–8.

142. Zivie, *Découverte à Saqqarah*, 151–173. J. Hoffmeier discusses this case in conjunction with the biblical Joseph (*Israel in Egypt: The Evidence for the Authenticity of the Exodus Tradition* [New York: Oxford University Press, 1997], 94).

143. Feucht, "The *H̱RDW N K3P* Reconsidered," 40–41.

144. It is uncertain whether Azariah and Zabud were sons of the same Nathan and whether this Nathan was the prophet at David's court.

grandfather's name included in their patronymic, suggesting at least three generations of dignitaries. This phenomenon is observable for the following names: Shaphan son of Azaliah son of Meshullam, Josiah's scribe (2 Kgs 22:3); Micaiah son of Gemariah son of Shaphan, an official of Jehoiakim (Jer 36:11); Gedaliah son of Ahikam son of Shaphan, the governor of Judah after the Babylonian conquest (2 Kgs 25:22); Baruch son of Neriah son of Mahseiah, Jeremiah's scribe, and his brother Seriah son of Neriah son of Mahseiah, Zedekiah's quartermaster (Jer 32:12; 51:59).[145]

Whereas some of the relationships illustrated in Table C are inferred and certain reservations remain,[146] the secure examples alone seem to indicate a general pattern for the monarchic state-organization, minimally for the periods specified. The evidence that certain families held key positions at the royal court implies that they resided in or near the palace complex. Thus, the writer's observation that Rehoboam's ילדים "grew up with him" (1 Kgs 12:8) can be understood literally. Apparently, the children of Solomon's closest officers and attendants were raised at court together with the princes. When Rehoboam ascended the throne, he presumably chose some of his officials from that group of ילדים. While a number of the older officials retained their posts, as evidenced by Adoram, whose tenure of office dates to the time of David (2 Sam 20:24; 1 Kgs 4:6, 12:18), one can imagine that the new king would appoint trusted men of his own generation to various positions. In light of the above reconstruction, it is conceivable that in a crisis Rehoboam would consult members of the ילדים and even follow their advice. It also seems reasonable that these new appointees, junior functionaries, would be overzealous in avoiding a policy that could be construed as indicative of their weakness.

Transmission of the Title?

If Rehoboam's ילדים are compared to the *ẖrdw n kȝp* of the Pharaohs, then possible origins of the Hebrew institution should be investigated. One avenue of transmission is direct borrowing from Egypt to Israel—in other words, adopting a foreign model. Two difficulties persist with this explanation: substantiating contact between Egypt and Israel during the period of the United Monarchy and bridging wide time gaps between the attestation of the term in Egyptian

145. While Baruch's position as scribe is not tied directly into an official role, his access to the palace complex and acceptance by Jehoiakim's ministers (Jer 36:8–19), as well as his brother's position, indicates that he belonged to a prominent court family (J. Muilenburg, "Baruch the Scribe" in J. Durham and J. Porter eds. *Proclamation and Presence* [Macon: Mercer University Press, 1983], 227–238; see Chapter 4-B).

146. See Chapter 2 – Prosopography.

records and its appearance in the Bible. The first issue is problematic primarily because Egyptian sources are silent on interconnections between Egypt and Israel in this period. The Bible, on the other hand, mentions trade connections (1 Kgs 10:28–29) and the marriage of Solomon to an Egyptian princess who came to live in Jerusalem (1 Kgs 3:1). Certainly a royal alliance through marriage would have presented opportunity for cultural exchange, including the adoption of palace customs associated with the *ḫrdw n kȝp*.[147] But despite the biblical evidence, the difficulties are not easily resolved.

Scholars continue to debate the historicity of these biblical records not only because the events are unconfirmed by Egyptian sources but because their credibility is questionable. In particular, the practice of wedding an Egyptian princess to a foreigner was most unusual. K. Kitchen, for one, accepts the feasibility of the marriage for the period of the 21st Dynasty (perhaps Pharaoh Siamun), a time of internal political weakness in Egypt. He maintains that, following the New Kingdom, Pharaohs did marry-off their spare daughters to non-Egyptians, as exemplified by the marriage of a daughter of Psusennes II to a Libyan.[148] The strength of Kitchen's evidence is questioned in a recent doctoral dissertation by P. Ash, especially on the matter of royal marriages with Libyans, who would not have been considered foreigners by the 21st Dynasty. Ash follows a school of thought that views the account of Solomon's marriage to an Egyptian princess as simply another legendary component of the idealized story written about Solomon centuries later by the Deuteronomistic writers.[149] But even if interconnections did take place between Israel and Egypt in this period, a weak point remains in this theory, namely that the title is last attested in Egyptian texts at the end of the 18th Dynasty, more than 300 years before Solomon's reign.

An alternate but related avenue of approach is positing indirect transmission of the Egyptian practice via the Canaanite city-states. During the New Kingdom, when Syria–Palestine was under Egyptian hegemony, local rulers regularly sent their sons and daughters to Egypt, in part as hostages and in part to be trained as obedient Egyptian vassals before being reinstated in their homeland.[150] Several Amarna letters indicate that Canaanite princes served as *ḫrdw*

147. See Mettinger (*Solomonic State Officials*, 140–157) and Williams ("A People Came Out of Egypt," *VTS* 28 [1975]: 238–252) on the influence of Egyptian literature in Israel; contrast Redford, *Egypt, Canaan, and Israel in Ancient Times*, 386–394.

148. Kitchen, "Egypt and East Africa," 116–120.

149. Ash, "Relationship Between Egypt and Palestine," 143–153. Ash details the current scholarly discussion on this and other issues pertaining to interconnections between Egypt and Israel at this time.

150. Redford, *Egypt, Canaan, and Israel in Ancient Times*, 198–199, 270.

at the Pharaoh's court. For example, Yahtiri, ruler of Gaza, explicitly states that as a child in Egypt he served the Pharaoh "standing at the gate," apparently as gatekeeper or guard (*EA* 296:25–29); Aziri prince of Amurru reminds the Pharaoh that he sent his sons for service to Egypt (*EA* 156:8–12);[151] Abdi-hiba, ruler of Jerusalem, who credits his position to the Pharaoh's benevolence, bears two Egyptian titles, *ruḫi šarri* and *úeú*, which he probably acquired as a young man in Egypt (*EA* 288:9–15).[152] Whereas the designation *ẖrd n kꜣp* is not attested in these Akkadian texts, the existence of the institution associated with this title is evident.[153]

Since the Amarna period corresponds to the latter part of the 18th Dynasty, this theory, like the one proposing direct Egyptian influence, is weakened by a wide time gap. More than 300 years separate the Canaanite material from the advent of any Israelite kingdom. Nevertheless, in favor of this proposal is ample data confirming continuity of Egyptian control over Canaan in the 19th and even into the 20th Dynasty (13th–12th centuries).[154] Accordingly, practices associated with the title *ẖrd n kꜣp* could still have been operational in one form or

---

151. Following Moran who reconstructs, "[my] sons" (*Amarna Letters*, 242).

152. Both terms appear to be Akkadian transliterations of Egyptian words: *ruḫi šarri* = *rḫ nswt*, "king's friend or acquaintance"; *úeú* = *wʿw*, "soldier" (H. Donner, "Der 'Freund des Königs'," *ZAW* 73 [1961]: 273–274; L. Oppenheim, "A Note on the Scribes in Mesopotamia," in H. Güterbock and T. Jacobsen eds. *Studies in Honor of Benno Landsberger* [Chicago: University of Chicago Press, 1965], 255 n. 5; see Chapter 4-D). Abdi-Hiba is the only Syro-Palestinian ruler to call himself by these titles (*EA* 285:6; 287:69; 288:10). In other instances, the term for Egyptian soldier, *wʿw*, is used solely to designate Egyptians (*EA* 108:16; 109:22; 150:6, 9; 152:47, 50;230:11; 287:47). Donner suggests that the Pharaoh conferred the designation *rḫ nswt* on Abdi-Hiba as an honorific title (p. 274). Cf. Moran, who thinks Abdi-Hiba was not in line for succession, but rather came to the throne due to his military position ("The Syrian Scribe of the Jerusalem Amarna Letters" in H. Goedicke and J. Roberts eds. *Unity and Diversity: Essays in the History, Literature and Religion of the Ancient Near East* [Baltimore: Johns Hopkins University Press, 1975], 156).

153. Other technical vocabulary, evidently, was exchanged between Egypt and Canaan. A number of Semitic military terms appear in Egyptian texts of the Amarna Age and several Egyptian words in the Amarna letters resemble Egyptian titles (W. Ward, "Comparative Studies in Egyptian and Ugaritic" *JNES* 20 [1961]: 39; Knudtzon, *Die El-Amarna-Tafeln* 2, 1549–1551).

154. Redford, *Egypt, Canaan, and Israel in Ancient Times*, 192–213. In addition to data from Egyptian documents reporting military victories of the Pharaohs, isolated written material from Canaan reflects Egypt's continued supremacy. For example, hieratic inscriptions on bowls from Lachish and Tel Seraʿ record taxes collected for Egyptian temples in Canaan in the late 13th and early 12th centuries (J. Černý, "Egyptian Hieratic" in O. Tufnell ed. *Lachish IV: The Bronze Age* [Oxford: Oxford University Press, 1958], 133, pl. 44; O. Goldwasser, "Hieratic Inscriptions from Tel Seraʿ in Southern Canaan," *TA* 11 [1984]: 77–87, pl. 4).

another. In the account of Wenamun (1:38–39), dated to the end of the 20th Dynasty, mention is made of a "youth" or "page," designated *ḫrd ꜥꜣ* (literally – "a great child") at the Phoenician court of Zakar-Ba'al.[155] The Israelite monarchy, which developed in a Canaanite setting, would have been familiar with the indigenous system, including Phoenician practices, since strong ties existed between David and Solomon and Tyre (2 Sam 5:11; 1 Kgs 5–9).[156]

Conclusions

Even the limited evidence presented here strongly suggests that the designation ילדים in 1 Kgs 12 should be understood as a technical term signifying membership in a special group.[157] Rehoboam's contemporaries, who were raised with him at the royal court, seem to belong to a palace household institution analogous to that of the *ḫrdw n kꜣp* of Egypt. Most probably, the ילדים were sons of officials and courtiers, both of royal and non-royal descent, who at the time Rehoboam ascended the throne served him in various capacities. Evidence for the existence of families of Israelite court officials spanning several generations supports this theory.

The title ילדים does not, however, specify any offices held by these junior functionaries or their exact relationship to the king. In addition, the question of origin and the transmission of the institution associated with the ילדים is not fully discernable. Possibly it developed independently in fulfillment of a need common to palace organizations. Analogies from the Book of Daniel seem to reflect a wider ancient Near Eastern tradition. It is more likely, though, that the practice from which the title ילדים arose reflects a connection with Egypt, possibly via an indirect route.

155. A. Gardiner, *Late Egyptian Stories* (Brussels: Édition de la foundation égyptologique, 1931), 65; J. Wilson, *ANET*, 26.

156. Aubet, *Phoenicians and the West*, 35–37, 95; Katzenstein, *History of Tyre*, 77–115; Briquel-Chatonnet, *Les relations entre les cités de la côte phénicienne et les royaumes d'Israël et de Juda*, 25–58.

157. The term ילדים plays a second role in this narrative. As a literary device the term refers to the immaturity and impetuousness of the younger advisors, a point the writer no doubt meant to emphasize as part of his ideological justification for the schism of Solomon's kingdom. Simultaneously, there is no reason to doubt that he utilized existing terminology to express the contrast between the two groups of royal advisors.

4
Function-Related Titles

A. אשר על הבית - Minister over the Royal House

Biblical Evidence

Probably the most prestigious title specifying a position in the state organization is that of אשר על הבית (*'šr 'l hbyt*), "the one who is over the house." Seven royal officials, six named and one unnamed, holding this title are mentioned in the Bible. An eighth court functionary is called נגיד הבית (*ngyd hbyt*), "ruler of the house." Ahishar, who is the first Israelite official entitled אשר על הבית, appears in the register of Solomonic appointees (1 Kgs 4:6).[1] For the period of the Divided Monarchy, the bible records three such officials from Israel: Arza, who served under King Elah and is listed as a casualty in a palace coup at Tirzah (16:9); Obadiah, who ministered in Samaria during the famine in the reign of Ahab (18:3); and an unnamed אשר על הבית, who together with the mayor of Samaria, the elders, and the guardians of the princes, assisted Jehu in exterminating the survivors of the house of Ahab (2 Kgs 10:5). In Judah, the crown prince Jotham is called על הבית when he becomes co-regent after his father Azariah is incapacitated by leprosy (2 Kgs 15:5 = 2 Chr 26:21).[2] Other Judahites who bear this title include Shebnah, who is the subject of an oracle by Isaiah in which the prophet denounces him and predicts his downfall (Isa 22:15), and Eliakim son of Hilkiah, who is listed as one of a delegation of three officials sent by Hezekiah to negotiate with the Assyrian officers besieging Jerusalem (2 Kgs 18:18 = Isa 36:3). One minister, Azrikam, is designated נגיד הבית. He is killed together with two other members of the court of Ahaz during the Syro-Ephramite war (2 Chr 28:7).

In addition, variations of the expression אשר על הבית refer to characters in the

---

1. In the Solomonic register the element אשר, "the one who," is absent from this and other titularies.

2. In Chronicles the title reads: על בית המלך. The nature of Jotham's office during his father's illness is problematic and will be discussed below.

Joseph stories who ministered to Pharaoh or his officials. Potiphar, a Pharaonic officer, appoints Joseph על ביתו, "over his house" (Gen 39:4). Later, Pharaoh elevates Joseph על ביתי "over my house" (41:40).[3] When Joseph's brothers are brought to his house they encounter at the doorway the man אשר על בית יוסף, "who is over the house of Joseph," (43:19).

Archaeological Evidence

To date only two provenienced inscriptions showing the title אשר על הבית are extant, one on a tomb inscription and the other on a bulla discovered accidentally on the surface.[4] Since both inscriptions lack a clear archaeological context they are dated paleographically, the tomb inscription to the end of the eighth century and the bulla to the end of the seventh or early sixth century. The tomb inscription, which was engraved above the door of a rock-cut tomb in Silwan, contains the title אשר על הבית in its first line. It is restored as follows: זאת [קברת...]יהו אשר על הבית, "this is the sepulchre of x-*yhw* who is over the house." One candidate proposed as the owner and occupant of the tomb is Shebnah (Isa 22:15–25), whose name is a hypocoristicon of *šbnyhw*. The bulla, which was found at Lachish, is impressed with the inscription לגדליהו אשר על הבית, "belonging to *gdlyhw* who is over the house." Its owner can tentatively be identified with either Gedaliah son of Ahikam, who became governor of Judah after the fall of Jerusalem (2 Kgs 25:22), or Gedaliah son of Pashhur, who was an official in the reign of Zedekiah (Jer 38:1). It should be realized, however, that since these inscriptions cannot be dated more accurately and in the case of Gedaliah there is no biblical corroboration for the title, the identifications remain conjectural.

Definition of the Title

The title אשר על הבית, like some others, does not clearly define the sphere of activity of office-holders. Primarily this lies in the imprecision of the key term, בית, which can denote a number of entities both in its absolute and construct nominal forms. For example, the absolute form commonly signifies a building

3. Joseph is never explicitly called אשר על הבית. See discussion below.

4. N. Avigad, "The Epitaph of a Royal Steward from Siloam Village," *IEJ* 3 (1953): 137–152; H. Hooke, "A Scarab and Sealing from Tell Duweir," *PEQ* 67 (1935): 195–197; de Vaux, "Le sceau de Godolias, maitre du palais," 96–102; O. Tufnell, *Lachish III: The Iron Age* (London: Oxford University Press, 1953), 348. Six additional bullae and one seal showing a PN followed by the designation אשר על הבית have appeared on the antiquities market. Three of the bullae bear the same PN and title but were stamped with two different seals. Avigad, *Hebrew Bullae*, 21–22; "A Group of Seals from the Hecht Collection," in *Festschrift R.R. Hecht* (Jerusalem: Koren, 1979), 119; Deutsch, *Messages from the Past*, 55–57. See Table A–2.

such as a house, palace, or temple: בית חדש, "a new house" (Deut 20:5); בית לדוד, "a palace for David" (2 Sam 5:11); הבית ליהוה, "the temple for God" (1 Kgs 6:1). The word בית can also have the sense family and dynasty, as בית נאמן, "an enduring family/dynasty" (1 Sam 2:35), or occasionally it can denote the house of an estate, as בית והון, "a house and riches" (Prov 19:14). When בית is in the construct state, the genitive often identifies the type of house or its owner: בית הסהר, "prison" (Gen 39:20); בית הבעל, "house of Baal" (1 Kgs 16:32), בית שאול, "house of Saul" (2 Sam 3:1). As a result of the wide range of usages of the term בית, scholarship is divided on the functions and jurisdiction of officials entitled אשר על הבית. Still it is generally agreed that occupants of this office were administrators of the highest status.[5]

Rank, Functions and Jurisdiction

Several factors are pertinent in evaluating the rank of royal officials. One criterion used is the place the functionary occupies on lists.[6] In the register of Solomonic appointees (1 Kgs 4), the most comprehensive official list and the earliest reference to this minister, the אשר על הבית, Ahishar, appears toward the end in eighth position. In contrast, in other cases, all of which refer to officials from the period of the Divided Monarchy, he is listed first, preceded only by persons of royalty. In the account of Jehu's revolt, the אשר על הבית heads a list of Ahab's functionaries, preceding the אשר על העיר, "the city governor," הזקנים, "the elders," and האמנים, "the guardians" (2 Kgs 10:5). In the context of the war between Pekah and Ahaz, the official designated נגיד הבית, Azrikam, is recorded second in a group of three Judahite casualties, appearing after the בן המלך, "the king's son," but before the משנה המלך, a personal attendant of the king (2 Chr 28:7). Finally, in the narrative of the Assyrian siege of Jerusalem in the reign of Hezekiah (2 Kgs 18–19), the אשר על הבית, Eliakim son of Hilkiah, is listed first each time as one of three delegates sent to the Assyrian officers and to the prophet Isaiah. In the former he precedes the scribe, in second place, and the herald, in third place (18:18, 26, 37); in the latter he precedes the scribe, in second place, and the elders of the priests, in third place (19:2).

Unfortunately, biblical official lists are unreliable indicators of rank. As shown by the aforementioned examples, those from the Divided Monarchy are fragmentary and only represent selected groups of officials. Even the more

5. The single occurrence of נגיד הבית is not illuminating since נגיד, when denoting an official, simply signifies a "leader or ruler" comparable, though not necessarily identical, to אשר על.

6. H.J. Katzenstein, "The Royal Steward," *IEJ* 10 (1960): 152; Mettinger, *Solomonic State Officials*, 88.

complete lists of royal functionaries from the United Monarchy are problematic and raise a number of issues. The Saulite and Davidic records do not contain any official by that title. The Solomonic list, in which this administrator first appears, shows him in eighth position in reference to other officials (1 Kgs 4:6). But in contrast to the MT, where one individual, Ahishar, holds this position, the Septuagint preserves the names of two such officers, Ahishar and Eliah (3 Kgs 4:6). In the LXX supplement, Ahishar is omitted and a different individual, Edram, "who is over his house," is mentioned (2:46h). To further confuse the matter, the order of officials in these three lists is inconsistent. Perhaps this is a sign of later tampering, evidence of a variant *Vorlage*, or an indication that the order was not necessarily based on rank.[7] On the other hand, the variations of the Solomonic list may imply that the status and position of the אשר על הבית underwent changes in the 10th century. As a result of these obstacles, the rank of the אשר על הבית cannot be determined from these biblical data and must rely primarily on information about his jurisdiction.

The jurisdiction of the אשר על הבית has been long debated by scholars. Arguments center on whether the realm of this minister was confined to the palace complex in the respective capitals or extended to royal holdings state-wide. Mettinger argues that the overall evidence points to a wider charge over the entire royal property.[8] In contrast, Rüterswörden and, most recently, Layton, maintain that the area of control of the אשר על הבית was restricted to the palace and its household.[9] Two biblical narratives are usually cited as holding the key to understanding the roles of the אשר על הבית. One refers to the authority conferred on the crown prince Jotham son of Azariah and the other relies on the pericope in Isaiah that deals with two royal ministers, Shebnah and Eliakim.

In the first episode, the Deuteronomist notes that when King Azariah became leprous, he moved to isolated quarters while his son Jotham assumed his duties:

וישב בבית החפשית ויותם בן המלך על הבית שפט את עם הארץ

He (Azariah) resided in the "house of freedom"[10] while Jotham the king's

7. E. Tov, *The Text-Critical Use of the Septuagint* (Minneapolis: Fortress Press, 1992), 303–304.

8. Mettinger, *Solomonic State Officials*, 70–110. Mettinger's thesis is an expansion of a theory by M. Noth ("Das Krongut der Israel. Könige und seine Verwaltung," *ZDPV* 50 [1927]: 217).

9. Rüterswörden, *Beamten der israelitischen Königszeit*, 77–85; S. Layton, "The Steward in Ancient Israel: A Study of Hebrew (*'ašer*) *'al-habbayit* in its Near Eastern Setting," *JBL* 109 (1990): 641–649.

10. The expression בית החפשית is difficult to define. For a discussion, see M. Cogan and H. Tadmor, *The Anchor Bible, II Kings* (Garden City: Doubleday, 1988), 166–167.

son was over the house, judging/ruling the people of the land[11] (2 Kgs 15:5).

In the Chronicler's parallel account, the wording varies somewhat: על הבית, "over the house," becomes על בית המלך, "over the king's house" (2 Chr 26:21). Usually it is assumed that Jotham's commission was equivalent to that of אשר על הבית[12] and that consequently the Chronicler's gloss, על בית המלך, should be understood as confirmation that the purview of this office was limited to the palace.[13] This argument, however, is problematic on several counts. First, it assumes that Jotham functioned as the אשר על הבית while Azariah still actively reigned and that he (Jotham) retained the office even after becoming co-regent and inheriting all the obligations of kingship.[14] Second, the description of Jotham's duties both in Kings and Chronicles, "judging/ruling the people," reflects the king's role, not that of a minister.[15] Third, the Chronicler's gloss can be viewed as an intentional distinction between Jotham's position as co-regent and that of the אשר על הבית. The Septuagint's translation of 2 Chr. 26:21, καὶ Ἰωάθαμ ὁ υἱὸς αὐτοῦ ἐπὶ τῆς βασιλείας, "and his son Jotham was over his kingdom," supports that contention. Thus, based on the evidence, it seems doubtful that Jotham occupied the position of אשר על הבית. Finally, even if Jotham did occupy that office, the expression בית המלך is not necessarily exclusive of royal holdings outside the palace; hence, the Chronicler's gloss cannot be used to define בית as solely referring to the palace in Jerusalem.[16]

---

11. The People of the Land seem to have been a privileged and powerful group in society. They attended the coronation of Joash (2 Kgs 11:14), they killed the conspirators in the palace coup against Amon (21:24), and they crowned Jehoahaz after Josiah's death (23:30). Perhaps the king had special obligations in judicial matters vis-à-vis this group (Cogan and Tadmor, *II Kings*, 167. For an in-depth discussion, see H. Reviv, *The Society in the Kingdoms of Israel and Judah* [Jerusalem: Bialik Institute, 1993], 149–156).

12. Cogan and Tadmor, *II Kings*, 167; Rüterswörden, *Beamten der israelitischen Königszeit*, 80; Avishur and Heltzer, *Studies on the Royal Administration*, 58.

13. Layton, "The Steward in Ancient Israel," 643.

14. The circumstantial clause of this verse, both in Kings and Chronicles, indicates that at the time Azariah was in isolation, Jotham carried out duties denoted by the phrase על הבית שפט את עם הארץ.

15. Katzenstein, "The Royal Steward," 152. Cogan and Tadmor also note that Jotham took over his father's judicial duties (*II Kings*, 167).

16. It should also be noted that Glueck's and Avigad's misidentification of the owner of a seal from Tell Kheleifeh inscribed ליתם, "belonging to *ytm*," as the crown prince Jotham and his alleged position as אשר על הבית, should be discarded (N. Glueck, "The Third Season of Excavation at Tell el-Kheleifeh," *BASOR* 79 [1940]: 13–15; N. Avigad, "The Jotham Seal from Elath," *BASOR* 163 [1961]: 18–22. Avigad had identified an object on the seal as bellows and based on the assumption that the seal belonged to Azariah's son, suggested that

The second text, Isaiah 22:15–25, mentions two individuals, Shebnah and Eliakim, who bear the title אשר על הבית. This passage of prophetic poetry, however, is far from lucid and poses more questions than resolutions.[17] The exact time-frame or context of the prophecy cannot be discerned, but apparently it precedes Eliakim's term as אשר על הבית, when Shebnah still held that post. Isaiah's message is a denunciation of Shebnah. It predicts that Shebnah will be replaced by a worthier man, Eliakim son of Hilkiah. Isaiah calls Shebnah קלון בית אדניך, "the shame of your master's house" (22:18), but he does not delineate a specific offense. He simply questions Shebnah's right to quarry a tomb for himself in the hills of Jerusalem, an indication perhaps that Shebnah was not a native Jerusalemite, since he did not already possess an ancestral burial place in the vicinity.[18]

Of note is the term סכן (*skn*) which Isaiah uses to refer to Shebnah in conjunction with his title אשר על הבית (22:15). The participial form of the verb סכן, defined as "one who provides service," occurs in the Bible only one other time, as feminine סכנת (*sknt*) in 1 Kgs 1:2, 4, a designation for David's personal attendant Abishag. It is commonly posited that סכן in Isaiah is a *hapax legomenon* denoting an official title parallel to אשר על הבית. Several scholars trace Isaiah's usage of סכן to an older Ugaritic and Syrian title *skn/sākinu*, a cognate appellation for a high royal official.[19] A close reading of Isa 22:15 in the context of the entire pericope, however, raises questions concerning the semantic relationship be-

---

when Azariah rebuilt Elat, he revived the copper industry and placed Jotham, the אשר על הבית, as head of mines and industry). Not only is the title אשר על הבית lacking from the seal but the name יתם seems to denote a different root, "orphan." Based on paleography, the seal appears to be Edomite, not Israelite (Naveh, *Early History of the Alphabet*, 102). Both Glueck and Avigad apparently recognized their error (Glueck, "Tell el-Kheleifeh Inscriptions," in H. Goedicke ed. *Near Eastern Studies in Honor of William Foxwell Albright* [Baltimore: Johns Hopkins Press, 1971], 225–226; Avigad, "Hebrew Epigraphic Sources," in *WHJP* 4/1, 43).

17. The enigmatic nature of the passage is borne out by the scope of scholarly interpretation. There is disagreement on who is condemned, why they are condemned, and what the metaphors really mean. See for example, J.B. Gray, *Isaiah* 1 (New York: Charles Scribner's Sons, 1912), 373–383; E.J. Kissane, *The Book of Isaiah* 1 (Dublin: Brown and Nolan, 1941), 250–255; O. Kaiser, *Isaiah 13–39: A Commentary*, (Philadelphia: Westminster Press, 1974), 148–159; J. Hayes and S. Irvine, *Isaiah the Eighth Century Prophet: His Times and His Preaching* (Nashville: Abington Press, 1987), 283–287.

18. Kissane's assumption (*Book of Isaiah*, 250) that Shebnah represented a political view contrary to one held by Isaiah is purely conjectural.

19. Mettinger, *Solomonic State Officials*, 71; Rüterswörden, *Beamten der israelitischen Königszeit*, 80–85; Layton, "The Steward in Ancient Israel," 647–648; Avishur and Heltzer, *Studies on the Royal Administration*, 58–59.

tween סכן and אשר על הבית. To begin with, the parallelism in the verse need not be viewed as synonymous:

> כה אמר אדני יהוה צבאות לך בא אל הסכן הזה על שבנא אשר על הבית
>
> Thus says the Lord YHWH of hosts: Go, come to that[20] סכן, to Shebnah who is over the house.

The term סכן in the first half of the verse can simply signify a general designation for a low level household or personal steward similar to סכנת. The demonstrative הזה, "that," referring to Shebnah, which follows the word סכן, should be understood in light of Isaiah's scornful tone that predominates in the prophecy.[21] The PN Shebnah and title אשר על הבית in the last segment seem to expand upon the earlier description by identifying Shebnah and his exact title. Quite possibly, the term סכן was chosen over another to heighten the sarcasm. In any case, the identification of סכן in Isaiah 22 as an archaic term of foreign origin that is equivalent to אשר על הבית cannot be sustained.[22]

Attempts to derive the roles of the אשר על הבית from Isaiah's description of Eliakim are also problematic. Isaiah's assertion that Eliakim will be entrusted with the key to the House of David and he alone will be charged with opening and closing is not revealing (22:22). In fact it is vague, not specifying whether the אשר על הבית holds keys to the palace-stores, other royal treasures, the entire acropolis complex, or royal property state-wide. Furthermore, the term מפתח, "key," in this passage can be understood metaphorically.[23] The same can be said of other images portrayed in verses 21–24. For example, Eliakim is likened to a father of the inhabitants of Judah and to a secure peg on which one hangs household vessels. To conclude, the range of the domain of the אשר על הבית cannot be defined with any degree of accuracy from the poetry in Isaiah 22.[24]

---

20. "That" instead of "this" following H.L. Ginsberg's view that the former better expresses contempt or displeasure ("Gleanings in First Isaiah" in *M.M. Kaplan Jubilee Volume* [New York: JTS, 1953], 255–256).

21. The reading על שבנא instead of אל שבנא has led several scholars to reorder this verse so that part two is the opening: על שבנא אשר על הבית. For a detailed explanation see, H. Wildberger, *Jesaja* (Neukirchen-Vluyn: Neukirchener, 1978), 831. However, in light of the frequent interchange of על and אל in the Bible (*BDB*, 41a, 757a), this exercise seems unnecessary. It is also possible, as Ginsberg suggests, that the writer wrote על in anticipation of the על of אשר על הבית (*Gleanings in First Isaiah*, 256).

22. The title סכן and its Aramaic, Ugaritic, and Akkadian cognates is discussed separately in Chapter 5–A.

23. Redford, "Studies in Relations between Palestine and Egypt During the First Millennium B.C.," 143 n. 5.

24. It should also be noted that a common association of Shebnah the אשר על הבית with

Ideally, the evaluation of the jurisdiction of the אשר על הבית should be based on data gleaned from administrative texts. However, the few letters that have survived on ostraca, primarily from Lachish and Arad, do not identify this official by title even once. The surviving bulla impressed with the title אשר על הבית was preserved without the document it sealed or even an archaeological context. Attempts to define the purview of this official based on an identification of the seal owner גדליהו with Gedaliah son of Ahikam, the governor of Judah after the fall of Jerusalem (2 Kings 25:22), are of limited value. First, the association of Gedaliah son of Ahikam with this seal is not secure and, even if correct, it does not necessarily follow that Nebuchadnezzar appointed Gedaliah governor due to his previous experience as the אשר על הבית.[25] Probably the pro-Babylonian political stand of the family of Ahikam, who supported Jeremiah in that policy, would have had a greater impact on Nebuchadnezzar's choice of a trustworthy governor. At best, the available archaeological evidence only hints at the administrative jurisdiction of this royal official. It does show, however, that this minister, along with a number of other court functionaries, owned seals inscribed with both a PN and title.

Despite the bleak picture painted here on the lack of information concerning the אשר על הבית, the scant biblical data do provide some material for elucidating the purview of this administrator. A clue pertaining to his mandate is found in the brief encounter with the unnamed אשר על הבית (2 Kgs 10:1–5). As previously mentioned, he heads a list of Samarian officials whose allegiance Jehu tests in the process of securing his kingship. In that list, the אשר על הבית is followed by the אשר על העיר, "the city governor," and the city elders. Perhaps Jehu purposely chose these individuals because they represented key spheres of power in Samaria. The jurisdiction of the אשר על הבית would have extended over the greater palace complex of the upper city, the acropolis, while the governor exercised control over municipal matters in the lower city; the elders would have represented the leadership of influential families in the region.[26] If this interpretation is correct, it follows that the אשר על הבית was the highest ranked court official.

---

the scribe by that name who served with Eliakim (2 Kgs 18; Mettinger, *Solomonic State Officials*, 71; Cogan and Tadmor, *II Kings*, 230) is an unfounded assumption. The name Shebnah appears frequently in epigraphic material from the late eighth century, at times with different patronyms. At least two persons with that PN are known from officials attested on *lmlk* type handles: שבנא בן שחר and שבניה בן עזריה (See the discussion on officials whose names appear on the *lmlk* handles in Chapter 6–B). Furthermore, it is far more likely that when Shebnah fell from favor he was dismissed rather than demoted to royal scribe (Ginsberg, "Gleanings in First Isaiah," 252–253).

25. Contra Layton, "The Steward in Ancient Israel," 641.

26. See Chapters 3–C and 4–I.

Notably, there appears to be an especially close relationship between the king and the אשר על הבית. King Elah is found drunk in the home of his אשר על הבית Arza when Zimri murders the two (1 Kgs 16:9). King Ahab and his אשר על הבית Obadiah work together to find sustenance for the livestock during the famine in Samaria (18:5–6). Eliakim's missions at the time of the Assyrian siege of Jerusalem indicate that the אשר על הבית can play the role of a diplomatic envoy.[27] Once he leads a delegation of three, including the scribe and herald, who meet with Sennacherib's officers (2 Kgs 18:18); later, he heads another delegation, this time with the scribe and the elders of the priests, to consult with Isaiah (19:2). As head of the delegation to the Assyrians, it seems that the אשר על הבית would have been in a position to negotiate military matters as well.[28] In this setting, Hezekiah's שר צבא, "commander of the army," is conspicuously absent. Possibly he was detained at Lachish or had been killed or captured in battle.[29] Perhaps, Eliakim the אשר על הבית, rather than another military officer, took his place. In Assyria, a minister associated with the administration of the palace could be given military authority under certain circumstances, as is evident from data on the *abarakku rabû* (see below). Conceivably, the commission of the אשר על הבית crossed similar administrative divisions.[30]

A review of the biblical material indicates that the activities of the אשר על הבית centered in the capital and its environs. Still, theories that his jurisdiction ex-

27. Katzenstein, "The Royal Steward," 152–153; Rüterswörden, *Beamten der israelitischen Königszeit*, 77; Layton, "The Steward in Ancient Israel," 641; cf. Mettinger, *Solomonic State Officials*, 71.

28. The Assyrians who confronted the Judeans were military officers. The *turtānu*, "viceroy," was the army commander (*AHW* 3, 1332; Cogan and Tadmor, *II Kings*, 229). The *rab ša rēši*, "chief eunuch," often led army units (Cogan and Tadmor, 229; H. Tadmor, "Rab-saris and Rab-shakeh in 2 Kings 18" in C.L. Meyers and M. O'Connor eds. *The Word of the Lord Shall Go Forth. Essays in Honor of D.N. Freedman* [Winona Lake: Eisenbrauns, 1983], 279–285). The *rab šaqî*, "chief butler," occasionally led troops but could have accompanied the king as a personal attendant, on this campaign also serving as spokesman since he knew the Judean language (*CAD* Š/2, p. 32; J.V. Kinnier-Wilson, *Nimrud Wine Lists* [London: British School of Archaeology in Iraq, 1972], 35; Cogan and Tadmor, 229–230 [Note that the definition "chief eunuch" for *rab šaqû* in Kinnier-Wilson is incorrect and should be, "chief butler" or "chief cup-bearer"). Note that Cogan's and Tadmor's assertion that the *rab šaqî* never participated in military campaigns cannot be sustained. According to the annals of Sargon II, on his campaign to Urartu, the *rab šaqî* and his troops were defeated by Ursa (ND 2463 in H. Saggs, "The Nimrud Letters, 1952 - Part IV; The Urartian Frontier," *Iraq* 20 [1958]: 200).

29. The text states that the Assyrian officers, together with a large force had arrived from Lachish (2 Kgs 18:17).

30. Cf. Cogan and Tadmor who note that Eliakim's position in this delegation may be due to his personal influence at court rather than his title (*II Kings*, 230).

tended over royal estates nationwide should not be dismissed outright[31] because crown lands and royal stores require overseers. A Chronistic record assigned to David's reign supports Mettinger's hypothesis on this matter. That register lists twelve stewards charged over the royal estates, including the storehouses, a variety of agricultural products and livestock (1 Chr 27:25–31).[32] Two individuals head the list: Azmaveth son of Adiel על אצרות המלך, "over the king's treasuries (in Jerusalem)," and Jonathan son of Uzziah על האצרות בשדה בערים ובכפרים ובמגדלות, "over the treasuries in the field, in the towns, in the villages and in the forts." Since these two ministers were responsible for the king's greater household, though not necessarily his residence, it has been argued that their offices were precursors of the position of the אשר על הבית. Possibly the two title-bearers in the Septuagint list of Solomonic officials represent the continuity of David's organization in the early years of Solomon.[33] Notably, the Chronicler's record enumerating the division of administrative overseers of David's royal estates is a unique biblical witness. From the time of Solomon through the period of the Divided Monarchy, both in Judah and in Israel, the אשר על הבית is the only official cited who **could** have been in charge of this realm or a part thereof. But whether several lower ranked officers reported to a local prefect or to one high ranking minister stationed at the royal court, presumably the אשר על הבית remains conjectural and may have differed from one administration to another.

From the discussion it is apparent that the biblical and epigraphic material provides only limited information from which to reconstruct the role of the אשר על הבית. Consequently, scholars have pursued potential comparative data from other Near Eastern cultures in an effort to further elucidate the important administrative position of this Israelite official.

Egyptian Evidence

Older theories generally posited Egyptian influence on the Israelite office of the אשר על הבית. One theory, proposed by R. de Vaux, is that the model for the אשר

31. As do Rüterswörden, *Beamten der israelitischen Königszeit*, 78 and Layton, "The Steward in Ancient Israel," 642–643.

32. As Japhet notes, there is no reasonable cause to doubt the authenticity of this record. The agricultural divisions that the stewards oversee reflect the economic conditions of the period, and their names seem appropriate to their special fields. In addition, there is no obvious Chronistic agenda to explain (*I & II Chronicles*, 472).

33. Katzenstein, "The Royal Steward," 149. Other options exist for explaining the two office-holders. Depending on the purview of this official, one could speculate that after Solomon's administrative reorganization, one אשר על הבית operated in Judah and another in Israel. Another possibility is that one of the two functioned as a deputy.

על הבית should be sought in the position of the Egyptian vizier, *ṯ3ty*, the highest official in the land second only to Pharaoh. De Vaux points to judicial, financial, military, and general governmental functions of the vizier in Egypt and claims that descriptions of Joseph at Pharaoh's court and Jotham and Eliakim in Jerusalem suggest comparable roles. He also posits that the more limiting title אשר על הבית reflects the Israelite position during the United Monarchy when it just represented the office of a royal steward.[34]

De Vaux's theory is generally not accepted, primarily because the biblical and Egyptian data do not support the contention that the roles of the vizier and the אשר על הבית were ever equivalent. The Egyptian vizier not only acted as the managing director of the *pr-nswt*, "royal palace," but he served as head of the civil administration. He appointed subordinate officials and was responsible for punishing incompetent ministers.[35] No evidence exists that the authority of the אשר על הבית ever extended over other civil officials. De Vaux's dependence on the Joseph stories for defining the function of the אשר על הבית is also problematic. Joseph's many titles, some of which appear to be honorific, are not reliable in delimiting the sphere of this office in the Israelite monarchy.[36] In addition, the nature of the account is legendary and numerous obstacles persist for dating it.

Another theory, advocated by Mettinger, is that the office of the אשר על הבית was modelled on that of the Egyptian *mr pr wr*, "overseer (*mr*) of the great (*wr*) house (*pr*)," who administered the crown property.[37] Mettinger contends that

---

34. De Vaux, "Titres et fonctionnaires," 400–403.

35. G.P.F. van den Boorn, *Duties of the Vizier: Civil Administration in the Early New Kingdom* (London: Kegan Paul International, 1988), 310–324. The vizier also bore the title *wr dw3 pr Ḏḥwti*, "greatest of the five of the house of Thoth." His designation as high priest of Thoth, god of law and order, complements his role as vizier (Gardiner, *Onomastica* I, 19*–20*).

36. Layton, "The Steward in Ancient Israel," 647 n. 66. W. Ward distinguishes Joseph's titles that define actual functions from those that are honorific ("The Egyptian Office of Joseph," *JSS* 5 [1960]: 144–150). One particularly interesting epithet, אב לפרעה (Gen 45:8), has been connected to the Egyptian designation *it-nṯr*, "father of the god" (*nṯr* = god = living king). It should be noted, however, that this Egyptian honorific title was held primarily by the Pharaoh's father-in-law or members of the priesthood (D. Redford, "A Study of the Biblical Story of Joseph," *VTS* 20 [1970]: 191), although occasionally, a valued high official such as a vizier bore the title (Gardiner, *Onomastica* I, 47*–54*). A parallel example from Israel could be the manner in which a king might address a prophet. For instance, the king of Israel addresses Elisha as אבי, "my father" (2 Kgs 6:21; 13:14). But this type of relationship is never attested between the king and the אשר על הבית.

37. The title "overseer of the great house" is expressed as *mr pr wr* or *imy-r pr wr*. *Imy-r* and *mr*, "overseer," are semantically equivalent; literally, *mr* = "in the mouth"; *imy-r* = "being in the mouth." This element is common in numerous titularies. A. Gardiner, *Egyptian Grammar* (Oxford: Oxford University Press, 1957), 553, 567, 577; Erman and Grapow, *Wörterbuch*, 1, 72–74; 2, 94). Sometimes in New Kingdom texts this overseer is designated,

the Hebrew title is a loan translation calqued on the Egyptian title *mr pr wr*, though the last element, *wr*, "great," is absent.[38] The Egyptian title, rendered "*Ober-Domänenvorsteher*" by Helck, signified from the 11th Dynasty (ca. 2000 BCE) onward one of the highest state officials, along with the army commander and royal scribe, outranked only by the vizier.[39] While the *mr pr wr* officiated at court, his jurisdiction extended over the royal residences with their respective property state-wide.[40] Occasionally, at the end of the 18th dynasty, the *mr pr wr* took over certain kingly duties during the minority of the Pharaoh. For example, Horemhab, the *mr pr wr*, governed Egypt during the early years of Tutankhamon (mid-14th century).[41] His far-reaching authority, however, can also be attributed to his influence at court and ambitious nature, as is borne out by the fact that eventually he became Pharaoh. Mettinger posits that בית in the Hebrew title carries a wide sense of "property," analogous to *pr* in the Egyptian title.[42] Like de Vaux, he cites the portrait of Joseph at Pharaoh's court to support his theory. He emphasizes Joseph's dominion over all the land of Egypt and his agrarian policy (Gen 41:40; 45:8; 47:14–26). Mettinger concludes that the biblical writers would not have entitled Joseph על הבית if his office differed from the Israelite minister.[43] A number of points, however, challenge these arguments. First, Joseph's designation never encompasses the entire titulary אשר על הבית. Second, variants of the title that appear in the story are sufficiently amorphous that when supplemented by details depicting Joseph's position, the result is a unique office, one nonexistent in the bureaucracy of monarchic Israel. Certainly Joseph's position in Potiphar's house, designated על הבית (Gen 39:4), is not equivalent to his high Pharaonic office expressed by the same Hebrew title (41:40). The former position is simply that of a steward on a private estate known by the Egyptian term *ḥry-pr*, "he who is over the house."[44]

Besides problems arising from Mettinger's use of the Joseph account, his

---

ꜥ3 n pr, "the great one of the house." In those cases the title does not precede a PN (Helck, *Verwaltung*, 102–103, 379).

38. Mettinger, *Solomonic State Officials*, 77–79.

39. W. Helck, "Domänenvorsteher," in *Lexikon* 1, 1120.

40. Helck, *Verwaltung*, 93–94. The purview of the office is enumerated in the titulary of *Mꜣꜣ-nḫt.f*, royal steward of Amenophis II, on his statue: "Manager of every royal building, manager of every royal field, manager of every royal barn in Upper and Lower Egypt" (p. 103).

41. Helck, *Militärführer*, 51–52.

42. Mettinger, *Solomonic State Officials*, 73–79. In the Egyptian title *pr* has the meaning "estate" (Gardiner, *Onomastica* I, 46*).

43. Mettinger, *Solomonic State Officials*, 77.

44. Faulkner, 174. Hoffmeier mentions this title in connection to Joseph and other Asiatic stewards of private estates (*Israel in Egypt*, 84).

analogy between the Egyptian title *mr pr wr* and the Hebrew title אשר על הבית has some merit. Yet despite the linguistic similarity, Egyptian influence on the Israelite office cannot be proven because equally valid parallels also exist between the Hebrew title and Akkadian and Ugaritic designations.

Mesopotamian Evidence

Several Akkadian titles similar to the Hebrew אשר על הבית deserve attention. On linguistic grounds, the title most closely resembling the Hebrew one is *ša muḫḫi bīti*, "administrator of a large household" (literally, the one who is over the house).[45] That designation, however, is held primarily by functionaries outside the royal court. A comparable title for a high court official is *ša muḫḫi ekalli*, "palace overseer" (literally, the one who is over the palace),[46] the equivalent of the Israelite title אשר על הבית if בית only means "palace." In order to evaluate the evidence for borrowing, the roles of the Mesopotamian officials must be examined and possible avenues of transmission established.

Assyrian and Babylonian sources indicate that a number of titles coexisted for royal officials who were involved with palace administration: *ša muḫḫi ekalli*, "palace overseer"; *rab ekalli*, "chief of the palace"; *ša pān ekalli*, "palace overseer" (literally, the one who is in the front/face of the palace);[47] and *abarakku rabû*, "chief steward."[48] Functionally, the first two titles cannot be distinguished, though the *rab ekalli* appears with a greater frequency in the Neo-Assyrian period. Some distinctions, however, have been observed between the first two and last two titles. Kinnier-Wilson classifies the *ša pān ekalli* and *abarakku rabû* as "controller of administration" and "royal treasurer" respectively.[49] Based on information gleaned from the eighth century Nimrud wine lists, he concludes that the *rab ekalli* or *ša muḫḫi ekalli* was the supreme major-domo who headed the *nīš ekalli*, "the palace personnel," and ranked second only to the king in authority over household matters. His responsibilities encompassed the staff as well as the buildings' maintenance.[50] A seventh-century archive of several *rab*

45. *CAD* B, 296–297. Akkadian *ša muḫḫi* (= Hebrew אשר על; *muḫḫi* = over [*CAD* M/2, 172]) is a construction found in other titularies as well—for example, *ša muḫḫi āli*, "city administrator." A lesser court functionary known as the *ša muḫḫi bītāni* supervised servants in the living quarters of the palace (Pečírková, "The Administrative Organization of the Neo-Assyrian Empire," 226).

46. *CAD* E, 62.

47. *CAD* E, 62; *AHW* 2, 818, 936–938.

48. *CAD* A/1, 33.

49. Kinnier-Wilson, *Nimrud Wine Lists*, 63, 105–110.

50. Kinnier-Wilson, *Nimrud Wine Lists*, 78, 95; Pečírková, "The Administrative Organization of the Neo-Assyrian Empire," 226.

ekalli from Fort Shalmaneser indicates that this official dealt with numerous transactions relating to the *ekal mašarti*, "great storehouse," including provisions for humans and animals, payment of workers, and delivery of supplies. There is also evidence that two or more individuals may have held this office simultaneously in certain periods.[51]

Kinnier-Wilson suggests that the Hebrew אשר על הבית is analogous to the *ša muḫḫi ekalli* or *rab ekalli*. He also proposes that the two top high officials in Hezekiah's delegation to Isaiah (2 Kgs 19:2), the אשר על הבית and the ספר, correspond to the hierarchy of the Assyrian king's household: *ša muḫḫi ekalli*, "the supreme major-domo," followed by the *ṭupšar ekalli*, "the royal scribe."[52] The same can be said regarding the delegation sent by Hezekiah to the Assyrians (18:18). As noted, in that scenario the role of Eliakim may be analogous to that of the *abarakku rabû*, a chief steward who under certain circumstances was empowered with military authority.[53]

It is not unreasonable to speculate that Judahite officialdom at the close of the eighth century was somewhat influenced by the Assyrian system. That is not to say that the role of the אשר על הבית, or any other official, was modeled after an Assyrian office. After all, the positions of Israelite monarchic officials, including that of the אשר על הבית, were in place during the United Monarchy, prior to any Assyrian or Babylonian presence in or active interconnections with the land of Israel. However, since Judah, and Israel beforehand, had been Assyrian vassals, they would have been familiar with particulars of the Assyrian organization[54] and may have adopted certain specific practices. Still, it must be realized that the empires of Mesopotamia and their respective administrative organizations, whether Babylonian or Assyrian, differed considerably from Israel in magnitude and complexity. As noted, the position of the *ša muḫḫi ekalli* or *rab ekalli* was complemented by that of other high palace officials. The lack of evidence for comparable ministers in Israel can probably be explained by a smaller and less complex organization that would have allowed the office of the אשר על הבית to encompass those of related positions.[55]

---

51. D. Oates, "Fort Shalmaneser An Interim Report," *Iraq* 21 (1959): 110.

52. Kinnier-Wilson, *Nimrud Wine Lists*, 98. Cf. de Vaux, *Ancient Israel*, 130.

53. Pečírková, "The Administrative Organization of the Neo-Assyrian Empire," 221; *ABL* 100.

54. As suggested above, the three-man Assyrian commission recorded in 2 Kgs 18:17–35 appears authentic, as does the designation for the Assyrian king, המלך הגדול, Akkadian *šarru rabû* (see, Cogan and Tadmor, *II Kings*, 229–231).

55. Individual ministers of cattle, grain, beer, wine, fruit, etc. attested from Assyria (Kinnier-Wilson, *Nimrud Wine Lists*, 73) are comparable to those listed by the Chronicler

Ugaritic Evidence

Most recently, attention has been focused on a Northwest semitic connection for the Hebrew title אשר על הבית based on an Ugaritic text containing a seemingly analogous expression. The introductory lines of the text contain a list of payments made to a group of named individuals, including a certain Yarimanu entitled *ʿl bt*: *ksp. d. šlm yrmn. ʿl. bt*., "silver which Yarimanu the steward paid."[56] If the expression *ʿl bt* is understood as constructed in apposition to the PN *yrmn*, then it can be regarded equivalent to the title על הבית.[57] Although a time differential of 300–400 years excludes the possibility that the Hebrew title was borrowed from Ugarit, this text provides a pre-Solomonic prototype of the title in a Levantine setting in which it may have been perpetuated until the rise of the Israelite monarchy.

Conclusions

The fragmentary bits of information available on the אשר על הבית, both biblical and non-biblical, cannot be assembled into a single composite picture illustrating this office's domain. Part of the problem seems to hinge on the evolution of the office itself and perhaps too on the personality of particular officials and their monarchs. Notably, the title אשר על הבית is absent in Chronicles and seems to be replaced by the expression נגיד הבית (2 Chr 28:7). Possibly in the post-exilic era the title נגיד הבית, usually associated with Temple overseers and already used in a related form in the Book of Jeremiah as part of the titulary of a priest,[58] also designated the minister over the royal house in references to the monarchic civil official.

Titles analogous to אשר על הבית in Egypt and Mesopotamia and even the partial title *ʿl bt* in the Ugaritic text do not clearly demonstrate modeling after any foreign system. Essentially the element אשר על of the title אשר על הבית seems to be more a generic expression reflecting normal Semitic morphology than a

---

for the reign of David (1 Chr 27:25–31). Assumably, overseers of such basic organizational units functioned during the Divided Monarchy as well.

56. *KTU* 4.755.

57. R.M. Good, "The Israelite Royal Steward in the Light of Ugaritic *ʿl bt*," *RB* 96 (1979): 580–582; "The Ugaritic Steward," *ZAW* 95 [1983]: 110–111. O. Loretz challenges Good's translation. He understands these lines as references to payment made by Yrmn "on the temple/palace account" ("Ugaritisch *skn–sknt* und hebraish *skn–sknt*," *ZAW* 94 [1982]: 124). Information in the text that payment was made to named individuals (and therefore not to the temple/palace) lends support to Good's interpretation.

58. The priest Pashhur is called פקיד נגיד בבית יהוה (Jer 20:1).

translation of any one foreign title.[59] Primarily the analogues show the range of functions of these types of officials in different Near Eastern states. The tasks performed by the אשר על הבית would have been essential for the administration of the palace, if not the greater royal estate. The fact that ministers of this class, with certain variations, are found throughout the region, suggests that the office in Israel could even have developed independently to fulfill specific needs. While it is possible that aspects of the position of the אשר על הבית reflect outside influence, a specific foreign model for the office is not discernable.

Despite the difficulties of defining the office of אשר על הבית, certain observations about this high ranking official are forthcoming:

(1) The bearer of the royal, as opposed to private, title is always attested in the biblical text in connection with a king or capital city.

(2) The element בית in the title refers minimally to the palace complex, but logically could have extended to royal property state-wide as suggested by Mettinger.

(3) The jurisdiction of this official, in Israel and elsewhere, could cross administrative divisions when deemed appropriate.

(4) Although the אשר על הבית may have occupied the highest administrative position, his office cannot be characterized as that of a vizier since no "second" to the king, who is charged over the entire bureaucratic organization, is known from monarchic Israel.

Based on the available evidence, it appears safest, if not most accurate, to translate the title אשר על הבית as "minister over the royal house" without further defining "royal house."

B. ספר – Scribe

Another key minister at court was the ספר. The designations ספר (*spr*, sing.) and ספרים (*sprym*, pl.) appear a number of times in the Bible and are attested in the archaeological record. Generally, the definition of this title, "scribe, secretary," including the basic roles of office-holders is not disputed. The origin of the appellation and the prototype for the position of the Israelite ספר, however, have been discussed at length and continue to be debated. These two issues will be reviewed briefly below. Subsequently, attention will focus on the various functions of persons entitled ספר within the hierarchy of Israelite officialdom. State scribes other than the royal court scribe will be examined as well.

---

59. Otherwise one would have expected an exact translation of an equivalent foreign title—for example, אשר על ההיכל for Akkadian *ša muḫḫi ekalli.*

Hebrew Corpus

The title ספר המלך, "scribe/secretary of the king," an explicit reference to a royal scribe, occurs in the Bible only once. Therefore, the determination that an individual who is simply entitled ספר is actually a royal minister must be derived from the context, which is not always revealing. Consequently, the exact number of these court officials, versus state office-holders outside the royal court or private professionals, is uncertain. Thirteen named persons in the Bible are known by the title ספר: Jonathan, David's "uncle" (1 Chr 27:32); Shemaiah, son of Nathanel the Levite (24:6); Seraiah (2 Sam 8:17; Sheva in 20:25; Shavsha in 1 Chr 18:16; Shisha in 1 Kgs 4:3); his sons Elihoreph and Ahiyah (4:3); Jeiel (2 Chr 26:11); Shebna (2 Kgs 18:18, 37; 19:2 = Isa 36:3, 22; 37:2); Shaphan, son of Azaliah son of Meshullam (2 Kgs 22:3, 8–10, 12 = 2 Chr 34:15, 18, 20); Elishama (Jer 36:12, 20–21); Baruch, son of Neriah (36:26, 32); Jonathan (37:15, 20); Ezra (Ezra 7:6, 11; Neh 8:1, 4, 9, 13); and Zadok (Neh 13:13). A 14th individual, Gemariah son of Shaphan, is usually included in this group, although the syntactical placement of his title, הספר, after his patronymic, Shaphan, can be interpreted as referring to the latter (Jer 36:10).[60] Two additional scribes are unnamed, one designated ספר המלך (2 Kgs 12:11 = 2 Chr 24:11) and the other (ה)ספר שר הצבא, "the scribe of the army commander" (2 Kgs 25:19 = Jer 52:25).[61] References to groups or families of scribes occur three times: Kenite scribal families at Jabez (1 Chr 2:55);[62] Levite scribes (2 Chr 34:13); and the royal scribes of Ahasuerus (Esth 3:12; 8:9).

The Hebrew corpus of epigraphic material containing the title ספר is surpris-

60. As already noted by Mettinger (*Solomonic State Officials*, 33 n. 44), commonly in titularies that include a patronymic, the title refers to the first name, the son. But occasionally, the reverse holds true as well, especially in cases of offices that are hereditary, like the priesthood (e.g. 1 Kgs 1:42; 2 Chr 24:20). In the latter examples, it is probable that the sons were also priests. Similarly, in cases of scribes, a strong possibility exists that sons followed in their fathers' footsteps.

61. The definite article prefixed to ספר occurs in Kings but not in the parallel account in Jeremiah. The grammatical construction in Kings, הספר שר הצבא המצבא את עם הארץ, renders the translation, "the scribe (who is) the army commander who recruits the people of the land," instead of, "the scribe of the army commander...," as in Jeremiah and LXX Jer 52:25; 2 Kgs 25:19. Of the two, the Jeremiah version seems more probable since it is doubtful that the army commander functioned simultaneously as the army's scribe or that the royal scribe (if that is the identity of הספר) held the office of army commander (following Mettinger, *Solomonic State Officials*, 20; Bergrich, "Sōfēr und Mazkīr," 3).

62. So too Japhet (*I & II Chronicles*, 67, 90). Contrast ספרים, "Siphrites," residents of Qiriath-sepher (W. Rudolph, *Chronikbücher* [Tübingen: J.C.B. Mohr, 1955], 25); "Sopherim" as a family name (J.M. Myers, *Anchor Bible I Chronicles* [Garden City: Doubleday, 1965], 12).

ingly small and, with one exception, consists of unprovenienced finds.[63] The one provenienced inscription that contains the term ספר, probably as a title designating the office, is an ostracon from Lachish (no. 3).[64] The ostracon was discovered in an archive in a gate-room at Lachish and is dated stratigraphically to the last days of the Judean monarchy.[65] No PN is attached to the ספר in this letter; rather, the title appears in a general reference to an army scribe.[66] A provenienced bulla that could have belonged to a scribe but does not bear any title was recovered in the City of David archive. It is inscribed לגמריהו בן שפן, "belonging to gmryhw son of špn." Shiloh believes that the seal-owner can be identified with the biblical Gemariah son of Shaphan the scribe.[67] Unfortunately, Gemariah did not include a title on his seal rendering any identification as conjectural.

Of the aforementioned biblical and epigraphic corpus, only certain scribes can be classified as state-officials with any degree of certainty. They include: Shemaiah the Levite and Seraiah during David's reign (1 Chr 24:6; 2 Sam 8:17; 20:25; 1 Chr 18:16); Elihoreph and Ahiyah under Solomon (1 Kgs 4:3); Jehoash's unnamed ספר המלך (2 Kgs 12:11 = 2 Chr 24:11); Jeiel the army scribe in the days of Uzziah (2 Chr 26:11); Shebna under Hezekiah (2 Kgs 18:18, 37; 19:2 = Isa 36:3, 22; 37:2); Josiah's scribe Shaphan and most probably his son Gemariah (2 Kgs 22:3, 8–10, 12 = 2 Chr 34:15, 18, 20; Jer 36:10); Elishama under Jehoiakim (Jer 36:12, 20–21); Jonathan and the unidentified scribe of the army commander in the reign of Zedekiah (Jer 37:15, 20; 2 Kgs 25:19 = Jer

63. The unprovenienced items include three seals and two bullae. The two bullae (*WSS* no. 417), stamped with the same seal לברכיהו בן נריהו הספר, have been associated with Jeremiah's scribe Baruch son Neriah (Avigad, *Hebrew Bullae*, 28–29; Deutsch and Heltzer, *Forty*, 37–38. The three seals are listed in *WSS* (nos. 21–23). Avishur and Heltzer suggest that scribes used their seals not only to seal their own personal documents but also some of those they wrote for other people (*Studies on the Royal Administration*, 45–46). Several other unprovenienced seals bearing the title ספר have been identified as Ammonite or Moabite (*WSS* nos. 862, 1007–1010; Deutsch and Heltzer, *Window*, 56–57).

64. The word ספר on Lachish Ostracon no. 3 ll. 9, 11, can be understood either as "letter, document" (H. Tur-Sinai, *The Lachish Ostraca* [Jerusalem: Bialik Institute, 1987], 53–55) or as the title "scribe" (Albright, *ANET*, 322; F.M. Cross, "A Literate Soldier: Lachish Letter III" in A. Kort and S. Morschauser eds. *Biblical and Related Studies Presented to Samuel Iwry* [Winona Lake: Eisenbrauns, 1985], 41–45). The context supports both readings, but grammatically (l. 9) the latter is preferable.

65. H. Torczyner (Tur-Sinai), *Lachish I: The Lachish Letters* (London: Oxford University Press, 1938), 11–14, 46–51; *Lachish Ostraca*, י"ז–כ"ב, 53–55; D. Ussishkin, "Excavations at Tel Lachish 1978–1983: Second Preliminary Report," *TA* 10 (1983): 134–136, 168.

66. Cross, "A Literate Soldier," 47.

67. Shiloh, "A Group of Hebrew Bullae from the City of David," 25–34, fig. 8:1 pl. 6:B.

52:25); the unidentified army scribe on the Lachish ostracon; and Ahasuerus' scribes (Esth 3:12; 8:9).[68] Of these, the three army scribes and the Levite scribe do not fit the narrower category royal scribe as a civil official.

Etymology and Evidence of Foreign Origin

Two topics that have been widely debated in connection with the royal secretary are the etymology of the title ספר and the potential foreign prototype for the Israelite office. The former issue, while not easily resolved, is fortunately not critical to the understanding of the role of this official. One point of contention is whether the Hebrew title ספר is a cognate of Akkadian *šāpiru*, "envoy, overseer, governor, ruler."[69] The difficulty revolves around semantic discrepancies between the two terms. It seems, though, that the Akkadian root *špr*, like the Hebrew root ספר, has a range of meanings that also encompasses a writing component.[70] For example, the verb *šapāru*, principally defined as "to send a person, a report, a message," has an extended meaning, "to write (a letter)," attested from the Old Akkadian through the Neo-Babylonian period;[71] the substantive *šipru* can carry the sense "commission, report, messenger."[72]

The wide semantic range of the root ספר is evident from the biblical evidence as well. According to Mettinger, the ultimate problem is that the definition of the position ס(ו)פֵר does not coincide with the basic meaning of the verb סָפַר, "count." A possible resolution is that the professional title is a denominative formation derived from the noun סֵפֶר, "book, document."[73] Notably, however, the designation ס(ו)פֵר is also used as a participle, "enumerator, recruit-officer," in those cases carrying the primary meaning of the verb (see below). Seemingly,

68. The status of some of these scribes is more certain than others. David's "uncle" Jonathan and Jeremiah's scribe Baruch may also have served as court scribes, although not enough evidence exists to include them in that category. Cf. Muilenburg, who postulates that Baruch had access to the secretariat at court and was received by the king's ministers (Jer 36) only because he himself was a royal official ("Baruch the Scribe," 231).

69. *CAD* Š/1, 453–458; *AHW* 3, 1172–1173. M. Tsevat thinks that the expression בשבט ספר in Judg 5:14 reflects the Akkadian meaning of *šāpiru*, "the staff of a ruler" ("Some Biblical Notes," *HUCA* 24 [1952–1953]: 107). It is equally possible, however, that the reference in Judges is to a military officer (cf. Jer 52:25) charged over enumeration and enrollment of troops (G. Moore, *A Critical and Exegetical Commentary on Judges* [Edinburgh: T. & T. Clark, 1895], 151).

70. For example, one definition of *šipru* is "message, communication" (*CAD* Š/3, 73–74). Hebrew סֵפֶר is probably a loanword from Akkadian *šipru* (*BDB*, 706–707; *HALOT* 2, 766).

71. *CAD* Š/1, 430–448; see especially pp. 440–446.

72. *CAD* Š/3, 73–76.

73. Mettinger, *Solomonic State Officials*, 44–45; for a discussion of this derivation and other less likely options, see pp. 42–44; *BDB*, 706–708.

these semantic distinctions are not irreconcilable, as the link between counting, recording and a written document forms a natural progression.[74]

The second issue of debate, whether the position of the royal secretary reflects borrowing, stems from the existence of four variant appellations for David's scribe: Seraiah, Sheva, Shisha, and Shavsha. The first name, שריה, is a common Yahwistic PN probably signifying "YHWH is ruler," and by itself does not present any obstacles.[75] But the discrepancy in the names, coupled by the non-Hebrew forms of the last three, has led to assorted explanations, including attempts to trace Sheva/Shisha/Shavsha to Akkadian,[76] Hurrian,[77] and Aramaic[78] PNs. Some of these theories in turn have led to suggestions that not only was the scribe in question a foreigner but the office itself may have been foreign as well.[79] Scholars who hold those opinions think that Seraiah is a Hebraized version of the foreign name. Others posit that only Seraiah is a PN while the remaining three names are actually corruptions of the Egyptian title *sš š'.t* or *sẖ š'.t*, "scribe of letters, secretary," misunderstood by the biblical writers as a PN.[80] However, while none of these theories can be ruled out entirely, most suffer from philological difficulties.[81] The proposal connecting Sheva/Shisha/Shavsha to the title *sš š't* falls short on other grounds as well. While aiming to

---

74. R.P. Dougherty, "Writing upon Parchment and Papyrus Among the Babylonians and Assyrians," *JAOS* 48 (1928): 113–114.

75. A number of other biblical persons are named שריה/ו: a priest (2 Kgs 25:18 = Jer 52:24) and two officials (2 Kgs 25:23; Jer 36:26).

76. First proposed by J. Marquart (*Fundamente israelitischer und jüdischer Geschichte* [Gottingen: Dieterich, 1896], 22).

77. B. Mazar, "King David's Scribe and the High Officialdom of the United Monarchy of Israel" in S. Ahituv and B. Levine eds. *The Early Biblical Period* (Jerusalem: Israel Exploration Society, 1986), 134–135.

78. E. Lipinski, "Royal and State Scribes in Ancient Jerusalem," *VTS* 40 (1986): 159.

79. It is possible, of course, that David's scribe was of Egyptian or Canaanite ancestry, since non-Israelites are found among David's other functionaries—for example, the stewards Obil the Ishmaelite and Jaziz the Hagrite (1 Chr 27:31). For a discussion on this topic, see Mazar, "King David's Scribe and the High Officialdom," 129–131.

80. De Vaux, "Titres et fonctionnaires," 398–399; expanded by A. Cody, "Le titre égyptien et le nom propre du scribe de David," *RB* 72 (1965): 387–393; Mettinger, *Solomonic Officials*, 27–29. Egyptian *sš* = scribe (the form *sẖ* reflects the pronunciation); *š't* = letter (Erman and Grapow, *Wörterbuch*, 475–481; Faulkner, *Middle Egyptian*, 246, 262).

81. For example, the Akkadian name associated with שושא, *Šamšu*, demands the phonetic shift medial *m* > *w*, a late phenomenon not found before the NB period; the equivalent Hurrian name proposed by Mazar ("King David's Scribe..."), *Šewiša*, is unattested and only works on the assumption that it is a hypocoristicon of the attested form *Šewi-šarri* (see Cody, "Le titre égyptien," 384–385); the connection of the Hebrew names to the Egyptian title *sẖ š'.t* requires the elimination of the consonant *ẖ* (cf. the Akkadian transliteration *šaẖšiẖa(šiẖa)*,

prove that the Israelite office was borrowed from Egypt, it indicates at most that the Egyptian term for scribe was known in Canaan, a fact already confirmed by the title's appearance in an Amarna letter.[82] Thus, regardless of Seraiah's ancestry, direct Egyptian modelling for the office of scribe is impossible to prove and, if borrowing did take place, indirect Egyptian influence via the Canaanite city-states is far more likely.[83] Moreover, the universal need for scribes in administrative systems and their functional similarities compounds the difficulty in tracing a model for the Israelite office, even if one existed.

Position and Functions of the Royal Scribe in Israel

The inclusion of the ספר in the Davidic and Solomonic lists of officials and in other records of groups of royal ministers eliminates any doubt that persons so entitled were among the highest ranking functionaries at court. In fact, in one Davidic register (2 Sam 8:17)[84] and in the Solomonic list of appointees (1 Kgs 4:3), the ספר is listed in second place, following the priest. While the fragmentary and seemingly corrupt lists of officials from the United Monarchy are not necessarily reliable indicators of hierarchal structure, the activities of the royal secretaries from the Kingdom of Judah confirm the prominent status of the ספר. For example, Hezekiah's scribe Shebna is one of a trio of high officials sent to negotiate with the Assyrians and later to meet with the prophet Isaiah (2 Kgs 18:18, 26, 37; 19:2 = Isa 36:3, 22; 37:2). His name consistently appears in sec-

---

EA 316:16) and the reduction of ʿto ʾ(see K.A. Kitchen, "Egypt and Israel During the First Millennium B.C.," *VTS* 40 [1986]: 112).

82. The term *šaḫšiḫa(šiḫa)* occurs in *EA* 316:16. W.F. Albright has shown it is equivalent to *sḫ šʿt* ("Cuneiform Material for Egyptian Prosopography," *JNES* 5 [1946]: 20–21 no. 53; previously, Knudtzon understood the designation as a PN [*Die El-Amarna Tafeln*, 919–920). The title is found in the postscript address of a letter written by the local chief of Yursa. It is utilized in the same way as the Akkadian title for royal scribe, *ṭupšar šarri*, attested in the letters of Abdi-Hiba of Jerusalem (*EA* 286:61; 287:64; 288:62; 289:47). Interestingly, the Egyptian title in the Amarna letter is preceded by the personal determinative, which Albright points out is commonly prefixed to titles as well as PNs in Canaanite documents. Thus, an appellation that was originally a title may have been misunderstood by Canaanites and later Israelite scribes as a PN, as in the case of David's scribe. In that light, Mettinger's view of direct borrowing from Egypt can be abandoned. His reasoning, "since we have to reckon with vivid contacts between Israel and Egypt in this very period" (*Solomonic State Officials*, 29), is quite baffling, especially for David's reign, since both Hebrew and Egyptian sources are silent on any contacts between Israel and Egypt.

83. On this issue, see Chapter 6 – Systems of Accounting, on the transmission of Egyptian hieratic numerals.

84. In the other Davidic register in 2 Samuel, (20:25), the scribe appears towards the end of the list preceding the priests. Compared to other records this is unusual.

ond place, following Eliakim the minister over the royal house and preceding Joah the herald.[85]

As is the case with other officials, a number of royal scribes make their sole appearance in lists of court functionaries or are mentioned in contexts that do not elucidate their roles (e.g. Seraiah, Elihoreph, Ahiyah, Jonathan). Interestingly, those duties usually considered primary for the ספר המלך, secretarial writing projects, are evident in connection with these office-holders only in the text of Esther. There, Ahasuerus' scribes are summoned twice to record royal edicts concerning the fate of the Jews (Esth 3:12; 8:9). From the monarchic period, the only ספר who can be considered a government functionary and who is explicitly mentioned in conjunction with a writing exercise is the Levite scribe Shemaiah son of Nethanel, a religious rather than civil official. He is credited with recording the organization of the priestly divisions, a task he performed in the presence of David, the king's officers and Israel's notables (1 Chr 24:6).[86]

It is noteworthy that the activities of two persons who bear the title ספר, Joash's unidentified scribe and Josiah's scribe Shaphan, fit the primary definition of the verb ספר, "count." The two enterprises with which these men were involved pertain to counting and the disbursement of Temple funds for repairs. In the case of Joash's ספר המלך, his task, carried out jointly with the high priest, was to count the silver that accumulated from donations in the Temple chest and to use it for wages of hired workmen and purchases of materials for the renovations (2 Kgs 12:11–13). An almost identical report is found of Josiah's repairs of the Temple and the roles played by his scribe Shaphan and the high

85. In a record of court emissaries sent by Josiah to the prophetess Huldah, the scribe, Shaphan, appears after the high priest Hilkiah and two other officials, Ahikam son of Shaphan and Achbor son of Micaiah (2 Kgs 22:12, 14). Since the official titles of Ahikam and Achbor are not indicated, it is difficult to speculate why their names precede Shaphan's. But both names do appear elsewhere in connection with prestigious court families (Jer 26:22, 24; 36:12; 2 Kgs 25:22). Possibly Ahikam or Achbor was the house minister, a higher office than the scribe, or perhaps they were sons-in-law of the king. As Cogan and Tadmor observe, it is unusual for a son to be listed before the father (*II Kings*, 282–283), although it seems doubtful that Ahikam was the son of a different Shaphan.

86. The description of Shemaiah recording these assignments in the presence of the king and his officers may reflect the Chronicler's philosophy of the integration of civil and religious personnel (Japhet, *I & II Chronicles*, 429). On the other hand, one can argue that since the king seems to have controlled certain matters involving the Temple, such as the dispersion of Temple funds (2 Kgs 12), his presence and that of other ministers would be expected at such occasions.

Jeremiah's scribe Baruch clearly performs writing duties. But for the purpose of this study, he cannot be regarded as a state-official since he functions as the private scribe/secretary of the prophet.

priest Hilkiah (22:3–6). Certainly these accounting duties would necessitate record-keeping by the scribes. The reason for the presence of a high civil official, the royal scribe, in concert with the most prominent religious functionary, the high priest, is not totally comprehensible. But it may be assumed that important projects concerning the Temple would involve both types of officials, perhaps as a system of balancing power or as a regulatory instrument of the central government.[87] The role of the ספר in these scenarios does indicate that he exercised some control over the Temple treasury.[88]

A related task carried out by scribes, in these cases army scribes, entails registering the people for military service. An annal from the time of Uzziah notes that his scribe Jeiel and Maasseiah the שוטר[89] oversaw the military muster (2 Chr 26:11). Probably Jeiel was a military scribe like the unidentified scribe of the army commander under Zedekiah, whose duties included mustering the people (2 Kgs 25:19 = Jer 52:25).

Another duty of the royal secretary was to read documents in the presence of the king or other ministers. The most famous reading takes place when a scroll of laws is discovered in the Temple by the high priest Hilkiah. Hilkiah hands the scroll to the scribe Shaphan who first read it to himself and then again out loud before Josiah. Although not explicitly mentioned, court scribes no doubt handled the king's domestic and foreign correspondence. Power over the realm of communication would have required not only skilled individuals but ones who could be trusted to relay communications accurately.[90] It is possible,

---

87. V. Hurowitz compares the biblical scenes with a similar one found in a letter to Esarhaddon ("Another Fiscal Practice in the Ancient Near East: 2 Kings 12:5–17 and a Letter to Esarhaddon (*LAS* 277)," *JNES* 45 [1986]: 289–294). In that letter, a royal functionary, Mār-Ištar, reports that he cannot check the gold available for repairs of the temple at Uruk because the temple administrators are away. The status of the royal functionary who wrote this letter is unknown, but notably, as in the biblical examples, royal as well as clerical personnel are involved in temple finances.

88. So too Rüterswörden (*Beamten der israelitischen Königszeit*, 85). Heaton's conclusion that these are "trivial chores" reflecting the near collapse of the kingdom (in Joash's reign) is totally unacceptable (*Solomon's New Men*, 48).

89. For a discussion of the title שטר see Chapter 5–C.

90. The influence of the royal scribe is reflected in a number of Akkadian and Hittite letters. For example, in several Amarna letters (i.e. nos. 286–289), postscripts addressed *ana ṭupšar šarri bēliya*, "to the scribe of the king my lord," contain entreaties of the sender that the scribe bring the message "with good words" to the king. These notations seem to indicate that the scribe was to improvise "good words" to further the cause of the sender. Apparently the manner in which the scribe delivered the message, not to mention the fact that he had the right to screen correspondence, rendered him great power over political matters. For a full discussion and additional examples, see L. Oppenheim, "A Note on the Scribes

however, that the practice of royal scribes reading documents before kings or their ministers may have been more a matter of protocol than a need arising from the illiteracy of the listeners.[91]

The aforementioned functions ascribed by the sources to the ספר project only a partial picture, as scribes appear mainly in political scenes. One scribal activity that is conspicuously absent is the writing of annals. Royal annals, known from the Bible as דברי הימים, apparently existed for both Israelite kingdoms in the period of the Divided Monarchy: ספר דברי הימים למלכי ישראל, "the Book of the Chronicles of the Kings of Israel," and ספר דברי הימים למלכי יהודה, "the Book of the Chronicles of the Kings of Judah." For the United Monarchy the evidence is limited to a book of records called ספר דברי שלמה, "the Book of the Acts of Solomon" (1 Kgs 11:41).[92] Despite the lack of evidence, it can be assumed that court scribes were responsible for keeping the annals.[93]

Another issue pertinent to the ספר המלך concerns the number of officials who served in that position simultaneously. The offices of other high functionaries, such as the minister over the royal house or the herald, are usually limited to a single office-holder. In the case of the ספר, most often it is difficult to discern whether more than one royal secretary functioned at court at any one time.

---

in Mesopotamia," 253–256; A. Rainey, "The Scribe at Ugarit," *Proceedings of the Israel Academy of Sciences and Humanities* 3 (1965), 143.

91. Note that later, when Josiah assembles the leaders and the people at the Temple to renew their covenant with God, the king himself reads the scroll (2 Kgs 23:2). Although it can be argued that in reality a scribe read, in the name of the king, there is no reason to presume illiteracy among the kings of Israel and Judah or even among government officials (cf. M. Haran, "On the Diffusion of Literacy and Schools in Ancient Israel," *VTS* 40 [1986]: 81–85). In support of arguments for literacy are several references in the Bible that imply literacy among the ruling class and prominent citizens (e.g. Jer 32:10, in which Jeremiah writes a deed for land purchase; Isa 38:9, which is possibly a colophon of a psalm of Hezekiah; see J.R. Lundbom, "Baruch, Seraiah, and Expanded Colophons in the Book of Jeremiah," *JSOT* 36 [1986]: 95). Officials other than scribes who brought messages to the king may also have been expected to read. For example, Jehudi son of Nethaniahu, the official who brings Jeremiah's scroll of doom to King Jehoiakim, reads it to the king (Jer 36:21). While it is possible that Jehudi was a scribe (so Mettinger, *Solomonic State Officials*, 31), he is not identified as such.

92. Lipinski notes that no record book is mentioned for David, and the book of the acts of Solomon was not initially annalistic in form. Therefore, the exact regnal years are missing for these kings, and the number forty, a conventional figure, served as a substitute. The first complete annals appear for Rehoboam and Jeroboam ("Royal and State Scribes in Ancient Jerusalem," 157–158).

93. Those scholars who interpret the position of the מזכיר as that of recorder maintain that he wrote the royal annals. But as shown below, any evidence that the מזכיר functioned as recorder dates to the Persian period at the earliest (see Chapter 4–C).

Primarily this is problematic because the titulary of the scribe generally does not distinguish different types of scribes and the profession seems to run in families.[94] For example, from the reign of Jehoiakim more than one scribe can be identified from the group of officials assembled at the Temple and palace secretariats: Elishama, Gemariah son of Shaphan, and perhaps his son Micaiah (Jer 36:10–20). Their precise scribal rank, however, is uncertain. The existence of two royal secretaries, Elihoreph and his brother Ahijah, the sons of David's scribe Seraiah/Shisha, is attested from the reign of Solomon; both are mentioned in the register of Solomonic officials (1 Kgs 4:3).[95] Possibly each scribe bore different obligations or, during the United Monarchy, one was responsible for matters pertaining to Judah and the other for northern Israel.[96]

---

94. In two cases mentioned, military scribes are distinguished (2 Kgs 25:19 = Jer 52:25; 2 Chr 26:11). Presumably, other scribes served at court in various capacities, probably in positions subordinate to the royal secretary. That arrangement seems pragmatic as several members of a scribal family could serve simultaneously.

95. The seemingly odd name Elihoreph has elicited several theories. Following a Greek gloss in 2:46h, "over the plinthion" (an instrument for determining the seasons by the length of the sun's shadow), Montgomery suggests reading על החרף, "over the year," instead of אליחרף. He posits that חרף, "autumn," the beginning of the year in the Semitic calendar is used here to signify the calendar year in general, the official over the חרף being equivalent to the Assyrian *limmu* official (*A Commentary on Kings*, 113–115, 118). Other scholars (e.g. de Vaux, "Titres et fonctionnaires," 399; Mettinger, *Solomonic State Officials*, 29–30), citing LXX versions in which the "ר" in אליחרף is omitted, rendering the reading Eliaph (B) and Eliab (L), connect the PN to the Egyptian god *Ḥ'py* (Apis). B. Mazar, who favors a Hurrian lineage for Seraiah, suggests that Elihoreph, like his father, bore a Hurrian name, חרף being the Hebrew equivalent for the deity *Harpa* ("King David's Scribe and High Officialdom," 137–138). But the name Elihoreph can also be viewed as Israelite. In the Bible חרף appears as the PN of a chief of the line of Judah (1 Chr 2:51) and חריף as a PN of the head of a family of returnees from Babylon (Neh 7:24). The name חריף/חרף is apparently a hypocoristicon of אליחרף, or חרף plus another theophoric element. If חרף is to be connected with the noun meaning "autumn," Elihoreph can signify, "God is mature/in his prime," an attribute of virility (cf. Job 29:4). Alternative proposals derive the name from different verbal meanings of חרף, "acquire" (D.M. Pike, "Israelite Theophoric Personal Names in the Bible and Their Implications for Religious History" [Ph.D. Dissertation, University of Pennsylvania, 1990], 148–149) or "reproach, sharp" (cf. *EM* 3, 289 – חריף). The latter interpretation seems less likely since its biblical usage has negative connotations. In light of the biblical evidence there is no compelling reason to emend the Hebrew text or to derive this PN from foreign DNs (so too J.H. Tigay, *You Shall Have No Other Gods: Israelite Religion in the Light of Hebrew Inscriptions* [Atlanta: Scholars Press, 1986], 77 n. 15).

96. Cf. Begrich, who suggests that perhaps they did not serve concurrently but rather one brother succeeding the other ("Sōfēr und Mazkīr," 8).

Evidence from Syria-Palestine, Mesopotamia and Egypt

As already noted, state scribes played a central role in administrative organizations throughout the ancient Near East. The term *spr* is attested in a number of non-Hebrew sources as the title for "scribe." In Ugaritic, as in Hebrew, *spr* is a general designation for scribe.[97] Only occasionally is a more specialized title attested, such as, *rb spr*, "chief scribe," the overseer of other state scribes.[98] The responsibility of Ugaritic scribes to keep the royal records is confirmed by the appearance of the scribe's signature on two administrative documents: *bsmn spr*, "PN the scribe," and *brqn spr*, "PN the scribe."[99] A ספר of the royal court is also mentioned in an Aramaic letter from a vassal of Necho II.[100] The West-Semitic root *spr* is attested in Egyptian and Akkadian texts as well. In an Egyptian letter it appears as *spr yd'*, "wise scribe," a Semitic expression quoted by the Egyptian scribe.[101] In Neo-Babylonian texts the term LÚ *si/epir* is used interchangeably with LÚ.KUŠ.SAR, "parchment writer," to signify scribes utilizing the alphabetic Aramaic script.[102] Possibly the term *si/epir* came into use in Akkadian from Old Aramaic.[103] In earlier Akkadian texts from Canaan, however, the predominant title for scribe is *ṭupšar šarri*, the East Semitic equivalent of ספר המלך.[104]

97. The term *spr* is found in a number of texts: e.g. *UT* 62:53; 127:59; 1039:30; 2116:23. For a list of the scribes of various texts, see M. Heltzer, *The Internal Organization of the Kingdom of Ugarit* (Wiesbaden: Dr. Ludwig Reichert, 1982), 158–159. In Akkadian texts from Ugarit the term for scribe is *ṭupšarru*.

98. *UT* 73:4 r.; A. Rainey, "The Social Stratification of Ugarit" (Ph.D. Dissertation, Brandeis University, 1962), 107. On the status of the scribe see Rainey ["Social Stratification," 107–109; "The Scribe at Ugarit," 126–147] and Heltzer [*Internal Organization*, 160–161]). One piece of evidence commonly used to demonstrate the high status of scribes at Ugarit is the occurrence of the title *ṭupšarru* as an added appellation for the *sukallu*, "vizier" (e.g. *PRU* III 15.113; VI 43, 45). In those instances, however, the appellation *ṭupšarru* could represent an honorific title, as in Egypt (see below).

99. *UT* 1039:30; 2116:23. More than 60 Akkadian tablets from Ugarit bear scribal signatures as well (*PRU* III, p. 236).

100. *KAI* 266:9 (Saqqara). In other Aramaic sources, where the title ספר plus a PN commonly appears at the end of texts as scribal authentications of a deed alongside the witnesses, the context is unclear (e.g. *KAI* 227:6 [Sfire]; 236:6 [Assur]).

101. Papyrus Anastasi I, 17:7 in A. Gardiner, *Egyptian Hieratic Texts* (Leipzig: J.C. Hinrichs, 1911), 58; trans. J. Wilson, *ANET*, 476. The root *spr* also appears as part of a GN (Papyrus Wilbour A 22:42 in W. Helck, *Die Beziehungen Ägyptens zu Vorderasien im 3. und 2. Jahrtausend v. Chr.* [Wiesbaden: O. Harrassowitz, 1971], 525, no. 283).

102. H.M. Kümmel, *Familie, Beruf und Amt im spätbabylonischen Uruk* (Berlin: Gebr. Mann Verlag, 1979), 136–137; Dougherty, "Writing Upon Parchment and Papyrus," 110–116; cf. *CAD* S, 225–226.

103. J. Lewy, "The Problems Inherent in Section 70 of the Bisutun Inscription," *HUCA* 25 (1954): 192–198.

104. The title *ṭupšar šarri* occurs in the postscript address of four Amarna letters from

In contrast to the Israelite and Canaanite material, Mesopotamian sources ofttimes distinguish various scribal offices. The titularies of officials who functioned as scribes indicate the different realms of their activity. For example, *ṭupšar Amurri*, probably the title of a scribe in charge of Amorite affairs, appears in a military context in some Mari letters.[105] Neo-Assyrian and Neo-Babylonian documents contain the titles *ṭupšar āli*, "scribe of the city (the mayor's office)";[106] *ṭupšar bīt ili*, "scribe of the temple";[107] *ṭupšar ekalli*, "scribe of the palace";[108] and *ṭupšar šarri*, "scribe of the king."[109]

Egyptian titles, like those from Mesopotamia, differentiate between classes of scribes, although honorific epithets must be separated from regular titles. As mentioned, the royal secretary in Egypt was entitled *sš šʿt*, "scribe of letters" (*šʿt*=document), in longer titularies expressed by *sš šʿt (n) nsw n pr-ʿ3*, "secretary of Pharaoh" or *sš šʿt n r Ḥk3 nt*, "secretary of Horus mighty bull (the king)."[110] In contrast, the appellation *sš nswt*, "scribe of the king" (= ספר המלך), is an honorific epithet commonly incorporated in the titularies of officials who are not court scribes. Apparently *sš nswt* signifies an academic degree of sorts.[111] Various titles of Egyptian temple scribes existed as well—for example, *ḥry sš(w) w3ḥ ḥtp-nṯr n nṯrw-nbw*, "chief (of the) scribe(s) who places offerings before all the gods"; and *sš ḥwt-nṯr*, "scribe of the temple."[112] A variety of titles are also attested for military scribes–for example, *sš nswt (n p3) msʿ*, "royal army scribe"; *sš mnfʒt*, "scribe of the infantry"; and *sš ẖnrt n p3 msʿ*, "scribe of the prison of the army."[113]

Abdi-Hiba, the ruler of Jerusalem: *EA* 286:61; 287:64; 288:62; 289:47. As noted above, a transcription of the Egyptian term for scribe, *šaḫšiḫa*, is found in *EA* 316:16.

105. *ARM* 1, 60:6; 2, 13:29 rev.

106. ND 1120 in D.J. Wiseman, "The Nimrud Tablets," *Iraq* 14 (1952): 65, pl 23. On the status of the city scribe, see Kinnier-Wilson, *Nimrud Wine Lists*, 9–10.

107. *ABL* 476:28. Based on information from Neo-Assyrian and Neo-Babylonian texts, Kinnier-Wilson considers the temple scribe as its chief administrator (*Nimrud Wine Lists*, 23).

108. Pečírková, "The Administrative Organization of the Neo-Assyrian Empire," 216, 222.

109. ND 1120 in Wiseman, "The Nimrud Tablets," 65, pl. 23. The king's scribe seems to be the chief scribe and the one closest to the king. See Kinnier-Wilson, *Nimrud Wine Lists*, 37, 63.

110. Faulkner, *Middle Egyptian*, 246, 262; Helck, *Verwaltung*, 277; Gardiner, *Onomastica* I, 21*. See Mettinger for an overview on the royal secretary in Egypt (*Solomonic State Officials*, 45–48).

111. Helck, *Verwaltung*, 61, 107.

112. Gardiner, *Onomastica* I, 47*, 58*.

113. A.R. Schulman lists at least a dozen different types of army scribes attested in New Kingdom sources (*Military Rank, Title, and Organization in the Egyptian New Kingdom* [Berlin: B. Hessling, 1964]: 4–5, 62–66).

Excursus: Scribes as Judicial Officers

State scribes in Egypt played various roles in the arena of the judiciary. Data from Ramesside texts indicate that scribes held key positions in the local courts of workmen communities, sometimes presiding in place of the chief workman or foreman who had judicial authority. In addition to their clerical duties, scribes regularly received petitions from litigants for whom they initiated legal proceedings. They also supervised oaths sworn by individuals involved in disputes. Often scribes played the role of prosecutor or defense attorney and occasionally even enforced court decisions. In matters pertaining to grave offenses, such as the great tomb robberies at Thebes, the local scribes, acting as informers, reported directly to the vizier. The *sš š't (n) nsw n pr-ʿ3*, "scribe of Pharaoh," sat on the Great *knbt*, the high court, together with other justices. In the late dynastic period, the high court, which no longer came under the presidency of the vizier, was actually in the charge of the chief scribe.[114] Notably, a scribe presented the grievances of the workers during the strikes in the reign of Rameses III, in essence acting as their advocate.[115]

While judicial roles are not mentioned in the Bible in connection with scribes, at least not with persons designated ספר,[116] their services would certainly have been essential in court proceedings. On this issue, the epigraphic material, specifically the late seventh-century ostracon from Meṣad Ḥashavyahu, is most enlightening.[117] The inscription describes the case of an agricultural worker, a reaper, who claims that his garment was confiscated by an overseer under false pretenses.[118] In protest of the injustice and in an effort to retrieve the garment, the reaper brought his case before the magistrate, the שר of Meṣad Ḥashavyahu.

Recent scholarship is generally in agreement that this document represents

114. Allam, "Egyptian Law Courts in Pharaonic and Hellenistic Times," *JEA* 77 (1991): 112–115. For a discussion of specific scribes at the workmen community of Deir el Medina, their titles and activities, see J. Černý, *A Community of Workmen at Thebes in the Ramesside Period* (Cairo: French Institute of Oriental Archaeology, 1973), 191–230. For the records of the great tomb robberies in the reign of Rameses IX, see Papyrus Abbott, trans. in J.H. Breasted, *Records of Ancient Egypt* 4 (Chicago: University of Chicago Press, 1906), 252–264.

115. Apparently, the workers of the necropolis at Thebes went on strike because their wages, in the form of grain and other food, were in arrears. According to Papyrus Turin, workers complained of hunger. The scribe Amennakht succeeded, at least initially, in procuring grain from the temple storehouses. For a complete discussion and translation, see W.F. Edgerton, "The Strikes in Ramses III's Twenty-Ninth Year," *JNES* 10 (1951): 137–145.

116. Some scholars posit that the שטר functioned in this capacity.

117. First published by J. Naveh, "A Hebrew Letter from the Seventh Century B.C.," *IEJ* 10 (1960): 129–139.

118. From the context of the letter it seems that the accusation leveled at this agricultural

a legal plea addressed to the highest officer of the fortress, the שר, who was also authorized to function as a judge.[119] V. Sasson argues convincingly that the format and language of the text reflect its judicial character.[120] A key statement in the inscription not fully discussed heretofore is one describing the circumstances of the reaper's oath. Apparently at the time the document was composed, the reaper testified under oath regarding his innocence: אמן נקתי מאשם, "truly (it is so), I am innocent of guilt" (ll. 11–12).[121] But according to the text, the witnesses, his fellow reapers, had not yet testified: וכל אחי יענו לי, "all my comrades will (can) testify for me" (ll. 10–11). Perhaps they would be summoned later by the שר to do so in court. A question arises concerning these proceedings: Since the reaper swore an oath before the case was presented to the שר, who administered or witnessed that oath? Two options exist. Although not mentioned, it is possible that a priest resided at the fort and attended the deposition. An alternate option is that the scribe himself witnessed the oath while composing the text in a legally accepted format based on the sworn testimony of the reaper.[122] This scenario is tenable in light of the evidence from Egypt that court scribes functioned as judicial officers in this capacity.[123]

---

worker was related to his performance, or lack of, on the job. Otherwise his summons of fellow reapers to testify to his innocence (ll. 14–17) is meaningless.

119. S. Yeivin, "The Judicial Petition From Mezad Hashavyahu," *BibOr* 19 (1962): 3–10; A. Lemaire, "L'ostracon de Meṣad Ḥashavyahu (Yavneh-Yam) replacé dans son contexte," *Semitica* 21 (1971): 57–79, esp. 76; D. Pardee, "The Judicial Plea from Meṣad Ḥashavyahu (Yavneh-Yam): A New Philological Study," *Maarav* 1 (1978): 33–66, esp. 55; V. Sasson, "An Unrecognized Juridical Term in the Yabneh-Yam Lawsuit and in an Unnoticed Biblical Parallel," *BASOR* 232 (1978): 57–62; K.A.D. Smelik, "The Literary Structure of the Yavneh-Yam Ostracon," *IEJ* 42 (1992): 55–61, esp. 60–61.

120. Sasson, "An Unrecognized Judicial Term," 57–62. Sasson's conclusions, based on comparative biblical usage, is that the word ואמלא in the letter is a judicial term and should be translated "so that I may be vindicated."

121. That the expression אמן is used in association with oaths (e.g. Num 5:21–22; Jer 11:5; Neh 5:12–13) has been noted by Naveh ("A Hebrew Letter from the Seventh Century B.C.," 133), S. Talmon ("*Amen* as an Introductory Oath Formula," *Textus* 7 [1969]: 127–129), J. Strugnell ("'Amen, I Say Unto You' in the Sayings of Jesus and in Early Christian Literature," *HTR* 67 [1974]: 177–181) and Lemaire ("L'ostracon de Meṣad Ḥashavyahu," 74). Talmon shows that אמן is an introductory formula of oaths, although only rarely preserved as such in the MT. He also maintains that the term אמנה is used synonymously to אמן, as illustrated by Achan's statement of guilt (Josh 7:20), the antithesis of the reaper's declaration of innocence (pp. 127–129).

122. Contra Naveh who believes the text was dictated verbatim by the reaper ("A Hebrew Letter from the Seventh Century B.C.," 136). The formal style of the composition, including the use of legal terminology, makes Naveh's view unlikely.

123. Smelik compares the role of the scribe to that of an attorney, comparable to customs

Conclusions

The evidence presented above reinforces the universality of state scribes in the administrative systems of the ancient Near East. While difficulties remain in interpreting the appellations of David's scribe and his possible heritage, certainly the office of scribe/secretary was sufficiently essential to governmental operations that its existence was not dependent on foreign modeling. Evidence of borrowing is scant, and that which exists points to indigenous Canaanites rather than to more distant Egyptians or Mesopotamians.

As gleaned from the biblical texts, scribes in Israel fulfilled a number of administrative duties, including accounting and public reading of documents. The royal scribe's proximity to the king and to his ministers and his involvement in important events indicates that he held prestigious rank at court, probably that of one of the highest officials. One problem particular to the Israelite material is distinguishing the different types of scribes. Comparative sources, especially those from Egypt and Mesopotamia, show a wide variety of classes of scribes. It is reasonable to suppose that in monarchic Israel such distinctions existed as well. The references to military and Levite scribes, scant though they are, support this assumption. Furthermore, the legal plea from Meṣad Ḥashavyahu might imply that scribes served as judicial officers.

C. מזכיר – Royal Herald

Biblical Corpus

A third high official at court was the מזכיר. The designation מזכיר (*mzkyr*) appears in the Bible in reference to three royal officials: Jehoshaphat son of Ahilud, who served David and Solomon (2 Sam 8:16 = 1 Chr 18:15; 2 Sam 20:24; 1 Kgs 4:3), Joah son of Asaph, who served under Hezekiah (2 Kgs 18:18, 37 = Isa 36:3, 22), and Joah son of Joahaz, who held that position in the reign of Josiah (2 Chr 34:8). The first, Jehoshaphat, is mentioned in both lists of Davidic officials and in the Solomonic list of appointees. The second, Joah son of Asaph, appears as one of a delegation of three ministers of state sent by Hezekiah to negotiate with the Assyrian officers during the siege of Jerusalem. The third, Joah son of Joahaz, is one of three royal officers charged with administering funds allocated for Temple repairs.

Definition of the Title מזכיר

Several factors contribute to difficulties in translating the title מזכיר and deriving

---

in classical Athens ("The Literary Structure of the Yavneh-Yam Ostracon," 61). That is also consistent with Egyptian customs.

the functions associated with that office. (1) The contexts in which these officials are found in the Bible do not clearly delineate their roles. This is further complicated by the fact that the מזכיר always appears together with other court functionaries. (2) Etymological and semantic considerations of the term מזכיר can lead in various directions. (3) Only three Israelite officials bearing this title are known, one from the period of the United Monarchy and two from Judah from late in the time of the Divided Monarchy. (4) The title מזכיר is unattested in Hebrew inscriptions; to date the archaeological record consists of a single Moabite seal inscribed with the title מזכיר.[124]

Despite, or as a result of, the aforementioned obstacles, scholars have formulated three separate theories defining the role of the royal מזכיר. Most scholarship on the subject of Israelite administration is divided between those who perceive this office as that of "herald" and those who view it as "recorder," the rendering in a majority of Bible translations. A minority opinion sees the מזכיר as the state prosecutor. Although several comprehensive studies of the term מזכיר, utilizing philological and comparative methods, have led a number of scholars to conclude that the title should be defined as "herald,"[125] recent translations of the title in the JPS *Tanakh* (1988), in Cogan and Tadmor *The Anchor Bible II Kings* (1988), and in Japhet *I & II Chronicles* (1993) preserve the more traditional interpretation "recorder." In light of this situation, it seems appropriate to review the evidence once again.

Since the contexts in which officials entitled מזכיר appear do not delineate the roles of the office, a lexical examination of the term is the next most reliable method in an attempt to define this title. The word מזכיר is a *hiphil* (*š* stem) participle of the verbal root זכר, "remember." As already noted by Mettinger, the *hiphil* stem of this verb is attested 40 times in the Bible, 9 times for the royal official.[126] In most of the 31 examples not referring to the royal official the causative form clearly has the sense of a *verbum-dicendi* (word of "speaking"), with the meaning "mention," "proclaim" or "utter."[127] Mettinger refers to sev-

---

124. The seal, engraved לפלטי בן מאש המזכר, "belonging to *plty* son of *m'š* the *mzkr*," was discovered in an Ammonite tomb. But based on paleographical and iconographic criteria, it has been identified as Moabite (M. Abu Taleb, "The Seal of *plty bn m'š* the *mazkir*," *ZDPV* 101 [1985]: 21–29).

125. Among others, de Vaux, "Titres et fonctionnaires," 395–397; Begrich, "Sōfēr und Mazkīr," 1–29; Mettinger, *Solomonic State Officials*, 19–24, 52–62; W. Schottroff, '*Gedenken und Gedächtnis' im alten Orient und im alten Testament* (Neukirchen-Vluyn: Neukirchener, 1964), 253–260.

126. Mettinger, *Solomonic State Officials*, 53.

127. Schottroff ('*Gedenken und Gedächtnis*', 253) and Mettinger (*Solomonic State Officials*, 53) maintain that all occurrences of the *hiphil* have the *verbum-dicendi* sense. It seems,

eral textual examples (Gen 40:14; Exod 20:24; 1 Sam 4:18; Isa 19:17; Jer 4:16; Ps 87:4), including a few with possible legal connotations (Gen 41:9; Num 5:15; 1 Kgs 17:18; Isa 43:26; Ezek 21:28–29; 29:16).[128] Of note is the idiom להזכיר שם, "to proclaim a name," often made in reference to God's name or that of another deity because its use frequently refers explicitly to speech (e.g. Exod 23:13; Josh 23:7; Isa 12:4; 49:1; Amos 6:10). A case in point not previously discussed is Exod 23:13: ושם אלהים אחרים לא תזכירו לא ישמע על פיך, "you shall not utter the name of other gods, they shall not be heard from your mouth." In this, as in a number of other examples, the act of speaking, indicated by a form of הזכיר, is reiterated by the use of another expression with parallel meaning, in this case ישמע על פיך.

While the element of speech is apparent in most of the biblical usages of the *hiphil* stem of זכר and is the means by which memory is effected, it must be stressed that in none is the act of writing explicitly alluded to. Adherents of the interpretation of מזכיר as "recorder" seem to rely primarily on post-exilic evidence. H. Eising, for example, links the title with ספר הזכרנות in Esth 6:1 and its Aramaic equivalent, ספר דכרניא, in Ezra 4:15.[129] The label ספר זכרון as a type of annals is also found in Mal 3:16. Although a מזכיר is never mentioned in conjunction with these books, it could be inferred from the three post-exilic biblical instances that an archivist had been entitled מזכיר.[130]

In another attempt to show that מזכיר means "recorder," Yeivin cites translations from the Septuagint and Targum that can be understood as defining the office as an annalist or archive keeper.[131] The LXX actually uses four different terms for the nine occurrences of the title מזכיר. One of these, ὑπομνηματογράφος, used in Chronicles and Isaiah, is the title of a Ptolemaic official who functioned

though, that in the cultic usage of the term מזכיר עון involving an offering (Num 5:15; Isa 66:3), the offering itself, rather than an utterance, is the means of recalling the transgression. In a few other cases as well, it is unclear whether the act of reminding involves speech.

128. Mettinger, *Solomonic State Officials*, 54–55. The possibility of a forensic use of the *hiphil* of זכר will be discussed below.

129. H. Eising, "זכר" in G.J. Botherweck and H. Ringgren eds. *Theologische Wörterbuch zum alten Testament* (Stuttgart: W. Kohlhammer, 1975), 584–585.

130. It must be noted that a related use of זכרון occurs in an early text (E), Exod 17:14. There, God commands Moses to record as a reminder in a document the fact that Amalek is condemned to extinction, כתב זאת זכרון בספר. (Interestingly, of more than 250 attestations of the root זכר, the one in Exod 17:14 and another in Exod 28:12 [P, in regard to the two inscribed stones on the ephod] are the only two examples of explicit connections made between writing and remembering in texts possibly of pre-exilic date.)

131. Yeivin, "Administration," 161. Yeivin also suggests that during the United Monarchy the מזכיר was charged with economic matters of state and the documents pertaining to them, and only later, when the royal steward attained high office, was the position of מזכיר limited to archivist. This proposal, however, lacks all proof.

as an annalist in the royal secretariat.[132] The other three, however, ἐπὶ τῶν ὑπομνημάτων, ἀναμιμνήσκων and ὑπομιμνήσκων, simply have to do with remembering or reminding, which can be applied to the role of a "herald" as well as a "recorder."[133] Targum Jonathan reads ממנא על דכרניא, which should probably be translated "record-keeper."

From the evidence presented above, it appears that a tradition concerning a record-keeping role for the Israelite מזכיר could have developed in the post-exilic period when the title was perhaps an appellation for professional annalists. This is not to say that the מזכיר of the First Temple Period never engaged in writing activities, but rather that his official title derived from a *verbum-dicendi* sense of זכר that focuses on his oral functions. Writing tasks, on the other hand, which no doubt included the recording of royal annals, were within the realm of the ספר, the royal scribe.

In light of the evidence, it seems safe to conclude that the primary duties of the royal מזכיר, at least initially, involved speech. In the process of delineating this official's specific tasks, the minority opinion, positing that the מזכיר represents an official prosecutor, demands evaluation. The main proponent of this theory, H. Graf Reventlow, interprets the title מזכיר as a technical term derived from a legal sense of זכר, as illustrated in the expression מזכיר עון\חטא (Gen 41:9; Num 5:15; 1 Kgs 17:18; Ezek 21:28–29; 29:16) and in the context of Isa 43:26.[134] The forensic sense evident in these examples, however, cannot be applied convincingly to the office of מזכיר.[135] A technical juridical understanding of the expression מזכיר עון is unjustified because the מזכיר עון is not a prosecutor.[136] Furthermore, while the term הזכרני, "remind me," in Isa 43:26 is used

---

132. See Mettinger for a comprehensive discussion on this and other LXX renditions (*Solomonic State Officials*, 21–25).

133. P.K. McCarter, for example, translates מזכיר as "herald" in 2 Sam 20:24 following the LXX *ἀναμιμνήσκων*; in 2 Sam 8:16 he translates it "remembrancer" after the LXX *ἐπὶ τῶν ὑπομνημάτων*, preserving the ambiguity of the Greek (*The Anchor Bible II Samuel* [Garden City: Doubleday, 1984], 433, 253).

134. H. Graf Reventlow, "Das Amt des Mazkir," *TZ* 15 (1959): 161–175. Interestingly, Rashi offers a similar interpretation for this office. He defines the מזכיר's duty as follows: מזכיר איזה דין בא לפניו ראשון לפוסקו ראשון, "He reminds (the king) which legal case coming before him has priority so that it is decided first" (2 Sam 8:16; 1 Kgs 4:3; 2 Kgs 18:18). Curiously, Rashi designates the מזכיר in Isa 36:3, the account parallel to 2 Kgs 18:18, also as a "recorder": כותב הזכרונות בספר דברי הימים, "(The one who) writes the remembrances in the book of chronicles."

135. At Mari, the person who administered oaths was called a *mušazkirum* (*ARM* 13, 143 r. 15, 17; *CAD* M/2, 263). Although the Hebrew term is an exact translation of the Akkadian (š stem participle of *zakāru* = מזכיר), evidence is lacking for any functional equivalency.

136. Schottroff, '*Gedenken und Gedächtnis' im Alten Testament*, 264–270.

in a legal sense, God calling upon Israel to testify on her own behalf, the same can be said for the verb ספר, "tell," found in parallel construction. But, since this usage of ספר does not transform the substantive סופר into a state-prosecutor, neither should the מזכיר be so designated. Most importantly, as Mettinger notes, there is no biblical evidence that an official state prosecutor served the king in his capacity as chief justice.[137]

In the final analysis, arguments favoring the definition "court herald" for the position of מזכיר seem most convincing. Although neither the biblical contexts of the title nor its attestation on a Moabite seal is revealing for deriving that meaning,[138] the identification rests on sufficient internal linguistic evidence and external comparative data. As mentioned, linguistic proof can be gleaned from a number of biblical examples where causative forms of זכר explicitly refer to vocalization, specifically to "announcing." In one case in particular, that interpretation is verified by the term השמיעו, "announce/proclaim," used in parallel construction to הזכירו (Jer 4:16). Clearly, making announcements is a key role of the court herald.

The Herald in Ugarit, Egypt and Mesopotamia

In support of the definition of מזכיר as "herald," textual material from the greater Near East testifies that the office of herald was widespread in the bureaucracies of the region. While Ugaritic, Egyptian, and Mesopotamian titles for herald vary slightly in meaning, each designation and its associated verbs, as Hebrew מזכיר, can denote some type of vocal expression. In Ugarit, the herald(s) is attested as *yṣḥ(m)*, from the root *ṣwḥ*, "shout, cry," or in Akkadian texts as *nāgiru.*[139] Heralds are listed among other royal dependents, *bnš mlk*, who served the king of Ugarit in return for land allotments.[140] More information on this official is available from Mesopotamia. There, the herald, designated

137. Mettinger, *Solomonic State Officials*, 55–56. It seems that Israelite citizens represented themselves or could attain the services of a specialist (see for example the letter from Meṣad Ḥashavyahu discussed in above in the excursus on Scribe). H.J. Boecker, who also supports a juridical understanding of certain usages of the verb זכר, thinks that anyone who served as a prosecutor or advocate would be called a מזכיר due to the nature of the activity. However, he does not extend this interpretation to the office of royal מזכיר, which he considers distinct and defines as "*Königssprecher*," ("Erwägungen zum Amt des Mazkir," *TZ* 17 [1961]: 211–216).

138. The appearance of the title מזכיר on a Moabite seal does prove that the designation was not confined to Israel or Judah in the pre-exilic period.

139. Cf. B. Margalit, who translates the term *ngr(t)* in the Keret Epic as "herald," instead of "carpenter" ("K-R-T Studies," *UF* 27 [1995]: 290–292; KTU I.16: IV: 3–12).

140. Heltzer, *Internal Organization*, 163–164; *KTU* 4.151, 4.69, 4609, 4692.

NIMGIR/*nāgiru*, appears in texts spanning the Sumerian through Neo-Babylonian periods.[141] The definition "herald" is derived from the verb *šasû*, "to exclaim, call"[142] or the noun *šisītu*, "a cry, proclamation,"[143] associated with the *nāgiru*'s activities.[144]

The functions of the *nāgiru* included announcing public proclamations, calling the populace to assembly, to arms, or for corvée labor.[145] Occasionally, the *nāgiru* performed guard-duty.[146] Beginning in the Old Babylonian period (19th century), this official is associated with military posts, and by the Middle-Assyrian period (14th century), he even attained the position of army commander.[147] The high status of the *nāgiru* at court in the Middle Assyrian period can be discerned from his place among palace officials in the Harem Edicts, where he is mentioned following the *rab ekalli* or *ša muḫḫi ekalli*, the palace managers at Assur.[148] In the Neo-Assyrian period, according to eponym lists, the *nāgir ekalli* appears as the second or third highest ranking official in the palace hierarchy, preceded only by the *turtānu*, "viceroy," and occasionally also by the *rab šaqî*, "chief cupbearer."[149] In this period he is known to function as provincial governor,[150] as a high military commander and as the officer associated with

141. See, E. Klauber, *Assyrisches Beamtentum* (Leipzig: J.C. Hinrichs, 1910), 64–69; for the most recent study on the *nāgiru* see, L. Sassmannshausen, "Funktion und Stellung der Herolde (NIMGIR/*nāgiru*) im Alten Orient," *Baghdader Mitteilungen* 26 (1995): 85–194.

142. *CAD* Š/2, 147, 152. It should be noted that in a few NA letters the verb *zakāru* is used with the expressions *amat šarri* and *abat šarri*, "royal decree," to mean "herald, announce" (e.g. *ABL* 186:13; 1214:r.6; see *CAD* Z, 20).

143. *AHW* 3, 1249; *CAD* Š/3, 122–124.

144. *CAD* N/1, 115–118. It is difficult to derive the meaning of *nāgiru* from the verbal form *nagāru* because it is rarely attested and cannot be clearly defined. Von Soden lists it under *nagāru* II, "ansagen," (*AHW*, 710), but *CAD* just notes "meaning uncertain" (p. 108).

145. For a wide-range of examples, see Sassmannshausen, "Funktion und Stellung der Herolde," 122–144.

146. Sassmannshausen, "Funktion und Stellung der Herolde," 145–149.

147. Sassmannshausen, "Function und Stellung der Herolde," 149–153.

148. E. Weidner, "Hof- und Harems-Erlasse assyrischer Könige aus dem 2. Jahrtausend v. Chr.," *AfO* 17 (1954–1956): 276:49; 286:95, 99. The royal *nāgiru* in the Middle Assyrian period is already designated *nāgir ekalli*, "herald of the palace," an appellation that is continued into the Neo-Assyrian period.

149. *RLA* 2 434 in *CAD* N/1, 118; *RLA* 2 428 in *CAD* Š/2, 32; Kinnier-Wilson, *Nimrud Wine Lists*, 35–36. Note that *rab šaqî* = chief cupbearer (*CAD* Š/2, pp. 30–32) not "chief eunuch" as defined by Kinnier-Wilson. Akkadian *rab ša rēši* = chief eunuch (Tadmor, "Rab-saris and Rab-shakeh in 2 Kings 18," 279–285).

150. See specifically Sargon's Annals (A. Lie, *The Inscriptions of Sargon II, King of Assyria* [Paris: P. Geuthner, 1929], 28–29).

home defense, specifically the city gates.[151] According to the military accounts of Sennacherib and his successors, the Elamite herald, like his Assyrian counterpart, also commanded royal troops. As such, he was considered a prize captive by the Assyrians in their Elamite campaigns.[152] L. Sassmannshausen posits that by this time the high rank of the palace herald hardly encompassed the role of announcer.[153]

In Egypt, the title for herald, *wḥm.w*, stems from the verb *wḥm*, "repeat," which refers to an action, or, when followed by the determinative , to speech.[154] The title *wḥm.w* actually means "spokesman," one who transmits information from one party to another.[155] Evidence from prior to the Middle Kingdom (1990 BCE) indicates that heralds served on the district level in the judiciary as investigators, reporters, and record keepers. During the Middle Kingdom, the *wḥm.w* is already associated with the palace, where he deals with matters of protocol in addition to his judicial duties.[156] By the Second Intermediate Period (1785 BCE), the herald's judicial role appears to have been integrated with the bureau of the vizier, from which he operated.[157] New Kingdom data focus on the activities of the chief royal herald, a high official entitled *wḥm tpy nswt n ḥm.f*, "first royal herald of his majesty."[158] As a court official he was charged with making reports to Pharaoh, announcing visiting dignitaries to the king and proclaiming royal commands. In the 18th Dynasty (1540–1300 BCE) the herald regularly accompanied the king on military campaigns, and his palace obligations expanded to overseeing the royal guard. During that period too, the herald was closely connected with the royal treasury, monitoring the collection of taxes and tribute. As in earlier periods, he continued to function in the judiciary, specifically in the *ꜥry.t*, "judgment-hall," of the palace. Some heralds were promoted to the highest offices (e.g. viceroy of Kush, vizier); others attained fame for their military achievements.[159]

151. Kinnier-Wilson, *Nimrud Wine Lists*, 12, 35–36.

152. Sassmannshausen, "Funktion und Stellung der Herolde," 154–158. See specifically, Oriental Institute Prism Inscription 3:82–88 in D.D. Luckenbill, *The Annals of Sennacherib* (Chicago: University of Chicago Press, 1924), 45.

153. Sassmannshausen, "Funktion und Stellung der Herolde," 169.

154. Faulkner, *Middle Egyptian*, 67; Erman and Grapow, *Wörterbuch* 1, 340–344.

155. S. and D. Redford, *The Akhenaten Temple Project 4: The Tomb of Re'a (TT 201)* (Toronto: University of Toronto, 1994), 29.

156. Redford, *Akhenaten Temple Project 4*, 29–30.

157. Helck, *Verwaltung*, 240–241.

158. Variations of the title "first herald" are attested as well as the office "deputy herald."

159. Gardiner, *Onomastica* I, 22*, 91*–92*; Helck, *Verwaltung*, 65–70; Redford, *Akhenaten Temple Project 4*, 31–32. Each army regiment also had its own herald, who could serve as captain as well.

The tasks of the palace herald are set forth neatly in the stele of Intef, the herald of Thutmose III, who is designated *wḥm-stny*, "royal reporter." Intef's many titles are enumerated before and after descriptions of his attributes and duties at court:[160] hereditary prince, seal bearer, companion, chief steward, overseer of the granary, overseer of works of the king's estate, scribe, and first herald. His responsibilities include: (1) managing the formalities and ceremonies at court; (2) communicating personal matters from the people and affairs of state to the Pharaoh; (3) acting as messenger of the judgment-hall and as originator of palace regulations; (4) inducting appointees and delineating their duties; (5) announcing to the people royal commissions; (6) communicating to Egyptians and to foreign countries matters of taxation; (7) generally being the "mouth-piece" of the palace; (8) exercising police control when accompanying the Pharaoh, including preparing his residence abroad; and (9) counting tribute.[161] Apparently, Intef's power, if accurately depicted, reflects his high status as bearer of several positions, both honorary and functional, though admittedly we cannot say whether they are all connected with his role as herald.

Functions of the Israelite Herald

The actual functions of the מזכיר are not mentioned in the Bible, but comparable to the heralds of other Near Eastern states, this Israelite minister seems to have been a high ranking government official. Jehoshaphat, David's מזכיר, holds the top civil position in one Davidic register of officials, where he is recorded after the highest military officer, Joab the chief army commander. He precedes the top cult functionaries, the priests Zadok and Abiathar and another civil official, the scribe Seraiah/Shavsha (2 Sam 8:16 = 1 Chr 18:15). In a different Davidic list, Jehoshaphat holds the second civil position, appearing after two military officers, Joab the army commander and Benaiah commander of Cherethites and Pelethites, and a civil official, Adoram the minister over the corvée. Again he precedes the scribe Sheva and the cult functionaries, the priests Zadok and Abiathar (2 Sam 20:24).

A change in status may be reflected in the Solomonic list of appointees. In that register Jehoshaphat the מזכיר, who apparently survived David and retained his office, is recorded in third place after Azariah the priest and the two scribes, Elihoreph and Ahijah; the army commander, now Benaiah, is listed following the מזכיר (1 Kgs 4:3). This shuffling of places may indicate reversals in status between the מזכיר and the ספר. J. Begrich attempts to harmonize this variance

160. It should be noted that while not all his other titles are repeated in each titulary, the designation "herald" appears throughout.

161. *Urk* IV, 963–975; translation in Breasted, *Ancient Records of Egypt* 2, 763–771.

by theorizing that originally, in all three lists, the מזכיר was in second place following the ספר. He shows that this reversal could have taken place when the text was copied from a prototype written in two columns.[162] Although tempting, this suggestion is speculative and may have been inspired by Begrich's conviction that the office of מזכיר, including its rank in the administrative hierarchy, was modelled after the Egyptian *wḥm.w*, who appears in certain lists after the scribe. Presently, as discussed in previous sections, the problematic nature of the biblical lists precludes deriving any firm conclusions based solely on their sequencing.

Later attestations of the מזכיר from the kingdom of Judah do not occur in lists of appointees, but appear amidst accounts of specific events from which possible functions of the office can be inferred. In the first of two such records, the מזכיר, Joah son of Asaph, appears in a wartime scene, the siege of Jerusalem by the armies of Sennacherib (701 BCE). He is mentioned as one of three officials who are charged by Hezekiah to meet with the Assyrian officers to negotiate a resolution to the crisis. Joah is listed third in this group of delegates, following the minister over the royal house, Eliakim, and the scribe, Shebnah (2 Kgs 18:18, 37 = Isa 36:3, 22). No individual tasks are delineated for the officers in Hezekiah's delegation, and their total dialogue with the Assyrian *rab šaqî* consists of a single remark requesting that he speak Aramaic not Hebrew. Due to a lack of details, the relationship between the role of the מזכיר in this episode and his official title, as well as that of the other officials, can only be surmised. One option is that the trio simply represented the king's highest functionaries who were dispatched on this crucial mission. A second option is that their presence actually served specific purposes, in that case the מזכיר could have functioned in at least two different roles. Perhaps the original intention was that he, as herald, would report Hezekiah's messages to the Assyrians and then relate theirs back to the king. An alternate explanation is that, comparable to the Neo-Assyrian *nāgirū* and the New Kingdom *wḥm.w*, the role of the Israelite herald by this time had evolved to encompass military duties, specifically those associated with the capital's defenses.[163] The herald's roles in the military realm would have made his presence essential at the negotiations. This interpretation is supported by the fact that the מזכיר did not participate in a subsequent dele-

162. Begrich, "Sōfēr und Mazkīr," 6–7.

163. Judah's recent vassalship under Assyria raises the possibility that her bureaucratic organization was influenced on some level by the Assyrian system. One of the functions of the *nāgir ekalli*, who is often ranked third in the central administration following the viceroy and chief butler, was with home defense, specifically the city gates (J. Pečírková, "The Administrative Organization of the Neo-Assyrian Empire," *ArOr* 45, 220–221; Kinnier-Wilson, *Nimrud Wine Lists*, 12, 35–36).

gation sent to the prophet Isaiah (2 Kgs 19:2). If he had acted solely as a spokesman in the delegation to the Assyrians, then his presence might be expected in the group sent to Isaiah as well, but if he functioned in some military capacity then he would not be needed in the meeting with Isaiah.

The other Judean מזכיר, Joah son of Joahaz, appears in the Chronicler's account of Josiah's cultic reforms (ca. 621 BCE) where he participates in the fiscal administration of the Temple repairs (2 Chr 34:8–13). Joah was one of three officials charged by the king to deliver moneys the Levites collected in Israel and Judah to the high priest Hilkiah and the overseers of the project. Here, as in the earlier episode, the מזכיר is listed in third place, in this instance following the scribe Shaphan and the governor of Jerusalem Maaseiah (34:8). In this case it is even less likely that his role was limited to reporting. One possibility, which assumes that the מזכיר's duties crossed over into the military sphere, is that he functioned as a guard entrusted with the safekeeping of the funds. A better option is that his position encompassed the duties of a treasurer, similar to Egyptian heralds.[164]

Was the Office of מזכיר *Modeled after an Egyptian Prototype?*

Having concluded that the evidence favors defining the royal official entitled מזכיר as herald,[165] it remains to reevaluate the long held view that the Israelite office was modeled after that of the Egyptian *wḥm.w*. Scholars who hold this opinion point to semantic correspondence of the two terms and similarity in rank of these functionaries, especially the seemingly routine placement on lists of the sequence scribe, herald.[166] In evaluating the semantic equivalency of the two titles, however, an important factor has been overlooked. The verb *wḥm*, "repeat," unlike זכר, is not explicitly related to "memory." A different Hebrew word, one semantically parallel to *wḥm*, is the verb שנה, which, like the Egyptian verb, is used in reference to both actions and speech (e.g. 1 Sam 26:8; 1 Kgs 18:34; Job 29:22; Prov 17:9). Similarly, a different Egyptian verb, *sḫꜣ*, "remember, mention, recall (to someone)," is analogous to זכר.[167] Thus, although the Egyptian and Hebrew titles stem from *verba-dicendi* and appear to designate the same office, semantically they are not equivalent. It should be noted too that

164. Begrich, "Sōfēr und Mazkīr," 19.

165. Rüterswörden's recent conclusion that the entity and functions of the מזכיר cannot be clarified seems overly cautious (*Beamten der israelitischen Königszeit*, 90–91).

166. Begrich, "Sōfēr und Mazkīr," 10–20; de Vaux, "Titres et fonctionnaires," 395–397; Mettinger, *Solomonic State Officials*, 58–61.

167. Faulkner, *Middle Egyptian*, 240; Erman and Grapow, *Wörterbuch* 4, 232–235.

the Ugaritic term for herald, *yṣḥ*, which derives from the verb *ṣwḥ*, "shout, cry," differs semantically from both the Egyptian and Hebrew designations.[168]

The second criterion, comparable ranking, used by proponents of the theory that the title מזכיר was borrowed from Egypt, is also questionable. An Egyptian document most often cited as proof is the record of tomb-robbery inquests from the reign of Rameses IX (ca. 1100 BCE). The herald, who appears in that text as a member of the inquest committee, is listed seven times in third position following the vizier and the scribe.[169] However, despite the consistency in that document, the sequence of these and other titles varies in several New Kingdom texts, thereby signaling caution as far as drawing conclusions about ranking.[170] Furthermore, as noted, the extant biblical lists are equally inconsistent. Initially in Davidic lists, the herald precedes the scribe, but subsequently, in a Solomonic list and in accounts of the kingdom of Judah, the scribe precedes the herald. A final objection to accepting the theory of direct borrowing of the Hebrew title from Egypt concerns chronological discrepancies. As Redford points out, the hey-day of the *wḥm.w* in the Egyptian royal administration was in the 18th Dynasty of the New Kingdom, before 1300. Thereafter the court title is only rarely attested in association with the vizier and disappears altogether by the late 21st Dynasty (ca. 950 BCE). It reappears in the Saite period (7th century BCE).[171]

Conclusions

Although the widely discussed Hebrew title מזכיר cannot be fully elucidated, a number of observations, based on the evidence presented above, help to define certain aspects of this office. (1) The position of מזכיר most probably represents that of court herald, not "recorder" as is often surmised. The usage of the *hiphil* stem of זכר in pre-exilic biblical texts generally shows a *verbum-dicendi* sense and only in post-exilic literature is the term definitively associated with annals, ספר

168. As noted above, the derivation of the Mesopotamian title *nāgiru* is unclear, but its meaning is inferred from connected terms, *šasû*, "exclaim, call," and *šisītu*, "proclamation, cry."

169. Papyrus Abbott in K.A. Kitchen, *Ramesside Inscriptions* 6 (Oxford: B.H. Blackwell, 1969), 468:10–13, 473:9–11, 480:1–5, 482:4–7, 487:13–14, 488:1–4, 490:4–6; trans. in T. Peet, *The Great Tomb-Robberies of the Twentieth Egyptian Dynasty* (Oxford: Clarendon Press, 1930), 37, 39, 42, 60.

170. Kitchen, "Egypt and Israel During the First Millennium B.C.," 113–114; Gardiner, *Onomastica* I, 38.

171. Redford, "Palestine and Egypt during the First Millennium B.C.," 144 n. 7; *Akhenaten Temple Project 4*, 33. Only military heralds are attested earlier.

הזכרנות. Importantly, the position of court herald is attested in Mesopotamia, Ugarit, and Egypt, suggesting that it existed in the Israelite monarchies as well.

(2) The Israelite מזכיר was a high ranking government official who seems to have served in various capacities. A dearth of data precludes tracing the evolution of the office over time, but the two contextual references from the reigns of Hezekiah and Josiah imply a wider scope of activities than a strict interpretation of the title might suggest. Information about Assyrian and Egyptian office-holders indicates that their jurisdiction crossed administrative divisions so that they functioned in the military realm as well.

(3) Questions as to whether the Israelite title and office of "herald" were borrowed directly from Egypt can tentatively be answered in the negative. While the inception of the position early in the monarchic period may indeed have been influenced by a non-Israelite source, there is no convincing evidence to that effect. In fact, the existence of semantic distinctions among the various titles for "herald" throughout the ancient Near East suggests that this office need not have been borrowed from anyone in particular but was designed to fulfill specific duties. The presence of the title מזכר on a Moabite seal indicates that the Hebrew designation was not restricted to Israel and Judah but may have been prevalent in various Palestinian states. On the other hand, Egyptian or Mesopotamian practices connected with this type of royal official could have influenced the roles of the Israelite מזכיר at one time or another to some extent. Of note is the potential for Assyrian inspiration in the eighth and seventh centuries when a close, though hostile, relationship existed between Assyria and Judah.

D. רע(ה) המלך – "Companion," Confidant of the King

Biblical Usage

In addition to the top echelon of civil officials at court, a number of lower ranked functionaries surrounded the king. One of these was the רע(ה) המלך. The designation רע/רעה/מרע (*r'/r'h/mr'*) of a king, which seems to be an old title, appears seven times in the biblical text, six times in reference to named individuals (Gen 26:26; 2 Sam 15:37; 16:16, 17; 1 Kgs 4:5; 1 Chr 27:33), and once in reference to an unnamed person (1 Kgs 16:11). In Gen 26, Abimelech, the King of Gerar, comes to Isaac with his army commander Phicol and מרעהו, "his *mr'*," Ahuzzath. In the account of Absalom's revolt against David, 2 Sam 15–16, Hushai, David's רעה, is mentioned in connection with his feigned defection to Absalom's camp. Hushai is also listed as רע המלך, "*r'* of the king," in a register of Davidic officials in 1 Chr 27. In the list of Solomonic appointees, 1 Kgs 4, Zabud son of Nathan the priest is entitled רעה המלך. An unnamed רע of King Basha is recorded in 1 Kgs 16 together with the heirs and redeemers of the king who were murdered by the usurper Zimri. This title is as yet unattested in any extra-biblical Hebrew inscriptional material.

The definition of the designation רע(ה) המלך, let alone the role in the monarchic organization of officials bearing that title, has been the subject of scholarly debate. Commonly, the title is translated "friend of the king," based on one of several usages of nominal forms derived from the verbal root רעה "to associate with." But רע has a wide semantic range, most frequently carrying the sense "companion, fellow, another person" (e.g. Exod 21:18; 1 Sam 15:28; Jer 6:21). Sometimes it simply refers to a person who is in spacial proximity to another (2 Sam 2:16). In the context of Judg 11:37–38 and Ps 45:15, the feminine form רעה can be translated as "attendant." Less often, רע carries the meaning "friend, intimate, lover" (e.g. Deut 13:7; Cant 5:16; Lam 1:2).[172] In one case, the רע of prince Amnon, Jonadab, serves as advisor (2 Sam 13:3). Possibly Jonadab was an attendant of the crown prince or a close friend who advised Amnon on his paramours, but it is unclear whether in this instance רע actually signifies a court title. The precise expression רע(ה) המלך, however, is found twice in lists of court officials, those of David and Solomon, and must therefore be understood as a technical term denoting a functionary of the king.

Most of the information on this title is gleaned from the references to Hushai the Archite, David's רע(ה) המלך. He is listed in 1 Chronicles 27 among different groups of administrators: military officers, tribal chiefs, various stewards, and royal counsellors. Hushai's name and title appear following that of Ahitophel, the king's advisor (27:33). He is called רעה המלך twice in the narrative of the rebellion of Absalom, 2 Samuel 15–17 (15:37; 16:16). During that revolt, he purposely pretends to desert David in order to thwart the counsel of Absalom's advisor Ahitophel. Hushai's deceptive advice prevails and the uprising against David is crushed. From this account it seems that at least one function of the רע(ה) המלך was to serve as advisor. One could argue, however, that Hushai's advice was sought because he was perceived as a traitor who was privy to valuable information and not because the רע(ה) המלך acted as a royal counselor. It is noteworthy that when Hushai first appears in Jerusalem proclaiming his fealty to Absalom, Absalom questions Hushai concerning his loyalty to *his* רע, King David (16:16–17). Referring to David as Hushai's רעה is curious. Mettinger suggests that the reference to David as רעה is a pun on Hushai's title רעה המלך.[173] But it is equally conceivable that a close relationship developed between the king and his רע even though the two were not of equal status.

The second Israelite רעה המלך, Zabud son of Nathan (the) priest, is listed in 1

172. *BDB*, 945–946; *HALOT* 3, 1253–1255.
173. Mettinger, *Solomonic State Officials*, 64.

Kgs 4:5 among Solomon's appointees.[174] Nothing else is known of Zabud but perhaps Azariah son of Nathan, the officer over the prefects listed before him, was his brother.[175]

A third, unnamed individual whose relationship to the king is noted as רעהו, is a victim in the assassination of the House of Basha (1 Kgs 16:11). Interestingly, the רע is murdered along with Basha's heirs and potential redeemers by the chariot-commander Zimri. In this case, however, the term רעהו may not refer to a court official. Although the possibility that this individual was indeed a royal official who remained loyal to his king and therefore lost his life in the revolt cannot be totally discounted, more convincing evidence exists that רעהו refers to a person or persons other than the functionary רע(ה) המלך. The latter is supported by the Peshitta, Targum, and Vulgate readings where רעהו appears in the plural and by a similar account in 2 Kings 10 that seems to further elucidate the issue. In the narrative of 2 Kings 10, the uprising of Jehu, the usurper slays all who remain of the House of Ahab in Jezreel: וכל גדליו ומידעיו וכהניו, "and all his magnates, his intimates, and his priests (10:11). If רעהו in the Basha account is to be read as plural, the term could be understood as comparable to מידעיו, "his intimates," and not as the title רע(ה) המלך.[176]

---

174. Some Mss read זכור instead of זבוד, the Septuagint omits "(the) priest."

175. J. Gray suggests that Zabud and Azariah were the sons of Nathan, the prophet who helped to secure the throne for Solomon. Nathan's sons were rewarded with government positions (*I and II Kings*, 133 [following the Septuagint, Gray deletes כהן, "priest," from Zabud's titulary]). A. van Selms thinks that Nathan was Solomon's nephew, the son of one of David's unnamed sons selected for the priesthood, as noted in 2 Sam 8:18 ("The Origin of the Title 'the King's Friend'," *JNES* 16 [1957]: 119). While neither reconstruction can be verified, Gray's is more logical in light of Solomonic appointees whose fathers were David's ministers.

176. Rüterswörden points out that the role of the מידעים in Israel may be similar to that of the מודדין in northern Syria (*Beamten der israelitischen Königszeit*, 74). Hebrew מידע (root ידע, "know, be intimate with") and Aramaic מודד (root יודד/ "love") are not directly related etymologically, but semantically, all three terms, מודד , מידע, and רע can have the sense "friend, intimate." In the Aramaic inscriptions of the Hadad statue of Panammu (*KAI* 214) and the treaty between KTK and Arpad (*KAI* 224), the context of מודד seems parallel to that of מידע in 2 Kgs 10:11 and רע in 1 Kgs 16:11. The Aramaic inscriptions, like the biblical texts, deal with assassinations of the royal family and its associates. In the treaty between KTK and Arpad, the king of KTK obliges the ruler of Arpad, in the event of a palace revolt, to avenge him by slaying not only the culprit but all his associates: ועקרה ושגבוה ומודדוה, "and his offspring, and his magnates, and his friends" (*KAI* 224:13–14). Apparently, the so called "friends of the king" are targeted, together with his kin and officers. The terms מודד, מידע, and רע in these usages, however, do not seem to describe the royal office of רע(ה) המלך, which is held by one individual at a time. Rather, the designations seem to resemble that of *mūdē šarri* from the Ras Shamra documents. The *mūdû-md(m)* from Ugarit, often construed as

Because of the lack of descriptive information in the Bible concerning the role(s) of the רעה) המלך(ה), scholars have regularly searched for comparative material from neighboring Near Eastern societies, especially Egypt.

Egyptian and Mesopotamian Evidence

Usually the Hebrew title is compared with the Egyptian *smr* or *rḫ-nswt*. One theory is that the רע המלך was functionally related to the Egyptian courtier *smr*, a personal attendant of the Pharaoh whose title is commonly followed by one or more adjectives such as "true, beloved, sole" and may have the meaning "friend."[177] Unfortunately, Egyptologists disagree about the definition of the term *smr*, some maintaining that it simply means "courtier" and does not specify any role.[178]

Several scholars posit that the designation רע(ה) המלך was borrowed from the Egyptian title *rḫ-nswt*, "acquaintance of the king."[179] The Egyptian verb *rḫ* is defined as, "to know, to have knowledge of, to be intimate with," and when followed by the determinative for person, it denotes the noun "wise man."[180] Functionally, however, the *rḫ-nswt* does not seem to be an advisor; instead, he appears as an attendant who accompanies the king on ceremonial occasions and tends to his personal needs. The *rḫ-nswt* appears connected to another court

"friends" or "acquaintances of the king," appear to have been members of a privileged group who paid an annual fee of 5–20 shekels of silver to the king or queen for their *mūdûtu* relationship. This status, which was hereditary, freed them from the jurisdiction of overseers of fields, chariots, and the *ḫazannu* (mayor, governor), and from various obligations such as quartering strangers, messenger service to Egypt and Hatti, and service to the palace overseer (Heltzer, *Internal Organization*, 161–163). But, despite the data available on the *mūdû*, their exact function at court and in the royal administration remains unclear (W. Thiel, "Zur gesellschaftlichen Stellung des *MUDU* in Ugarit," *UF* 12 [1980]: 349–356; P. Vargyas, "Le *MUDU* à Ugarit. Ami du roi?" *UF* 13 [1981]: 165–179). At present, too little is known of the Israelite מידע or the Syrian מודד to connect them with any certainty to the *md* from Ugarit, nor should the *mūdē šarri* be connected to Egyptian *rḫ-nswt*, "the acquaintance of the king" (Kitchen, "Egypt and Israel During the First Millennium B.C.," 115 n. 52; contra Rüterswörden, p. 75). It should be noted that the expression "friends of the king" is also known from Hellenistic sources (1 Macc 2:18; 13:36; 14:39; 2 Macc 8:9), where such persons appear to be privileged members of the royal court (J. Goldstein, *The Anchor Bible I Maccabees* [Garden City: Doubleday], 232).

177. Donner, "Der 'Freund des Königs'," 271–272.

178. Helck, "Beamtentum," in *Lexikon* 1, 672–675; Kitchen, "Egypt and Israel During the First Millennium B.C.," 115. Contra Faulkner, *Middle Egyptian*, 229.

179. De Vaux, "Titres et fonctionnaires," 404–405; Mettinger, *Solomonic State Officials*, 67–68; Rüterswörden, *Beamten der israelitischen Königszeit*, 75–76.

180. Faulkner, *Middle Egyptian*, 151.

title, *imy-ḫnt*, literally, "the one who is in the face of (the king)."[181] When the latter functioned in the palace it was in the capacity of Pharaoh's chamberlain.[182] Recently, the title *rḫ-nswt* has been defined as "king's intimate," a sense more in keeping with the verbal meaning as well as the apparent role of this functionary.[183] While the assumption that the Hebrew title רעה המלך is connected to Egyptian *rḫ-nswt* is problematic because no direct etymological relationship exists between רע and *rḫ* (Egyptian *ḫ* = Hebrew *ḥ*; Egyptian ʿ = Hebrew ʿ), the term רע may reflect a loose translation of *rḫ*.[184]

If the Egyptian title *rḫ-nswt* is connected in some way to the Hebrew title רע(ה) המלך, then an avenue of transmission needs to be established. The most convincing proposal focuses on Canaanite borrowing during the Late Bronze Age when Canaan was under Egyptian hegemony. A term resembling *rḫ-nswt*, Akkadian LÚ *ruḫi šarri*, is found in an Amarna letter (*EA* 288:11). In this letter, the ruler of the city-state Jerusalem, Abdi-hiba, expounds on his loyalty to Pharaoh:

a-mur a-na-ku la-a LÚ *ḫa-zi-a-nu*
LÚ *ú-e-ú a-na šarri bēli-ia*
a-mur a-na-ku LÚ *ru-ḫi šarri*
ù ú-bil bilat šarri a-na-ku (ll. 9–12)

See, I am not (only) a *ḫazannu* (mayor)
(I am) a soldier of the king my lord
See, I am a *ruḫi* of the king
and a tribute bearer of the king.[185]

Abdi-hiba maintains that he is not merely a native local ruler, but an Egyptian soldier, a *ruḫi* of the king and a tribute bearer.[186] He furthermore credits his

---

181. Helck, *Verwaltung*, 279.

182. Gardiner, *Onomastica* I, 23*. Helck thinks that the designation *rḫ-nswt* is only an honorific epithet conferred on various officials (*Verwaltung*, 279–280).

183. Quirke, "The Regular Titles of the Late Middle Kingdom," 118.

184. Mettinger, *Solomonic State Officials*, 68 (Mettinger mentions other possibilities as well).

185. Following Moran, *ūbil* is understood as a construct nominal form (cf. *ūbilī*, *EA* 287:55; *Amarna Letters*, 331). It can also be read as a verb: "I carried (the tribute)."

186. There seems no reason to follow Rüterswörden that Abdi-heba presents himself with lowly designations (*Beamten der israelitischen Königszeit*, 76). Quite the contrary, Abdi-hiba appears proud of his roles in the Pharaoh's service. Abdi-hiba's denial that he is a *ḫazannu* cannot be taken literally. In numerous Amarna letters the native local rulers refer to themselves and each other as *ḫazannu* and credit their mayorship to the Pharaoh (e.g. *EA* 117:37; 144:5; 161:51–53; 212:8). Apparently Abdi-hiba wishes to enumerate his other titles as well, especially the Egyptian ones.

patrimony to the mighty arm of the Pharaoh, who, rather than his parents, secured his position. Following Redford, Abdi-hiba was probably one of a number of sons of Syro-Canaanite rulers sent to Egypt as children to be trained at court to serve the Pharaohs and later reinstated in their homelands as loyal vassals.[187] The titles that Abdi-hiba claims for himself in the letter may actually reflect those he acquired while in Egypt, especially *ruḫi šarri* and *úeú*. In that light, the designation *ruḫi šarri* is probably a transcription of the Egyptian term *rḫ*, comparable to *úeú* (=Egyptian *w'w*), soldier.[188] An alternate solution, that *ruḫi* is an Akkadian transliteration of the Canaanite term רע/ה,[189] is less likely since the expression רע(ה) המלך is unattested in Late Bronze inscriptions. Moreover, if a Semitic term was sought, Akkadian *rū'u* or *ibru*, "companion, friend," would have been a better choice.[190]

An Akkadian title that may be comparable to "friend of the king" is *bēl dumqi*. The expression appears in a Mari letter listing the king of Eshnunna, his palace personnel, and *bēl dumqi*, "friend."[191] Admittedly, this one example is of limited value since no information is provided about the title-bearer. Two other terms, *rū'u* and *ibru*, are also worth mentioning. Both nouns denote "comrade, fellow, friend, person of same status,"[192] analogous to Hebrew רע. Like Hebrew רע, they have a wide semantic range. The designations *rū'u* and *ibru* of the king are rare as well. One possible example appears in the epic of Tikulti Ninurta as *rū'uašu*, "his friend." The inscription is too fragmentary, however, to reveal the context or to indicate whether the reference is in fact to the king's (Tikulti Ninurta)

---

187. Redford, *Akhenaten Temple Project* III, 16–17. Similarly, Yahtiri, ruler of Gaza(?), explicitly states that as a child in Egypt he served the Pharaoh "standing at the gate" (*EA* 296:25–29). Aziri, a Syrian prince, reminds the Pharaoh of the sons he sent for service (*EA* 156:8–12). Amanhatpi, the mayor of the Syrian city of Tusulti (*EA* 185, 186), has an Egyptian name, which he could have acquired as a foreign prince serving in Egypt (Albright, "Cuneiform Material for Egyptian Prosopography 1500–1200 B.C.," 9–10). Knudtzon (*Die El-Amarna Tafeln* II, 1282) and Moran (*Amarna Letters*, 265–268) posit instead that Amanhatpi is a native Egyptian turned traitor. For a discussion of Egyptian and foreign children at the Pharaonic court, see Chapter 3-D.

188. De Vaux, "Titres et fonctionnaires," 404.

189. Yeivin, "Peqidut," 546. For further discussion, see Mettinger, *Solomonic State Officials*, 67–68; Rüterswörden, *Beamten der israelitischen Königszeit*, 75–76.

190. However it should be noted that in Akkadian orthography *ḫ* can replace ', as in foreign names where on occasion *ḫ* takes the place of ' (*GAG* 25:a, c). The term *ibrum* is actually attested in *EA* 126:16 as a designation for Rib-Hadda's fellow mayors.

191. *ARM* 4 26:11; *CAD* D, 183 (both translate the title as "notables," in the plural). There seems no reason to take *be-el du-um-qi* as a plural. See L. Oppenheim, who compares the expression to the Hebrew and Egyptian titles ("The Archives of the Palace of Mari II: A Review Article," *JNES* 13 [1954]: 143).

192. *AHW*, 363–364, 998; *CAD* I-J, 5–7.

"friend."[193] Another example, found in the annals of Esarhaddon, refers to Taharqa king of Kush as the *ibru* of Ba'lu king of Tyre. In that account, Esarhaddon apparently makes jest of the defeated Ba'lu for having relied on his *ibru* Taharqa. In this instance, the expression "his friend" is either used sarcastically or more likely, has the sense "his ally."[194] A final case may actually offer some insight into the position of the Israelite רע(ה) המלך. On a *kudurru*, a boundary stone, of Nebuchadnezzar I, a certain Bau-šum-iddina is entrusted to measure land granted by the king to the priest Nusku-ibni. Among Bau-šum-iddina's qualifications mentioned is his role as *ibru* of the king:

> *Ba-ú-šùm-iddina mār Hu-un-na i-bir bēli-šu*
> *na-an-za-az maḫ-ḫar šarri*
> *ki-zu-ú ša ultu ul-la at-mu-šú na-as-qu-ma*
> *šú-zu-uz-zu ina maḫ-ri šakkanak Bābli*[ki]
> *ša-kìn Bīt-sin-še-me.*[195]

> PN son of PN the *ibru* of his lord (the king)
> who stands before the king,
> the servant[196] whose counsel was always chosen and
> who was placed (elevated) before the ruler of Babylon,
> (as) governor of GN.

The *ibru* of the king in this context appears to be a royal attendant whose advice was greatly valued and who consequently was promoted to governor.[197] The translation of *ibru* as "intimate" rather than as "friend" is an interpretation that seems to describe accurately the function of this official vis-à-vis his king.[198]

Conclusions

A few observations are in order concerning the position of the Israelite official entitled רע(ה) המלך. Although the title does not clearly denote a function, nevertheless, it does not seem to be merely an honorary epithet applicable to various

---

193. W.G. Lambert, "Three Unpublished Fragments of the Tikulti-Ninurta Epic," *AfO* 18 (1957–1958): 46 l. 34; P. Machinist, "The Epic of Tikulti-Ninurta I: A Study in Middle Assyrian Literature" (Ph.D. Dissertation, Yale University, 1978), 132–133.

194. *CAD* I-J, 6.

195. W. Hinke, *A New Boundary Stone of Nebuchadrezzar I from Nippur* (Philadelphia: University Museum, 1907), 146.

196. *kizû* is defined as "groom or personal attendant" (*CAD* K, 478).

197. That Baušumiddina was governor of Bitsinšeme is made explicit in III:9 (Hinke, *A New Boundary Stone of Nebuchadrezzar I*, 148).

198. *CAD* I-J, 6.

courtiers or different offices.[199] The biblical examples of רע(ה) המלך indicate that a certain royal functionary during the period of the United Monarchy was called by that title. Whether or not the title and its accompanying office disappeared with the division of the kingdom, is unknown. The appearance of this title in the reign of David may reflect the adaptation of aspects of the local Canaanite administrative organization by the newly formed Israelite monarchy. The somewhat similar title *rḫ-nswt* in the Jerusalem Amarna letter and the biblical attestation of מרעהו as a designation for Abimelech's official Ahuzzath, may point in that direction.[200]

The internal biblical evidence implies that the רע(ה) המלך functioned at court as an advisor, but not per se in place of one, since the advisor to the king, יועץ למלך, is listed in addition to the רע המלך in a Davidic record in Chronicles. Yet it remains obscure whether counseling was the primary role of the רע(ה) המלך or just an outgrowth of his duties as a personal attendant that placed him in close ties to the palace and the monarch. Rüterswörden's view that this official was a *Vertrauensperson,* "a confidant," seems most accurate.[201] The example of the *ibru* of Nebuchadnezzar I lends support to that contention.[202] Possibly, the רע(ה) also tended to various personal needs of the king comparable to the *rḫ-nswt* of the Pharaoh, although a secure connection between these two offices cannot be achieved satisfactorily. The occurrence of potentially similar titles in various states in the region does suggest that such a position, albeit with distinctions, was widespread.

E. משנה ל/המלך – "Second" to the King, Personal Escort

Etymology and Usage

Another court functionary in the suite of the king was the משנה המלך. The designation משנה ל/המלך (*mšnh l/hmlk*) appears three times in the biblical text, in 1 Sam 23:17, Esth 10:3, and 2 Chr 28:7. In 1 Samuel, Jonathan assures the fleeing

199. Contra de Vaux and Gray (*Ancient Israel*, 123; *I and II Kings*, 133).

200. Van Selms' argument that Ahuzzath, as well as other persons designated רע(ה) in Hebrew or *ibru* in Akkadian, functioned in the capacity of "best man" ("The Origin of the Title 'the King's Friend'," 118–123), is unconvincing. While the term can be interpreted as "best man" in certain instances and has been so translated in the Septuagint and Targumim, that understanding is rarely if ever evident from the context.

201. Rüterswörden, *Beamten der israelitischen Königszeit*, 73.

202. After this study was completed, Victor Hurowitz brought to my attention his similar association of the Akkadian title *ibir bēlišu* in this text with the biblical title רע המלך (*Divine Service and Its Rewards: Ideology and Poetics in the Hinke Kudurru*, [Beer-Sheva: Ben-Gurion University of the Negev Press, 1997], 100).

David that Saul will not harm him, that he (David) will be king over Israel while he (Jonathan) will be David's משנה. At the end of the Book of Esther, King Ahasuerus elevates Mordecai to the position of משנה למלך. In 2 Chronicles the משנה המלך, Elkanah, is recorded third among three individuals at the court of Ahaz murdered by Zichri, Pekah's Ephramite champion-warrior. The first two casualties on that list are Maaseiah בן המלך, "son of the king," followed by Azrikam נגיד הבית, "minister over the royal house." Although none of these examples defines the role of the משנה, the contexts imply that the term is indicative of a court title.

Aside from the rare expression משנה of the king, the term משנה is widely attested in the biblical material in construct position to other nouns. The word משנה, a nominal form of the verbal root שנה, "to repeat," is defined as "second (in rank or age), substitute, double, copy."[203] Its usage "second in rank" seems to denote "deputy or assistant" as: כהן משנה, "deputy priest" (2 Kgs 23:4; 25:18; Jer 52:24); Levite assistants, משנים, or those of the second order (1 Chr 15:18; 16:5; Neh 11:17);[204] משנה על העיר, "deputy governor" (Neh 11:9); and deputy, המשנה, of a chief, הראש (1 Chr 5:12; 2 Chr 31:12). At times משנה designates the one next to the eldest in age, הבכור ומשנהו (1 Sam 8:2; 17:13; 2 Sam 3:3). Twice משנה characterizes a type of chariot: Joseph rides in Pharaoh's משנה chariot (במרכבת המשנה, Gen 41:43); the mortally injured King Josiah is driven to Jerusalem in his משנה chariot (על רכב המשנה, 2 Chr 35:24).

With the possible exception of רכב משנה, the above examples of the term משנה in construct position to a noun other than "king" are not especially helpful in elucidating the role of the משנה המלך. There is no evidence that any Israelite king had a deputy or an official designated second in command of the kingdom, certainly not bearing that title.[205] That conclusion is partially borne out by the case of Elkanah, who as the משנה is listed third following the בן המלך and נגיד הבית (2 Chr 28:7). If placement on this list is indicative at all of status then it follows that the משנה was an official of lower status than the minister over the royal house.

Foreign Analogues

Since the title משנה המלך is poorly attested and does not appear on any known

203. *BDB*, 1041; *HALOT* 2, 650.

204. Japhet, *I & II Chronicles*, 303.

205. The implication that Joseph was second to Pharaoh in Egypt (Gen 41:40) cannot be used as evidence that such a position existed in Israel. First, the term משנה is not used in that Genesis account and second, as noted, Joseph's position in Egypt does not seem to reflect an actual office. The LXX translation of משנה in 2 Chr 28:7 and Esth 10:3 as διάδοχος, "deputy, successor," is unsupported by biblical data.

Hebrew seals or inscriptions, any hints that may be gleaned from foreign analogues are worth pursuing. Akkadian, Ugaritic, and Egyptian sources are of limited value in this investigation. A cognate of Hebrew משנה is found in the Akkadian noun *šanû*, which occurs as LÚ.2 or *amēl šanî* and is defined as "second-in-command, deputy, assistant."[206] Like משנה, the term is used primarily to denote the deputy of a specific official or the second-in-command of an entity such as a palace, city, or country. Occasionally, LÚ.2 is not in construct position to another noun and can be translated simply as "the deputy." In rare cases the individual appears as "PN LÚ.2-*i ša mār šarri*," PN *šanû* of the king's son, or crown prince.[207] Since "deputy of the king's son" is an unlikely position, the Akkadian expression poses a similar problem as Hebrew משנה המלך.[208]

Ugaritic *ṯnn*, a nominal form related to *ṯn* and *ṯny* (=שני), "two, twice, repetition," is a technical term for a kind of soldier.[209] It has been identified with the *šanannu* charioteers of Alalakh, possibly the archers.[210] The Semitic term was borrowed into Egyptian as *śnn* (š=ś), and there too it appears to signify a chariot-warrior, archer.[211] It is noteworthy that in Egyptian the term *śnw*, "two," a cognate of שני, when written with the determinative for person means "companion, fellow."[212] In context it sometimes refers specifically to a companion who is spatially close-by.[213]

Functions of the משנה המלך

One suggestion connects the Hebrew משנה המלך with charioteers. Just as the שליש is identified as the "third man on the chariot, the shield-bearer," so the משנה is identified with the second charioteer, possibly the driver.[214] The proposal that the משנה המלך was the king's driver is feasible but cannot be proven from the biblical examples. Nothing is known of Elkanah the משנה of King Ahaz (2 Chr 28:7), though one might imagine that he drove a chariot carrying Maaseiah and Azrikam and the three met their deaths in an attack. More can be said of Mor-

206. *CAD* Š, 397–398; *AHW* 3, 164–165.

207. *ADD* 129; 694.

208. C.H. Johns suggests, without evidence, that the *šanû* is a business representative or agent (*ADD* 2, 159).

209. *UT*, 504.

210. Wiseman, *Alalakh Tablets*, 11.

211. Gardiner, *Onomastica* I, 28*. For a brief discussion, see Ward, "Comparative Studies in Egyptian and Ugaritic," 39.

212. Faulkner, *Middle Egyptian*, 230.

213. "The story of the Shipwrecked Sailor" ll. 42, 101 in A.M. Blackman, *Middle Egyptian Stories* I (Brussels: Édition de la foundation égyptologique, 1932), 41–48.

214. Yeivin, "Peqidut," 560.

decai and Jonathan. Both had proven themselves trustworthy and loyal, Mordecai by saving King Ahasuerus from two would-be assassins and Jonathan by repeatedly rescuing David, the future king, from the wrath of Saul. While the story of Esther is set in the Persian court and משנה המלך could reflect a non-Israelite title, the term in the David and Jonathan saga logically could be indicative of an Israelite court official. In either case it seems doubtful that Mordecai or Jonathan would have served as charioteers since they never do so prior to attaining the title משנה, instead they appear as functionaries in close proximity to the king.[215]

As noted, the Egyptian term *śnw* can designate a companion who is close by. Although this usage of שנה is not explicitly attested in biblical Hebrew, it may define the type of chariot called מרכבת המשנה, usually assumed to be the king's second chariot. As mentioned, Joseph was privileged to ride in Pharaoh's משנה chariot and Josiah traveled in one to Jerusalem after being wounded at Megiddo. The function of this chariot can be clarified by the Josiah account (2 Chr 35:23–24). After the king is mortally wounded in battle, his servants first transfer him to his רכב המשנה and only then transport him to Jerusalem. Apparently, the chariot in which he was shot was damaged but his רכב המשנה was nearby as a backup. This chariot was probably called משנה not because the king had only two chariots (presumably he had more) but because it rode alongside the chariot carrying the king. Evidence of such a reserve chariot also comes from Assyria.[216]

Similarly, it is conceivable that the official entitled משנה המלך was an individual serving in close proximity to the king. Perhaps he was his personal escort who accompanied him and simultaneously functioned as a bodyguard. This interpretation would account for the slaying of Ahaz's משנה Elkanah, together with the son of the king, perhaps the crown prince, during the Syro-Ephramite war, when Pekah sought to depose Ahaz in order to replace him with a king sympathetic to an anti-Assyrian alliance. Eliminating Ahaz's heir would have been necessary as part of the plot. The משנה המלך may have been temporarily assigned to the king's son at the time of the murder.

Conclusions

The title משנה המלך remains difficult to interpret. Comparative material is not illuminating but does show a similar title among Assyrian functionaries. While not explicitly defining the position, the internal biblical evidence suggests that persons entitled משנה המלך served in close proximity to the king. Naturally, such

---

215. In Jonathan's case, he only alludes to his role as משנה for a future time when David is king.

216. Kinnier-Wilson, *Nimrud Wine Lists*, 52–53.

individuals would have earned the monarch's utmost trust by having proved their loyalty, as had Jonathan and Mordecai. Possibly, functionaries holding this title acted as the king's personal escort.

F. יועץ למלך – Advisor to the King

Biblical Evidence

A third royal functionary, designated יועץ למלך (*yw'ṣ lmlk*), "advisor, counselor to the king," appears with this specific official title in the Bible only in connection with David's reign. To date the title is unattested in inscriptions. In the Bible it is ascribed to four individuals: Ahitophel, Jonathan, Jehoiada, and Abiathar (2 Sam 15:12; 1 Chr 27:32–34). These four men are listed in a Chronistic record of David's administrative organization[217] but of the four, only Ahitophel is mentioned outside Chronicles in the capacity of royal advisor. Others who served as royal advisors but do not bear this exact title include members of the House of Ahab who counseled Ahaziah of Judah: the king's mother, Athaliah, and additional unnamed relations of Ahab (2 Chr 22:3–4). Another group of unnamed counselors is mentioned in connection with Artaxerxes (יועציו, "his advisors," Ezra 7:28; 8:25). An allusion to the position of יועץ למלך is found in a sarcastic retort to the unnamed prophet who admonished Amaziah for worshipping Edomite gods: הליועץ למלך נתנוך, "have we appointed you advisor to the king?" (2 Chr 25:16). Additional references to counselors are general and seem to encompass various leadership roles with no indication that the individual's assigned duty was to advise the king.[218]

Scant information relating to rank or specific duties is available on office-holders entitled יועץ למלך. In general, monarchs who sought advice turned to various ministers of state, ofttimes referred to in the biblical text by imprecise designations (e.g. שרים, עבדים). Usually it reads וַיִּוָּעַץ המלך, "the king took counsel," plus the name of the group he consulted, though occasionally the latter is omitted altogether.[219] For example, Jeroboam consults an unnamed body of functionaries before he establishes the calves at Dan and Bethel (1 Kgs 12:28);

217. The section of the list containing the names of these four advisors is appended to the register of David's stewards. The list seems to supplement the information in 1 Chr 18:15–17, a parallel to 2 Sam 8:16–18 (Japhet, *I & II Chronicles*, 473).

218. For example, in Isaiah the term יועץ appears in parallel construction with שפט, "judge, ruler," or together with other שרים, "officers" (1:26; 3:3; 19:11). Similar usages of the participle יועץ and the verb יעץ, "advise," are attested elsewhere. Some refer to persons of authority at the palace or the Temple, while others are unspecified (e.g. Ezek 11:2; Mic 4:9; Job 3:14; 12:17; 1 Chr 26:14).

219. When the group the king consults is mentioned, one of three prepositions signifying

Jehoshaphat confers with the people (העם) regarding military and cultic activities during the battle with Ammon and Moab (2 Chr 20:21);[220] an unnamed Aramean king takes counsel with his עבדים concerning war with Israel (2 Kgs 6:8); Amaziah consults an unnamed group of advisors to plan his campaign against Joash and Israel (2 Chr 25:17); Hezekiah confers with his officers (שרים) and the assembly in Jerusalem regarding the Passover celebration (30:2); Hezekiah together with his officers and mighty warriors (גבורים) plans strategies for sealing the water sources outside Jerusalem in wake of an impending war with Assyria (32:3). In a few cases the identity of individuals the king consults is more definite, for example, David confers with שרי האלפים והמאות לכל נגיד, "officers of thousands and hundreds, with every chief," about transferring the ark to Jerusalem (1 Chr 13:1); Rehoboam consults the זקנים and the ילדים at Shechem on the issue of reducing corvée requirements in Israel (1 Kgs 12:6, 8 = 2 Chr 10:6, 8).[221]

Based on the biblical data, it seems that different royal officials and functionaries acted as advisors to the king. The יועץ למלך may have borne the official title of counsellor but he apparently did not carry that duty alone. In addition, two or more persons bearing this title may have served concurrently, as is implied in the Chronicler's record, which lists Jonathan and Ahitophel as advisors followed by Jehoiada and Abiathar in that role (1 Chr 27:32–34). Evidence from the Persian court suggests that a body of official advisors surrounded the king, in the case of Artaxerxes seven individuals: מלכא ושבעת יעטהי, "the king and his seven advisors" (Ezra 7:14–15). Presumably, the expertise required for a particular situation dictated whom the king consulted. Perhaps, the יועץ למלך (pl. יועצי) functioned as a general advisor(s). In any case, as proposed by P. Boer, this minister probably belonged to the circle of officials called שרים.[222]

Unfortunately, little is known of the four named persons designated royal advisors or those others who appear anonymously. The first יועץ listed in the Davidic record of officials in Chronicles is Jonathan, recognized as a man of understanding, a scribe, and one of two court functionaries who attended (was with) the princes (1 Chr 27:32).[223] His position as counsellor may or may not

---

"with" precedes it: עם (1 Chr 13:1; 2 Chr 32:3); את (1 Kgs 12:6, 8 = 2 Chr 10:6, 8); אל (2 Kgs 6:8; 2 Chr 20:21).

220. The reference to the populace in this context seems to reflect the Chronicler's idea of "democracy" (Japhet, *I & II Chronicles*, 797). Probably, Jehoshaphat consulted his military leaders and priests, not "the people" as a whole.

221. See Chapter 3–C & D for discussions on the ילדים and זקנים in this episode.

222. P. Boer, "The Counsellor," *VTS* 3 (1955): 49.

223. The other is Jehiel the Hachmoni (1 Chr 27:32). It is unclear whether or not Jonathan served as royal scribe in addition to Sheva (2 Sam 20:25). A controversial issue regarding Jonathan is his relationship to David. He is designated דוד דויד, which can be defined as

be related to his other roles.[224] The second יועץ is Ahitophel,[225] who defected from David's court to join Absalom in his revolt against his father. That Ahitophel was David's advisor is explicitly stated early in the account of the rebellion (2 Sam 15:12) and it is clear that he continued in the role of advisor while in the service of Absalom (16:15–17:14). Apparently Ahitophel was a wise counselor, for had Absalom followed his advice to pursue David the night he fled Jerusalem, the revolt could have succeeded. Instead, Hushai, David's רעה/רע who feigned loyalty to Absalom, thwarted Ahitophel's plan for immediate action, thereby salvaging David's kingship. The length of Ahitophel's term as David's advisor is unclear. He may have served together with Jonathan, perhaps in a distinct capacity, or following him. In any case, after Absalom's defeat David appointed new advisors, probably Jehoiada son of Benaiah and Abiathar (1 Chr 27:34).[226] Nothing is mentioned about their activities as advisors.

Mesopotamian and Canaanite Evidence

In Akkadian texts, the advisor(s) of the king is called *māliku(ū)*. In Assyrian and Babylonian documents, the term is attested primarily in the plural, as one group

---

David's uncle, a person "beloved" by David or a "kinsman" of some sort of David (*BDB*, 187; *HALOT* 1, 215; see especially Amos 6:10). Differing understandings of the word have yielded various possible identifications: an uncle of David not mentioned elsewhere; David's nephew, Jonathan son of Shimei (2 Sam 21:21; Japhet [*I & II Chronicles*, 468, 479] translates "uncle" but notes that Jonathan could be David's nephew); David's closest friend, Jonathan son of Saul (E.L. Curtis, *A Critical and Exegetical Commentary on the Books of Chronicles* [New York: Charles Scribner's Sons, 1910], 294). Of these three possibilities, the last seems impossible, since David did not ascend the throne until after the death of Saul and Jonathan. The first option is conceivable, as is the second, because David regularly appointed his nephews to state positions (e.g. Joab, Abishai, Asael).

224. Rüterswörden notes an interesting parallel between the depiction of Jonathan in Chronicles and Aḥiqar in an Aramaic text from Elephantine (*Beamten der israelitischen Königszeit*, 107). Aḥiqar is described as, ספרא חכימא יעט אתור כלה, "the wise scribe, counsellor of all Assyria" (B. Porten and A. Yardeni, *Textbook of Aramaic Documents from Ancient Egypt*, 3 [Jerusalem: Hebrew University, 1986–1993] C1.1 A.l.12). Practically speaking, it is not surprising that a royal advisor was literate, and certainly he would be expected to be clever.

225. Ahitophel is the only name directly prefixed to the designation יועץ למלך.

226. If the components of his name were reversed in the text, Jehoiada son of Benaiah could actually refer to Benaiah son of Jehoiada, a mighty warrior who attained the rank of overseer of David's body guard. Jehoiada could also have been a son of Benaiah the war hero or even his father (1 Chr 11:22–25; Japhet, *I & II Chronicles*, 480). Abiathar may refer to David's priest by that name (2 Sam 20:25), or according to Japhet, his inclusion may reflect the Chronicler's compensation for excluding Abiathar from the list of David's priests (1 Chr 18:16 mentions Abimelech instead). If the latter is correct, then Abiathar did not really serve as advisor at all.

of royal functionaries among others, "counselors of the king."[227] For example, the following are listed together: ***rabûtišu šībī mālikī zēr bīt abišu šakkanakkī u rēdê*** *muma'irūt mātišu*, "his high officials, the elders, the advisors, the men of his father's house, the military governors and the administrators who govern his country."[228] Even when mentioned separately, as those whose advice the king seeks or doesn't seek, the *mālikū* generally appear as a group.[229] Occasionally, one particular advisor is mentioned, indicating perhaps that in certain situations one special individual bore that title.[230] A detailed description of a *mālik šarri*, "advisor of the king," is found in reference to Išum, the advisor of the god Nergal, king of the underworld. Išum is portrayed as the intercessor who spares life, the one who loves truth and the one who makes the heart of the all-powerful Nergal as calm as pure well water.[231] Although this example pertains to an advisor of a god, his attributes probably reflect those of any wise royal counselor.

The expressions *mālikū* and *mālik šarri* also appear in an Amarna letter from Canaan (*EA* 131:21, 23). There, the *rābiṣū*, the Egyptian commissioners in Canaan, are called the *mālikū* of the Pharaoh. It seems, however, that the Akkadian definition of *māliku* as "advisor" should not be applied to the Canaanite usage.[232] As shown by J. Renger and C. Zaccagnini, the use of the verb *malāku* in documents from Syria, Palestine and Ugarit better fits the West Semitic meaning of the root *mlk*, "rule, have power over."[233] It follows then that the title *mālik šarri* in EA 131 should be defined as "commissioner, governor of the king," synonymous to *rābiṣu* and *sūkini/a*, the other titles held by Pawuru, one of the *mālik šarri* mentioned in this letter.[234]

Conclusions

Based on the aforementioned observations, it is difficult to describe accurately

---

227. *CAD* M/1, 162–164; *AHW* 2, 595.

228. *TCL* 3 33 in *CAD* M/1, 163.

229. They appear as a group in various genres of literature. See *CAD* M/1, 163–164.

230. A ***rabû mālik šarri*** is listed in a Babylonian *kudurru* inscription (*MDP* 2 pl. 23, 6:2 in *CAD* M/1, 163).

231. *ZA* 43 1:16–17 in A. Livingstone, *Court Poetry and Literary Miscellanea* (Helsinki: Helsinki University Press, 1989), 74 no. 32.

232. Contra Moran, *Amarna Letters*, 212.

233. For example, *EA* 90, 114, 136; RS 15.137. J. Renger, "Zur Wurzel MLK in akkadischen Texten aus Syrien und Palästina" in R. Archi, ed. *Eblaite Personal Names and Semitic Name-Giving* (Rome: Italian Archaeological Mission in Syria, 1988), 165–172; C. Zaccagnini, "Notes on the Pazarcik Stela," *SAAB* 7 (1993): 53–72, esp. 56–57.

234. Pawuru is entitled *rābiṣu* in *EA* 287:45, *sūkina* in 362:69 and by an Egyptian term *irpi* (=*iry p't*), "prince," in 289:38. Note that Knudzon wavers between the two definitions (*Die El-Amarna-Tafeln* 1, 559).

the position of the יועץ in the hierarchy of Israelite officials. Certainly, as the title indicates, the office existed in the realm of the royal court and entailed counseling the king, probably on various issues. It remains uncertain, however, whether these office-holders comprised a group or functioned individually, whether they held other titles concurrently and whether the title as a distinct position disappeared after the reign of David. Notably, persons officially entitled יועץ למלך do not appear in the Solomonic list of officials or any subsequent list. Possibly the office was absorbed by others under different titles or was assigned to a group of courtiers, comparable to the *mālikū* in Mesopotamia.

G. אשר על המס – Minister over the Corvée

Biblical Evidence

Probably the most unpopular royal official, at least among the populace, was the אשר על המס. The term מס (*ms*) is defined as conscripted labor or corvée and is used to refer to the abstract concept as well as to actual work gangs.[235] Essentially, מס is a form of taxation levied by the central authority that obligates the populace to work on government projects for a certain number of months a year. In Israel, the officer in charge of this operation was called אשר על המס, "the one who is over the corvée." Only one named biblical royal official bears this title, Adoram (=Adoniram, Hadoram) son of Abda, who served under three kings. Adoram was appointed by David (2 Sam 20:24) and remained in office during the kingship of Solomon (1 Kgs 4:6; 5:28) and the beginning of the reign of Rehoboam (1 Kgs 12:18 = 2 Chr 10:18).[236] Adoram was stoned to death when Rehoboam sent him to Israel after the North had seceded from Judah to form a separate kingdom. Another person who held a similar position, albeit one of a more limited purview, was Jeroboam son of Nebat. According to 1 Kgs

235. *BDB*, 586–587; *HALOT* 2, 603–604.

236. If Adoram attained his office late in David's reign and then served throughout Solomon's reign (40 yrs. according to 1 Kgs 11:42, although that may not represent an accurate number), it is possible that he was not too advanced in age to keep the position when Rehoboam first ascended the throne. Although the patronym Abda appears only once (1 Kgs 4:6), it is generally assumed that the three similar names, Adoram, Adoniram, and Hadoram belong to one individual. The variations of these names can be explained two ways: 1. Adoram and Hadoram contain shortened forms of the theophoric name Hadad/Adad, the Semitic storm god (*hd*=*hadd* is attested in Ugaritic [*UT* no. 749]; Adoniram is a corrupt form of that name. 2. The root of Adoram/Adoniram is *ad*, "father" (Ugaritic) and the names mean "the/my (divine) father is exalted." The form Hadoram, which appear in Chronicles, was a later revision (an *ʾ*>*h* interchange). For a discussion of these names, see B. Mazar, "Adoram" in *EM* 1, 116–117; Mettinger, *Solomonic State Officials*, 133; Pike, "Israelite Theophoric Personal Names," 128–132.

11:28, Solomon appointed him לכל סבל בית יוסף, "over all the forced labor of the House of Joseph."[237]

The rank of the אשר על המס in the administrative hierarchy is difficult to define. In a Davidic register, Adoram is listed following two military officers, the chief army commander and the commander over the Cherethites and Pelethites, but before the herald (2 Sam 20:23–24), a high civil official. In Solomon's list of appointees, however, he is in last place following the minister over the royal house (1 Kgs 4:6). If these registers are understood as indicators of rank, then the change in placement could imply that during David's reign the minister over the corvée was the top civil official but that under Solomon the office became low-level. That scenario seems highly doubtful, since the institution of corvée was an integral component of Solomon's administrative organization.[238]

237. Both מס and סבל, "load, burden," in these contexts refer to forced labor (*BDB*, 687; *HALOT* 2, 741; cf. Gen 49:15; Exod 1:11; 1 Kgs 5:29; Ps 81:7). In the case of 1 Kgs 11:28, סבל was levied at the population of north Israel, non-Judahites. A. Rainey derives two distinct administrative entities, based on the two terms ("Compulsory Labour Gangs in Ancient Israel," *IEJ* 20 (1970): 200–202). He claims that מס, corvée, belongs to the institution charged with the labor gangs in Lebanon who provided lumber for the construction of the Temple, while סבל, levy, is associated with an office in charge of the "porters" and "quarriers" who worked on the Temple project in Israel (1 Kgs 5:27–30). This division, however, seems unnecessary, especially in light of the fact that the term מס is used elsewhere to describe labor in Israel, as the building of Hazor, Megiddo, Gezer, and Jerusalem's fortifications (9:15). Admittedly, the discrepancy in the numbers of Solomon's work-gangs, 30,000 workers (5:27) vs. 150,000 workers (5:29) is problematic. Rainey's solution, however, is not tenable. The notion of 10,000 Israelites serving in Lebanon each month, as foresters or at related tasks, is unrealistic. The numbers for that type of operation are inflated even for three months a year, let alone for twelve months year-round (cf. a total of 60 men working 30 forests in Umma [P. Steinkeller, "The Foresters of Umma: Toward a Definition of Ur III Labor" in M. Powell ed., *Labor in the Ancient Near East* (New Haven: American Oriental Society, 1987), 76–90]). The 150,000 porters and quarriers are usually explained as the insertion of a secondary source (Montgomery, *The Book of Kings*, 137; Gray, *I and II Kings*, 147; Mettinger, *Solomonic State Officials*, 135). Another possibility is that these workers, whose ethnicity is unspecified, represent non-Israelites recruited in addition to Israelites. But either way, the number 150,000 is fantastic and cannot be taken at face value (cf. a total work force of 8368 quarriers and auxiliary personnel sent on a major expedition to Wadi Hammamat in year 3 of Rameses IV [C. Eyre, "Work and the Organization of Work in the New Kingdom" in *Labor in the Ancient Near East*, 180–182]). Actually, the number 150,000 more closely represents the entire population of western Palestine at the beginning of the Iron Age II (M. Broshi and I. Finkelstein, "The Population of Palestine in Iron Age II," *BASOR* 287 [1992]: 47–60, esp. 55). The total figure of eligible workers would have been far less.

238. Public service on construction projects most certainly accounts for the monumental architecture credited to Solomon. According to the writers of Kings, in addition to the Tem-

As previously noted, the monarchic lists of officials are fragmentary, and Solomon's list in particular is corrupt. Therefore, while the precise rank of the minister over the corvée cannot be determined, his position, like that of the minister over the royal house, should not be considered low-ranking.

The function of the אשר על המס, although not delineated, presumably entailed overseeing the entire corvée system.[239] Subordinate officials, such as Jeroboam,

---

ple, the fortifications of Jerusalem and the royal cities of Hazor, Megiddo, and Gezer were built with corvée labor (1 Kgs 9:15). Material remains dated by a number of archaeologists to the 10th century, such as those at Hazor, Megiddo, and Gezer, support the biblical data (Mazar, *Archaeology of the Land of the Bible*, 375–397; Dever, "Archaeology and the 'Age of Solomon'," 217–251; A. Ben-Tor, "Excavating Hazor, Part I: Solomon's City Rises from the Ashes," *BAR* 25 (1999): 26–37, 60).

239. According to the report in Kings on the construction of the Temple, the system was organized as follows: the levy applied to all eligible Israelites and a total of 30,000 men, in three shifts of 10,000, served three or four months each year (1 Kgs 5:27–28). It is unclear whether Israelites served one month of every three or three consecutive months each year. The phrase חדש יהיו בלבנון שנים חדשים בביתו, "one month they would be in Lebanon, two months in his house," can be interpreted two ways, depending on who is the subject of the suffix "his." If "in his house" refers to the house of the king, then workers served one month in Lebanon and two months in Jerusalem. Alternatively, if the word בביתו refers to the worker's home, then laborers spent one month away on duty for every two months at home. The latter explanation is adopted by most commentators on the assumption that בביתו = the worker's home or that the "ו" of בביתו is a dittography and the word should read בבית. Following Mettinger, it seems that the MT should be retained and בביתו understood as the house of the king—in other words, the palace complex (including the Temple) that was in a state of construction (*Solomonic State Officials*, 135). This interpretation is supported grammatically since בביתו, rendered with a singular suffix, does not agree with the preceding verb יהיו, in the plural (although cases of non-agreement are not unprecedented). If בביתו is understood as the king's house, then the corvée obligation equals three consecutive months per year, one month in Lebanon and two in Israel (see note 237).

A later narrative claims that Solomon did not levy forced labor on Israelites, rather only on the remaining indigenous Canaanite population (1 Kgs 9:20–22 = 2 Chr 8:7–9). The term for corvée in that account in Kings is מס עבד, which some scholars consider distinct from מס. I. Mendelsohn, for example, thinks that מס עבד refers to permanent corvée imposed on non-Israelites, thus making them state slaves ("State Slavery in Ancient Palestine," *BASOR* 85 [1942]: 16–17). A. Biram, building on Mendelsohn's argument, maintains that the element עבד of מס עבד indicates servitude, the lot of conquered populations according to Deut 20:11 ("*Mas 'obed*," *Tarbiz* 23 [1952]: 137–142 [Hebrew]). Mettinger, who agrees with this interpretation, defines עבד as "eternal," based on a different root, אבד II, found in Arabic (*'bd*) and Ugaritic (*ubdy*; pp. 131–132; *HALOT* 1, 3). None of the aforementioned theories is convincing, especially since the biblical records use both expressions to describe Canaanites who became corvée laborers (מס is used in Josh 17:13; Judg 1:28, 30, 33, 35; 2 Chr 8:8; מס עבד is found in Josh 16:10; 1 Kgs 9:21). Mettinger's theory is particularly weak since neither עבד or אבד is found in biblical Hebrew with this meaning. N. Avigad, in contrast,

who oversaw the corvée for the region of Ephraim and Manasseh, would have served under this minister. The נצבים, "district prefects," who were responsible for the taxation of their geographical locale and the provisioning of the palace for one month each year (1 Kgs 4:7), probably coordinated the corvée for their respective district.[240] In addition, hundreds of lesser officials, foremen, were needed to oversee local labor gangs. The five-hundred and fifty שרי הנצבים, "officers of the prefects," mentioned as על המלאכה, "over the work (gangs)," seem to fit that category (1 Kgs 9:23; cf. 250, 2 Chr 8:10).[241]

Nothing is mentioned explicitly in the Bible about any corvée ministers or a corvée system after the murder of Adoram (1 Kgs 12:18). However, evidence exists that the practice of imposing corvée obligations did not end with the division of Solomon's kingdom but continued, at least in Judah, until the end of the monarchic period. Data from the reigns of Asa and Jehoiakim are revealing in this connection. In the early ninth century, Asa drafted all Judah in order to build Geba and Mizpah as buffers against the North: והמלך אסא השמיע את כל יהודה אין נקי, "then king Asa called all Judah (to labor), no one was exempt" (1 Kgs 15:22).[242] In an oracle of Jeremiah dated to the end of the seventh century, Jehoiakim is rebuked for injustices practiced against the laborers who built the king's new palace. Jeremiah's accusation ברעהו יעבד חנם, "he makes his fellow work without pay," seems to refer to the king's use of conscripted labor instead of hired workers, a royal prerogative the prophet apparently opposed (Jer

notes that no semantic differences are evident between the two expressions and the word עבד, "labor, laborer" is probably a gloss ("The Chief of the Corvée," *IEJ* 30 [1980]: 172). The discrepancy between the two accounts of Solomon's corvée policy may be the result of a later writer's attempt to present Solomon in a more positive light. As Japhet notes, it is an apologetic remark phrased in an apologetic tone (*I & II Chronicles*, 624–625). The appeal of northerners to Rehoboam at Shechem to lighten their work load and the subsequent secession of the North from Solomon's kingdom seems to support the earlier account.

240. See Chapter 4–H.

241. Thousands of supervisors, 3,300, are mentioned in 1 Kgs 5:30 (cf. 3,600, 2 Chr 2:1) in association with the 150,000 porters and quarriers (see note 391). In the expression שרי הנצבים the שרים should be viewed as subordinates of the נצבים (Noth, *Könige*, 219; Gray, *I and II Kings*, 156) rather than as chief officers, following Montgomery (*The Books of Kings*, 137) and Japhet (*I & II Chronicles*, 618, 625). The construct relationship of the two nouns is comparable to that of שרי המלך, "officers of the king," in which the genitive noun designates the higher ranking.

242. In 2 Chr 16:6 Asa's muster is expressed by the verb לקח, "took," instead of השמיע. In Akkadian sources, the *nāgiru* "calls" the people for corvée labor (*CAD* N/1, 116–117; see Chapter 4–C). An unprovenienced seal incised on both sides, dated to the seventh century, bears this title. One side reads: לפלאיהו אשר על המס, "belonging to *pl'yhw* who is over the corvée"; the other side bears the owner's PN and patronym, לפלאיהו מתתיהו (Avigad, "The Chief of the Corvée," 170–171).

22:13).[243] Jeremiah's words echo Samuel's warning concerning the evils of a monarchic system (1 Sam 8:11–17).[244]

In addition to building projects, corvée obligations also included agricultural labor on crown lands. This is clearly delineated in Samuel's "manner of the king": "He (the king) will take your sons...to plow his field and to reap his harvest" (1 Sam 8:11–12). It is likely that the letter from Meṣad Ḥashavyahu reflects the lot of an Israelite worker fulfilling that duty. The laborer, a reaper who pleads for the return of his garment, was allegedly punished unfairly for not satisfying his quota.[245] Probably one of the responsibilities of the שר of the fortress of Meṣad Ḥashavyahu was to oversee the agricultural workers at the site.[246] As such, he would have been in charge of the מס for a specified locale. The officer entitled אשר על המס would have overseen the central operation, as did Adoram. Possibly, similar titles were held by supervisors of local work-gangs.

Evidence from Akkadian Sources

The equivalent terms for מס and סבל in Akkadian are *massu* and *sablu*, the latter of West Semitic origin.[247] No semantic distinction is evident between the two terms, but each is attested in sources of different societies—*massu* in documents from Alalakh and Canaan and *sablu(m)* in the Mari correspondence. Both *massu* and *sablu* are used in reference to corvée workers. In a text from Mari, *sablu(m)* designates a party of young men and women brought by the governor to fulfill the quota of laborers from his district.[248] These work-gangs served on construction projects as well as on agricultural operations.[249] Administrative texts from Alalakh contemporaneous to the Mari letters refer to corvée laborers

243. J. Bright, *The Anchor Bible Jeremiah* (New York: Doubleday, 1965), 145; W.L. Holladay, *Jeremiah 1, A Commentary on the Book of Jeremiah* (Philadelphia: Fortress Press, 1986), 594.

244. It seems that the corvée system continued even after the fall of the monarchy in the Persian period, as evidenced by Nehemiah's policy of drafting settlers to rebuild Jerusalem's walls (Neh 3).

245. I. Mendelsohn, "On Corvée Labor in Ancient Canaan and Israel," *BASOR* 167 (1962): 33–34. Mendelsohn argues convincingly that if the reaper was a tenant farmer or hired agricultural worker, more effective punishment, such as withholding wages, would have been imposed for idleness.

246. See Chapter 4–I.

247. *CAD* M/1, 327; S, 4; *AHW*, 619, 999. For the West-Semitic origins of the term, see P. Artzi, "*Sablum* = סבל," *BIES* 18 (1954): 66–70; for its relationship to *zabālu*, "to transport, carry," see M. Held, "The Root ZBL/SBL in Akkadian, Ugaritic and Biblical Hebrew," *JAOS* 88 (1968): 90–96.

248. *ARM* 3, 38: 5–14.

249. *ARM* 2, 88:9–10; 67:5.

but employ the term *massu*.[250] Corvée workers, *awīlū massī*, are mentioned in conjunction with the city or town in which they served, or together with the leader of the group. Under the system at Alalakh, they received wages in the form of provisions from royal stores.[251] The *massu* laborers also appear in an Amarna letter from Megiddo, where they are recruited by Biridiya, the *ḫazannu*, "city ruler," to plow fields belonging to the Pharaoh's property.[252] In these examples, the individuals responsible for organizing the corvée do not seem to bear a special function-related title comparable to the Hebrew designation.

Conclusions

Officials entitled אשר על המס or those holding related positions, such as שרי הנצבים or appointees over the סבל, are attested in the Bible only for the period of the United Monarchy. Nevertheless, evidence from the Kingdom of Judah indicates that the practice of forced labor, the corvée, existed there throughout the monarchic period. Comparable institutions, designated by cognate terms, from 18th century Mari and Alalakh and 14th century Canaan, show that the system enjoyed a long history in the region. Its adoption into the state-organization of the Israelite monarchy can probably be attributed to Canaanite influence. The establishment of an office of אשר על המס would have followed naturally.[253]

H. נצב/נצבים, על הנצבים – Prefect(s), Overseer of the Prefects

Not all government officials served at the royal court. Officials belonging to the group called נצבים were among those who were stationed outside the capital. Before examining the roles of these administrators, the title נצב and the related form נציב require some clarification.

---

250. Alalakh Stratum 7. One text comes from a later stratum, AT 161, dated to the 15th century (Str. 4).

251. D.J. Wiseman, *Alalakh Tablets*, 259:15–17; 265:7; 268:14; "Supplementary Texts from Alalakh," *JCS* 8 (1954): 19, 21; "Ration Lists from Alalakh VII," *JCS* 13 (1959): 25, 27-28. Wiseman's original reading, *ku-si/zi*, was corrected by W. Moran to *ma-si/zi* ("The Hebrew Language in Its Northwest Semitic Background" in G.E. Wright ed. *The Bible and the Ancient Near East. Essays in Honor of William Foxwell Albright* [London: Routledge and Kegan Paul, 1961], 57). For a discussion of these texts, see Rainey, "Compulsory Labour Gangs in Ancient Israel," 192–195.

252. *EA* 365: 10–14, 22–25. F. Thureau-Dangin, "Nouvelles lettres d'El-Amarna," *RA* 19 (1922): 97–98; A. Rainey, *El Amarna Tablets 359–379* (Neukirchen-Vluyn: Neukirchener, 1970), 24–27.

253. Possibly Adoram was an indigenous Canaanite hired by David to be his corvée overseer.

The Titles נצב *and* נציב

The designations נִצָּב and נְצִיב (pl. נִצָּבִים and נְצִיבִים), literally, "one who is stationed," are two nominal constructions of the verbal root נצב, "take a stand": נִצָּב is a niphal participle and נְצִיב is a noun (*qetil* pattern).[254] Although derived from the same root, it is not certain, however, that the two titles are equivalent or interchangeable, as is often assumed. An examination of the distribution of נצב and נציב in the biblical material indicates a pattern of sorts, implying perhaps that two distinct positions are represented by these terms.

The titles נצב/נצבים and על הנצבים, with one possible exception, appear exclusively in connection with Solomon's reign. One of Solomon's high officials, Azariah son of Nathan, is entitled על הנצבים (1 Kgs 4:5). A group of 11 or 12 individual נצבים[255] is listed in the same record of appointees; each is charged over a geographical region in Israel (4:7–19). The term נצבים in this context is translated as "prefects, governors." All of the נצבים are under the supervision of the minister entitled על הנצבים, "(the one who is) over the prefects." Other officers designated שרי הנצבים are mentioned as overseers of corvée labor gangs (5:30; 9:23 = 2 Chr 8:10). One problematic occurrence of נצב is found in an account relating events from Jehoshaphat's reign. A נצב מלך, "*nṣb* of (the) king," from Edom is referred to in conjunction with the wreckage of a fleet of ships bound for Ophir (1 Kgs 22:48). Following variations in some Mss that read נציב, scholars usually emend the MT.

In contrast to the designation נצבים/נצב, the term נציב (pl. נציבים) seems to be used as a title for military officers stationed primarily in occupied territory. Some scholars have suggested that it means "garrison,"[256] though a distinction between "officer(s)" and "garrison(s)" can rarely be ascertained. For example, in Giv'at HaElohim (Gibeah) there were נצבי פלשתים, "*nṣbym* of the Philistines" (1 Sam 10:5); one נציב פלשתים was in Bethlehem (1 Chr 11:16); David installed

254. *BDB*, 662; *HALOT* 2, 714–717. As a verb *nṣb/naṣābu*, "place, settle," is attested in Ugaritic (*UT* no. 1685) and in Amarna Akkadian (*EA* 147:11; 148:42; 151:42). In the Bible the verbal form is sometimes used to describe an official position. For example, in reference to Doeg the Edomite, an official of Saul, it says: והוא נצב על עבדי שאול (1 Sam 22:9). The meaning of נצב can be interpreted two ways: 1. Doeg was actually standing by Saul's servants (H.W. Hertzberg, *I and II Samuel* [Philadelphia: Westminster Press, 1964], 186); 2. Doeg was presiding (in some way) over Saul's servants (P.K. McCarter, *The Anchor Bible, I Samuel* [Garden City: Doubleday, 1980], 360). The latter, which corresponds better to Doeg's exercise of power, compares to the description of the steward of Boaz's estate: הנצב על הקצרים, "who was appointed over the reapers" (Ruth 2:5–6).

255. The prefect of district six and the prefect of district 12 may represent the same person (see below).

256. *BDB*, 662; *HALOT* 2, 717; Gray, *I and II Kings*, 135.

(וישם) נציבים in the vassal states of Aram-Damascus (2 Sam 8:6) and Edom (8:14 = 1 Chr 18:13); Jehoshaphat installed (ויתן) נציבים in Judah and in the cities of Ephraim that his father Asa had captured (2 Chr 17:2). That the term נציב can refer to a person rather than an entity is clear from 1 Sam 13:3, where it states that Jonathan killed the נציב פלשתים who was in Geba (Gibeah). Conversely, in no example does נציב/נציבים definitely refer to an entity, a garrison, rather than to a person, an officer. If we accept the emendation נציב for נצב in 1 Kgs 22:48, then that example too is of an officer stationed in occupied territory. In that account, an officer of Jehoshaphat was apparently stationed as ruler in Edom; he was also the overseer of a shipping expedition to Ophir.[257]

Based on the aforementioned samples of usages of נציב/נציבים, it seems that the designation refers to military commanders (or installations) rather than to civil officials, as are Solomon's district governors, the נצבים. The military nature of the office (or entity) is especially evident in the example from Jehoshphat's reign where the נציבים are mentioned in conjunction with חיל, "military forces."[258] One exceptional use of the title נציב that is synonymous to נצב occurs in 1 Kgs 4:19, the end of the list of Solomon's prefects. In that instance נציב clearly signifies a prefect: ונציב אחד אשר בארץ, "and one *nsyb* who is in the land (of Judah?)." This problematic reference, however, could represent a later interpolation, at a time when the subtle distinction between the terms נצב and נציב was already lost.[259]

In keeping with the focus of this study, civil officials, the discussion below

---

257. In that context, the position of the title-bearer is difficult to explain: ומלך אין באדם נצב מלך, "There was no king in Edom, a *nṣb* (acted as) king" (1 Kgs 22:48). Usually, scholars connect this verse to the next one, either retaining or deleting the RN Jehoshaphat at the beginning of the verse, so that the term נציב/נצב is in construct state to מלך and reads, "the *nṣb/nṣyb* of King Jehoshaphat" (Montgomery, *Books of Kings*, 343; Gray, *I and II Kings*, 457–458; Aharoni, "*nṣyb, nṣybym, nṣb, nṣbym*" in *EM* 5, 914).

258. Jehoshaphat's military measures appear to be part of a general strategy to centralize the government and strengthen Judah following a period of weakness under Asa. Asa's reign was marked by warfare with Baasha of Israel, dependence on foreign aid from Ben-Hadad of Damascus, and finally the king's illness (1 Kgs 15:17–24; 2 Chr 16).

The title שרי המדינות, "officers of the provinces" (1 Kgs 20:14–15, 17, 19), used in connection with Ahab's reign, may be a northern equivalent showing Aramaic influence (Mettinger, *Solomonic State Officials*, 124–125). However, since only נערי שרי המדינות, "the squires/soldiers of the officers of the provinces," are mentioned in the text, it is difficult to define the title.

259. This loss of distinction also seems indicated in 2 Chr 8:10 (the parallel account to 1 Kgs 9:23), where the K is הנציבים and the Q is הנצבים. Noth thinks 1 Kgs 4:19b is a later addition lacking a named official (*Könige*, 74); Mettinger considers it a gloss (*Solomonic State Officials*, 111, 122); neither scholar, however, distinguishes between the terms נצב and נציב.

will center on the designations נצב/נצבים and על הנצבים, the titles for the district prefects in Israel and their overseer.

Biblical Evidence

The functions of Solomon's נצבים in the administrative organization are delineated in the sources concerned with his reign. The Solomonic list of officials in 1 Kings 4 is composed of two types of royal appointees: the court שרים, prominent functionaries who served in the greater palace complex, including the Temple; and the נצבים, who represented the government outside Jerusalem, one in each administrative district in Israel. Officials who belonged to the latter group are registered by their name and region.[260] Each נצב, charged over one district, was responsible for the taxation of his geographical area. According to the text, the prefect's responsibility was לכלכל, "to provision," the palace household for one month of the year (4:7; 5:7). An overseer of the נצבים, called על הנצבים, is listed together with the high officials stationed at court. His responsibilities probably entailed all aspects of supervision relating to the district prefects. Since the prefects were accountable for supplying the palace twelve months a year on a rotating basis, it can be assumed that their superior coordinated the system from the central headquarters in Jerusalem, thereby guaranteeing its efficacy.

One difficulty in understanding Solomon's taxation system hinges on the number of district prefects identifiable in 1 Kings 4. Evidently the writer wished to convey a division of twelve, a requirement if each prefect and his region were

260. In five cases only the patronymic is recorded: בן חור, בן דקר, בן חסד, בן גבר, בן אבינדב. Possibly this phenomenon is a result of damage to the *Vorlage* or another problem in transmission (W.F. Albright, "The Administrative Divisions of Israel and Judah," *JPOS* 5 (1925): 25–26; Noth, *Könige*, 60). Another explanation is that these positions were inherited, and as at Ugarit, simply the family name was listed (Alt, *KS* III, 198–213). Alt's theory presupposes that these officials were locals who previously served in the Canaanite administration. Notably, though, not all the corresponding districts consist of former Canaanite territory.

The 12 administrative districts incorporated both Israelite tribal lands and those cities and regions that David conquered from the indigenous population. Topographical issues pertaining to these districts are beyond the scope of this inquiry. For an examination of those issues, see, among others, Alt, *KS* II, 76–89; Albright, "The Administrative Divisions," 17–54; F.M. Cross and G.E. Wright, "The Province and Boundary Lists of the Kingdom of Judah," *JBL* 75 (1956): 202–226; Z. Kallai-Kleinmann, "The Town Lists of Judah, Simeon, Benjamin and Dan," *VT* 8 (1958): 134–160; "Note on the Town Lists," *VT* 11 (1961): 223–227; Gray, *I and II Kings*, 136–140; G.E. Wright, "The Provinces of Solomon," *EI* 8 (1967): 58*–68*; Mettinger, *Solomonic State Officials*, 112–126; A. Caquot, "Préfets" in *Dictionnaire de la bible: Supplément*, 8 (Paris: Letouzey Ané, 1972): 276–283; Y. Aharoni, *The Land of the Bible: A Historical Geography* (Philadelphia: Westminster Press, 1979), 309–317.

responsible for 1/12 of the yearly maintenance; 1 Kings 4:7 indicates that Solomon appointed twelve נצבים. Notably, however, a נצב for Judah is not explicitly mentioned. Scholars are divided on how best to understand this omission. Some solve the problem by viewing districts six and twelve as doublets of each other.[261] This approach is justifiable because the territories of those districts seem to overlap—both encompass the land of Gilead (4:13, 19a)—and the two district prefects have the element Geber in their PNs. Proponents of this theory argue that "the son of Geber" (4:13) is simply a variant of Geber son of Uri (4:19a). Furthermore, these scholars tend to regard the unnamed prefect, ונציב אחד אשר בארץ, "and one prefect who is in the land" (4:19b), as actually representing the twelfth נצב who is over Judah. One candidate for the unidentified prefect of Judah is Azariah son of Nathan, the overseer of the other נצבים (4:5).[262]

Other scholars, who advocate an alternate solution, outline the borders of Israel's twelve districts from the data provided in verses 8–19a, but exclude Judah.[263] Such a division assumes that Judah was administered differently from the rest of Israel. This opinion is also held by Wright, who adds that Judah too was divided into districts and that they are reflected in the province lists recorded in the book of Joshua (15; 18).[264] Dates for the town lists in Joshua, however, are hotly debated, and these records cannot be utilized as proof texts. While the controversy over Judah's inclusion or exclusion from Solomon's dis-

261. For example, Albright, "The Administrative Divisions of Israel and Judah," 26–28; Montgomery, *Books of Kings*, 121–122; Gray, *I and II Kings*, 135; Mettinger, *Solomonic State Officials*, 121–122. The GN Judah, which appears in the LXX, may have been omitted in the MT through haplography.

262. Mettinger, *Solomonic State Officials*, 123; cf. Gray who suggests that Judah's prefect was the royal house minister (*I and II Kings*, 140).

263. For example, Alt, *KS* II, 76–89; de Vaux, *Ancient Israel*, 133–136; Aharoni, *Land of the Bible*, 309–317. Aharoni identifies three districts in Transjordan and notes that Gilead is simply a general name for the entire region. Alt (p. 83) and de Vaux (p. 134) follow the LXX B, reading Gad for Gilead in 4:19a. M. Ottosson, who opposes a textual emendation, thinks that verse 19 reflects pre-Solomonic conditions under which Gilead, Israelite territory in Transjordan, was considered one entity. Building on that premise, he interprets 19b, ונציב אחד אשר בארץ, as referring back to the prefect charged over the entire land of Gilead (*Gilead: History and Tradition* [Lund: Gleerup, 1969], 218–220).

P. Ash, expanding on Albright's suggestion that Judah's absence from the list reflects its northern origin ("Administrative Divisions," 36), proposes that refugees from Israel who wished to establish their leadership rights in Judah linked one-time administrators from the North to a Solomonic system. He maintains though that the data in the list is not accurate for the period of Solomon because it does not represent an archival source from the 10th century. Instead, it is the garbled product of oral and scribal transmission ("Solomon's? District? List," *JSOT* 67 [1995]: 67–86 esp. 84–85).

264. Wright, "The Provinces of Solomon," 67*–68*.

tricts cannot be resolved satisfactorily, it is clear from the record in 1 Kings 4 that only lands inhabited by Israelites were part of this organizational system.[265] Notably, as previously mentioned, Israelite officers entitled נציבים stationed in vassal states (2 Sam 8:6, 14; 1 Kgs 22:48) held positions that seem distinct from those of the district prefects.

A matter less complicated is the human composition of the group of twelve prefects. Some of the names on the list may be identifiable with persons known elsewhere in the Bible or with their families. The overseer of the prefects, Azariah son of Nathan, could be the son of Nathan the prophet at David's court and/or the brother of Zabud son of Nathan the "companion" of the king (4:5). Two of the נצבים were Solomon's sons-in-law: the son of Abinadab was married to Taphath (4:11), and Ahimaaz was married to Basemath (4:15). Possibly, Ahimaaz was the son of Zadok the priest (2 Sam 15:27). Another prefect, Baana son of Ahilud (1 Kgs 4:12), may have been the brother of David's and Solomon's מזכיר, Jehoshaphat son of Ahilud (2 Sam 8:16; 1 Kgs 4:3). A fourth, Baana son of Hushi (4:16), could have been the son of David's רעה, Hushi the Archite (2 Sam 15:37). Although few of these family relationships can be proven, they are reasonable proposals in light of the existence of other sons of David's dignitaries in Solomon's administrative organization.[266]

In addition to the overseer of the prefects and the twelve district prefects, other נצבים are mentioned in connection with Solomon's reign. Some questions exist concerning officers entitled שרי הנצבים who were involved in the supervision of corvée labor (1 Kgs 5:30; 9:23). Since their numbers are far greater than the twelve district prefects (3300 in 5:30; 550 in 9:23; 250 in 2 Chr 8:10), they are evidently different types of officials.[267] Defining their identity depends somewhat on the interpretation of the title שרי הנצבים. The two words can be

---

265. Contra Rüterswörden, who implies that Solomon treated Israel (northerners) comparable to his עבדים, "vassal states," such as Edom, Moab, Ammon, Aram (*Die Beamten der israelitischen Königszeit*, 109).

266. See Table A–1. As far as ethnic origins of Solomon's prefects are concerned, they cannot be properly identified due to the lack of theophoric elements in most of their PNs. While former Canaanite administrators seem to have been incorporated into the body of officials of the United Monarchy, the lineage of most of these men remains speculative.

267. The number 3,300 for corvée officers in 1 Kgs 5:30 seems rather large. Gray suggests that it actually represents the number of workers under each supervisor (*I and II Kings*, 147). That suggestion, however, is impossible because it would bring the number of workers to at least 825,000 (3300 × 250), an astronomical number far beyond the entire population of Solomon's kingdom. Recent studies estimate the population of western Palestine at the beginning of the Iron Age II to be approximately 150,000 (Broshi and Finkelstein, "The Population of Palestine in Iron Age II," 47–60, esp. 55). The number of eligible workers would have been far less.

translated "chief officers," that is, those in charge of other officers,[268] or "officers of Solomon's prefects," referring to officers subordinate to the twelve prefects.[269] Sustaining the former understanding is difficult, since it presumes the existence of another, larger group of lower ranked officials over which this group of chief officers was charged. In contrast, the latter interpretation makes perfect sense in view of the roles of the twelve district prefects, who would be the superiors of these officers. First, it can be assumed that each of the twelve prefects had under his charge lesser functionaries, who in turn oversaw various operations in the district. One of the chief responsibilities of the נצבים was implementing Solomon's taxation system. The corvée, which was central to that system, required officials to oversee labor gangs. The שרי הנצבים, who are described as על המלאכה, "over the labor," fit that role.

Evidence from Mesopotamia and Egypt

Solomon's division of Israel into twelve administrative districts, each headed by a prefect, has raised questions concerning a prototype. Mesopotamian as well as Egyptian models have been suggested. Y. Aharoni views the Israelite organization as continuing an old Near Eastern tradition originating in the Ur III period. Assuming that the provisioning of Solomon's household actually refers to Temple maintenance, he cites as an example W. Hallo's construct of a Sumerian amphictyony that supplied the temples of Nippur.[270] However, based on additional evidence, Hallo's notion of a Sumerian amphictyony has recently been discredited.[271] Another parallel is drawn by R. Dougherty from sixth-century sources of the Neo-Babylonian and Persian periods, in which certain officials are designated overseers of the *quppu*, "store, treasury (literally, basket)," of the king at Erech.[272] Of the four officials cited in these texts, none

---

268. Japhet, *I & II Chronicles*, 625. For 1 Kgs 9:23 the LXX translation is equivalent to השרים הנצבים, "the officers, those in charge."

269. Noth, *Könige*, 219; Gray, *I and II Kings*, 156. The expressions שרי המלך, "officers of the king" (Esth 1:18) and שרי פרעה, "Pharaoh's officers" (Gen 12:15), among others, show comparable constructions.

270. Aharoni, *Land of the Bible*, 316; W. Hallo, "A Sumerian Amphictyony," *JCS* 14 (1960): 92–93. Under this system 12 cities participated in any one year. The *ensi*, ruler, of each city had a one month *bala*, "turn of service." From year to year different groups took part.

271. P. Steinkeller, "The Administrative and Economic Organization of the Ur III State: The Core and the Periphery" in M. Gibson and R. Biggs eds., *The Organization of Power: Aspects of Bureaucracy in the Ancient Near East* (Chicago: Oriental Institute of the University of Chicago, 1987), 27–30.

272. R. Dougherty, "Cuneiform Parallels to Solomon's Provisioning System," *AASOR* 5 (1923–1924): 23–29. The officials bear titles that are variants of the following two: LÚ *ša*

is mentioned in connection with more than one month of a particular year. Dougherty infers that each officer was responsible for a certain month(s) of the year, although the month connected with each of these four officials varies from year to year.[273] This correlation is problematic on several counts. Aside from the late date of the texts, the basic structure of twelve districts (one per month) is not evident. In addition, it is unclear whether each official was actually in charge of a district or what his duties were beyond the deliveries of goods to the palace.

A more tenable analogy is made by D. Redford, based on an Egyptian text from the reign of Shishak that records a yearly levy of supplies earmarked for the temple of Arsaphes in Herakleopolis.[274] The inscription is arranged in twelve monthly sections, plus one for the five epagomenal days. It lists for each month the officials and towns responsible for provisioning the temple, plus the duty amount. Although this twelve-part division of towns and their maintenance obligations is certainly comparable to Solomon's system, a number of discrepancies exist. Shishak's setup seems to have been created to cope with a local problem in a certain region, the provisioning of a temple that previously had been neglected. In contrast, Solomon's administrative organization represents a wide-scale national system. In addition, as with the Ur III example, the Egyptian case deals with temple rather than palace supplies.[275] While these discrepancies do not preclude foreign influence on Solomon's system, neither do their similarities necessitate direct borrowing from Egypt. Redford himself points out that Solomon's taxation system bears general affinities with the Egyptian system in Canaan in the New Kingdom. Under that system Canaanite city-states were assigned an annual levy, *ḥtr*, to provision Egyptian garrisons, though admittedly, there is no evidence of twelve monthly divisions.[276]

A different background to the affinity between Shishak's and Solomon's tax-

---

muḫḫi quppu ša šarri, "the one who is over the basket of the king"; LÚ *rēš šarri ša eli quppu*, "the chief officer of the king who is over the basket" (pp. 25–26).

273. Dougherty, "Cuneiform Parallels to Solomon's Provisioning System," 26.

274. Redford, "Studies in Relations between Palestine and Egypt," 141–156, esp. 153–156.

275. Redford suggests that the quotas listed for Solomon's household (1 Kgs 5:2) actually represent Temple offerings ("Studies in Relations between Palestine and Egypt," 155).

276. Redford, "Studies in Relations between Palestine and Egypt," 155. Hieratic inscriptions on bowls from Lachish and Tel Sara', dated to the late 19th and 20th dynasty, record harvest taxes apparently bound for Egyptian temples in Canaan and probably used to supply garrisons (Černý, *Lachish* IV, 132–133, pl. 47; Goldwasser, "Hieratic Inscriptions from Tel Sera' in Southern Canaan," 83–87, fig. 1 pls. 4–5). Cf. *EA* 365, an account of field workers fulfilling the corvée obligations of the king of Megiddo.

ation systems is proposed by A. Green.[277] Green posits that instead of Solomon borrowing from Egypt, the reverse occurred, that Shishak was influenced by an Israelite innovation. Green argues that Solomon's system was probably in place by the time Shishak ascended the throne. In addition, he notes that Egyptian taxation systems prior to Shishak varied sufficiently to preclude earlier models.[278] Finally, he suggests that Jeroboam, a high Israelite corvée officer, could have brought the blueprint for Solomon's organization to the Egyptian court when he fled Israel and took refuge with Shishak (1 Kgs 11:40). While Green's scenario is possible, the discrepancies in the two systems mentioned above remain problematic.

Conclusions

The evidence presented above, while showing that both titles, נצב/נצבים and נציב/נציבים, designate administrators charged over specific regions, does not indicate that both terms are definitely equivalent or interchangeable. It is feasible that the term נצב/נצבים signified civil officials, while the term נציב/נציבים signified military officers, though the distinction is blurred by exceptional usages. It is clear, however, that the על הנצבים and the twelve נצבים appointed by Solomon were civil officials. The overseer, who quite possibly served as prefect of Judah, was stationed in Jerusalem to coordinate the provisioning of the palace household while the prefects were located in the districts of Israel as agents of the central government, each charged over the taxation of one geographical district. After the division of the kingdom, some of the duties of the על הנצבים may have been absorbed by the office of the אשר על הבית.

The search for an Egyptian or Mesopotamian model for Solomon's organizational system seems unnecessary.[279] As shown, taxation systems of some kind or another based on twelve monthly divisions were not unique to any one state in the region. However, this particular type of institution devised for the purpose of national administration appears to be limited to Israel, although Solomon may have built his particular structure on a preexisting basic taxation system that had been operative in Canaan at an earlier time.

277. A. Green, "Israelite Influence at Shishak's Court?" *BASOR* 233 (1979): 59–62.

278. Green's comparison of Solomon's 12 monthly divisions with that of post-Shishak annual levies, in particular that of Osorkon, is not totally convincing. Osorkon divided the obligations for daily provisioning of oil and offerings for the temple into four-month and two-month partitions (Caminos, *Chronicle of Prince Osorkon*, 85, 93).

279. So too Mettinger, *Solomonic State Officials*, 127.

I. שר העיר, אשר על העיר – Governor of the City

Biblical Evidence

Another royal appointee who functioned as a local administrator in cities and forts is the שר העיר. The title שר העיר (*śr h'yr*), "governor of the city" is attested in the Bible in conjunction with four persons: Zebul, the governor of Shechem during the kingship of Abimelech (Judg 9:30); Amon, the governor of Samaria in the reign of Ahab (1 Kgs 22:26 = 2 Chr 18:25); Maaseiah, the governor of Jerusalem in the reign of Josiah (2 Chr 34:8); and Joshua, a governor for whom a city gate was named (2 Kgs 23:8). The collective designation שרי העיר (*śry h'yr*) is found once in the account of Hezekiah's Passover celebration (2 Chr 29:20). One unnamed governor of Samaria at the time of Jehu's coup bears a similar title: אשר על העיר (*'šr 'l h'yr*), "the one who is over the city" (2 Kgs 10:5).

The meaning of the title שר העיר is not usually debated but is understood as a designation for a high official in the municipal administration. The term שר, alone, is a general label for "official" (e.g. 2 Kgs 24:12, 14), but in titles where it stands in construct state with a qualifying noun, like city, it denotes a specific official position. Usages of שר in Hebrew titularies cross civil, military, and religious administrative divisions and can indicate any of the following: the highest ministers of state (1 Kings 4:1–6); a magistrate (Ezek 22:27); different classes of military officers, such as army general (2 Sam 2:8) and captain of the chariotry (1 Kgs 16:9); and the head of a class of religious personnel, such as priests (2 Chr 36:14) and Levites (35:9). The biblical writers also use this title of foreigners: for example, the Philistine chieftains or princes (1 Sam 29:3); the chief of domestic courtiers in Egypt, such as the chief butler and chief baker (Gen 40:2); and an institutional overseer, such as of an Egyptian prison (39:21). In the case of שר העיר, the definitive element in the title, the genitive עיר, clearly delineates the area over which this official is charged—namely, an urban center, often a capital city. Although the overall jurisdiction of the שר העיר is understood, his specific roles require some clarification.

The biblical context for officials entitled שר העיר provides bits of data concerning their functions. For the pre-monarchic period one שר העיר is recorded—Zebul, the governor of Shechem (Judg 9:30) at the time of Abimelech son of Gideon, a local ruler in the hill country of Manasseh. Zebul is also called the פקיד (*pqyd*), "officer," of Abimelech (9:28), an indication that he was a subordinate of Abimelech and had probably been appointed governor by him.[280] Perhaps because of his subservient position, Zebul remained loyal to Abimelech throughout his harrowing reign.

280. One sense of the verb פקד is "appoint" (*BDB*, 823).

More information can be gleaned from references to שר העיר in the monarchic period. Amon, the governor of Samaria in the reign of Ahab (1 Kgs 22:26 = 2 Chr 18:25) together with Joash, a member of the royal family,[281] is charged with the arrest and incarceration of Micaiah son of Imlah, the prophet who predicted Ahab's death and the defeat of Israel at the hands of the Arameans (1 Kgs 22:17–28). According to this account, the governor's jurisdiction (and that of the prince) included the supervision of political prisoners.

The unnamed governor of Samaria at the time of Jehu's coup, designated אשר על העיר,[282] is one of a group of Samaria's leaders who at Jehu's request murdered the remaining descendants of the house of Ahab as a pledge of loyalty to the usurper (2 Kgs 10:5). Notably, he is listed after the minister over the royal house but before the elders and guardians of the princes.[283] Apparently his status was below that of the house minister, probably the highest royal official whose authority extended over the palace complex, but higher than the other dignitaries mentioned.

Two city governors are mentioned in conjunction with the reign of Josiah. The first, Maaseiah, is one of three royal officials who administers the funds for the Temple repairs (2 Chr 34:8). The other officials assigned to this project are the scribe Shaphan son of Azaliah and the herald Joah son of Joahaz.[284] The precise role of Maaseiah in connection with Temple repairs is unclear but may be related to the collection and administration of funds. His place on this list of officials, following the scribe but preceding the herald, could conceivably imply that his rank was above that of the herald. The second city governor, Joshua, appears in reference to the destruction of a *bamah* situated by a city gate named for him.[285] The time period of the tenure of Joshua's office is unknown, but it

---

281. See Chapter 3–A for a discussion of the title בן המלך.

282. There is no biblical evidence that the designations שר העיר, literally, "the official of the city," and אשר על העיר, "the one who is over the city," were distinct positions. However, since in Mesopotamia and in Egypt often two and even three officials jointly presided over the city government, each holding a different title (see below), the possibility of two diverse positions cannot be excluded.

283. See Chapter 3–C for a discussion on these elders.

284. In the Deuteronomistic account of this event only Shaphan the scribe is mentioned (2 Kgs 22:3–4). See chapter 4–B & C for discussions of the possible roles of the scribe and herald in conjunction with this project.

285. It is not totally clear from the biblical context whether the city gate named for Joshua was in Jerusalem or in another city where bamot were destroyed as part of Josiah's religious reform. No Jerusalem city gate by this name is known from other sources. Y. Yadin suggests that the reference is to the city gate of Beer-sheba ("Beer-Sheba: The High Place Destroyed by King Josiah," *BASOR* 222 [1976]: 8–9). There is no evidence, however, that the urban center of Beer-Sheba was occupied in the mid-seventh century. The pottery of

may be assumed that he distinguished himself in some way to have a gate bear his name.

In addition to these city governors, the collective title, שרי העיר, is attested once in the Chronicler's account of Hezekiah's special Passover celebration. The שרי העיר join the king in bringing sacrificial animals up to the Temple (2 Chr 29:20). In contrast to other attestations of the title in the singular, the collective designation in this episode seems to be a general label for municipal officials or notables of Jerusalem.[286] Since there is no mention of other cities or any indication that officials outside of Jerusalem were involved in the ritual, it cannot be assumed that the reference שרי העיר is to a number of governors from different towns. It may be that only the singular, שר העיר, acquired specific meaning and evolved into a function-related title.

A title that may be similar to שר העיר is שר פלך (*śr plk*), "governor of the district of," plus GN, found in biblical records of the Persian period. In the book of Nehemiah, several persons who participate in the repairs of Jerusalem's walls are entitled שר פלך. Following their PNs and title שר are GNs of cities and towns. These include: חצי פלך ירושלם, "half the (or, the half) district of Jerusalem"; פלך בית כרם, "district of Beth-Kerem"; פלך המצפה, "the district of Mizpah"; חצי פלך בית צור , "half the district of Beth-Zur"; חצי פלך קעילה, "half the district of Keilah" (Neh 3:9–19). The term פלך, "round, circuit," seems to denote a circumscribed area.[287] As a political entity it signifies an administrative district such as a city or a city together with its outlying regions.[288] Notably, פלך is a post-exilic term not found in reference to the נצבים of Solomon's districts.

---

the final destruction stratum, Beer-Sheba II, fits well into the repertoire of ceramics from the latter part of the eighth century (T.L. McClellan, "Quantitative Studies in the Iron Age Pottery of Palestine" [Ph.D. Dissertation, University of Pennsylvania, 1975], 393).

286. S. Japhet prefers "notables," as they are more representative of the people (*I & II Chronicles*, 925).

287. Akkadian and Ugaritic cognates, *pilakku* and *plk*, respectively, carry the primary meaning "spindle," hence the derivation, "round, circuit" (*AHW*, 863; *UT* no. 2050).

288. J. Blenkinsopp, *Ezra-Nehemiah: A Commentary* (Philadelphia: Westminster Press, 1988), 235. In one instance, the GN Mizpah is not designated פלך (Neh 3:19), perhaps specifying the immediate city rather than entire district. For a different understanding of פלך see A. Demsky, "Pelekh in Nehemiah," *IEJ* 33 (1983): 42–244. Demsky interprets פלך as an administrative term associated with taxation, a work duty or conscripted labor comparable to מס עבד (*ms ʿbd*) or סבל (*sbl*). He derives the Hebrew usage from the secondary meaning of Akkadian *pilku* (*AHW*, 863 – *pilku* I = district; *pilku* II = service). Thereby, the שר of a certain פלך is the officer in charge of that particular work force.

Epigraphic Evidence

The precise title שר העיר is only attested on bullae lacking provenience.[289] A possible equivalent to that title, לשרער, "belonging to (the) city governor," is incised on four jars from Kuntillet 'Ajrud.[290] However, since Kuntillet 'Ajrud is a way-station in the Sinai and cannot be considered an urban center that would house a governor, it has been argued that this inscription signifies a PN rather than a title, albeit one as yet unattested elsewhere.[291] A problem with that contention lies in its narrow definition of the term עיר, which actually covers a broad spectrum of settlements, from fortified cities, ערים בצרות, to rural towns, ערי השדה.[292] Possibly Kuntillet 'Ajrud fell into the latter category. Furthermore, the שר in question may have been a regional governor, with the way station one of several habitations in the Sinai under his purview, or he may have had no official connection to this site.

In addition, an ostracon from the Judean fort of Meṣad Ḥashavyahu contains a letter addressed to השר, "the governor," but without the specifying genitive, עיר.[293] The inscription, a legal plea in letter form, was written on behalf of an

289. Avigad, *Hebrew Bullae*, 31, 10a,b; G. Barkay, "A Second Bulla of the 'Governor of the City'" *Qadmoniot* 10 (1977/78): 69–71 (Heb). The two bullae, impressed with the same seal, bear the title שר הער but no personal name. The seal's iconography is Assyrian in style showing two authority figures, one perhaps the king and the other an official. Another unprovenienced bulla reads לשר, "belonging to the governor," without the genitive "city" (Diringer, *Le iscrizioni*, no. 99). Three aniconic bullae, two of which include PNs, were recently published by Deutsch (*Messages from the Past*, 62–64). These bullae, like others that have appeared on the antiquities market, have not been authenticated.

290. M. Meshel, *Kuntillet 'Ajrud – A Religious Center from the Time of the Judaean Monarchy on the Border of Sinai* (Israel Museum Catalogue 175; Jerusalem, 1978), 18 no. 21. Note the defective orthography of ער, which is more common in the 8th than in the 7th century (e.g. Siloam Tunnel inscription: אש – for איש, ים – for יום and Arad Ostracon no. 40: ים – for יום [8th century]; cf. Ostraca Lachish no. 4 & Arad no. 24: עיר [late 7th/early 6th century]).

291. Avigad, *Hebrew Bullae*, 32 n. 31.

292. *BDB*, 746; *HALOT* 2, 821–822.

293. J. Naveh, "A Hebrew Letter from the Seventh Century B.C.," 129–139; "More Hebrew Inscriptions from Meṣad Ḥashavyahu," *IEJ* 12 (1962): 27–32. Not all scholars agree that Meṣad Ḥashavyahu was under Judean control. N. Naaman argues that it was an Egyptian fortress staffed by mercenaries of mixed origin: Greek, Phoenician, and Judean ("The Kingdom of Judah Under Josiah," *TA* 18 [1991]: 44–47). At present, his theory remains unproven. The Hebrew inscriptions from Meṣad Ḥashavyahu, including Yahwistic personal names, strengthen the contention that the fortress was Judahite. Foreign evidence from the site consists of East Greek pottery of the Middle Wild Goat Style, prevalent in the last quarter of the seventh century (Naveh, "The Excavations at Meṣad Ḥashavyahu: Preliminary Report," *IEJ* 12 [1962]: 97–99). Note that R. Wenning identifies the pottery as Late Wild Goat Style dated to the early sixth century ("Meṣad Ḥašavyāhū, Ein Stützpunkt des Jojakim?" in *Vom Sinai zum Horeb*, F.L. Hossfeld, ed. [Würzburg: Echter, 1989], 181–189).

agricultural worker, a reaper, who protests the unjust confiscation of his garment by an overseer. The case of the reaper presented in the letter is addressed to an official entitled השר. Although the unnamed officer is only designated השר, instead of שר העיר, it is assumed that he governed the fortress of Meṣad Ḥashavyahu.[294] Y. Suzuki proposes that this שר was a royal appointee who held three positions simultaneously: supervisor of the corvée, military commander, and judge.[295] That phenomenon would not be surprising in view of the various duties held by שר העיר title-bearers mentioned in the Bible. Probably a small enclave like Meṣad Ḥashavyahu would have had only one high official with multiple roles, and it is natural that appeals such as that recorded on this ostracon were directed to the שר for arbitration. The authority of the שר over corvée labor, a possibility not made explicit in the text, could also have been within the realm of a governor of an outpost.[296] Admittedly, though, the precise rank of the שר of Meṣad Ḥashavyahu cannot be ascertained from his generic title.

Canaanite and Mesopotamian Evidence

The element *śr* as part of the titulary of the chief administrator of a city or town is not found in Semitic languages aside from Hebrew. A common Aramaic, Ugaritic, and Akkadian semantic equivalent is the term *rb/rabû*, "great, chief."[297] In Ugaritic a title comparable to Hebrew שר העיר is *rb qrt*, "chief of the city." The title *rb qrt*, but without a PN, appears in a text listing various craftsmen of different towns who belong to the circle of *bnš mlk*, "the king's personnel."[298] Another designation for mayor in Ugaritic is *skn qrt*, or in Akkadian texts, *šakin āli* (*qrt* and *āli* = city). The Ugaritic term *skn*, which has the basic meaning "provider," can denote a variety of officials including governor.[299] In its present

---

Greeks, known as כתים (*ktym*) from the Arad inscriptions (nos. 1–2, 4–5, 7–8, 10–11, 14), probably resided at Meṣad Ḥashavyahu, but it is unclear whether they functioned as mercenaries or merchants (J. Waldbaum, "Early Greek Contacts with the Southern Levant, ca. 1000–600 B.C.: The Eastern Perspective," *BASOR* 293 [1994]: 60–61).

294. השר may be an abbreviation for שר העיר. Cf. the Egyptian *śr* of Buhen discussed below.

295. Y. Suzuki, "A Hebrew Ostracon from Meṣad Ḥashavyahu: A Form-Critical Reinvestigation," *Annual of the Japanese Biblical Institute* 8 (1982): 33–36.

296. Cf. with the Egyptian *śr* of Buhen discussed below.

297. See chart in Rüterswörden (*Beamten der israelitischen Königszeit*, 57). *Targum Onkelos*, for example, renders שר as רב.

298. *KTU*, 4.141, r. 3. The *bnš mlk* group of royal dependents was composed of various professionals who were compensated for their services by the crown with goods and privileges. See Heltzer, *Internal Organization*, 3–15, 23–48. It is unclear whether any relationship exists between the governor, probably of Ugarit, and the craftsmen listed in this text.

299. Gordon, *UT*, 449–450; S. Segert, *A Basic Grammar of the Ugaritic Language* (Berkeley: University of California, 1984), 195. The Akkadian term *šakin* is not derived from the same

usage it is commonly found preceding town names.[300] One *skn qrt* is recorded exercising judicial authority in a land case.[301] Two such officials are listed on a register of rations allocated to the *bnš mlk*.[302] In Akkadian texts from Ugarit, the appellation for this class of official is *ḫazannu*, the title for the mayor of a town, a village or a quarter of a larger city.[303] Occasionally, the term *āli* follows the title *ḫazannu*.[304] In the Amarna letters, the local city rulers often refer to each other as *ḫazannu* (e.g. *EA* 89; 118; 286; 287). From the correspondence it is clear that they are under the control of the *rābiṣū*, Egyptian administrators appointed by the Pharaoh (e.g. *EA* 129; 211; 315). Not enough information is available from the Canaanite material to discriminate functional distinctions between bearers of the three titles: *rb qrt*, *skn qrt*/*šakin āli* or *ḫazannu*, but all seem to be royal appointees.[305]

In Neo-Assyrian and Neo-Babylonian records, four different titles signify municipal rulers: *bēl āli*/LÚ.EN.URU, "lord of the city"; *rab āli*/LÚ.GAL.URU,[306] "chief or overseer of the city"; *ša muḫḫi āli*/LÚ *ša* UGU.URU, "the one who is over the city"; and *ḫazannu*, "mayor."[307] Functional distinctions between these designations are difficult to discern. The title *bēl āli* sometimes signifies a city ruler of vassal status.[308] The *bēl āli* seems to have been responsible for providing troops[309] and performing policing duties.[310] It should be noted that the label *bēl*

---

verbal root as Ugaritic *skn* (see Chapter 5–A). For a discussion of the term *skn* in titularies and various textual examples, see Heltzer, *Internal Organization*, 141–152, esp. 150–152.

300. *KTU* 4.288; 4.160; 4.609.

301. Iribilu, the *skn* of Riqdi, seizes the land of two women (RS 17.61). See the discussion in M. Heltzer, *The Rural Community in Ancient Ugarit* (Wiesbaden: Dr. Ludwig Reichert, 1976), 55–56.

302. *PRU V* 19–21.

303. *CAD* H, 163–165.

304. RS 15.137:15.

305. As Heltzer points out, there is no evidence that any of these officials were locally elected (*Internal Organization*, 151).

306. The *rab āli* should be distinguished from the *rab ālāni*, seemingly a "village manager or inspector" under the provincial authority (*ABL* 414; 424; 506; Kinnier-Wilson, *Nimrud Wine Lists*, 96; S. Parpola, *The Correspondence of Sargon II, Part I, Letters from Assyria and the West* [Helsinki: Helsinki University Press, 1987], 224; G.B. Lanfranchi and S. Parpola, *The Correspondence of Sargon II, Part II, Letters from the Northern and Northeastern Provinces* [Helsinki: Helsinki University Press, 1990], 233).

307. *CAD* A/1, 388–390; H, 163–165; *AHW*, 39, 119, 338–339.

308. *ABL* 136 and 526 in Parpola, *Correspondence of Sargon II, Part I*, nos. 146–147, 118–119.

309. *ABL* 342 in Lanfranchi and Parpola, *Correspondence of Sargon II, Part II*, no. 217, 154–155.

310. In *ABL* 590 the *bēl āli* is involved in a manhunt; in *TCL* 9 67 he carries out policing

āli, as a singular or collective, can also indicate city notable(s) comparable to Hebrew בעלי plus GN (e.g. Judg 9:2; 1 Sam 23:11; 2 Sam 21:12).[311] The *rab āli*, another city administrator, is sometimes mentioned together with the *ḫazannu*.[312] Although either can function alone as chief executive of the city, there is evidence that in the Assyrian capitals and certain provincial capitals two or three officials may have ruled concurrently. When a triarchy existed it included the *rab āli* or *ša muḫḫi āli*, the *ḫazannu* and the *ṭupšar āli*, "city scribe."[313] Sometimes the municipal hierarchy consisted of a *ḫazannu*, his *šanû* (second), and *šalšu* (third).[314] Notably, the Hebrew title אשר על העיר (2 Kgs 10:5) is an exact translation of *ša muḫḫi āli*, a title attested only in the Neo-Assyrian and Neo-Babylonian periods.

The oldest of the aforementioned Akkadian titles is *ḫazannu*, an appellation connected with GNs of towns as early as the Ur III period. An Ur III seal bears the title *ḫazannu* followed by a GN.[315] In a few OB texts the *ḫazannu* is mentioned together with the city elders in their role as witnesses.[316] Nuzi records indicate that the jurisdiction and responsibilities of the *ḫazannu* extended into the outlying territory around his town.[317] Neo-Babylonian legal texts show that the *ḫazannu* functioned as judge together with the *sartennu*, a chief justice.[318] As indicated by the Israelite officials שר העיר and אשר על העיר, no clear distinction is evident between the Akkadian titles *rab āli, ša muḫḫi āli* and *ḫazannu*. The *bēl āli*, on the other hand, differs from the other three in that he is often a municipal chief of vassal status.

Egyptian Analogues

In Egyptian the titulary of the mayor is expressed by the term *ḥ3ty-ʿ*, "local prince or headman" (literally, "foremost in position").[319] Originally holders of this title were independent princes and the position was inherited. By the be-

duties (Lanfranchi and Parpola, *Correspondence of Sargon II, Part II*, nos. 100, 103, 79–81).

311. *ABL* 387 in Lanfranchi and Parpola, *Correspondence of Sargon II, Part II*, no. 203, 147.

312. *ADD* 59:15 in T. Kwasman and S. Parpola, *Legal Transactions of the Court of Nineveh, Part I*, 79 no. 91.

313. The difference in status between the *ša muḫḫi āli* and the *ḫazannu* cannot be discerned from their place on lists since the order is inconsistent.

314. Kinnier-Wilson, *Nimrud Wine Lists*, 7–9; for example, *ABL* 530; 710; *ADD* 160.

315. *CAD* H, 164. The unpublished seal is inscribed *ḫa-za-an-num Marad.da*[ki].

316. For example, *ARM* 3 73:9, Wiseman, *Alalakh Tablets*, 2:27.

317. *CAD* H, 164–165 (transliteration and translation of E.R. Lacheman, "Nuziana II," *RA* 36 [1939]: 115).

318. *CAD* H, 164 (transliteration and translation of *An Or* 8 74:6).

319. Faulkner, *Middle Egyptian*, 162; Gardiner, *Egyptian Grammar*, 51; *Onomastica I*, 31*.

ginning of the New Kingdom the term *ḥ3ty-ʿ* came to signify "mayor," an official of the state under the authority of the vizier.[320] Accounts of the office of the vizier enumerate the various local administrative duties of the *ḥ3ty-ʿ*. These include: overseeing cultivation and harvesting; the collection and transportation of taxes; accounting for deliveries of grain and other commodities; maintenance of local temples; and law enforcement.[321] Some of these functions are comparable with those mentioned in reference to two biblical mayors, Amon and Maaseiah, and the שר of Meṣad Ḥashavyahu. Amon the שר העיר of Samaria was charged with the imprisonment of the prophet Micaiah (1 Kgs 22:26 = 2 Chr 18:25); Maaseiah the שר העיר of Jerusalem helped administer Temple repairs (2 Chr 34:8); and the שר of the fortress of Meṣad Ḥashavyahu was petitioned to arbitrate the legal dispute between a reaper and his overseer.[322]

It is noteworthy that the Egyptian governor of the Nubian fortress of Buhen, the highest official of the town, is designated *śr*. His rank is adduced from evidence that the title was held by one individual at a time. In one instance the *śr* of Buhen is also entitled *s3b (iry) Nḫn*, "warden of Nekhen," a rank carrying judicial authority. Another officer at the fortress, entitled *ṯsw n Bhny*, "the military commander of Buhen," seems to have been subordinate to the *śr*.[323] The position of the *śr* of Buhen is an interesting parallel to that of the שר of Meṣad Ḥashavyahu, whose judicial powers are evident from the ostracon's text. It also indicates that the Egyptian title *śr*, normally a general term for "official," could designate a specific rank.

Conclusions

In the Bible, the title for the highest municipal administrator is שר העיר or in one case אשר על העיר. These titles appear in references to governors of Shechem (pre-monarchic), Samaria and Jerusalem, but lesser urban centers were undoubtedly administered by this class of official as well. In the letter from Meṣad Ḥashavyahu, an abbreviated form of these titles, השר, seems to designate the

320. Egyptologists debate the date of the transition of the position of *ḥ3ty-ʿ*. Helck and Gardiner date it to the 12th Dynasty (1990–1785 BCE), when the government became more centralized (Helck, *Verwaltung*, 211; Gardiner, *Onomastica I*, 31*). Van den Boorn supports a later date, the beginning of the 18th Dynasty (1540 BCE), maintaining that as late as the 17th Dynasty the office was still inherited (*Duties of the Vizier*, 354).

321. Helck, "Bürgermeister" in *Lexikon 1*, 875–880; *Verwaltung*, 113–114; Van den Boorn, *Duties of the Vizier*, 104, 234, 243.

322. Naveh, "A Hebrew Letter from the Seventh Century B.C.," 136.

323. H.S. Smith, *The Fortress of Buhen: The Inscriptions* (London: Egypt Exploration Society, 1976), 78–79. These inscriptions date to the late Middle Kingdom (late 19th–early 18th century).

highest officer of the small fortress. Often the titles of officials charged over urban centers are lacking, for example, Eliashib at Arad and Jehoshaphat's sons at various Judean fortified towns, but it may be assumed that they fit one of the three attested forms. Notably, the governors of capital cities perform duties jointly with state-officials on matters pertaining to the central government, such as the incarceration of dissidents and the regulation of Temple funds. That these governors in particular were influential officials is evident from the revolt of Jehu, where the allegiance of the אשר על העיר is demanded in addition to loyalty from royal ministers and courtiers.

Evidence about municipal officials from Canaanite, Mesopotamian, and Egyptian sources is illuminating for linguistic purposes and for understanding state-organizations. Comparable officials from Ugarit and Mesopotamia bear similar titles, in the case of *ša muḫḫi āli*, the Hebrew title אשר על העיר is an exact translation. Although the standard Egyptian term for mayor differs in meaning, the title *śr* for the commander of the fort of Buhen is particularly interesting since it is parallel to the Hebrew designation השר. Many of the foreign examples are also analogous when comparing the functions of these officials. A significant discrepancy, however, exists in the number of officials who served at any one time. Whereas in Mesopotamia at times two and three high ranking officials comprised the municipal bureaucracy, no evidence exists for more than a single office-holder in Israelite cities.

Excursus: The Term *Śr*

The term *śr* is imbued with difficulties, beginning with its etymology. Related forms of the noun *śr* are attested in Akkadian (*šarru*), Ugaritic (*šr*), Phoenician (שר), Ekronite (שר), Hebrew (שר) and Egyptian (*śr* ).[324] But as far as is known, the only languages in which it carries the meaning "official" are Hebrew and Egyptian. In Egyptian the semantic range of *śr* is comparable to that in Hebrew. Rüterswörden, in his study of Hebrew examples and usages of the term שר, dismisses any potential significance to the affinity between the Egyptian and Hebrew terms.[325] In view of the nature of this study, a more detailed examination of the etymological and semantic relationship between the Hebrew and Egyptian words is in order.

---

324. *HALOT* 3, 1351. For the recently discovered 7th century Philistine example, see S. Gitin, T. Dothan and J. Naveh, "A Royal Dedicatory Inscription from Ekron," *IEJ* 47 (1997): 9–11.

325. Rüterswörden, *Beamten der israelitischen Königszeit*, 62–63.

Etymology and Semantics

The Hebrew noun שַׂר is defined as "chief, ruler, commander, official." It appears in verbal form as a denominative, שָׂרַר, "to be a ruler, to govern."[326] Usually it is connected etymologically to Akkadian *šarru*, "king," which was expressed in Old Akkadian as *śarru*.[327] A verbal form, *šarāru*, with the meaning "to rule," however, is not attested in Akkadian. Notably, *šarru* has a much narrower semantic range than Hebrew שַׂר. The Akkadian term is not used as an appellation for a government official but refers exclusively to a king.[328] Rare occurrences of *śr* in Ugaritic, Phoenician, and a late Philistine dialect also seem to carry the sense "king" or "prince."[329] Normally the West Semitic designation for king is *mlk*, in Ugaritic and Aramaic as well as in Hebrew.[330] Interestingly, biblical examples of שַׂר that may be understood to mean "king," are designations for angelic figures in the book of Daniel, dated to the second century (Dan 10:20–21: שַׂר פָּרַס, "ruler of Persia"; שַׂר יָוָן, "ruler of Greece"; מִיכָאֵל שַׂרְכֶם, "Michael your ruler").

The etymological relationship of Egyptian *śr* to Akkadian *šarru* or to the Hebrew term is uncertain. Although there are many Semitic loan words in Egyptian, it is questionable whether *śr* belongs in that category.[331] Often, Semitic loanwords experienced certain phonetic shifts in Egyptian. Up until the 13th Dynasty, the Semitic phoneme /r/ shifted to /ȝ/ in Egyptian,[332] a phenomenon not evident in the word *śr*, which is already attested in the Fifth Dynasty

---

326. *BDB*, 978–979; *HALOT* 3, 1350–1353, 1362.

327. In phonetic shifts of sibilants Akkadian š > Hebrew ś or š (*GAG*, 29–31 no. 30; A. Goetze, "The Sibilants of Old Babylonian," *RA* 52 (1958): 139; I.J. Gelb, *Glossary of Old Akkadian* [Chicago: University of Chicago Press, 1957], 286–289).

328. In Akkadian, official = *rabianu/rabānu* (*AHW*, 934–935). Interestingly, at Ebla the Sumerian term LUGAL, which is used in Akkadian parallel to *šarru*, does not designate "king" but rather the highest official (Sumerian EN = king). The term *šarru*, however, is unattested and the Eblaite title corresponding to LUGAL is unknown (G. Pettinato, *The Archives of Ebla: An Empire Inscribed in Clay* [Garden City: Doubleday, 1981], 122–133; P. Matthiae, *An Empire Rediscovered* [London: Hodder and Stoughton, 1980], 182).

329. *CTA* 12 in N. Wyatt, "Atonement Theology in Ugarit and Israel," *UF* 8 (1976): p. 421; *KAI* 14:17; 15; 16 (the reading *śr* is not quite certain as the "r" could be a "d"). In the Ekron inscription שַׂר is the title of the ruler, אכיש, who is referred to as "king" in the Assyrian annals (Gitin, "Royal Dedicatory Inscription," 9–11).

330. Cf. lexical text, *malku=šarru* (A. Kilmer, "The First Tablet of MALKU=ŠARRU Together with Its Explicit Version," *JAOS* 83 [1963]: 424–425).

331. F. Calice, *Grundlagen der ägyptisch-semitischen Wortvergleichung* (Vienna: Orientalischen Institutes des Universitat, 1936), 80 no. 305.

332. W. Ward, "Some Effects of Varying Phonetic Conditions on Semitic Loan Words in Egyptian," *JAOS* 80 (1960): 323.

(mid-third millennium).[333] Furthermore, the inconsistency of sibilant shifts between Semitic and Egyptian complicates any attempts to determine borrowing in this case. Semitic *ś* is rendered by Egyptian *ś* or *š* but more often by *ś*, while Semitic *š* is represented more frequently by Egyptian *š*.[334] An alternate possibility, that Hebrew שר is an Egyptian loanword, is equally troublesome since the derivation of the Hebrew word from Akkadian *šarru* is consistent with other East/West Semitic formations. In addition, Egyptian *ś* appears in Hebrew primarily as *š*, although occasionally it remains *ś*.[335] At present, these difficulties preclude arriving at a precise understanding of the etymology of the term *śr*.

Despite the enigmatic etymological relationship between Hebrew שר and Egyptian *śr*, the semantic parallels are easily recognizable. The Egyptian term has a wide semantic range similar to that of the Hebrew. Egyptian *śr* carries the following meanings: "prince, noble, royal advisor, royal official, military official and magistrate." Most often the word appears as a collective, *śrw*. As in Hebrew, a denominative verb defined as "to be a prince" is attested in Egyptian.[336] An observable distinction between the usage of the term *śr* in Egyptian and שר in Hebrew is that in Egyptian the title is a general designation for a government official and is not usually followed by a qualifying noun.[337] In the Middle Kingdom, and with rare exceptions in the New Kingdom, *śr* is not employed as a regular title associated with specific duties. When it does appear followed by a qualifying phrase, the appellation seems to be an epithet rather than a title: in the singular it refers to the subject, for example, *śr m-ḥ3t rḫyt*, "official before the

333. The designation *śr* appears in the Pyramid Texts, see Erman and Grapow, *Wörterbuch* 4, 188; *Beligennen* 4, 33.

334. J.E. Hoch, *Semitic Words in Egyptian Texts of the New Kingdom and Third Intermediate Period* (Princeton: Princeton University Press, 1994), 409. Among Egyptian transliterations of Canaanite toponyms, for example, the GN שוכה (*swkh*) appears in a text of Thutmose III as *s3k3* (W. Helck, *Die Beziehungen Ägyptens zu Vorderasien im 3. und 2. Jahrtausend* [Wiesbaden: O. Harrassowitz, 1971], 537, 557). Other cases include: *ś'r* = שער (*ś'r*), "barley"; *ś'rt* = Heb. שער (*ś'r*), "wool, animal hair"; *śg* = Heb. שק (*śq*), "sackcloth" (Hoch, pp. 255–256, 269, nos. 358, 359, 383).

335. W. Leslau, "Semitic and Egyptian Comparisons," *JNES* 21 (1962): 46–47. Note the non-shift—Egyptian *rś*, "wake up," and Hebrew נשא (*nś'*), "lift" (no. 21).

336. Erman and Grapow, *Wörterbuch* 4, 188–190; Faulkner, *Middle Egyptian*, 235. *Śr* with the meaning "prince" is attested from the Old Kingdom onward; the meaning "official" first appears in the early Middle Kingdom. For a discussion of *śr* and *śrw* in Middle Kingdom epithets, see Doxey, *Egyptian Non-Royal Epithets in the Middle Kingdom*, 157–159.

337. The title *śr*, appended to a PN, is attested on a seal (Martin, *Egyptian Administrative and Private-Name Seals*, no. 320). Rüterswörden dismisses the possibility of a significant connection between Egyptian *śr* and Hebrew שר primarily because of the general meaning of the Egyptian term (*Beamten der israelitischen Königszeit*, 62–63).

people"; in the plural it functions in a comparative statement, the subject as compared to other *śrw*, for example, *ḫnty śrw r..*, "foremost of the officials to..."[338] Although the term *śr* does not denote rank or power, evidence exists of a hierarchy of *śrw*: *śr m sꜣ ʿm śr tpy nfryt r śr n nfryt*, "(any) official, from the highest (first) official to the lowest official."[339]

Occasionally, in the New Kingdom, *śr* appears in a more definitive title, for example, *śr n ḳnbt*, "official of the judgment hall."[340] The judicial role of the *śrw* can be gleaned from the context in several texts. A case in point is the legal proceedings surrounding suspected tomb robbers at the Theban necropolis in the reign of Rameses IX (last quarter of the 12th century).[341] The investigation and trial were conducted by a number of high officials, including the vizier and the city governor. Notably the *śrw* accompany one of the defendants, a coppersmith named Pekharu, to the tomb he was accused of looting and there probe his testimony.[342] Later, in court, the vizier presents the evidence to the assembled *śrw* and they pass judgment, in this case finding the craftsmen innocent.[343] In the Third Intermediate Period too, *śr* appears now and then in the titulary of court officers: *śr n tꜣ ḳnbt ʿꜣt nt niwt*, "official of this great judgment hall of the city (capital)."[344]

In spite of the differences between usages of the designations *śr* in Egyptian and שר in Hebrew, important similarities are noteworthy. Like the Egyptian term, Hebrew שר is used as a general appellation for a chief or government official, both for Israelites and foreigners. Sometimes an ethnic identity or GN is appended to the collective, שרי, "officials of."[345] The neutral, non-specific usage, שר or שרים alone, is attested in the biblical texts far more frequently than titularies in which שר is followed by a qualifying noun denoting particular duties.

A significant parallel between the functions of Israelite שרים and Egyptian *śrw* is in the realm of the judiciary. In the monarchic period judicial authority, formerly the sole purview of Israel's elders, was allocated in part to royal appoin-

338. Ward, *Index of Egyptian Administrative and Religious Titles*, 153; Doxey, *Egyptian Non-Royal Epithets in the Middle Kingdom*, 172.

339. Van den Boorn, *Duties of the Vizier*, R10, 88–89.

340. Helck, *Verwaltung*, 62.

341. Papyrus Abbott in G. Maspero, *Une enquete judiciare à Thebes au temps de la XXe dynastie* (Paris: Imprimerie nationale, 1871); Breasted, *Ancient Records of Egypt* 4, nos. 509–535.

342. Papyrus Abbott 5:1–8.

343. Papyrus Abbott, 7:8–15.

344. Allam, "Egyptian Law Courts," 115.

345. For example, Midian (Judg 8:3), Jezreel (2 Kgs 10:1), Israel (2 Chr 21:4), Jerusalem and Judah (Jer 34:19), Babylon (2 Chr 32:31).

tees, at least in matters of state law (e.g. Isa 1:23; Jer 26:10; Ezek 22:27; Hos 5:10).[346] A biblical scenario comparable to the tomb robbery case cited above is the account of the trial of Jeremiah following his prophecy of doom in the Temple courtyard (Jer 26). Having heard the news of Jeremiah's arrest, the שרים of Judah go up from the palace to the Temple gate where they sit in judgment. After weighing the evidence, the accusations of treason pronounced by the priests and prophets and Jeremiah's defense of his divine mission, the שרים declare that Jeremiah is innocent.

Other, more definitive Hebrew titles are sometimes formed with the element שר. In most cases, the second element denoting an area of jurisdiction is a military designation.[347] A few titles that incorporate שר are not distinguishably military or civil;[348] two denote Temple officers.[349] Occasionally, the collective designation שרים refers to a heterogeneous group of civil officials of varying rank. This is evident from the register of Solomonic appointees listed under the heading שרים (1 Kgs 4:2–6).[350]

Interestingly, when the biblical writers mention specific foreign officials, they utilize the term for "official" appropriate to that individual's native language. Titles of Egyptians are prefixed by the element שר: שר הטבחים, "captain of the guard" (Gen 37:36); שר בית הסהר, "warden of the prison" (39:21); שר המשקים, "chief butler" (40:2); and שר האופים, "chief baker" (40:2).[351] Likewise, titles of Philistine and Canaanite officers are rendered with the element שר—for example, Phicol the שר צבא, "army commander," of Abimelek king of Gerar (Gen

346. See Chapters 3–C & 4–J.

347. For example, שר החיל, "army commander" (2 Sam 24:2); שרי אלפים שרי מאות, שרי חמשים, שרי עשרות, "commanders (of units) of thousands, commanders of hundreds, commanders of fifties, commanders of tens" (Exod 18:21); שר מחצית הרכב, "commander of half the chariot force" (1 Kgs 16:9).

348. For example, שר העיר, "mayor or governor" (above); שרי הנצבים, "officers of the prefects" (1 Kgs 5:30); שרי הרצים, "officers of the (palace) guard" (2 Chr 12:10).

349. שרי הלוים, "officers of the Levites," and שרי הכהנים, "officers of the priests" (2 Chr 35:9; 36:14).

350. McKenzie's contention that the title שר always signifies a military or militarily related post cannot be supported in light of the Solomonic list ("The Elders in the Old Testament," 394).

351. Rüterswörden maintains that these appellations are not translations of Egyptian titles but rather reflect Hebrew expressions. He notes that specific Egyptian titles did not contain the element *śr* (*Beamten der israelitischen Königszeit*, 47–54). Although Rüterswörden is probably correct in that these titles are not Egyptian in origin (see Redford, "A Study of the Biblical Story of Joseph," 191–192), he misses the point. Apparently, the biblical writers differentiated between terms for "official," seemingly based on knowledge of national usage. Whether they were aware that Egyptians did not normally incorporate *śr* in definitive titles is uncertain, but they probably knew that the term *śr* in Egyptian means "official."

21:22; 26:26) and Sisera the שר צבא of Jabin king of Hazor (Judg 4:2, 7).[352] In contrast, titles of Assyrians and Babylonians are prefixed by the element *rb*:[353] רב סריס, "chief eunuch" (2 Kgs 18:17); רב שקה, "chief butler" (18:17); רב טבחים, "chief of the guard" (25:8).[354]

Conclusions

The etymology of the term *śr*, including its diffusion into Akkadian, Ugaritic, Hebrew, and Egyptian remains elusive. However, certain tentative conclusions can be drawn concerning its cultural applications. Clearly, in Akkadian, and perhaps in Ugaritic and Phoenician, *šarru/šr* is an appellation reserved for royalty. In Egyptian and in Hebrew, in addition to signifying a prince or some type of chief, the title is a general designation for a government official or notable. In Israelite usage, in contrast to Egyptian, the element שר in titularies is commonly formulated with substantives. Seemingly, the term *śr* branched out in three directions: in Mesopotamia its semantic range remained restricted, referring only to "king"; in Egypt it broadened and was applied to "prince," "notable" and "royal official"; in Israel it encompassed the same meanings as in Egypt but took on an extra more specialized dimension in its usage with substantives. Notably, the Hebrew meaning "official" does not appear to have been borrowed from other Semitic languages and, unless it developed in Israel independently, it was the result of Egyptian influence transmitted indirectly via the Canaanites and/or Philistines, who had adopted it while under Egyptian hegemony during the New Kingdom.[355]

352. If the biblical usage of the term שר for Canaanite and Philistine officers represents the actual local appellation then it is not impossible that the title was adopted as a result of Egyptian influence. Canaanites may have borrowed the title while under Egyptian rule during the New Kingdom; Philistines, who regularly manned Egyptian garrisons in southern Canaan in the 13th–11th centuries, may have done likewise. The usage of שר with the meaning "ruler, king" in the seventh-century Philistine inscription from Ekron is probably the result of later Assyrian influence.

353. The appellations in Jer 39:3, 13 that include the element *śr*, *śr-'ṣr* and *śr-skym*, seem to be Akkadian PNs formulated with the term *šarru*, "king." See, Bright, *Jeremiah*, 243.

354. In addition, the captain of the ship on which Jonah traveled (1:6), who is an officer of unknown ethnic origin, is entitled רב חבל.

355. Contrast Begrich, who suggests that the expanded usage of the Hebrew word was the result of direct Egyptian influence during the United Monarchy ("Sōfēr und Mazkīr," 14–15). His theory is accepted by Mettinger (*Solomonic State Officials*, 3).

J. שפט – Judge

Some officials who served in the judiciary were administrators of the central government. The title שפט, however, carries a wide semantic range whose broader meaning needs to be delineated.

The Meaning of שפט

The term שפט (*špṭ*), plural שפטים (*šptym*), is attested in the Bible about 60 times. It is a substantive formed from the verbal root שפט, defined as "to judge, govern." The title can designate various positions of authority, including "judge, officer, chief and king."[356] The use of שפט in parallel construction with other titles, such as שר, "official" (Mic 7:3; Zeph 3:3; Ps 148:11), and מלך, "king" (Hos 7:7; Ps 2:10), confirms its broader meaning, "one who governs."[357] According to the writer(s) of Judges (2:16–19), in the pre-monarchic period the chieftains or petty princes who ruled in the hill country of Ephraim and Manasseh were known as שפטים.[358] However, the duties of the שפט could entail judging, as is implied in reference to Samuel and his sons: Samuel traveled outside his home base at Ramah to Bethel, Gilgal, and Mizpah as a circuit judge (1 Sam 7:16); his sons, who were stationed at Beer-sheba, are accused of taking bribes and thwarting justice (8:1–3). Although the juridical, more specialized aspect of שפט is not always distinguishable from its broader sense, in certain contexts the term clearly refers solely to the office of judge and to activities related to the judiciary. The latter, more specific usage of שפט is the focus of the study below, with special emphasis on occurrences of the title as applied to officials in the monarchic period.

---

356. *BDB*, 1047–1048; *HALOT* 4, 1622–1626.

357. The phrase שר ושפט (Exod 2:14) is usually understood as a hendiadys, "an officer in authority" (M.C. Rozenberg, "The Stem *špṭ*: An Investigation of Biblical and Extra-Biblical Sources" [Ph.D. Dissertation University of Pennsylvania, 1963], 63–64; Weinfeld, "Judge and Officer," 68). Rozenberg (p. 198) considers it parallel to the Akkadian phrase *šarru u šāpiṭu* attested in a Neo-Assyrian letter from the time of Assurbanipal (no. 1431 in L. Waterman, *Royal Correspondence of the Assyrian Empire* [Ann Arbor: University of Michigan Press, 1930], 496–499). That interpretation, however, is debatable, as the two so-called parallel terms, both in Hebrew and Akkadian, can be understood as representing two positions of authority, "officer and judge," even if they are related. Similarly, in Amos 2:3 שופט ושריה refers to separate offices.

Other titles used in association with שפט further illustrate its broader meaning of "ruler, official," although not all are necessarily synonymous: נשיא, "prince" (2 Chr 1:2); יעציך, "your advisors" (Isa 1:26); מחקקנו, "our leader" (33:22); רוזנים, "officials" (40:23).

358. Other leadership titles are attached to individual chieftains: מושיע, "redeemer" (Judg 3:15); נביא/ה, "prophet/prophetess" (4:4; 6:8); ראש, "chief" (11:8).

Biblical Evidence

The verb שפט with the meanings "arbitrate," "judge" and "execute justice" is used in the Bible to describe activities of both God and humans. YHWH arbitrates between individuals (Gen 16:5; 1 Sam 24:13, 16) and between nations (Judg 11:27; Isa 2:4 = Mic 4:3); the עדה, an assembly of Israelites, is authorized to judge between a murderer and an avenger (Num 35:24). As a substantive, שפט or שפטים occurs several times in a judicial context (e.g. Deut 1:16; 16:18; 17:9, 12; 19:17–18; 21:2; 25:2; 2 Sam 15:4; Isa 16:5; 2 Chr 19:5–6). In a few additional cases where the appellation implies "judge," it is found in concert with other titles signifying leadership, such as שטרים, זקנים, ראשים, "officers, elders, chiefs" (Josh 23:2; 24:1; Ezra 10:14).[359]

In Deuteronomy, the contextual placement of officers designated שפטים clearly defines their roles as judges. Moses' instructions at the opening of the book include the appointment of chiefs, military officers and other officials (1:15). The שפטים, apparently chosen from among these leaders, are commanded to hear cases and to deal impartially in their judgments (1:16–17; 16:19–20).[360] These judges, along with other officials called שטרים, are stationed at the gate of each city (16:18), the meeting and market place of fortified settlements (cf. 1 Kgs 22:10; 2 Kgs 7:1; Ruth 4:1–12).[361] In the high court, the שפט, a

---

359. To date the title שפט is unconfirmed in epigraphic material. An unprovenienced seal inscribed לשפט (*WSS* no. 381, 160–161) is apparently a PN (short form) comparable to other seals with the name שפט plus a patronymic (*WSS* nos. 382–383, 161). Avishur and Heltzer suggest, however, that the inscription on this seal signifies a title (*Studies on the Royal Administration*, 93–94).

360. Similar instructions to judges are found in Hittite and Egyptian texts. For a summary, see Weinfeld, "Judge and Officer," 76–81.

361. The term בכל שעריך, "at all your gates," (Deut 16:18) indicates that the law pertaining to the appointment of judges applies to all walled cities, similar to the statement in 2 Chr 19:5, בכל ערי יהודה הבצרות לעיר ועיר, "at all the fortified cities of Judah, city by city" (Weinfeld, "Judge and Officer," 66). In contrast, S. Japhet (*I & II Chronicles*, 773, 775), K.W. Whitelam (*The Just King* [Sheffield: University of Sheffield, 1979], 192) and J. Tigay (*Deuteronomy*, xxii), among others, interpret the Deuteronomic law as inclusive of all settlements, unfortified as well as fortified. Tigay considers "gates" a metonymy for all settlements. There is no reason, however, to presuppose an extended meaning for שעריך. All persons mentioned in the text in association with the term שעריך are precisely the people one expects to congregate in urban centers: aliens, orphans, widows, the needy, and Levites (e.g. Exod 20:10; Deut 5:14; 12:12; 14:28–29; 15:7; 16:14, 26:12). Many are probably non-landowners in search of food and shelter. Weinfeld (p. 66 n. 5) notes a parallel reference in an Ugaritic text: *gr hmyt ugrt*, "the strangers in the walls of Ugarit" (*UT* 2:27–28). In addition, the term שעריך appears in connection with sites at which certain practices are permitted or prohibited, in contrast to the chosen cult place (Deut 12:15, 17; 16:5–6). Since Jerusalem, a fortified city, is the chosen site in question, the other settlements used in the comparison are probably also fortified.

lay person, shares the bench with religious personnel, priests and Levites (Deut 17:9; cf 2 Chr 19:8). Noticeably, the שפטים are present in some legal matters but absent in others. For example, they oversee the flogging of offenders (Deut 25:2) and assist the elders in cases where a homicide cannot be avenged because the murderer is unknown (21:2). But other cases—a rebellious son (21:19), a bride accused of not being a virgin (22:15–19) and a levirate marriage (25:7–9)—are brought before a council of elders, without mention of judges.

While the judicial functions of the שפטים in Deuteronomy are evident, their precise position in the administrative system and their relationship to other officials and notables is somewhat blurred. Primarily the debate centers around the selection of judges. Are they representatives of the people, as elders, or are they state appointees similar to other royal functionaries? Rüterswörden, following Köhler, argues the former, maintaining that judges were chosen by the populace rather than by the crown.[362] He points out that the designation שפטי המלך, "judges of the king," is absent from official lists. His argument bears little weight, however, since the extant lists of royal officials are fragmentary. Weinfeld, and more recently, Reviv hold the view that judges were state officials. They claim that in monarchic Israel, as in neighboring Near Eastern cultures, the legal system was jointly in the hands of agents of the central government and the elders.[363] References to שפטים as שרים in Exod 18:21–22 and Deut 1:15–16 imply that some שרים were appointed to be שפטים.[364]

That the expression שעריך in Deuteronomy can refer to walled cities with gates is clear from the injunction to inscribe the doorposts of gates as well as those of houses (Deut 6:9; 11:20). Lastly, in the Iron Age IIB-C, the period of the Divided Monarchy, even small settlements were often fortified and a large portion of farmers dwelled in those towns (Mazar, *Archaeology of the Land of the Bible*, 403–462, esp. 415–416, 435–437). Those who lived on surrounding farmsteads would have gone to the walled centers for their business dealings, including judicial proceedings.

362. Rüterswörden, *Beamten der israelitischen Königszeit*, 112–113. L. Köhler maintains that the judiciary remained within the purview of assemblies of towns and villages and that Deuteronomy functioned as a source of unification of the justice system, comparable to the worship system, that exhibited regional divergences in law codes (*Hebrew Man*, [trans. P. Ackroyd, London: SCM Press, 1953], 149–175).

363. Weinfeld, "Judge and Officer," 67–71; Reviv, *Elders in Ancient Israel*, 92–94. These biblical designations are significant, whether one assigns the sources to the early or late monarchic period. In either case, the title שפטים is not equated with זקנים but rather with שרים.

364. As discussed in connection to שר העיר, at least in certain cases שרים were empowered with judicial authority even when they were not specifically designated שפטים (e.g., the שר of Meṣad Ḥashavyahu, the שרים who tried Jeremiah [Jer 26:10–16]). That is not to say that all שרים functioned as judges or that those specifically entitled שפטים held other positions. In fact, in the monarchic period שפטים are never described as performing non-judicial duties,

Textual evidence of kings exercising the prerogative of appointing judges, however, is scant, as only David and Jehoshaphat are explicitly mentioned (2 Sam 15:3–4; 1 Chr 23:4; 26:29; 2 Chr 19:5–8). Nevertheless, these accounts deserve attention, especially the narrative describing Jehoshaphat's so-called "judicial reform." The Davidic record indicates that 6,000 שטרים ושפטים, "officers and justices," were selected from Levitical families for "external duties," that is tasks outside the Temple complex. Jehoshaphat's judicial appointments fall into two categories: those assigned to provincial courts in fortified cities and those who sat on the high court in Jerusalem. Members of the Jerusalem court apparently were chosen from among Levites, priests, and heads of families (elders), but the social status of the provincial judges is not specified. Whatever their original societal position(s), these individuals became royal appointees assigned by the crown to specific judicial posts. In that capacity, they should be regarded as state officials under the jurisdiction of the king.[365]

A topic commonly discussed in connection with Jehoshaphat's judicial organization is its inception and operation. Evidently, with the establishment of the monarchy, the king bore the responsibility to provide an effective judicial system (1 Sam 8). As suggested by the conditions preceding Absalom's revolt, especially his promises to hear the legal pleas of dissatisfied Israelites, David seems to have been lax in this regard, or at least so Absalom insinuated (2 Sam 15:3–4). Quite possibly, David simply had not provided judges for the courts nor had he compensated by hearing the cases himself.[366] In light of information about royal involvement with the legal system during David's reign, Jehoshaphat's legal structure should not be viewed as necessarily innovative or modeled after a foreign system.[367] Rather, the institution of his judicial organization

---

with the exception of the king who was the chief justice. This observation weakens Rozenberg's assumption that the administration of justice was only one of many functions of the שפטים described in Deuteronomy ("The Stem *špṭ*," 68–73).

365. The general issue of Levitical descent of monarchic officers and judges in Chronicles is problematic and may actually reflect conditions of the Chronicler's own time (see Japhet, *I & II Chronicles*, 454–455). On the other hand, kings appointing officers and judges, regardless of their social standing, is certainly within the realm of royal authority.

366. R. Wilson, "Israel's Judicial System in the Preexilic Period," *JQR* 74 (1983): 242–243. Abshalom's comment, ושמע אין לך מאת המלך, "but you do not have a hearer from the king," may indicate that judges were not provided, not by way of the king in his role as chief justice nor through his officials. As noted by Weinfeld ("Judge and Officer," 80 n. 90), the verb "to hear" and the substantive "hearer" are commonly used in Egyptian to mean "judge" (*sḏm/sḏmw*).

367. Cf. G.C. Macholz, who believes that royal officials were first given judicial powers at the time of Jehoshaphat ("Zur Geschichte der Justizorganisation in Juda," *ZAW* 84 [1972]: 314–340). The edict of Haremhab (mid14th century) is sometimes designated as the proto-

can be understood as one of several measures undertaken periodically by monarchs to revitalize aspects of the state administration and reinforce royal authority.[368] By appointing provincial judges, Jehoshaphat may have attempted to secure a judiciary answerable to the crown, at least in state affairs. The high court in Jerusalem, headquartered within royal view, would deal with difficult cases referred to it by the local courts.[369]

Courts administered by state-appointed justices, however, did not eliminate the judicial power of local councils. The coexistence of two judicial components, one comprised of elders and another of government officials, who ofttimes cooperated in the decision-making process, is supported by biblical data. Traditional law involving family matters on the local level remained within the authority of the elders exclusively, while legal issues affecting the state required representation of the central government through monarchic officials. In the treason trial of Jeremiah royal officers presided, but certain elders, who apparently participated in the proceedings, introduced a precedent case in order to free the prophet (Jer 26:10–19). Similarly, in intercity matters, such as the case of an unidentified murder, judges and elders worked cooperatively (Deut 21:2).[370] The judges oversaw the measuring of distances between the corpse and surrounding cities so that the elders of the closest town, to which responsibility

---

type for Jehoshaphat's judicial system (Albright, "The Judicial Reform of Jehoshaphat," 78–82; Macholz, 330–333). Although definite similarities exist between the Egyptian text and the Chronicler's account, especially in depictions of the composition of the courts and in the admonition to the judges, temporal considerations, among others, make the possibility of borrowing unlikely (for a detailed discussion see: Weinfeld, "Judge and Officer," 78–81; Whitelam, *Just King*, 203–205). In addition, as Weinfeld notes, both judicial systems show features common in other Near Eastern cultures (e.g. the Hittites), indicating widespread practices that cannot be traced to any one system (pp. 75–76).

368. Jehoshaphat's concern over royal authority is evident from the following acts: he stationed military units in Judahite cities and assigned officers (2 Chr 17:2); his own sons were given control over certain cities (21:2–3); he built additional forts and store-cities (17:12); he sent officers throughout Judah to teach religious law to the people (17:7–9). Jehoshaphat's religious reforms, like Hezekiah's and Josiah's, promoted uniformity of practice and focused on Jerusalem as the seat of power for cultic as well as political and economic matters.

369. According to the Chronicler, jurisdiction in the high court was divided between cultic and state concerns. The high priest oversaw דבר יהוה, "matters of the YHWH," while a leader of the house of Judah was in charge of דבר המלך, "matters of the king" (2 Chr 19:11). Wilson suggests that some of the unusual features of Jehoshaphat's judicial system, including the distinction between sacred and secular law, are reflections of the exilic and post-exilic periods ("Israel's Judicial System in the Preexilic Period," 246–248).

370. Although it is not stated in Deuteronomy that judges were state appointed, a clear distinction between זקנים and שפטים is made in this example.

was assigned symbolically, could perform the expiatory rite of beheading a heifer. As mentioned, the high court in Jerusalem, staffed by royal appointees from the ranks of distinguished groups in society, included local dignitaries, most probably chosen from the circle of elders.

Mesopotamian, Hittite, Ugaritic and Egyptian Evidence

In Mesopotamian texts from the Old Akkadian through the Late Babylonian period, the term for judge is expressed by the word *dayyānu*/LÚ.DI.KU$_5$.[371] In contrast, the term *šāpiṭu*, a cognate of Hebrew שפט, is usually not a precise title, but like many biblical usages of שפט an undefined designation for one who bears administrative authority on a larger scale.[372] The judicial roles of the *dayyānu*, on the other hand, are clearly delineated in Mesopotamian sources. In Old Assyrian documents the *dayyānū* hear cases and pass sentences.[373] In one case they are identified as the judges of the temple of Assur.[374] Similarly, they are mentioned in Old Babylonian law codes as the executors of legal decisions.[375] Notably, one law in Hammurabi (no. 127), comparable to Deut 25:2, specifies that corporal punishment be administered in the presence of a *dayyānu*.

---

371. *CAD* D, 28–33; *AHW* 1, 167–168.

372. *CAD* Š/1, 459; Rozenberg, "The Stem *špṭ*," 170–215; contra *AHW* 3, 1173 "Richter" (*šāpiṭu* is derived from the verb *šapāṭu* A [i-class], "rule" [*CAD* Š/1, 450; *AHW* 3, 1172]; cf. *šapāṭu* B [a/u-class], "discipline" [*CAD* Š/1, 451; *AHW* 3, 1172]). At Mari, it seems that the office of *šāpiṭu* refers to the provincial governor (see especially *ARM* IV 81, 98, 112). Notably, the title only occurs alone in titularies not containing a PN (J. Safren, "New Evidence for the Title of the Provincial Governor at Mari," *HUCA* 50 [1979]: 1–15). In a foundation inscription from Mari the term *šāpiṭu* describes the role of the god Šamaš: *ša-pi-iṭ ilī u a-wi-lu-tim*, "the *šāpiṭu* of gods and mankind" (l. 3). A few lines below in the same inscription, he is designated, *da-ia-an ša-ki-in na-pi-iš-tim*, "the judge of living beings" (l. 9). Since the entire text depicts Šamaš as a champion of justice, it seems reasonable to interpret *šāpiṭu* in this context as "judge," parallel to *dayyānu* (G. Dossin, "L'inscription de fondation de Iadun-Lim roi de Mari," *Syria* 32 [1955]: 12; *CAD* Š/1, 459). Cf. Speiser, who understands *šāpiṭu* and *dayyānu* as signifying different functions ("The Manner of the King" in *WHJP* 3, 281) and Rozenberg, who translates *šāpiṭu* as "authority" (pp. 173–175). Rozenberg supports his argument by pointing to the lack of a personal determinative, L, before the word *šāpiṭu*. This, however, seems inconsequential, especially since the L determinative is also absent before the word *dayyānu*.

373. *Tübinger* 2 in G. Eiser and J. Lewy, "Die altassyrischen Rechtsurkunden von Költepe," *MVAG* 35/3 (1931): 79–80 no. 325a:11–13.

374. VAT 9215 in Eiser and Lewy, "Die altassyrischen Rechtsurkunden," 75–78 no. 325:32.

375. Lipit-Ištar, no. 30; Hammurabi, nos. 5, 9, 13, 127, 168, 172, 177. For a detailed discussion of the *dayyānū* and the structure of the court in the OB period, see A. Walther, *Das altbabylonische Gerichtswesen* (Leipzig: J.C. Hinrichs, 1917), 5–45.

It is sometimes difficult to determine whether the *dayyānū* were local representatives or officials of the central government who often shared judicial authority with local agents.[376] The dilemma is resolved when the title *dayyānu* is followed by a qualifying genitive, as *dayyānū šarrim*, "the judges of the king," attested in Old Babylonian sources.[377] According to Middle Assyrian Laws, royal officers (1 SUKAL *ša pāni* LUGAL, "one high minister who is before the king"; *qēpūtu ša* LUGAL, "officials of the king"), in concert with municipal officials (DUB.SAR URU, "the scribe of the city"; LÚ.ÍL, "the herald"), functioned as judges in legal proceedings involving property in Assur. When the case dealt with property in another city, the mayor (*ḫazannu*) and three city notables (3 GAL.MEŠ *ša* ERI) handled it.[378] In first millennium texts, especially in Neo-Assyrian and Neo-Babylonian letters, officials bearing other titles signifying special judgeships are also attested. One title belongs to the *sartennu*, the chief justice, and another to the *sukallu*, a vizier-like high official who frequently presides over the court with the *sartennu*.[379] These distinguished judges apparently functioned in the higher courts of the central authority, which often dealt with cases too difficult for local officials.[380] One particular *sartennu*, Šumma-ilu, may have been a *šangû*-priest (temple administrator), thereby intimating a priestly background for the office.[381] When the *dayyānū* are mentioned together with the *sukallu* or the *sartennu*, they are listed last, indicating their lower rank.[382] Occasionally, the *ḫazannu* also participated in judicial proceedings.[383]

---

376. For the judicial role of the Mesopotamian elders, see Chapter 3–C.

377. For example, in the First Babylonian Dynasty a royal official presided over the court (*BE* 6/1 10:8 in *CAD* D, 29).

378. Middle Assyrian Laws B, no. 6. Corporal punishment is carried out by the mayor and five city notables (no. 18). M. Roth, *Law Collections from Mesopotamia and Asia Minor* (Atlanta: Scholars Press, 1995), 177.

379. *CAD* S, 185–186; *ABL* 716. On the office of *sukallu* see Kinnier-Wilson, *Nimrud Wine Lists*, 36–37.

380. A case in point is recorded on a tablet from Ninveh (BM 123360). It outlines the case of thieves brought before local officials for judgment. Apparently the local authorities were not empowered to investigate the charge and planned to refer the case to the central authority of the *sukallu* and the *sartennu*. At that point the thieves, who were trying to avoid sentencing by the higher officials, confessed and were fined by the local officials (J.N. Postgate, "More 'Assyrian Deeds and Documents,'" *Iraq* 32 [1970]: 131–133).

381. A *šangû*-priest named Šummu-ilu, is mentioned in *ADD* 374, rev. 11 (p. 286). In BT 118 (B. Parker, "Economic Tablets from the Temple of Mamu at Balawat," *Iraq* 25 [1963]: 95) a *sartennu* also called Šumma-ilu seems to have another title, restored by Kinnier-Wilson as *šangû* based on *ADD* 374, a contemporaneous text (*Nimrud Wine Lists*, 22). It is uncertain, however, whether the two occurrences of the same name refer to the same person.

382. *VAS* 4, 87; 5, 156; 6, 99 in *CAD* D, 31.

383. See Chapter 4–I.

As already noted in the discussion on elders, in the Hittite and Ugaritic judicial systems local representatives played a major role. In the case of Ugarit, however, insufficient information is available on the role of persons entitled *dayyānu* in the administrative organization.[384] In the Hittite system, it is clear that officers of the king represented the government in local courts. As mentioned, the *auriyaš išḫaš* (=*bēl madgalti*), "the commander of the guard," a regional military governor, functioned as judge in concert with town officials and a body of elders.[385] Apparently, priests also took part in the judicial process. But as in Israel, the king acted as chief justice.[386]

Evidence for the Egyptian system of justice, even more than other systems of Near Eastern societies, shows courts comprised of both state officials and religious personnel. Middle Kingdom records show that officials who functioned as judges acquired the title *sḏmw*, literally, "hearers."[387] In the period of the New Kingdom, the vizier, who headed the state-administrative apparatus, was in charge of the judiciary. Local *ḳnbt* councils, comprised of prominent men in the community, such as local office-holders and professionals, convened when necessary to render legal decisions. Occasionally outside officials were included on the bench, especially in difficult cases. Even *ḳnbt* councils associated with temples were active in secular affairs, often dealing with cases that arose among workers on their lands. A *ḳnbt ꜥ3t,* "great" *ḳnbt,* functioned in the capital city as a supreme court. Its membership, comparable to Jehoshaphat's Jerusalem court, was composed of lay officials and priests.[388] But unlike the Israelite bureaucracy which lacked a vizier, the Egyptian high court was headed by the vizier. The *ḳnbt ꜥ3t* dealt with important cases that exceeded the authority of the local courts, such as serious crimes involving high officials, litigations over large

384. Heltzer, *Internal Organization*, 166; *PRU* III 16.132:26, 156:20. The Ugaritic term *ṯpṭ*, the equivalent of Hebrew שפט, is not attested as an agent noun meaning "judge." Although the verb *ṯpṭ*, used in parallel construction to *d-n*, has the sense "to deal justly, uphold rights," the nominal forms seem to carry the broader meaning "authority, ruler" (Rozenberg, "The Stem *špṭ*," 215–217, 232).

385. Weinfeld, "Judge and Officer," 81. Although the *auriyaš išḫaš* at times was responsible for cultic matters (A. Goetze, *ANET*, 210–211), there is no evidence that he was a priest.

386. The edict of Muršiliš stipulates that the priest investigate the case. If it is too difficult he refers it to the king for judgment (Von Schuler, *Hethitische Dienstanweisungen*, 57).

387. W. Helck, "Richtertitel" in *Lexikon* 5, 255–256.

388. Pharaoh Haremhab in the latter half of the 14th century appointed priests and lay officials as judges (text in Pfluger, "The Edict of King Haremhab," 260–276). Apparently, his aim was to eliminate corruption and assure loyalty to the crown while simultaneously mending relations between the priests of Amun and the crown following the collapse of Akhenaten's Aten cult.

estates, etc.[389] Notably, technical proceedings were in the hands of professional court scribes.[390] Texts from the Third Intermediate and Saite periods continue to list judges of the *ḳnbt ʿ3t* of Thebes with priestly titles. By that time, however, the chief scribe instead of the vizier was in charge of the supreme court.[391]

Conclusions

Some tentative conclusions can be drawn concerning the title שפטים/שפט. Initially, it is evident that the term not only functions as a general designation for a figure of authority but is also the Hebrew title for judge. Although the social origin of the שפט is not always discernable, there are examples of שפטים chosen from the ranks of heads of families (2 Chr 19:8), שרים (Ex 18:21–22; Deut 1:15–16) and Levitical families (1 Chr 23:4; 26:29). Regardless of origin, at least in the monarchic period they appear to be government officials probably appointed by the king and answerable to him. But even during the monarchy, the שפטים do not replace the elders in their judicial roles entirely. Rather, like their Hittite and Mesopotamian counterparts, they often cooperate with them in the legal process.

On the matter of Jehoshaphat's judiciary, certain observations are noteworthy. Jehoshaphat's judicial organization should not be viewed as revolutionary but as one component of his administrative reorganization. Most importantly, there is insufficient evidence to support the notion that Jehoshaphat created the office of state-appointed judgeship or that he modeled Israel's judiciary after an Egyptian system. Several aspects of Israel's judiciary are present in other systems of the region, but no traceable lines of borrowing are visible. One common feature is the mixed lay and ecclesiastical composition of some courts, clearly manifest in Egyptian documents and evident to a lesser extent in Mesopotamian and Hittite sources.

K. שער – Gatekeeper

The last function-related title discussed in this study is that of gatekeeper, a position that could refer to either a military or civil office. But since the title שער is never directly associated with a military classification and may therefore signify a civil post, it is included.

---

389. Allam, "Egyptian Law Courts," 110–112.

390. See Chapter 4–B.

391. The title of an official of the great *ḳnbt*, *śr n t3 ḳnbt ʿ3t nt niwt*, "official of the great *ḳnbt* of the capital," is often combined with the title *it-nṯr*, "god's father." The priestly title seems to indicate that these judges were chosen from the clergy of Amun (H. de Meulenaere, "Notes de prosopographie thébaine," *CdE* 57 [1982]: 223–224; Allam, "Egyptian Law Courts," 115).

Hebrew Corpus

The designation שער (*š‘r*), "porter, gatekeeper," (pl. שערים, *š‘rym*), is derived from the noun שער, "gate." As a title it appears alone or with a qualifying noun denoting the structure to which the gate belongs. It is attested in the Bible primarily in conjunction with Temple personnel.[392] Since titles connected with Temple officials are outside the focus of this study, שערים in that context will only be mentioned if information about them can supplement knowledge of the civil officers. The title שער does occur twice in non-cultic settings, where it refers to porter(s) of city gates, once without and once with the qualifying noun "city": השער, "the gatekeeper" (2 Sam 18:26) and שער(י) העיר, "the gatekeeper(s) of the city" (2 Kgs 7:10–11). To date one unprovenienced inscription bearing the title שער has appeared on the antiquities market.[393]

Position of Gatekeeper

The title gatekeeper, often followed by a qualifying noun, is found in the corpus of titularies of all states in the region. Porters of city gates, palace gates and temple gates are the most common. Since the Jerusalem Temple was the focus of attention of the post-exilic writers of Ezra-Nehemiah and Chronicles, cultic personnel associated with it, including families of gatekeepers, are mentioned frequently. Obviously city gates, doorways to palaces, and other non-cult related structures also required gatekeepers. Therefore it is somewhat surprising that in non-cultic contexts the title שער appears so rarely in the Bible. When it does, however, as in the two cases of city gatekeepers, the roles of these functionaries are fairly clearly delineated.

The first of two unnamed porters of city gates is mentioned in the narrative recounting the end of Absalom's revolt (2 Sam 18). According to the account, David was sitting in the piazza between the inner and outer city gates, בין שני השערים, of Mahanaim awaiting news of the outcome of the battle between his troops and Absalom's (18:24).[394] A צופה, "watchman," who was standing on the

---

392. The gatekeepers of the Temple are identified both as Levites and non-Levites. In Ezra and Nehemiah they constitute an independent group of Temple personnel, non-Levites (e.g. Ezra 2:42, 70; 7:7; 10:24; Neh 7:72; 11:19; 13:5). In contrast, in Chronicles they are presented as Levites (1 Chr 23:3–5). For a discussion on the ancestry and organization of the Temple gatekeepers, see Japhet, *I & II Chronicles*, 214–217.

393. A bulla of unknown provenience that remains unauthenticated is inscribed with the designation שער plus a different qualifying noun: לעזריהו שער המסגר, "belonging to *‘zryhw* the porter of the prison." This precise title is unknown from the biblical record. For a discussion of the bulla, see N. Avigad, "Hebrew Seals and Sealings," *VTS* 40 (1986): 10 and Deutsch and Heltzer, *Forty*, 41–42).

394. At large cities an outer gate with towers led to a piazza which in turn led to an inner

watchtower of the gate and spotted a runner approaching the city inquired of the king whether to allow the runner to enter. Later, the watchman spotted another runner. This time, according to the MT, he reported it to השער, "the gatekeeper," rather than to the king (18:26). Possibly the watchman called to the gatekeeper the first time as well, and he (the gatekeeper) in turn requested instructions from David.[395] It is unclear whether the functions of the שער and the צופה were interchangeable, since manning the city gate could also entail similar activities as keeping watch from the tower. The second example of gatekeeper indicates that more than one was on duty at a time. This narrative deals with the adventure of a band of lepers isolated outside Samaria during one of the wars between Israel and Aram (2 Kgs 7).[396] The lepers, having discovered that the Arameans had abandoned their camp, returned to Samaria to inform the king. In order to convey their message, they call to שער העיר, "(the) gatekeeper of the city" (usually read שערי העיר, "(the) gatekeepers of the city," 7:10).[397] The שערים in turn report the information to the king (7:11). The procedure described in this account is comparable to the scenario recorded in 2 Sam 18. From the two episodes it is clear that gatekeepers functioned as guards and messengers on matters pertaining to the gate. They were the first group of officers that an outsider would encounter upon approaching a city. Entry to the city, however, may have required the permission of a higher authority.

Nothing is known from the biblical record about the organization, number, or hierarchy of the many gatekeepers whose services would have been required at the gates of urban centers. Certainly large cities, such as Jerusalem and Lachish, which featured an acropolis surrounded by secondary fortifications in addition to the main fortifications of the lower city, would have employed nu-

---

gate complex often consisting of six chambers (see Mazar, *Archaeology of the Land of the Bible*, 384, 428–429, figs. 9.10, 10.16). The scenario in 2 Sam 18 provides a *Sitz-im-Leben* for the canopied structure discovered between the outer and main inner gates at Tell Dan. The structure probably housed a seat that was occupied by the king or another dignitary presiding over events taking place at the city gate (cf. 2 Sam 19:9; A. Biran, *Biblical Dan* [Jerusalem: Israel Exploration Society; Hebrew Union College, 1994], 238–241, figs. 197–199, pl. 44).

395. An alternate possibility, following the LXX B, is that the word הַשֹּׁעֵר should be read הַשַּׁעַר, "the gate," implying that the watchman called to David who was sitting at the gate. Another option, following the LXX L, is to read מעל השער, "on the gate," thus referring to the place from which the watchman called (so McCarter, *II Samuel*, 398, 403). Since the MT reading is logical, there seems no reason to reject it.

396. The precise time-period of this account, the siege of Samaria, is uncertain because no Israelite king is named. Cogan and Tadmor suggest the reign of Jehoahaz in the last quarter of the ninth century as a possible date (*II Kings*, 85).

397. The reading שערי in place of שער is suggested by the subsequent plural form of להם, "to them," and by the usage of the plural, שערים, in verse 11 (so too the Peshitta and Targum).

merous gatekeepers. The same situation must have prevailed in and around palace complexes. In reference to Temple gatekeepers, the Chronicler states that they were supervised and organized by גברי השערים, "chief gatekeepers" (1 Chr 9:26). Probably overseers existed among the city and palace gatekeepers as well.

Ugaritic, Mesopotamian and Egyptian Evidence

In sources from Ugarit the term for gatekeeper(s) is *ṯǵr(m)*, in Ugaritic documents, and LÚ *atû*, in Akkadian texts. Title-bearers are attested individually or in groups; sometimes their PNs are included.[398] Occasionally the title *ṯǵr* is followed by a qualifying noun, for example, *ṯǵr hkl*, "gatekeeper of the palace."[399] In a dedicatory building inscription, an individual named *B'lṣdq*, who is designated *ṯǵr mlk*, "gatekeeper of the king," bears an additional title *skn bt mlk*, "steward of the house of the king": *b'lṣdq skn.bt mlk.ṯǵr mlk*. It is unclear whether this person held the two positions concurrently or at different times.[400] Apparently gatekeepers at Ugarit belonged to the circle of *bnš mlk*, receiving rations as royal dependents while serving at the royal court.[401]

In Akkadian, the designation for gatekeeper or doorkeeper is expressed by several terms: LÚ *atû*, LÚ *pētû* (LÚ.Ì.DU_8) and *mār abulli* (DUMU KÁ.GAL).[402] The title LÚ *atû* (LÚ.Ì.DU_8) is found in texts of varying genres and in different contexts. As an official title it is attested in administrative and legal texts. One administrative document from the Middle Babylonian period mentions the guard duty of a gatekeeper of prison doors.[403] From Neo-Assyrian texts it is

398. Rainey, "The Social Stratification of Ugarit," 150, 164). Heltzer, *Internal Organization*, 169. Rainey and Heltzer list a number of texts in which the title appears (e.g. *UT* 169:r. 5; 171:11; 300:r. 7; 1024:2; 1069:3.

399. In reference to two persons, *UT* 1056:8, 9.

400. RS 15.177. Layton interprets "gatekeeper" as a function of the *skn bt mlk*, citing as a "distant echo" the סכן in Isa 22, who opens and shuts with the key to the house of David ("The Steward in Ancient Israel," 644). Heltzer maintains that this text indicates that the gatekeeper could also function as the major-domo of the palace-economy (*Internal Organization*, 170). These connections between *skn* and *ṯǵr* are unconvincing, especially since the gatekeeper is widely known as a lesser functionary whose position is distinct from that of the *skn*. In the case of *b'lṣdq*, it seems more likely that he bears the title *ṯǵr* because he occupied that position previously and is still recognized by that appellation.

401. *UT* 171:11; 1024:r. 2.

402. *CAD* A/2, 516–518. The term *atû* is of uncertain origin, possibly representing a Sumerian loanword (*AHW* 1, 88). The term *pētû* is derived from the verb *petû/patû*, "to open" (*AHW* 2, 858–861). The title *mār abulli* contains the Akkadian term for "gate" or "entrance," *abullu* (*CAD* A/1, 82–88).

403. *BE* 14 129:5 (in *CAD* A/2, 517).

clear that gatekeepers belonged to the category of royal officials. In a list of court personnel from Nineveh, three persons are entitled LÚ *atû*; two others appear on a list of lodgings for officials.[404] Another Neo-Assyrian list of officials includes a LÚ.Ì.DU_8 *ša qanni*, "gatekeeper of the temple/palace complex."[405] A Neo-Babylonian text names the gatekeeper of a *bīt šutummu*, "storehouse."[406] In Assyria there existed a hierarchy of gatekeepers, some attained the rank *rab atû*, "chief gatekeeper."[407]

In Neo-Assyrian texts from Nimrud, gatekeepers are most often designated by the title *pētiūte* (*pētû*) and *rab* (chief) *pētiūte*. They are mentioned together with other municipal officials such as the magistrates of the city (*ḫazannu*, *ša muḫḫi āli*, *rab āli*), the town elders (*šībūti*), and the city scribe (*ṭupšar āli*).[408]

The third term for gatekeeper, *mār abulli* or *rab abulli*, is found primarily in Old Babylonian documents. In one case the *mār abulli* acts as a messenger, delivering a tablet.[409] In another case, the gatekeepers, designated *ša abulli*, collect a gate toll.[410] One Neo-Assyrian text designates a gate official by the title *rab abulli*. That particular gatekeeper is associated with the chariotry, perhaps in the capacity of a guard.[411]

The Egyptian term for gatekeeper or doorkeeper is *iry-ʿ3*, literally "belonging to the door."[412] It is widely attested in New Kingdom texts but is traceable to the Middle Kingdom. The title is found in reference to persons serving in private households as well as functionaries in temples and at the royal court.[413] In the palace complex doorkeepers appear in the reception chamber, the harem,

404. *ADD* 857 ii 24, r. 22, 28; 860 i 17, ii r. 4 (in F.M. Fales and J.N. Postgate, *Imperial Administrative Records, Part I, Palace and Temple Administration* [Helsinki: Helsinki University Press, 1992], 9–10, 16, 18).

405. H.W.F. Saggs, "The Nimrud Letters 1952 Part II," *Iraq* 17 (1955): 139, no. 20:32.

406. *YOS* 7 78:3 (in *CAD* A/2, 517).

407. For example, *ADD* 372 rev. 11; 425 rev 14; 453 rev. 12 (in Kwasman and Parpola, *Legal Transactions of the Royal Court of Nineveh, Part I*, 279, 228). These chief gatekeepers are listed among other officials as witnesses of real estate transactions.

408. Kinnier-Wilson, *Nimrud Wine Lists*, 7.

409. *CT* 2 19:9, 26 (in *CAD* A/1, 88). Although this official is not explicitly mentioned in the Laws of Eshnuna (nos. 51 & 52) in connection with regulations governing the checking of slaves entering and leaving the city gate, the implication is that gatekeepers functioned in that capacity as well (Roth, *Law Collections from Mesopotamia and Asia Minor*, 57).

410. *VAS* 7 54:10 (in A. Goetze,"Old Babylonian Documents from Sippar in the Collection of the Catholic University of America," *JCS* 11 [1951]: 36, no 28:6).

411. *ABL* 493 r. 17 (in *CAD* A/1, 88).

412. The adjective *iry* is the first element in a number of titularies that is compounded with different nouns indicating an area of jurisdiction (Faulkner, *Middle Egyptian*, 25, 37; Černý, *A Community of Workmen*, 161).

413. Gardiner, *Onomastica* I, 90*.

the treasury, the barn, and, in the offices of officials such as the vizier. Texts that describe the functions of the *iry-ʿꜣ* indicate that title bearers were guards, sometimes patrolling workers. In artistic representations the doorkeepers are often depicted with weapons in hand.[414] At the workmen community of Deir el-Medina at the Theban necropolis, two and occasionally three of these functionaries were employed.[415] The title *ḥry iry-ʿꜣ*, "chief doorkeeper," is also attested. Doorkeepers at Deir el-Medina were low-ranking officials who were not considered part of the workmen gang. Some apparently attained higher positions as guardians of the tomb, a distinct title. Notably, the doorkeepers acted as messengers, court bailiffs, and distributors of supplies for the workmen.[416]

Conclusions

The definition of the Hebrew title שער and the functions of title bearers seem relatively clear. Primarily, the duties of this official involved guarding entrance ways, those belonging to cities and to smaller complexes such as palaces and the Temple. This information accords well with data from Mesopotamian and from Egyptian records. Apparently, though, gatekeepers also carried out other functions, such as delivering messages and distributing goods. From the extant material, it cannot be determined, however, what rank these functionaries held in the Israelite administrative hierarchy.

414. W. Helck, "Türhüter" in *Lexikon* 6, 787–789.
415. Černý, *A Community of Workmen*, 161–165.
416. Černý, *A Community of Workmen*, 168–173.

5
Miscellaneous Designations

A. סכן/סכנת – Household Steward, Personal Attendant

Biblical Evidence

A few general designations that do not seem to fit the classification "official title" appear in connection with courtiers or other persons involved in the monarchic organization. The terms סכן and סכנת fall into this category. The participle סכן, feminine סכנת, is attested in the Bible twice as an appellation for persons connected to the king: Shebnah, the minister over the royal house, is referred to as a סכן by Isaiah (Isa 22:15); Abishag, David's personal attendant, is called a סכנת (1 Kgs 1:2, 4). These substantives are derived from the verb סכן, "give or derive benefit."[1] As noted in the discussion on the אשר על הבית, the title סכן, in association with the royal official Shebnah, has elicited lengthy discussions, primarily in light of cognate titles in Ugaritic, Aramaic, and Akkadian. The definition of סכנת as a designation for Abishag, albeit less controversial, is also debated. An evaluation of the title in connection to Israelite officialdom seems pertinent.

The role of Abishag as a סכנת to the aged David is spelled out in the text. She is engaged to keep the king warm, that is, to attend to his personal needs and to sleep with him.[2] Two expressions portray her status: ועמדה לפני המלך ותהי לו סכנת, "she will minister to (literally – stand before) the king and be a *sknt* to him" (1 Kgs 1:2). The phrase לעמד לפני, "to stand before," is commonly used of courtiers in attendance on a king.[3] A parallel term, לשרת, "to minister to, serve" appears with the second mention of סכנת in reference to Abishag: ותשרתהו ותהי למלך סכנת, "she ministered to him and became a *sknt* to the king" (1:4). Based on the context, סכנת must mean something like "personal attendant." Alternate sugges-

1. *BDB*, 698; *HALOT* 2, 755.

2. Gray, *I and II Kings*, 77.

3. The expression describes the status of the זקנים vis-à-vis Solomon and the ילדים vis-à-vis Rehoboam (1 Kgs 12:6, 8). The equivalent phrase, with the same idiomatic meaning, in Akkadian is *ina pān* (PN) *i/uzuzzu*, "to stand before (someone)" (*AHW* 1, 409).

tions, postulating that Abishag was in charge of the administration of the household, are not supported by the text.[4] There are no indications whatsoever that she held managerial duties relating to palace supplies or personnel. On the other hand, as a personal attendant to the king who ministered to him day and night, her status was probably higher and her responsibilities greater than those of a simple handmaiden, a נערה.

The term סכן in Isa 22:15 is more difficult to explain because it is found in parallel construction to the title אשר על הבית. However, as shown in the discussion on the אשר על הבית, the two designations need not be interpreted as synonymous. Nevertheless, scholars generally consider סכן in Isaiah as a *hapax legomenon* synonymous to אשר על הבית. Their position is predicated on the assumption that the use of the term in the Bible reflects knowledge of an older West Semitic title, *skn/sākinu*, seemingly a cognate appellation for a high royal official.[5]

The Root skn *in Ugaritic, Aramaic and Phoenician*

Ugaritic *skn/ sākinu* (in alphabetic texts/in Akkadian texts) is widely attested in titles of various types of officials. Its underlying meaning is derived from the verb *skn/sakānu,* a cognate of Hebrew סכן.[6] In the Akkadian texts from Ugarit, a seeming semantically equivalent title but one derived from a different verbal root, *škn/šakānu,* "establish, organize, appoint," appears as LÚ.MAŠKIM/LÚ. GAR-*kin* (= *šakin*).[7] The title is usually followed by a genitive noun defining the

4. Yeivin posits that סכן and סכנת are derived from the noun מסכנות, "store-places." Consequently, functionaries so entitled should be viewed as household stewards ("Peqidut," 547–548). O. Loretz thinks that Abishag held an administrative title ("Ugaritisch *skn* - *sknt* und hebräisch *skn* - *sknt*," *ZAW* 94 [1982]: 126–127). M.J. Mulder suggests that she functioned as a substitute for the aging Bathsheba ("Versuch zur Deutung von *sokènèt* in Kön. I 2,4," *VT* 22 [1972]: 53–54). Both Loretz and Mulder base their conclusions on Ugaritic *sknt.* However, the Ugaritic text they use as a model (*KTU* 4.135:1–2) simply records a debt of 20 shekels of silver for a *sknt* from Siyanu. It does not delineate her functions.

5. Mettinger, *Solomonic State Officials,* 71; Rüterswörden, *Beamten der israelitischen Königszeit,* 80–85; Layton, "The Steward in Ancient Israel," 647–648; Avishur and Heltzer, *Studies on the Royal Administration,* 58–59.

6. *HALOT* 2, 755; *AHW* 2, 1011; *CAD* S, 76–77. The verb *sakānu* is attested in the Amarna letters from Jerusalem (e.g. *EA* 285:26; 286:35, 38; 287:13, 17, 40; 288:48).

7. The reading LÚ.GAR-*kin* (*kin* = a phonetic complement) instead of ŠA.KIN, as a pseudo-logogram, is preferred more recently (R. Borger, *ABZ,* 207). Its Akkadian rendering, *šakin,* is a noun in the construct state not a participle. For a discussion, see *UT,* 490 (*skn*); *AHW* 3, 1141 (*šaknu*); *CAD* Š/1, 116 (*šakānu*), 180 (*šaknu*); A. Rainey, "LÚ MAŠKIM at Ugarit," *Or NS* 35 (1966): 428; "Observations on Ugaritic Grammar," *UF* 3 (1971): 171; "More Gleanings from Ugarit," *IOS* 5 (1975): 26; H. Kümmel, "Ugaritica Hethitica," *UF* 1 (1969): 160. Rainey notes that while in the Amarna letters *rābiṣu* is the reading for LÚ.

realm of the office. Rainey and Heltzer examine these various terms as part of their study of Ugaritic royal administration.[8] Three classes of officials can be distinguished: (1) LÚ.GAR KUR/*šakin māti*, "*šakin* of the land (of Ugarit)";[9] (2) *skn bt mlk*, "*skn* of the house of the king"; and (3) *skn qrt/āli*, "*skn* of the town."

The first class of officials, the *šakin māti*, was the highest minister of the kingdom after the king. He frequently functioned in the diplomatic realm, as attested in correspondence between this Ugarit official and neighboring kings or other similarly entitled ministers of state.[10] His role encompassed judicial and police matters as well, the latter often in connection with foreign commercial relations.[11] The position of the *šakin māti* closely resembles that of a "vizier," an observation already made by Alt.[12]

The second category of Ugaritic *skn*, the *skn bt mlk*, designates a palace official, perhaps a royal major-domo.[13] The title is attested in a dedicatory building inscription: *bʿlṣdq skn.bt mlk.ṯġr mlk*, "PN *skn* of the house of the king, gatekeeper of the king."[14] In an Akkadian document, an official named Matenu is called "*šakin* of the king."[15] Rüterswörden notes that in a second text Matenu is designated "*abarakku* of the king," an Assyrian title for steward.[16] A more specific

---

MAŠKIM, *rābiṣu* and *sākinu* may be two terms for the same type of official ("LÚ MAŠKIM at Ugarit," 426–428).

8. Rainey, "The Social Stratification of Ugarit," 92–96; Heltzer, *Internal Organization*, 141–152.

9. It is unclear whether in Ugarit LÚ.MAŠKIM/LÚ.GAR-*kin* (of X) was pronounced *šakin*, following the Akkadian, or *sākin*, following the Ugaritic. That *sākinu* = *šakin māti* is evident from *PRU* III 15.182:6, 10, where the title appears once as a logogram and once spelled syllabically.

10. For example, *PRU* III, 11.730; 19.19; *PRU* IV, 17.425; 17.393 (listed in Rainey, "The Social Stratification of Ugarit," 95–96; Heltzer, *Internal Organization*, 142).

11. Heltzer, *Internal Organization*, 145–146.

12. A. Alt, "Hohe Beamte in Ugarit" in *Studia Orientalia* 19 (1954): 1–11.

13. Heltzer, *Internal Organization*, 149–150. The title *šakin bīt šarrati*, "*šakin* of the queen," is attested as well (e.g. RS.8.208).

14. RS 15.177. Layton interprets gatekeeper as a function of the *skn bt mlk*, citing as a "distant echo" the סכן in Isa 22, who opens and shuts with the key to the house of David ("The Steward in Ancient Israel," 644). This connection is unconvincing since the *ṯgr(m)*, "gatekeeper(s)," is a known, lesser functionary whose title is widely attested. Possibly *bʿlṣdq* bears the title "gatekeeper" because he occupied that position previously and is still known by that appellation.

15. RS 17.325.

16. RS 17.86+241+208; Rüterswörden, *Beamten der israelitischen Königszeit*, 84–85. The official named Matenu appears to be the same person in both texts (*Ugaritica* 5, 262–264).

form of this title is also attested: *šakin ekallim*, "overseer (steward) of the palace."[17]

The third class of *skn*, the *šakin qrt/āli*, exercised power locally over a town or group of villages.[18] Whereas the functions of persons entitled *skn/saknu* are not always determinable, the Ugaritic material proves that the designation was incorporated in the titles of distinct classes of officials.

The title *skn bt mlk* also appears in an eighth- or ninth-century Aramaic inscription from Hamath: אדנלרם סכן [ב]ית מלכה, "PN *skn* of the house of the king."[19] In a mid-eighth-century Phoenician inscription from Cyprus, the title *skn* is written in construct state with a GN and is associated with a royal official: ...ו סכן קרתחדשת עבד חרם מלך צדנם, "PN *skn* of *qrthdšt* (Cypriot Carthage) servant of Hiram king of the Sidonians.[20] The *skn* of this Tyrian colony on Cyprus seems to be a local governor in the service of Hiram II king of Tyre (739–730).[21] These examples affirm the survival of the title *skn* into the first millennium.

Akkadian šaknu

As noted above, the Akkadian term corresponding to *skn/sākinu* is *šaknu*, "an appointed person." Like the title *skn/sākinu*, the Assyrian and Babylonian title *šaknu* can designate distinct classes of officials. Title-bearers fall into two main categories: (1) provincial governor, the highest office in the provincial authority, and (2) subordinates of the governor or of other high officials.[22] The governor *šaknu* had jurisdiction over a certain geographical area specified in his titulary: PN *šaknu ša* GN.[23] His authority could entail civic and military responsi-

---

17. *PRU* 3:112. The person bearing this title, Takulinu, also appears in the Ugarit letter from Aphek where he holds the higher title of governor, *šakin māti*. Apparently he was promoted (I. Singer, "Takuḫlinu and Ḫaya: Two Governors in the Ugarit Letter from Tel Aphek," *TA* 10 [1983]: 15).

18. Heltzer, *Internal Organization*, 150–152.

19. *KAI* 203.

20. G. Cooke, *A Text-Book of North Semitic Inscriptions* (Oxford: Clarendon Press, 1903), 52 no. 11. The name *Qrthdšt*, literally "new city," was later given to the North African city of Carthage.

21. Aubet, *Phoenicians and the West*, 42–43, 122.

22. *CAD* Š/1, 191.

23. The role of the *šaknu* as provincial governor sounds somewhat similar to the position of the LÚ.MAŠKIM (*rābiṣu/sukina*) mentioned in the Amarna letters. From the Jerusalem letters of Abdi-hiba, for example, we know that Addaia was the Egyptian provincial governor over southern Canaan (*EA* 285:24); he was succeeded by Pauru (*EA* 287:45). Both these men are designated *rābiṣ šarri*, "*rābiṣu* of the king (Pharaoh)." Apparently, Syria-Palestine was divided into geographical zones, with an Egyptian governor answerable to the Pharaoh over each.

bilities.[24] Titleholders of the second category include individuals who functioned as managers of large households or palaces, such as the *šaknu* of the palace at Nuzi, and various military officers, such as the *šaknu* in charge of cavalry, stables, or troops in general. But in its widest usage, the term *šaknu* designates officials of lesser rank.[25]

Conclusions

Based on the evidence it appears that the limited internal biblical evidence only supports a general definition of the designation סכן. The usages of סכנת in the book of Kings and סכן in Isaiah suggest that this title may have been a technical term for a range of court functionaries. Akkadian *šaknu* is used similarly. A clear understanding of סכן in Isaiah, however, is somewhat blurred because the term, while not obviously synonymous to אשר על הבית, is utilized to depict a person holding that office. Since non-Hebrew West Semitic usages of the term *skn/sākinu* sometimes indicate a stewardship of sorts, this meaning was probably intended for סכן in Isaiah, but not necessarily as a specification for the top ranking minister. As shown, non- Hebrew attestations of *skn* encompass a wide semantic expanse and the significance of any particular title is always dependent on the genitive constructed to this term. Isaiah's derogatory tone vis-à-vis Shebnah suggests that his application of סכן should not be understood in its more prestigious connotation.

B. נער/נערה – Estate Steward, Squire, Handmaid

Another general designation—one also held by certain court attendants and administrators of royal estates—is the term נער/נערה. The term נער (*n'r*), plural נערים (*n'rym*), has a wide semantic range that can be divided into two main categories: one signifying age or a stage of life and the other indicative of occupation or social status. Some common definitions of נער include: "boy, youth, servant, and retainer." The feminine form, נערה (*n'rh*), plural נערות (*n'rwt*), is similarly defined: "girl, young woman, female attendant, and handmaid."[26] These broad classifications, however, do not encompass the many variant usages of the designation which can be broken down into more specialized

24. R.A. Henshaw, "The Office of *šaknu* in Neo-Assyrian Times," *JAOS* 87 (1967): 519, 525.

25. *CAD* Š/1, 190–191; J.N. Postgate, "The Place of the *šaknu* in Assyrian Government," *AnSt* 30 (1980): 67–76.

26. *BDB*, 654–655; *HALOT* 2, 707–708. In one case נערה, a wife of Ashhur, is a PN (1 Chr 4:5–6). The abstract forms נער, נערות, נערים are defined as "youth."

meanings. Usually the term נער, a generic designation rather than a function-related title, is not included in studies on government officials. But as will be shown, several examples in the biblical text and epigraphic material indicate that persons entitled נער/נערה served the king or his ministers in some capacity, either inside or outside the palace complex.

Biblical Usage

As an indicator of age, the designation נער can refer to an infant (e.g. Moses in Exod 2:6; Samson in Judg 13:8), a young child (e.g. Samuel in 1 Sam 1:24), or a youth in his teens (e.g. Ishmael in Gen 21:12; Joseph in 37:2; Josiah in 2 Chr 34:3). The feminine, נערה, commonly alludes to a young woman of marriageable age (e.g. Gen 24:16; 34:3; Deut 22:15, 23–29; Judg 21:12; Esth 2:2–4).[27] Frequently, the term נער is used opposite זקן, "elder," in a merism construction to express totality, "all the people": מנער ועד זקן, "from youngsters to old people" (Gen 19:4; Josh 6:21; Esth 3:13).[28]

In a few instances, the term נער/נערה is suggestive of a person's inexperience in a certain role rather than a mark of age or status. Solomon calls himself a נער קטן, "a young *n'r*," when praying to God for guidance early in his reign (1 Kgs 3:7).[29] While one purpose of his diminutive self-evaluation is to convey modesty, the description of the huge task of kingship and his own inexperience in that area as compared to his father reflects reality. Similarly, when David offers to battle Goliath, Saul attempts to dissuade him by saying that he (David) is a נער, while Goliath has been a man of war since נעריו, "his youth" (1 Sam 17:33). In this case too, the designation נער appears to refer more to David's lack of experience as a warrior than to his young age.[30]

In other usages נער/נערה may be indicative of a son's or daughter's dependent status within the family. Jesse's sons living in their father's household and David's sons at court are called נערים (1 Sam 16:11; 2 Sam 13:32; 14:21).[31] H.P. Stähli

27. Frequently the qualifier בתולה, "virgin," or מארשה, "betrothed," follows the term נערה.

28. Contrast J. MacDonald, who understands that expression as a military designation ("The Status and Role of the Na'ar in Israelite Society," *JNES* 35 [1976]: 166–168).

29. Cf. L. Stager, who understands the phrase נער קטן as signifying Solomon in the role of youngest son of David and Bathsheba ("The Archaeology of the Family in Ancient Israel," *BASOR* 260 [1985]: 26). H.P. Stähli sees Solomon's self-evaluation as a product of the wisdom literature school (*Knabe, Jüngling, Knecht: Untersuchung zum Begriff* נער *im alten Testament* [Frankfort: Peter Lang, 1978], 113–117).

30. MacDonald posits that Saul's reference to David as a נער acknowledges his rank as a soldier, admittedly at the beginning of his career ("The Status and Role of the Na'ar," 160). Based on the context of the narrative this explanation is unacceptable.

31. Although the ages of these נערים are not stated, from the context it does not seem that they are children.

restricts this usage of נער to unmarried sons who have not yet established a household.[32] But as seen in the case of Absalom, who is called a נער despite having fathered three sons and a daughter (2 Sam 14:21, 27; 18:29), bachelorhood is not a prerequisite.[33] The circumstances of a daughter designated as a נערה seem to be comparable. A woman residing with her parents is known as a נערה (Deut 22:15–16, 28–29), although sometimes it is obscure whether the term signifies her status as a dependent of her father or merely denotes that she is of marriageable age. In addition, on occasion a woman is called a נערה even after marriage, albeit in cases where her status is liminal, for example, when the marriage is in limbo because of her questionable virginity (22:13–22) or in the case when a woman returns to her father (the Levite's concubine in Judg 19).[34]

Most often, the term נער/נערים or נערה/נערות designates a person's occupation or role in society unrelated to age. Generally the title refers to some type of attendant in the service of someone of higher standing.[35] Several נערים and נערות attend kings or other members of the royal family. Examples include: Pharaoh's daughter (Exod 2:5); the princes Amnon (2 Sam 13:17) and Absalom (2 Sam 13:28–29); Sennacherib (2 Kgs 19:6); Ahasuerus (Esth 2:2; 6:3); and Esther (Esth 4:4, 6).[36] As servants at court these נערים/נערות should be classified as royal functionaries.[37] Although their specific duties are not always delineated, they

---

32. Stähli, *Knabe, Jüngling, Knecht*, 96–100.

33. Stager observes that once the head of a household dies the son who assumes his role is no longer designated a נער ("The Archaeology of the Family in ancient Israel," 26). This observation, however, may be a generalization. For example, Jeroboam is referred to as a נער when Solomon takes note of his superiority in the work-force, although earlier in the text the writer states that Jeroboam is the son of a widow and as such, of independent status (1 Kgs 11:26, 28). An additional reference calling him a גבור חיל could indicate that he was a person of means, having inherited property from his father (Gray, *I and II Kings*, 294). Alternatively, it could signify that he was a mighty warrior.

34. Notably, Ruth is called a נערה, once by Boaz's overseer who knew that she came with Naomi but may not have known that she was previously married (Ruth 2:6) and again when Boaz is officially named as the redeemer who will marry Ruth (4:12). In these cases too the status of the נערה is liminal.

35. A form of the term משרת, "one who serves," is sometimes found in apposition to נער (e.g. 2 Sam 13:17; Esth 2:2; 6:3). MacDonald claims that in general נערים were of high birth ("The Status and Role of the Na'ar," 147, 150). However, since their lineage is rarely revealed, this is only an assumption.

36. Some of these נערים may carry a military title, see below.

37. Other נערים and נערות mentioned in the Bible minister to non-royal individuals of high status and/or wealth. Abraham has נערים in his service who accompany him on his trips (Gen 22:3). Baalam the seer travels with נערים (Num 22:22). The blind Samson is guided by a נער. Saul, as a member of an important Benjaminite family, roams the countryside with his נער (1 Sam 9:27). Likewise, David's wandering band includes נערים who function as

all operate in close proximity to their master or mistress. Absalom's נערים, for example, were armed guards who upon their master's order murdered the crown prince Amnon.[38]

Occasionally, laborers and overseers of estates are called נערים or נערות. Boaz's field-workers, both male and female, are so designated (Ruth 2:8–9, 21, 23). In two cases נערים hold supervisory positions: the overseer of Boaz's harvesters (Ruth 2:5–6) and the steward of Saul's estate, Zibah (2 Sam 9:9–11; 16:1–4; 19:18).[39] Not much is known of Boaz's unnamed נער and his duties seem to be in the private realm. More information is available on Zibah. He is the father of 15 sons, which certifies his maturity, and he manages 20 עבדים, "servants," a sizable household (2 Sam 9:9). As the administrator of Mephibosheth's property he cultivates the land and sends provisions to his master while he (Mephibosheth) dines at court at David's table (9:10). Later, when David flees Jerusalem in the face of Absalom's rebels, Zibah provides supplies for David and his men (16:1-4). Clearly, Zibah is a powerful figure who appears to have full control of Saul's estate. His position may be categorized as that of a royal functionary, a steward of royal lands.[40] Thus the biblical evidence indicates that the designation נער can be applied both to higher ranked personnel as well as to mere attendants of the royal family. The archaeological record also seems to support this contention.

---

scouts and runners (25:5). Joshua as Moses' assistant is called a נער (Exod 33:11). Moses also has נערים who assist as cult officiants (24:5). The prophet Elishah has a נער, Gehazi, who assists him and acts as a messenger (2 Kgs 4:12). A נער of a priest collects the offerings (1 Sam 2:13, 15). Women of affluent families, such as Rebekah and Abigail, are accompanied by נערות, who presumably tend to their needs (Gen 24:61; 1 Sam 25:42).

38. The designation נערים is commonly found in military contexts in reference to soldiers. In this category are included: David's fighting men (1 Sam 21:3; 25:8–9; 2 Sam 1:15; 4:12); Abner's and Joab's elite troops (2 Sam 2:14); a unit of 400 Amalekite warriors (1 Sam 30:17. Their designation, איש-נער, usually translated "young men," more likely signifies a special unit or type of soldier [MacDonald, "The Status and Role of the Na'ar," 163]); and the soldiers of provincial governors (1 Kgs 20:14–19). Sometimes, the particular role of the נער in the military is indicated by a qualifying word or phrase, for example, נשא כלים, "armor-bearer" (Judg 9:54; 1 Sam 14:1; 2 Sam 18:15) and מרגלים, "scouts" (Josh 6:23). In the case of Amnon's נערים, it is unclear whether they belonged to a special military unit or were simply the prince's armed guards.

39. J. MacDonald considers the נער who accompanied the Levite and his concubine in this category ("The Role and Status of the *ṣuḫāru* in the Mari Correspondence," *JAOS* 96 [1976]: 60). He posits that he was a steward in charge of the Levite's property (Judg 19:19). This connection, however, is not explicit, and the נער is simply mentioned together with the other members of the party.

40. It is quite possible that Zibah was appointed steward of Saul's property while Saul was still king.

Epigraphic Evidence

Hebrew inscriptions containing the title נער consist of provenienced and unprovenienced pieces. The provenienced items include one ink inscription with two such title-bearers and four *lmlk* type handles impressed with an identical personal seal.[41] In each case the formula that appears is PN the *n'r* of PN. The inscribed potsherd, Arad no. 110, was discovered along with other pieces of the same jar outside the fort. It is dated paleographically to the beginning of the sixth century. The context of the find, several sherds from one container, indicates that the inscription is not a true ostracon but rather a jar label, that is, a message written on a complete jar. The writing consists of two lines, the first mentions שמיה משלם נער אלנתן, "*šmyh* [son of] *mšlm* the *n'r* of *'lntn*," and the second מכי נער גדליה, "*mky* the *n'r* of *gdlyh*."[42] Since the two נערים listed on the jar served different men, it seems unlikely that they (the נערים) sent the jar. On the other hand, they may have been assigned to Arad for service, and the jar was shipped to them by their overlords from a central location, perhaps Jerusalem.[43] Interestingly, the names אלנתן and גדליה belong to important royal officials of that time.[44] Any association between those officials and the names on this inscription, however, is purely conjectural.

More significant information can be derived from the seal impression לאליקם נער יוכן, "belonging to *'lyqm* the *n'r* of *ywkn*," stamped on the four jar handles, two unearthed at Tell Beit Mirsim, one at Beth Shemesh and another at Ramat Raḥel.[45] These handles, identified as belonging to *lmlk* jars, are assigned to

---

41. The formula PN נער PN also appears on four unprovenienced seals (see Table A-2; *WSS*, nos. 24–26; Deutsch and Heltzer, *Forty*, 51–53). In addition, an unprovenienced ostracon includes the title נער plus a PN among a list of names (Deutsch and Heltzer, *New Epigraphic Evidence*, 92–102).

42. A. Rainey, "Three Additional Texts" in *Arad Inscriptions*, 122–123.

43. Stager suggests that these two נערים were at Arad on military or other governmental duty ("The Archaeology of the Family in ancient Israel," 25–26). The second line of the inscription shows a *qof* of what could be the first letter of another name following the PN גדליה. It is unclear, however, whether the missing word is the patronym of גדליה or the name of a third individual.

44. As already noted by Rainey ("Three Additional Texts," 122–123), the possibilities include the following: Elnathan father of Nehushta mother of Jehoiachin (2 Kgs 24:8); Elnathan son of Achbor (Jer 36:12); אלנתן father of כניהו the army commander (Lachish Letter no. 3); Gedaliah son of Pashhur (Jer 38:1); Gedaliah son of Ahikam (2 Kgs 25:22; Jer 40:5, not cited by Rainey). In the case of Elnathan, where a patronym appears only once, the aforementioned references can belong to one person or several.

45. W.F. Albright, *The Excavation of Tell Beit Mirsim I: The Pottery of the First Three Campaigns* (*AASOR* 12; New Haven, 1932), 78, pl. 40:5; *The Excavation of Tell Beit Mirsim III: The Iron Age* (*AASOR* 21–22; New Haven, 1943), 66–67, figs 5–6; E. Grant and G.E. Wright, *Ains Shems Excavations V* (Haverford, 1939), 80, fig. 10a:2; Y. Aharoni, *Excavations at Ramat Raḥel:*

the reign of Hezekiah in the last quarter of the eighth century.[46] The seal of אליקם is one of several personal seal-impressions on handles that conform to those of storage jar style no. 484. Jars of this type regularly bear stamps with a royal symbol on one or more of their four handles and occasionally a personal seal-impression as well. Only in the case of אליקם, however, is the PN on the stamp followed by a title.[47] Despite the general absence of titles, current scholarship holds that the individuals whose names appear on the jar handles were associated with the monarchic state-organization and perhaps in some way with the *lmlk* project.[48] If this theory is correct, then אליקם the נער of יוכן must also have functioned in some administrative capacity.

Any reconstruction of the role of אליקם should be understood as conjectural due to the lack of concrete evidence. Still, bits of data gleaned from the Bible and the epigraphic material produce a tentative picture that deserves attention. Recently P. Bordreuil and F. Israel suggested that the owners of the seals inscribed לאליקם נער יוכן and לאליקם עבד המלך and Elyakim the minister over the royal house under Hezekiah (2 Kgs 18:18) were all one and the same person. They posit that the three titles represent Elyakim's promotion in the administrative hierarchy, from נער to עבד to אשר על הבית.[49] Although the seal of אליקם with the title עבד is not considered in this study because it is unprovenienced, still the observation that one person named אליקם was promoted may be valid, based on the remain-

---

Seasons 1961–1962 (Rome, 1964), 33, fig. 37:6, pl. 40:4. The two handles from Tell Beit Mirsim (nos. 623 & 860) belong to two separate storage jars. Each of the אליקם handles was found together with *lmlk* handles of the two-winged variety stamped למלך חברן, "*lmlk* Hebron." Based on size, shape, and color of clay, each אליקם handle was matched with a *lmlk* handle (no. 623 with no. 580; no. 860 with no. 867) apparently originating from the same vessel (D. Ussishkin, "Royal Judean Storage Jars and Private Seal Impressions," *BASOR* 223 [1976]: 6–11).

46. Ussishkin, "Royal Judean Storage Jars and Private Seal Impressions," 6–13. Ussishkin illustrates convincingly that the אליקם handles, like others impressed with PNs, belong to *lmlk* jars. Originally W.F. Albright dated the handles to the beginning of the sixth century to the reign of Jehoiachin ("The Seal of Eliakim and the Latest Preexilic History of Judah, with Some Observations on Ezekiel," *JBL* 51 [1932]: 84, 101–103). His dating was based on the assumption that יוכן, a hypocoristicon of Jehoiachin, should be identified with the penultimate king of Judah. The נער ,אליקם was therefore the steward in charge of his royal estate. In general scholars adopted Albright's mistaken dating and it is still found in works as recent as 1993 (Ahlström, *History of Ancient Palestine*, 762).

47. An unprovenienced handle that bears a seal-impression with a PN and the title בן המלך has been linked to the *lmlk* jars. This association, however, is unproven (see Chapter 3–A).

48. See Chapter 6 – *LMLK* Impressions.

49. P. Bordreuil and F. Israel, "À propos de la carrière d'Elyaqim: du page au majordome (?)," *Semitica* 41/42 (1991–1992): 81–87.

ing evidence (from נער to אשר על הבית). One reason to associate the two attestations of the name with one person is that the PN אליקם is not especially common in the Hebrew onomastica of the eighth century. In fact it does not reappear in the Bible until the latter half of the seventh century (2 Kgs 23:34), and of the three other seal owners bearing that name, none of their seals are dated to the eighth century.[50]

Furthermore, as shown from the biblical examples, a נער could be the steward of a large estate or an overseer of agricultural workers. These responsibilities certainly would help to prepare a minister to take charge of the royal compound.

Since the stamp of אליקם the נער appears on *lmlk* storage jars, an association must also be established between the role of a נער and the *lmlk* enterprise. In addition, יוכן, the superior of אליקם, according to the seal, must fit into the picture as well, possibly as a high royal functionary linked to the project. A hint pertaining to the latter may exist in the Bible. Notably, the overseer of tithes in the reign of Hezekiah is a Levite named כנניהו, "Conaniah" (2 Chr 31:12). Since the name יוכן can be a hypocoristicon of כנניהו, in this case the two names may represent the same individual.[51] Although the identification of יוכן, the superior of אליקם, with the Levite Conaniah is conjectural, especially since his patronymic is lacking, the time-frame and circumstances support the connection.

The Chronicler recounts that following Hezekiah's religious reformation the people in their zealousness contributed an overabundance of tithes (agricultural products, wine, oil, and sacrificial animals). What could not be consumed by the clergy was heaped in great mounds that grew so large that Hezekiah ordered storehouses to be prepared in or by the Temple to accommodate the provisions (2 Chr 31:5–11). Interestingly, this massive collection is the only one recorded for the period of the Divided Monarchy; its unparalleled achievement is reminiscent of Hezekiah's extensive *lmlk* operation.[52] Possibly, the account in Chronicles actually is based on records of the *lmlk* enterprise, while its religious coloring reflects the ideology of the Chronicler's own time. In that case, Conaniah the overseer, whose name appears on the seal of אליקם as יוכן, could be an appointee of Hezekiah charged over a major aspect(s) of the *lmlk* project, probably in Jerusalem. Simultaneously, his name on *lmlk* handles could indi-

50. *WSS*, nos. 69, 437, 438.

51. The roots כון and כנן are interchangeable (*BDB*, 487; on the relationship of ע"ו and ע"ע verbs see, *GKC*, 219). Another form of the name Conaniah is Jehoiachin. Outside the book of Kings, alternate forms of יהויכין include: כניהו (Jer 22:24, 28; 37:1), יכניהו (Jer 24:1; 27:20), יכניה (1 Chr 3:16–17) and יויכין (Ezek 1:2).

52. For an in depth discussion, see Chapter 6 – *LMLK* Impressions.

cate that he was a recipient of a royal land grant.[53] His subordinate, אליקם, would have held certain administrative responsibilities connected to production, packaging, and shipping of the produce from its estate of origin.

The fact that a נער owned a seal bearing that title implies that he was not a mere servant or attendant. One use for the seal would have been to stamp containers of products shipped under the supervision of the נער. Previously it was argued that נערים operated only in private capacities rather than as royal functionaries.[54] That conclusion, however, is debatable in light of the current evidence.

The n'rm/n'rn *in Ugaritic and Egyptian Texts*

The Semitic term *n'r* (pl. *n'rm;* fem. *n'rt*) is attested in Ugaritic texts;[55] in Egyptian sources the word appears as *n'rn* (masc. pl.).[56] In some usages the Ugaritic term, like its Hebrew cognate, signifies a youth or the dependent status of a son. For example, in a list of family members of work teams the sons of one family are divided into two groups, *bnh b'lm*, "sons (who are) owners, lords," and *n'rm*, the former apparently designating independent, perhaps married, sons and the latter indicating those still living at home, probably unmarried.[57] At times the occupations of a *n'r* are mentioned: for example, a baker's assistant, *n'r d'apy,* is mentioned in a text listing personnel.[58]

---

53. Rüterswörden notes that the service of priests to the crown—for example Abiathar (1 Kgs 2:26) and Amaziah (Amos 7:17)—was apparently rewarded by land grants (*Beamten der israelitischen Königszeit*, 125).

54. Avigad, "New Light on the *Na'ar* Seals" in F.M. Cross, W.E. Lemke, and P.D. Miller eds. *Magnalia Dei, the Mighty Acts of God. Essays on the Bible and Archaeology in Memory of G.E. Wright* (Garden City: Doubleday, 1976), 297–298; "Titles and Symbols on Hebrew Seals," 303.

55. For example, *n'r* (*UT* 2094:3); *n'rm* (169:12); *n'rt* (119:17; 2080:4–5); in Akkadian texts, LÚ *na-ḫi-ru* (PRU 6.136).

56. Papyrus Anastasi I 17:2–4 in J. Wilson, *ANET* 476; Merneptah Stele in A. Mariette, *Karnak* (Leipzig: J.C. Hinrichs, 1875), pl. 54:45; Kadesh Captions no. 11 in Wilson, *ANET*, 256.

57. *UT* 2080:4–5.

58. *UT* 2094:3. Gordon reconstructs 2066:4–5 to read, "two sons of Iwrḫz, *n'rm*, potters" (p. 284).

In many of the Ugaritic instances the context is military and the title refers to able and experienced soldiers (*UT* 169:12; 113:60). *N'rm* sometimes belong to the class of *maryannu*, "noble chariot warriors" (*UT* 1031:3; on *maryannu* as "chariot-warriors," see W.F. Albright, "Mitannian *maryannu* 'chariot-warrior', and the Canaanite and Egyptian Equivalents," *AfO* 6 [1930–1931]: 217–221; on their role in Ugarit and connection to Hebrew *n'rm*, see A. Rainey, "The Military Personnel of Ugarit," *JNES* 24 [1965]: 21).

In Egyptian documents *n'rn*, a Semitic loanword, signifies the Asiatic term for "soldier," although it is not a military title or rank per se (Erman and Grapow, *Wörterbuch* 2, 209; Koch,

The ṣuḫāru/ṣuḫārtu *in Akkadian Texts*

Detailed comparative studies of the Akkadian term *ṣuḫāru* and the Hebrew term נער have been made by J. MacDonald and H.P. Stähli and therefore require only a brief summary.[59] These analyses have shown that the word *ṣuḫāru* and its related forms are attested in usages parallel to those of biblical נער.[60] Like the Hebrew term, the substantive *ṣuḫāru* (fem. *ṣuḫārtu*) has a wide semantic range. It can signify a young child or an adolescent as well as a servant or an employee. Unmarried sons and daughters are so designated as an indication of their dependent status. Women, however, can retain the title even after marriage, perhaps a reflection of their dependent status as wives.[61]

The designation *ṣuḫāru/ṣuḫārtu* is common in the Mari correspondence where these persons play a variety of roles. MacDonald divides them into the following main categories: personal attendant (male or female), military figure,[62] guard, overseer, envoy (including royal envoy), informant, and professional.[63] Although it is often difficult to ascertain the social status of the *ṣuḫāru* from the context of the letters, apparently some held important positions in the service of kings, royal officials, or private individuals.[64] In one case the *ṣuḫāru*

Semitic Words in Egyptian Texts, 182–183; Schulman, *Military Rank, Title and Organization in the Egyptian New Kingdom*, 24). The *n'rn* mentioned in Papyrus Anastasi I (17:2–4) are Canaanite warriors targeted for attack by the Egyptians (Wilson, *ANET*, 476). In the Merneptah Stele inscription the term *n'rn* seems to be used in parallel construction to the word *iзyw*, "veteran," an indication that they were experienced soldiers (in Mariette, *Karnak*, pl. 54:45). A unit of *n'rn* fought in the battle at Kadesh and probably rescued the army of Rameses II from total destruction by the Hittites (Kadesh Captions, no. 11 in Wilson, *ANET*, 256).

59. MacDonald, "The Role and Status of the *ṣuḫāru*," 57–68; Stähli, *Knabe, Jüngling, Knecht*, 249–274.

60. *CAD* Ṣ, 229–235; *AHW* 3, 1108–1109. The term *ṣiḫru* (fem. *ṣiḫirtu*) is used as a noun meaning "child, servant" or as an adjective defined as "small, young, few" (pp. 179–185). The noun *ṣiḫḫirūtu* means "servants," while as an adjective it is defined as "small, young" (pp. 174–176). The verb *ṣeḫēru* means "to be young, small, to reduce in size" (pp. 120–124). In the MB and NB periods the term *ṣuḫurtu/ṣaḫurtu* was used to designate a class or profession, or adolescence as an age group (pp. 237–238).

61. Stähli, *Knabe, Jüngling, Knecht*, 252–254, 272–274.

62. Stähli argues against a military role for the *ṣuḫāru* maintaining that the Canaanite/Israelite usage was a later development (*Knabe, Jüngling, Knecht*, 273). Although the title *ṣuḫāru* in Mari is not explicitly a military designation, *ṣuḫārū* are clearly found in military contexts (e.g. *ARM* 14, 2:24r.; 70:6r.)

63. Dozens of Mari letters are cited by MacDonald.

64. Cf. M.D. Pack, who categorizes *ṣuḫārū* as a title of a non-administrative functionary ("The Administrative Structure of the Palace at Mari," Ph.D. Dissertation University of Pennsylvania, 1981, 255–306). Pack argues that the *ṣuḫārū* were always employed or subordinate to someone else, such as the king or a variety of royal officials (p. 288). At the same

seems to be charged with the supervision and protection of agricultural workers, similar to the duties of Ziba and Boaz's steward.[65] Interestingly, the duties of a *ṣuḫāru* of a cup-bearer entail overseeing the transportation of wine,[66] a responsibility that suggests one possible *Sitz-im-Leben* for the seals of Israelite נערים. In another case the *ṣuḫāru* is associated with cooking or baking,[67] analogous to the Ugaritic example of the *n'r d'apy*.

Conclusions

Based on the examples cited above, the following tentative conclusions can be drawn. Aside from indicating "youth" or a dependent status within the family, the designation נער can function as a technical term denoting occupation and status in society. While the title crosses civil, military, and religious divisions, it always describes an individual who is in the service of another person of higher standing. The status of a נער/נערה can vary from quite lowly, such as that of a household servant, to considerably high, such as that of an administrator. In either case, the title can designate a private servant or an employee of the monarchy. As mentioned, royal attendants entitled נערים/נערות served at Israelite and foreign courts. Other נערים were administrators connected with enterprises of the central authority, such as stewards of royal lands. The case of אליקם, which appears to associate the role of a נער with the *lmlk* operation, is probably an example of that. Any connection between אליקם the נער and Elyakim the house minister, however, remains speculative, as does the identification of יוכן with Conaniah the Levite.

Comparative material from Ugarit reveals that the designation *n'r/n'rm* was of Northwest semitic origin. Although the extant Ugaritic evidence is sparse, it indicates that the term was used similarly. In Mesopotamia, the semantically equivalent term is *ṣuḫāru/ṣuḫārtu* and its related forms. It is widely attested, especially at Mari, where the range of meanings for persons entitled *ṣuḫāru* closely corresponds to that of the Israelite נער.

---

time he states that a number of *ṣuḫārū* formed part of the palace administration at Mari (p. 306). In light of the fact that some *ṣuḫārū* did function in the bureaucratic organization, I conclude that the title can indeed designate an administrative functionary.

65. *ARM* 5, 30.

66. *ARM* 13, 149.

67. *ARM* 13, 101:30–32.

C. שֹׁטֵר – "Officer"

Etymology and Biblical Evidence

A third non-specific designation, שֹׁטֵר, appears in connection to various types of offices, some components of the monarchic system. The title שֹׁטֵר (šṭr) is attested in the Bible 25 times, 23 appearing as the collective שֹׁטְרִים (šṭrym). The term is distributed primarily in the Pentateuch, in Exodus, Numbers, and Deuteronomy, and in Joshua and Chronicles; a single example occurs in Proverbs. Only once, however, is the title attached to an individual (2 Chr 26:11). Often שׁוֹטְרִים are mentioned in concert with other officials or notables holding civil, military, and religious leadership positions. Contextual information concerning the functions of שׁוֹטְרִים is scant. As a result, translations frequently leave the definition of the designation undetermined, simply rendering it as "official." When a more specific meaning is provided, such as "secretary" or "constable," it is derived primarily from etymology and usages from later sources.

The etymology of the Hebrew term שֹׁטֵר/שֹׁטְרִים is generally connected to the root šṭr, attested in Akkadian in the verb šaṭāru, "write, copy, decree in writing, register, assign" and the noun šaṭāru(m), "document, copy."[68] Notably though, Akkadian has no noun from this root meaning "scribe" (=ṭupšarru) or any other profession. In Hebrew, on the other hand, the root שֹׁטֵר is never found as a verbal form, either with the meaning "to write" or anything else, nor is the שֹׁטֵר(וֹ) ever explicitly associated with writing activities.[69] Interestingly, a variant nominal form of šṭr, mśtyr, is attested in two Egyptian documents from the reign of Thutmose III (1490–1436 BCE) registering shipments of ivory and lumber.[70] The term mśtyr, apparently of Semitic origin, refers to the building or building complex at the dockyard in which goods were stored. Based on usages of the Semitic root šṭr it has been translated "office, chancellery."[71]

Several functions are attached to the שׁוֹטְרִים in postbiblical sources. That their roles were viewed as involving writing is reflected in the Greek and Syriac translations of the Hebrew title, which renders it "scribes" (LXX – γραμματεύς;

---

68. *CAD* Š/2, 221–241; *AHW* 3, 1203–1204.

69. In Job (38:33) the substantive מִשְׁטָר, "authority," appears parallel to חֻקּוֹת, "laws," perhaps indicating a written law code. Cf. Aramaic and Syriac שְׁטָרָא, "document, contract" (*BDB*, 1009; *HALOT* 4, 1475–1476).

70. Papyrus Leningrad 1116B and Papyrus British Museum 10056, cited in S.R.K. Glanville, "Records of a Royal Dockyard of the Time of Thutmosis III," *ZAS* 66 (1930): 108, 113; *ZAS* 68 (1932): 17.

71. Glanville, "Records of a Royal Dockyard," 17; Hoch, *Semitic Words in Egyptian Texts*, 154–155.

Peshitta - ספרא).[72] M. Weinfeld notes that frequently in contexts where the שטרים are mentioned with judges, the rendering in the LXX, γραμματοεισαγωγεῖς, is a combination of two titles known from the Ptolemaic Egyptian court, γραμματεύς and εισαγωγεῖς (Deut 1:15; 16:18; 29:9; 31:28).[73] Of the two, the εισαγωγεῖς was a royal functionary who represented the central government while working with the local judiciary. One of his functions, apparently, was to introduce cases to the judges. The court scribe, γραμματεύς, seems to have continued to fulfill various roles in legal proceedings as he had earlier in the New Kingdom.[74] Based on the Akkadian meaning of *šṭr* and additional usages in later literature, including rabbinic texts (e.g. שוטרי הדיינין - Tosephta Sanhedrin 3:9), Weinfeld concludes that the biblical שטרים were court recorders, constables, and messengers comparable to the personnel of Egyptian and Mesopotamian courts.[75]

Although etymological relationships with non-Hebrew terms and usages in postbiblical sources may be valuable in elucidating the role(s) of the biblical שטרים, this comparative material must also be supported by internal biblical evidence to be convincing. The following picture emerges from bits of data gleaned from applications of the term in the Bible. The title שטר, which is found together with titles designating government officials and notables not appointed by the state, can fall into either of these categories. According to the Chronicler, at least some of the שטרים were Levites. In a few instances they constitute a Levitical division corresponding to other functional units such as gatekeepers, scribes, judges and musicians (1 Chr 23:4–5; 26:29; 2 Chr 19:11; 34:13).[76] The

---

72. The LXX translates שטרים in Numbers, Deut 20, Josh, 1 Chr and 2 Chr 19 as "scribes." Notably, however, in 2 Chr 26:11 and 34:13 the term is interpreted as "judges."

73. Weinfeld, "Judge and Officer," 83–86.

74. See most recently, Allam, "Egyptian Law Courts," 119–127.

75. Weinfeld, "Judge and Officer," 84. According to A. Walther, in the Old Babylonian period, six titles, besides those belonging to judges, can be traced to officials in the legal courts: the *rābiṣu* functioned as an attorney; the *akil* or *šāpir dayyāni* was an attendant who held different administrative duties; the *rēdû* was another attendant who also served as constable; the *ṭupšarru* performed secretarial duties; the *parkullu*, "sealcutter," was a notary; the *gallābu*, "barber," executed corporal punishment (*Das altbabylonische Gerichtswesen*, 168–180). In Egypt in the New Kingdom the *sš* was the court scribe who also functioned as prosecutor and advocate; the *šmsw* were court attendants who fulfilled various tasks such as house-searches and seizure of goods (Allam, "Egyptian Law Courts," 110–115).

In a recent study, Avishur and Heltzer derive a military/policing function for the שטר based on usages of the title in Punic sources (*Studies on the Royal Administration*, 94–99).

76. As Japhet observes, the concept that Levites served as officials of the crown is peculiar to Chronicles (*I & II Chronicles*, 453, 779). However, the notion is compatible with views that Temple personnel, both priests and Levites, were state functionaries who answered to the king. See, for example, Ahlström, *Royal Administration and National Religion in Ancient Palestine*, 44–74.

sphere of duty of Levites who served as ש(ו)טרים, like those who were judges, encompassed tasks outside the Temple: למלאכה החיצונה על ישראל, "for external duty over Israel" (1 Chr 26:29).

In other cases, the שטרים are recognized as state appointees "ministering to the king" (27:1), seemingly not of Levitical descent. One שטר identified as Maaseiah is mentioned together with military personnel, including a scribe named Jeiel, as a subordinate of King Uzziah's officer named Hananiah (2 Chr 26:11). An inferior status is also indicated of the שטרים in 1 Chr 27:1, where the group's superiors consist of officers of thousands and officers of hundreds.[77]

In the Pentateuch traditions and in Joshua, the שטרים hold different positions of authority. In Exodus they are mentioned in conjunction with the נגשים (*ngśym*), "taskmasters," as "foremen" who communicate orders between Pharaoh and the Hebrew slaves and are responsible for brick production (5:10–19).[78] While they are clearly subordinate to the Egyptian taskmasters, the שטרים seem to hold the highest rank among the Israelites. In Numbers the שטרים belong to the 70 elders of Israel who assist Moses (11:16), unquestionably a prominent group. In Deuteronomy the שטרים appear together with judges, elders, and military officers. They are stationed with judges at city gates (16:18)[79] and inform recruits of exemptions from military service (20:5–9). Their involvement in judicial procedures and military recruitment may reflect monarchic practices. The שטרים are mentioned with clan notables and elders (29:9; 31:28); once they appear at the end of a list of military officers chosen from those ranks (1:15). In Joshua, as in Numbers and Deuteronomy, they are categorized as leaders alongside the elders, clan heads, and judges (8:33; 23:2; 24:1). When Joshua leads the Israelites across the Jordan, the שטרים convey his orders to the people (3:2–4). That the title שטר signifies leadership status is also evident from

---

77. Tigay suggests that the inferior status of the שטרים in Chronicles may be based on an interpretation of its usage in Deuteronomy. The term itself may be a resurrected pre-monarchic, rather than a monarchic, designation (*Deuteronomy*, 345 n. 61). Contrast A. Rofé, who in a recent unpublished paper suggests that the title שטר is a catachronistic invention—that is, a root borrowed from a cognate language, formed into a noun to designate an archaic but unattested term. The motive is to avoid an anachronism, in this case ספר—the equivalent functionary ("Notes on Biblical Historiography and Historical Thought," 1999).

78. M. Sekine equates the שטרים of Exod 5 with השעיהו, the officer in charge of the corvée laborers mentioned in the ostracon from Meṣad Ḥashavyahu. He also assumes that the term שטר first came into use in the seventh century and reflects a later addition to the JE account of Exod 5. ("Beobachtungen zu der Josianischen Reform," *VT* 22 [1972]: 363–364). Neither of Sekine's points, however, can be proven. Certainly, it cannot be shown that agricultural supervisors were known as שטרים based on the role of השעיהו since he does not bear a title.

79. For a discussion of the meaning of שעריך, see Chapter 4–J.

Proverbs where the term appears parallel to קצין (*qṣyn*) and משל (*mšl*), designations for rulers (6:7).

Conclusions

Based on the biblical material, a few observations can be made concerning the roles of Israelite שטרים. (1) The realm in which these functionaries operated is non-cultic; even in the Chronicler's account the Levite שטרים operate outside the Temple. (2) In many instances their duties are related to the judiciary, although specific tasks are not mentioned. Sometimes the context is military. (3) The rank of the שטרים vis-à-vis other officials is not always obvious but in a few cases their status is clearly subservient. (4) Occasionally, שטרים appear as leaders of the highest rank. (5) In accounts of the monarchic period, שטרים are attested in Chronicles but never in the books of Samuel or Kings. (6) Outside Chronicles, it seems that the title שטר can be held by both state officials and local representatives.[80]

In sum, it seems that the title שטר is a non- specific designation for various types of officials, somewhat analogous to the title שר. Apparently, the שטרים worked with judges, military commanders, and labor overseers in different capacities. In some cases they were assistants,[81] but in other instances their status may have been equivalent to these officers. It is difficult to ascertain if the original meaning of the root *šṭr*, "write," determined some or any of the activities of Israelite שטרים. Notably, as Van der Ploeg observes, their duties frequently entailed speaking, but writing is never mentioned explicitly.[82] Nevertheless, based on the biblical context in which some of the שטרים appear and translations of the term in the post-biblical period, a case can be made that these officers functioned as court secretaries, constables, and other attendants. Even the שטרים pictured in Exodus 5 reflect record-keepers of sorts.[83] The Semitic term *mśṭyr*

---

80. Rüterswörden does not accept the Chronicler's categorization of the שטרים as state officials or the possibility that they are designated as such in Deut 16:18. Rather, he sees them purely as representatives chosen by the people (*Beamten der israelitischen Königszeit*, 111). However, as discussed above, there is no valid reason to dismiss the Chronicler in this matter and certainly the שטרים of Deut 16:18, who appear together with the שפטים, "judges," can be interpreted as state appointees.

81. J. Van der Ploeg sees the שטרים generally as assistants to other higher officials ("Les šoṭerim d'Israël," *OTS* 10 [1954]: 195–196).

82. Van der Ploeg, "Les šoṭerim d'Israël," 196. He also suggests that the titles מזכיר and שטר may be related functionally (pp. 194–195).

83. N. Sarna notes that logs of foremen of work-gangs are extant from ancient Egypt (*The JPS Torah Commentary Exodus* [Philadelphia: Jewish Publication Society, 1991], 28); K. Kitchen discusses a number of Egyptian documents and paintings from the Old, Middle, and New Kingdoms that delineate brick production. These sources detail material, produc-

in Egyptian texts is another witness of the variant usages of the root *šṭr*. In that case, the record keeping function of the building may have given rise to its name, although the origin of the term and its application is as yet uncertain. Possibly, nouns formed from the root *šṭr* developed along two lines: one closer to the original meaning and another with a wider semantic range.[84]

D. סריס – "Eunuch," Palace Attendant

The only clearly foreign title in the corpus of Israelite official titles, that of סריס, was held by a certain class of royal functionaries. The designation סריס (*srys*; pl. סריסים [*srysym*]) occurs in the Bible in reference to individuals at both Israelite and foreign courts. It is normally agreed that the West Semitic term is a loanword from Akkadian *ša rēši* (pl. *šūt rēši*; Sumerian LÚ.SAG), literally, "(one) of the head, chief."[85] The Akkadian title is often associated with eunuchs. However, while evidence from Akkadian sources clearly proves that the term can signify "eunuch," some scholars argue that the basic or broader meaning of *ša rēši* is simply "officer" and that the specialized sense "eunuch," which developed later, is not indicative of all title-bearers.[86] Disagreement concerning the term סריס centers on the definition of the Akkadian title as much as on the Hebrew usage. The main point of contention is whether סריסים were all

---

tion quotas, workers and supervisors. Foremen in charge of small work-gangs are mentioned in a Middle Kingdom text, the Reisner Papyrus. In the workmen community of Deir el-Medina, foremen were appointed from the ranks of the workers, similar to the Hebrew שטרים. Other texts indicate that higher officials, comparable to the נגשים, were in charge of several work-gangs ("From the Brickfields of Egypt," *Tyndale Bulletin* 27 [1976]: 136–147).

84. Hoch, *Semitic Words in Egyptian Texts*, 155.

85. *BDB*, 710; *HALOT* 2, 769–770.

86. The clearest evidence that *ša rēši* means "eunuch" comes from a reference to a ritual stating that the *šūt rēši* have no semen and cannot father children (*CT* 23, 10:14 in *CAD* N/2, 234). In support of the definition, see H. Tadmor, "Rab-saris and Rab-shakeh in 2 Kings 18," 279–285; "Was the Biblical *sārîs* a Eunuch?" in Z. Zevit, S. Gitin and M. Sokoloff eds. *Solving Riddles and Untying Knots* (Winona Lake: Eisenbrauns, 1995), 317–318; A.K. Grayson, "Eunuchs in Power: Their Role in the Assyrian Bureaucracy" in M. Dietrich and O. Loretz eds. *Vom alten Orient zum alten Testament* (Neukirchen-Vluyn: Neukirchener, 1995), 85–98; Kinnier-Wilson, *Nimrud Wine Lists*, 46–48; Heltzer, *Internal Organization*, 170–173. Von Soden supports the more general meaning "officer," see *AHW* 2, 974. L. Oppenheim ("A Note on *ša rēši*," *JANES* 5 [1973]: 325–334) and P. Garelli ("Remarques sur l'administration de l'empire assyrien," *RA* 68 [1974]: 133–137), while acknowledging that some *šūt rēši* were eunuchs, like those who served in the harem or certain other areas of the palace, do not define the title as "eunuch" in all cases. It is beyond the purview of this study to attempt to answer the difficult question whether all *šūt rēši* were eunuchs.

necessarily eunuchs.[87] As part of this inquiry the interpretation of the term סריס as "eunuch" will be reevaluated in light of biblical ideology concerning castration. The primary focus, however, is to categorize the term as an official title and to isolate the functions and rank of title-bearers within the monarchic organization.

Biblical Evidence

Royal functionaries entitled סריס/סריסים appear in the Bible in the service of both Israelite and foreign kings. Of those serving in Israel, most are mentioned in connection with the following six kings: David, Ahab, Jehoram of Israel, Josiah, Jehoiachin, and Zedekiah.[88] The סריסים of David's reign are listed in Chronicles among several groups of royal dignitaries assembled in Jerusalem to hear the king's speech concerning Solomon's election and the building of the Temple. The assembly consists of various categories of Israelite שרים: officers of the tribes, officers of royal departments, military commanders, stewards, סריסים, and mighty warriors (1 Chr 28:1).[89] In a narrative set at the city gate of Samaria preceding an Israelite-Aramean war, Ahab summons a סריס to fetch the prophet Michiah in order that he will predict the outcome of the battle (1 Kgs 22:9 = 2 Chr 18:8). Ahab's סריס seems to be serving as the king's attendant. In a scene from the last days of Jehoram, a group of two or three סריסים surface in the queen mother's (Jezebel's) apartment. Jehu the usurper orders them to thrust her out the window, which they do (2 Kgs 9:32). In another incident, Jehoram, or a later king,[90] assigns a סריס to the Shunamite woman to supervise the return of her land and its produce (8:6). An account of the reform of Josiah refers to a chamber near the entrance of the Temple that belongs to a סריס named

87. Tadmor, "Was the Biblical *sārîs* a Eunuch?" 319–320. Most Bible translations show varying interpretations of the term within the biblical corpus. The *JPS Tanakh*, for example, translates סריס as "eunuch" in all its occurrences except in the Joseph stories and in Daniel. Other translations more frequently render סריס as "officer, courtier."

88. The designation סריסים is also found in Samuel's warning about the demands of the king (1 Sam 8:15). The prophet states, among other things, that the king will confiscate the people's land and allocate it to his סריסים and עבדים. Note that McCarter translates the term as "officers," in keeping with his understanding of the broader definition of the Akkadian as well as the Hebrew (*I Samuel*, 158–159).

89. Japhet translates סריסים as "palace officials" (following the *NEB* and *RSV*), but notes in her commentary that the title means "eunuchs" (*I & II Chronicles*, 481, 486).

90. The Israelite king in this narrative is unnamed and cannot be accurately identified from the context, despite the textual placement of the pericope among the records of Jehoram's reign. Cogan and Tadmor suggest that the entire account of the siege and famine of Samaria should be assigned to a later king, Jehoahaz son of Jehu (*II Kings*, 85).

Nathan-melech, an officer who is in charge of the "precincts" (23:11).[91] In a record of the first exile to Babylon in the reign of Jehoiachin, the list of deportees includes: the king, the queen mother, the royal servants (עבדים), the officers (שרים), and the סריסים (24:12). Another register of the same exile consists of the following individuals and groups: the king, the queen mother, the royal wives, the סריסים, and the nobles of the land (24:15). A third record, referred to in the letter Jeremiah sent to Babylon, reads: the king, the queen mother, the סריסים, the שרים, and the craftsmen and smiths (Jer 29:2). Later, in the reign of Zedekiah, סריסים, along with the officers of Judah and Jerusalem, the priests, and the people of the land, are the object of Jeremiah's condemnation (34:19). A lengthy narrative in Jeremiah tells of a Nubian סריס named Ebed-melech, a palace servant, who rescued the prophet from his pit prison (38:7). When Jerusalem falls, the Babylonian commander Nebuzaradan delivers important prisoners to his king, among them an unidentified סריס who is a commander (פקיד) over the soldiers (2 Kgs 25:19 = Jer 52:25). After the fall of Jerusalem and the murder of Gedaliah, a list of survivors taken to Egypt includes: men, soldiers, women, children, and סריסים (Jer 41:16).

Several of the aforementioned examples show סריסים in lists, together with other classes of royal functionaries. Apparently as a group they belong to a category separate from those of עבדים and שרים. In two cases they attend women, Jezebel and the Shunamite, but it is unclear whether their primary role is to serve women or whether as servants of the king they tend to the needs of various persons. Alternatively, in the cases of Ahab and Zedekiah, סריסים minister directly to the king. In records of deportees, סריסים and other officials are mentioned in association with the entire royal family. In three of four such lists, the place of the סריסים in the list is following the women or children. Based on these examples, it seems safe to conclude that generally the סריס was a personal attendant who served different members of the royal family. That he was also a eunuch is not indicated.[92] Although it was customary in some cultures of the region to employ emasculated males as harem courtiers, this was not universal (see below). In two cases cited above, the סריס appears to be a higher official:

---

91. The interpretation of the term פרורים, "precincts," is problematic. Perhaps it is equivalent to פרבר (1 Chr 26:18), a Persian loanword meaning "court, vestibule, summer-house" (*BDB*, 826; *HALOT* 3, 962; cf. Cogan and Tadmor, *II Kings*, 288–289).

92. It should be noted that the Hebrew term סריס can signify "eunuch." This usage is attested in an exilic prophetic text: ואל יאמר הסריס הן אני עץ יבש, "Let not the *srys* say I am a dried up (wilted) tree" (Isa 56:3). In this prophecy of redemption Isaiah states that if the eunuch abides by the laws, God will grant him a name more enduring than progeny (56:5). Tadmor's position, that this meaning of סריס was not newly acquired in the Babylonian exile, is reasonable, though unproven ("Was the Biblical *sārîs* a Eunuch?" 322).

Nathan-melech was in charge of a certain area, either inside or outside the palace; the unnamed סריס who was captured by the Babylonians was an army officer. These two סריסים evidently attained more prestigious positions.

Biblical references to סריסים at non-Israelite courts consist of Persian, Babylonian, and Egyptian examples. Egyptian סריסים appear in the Joseph stories as Pharaoh's courtiers. They include a chief of the guards, a chief butler, and a chief baker. The butler and baker are imprisoned with Joseph (Gen 40:2, 7); the chief of the guards is the famous Potiphar whose wife attempts to seduce Joseph (37:36; 39:1). The translation "eunuch" for these סריסים is problematic, primarily because Egyptians did not practice castration on humans and no evidence exists that eunuchs served at Egyptian courts before the Persian period.[93] This difficulty can be overcome by one of two proposed solutions. Either the biblical writer was ignorant of Egyptian customs or he defined the term סריס as a generic designation for "officer, courtier."

Two references are attested in the Bible for סריסים in Babylon. The first, found in the context of Isaiah's reprimand of Hezekiah for displaying his treasures before the Babylonian ambassador, is the prophet's prediction that Hezekiah's offspring will serve as סריסים in the palace at Babylon (2 Kgs 20:18 = Isa 39:7). The second reference, set in Nebuchadnezzar's palace, is to a רב סריס, "chief *srys*," who was responsible for the welfare of Daniel and other foreign youths serving at court (Dan 1:3, 7–11, 18). These examples too indicate that סריסים functioned within the palace, though the status eunuch, albeit a possibility, is not implied.

Examples of Persian סריסים are found in the book of Esther. They all function in the palace, either in connection with the harem or as personal servants of the king. A group of סריסים is instructed by Ahasuerus to bring Vashti before him (Esth 1:10, 12, 15); a סריס named Hegai is the harem guard who cares for Esther when she first arrives (2:3, 15); a second סריס named Shaashgaz guards the king's concubines (2:14); a third סריס named Hathach is Esther's servant after she becomes queen (4:5); two סריסים named Bigthan and Teresh, guards of the threshold, plot to assassinate the king (2:21; 6:2); Ahasuerus' סריסים escort Haman to Esther's banquet (6:14); another סריס named Harbonah suggests that Haman be impaled on the stake he built for Mordechai (7:9). Since eunuchs are known to

---

93. Contrary assertions by Greek authors seem to reflect customs of their own period (A.T. Sandison, "Eunuchen" in *Lexikon* 2, 46–47; G.E. Kadish, "Eunuchs in Ancient Egypt?" in *Studies in Honor of John A. Wilson* (Chicago: University of Chicago Press, 1969), 55–62; Redford, "A Study of the Biblical Story of Joseph," 200–201). Tadmor correctly points outs that Potiphar's marital state is in itself not an obstacle to defining סריס as eunuch. He notes examples from several cultures where eunuchs of higher status married and adopted children ("Was the Biblical *sārîs* a Eunuch?" 321 n. 17).

have served in Persian courts, it can be safely assumed that of the aforementioned סריסים, at least those connected with the harem were indeed eunuchs.[94]

In sum, the biblical data, both of סריסים in Israel and at foreign courts, indicate that in most instances persons bearing this title functioned as personal attendants within the palace in close proximity to the royal family. Even those holding specialized roles served in the palace complex (e.g. butler, baker, guard). Only occasionally are סריסים found as officials in administrative positions (e.g. army officer, officer of precincts). In all but a few examples in Esther, the definition "eunuch" is not evident nor is it required for the sense of the context. Admittedly, though, in cases where these functionaries are associated with women and their living quarters, the interpretation "eunuch" is plausible.

In light of the uncertainties surrounding the status of the סריס, it seems appropriate to examine biblical ideology concerning castration. One of the Deuteronomic laws clearly stipulates that a male whose testes are crushed or whose member is cut off is not admitted to the congregation of YHWH (Deut 23:2). Apparently genital mutilation in general was regarded negatively in Israel, so much so that among Israelite punitive regulations, none calls for castration.[95] Even the gelding of animals, a common ancient Near Eastern practice, is forbidden, and sacrificial animals whose testicles were maimed could not be brought for offerings (Lev 22:24). Although the knowledge of and compliance with these laws in the monarchic period are uncertain factors, their existence alone raises serious doubts that castration was practiced in Israel for the purpose of creating palace eunuchs.

Assuming that castration was not practiced among Israelites, it still seems that the designation סריס cannot be understood specifically as a title for "palace attendant." Rather, it appears to signify a class of functionaries whose members served primarily as palace attendants for members of the royal family. Importantly, those few who rose to higher positions, as the official over the precincts and the army officer, retained the title סריס instead of acquiring the more role-appropriate designation שר. These observations, coupled by the fact that the term סריס is the sole clearly foreign title in the corpus of Israelite official titles, raise the possibility that סריסים were non-Israelites, foreigners imported from Syria and/or Mesopotamia to serve at the royal courts of Israel and Judah. Notably, the two named סריסים in Judah, Ebed-melech and Nathan-melech, do not show PNs with Yahwistic theophoric elements, a highly common charac-

94. See Tadmor's discussion and references ("Was the Biblical *sārîs* a Eunuch?" 322 n. 21). Based on Persian customs, probably Ahasuerus' personal סריסים were eunuchs as well.

95. Cf. Middle Assyrian laws which stipulate castration as corporal punishment for adultery and homosexuality (nos. 15, 20 in T. Meek, *ANET*, 181; *KAV* 1, 2:54, 97).

teristic among Israelite PNs in the late monarchic period. Ebed-melech, who is identified as a Nubian, is certainly a foreigner, and Nathan-melech, whose ethnicity is unknown, could have been foreign as well.[96] A second issue, whether all סריסים were eunuchs or whether the title in Israel was applied to imported palace servants both emasculated and non-emasculated, cannot be resolved with certainty. However, if in Israel as elsewhere eunuchs were considered desirable as royal attendants because of their special loyalty and if they were not available locally, then they may have been imported for that trait.

Ugaritic, Mesopotamian and Egyptian Evidence

More information is available on the *ša rēši* from Ugarit and Mesopotamia. Palace personnel designated LÚ.MEŠ *rēši* (or *ša rēši*) are attested in Akkadian texts from Ugarit. Some are specifically designated *ša rēš šarri*, "'eunuch' of the king," or *ša rēš ekalli*, "'eunuch' of the palace." The LÚ.MEŠ *ša rēši* in Ugarit served as witnesses at court, they could own slaves and other property, and they could become members of the *bnš mlk*, "royal dependents."[97]

In Mesopotamia persons entitled *ša rēši* (LÚ.SAG) held various positions at court, some of the highest status. A bulla from Khorsabad inscribed in Aramaic bears the name and title of this functionary from the reign of Sargon II: [ל]פנאסר[ל]מר סרס ז[י] סרגן, "belonging to *pn'srlmr* the *srs* of Sargon."[98] Palace *šūt rēši* served in the *bītānu*, "inner court," as well as in the *bābānu*, "outer court."[99] That many functioned specifically in the harem as eunuchs is known from Middle Assyrian Palace and Harem Edicts that enumerate provisions for examining the *ša rēš šarri* before his admission to the harem to confirm that he is in fact a eunuch.[100] In many cases *šūt rēši* are senior officials and army officers. Grayson lists 19 persons from the ninth and eighth centuries, many of whom bore such titles as governor, palace major-domo and herald.[101] The *rab ša rēši*, "chief 'eunuch'," often turns up as army commander in the Assyrian army.[102] Those

---

96. The possibility that a Nubian was a eunuch is also problematic as their customs were comparable to the Egyptians'. Perhaps this unfortunate Nubian was initially sold into servitude in Syria or Mesopotamia and thus met his fate.

97. For a list of texts, see Heltzer, *Internal Organization*, 170–173.

98. *WSS*, no. 755.

99. Kinnier-Wilson, *Nimrud Wine Lists*, 46–47; Grayson, "Eunuchs in Power," 94.

100. E.F. Weidner, "Hof- und Harems-Erlasse assyrischer Könige aus dem 2. Jahrtausend v. Chr.," 276–277 no. 8:48–51.

101. For a discussion and list of these individuals, see Grayson, "Eunuchs in Power," 93, 98.

102. Grayson lists several examples from Neo-Assyrian texts ("Eunuchs in Power," 93 n. 49). Cf. Sennacherib's רב סריס at Jerusalem's walls in the reign of Hezekiah (2 Kgs 18:17).

scholars who claim that all *šūt rēši* are eunuchs refer to the beardless figures in reliefs to further their argument.[103]

In contrast to Syrian and Mesopotamian customs, there is no evidence that castration was practiced on humans in Egypt, not for punitive measures or to create courtiers for the palace harem.[104] The absence of harem eunuchs at Egyptian courts deserves comment. Apparently the private living quarters of the Pharaoh occupied by his wives, concubines, and children were serviced by non-emasculated males. Two titles in particular are attested for functionaries of the Middle and New Kingdom who were attached to the inner palace: *iry-ʿt n k3p*, "hall-keeper of the harem/inner palace," and *imy-r ʿẖnwty n k3p*, "chamberlain/overseer of the harem, inner palace."[105] The chamberlain of the harem oversaw maintenance, including provisioning of the kitchens while the hall-keeper of the harem usually served as a personal attendant to a member of the royal family.[106] The Egyptian evidence implies that the use of eunuchs in the inner palace, including in the women's residence, was not a requisite that can be assumed.

Conclusions

Based on biblical and comparative material, the designation סריס seems to fit a class or type of functionary rather than denoting a specific office. The internal biblical evidence concerning סריסים at Israelite courts indicates that these functionaries, with few exceptions, served as palace attendants for various members of the royal family. While there is no explicit testimony in the Hebrew data from the pre-exilic period that the סריס was a eunuch, the context in which this courtier sometimes appears, in the service of women, may imply that status. However, in light of Israelite law, it seems highly unlikely that the society pro-

---

103. Among others, Tadmor, "Was the Biblical *sārîs* a Eunuch?" 317–318; Grayson, "Eunuchs in Power," 93. Contrast, Oppenheim, "A Note on *ša rēši*, 333–334; Garelli, "Remarques sur l'administration de l'empire assyrien," 133–137.

104. Sandison, "Eunuchen," 46–47. Sandison notes that no word for "harem eunuch" even exists in Egyptian. Other terms, which have been interpreted as signifying "castrated male" in certain contexts, are discussed by Kadish and in almost all cases are dismissed. Of two exceptions, one refers to enemies of Egypt–non-Egyptians, and the other appears in the myth of the struggle between Horus and Seth in which the latter has his testicles severed temporarily (Kadish, "Eunuchs in Ancient Egypt?" 60–61).

105. Faulkner, *Middle Egyptian*, 25, 48; Erman and Grapow, *Wörterbuch* I, 160, 226–227; Gardiner, *Onomastica* I, 44*–45*.

106. Helck, *Verwaltung*, 252–256; Quirke, *The Administration of Egypt in the Late Middle Kingdom*, 87–90. In the New Kingdom the *imy-r ʿẖnwty* also served as tutors for the princes. Notably, a number of them bore the title *ẖrd n k3p*, "child of the harem," indicating that in their youth they themselves were raised in the palace quarters (see Chapter 3–D).

duced eunuchs from its own population. On the other hand, it is quite feasible that eunuchs were imported from Syria and/or Mesopotamia, where they clearly functioned in palace settings. The absence of Yahwistic PNs among the named סריסים in the Bible supports that contention somewhat, although admittedly, the limited data hardly comprise adequate proof. Finally, the less likely possibility that סרים simply refers to a palace functionary who is a foreigner, not a eunuch, cannot be totally dismissed.

6
Aspects of Administration Revealed in Inscriptions

Land Grants, Supply Networks and Regional Administration

A. Samaria Ostraca

In addition to the corpus of seals engraved with short texts of mostly PNs and a few titles, the epigraphic remains from Israel include ostraca displaying longer texts, often on administrative matters. The collection of ostraca from Samaria, which fits this category, was the first archive of Hebrew inscriptions to be uncovered in an archaeological excavation. Since its discovery in 1910 in what was once a storehouse in the palace complex at Samaria, this corpus of inscribed pottery sherds has been the topic of much scholarly discussion. Various issues relating to the data contained in the texts have been and continue to be debated. These include questions of chronology, the role of persons appearing in the inscriptions, philological considerations, and implications of the material for understanding Israelite administration. In light of the focus of the present study, the arguments surrounding these ostraca will be summarized below and their validity reexamined.

Corpus and Chronology

The corpus of ostraca from Samaria consists of 102 pieces, 63 of which were initially published by G.A. Reisner and the balance of readable inscriptions by I.T. Kaufman in his dissertation.[1] Most of the 102 ostraca are at least partially readable with only 25 totally illegible.[2] With two exceptions, the inscriptions are categorized as ostraca because the text is written to fit the surface of the pottery sherds. The two exceptional sherds, nos. 62 and 63, are jar labels, heavy ceramic fragments of containers that were inscribed with information on the jar

1. G.A. Reisner et al., *Harvard Excavations at Samaria 1908–1910, I* (Cambridge: Harvard University Press, 1924), 227–246; I.T. Kaufman, "The Samaria Ostraca: A Study in Ancient Hebrew Paleography" (Ph.D. Dissertation, Harvard University, 1966), 145–147.

2. See, most recently, *HDAE* 1, 89–109; 2, pls. VI–VIII.

contents while intact.[3] All the ostraca were discovered in a building situated between the palace and the casemate wall designated by the excavators as the 'Ostraca House.' Their precise provenience is the fill of the floor of a complex of store-rooms.[4]

One issue widely debated in connection with this archive is the chronology of the texts. Typical methods for dating ceramics, namely stratigraphy and pottery typology, are helpful but inconclusive in this instance. The sherds of the ostraca themselves resemble several pottery types prevalent from the mid-ninth to mid-eighth century, primarily those dating to ca. 800 BCE (Samaria Period IV).[5] Their findspot provides a *terminus ad quem*, as the ostraca predate the construction of the building several years prior to the Assyrian destruction of Samaria in 721/722.[6] Additional useful information for dating is derived from the contents of the texts and the script. Paleographical analysis, while not an exact science, has narrowed the date of the ostraca to between the first and third quarter of the eighth century.[7] Four regnal years recorded on the ostraca narrow the potential reigns to certain kings who ruled the requisite number of years. Two distinct formulas distinguishable in the inscriptions raise the possibility that two separate reigns are involved. As these combined data have elicited much discussion, they require a detailed examination.

Four year-dates signifying regnal years appear in the inscriptions: nine, ten, fourteen(?),[8] and fifteen. Consequently, if the ostraca date to the reign of one

3. Reisner, *Harvard Excavations at Samaria*, 238.

4. Reisner, *Harvard Excavations at Samaria*, 227; Kaufman, "The Samaria Ostraca," 101–110; "The Samaria Ostraca: An Early Witness to Hebrew Writing," *BA* 45 (1982): 231–232.

5. J.W. Crowfoot, K.M. Kenyon and E.L. Sukenik, *Samaria-Sebaste I. The Buildings at Samaria* (London: Palestine Exploration Fund, 1942), 105.

6. Kaufman, "The Samaria Ostraca: An Early Witness to Hebrew Writing," 232–233. For a detailed discussion of the pottery, see Kaufman, "The Samaria Ostraca," 110–121.

7. S.A. Birnbaum, I.T. Kaufman, and F.M. Cross date the ostraca to the second quarter of the eighth century ("The Dates of the Gezer Tablet and the Samaria Ostraca," *PEQ* 74 [1942]: 108; "The Samaria Ostraca: An Early Witness to Hebrew Writing," 234; "Ammonite Ostraca from Heshbon: Heshbon Ostraca IV-VIII," *AUSS* 13 [1975]: 8; Cross originally supported a later date ["Epigraphic Notes on Hebrew Documents of the Eighth-Sixth Centuries B.C.," 35], but subsequently changed his mind); Y. Aharoni dates the ostraca to the first half of the eighth century and based on distinctions of certain letters, he presumes two successive reigns (*Land of the Bible*, 366). See below.

8. Originally, the regnal year on ostracon no. 63, the questionable year-date, was read as 17, based on a sign resembling a "t" situated between the hieratic symbols for ten, Λ, and two, ||, which Reisner interpreted as a "five" (*Harvard Excavations at Samaria*, 238). Kaufman observed, however, that the crossbar of the "t" is simply a groove in the pottery surface. He reads the year date as either 13 or 14, hieratic ten plus three or four vertical strokes ("The

king, that king must have ruled minimally for fifteen years. In addition, it is observable that, in general, the texts dated to years nine and ten are formulated differently than those dated to year 15.[9] Several theories regarding the date of the ostraca have been proposed in light of this information. Some scholars, based on the stylistic distinctions, especially the shift from expressing numerals by their Hebrew names to depicting them in Egyptian hieratic numerals, assign the ostraca of years nine and ten to one king and those of year 15 to another. Two sets of candidates have been proposed: Jehoahaz and Jehoash (reigned 17 and 16 years respectively, late 9th-early 8th century);[10] and Jehoash and Jeroboam II (reigned 16 and 41 years respectively, early-mid 8th century)[11]. Other scholars, who do not consider the variations as necessarily indicative of a new administration, date all the ostraca to a single reign, that of Jeroboam II.[12] At present it cannot be proven one way or another whether the year dates on the ostraca refer to the reigns of one king or two, although stylistic

Samaria Ostraca," 140). Lemaire reads the date as year 12, ignoring the "t" mark altogether (*IH*, 37).

9. Those dated to year nine or ten consist of the following: a year date expressed in words, בשת התשעת, "in the ninth year," or בשת העשרת, "in the tenth year"; a GN prefixed by the preposition מ (*mem*); a PN prefixed by the preposition ל (*lamed*); and a product, either a jar of wine or oil. In contrast, those ostraca dated to year 15 include: the year-date expressed in hieratic numerals, 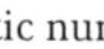 ; a GN prefixed by the preposition מ; a PN prefixed by the preposition ל; a second PN with or without a patronym; and a second GN. In a few cases additional PNs appear on both groups of ostraca; occasionally the ostraca of year 15 also show a product.

10. W.H. Shea, "Israelite Chronology and the Samaria Ostraca," *ZDPV* 101 (1985): 9–20. Previously, Shea had suggested that the ostraca be assigned to the reigns of Menahem and Pekah, more than 60 years later ("The Date and the Significance of the Samaria Ostraca," *IEJ* 27 [1977]: 17–22).

11. Aharoni assigns the ostraca of years nine and ten to Jehoash and those of year 15 to Jeroboam II, based on paleographical distinctions as well (*Land of the Bible*, 366). A. Rainey suggests the reverse, assigning the ostraca of year 15 to Jehoash and those of years nine and ten to Jeroboam II, counting the latter's years as coregent ("Toward A Precise Date for the Samaria Ostraca," *BASOR* 272 [1988]: 71).

12. Cross, "Ammonite Ostraca from Heshbon," 8; Kaufman, "The Samaria Ostraca: An Early Witness to Hebrew Writing," 235. Previous theories date the ostraca to the reigns of Ahab (Reisner, *Harvard Excavations at Samaria*, 227; Albright, "The Administrative Divisions of Israel and Judah," 42; Albright subsequently changed his mind and lowered the date to the reign of Jeroboam II [*Archaeology and the Religion of Israel* (Baltimore: Johns Hopkins Press, 1953), 41]), Jehoahaz (B. Mazar, "The Historical Background of the Samaria Ostraca," *JPOS* 21 [1948]: 123) or Menahem (Y. Yadin, "Ancient Judean Weights and the Date of the Samaria Ostraca," *SH* 8 [1961]: 22–25). The reign of Ahab in the mid-ninth century is premature paleographically, as is Jehoahaz's reign in the late ninth century. Menahem's reign, Yadin's proposal, was based on his incorrect interpretation of the numer-

distinctions in the texts seem hardly significant enough to be used as a determining factor. Different modes of expressing numerals, for instance, are common in a single period, as is evident from date formulas in the Arad letters.[13] On the other hand, the provenience of the ostraca and their paleography favor a date in the first half of the eighth century. Therefore, the reign of Jeroboam, or the last years of Jehoash and the early years of Jeroboam, is preferable to that of earlier kings.

Who are the Persons Named on the Samaria Ostraca?

A topic even more controversial than the date of the Samaria ostraca is their significance as reflexes of Israelite administrative practices. Yet despite prevailing disputes, a number of interpretations have been accepted. It is generally agreed that the ostraca record deliveries of jars of wine and oil to the palace at Samaria from estates in the region of the capital. GNs of towns on the ostraca of years nine and ten or clan districts on the ostraca of year 15, prefixed by the preposition מ (*mem*), "from," indicate the place of origin of the products.[14] Two groups of PNs are mentioned in the inscriptions: PNs prefixed by the preposition ל (*lamed*) and PNs appearing without the preposition. Those without a ל, commonly called "non l-men," are usually identified as tenants or stewards of individual estates.[15] An exception to this understanding is a recent proposal that the "non l-men" on the ostraca from year 15 are military recruits.[16]

In comparison to discussions on the "non l-men," the identity of the men whose PNs are prefixed by the preposition ל, commonly designated "l-men," is intensely debated. The particle ל has a wide semantic range.[17] On personal seals ל plus a PN signifies possession, "of, belonging to PN." Similarly, the *lmlk* impressed handles signify "of, belonging to the king." However, the ל prefixed to a PN can also signify the preposition "for, to," thus designating the PN following

als as Aramaic or Phoenician types, thus reading year 15 as year 9. Menahem's 10-year reign could not account for regnal year 15.

13. For example, among four Arad letters from Stratum VI (nos. 7, 8, 17, 20), the last years of the Judean monarchy, three bear date formulas expressed in words (nos. 7, 8, 20), while one shows the use of hieratic numerals (no. 17). For a discussion of this and related phenomena, see Arad and Other Judean Inscriptions below.

14. For a discussion of the GNs and their locations, see Aharoni, *Land of the Bible*, 356–369, map no. 29.

15. Y. Yadin, "Recipients or Owners: A Note on the Samaria Ostraca," *IEJ* 9 (1959): 186; Cross, "Ammonite Ostraca from Heshbon," 10; Rainey in Aharoni, *Land of the Bible*, 365. Each of the "non l-men" appears in association with only one GN.

16. Shea, "Israelite Chronology and the Samaria Ostraca," 18.

17. *BDB*, 510–518; *HALOT* 2, 507–510.

the ל as the recipient. For example, an ostracon from Heshbon lists the distribution of various agricultural products, livestock, and silver to the king and five other individuals; the PN or title of each recipient is prefixed by ל.[18] In the case of the Samaria ostraca, scholarship is divided on whether the "l-men" represent the senders of the commodities or their recipients. The resolution of this difficulty is essential to the comprehension of the texts.

Five distinct theories have been put forth regarding the identity of the "l-men" and the consequent *Sitz-im-Leben* of the ostraca. Those scholars who interpret the "l-men" as senders of the commodities understand the ostraca as receipts for taxes paid to the crown in the form of wine and oil from the estates of wealthy landowners.[19] In contrast, scholars who view the "l-men" as recipients define their roles as one of the following: tax collectors;[20] administrators of royal estates;[21] functionaries at court who are provisioned by products from their own estates;[22] or military officers (year 15 "l- men").[23] These five theories can be characterized as follows:

(1) The ostraca are records of taxes paid to the government by landowners, "l-men."
(2) The ostraca are records of tax payments sent to tax officials, "l-men."
(3) The ostraca are records of produce from royal estates sent to administrators of those estates, "l-men."
(4) The ostraca are records of commodities from the estates of officials sent to them in the capital where they ("l-men") reside.
(5) The ostraca of year 15 are records of individual recruits sent from their respective clans to serve under officers ("l-men") in Samaria.

These possible interpretations of the Samaria ostraca can be narrowed to those options that are most feasible and that are supported by comparative data from other Hebrew texts and/or non-Hebrew sources. Of the five theories, the second, third, and fifth have little to recommend them. Originally, W.F.

---

18. Cross, "Ammonite Ostraca from Heshbon," 1–7, Ostracon IV. For a discussion of this usage of the preposition ל in the Bible, see A. Rainey, "Semantic Parallels to the Samaria Ostraca," *PEQ* 102 (1970): 45–51.

19. Yadin, "Recipients or Owners," 186; Cross, "Ammonite Ostraca from Heshbon," 8–10; Kaufman, "The Samaria Ostraca: An Early Witness to Hebrew Writing," 235–237.

20. Albright, "The Administrative Divisions of Israel and Judah," 40–41; Shea, "The Date and Significance of the Samaria Ostraca," 25–27.

21. Noth, "Das Krongut der israelitischen Könige und seine Verwaltung," 229–230.

22. A. Rainey, "The Samaria Ostraca in the Light of Fresh Evidence," *PEQ* 99 (1967): 35–41; "The *Sitz im Leben* of the Samaria Ostraca," *TA* 6 (1979): 91–94; Lemaire, *IH*, 76.

23. Shea, "Israelite Chronology and the Samaria Ostraca," 18.

Albright posited that the "l-men" were tax collectors to whom wine and oil were sent as tax payments from private estates.[24] Later, this theory was adopted by B. Mazar and W. Shea.[25] A close look at the data, however, reveals that not only could an "l-man" receive goods from several GNs in one year, but different "l-men" would receive the revenues from the same GN in the same year.[26] As pointed out by Y. Yadin, F.M. Cross, and A. Rainey, if these men were tax-collectors, such a system would result in administrative chaos.[27] Similarly, Noth's theory (no. 3), that the GNs signify crown lands and the "l-men" are their administrators subordinate to the אשר על הבית, "the minister over the royal house,"[28] has been disregarded. The main problem with this interpretation is that the amounts of shipments of commodities to Samaria are far too small to be representative of the income from royal lands.[29]

More recently Shea drafted an alternate theory for the ostraca of year 15. He postulates that since those ostraca are formulated differently from those of years nine and ten, generally lacking mention of a commodity but including a "non l-man" and a clan name, they served a different purpose. Shea maintains that these ostraca do not record commodities at all but rather military recruits, "non l-men," sent from their respective clans to military officers at the capital, "the l-men." He sees the historical setting for this scenario as the reign of Jehoash, a time when Israel prevailed militarily over Aram and a time when young men were conscripted. Shea's theory is problematic on several counts. First, he ignores the fact that "non l-men" also appear on ostraca listing commodities (no. 1 and no. 2 from year ten). Second, he assumes that if commodities were the objects of discussion, they would certainly have been enumerated on the ostraca from year 15. Shea is correct in that information of this type is important for record- keeping if two or more commodities are in question. But if only one commodity was transferred in year 15 from those estates, as seems to be the case for year nine, then its notation for accounting purposes is not essential.[30] Finally, a serious weakness in Shea's argument is that if the "non l-men" repre-

24. Albright, "The Administrative Divisions of Israel and Judah," 40–41.

25. Mazar, "The Historical Background of the Samaria Ostraca," 127; Shea, "The Date and Significance of the Samaria Ostraca," 26–27.

26. For example, גדיו received from four different places (ostraca nos. 4, 16, 17, 18) while שמריו received from three places (ostraca nos. 13, 14, 21); payments from the same GN, שמידע, were apparently sent to three individuals (ostraca nos. 29–39).

27. Yadin, "Recipients or Owners," 185; Cross, Ammonite Ostraca from Heshbon," 9; Rainey, "The *Sitz im Leben* of the Samaria Ostraca," 91.

28. Noth, "Das Krongut der israelitischen Könige," 229–230.

29. Cross, "Ammonite Ostraca from Heshbon," 9.

30. Notably, the ostraca dated to year nine only mention wine.

sent military draftees, their numbers would expectedly be greater than the few attested from each clan, mostly one or two and a maximum of eight men.[31]

Theories worthy of more serious consideration are the one put forth by Yadin, Cross, and Kaufman (no. 1 above) and the one proposed by Rainey (no. 3 above). In their interpretations, the definition of the particle ל plays the key role. Yadin, Cross, and Kaufman all understand the ל prefixed to the PNs on the ostraca as indicative of ownership, comparable to the usage of ל on personal seals, the *lmlk* impressions, and the incised handles from Gibeon.[32] Therefore, they suggest that the "l-men" were the owners of the estates designated by a GN and the commodities represent their taxes sent to Samaria. That some "l-men" are associated with two, three, or four GNs is due to the fact that their landholdings consist of royal grants in addition to patrimonies. In light of this explanation, the ostraca functioned as receipts for tax payments.[33] Kaufman notes that the information on the ostraca was probably copied from labels on the wine and oil jars. Those labels, like the inscriptions on the Gibeon handles, would have included minimally the PNs of landowners, prefixed by the preposition ל, and the GNs of the estates from which the products originated.[34]

Although the aforementioned theory is plausible, it is difficult to support in light of the texts' contents.[35] If the commodities listed on the Samaria ostraca refer

---

31. Eight men from שמידע is an exceptionally large number compared to those from other places.

32. J.B. Pritchard, *Hebrew Inscriptions and Stamps from Gibeon* (Philadelphia: University Museum, 1959), 1–17.

33. Yadin, "Recipients or Owners," 184–187; Cross, "Ammonite Ostraca from Heshbon," 8–10; Kaufman, "The Samaria Ostraca: An Early Witness to Hebrew Writing," 236–237.

34. Kaufman, "The Samaria Ostraca: An Early Witness to Hebrew Writing," 237. Rainey argues, contra Kaufman, that grammatically, the sender's PN prefixed by the preposition ל, juxtaposed to the GN of the place of origin prefixed by the preposition מ, is an odd construction ("The *Sitz im Leben* of the Samaria Ostraca," 93). His argument, while valid based on extant sources, does not draw on comparable texts, jar labels. The two Samaria jar labels are only partially preserved and while neither contains both a GN prefixed by מ and a PN prefixed by ל, the full inscription could be so reconstructed. For example, ostracon no. 62 reads: ין שמיד[ע], "wine (of) *šmydʿ*." One might expect a missing PN on that jar label to be prefixed by a ל as an indicator of the owner of the wine, "wine of GN belonging to PN," comparable to the inscription appearing on a Gibeon handle: גבען לחנניהו לגדד, "(wine of) Gibeon belonging to *gdd*, belonging to *ḥnnyhw*" (Pritchard, *Hebrew Inscriptions and Stamps from Gibeon*, 6 no. 51). Ostracon no. 63, the second jar label, reads, בשת 14(?) משמידע, "in the 14th(?) year from *šmydʿ*." In this case, an attached PN could be preceded by a ל to show ownership of the unspecified commodity. It seems that a grammatical argument is inconclusive.

35. It should be noted that Lemaire's and Kaufman's comparison of Egyptian jar labels

to taxes from private estates they are indeed meager amounts, mostly one and occasionally two containers. This phenomenon would be indicative of relatively small estates that are assessed only one or at most two jars of wine and/or a jar of oil. In comparison, an oil tax list from Ugarit shows larger amounts distributed more unevenly: the 68 jars of oil collected from the village of *Slmy*, for example, come from individual households assessed between one and four containers each.[36]

A more convincing argument is offered by Rainey, who draws extensively on comparative material from Ugarit.[37] Apparently at Ugarit, income from tracts of land granted by the king to his functionaries in exchange for their service was customarily used to support those individuals while they resided at court. Notably, documents from Ugarit recording deliveries for designated personnel are worded similarly to the Samaria ostraca. Recipient names are prefixed by the preposition *ana*, "to, for," in Akkadian texts, and *l*, "to," in Ugaritic texts; the GN of the product's place of origin is indicated by the Ugaritic prefix *b*, "from" (= Heb. מ), written in juxtaposition to *l*.[38]

Although the Israelite system of the Iron Age II does not necessarily match Late Bronze Age Ugaritic practices, testimony from the books of Samuel and Ezekiel

---

from the palace of Amenhotep III to the Samaria ostraca is of little value for the issue at hand (*IH*, 68–69; "The Samaria Ostraca: An Early Witness to Hebrew Writing," 237; W.C. Hayes, "Inscriptions from the Palace of Amenhotep III," *JNES* 10 [1951]: 35–56, 82–111). The Egyptian jar labels, while demonstrating that the practice of recording information about commodities on containers existed in Egypt, seem to reflect a quite different context. They contain the following data: the regnal year in which the contents were packaged; the name of the commodity; a modifying adjective describing the product type, color, or grade; the quantity; the occasion or purpose for sending it; the GN of origin; the name of the donor; and the name of the specialist who oversaw production/packaging. Although some of those data are found on the Samaria ostraca as well, the Egyptian texts, in contrast to the Hebrew ones, are explicit about the purpose of the shipments and the identity of the senders. Clearly, they are festival jars, filled with a variety of foods, drinks, and oils, sent from different parts of the kingdom to Thebes in honor of the celebration of Amenhotep III's *Sed*-festivals (jubilees). The estates from where they originate are royal and temple lands, the donation often coming from functionaries or members of royalty holding privileges in connection with those estates. If the documents from Samaria were equally lucid the present exercise would be unnecessary.

36. *PRU II*, 82 in Heltzer, *Rural Community in Ancient Ugarit*, 42.

37. For references to Ugaritic texts as well as a detailed discussion of other material, see A. Rainey, "Administration in Ugarit and the Samaria Ostraca," *IEJ* 12 (1962): 62–63; "The Samaria Ostraca in the Light of Fresh Evidence," 32–41; "The World of Sinuhe," *IOS* 2 (1972): 374–375.

38. See especially *UT* 1098 (Rainey, "The Samaria Ostraca in the Light of Fresh Evidence," 37).

suggests that comparable practices did exist in monarchic Israel. Samuel's warning concerning the manner of the king: ואת שדותיכם ואת כרמיכם וזיתיכם הטובים יקח ונתן לעבדיו, "your best fields and vineyards and olive groves he (the king) will take and give to his servants" (1 Sam 8:14), indicates that the royal prerogative of allotting land to functionaries was customary in Israel.[39] Saul as king raises the issue of land grants when warning his men that they, as Benjaminites, would be deprived of that privilege under David (22:7). Ezekiel, in discussing inheritance laws applicable to royal property, specifies that grants of crown lands awarded to royal functionaries are temporary and must revert back to the royal family in the year of release, שנת הדרור (Ezek 46:17).[40] In addition, the account of Jonathan's son Mephibosheth at David's court supports the theory that courtiers furnished some of their own supplies. Mephibosheth, who was a regular at David's table, was provisioned by income from his family estate, which was administered by his steward Ziba (2 Sam 9:7–10). Similarly, the "l-men" of the Samaria ostraca could have received wine and oil shipments from their various landholdings, including those allotted to them by the king from large royal estates that he subdivided. The small amounts of commodities reflected in the texts would fit such a scenario, especially if these functionaries were in residence at the palace only part time.[41] Like Ziba, the steward of Mephibosheth's estate, the "non l-men" would have fulfilled parallel duties, either as overseers or tenants.

One argument raised against Rainey's theory is that it does not take into account those ostraca that note commodities but do not mention any "l-men" (nos. 53, 54, 55, 61, 72).[42] In response, Rainey posits that the wine and oil listed on those ostraca represent produce from crown lands bound for the palace but not for any particular individual.[43] Interestingly, the GN that appears on four of those ostraca is כרם התל (*krm htl*), the same GN found on two ostraca from year 15 each listing a different "l-man" (nos. 56 and 58).[44] The implication is that כרם

39. Even if this text is hyperbolic and patrimonies were not commonly confiscated (cf. 1 Kgs 21), it seems reasonable to assume that territory acquired in battle or by other legal means was divided between the crown and the king's officers (cf. I. Mendelsohn, "Samuel's Denunciation of Kingship in the Light of the Akkadian Documents from Ugarit," *BASOR* 143 (1956): 17–22, esp. 19–20).

40. According to Lev 25:10, this refers to the fiftieth year, the jubilee.

41. Already noted by Rainey ("The Samaria Ostraca in the Light of Fresh Evidence," 39).

42. Yadin, "Recipients or Owners," 65; Kaufman, "The Samaria Ostraca," 152–154.

43. Rainey, "The *Sitz im Leben* of the Samaria Ostraca," 91–92.

44. The GN on ostracon no. 56, התל, is assumably equivalent to כרם התל.

התל is a royal estate, parcels of which were allocated to different government officials.

The Status of Persons Appearing in the Texts

At present, the evidence appears to favor the interpretation that the Samaria ostraca are records of commodities, namely wine and oil, delivered from the local estates of royal functionaries to a central storehouse in the palace complex for the use of those functionaries, the "l-men," while they reside at court. Having tentatively accepted this identification of the "l-men," it seems worthwhile to attempt to recover other information about these individuals. B. Rosen began this task in his study of the wine and oil distributions recorded in the texts of years nine and ten.[45] The results of his analysis reveal a number of interesting facts:

(1) The two commodities, wine and oil, are not evenly distributed. Approximately 26 jars of wine are mentioned in comparison to 10 containers of oil, a ratio of 2.6:1.

(2) The six named "l-men" recipients can be divided into two groups of three based on the commodity(s) and quantity each receives. Those three men who comprise Group A are supplied with both oil and wine, the amount of wine exceeding the amount of oil. The three recipients of Group B are provisioned only with small amounts of wine. Notably, when the crown, rather than an "l-man," is the recipient, an equal proportion of wine and oil is listed.

(3) Persons of Group A each received wine and oil from two or more estates, while persons of Group B each received wine from only one estate.

(4) Of the three members of Group A, none bears a name with a clearly non-Yahwistic theophoric element.[46] In contrast, all three members of Group B bear names with non-Yahwistic theophoric elements, either Baal or Horus.[47] Based on comparative evidence from Ugarit and Crete, Rosen constructs a hierarchal system for the "l-men." The data from Greek and Ugaritic sources indicate that the higher the status of a functionary, the greater his allotment of

45. B. Rosen, "Wine and Oil Allocations in the Samaria Ostraca," *TA* 13 (1986): 39–45.

46. Two names are Yahwistic, גדיו (2:2; 4:2; 5:2; 6:2–3; 7:2; 16a,b:2; 17a,b:2; 18:2) and שמריו (1:1–2; 13:2; 14:2; 21:1–2). The third, depending on the restoration of either אדנעם (8:2; 9:2; 10:2–3; 11:2; 19:4; Kaufman, "The Samaria Ostraca," 135–136; *IH*, 48), אחנעם (Reisner, *Harvard Excavations at Samaria*, 233) or אבנעם (*HDAE*, 92), is not clearly identifiable with a particular deity.

47. The two Baal names are בעלא (3:3) and בעלזמר (12:2–3); the name אשחר (13:3) is probably of Egyptian derivation, *ḥr* signifying the deity Horus. For a discussion of the names, see Lemaire, *IH*, 49–50; Tigay, *You Shall Have No Other Gods*, 65–66 nn. 5–6, 9 and p. 72 n. 43; cf. S. Ahituv, "Pashhur," *IEJ* 20 (1970): 95–96.

oil and wine. In fact, certain low level functionaries receive wine but no oil at all.[48] Applying the statistics from non-Israelite societies to Israel, Rosen suggests that the "l-men" of Group A were higher level officials than those of Group B.[49]

The observation that members of Group A and B are distinguishable by their names raises some intriguing questions pertaining to their identity. One possibility is that the non-Yahwistic names signify non-Israelites residing in the environs of Samaria. Positions held by these individuals at court would expectedly be less prestigious than those of Israelites. Another prospect is that persons with non-Yahwistic theophoric elements in their names were Israelites, but perhaps members of a different social class.[50] This issue may be somewhat elucidated by evaluating the onomasticon of the "l-men" compared to that of the "non l-men."

Regardless of which theory one follows, it is generally agreed that the "non l-men" held lower ranking positions than the "l-men." The "non l-men," although untitled, are commonly viewed as tenants or stewards of estates belonging to the crown or to royal officials.[51] Distinctions in the PNs of the "non l-men" group as compared to the PNs of the "l-men" group call for comment. A minimum of forty individuals are mentioned on the Samaria ostraca: 17 "l-men" bearing 15 different PNs; 23 "non l-men" bearing 20 different names.[52] As noted, among the "l-men," two persons have Baalistic PNs and

48. Rosen, "Wine and Oil Allocations in the Samaria Ostraca," 42–43, Table 2 (Hagia Triada); Table 3 (RS 20.425).

49. Rosen, "Wine and Oil Allocations in the Samaria Ostraca," 42–44.

50. Tigay notes that it cannot be assumed that polytheism was characteristic of the lower classes since biblical accusations of such practices are generally directed at the upper classes (e.g. 1 Kgs 11:4–10; 15:13; 16:31–33; 2 Kgs 1:2; 21:2–7; Tigay, *You Shall Have No Other Gods*, 10). He does not take into account, however, that the focus of the biblical writers is primarily on the behavior of the leaders of Israelite society. They rarely draw attention to less influential groups. Therefore, the possibility remains that non-Yahwistic names were more prevalent among certain circles or families of the middle and lower social strata. Conceivably, some individuals from those classes rose to higher positions.

51. In contrast, Egyptian jar handles inscribed with the name of the estate of origin of a certain product often include the PN and title of the person charged with the production or packaging of the product. For example, a common title that appears in connection with wine is *ḥry k3mw*, "chief of the vineyard" (Hayes, "Inscriptions from the Palace of Amenhotep III," 101–102; F.L. Griffith, "The Jar Inscriptions" in W.M.F. Petrie ed. *Tel El Amarna* [Warminster: Aris & Phillips, 1974], 33). Interestingly, from the time of Amenhotep III several names belonging to vineyard stewards are Semitic, suggesting that these persons were Asiatic.

52. Since patronyms are not consistently used for all individuals, names that repeat, at times without patronymics and at times with patronymics, are only considered as part of

a third seems to bear a Horus PN. Five others have Yahwistic names and nine bear PNs not showing a DN.[53] In contrast, among the "non l-men" probably as many as six have Baalistic PNs,[54] four bear Yahwistic PNs[55] and 13 have PNs not specifying a DN. These statistics yield the following percentages: 17.6% of the "l-men" bear PNs with non-Yahwistic theophoric elements (all of Group B); 26% of the "non l-men" bear PNs with non-Yahwistic theophoric elements;[56] 29.4% of the "l-men" bear PNs with Yahwistic theophoric elements; 17.3% of the "non l-men" bear PNs with Yahwistic theophoric elements.[57] Clearly, there is a lower frequency of Yahwistic PNs and a higher frequency of non-Yahwistic PNs among the "non l-men" group than among the "l-men" group. The figures for both "l-men" and "non l-men," although admittedly limited, imply that

---

these data when they include a patronym, thus distinguishing one person from another. Therefore, the total of 40 individuals is conservative and could in reality be greater. The interpretation that xy signifies a PN plus patronym is based on the assumption that the word "בן" (son of), which never appears on the Samaria Ostraca between two names, is understood (contra Yadin, "Recipients or Owners," 187). This type of abbreviated writing is common on personal seals and is also attested in ink inscriptions other than the Samaria Ostraca, for example, Murabba'at Papyrus B and Arad no. 110. In the latter, the person's title, written as a singular noun, confirms that one individual is indicated: שמיה משלם נער אלנתן. Duplicate names found on the Samaria Ostraca include the following: three or four (see below) "non l-men" are named בעלא; two are named גרא; and two are named אשא. Among the "l-men," three bear the name חלץ. Apparently, certain PNs were popular in different regions in different periods (cf. the frequency of certain names from comparably sized Judean onomastica: five persons bear a form of the name נחם and three of the name שלם on personal seal-impressions from *lmlk* handles; three persons named שמעיהו are known from the bullae from the City of David).

53. The Yahwistic PNs include: שמריו (1:1–2; 13:2; 14:2; 21:1–2), גדיו (2:2; 4:2; 5:2; 6:2–3; 7:2; 16:2; 17:2; 18:2), ידעיו (42:2; 48:1), אר/ביו (50:2) and בדיו (58:1).

54. Three persons are named בעלא (*b'l'*): בעלא (בן) אלישע (1:7); בעלא (בן) בעלמעני (27:3); בעלא (בן) זכר (31a:3; 31b:3). A possible fourth person, בעלא מאלמתן, "*B'l' from 'lmtn*" (28:3) may be distinguished by his hometown rather than a patronym (the GN does not refer to the estate he services, cf. nos. 29 and 45). A fifth individual is named אבבעל (*'bb'l*, 2:4) and a sixth is called מרבעל (*mrb'l*, 2:7). A seventh person bears the name אלבא (*'lb'*, 1:6), but that PN should probably be translated "God came" (Tigay, *You Shall Have No Other Gods*, 75 n. 3), although Lemaire suggests it may be a hypocoristicon of *'lb'l*, "God is Baal" (*IH*, 49).

55. The Yahwistic PNs include: ידעיו (1:8); אדניו (42:3); יונתן (45:3); עבדיו (50:2). A fifth possibility is אביו (52:2), but in light of לאביו on ostracon no. 50, it is highly likely that a "*l*" is missing from the end of the previous line, which is illegible and the name belongs to an "l-man."

56. These statistics include those names that are possibly foreign, one for the "l-men" group and one for "non l-men" group.

57. These statistics only take into account those PNs clearly Yahwistic.

among persons of higher status, PNs with non-Yahwistic theophoric elements were less prevalent.

Conclusions

The Samaria ostraca are a significant source for the study of Israelite officialdom. They provide a glimpse into the record-keeping practices of the Northern Kingdom in the mid-eighth century. While currently the identity of certain persons mentioned in the texts is still uncertain, the evidence suggests that officials residing at the royal court were partially provisioned by produce from their own estates. In addition, a hierarchal system is indicated for persons mentioned in the texts. The "l-men" were of higher status than the "non l-men" and among the "l-men" there existed at least two groups of distinct rank. Interestingly, the data also imply that naming customs may have been influenced by social standing or by national origin. Unfortunately, information on the offices held by the "l-men" at court is totally lacking and none can be associated with any biblical characters.

B. *LMLK* Seal Impressions

Jar handles stamped with royal or personal seals are another important type of epigraphic source material from Israel. The *lmlk* seal impressions comprise the largest assemblage of archaeological data associated with an enterprise of the central government. Scholarship on the *lmlk* phenomenon, which spans a century or more, has produced a number of theories concerning various issues relating to the seals and the vessels on which they appear, including chronological, typological, and functional considerations. Moreover, handles belonging to *lmlk* jars stamped with personal seals, commonly designated "private seal-impressions" or more recently "official seal- impressions," have raised additional questions. In the last 20 years or so scholarly investigations have solved some of these problems, most importantly the accurate dating of the vessels. Many issues, however, remain open. In light of the significance of the *lmlk* jars to the subject of officials and administration, it seems worthwhile to review the main points and to reconstruct possible scenarios for the *Sitz-im-Leben* of this enterprise.

Corpus and Typology

The latest figures compiled by A. Vaughn in his dissertation bring the number of *lmlk* handles to 1716.[58] These handles belong to large four-handled storage

58. Vaughn, "The Chronicler's Account of Hezekiah," 219, 231–251.

jars cataloged by O. Tufnell as Type 484.[59] Tests of the chemical composition of a sampling of handles from different sites revealed a degree of homogeneity that is indicative of a single place of manufacture. Although no specific site has been identified, its general location is isolated to the Shephelah.[60]

The *lmlk* seal impressions, for which no seals have been found to date, do not display uniformity and, accordingly, have been classified by certain characteristics. Most of the impressions bear the following features: a representation of a four-winged scarab beetle or a two-winged solar disc as the central design; the designation למלך inscribed above the scarab or solar disc; and one of four GNs (זיף, סוכה, חברן, ממשת) inscribed below the scarab or solar disc.[61] Originally, D. Diringer distinguished a three-class typology based on iconographic, stylistic, paleographic, and orthographic distinctions.[62] As the corpus of *lmlk* seal impressions grew, modifications were made to Diringer's class divisions by P. Lapp,[63] Y. Aharoni,[64] P. Welten,[65] and most recently by A. Lemaire, whose typology is currently in use.[66] Notably, there exist a few unusual classes among these seals: IIc – lacks the designation למלך but bears a GN inscribed above the two-winged solar disc; XII – contains the word למלך but does not include a GN; OII – has neither the word למלך nor a GN but consists solely of a two-winged solar disc

59. Tufnell, *Lachish III*, 315–316, pl. 78:1, 5, 11. Several *lmlk* jars have been fully restored (Ussishkin, "Royal Judean Storage Jars and Private Seal Impressions," 1–2; "Excavations at Tel Lachish (1973–1977)," 76–80; "Excavations at Tel Lachish 1978–1983," 162–163). Four exceptional *lmlk* handles belong to *pithoi*, one from Beer-sheba Stratum II (A. Rainey, "Wine from the Royal Vineyards," *BASOR* 245 [1982]: 60) and three unprovenienced handles (Vaughn, "The Chronicler's Account of Hezekiah," 251).

60. Mommsen, Perlman and Yellin, "The Provenience of the *lmlk* Jars," *IEJ* 34 (1984): 89–113.

61. The letters H, S, Z, M used in the classification system of *lmlk* seals signify the four GNs, Hebron, Socoh, Ziph and Mmšt respectively.

62. D. Diringer, "On Ancient Hebrew Inscriptions Discovered at Tell ed-Duweir (Lachish) II," *PEQ* 73 (1941): 91–102.

63. P. Lapp, "Late Royal Seals from Judah," *BASOR* 158 (1960): 11–22.

64. Y. Aharoni, *Excavations at Ramat-Raḥel, Seasons 1959 and 1960* (Rome: Centro di Studi Semitici, 1962), 46.

65. P. Welten, *Die Königs-Stempel. Ein Beitrag zur Militärpolitik Judas unter Hiskia and Josia* (Wiesbaden: Harrassowitz, 1969), 35–46.

66. A. Lemaire, "Classification des estampilles royales judéennes," *EI* 15 (1981): 54*–60*, pl. 8. Seals classified Types Ia and Ib show a four-winged scarab, the designation למלך engraved above the symbol and one of four GNs engraved below. Seals classified Types IIa and IIb show a two-winged disc, the designation למלך engraved above the symbol and one of four GNs engraved below. Sub-classes a and b are distinguished on stylistic, paleographic, and orthographic criteria. In seals Type IIa and IIb, the latter shows divided GNs, half the letters flanking each side of the symbol's tail (e.g. HIIb חב–רן).

representation.[67] The latter variety seems to imply that the key identifying element of the *lmlk* seal impression is the scarab or solar disc emblem.

Chronology, Distribution and Archaeological Context

Prior to Ussishkin's renewed excavations at Lachish in the 1970s, there were three schools of thought on the chronology of the *lmlk* jars. Their theories were linked to three issues: (1) the dating of the stratigraphy at Lachish, primarily that of Stratum III, which housed the handles; (2) attestations of two distinct symbols on jar handles from the same site;[68] (3) distinctions in paleography. One group of scholars, following J. Starkey's assertion that the pottery types of Strata III and II were sufficiently similar to postulate a destruction of 597 BCE and 586 BCE respectively, dated the jars to the reign of Josiah at the end of the Judean monarchy.[69] Another group of scholars sided with O. Tufnell in dating the destruction of Stratum III to 701 BCE, the Assyrian campaign of Sennacherib. Tufnell's conclusions were based on the identification of new pottery types from Stratum II that indicated a time-gap greater than 10 years between Strata III and II. This school of thought assigned the jars to the reign of Hezekiah.[70] A third group of scholars postulated that the *lmlk* seal impressions spanned a wider time-period, from the late eighth century through the early sixth century. Albright, who held this opinion, based his conclusions on the considerable paleographic variations he observed on the seals.[71] Welten, who also supported that position, argued chronology on the strength of the two distinct symbols. He dated seals with the four-winged scarab to the reign of Hezekiah, while those bearing the two-winged sun disc he assigned to the reign of Josiah.[72]

The issue of chronology was resolved with renewed excavations at Lachish that expanded the original dig areas and reevaluated the ceramic remains. The results, which showed clear differentiation between the pottery of Strata III and

---

67. Lemaire, "Classification des estampilles royales judéennes," 57*.

68. The two symbols are never found together on the same jar handle or on separate handles of a single jar.

69. J. Starkey, "Excavations at Tell ed-Duweir," *PEQ* 69 (1937): 236; G.E. Wright, "Review of Lachish III," *JNES* 14 (1955): 188–189; *VT* 5 (1955): 100–104; K. Kenyon, "The Date of the Destruction of Iron Age Beer-Sheba," *PEQ* 108 (1976): 63–64; Lapp, "Late Royal Seals," 18–22; F.M. Cross, "Judean Stamps," *EI* 9 (1969): 20*–21*; J. Holladay, "Of Sherds and Strata" in Cross, *Magnalia Dei*, 266–267.

70. Tufnell, *Lachish III*, 55–58, 94–98; Y. Aharoni and R. Amiran, "A New Sub-Division of the Iron Age in Palestine," *IEJ* 8 (1958): 182 n. 42, chart p. 183; Aharoni, *Land of the Bible*, 340–342; A. Rainey, "The Fate of Lachish During the Campaigns of Sennacherib and Nebuchadrezzar" in *Lachish V*, 47–60.

71. Albright, *Tell Beit Mirsim III*, 74–75.

72. Welten, *Königs-Stempel*, 104.

II and also revealed an intermediate level, confirmed Tufnell's dating. Ussishkin's discovery of the Assyrian siege ramp and battering rams, similar to those pictured in Sennacherib's reliefs at Nineveh depicting the capture of Lachish, buttressed the ceramic evidence.[73] The findings at Lachish, supported by comparable eighth century material from other Judahite sites, such as Tel Batash (Timnah) Stratum III and the City of David Stratum 12, fix the chronology of the jars to the late eighth century.[74] Notably, with few exceptions, *lmlk* handles are absent from seventh century strata.[75]

The distribution of the *lmlk* jars at eighth century sites is widespread. Vaughn lists 65 sites for the 1361 provenienced handles[76] (see Distribution Map). While the greatest concentration of handles are traceable to cities and towns in the Shephelah and Judean Hills, a number were found at Judean Desert settlements and a few isolated handles appeared at Negeb, Coastal Plain and even northern sites. The site that produced the most handles is Lachish (407), the largest city in the Shephelah and one classified as a royal regional administrative center.[77] Jerusalem and Ramat Raḥel rank second (275) and third (160) for quantity of handles. These three urban centers alone account for about ⅔ of the total provenienced pieces. A large number of handles originates from several cities north of Jerusalem, namely, Gibeon, Mizpah, and Gibea (total 195) and from urban settlements in the Shephelah north of Lachish such as, Mareshah, Tel Judeideh, Azekah, and Beth Shemesh (total 124). From sites in the northern Negeb, the fortress of Arad produced the most handles (ten), but notably, the

73. D. Ussishkin, "The Destruction of Lachish," *TA* 4 (1977): 36–54; "Excavations at Tel Lachish (1973–1977)," 64, 67–74.

74. G.L. Kelm and A. Mazar, "Three Seasons of Excavations at Tell Batash," *BASOR* 248 (1982): 29–30; Y. Shiloh, *Excavations at the City of David I* (Jerusalem: Institute of Archaeology, 1984), 28; "Judah and Jerusalem in the Eighth-Sixth Centuries B.C.E." in S. Gitin and W. Dever eds. *Recent Excavations in Israel: Studies in Iron Age Archaeology* (*AASOR* 49; Winona Lake: Eisenbrauns, 1989), 97–105, esp. chart p. 103.

75. One two-winged type *lmlk* handle was found at the seventh-century site of Horvat Shilḥah (A. Mazar, "The 'Border Road' between Michmash and Jericho and Excavations at Horvat Shilḥah," *EI* 17 [1984]: 247–248, fig. 5:20 [Hebrew]). Mazar notes that some eighth-century jars, especially from sites not destroyed by Sennacherib, survived into the seventh century and continued to be used.

76. Vaughn, "The Chronicler's Account of Hezekiah," 219, 231–251. Only 355 handles are unprovenienced.

77. Lachish is classified with Jerusalem and Samaria as a royal city as well as a regional administrative center, based on its construction plan, which features a palace-fort on the acropolis separated by an enclosure wall from the rest of the city. For a classification of the four types of Israelite cities, see Z. Herzog, "Israelite City Planning," *Expedition* 20:4 (1978): 43.

lmlk jars are conspicuously rare in the rest of the Negeb: Aroer (3), Beer-Sheba (2) and Tell 'Ira (1). Interestingly, border sites in Israel and Philistia have produced a fair amount of handles: Gezer (37); Tell 'Erani (15); Timnah (11); Tell es-ṣafi (Gath; 6); Ekron (3); Ashdod (1). The latter provide a *terminus a quo* for the *lmlk* jars, at least for those circulating outside of Judah proper, as those sites would not have been under Judah's influence before the decline of Assyrian control in the region in the reign of Hezekiah.[78] A few handles even found their way to sites in North Israel: Jezreel (2) and Kfar Ata, near Haifa (1).[79]

While *lmlk* handles are widely distributed at dozens of sites, the archaeological context of concentrations of handles is in the remains of public buildings. At Lachish, for example, where most finds were recovered *in situ*, contexts, including those of the ten restored *lmlk* vessels, were gatehouse chambers, storerooms associated with the gatehouse, and city walls and buildings on the main road from the gate into the city.[80] At Tel Batash too, a collection of *lmlk* handles and jar sherds was discovered in a large storage complex.[81] Notably, however, Tufnell observes that at Lachish at least one example of a *lmlk* vessel was found in nearly all rooms of Stratum III (in public and non-public buildings), the occupation level destroyed by Sennacherib.[82]

Symbolism

The designation *lmlk*, "belonging to the king," clearly indicates that the seals should be classified as royal seals and that their impression on jars signifies royal property.[83] Questions pertaining to the symbolism of the four-winged scarab beetle and the two-winged solar disc are more complex. Apparently the existence of handles marked with a seal engraved solely with the solar disc, thus devoid of any accompanying inscription, implies that the emblem alone can be understood as a sign of Judahite kingship.[84] One theory concerning these symbols that deserves attention was proposed by A.D. Tushingham. He identifies

---

78. 2 Kgs 18:8. Probably, those sites came under Judah's influence around 705 BCE after the death of Sargon II.

79. Vaughn, "The Chronicler's Account of Hezekiah," 248–249.

80. Tufnell, *Lachish III*, 124, 315, 340–341; Ussishkin, "Royal Judean Storage Jars and Private Seal Impressions," 1; "Excavations at Tel Lachish (1973–1977)," 76–77.

81. Kelm and Mazar, "Three Seasons of Excavations at Tell Batash," 28–29.

82. Tufnell, *Lachish III*, 315, 340.

83. A number of *lmlk* handles are incised with concentric circles or an X over the seal impression. It is generally assumed that those marks canceled the royal status of the jars, perhaps allowing them to be used for other purposes (e.g. Welten, *Königs-Stempel*, 189–190; Ussishkin, "Excavations at Tel Lachish 1978–1983," 163, fig. 28).

84. Welten suggests that it may be analogous to a coat-of-arms (*Königs-Stempel*, 171).

each symbol as the royal insignia of one Israelite kingdom, the four-winged scarab belonging to Israel and the two-winged solar disc to Judah.[85] He derives the association of the four-winged scarab with Israel from other similar depictions on seals, showing a scarab beetle pushing a solar ball, that may have been used as state seals for the kingdom of Israel.[86] Tushingham traces the originally Egyptian motif of the scarab (the symbol of Khepri, god of the rising sun) to the Syrian cultural world, from where it could have been transmitted to Israel, probably via the Phoenicians in the ninth century.[87] By a process of elimination, the two-winged solar disc symbol is assigned to Judah. Tushingham shows that it too originated in Egypt (a symbol of the god Horus of Edfu) but found its way to Syria, where variations of the motif were adopted as emblems of kingship.[88]

While the evidence is too scant to substantiate Tushingham's theory, his proposal does offer one option for understanding the background of these two symbols, one of which appears on every *lmlk* seal impression. The fact that depictions of four-winged scarabs and two-winged sun discs resembling those on the *lmlk* handles are also found on Israelite private seals is not critical to the validity of the argument because these motifs are not restricted to kingship.[89] Also, for personal seals, connections between iconography and text cannot normally be assumed, as many seals probably were produced in one workshop and

---

85. A.D. Tushingham, "A Royal Israelite Seal (?) and the Royal Jar Handle Stamps (part one)," *BASOR* 200 (1970): 71–78; (part two) *BASOR* 201 (1971): 23–35.

86. An unprovenienced scaraboid type seal is engraved with a four-winged beetle pushing a solar ball (Tushingham, "A Royal Israelite Seal (?) (part 1)," figs. 1–3); nine bullae discovered at the palace at Samaria were impressed with a similar seal (Crowfoot, Kenyon and Sukenik, *Samaria-Sebaste,* I, 108; III, 88, nos. 29–37, pl. 15).

Notably, three Ammonite seals show the same beetle, but flanked by what appear to be standards. One of the seals is inscribed, למלכמאור עבד בעלישע, "belonging to *mlkm'wr* the servant of *b'lys',*" the genitive being the PN of a late seventh century Ammonite king (Jer 40:14). The two other seals may also belong to royal officials. R.W. Younker, who accepts Tushingham's interpretation of the scarab as the royal symbol of Israel, posits that the Ammonites, like Israel, adopted the scarab as a royal motif, their inspiration coming from Israel ("Israel, Judah, and Ammon and the Motifs on the Baalis Seal from Tell el-'Umeiri," *BA* 48 [1985]: 173–177).

87. Tushingham, "A Royal Israelite Seal (?) (part one)," 71–77.

88. The closest parallels to the winged sun disc on the *lmlk* impression are found on ivory plaques from Nimrud and on the Bar-Rakkab orthostat from Zinjirli, both dated to the eighth century (Tushingham, "A Royal Israelite Seal (?) (part two)," 26–33). Y. Yadin identifies the winged sun disc on the Zinjirli stele with the god El ("Symbols of Deities at Zinjirli, Carthage and Hazor" in *NEATC,* 199–216).

89. For various examples, see Sass, "The Pre-Exilic Hebrew Seals," 212–214 nos. 77–90, 238–239 nos. 147–151.

inscribed with the PN of the seal owner by a different engraver at the time of purchase, perhaps in another geographical locale.[90]

Another puzzling issue related to the scarab and winged sun disc is the rationale underlying the coexistence of two royal emblems for the *lmlk* jars. If in fact the symbols represent the two Israelite states, then it can be argued that the symbol of Judah alone should have sufficed for a Judahite enterprise, especially at a time when the Kingdom of Israel no longer existed. Originally Tushingham suggested that the usage of the symbols reflected Josiah's assertion that he was the ruler of a reunited kingdom encompassing the territories of both Israel and Judah.[91] More recently, in light of the secure dating of the *lmlk* jars to the late eighth century, he adjusted his theory, claiming that Hezekiah utilized the insignia of the North to symbolize reunification while the Judahite emblem was confined to Jerusalem proper, where it was used until the reign of Josiah.[92] Although Tushingham's chronological argument is not supported archaeologically, his underlying thesis that the symbols signify a reunited kingdom may be applicable to the reign of Hezekiah only. The Chronicler's report that Hezekiah sent couriers throughout Israel, including Ephraim and Manasseh, to invite the people to Jerusalem to celebrate the Passover, accords with a plan to incorporate the former kingdom of Israel into Judah's domain (2 Chr 30:1–9).[93] Adopting the royal insignia of the North as one of Judah's state symbols may have served to unify the populace of Judah, a percentage of which by this time was probably of northern origin.[94] The designation *lmlk* as a superscription on most of the royal seals would certify that both the scarab and the winged sun disc qualified as state symbols.

This explanation, rationalizing the coexistence of two royal emblems, still does not adequately explain the use of both for a single project. It would seem that the utilization of two distinct icons held some differentiation purpose. At least two potential explanations exist for this phenomenon, although admittedly, neither can be proven. One possibility is that the four-winged scarab and the two-

---

90. A. Lemaire, "Les critères non-iconographiques de la classification des sceaux nord-ouest sémitiques inscrits" in Sass, *Studies,* 18–21; Uehlinger, "Northwest Semitic Inscribed Seals," 275–276.

91. Tushingham, "A Royal Israelite Seal (?) (part two)," 33–35.

92. A.D. Tushingham, "New Evidence Bearing on the Two-Winged LMLK Stamp," *BASOR* 287 (1992): 61–64.

93. Welten, among others, maintains that this narrative in Chronicles is not historically accurate for the reign of Hezekiah, but his arguments are not compelling (*Königs-Stempel,* 159).

94. On the migration of northerners to Judah, see M. Broshi, "The Expansion of Jerusalem in the Reigns of Hezekiah and Manasseh," *IEJ* 24 (1974): 21–26.

winged sun disc each denotes a certain product stored in the jars, one wine and the other oil. A second possibility, one that conforms to the theory that the jars stocked wine only, is that the two symbols represent two types or grades of wine. Variant types or grades of wine are known from other Hebrew inscriptions. For example, on the Samaria ostraca, some of the wine is designated יין ישן, "aged wine;"[95] wine on one Arad ostracon is called יין האגנת, "wine of the *'gnt* vessels;"[96] a Lachish decanter is labeled יין עשן, "smoked wine;"[97] and on a decanter from el-Qom the wine is marked יין כחל, "blue or dark wine."[98] Interestingly, handles showing the two-winged solar disc stamps predominate over the four-winged scarab stamps in finds from Jerusalem, in the corpus of handles from Ramat Raḥel, and in the handles from cities north of Jerusalem.[99] If this symbol designates jars containing the more desirable type or grade of wine, its concentration in the vicinity of royal residences is understandable. On the other hand, the prevalence of a higher grade of wine at north Judean sites such as Gibeon and Tell en-Naṣbeh (Mizpah) is not as easily explained.

The Four GNs

Several proposals have been put forth on the significance of the four GNs found on *lmlk* seals: חברן (Hebron); שוכה (Socoh); זיף (Ziph); and ממשת (Mmšt):[100]

95. Samaria Ostraca nos. 1, 3–15, 101. In other cases the wine is simply called, יין.

96. This designation indicates a type of wine kept or diluted in special bowls. Aharoni, *Arad Inscriptions*, no. 1:9–10, 12, 14, 144.

97. Ussishkin, "Excavations at Tel Lachish (1973–1977)," 83–84, inscription no. 25, fig. 26, pl. 27; A. Demsky, "A Note on 'Smoked Wine'," *TA* 6 (1979): 163.

98. N. Avigad, "Two Hebrew Inscriptions on Wine-Jars," *IEJ* 22 (1972): 1–5; A. Demsky, "'Dark Wine' from Judah," *IEJ* 22 (1972): 233–234; S. Paul, "Classifications of Wine in Mesopotamian and Rabbinic Sources," *IEJ* 25 (1975): 42–44. Avigad posits that the term כחל designates the location of the vineyard, while Demsky and Paul maintain that it indicates a type of wine based on the dark color. Demsky's and Paul's arguments, based on comparable differentiation of wine in Mesopotamian and rabbinic texts and the usage of the root כחל/חכל to signify a dark color in biblical Hebrew (Akkadian cognate = *eklu*), are more convincing.

99. 92% of the handles (235 of 254) from Jerusalem are of the two-winged solar disc variety (G. Barkay, "Northern and Western Jerusalem in the End of the Iron Age" [Ph.D. Dissertation Tel Aviv University, 1985], 406, 424); at Ramat Raḥel the solar disc symbol constitutes more than 85% of the total amount of handles (Aharoni, *Ramat Raḥel, Seasons 1961 and 1962*, 63); at Gibeon 87% and at Tell en-Nabeh 78% of the handles bear the solar disc symbol (Pritchard, *Hebrew Inscriptions and Stamps from Gibeon*, 18–20).

100. No GN ממשת exists in the Bible or in other epigraphic source of the pre-exilic period. The most convincing explanation for identifying ממשת was offered by H.L. Ginsberg who proposed that it is an abbreviation for ממשלת (*mmšlt*), "government," an administrative designation for Jerusalem ("MMŠT and MṢH," *BASOR* 109 [1948]: 20–21). The fact that a large percentage of *lmlk* impressions from northern sites in Judah bear the GN ממשת further

(1) the four GNs represent centers of administrative districts; (2) the four GNs signify defensive zones; (3) the four GNs designate royal estates.

The first theory was introduced by C. Clermont-Ganneau and later adopted with variations by other scholars, including W.F. Albright and Y. Aharoni.[101] Aharoni, who presents the most detailed explanation, suggests that Hezekiah in the process of centralizing the royal administration reorganized Judah's 12 administrative districts (Josh 15:21–62) into four, apparently for more efficient tax collection.[102] He assumes that the four GNs on the *lmlk* seal impressions signify the main store cities of each district where the taxes were concentrated. Under this system the 12 original districts were divided into four groups, each composed of three former districts and united around one of the four sites.[103] While Aharoni's interpretation is plausible, several weaknesses are apparent. First, it presumes a reorganization of Judah's districts unattested in the Bible. More importantly, of the three known sites, Hebron, Socoh, and Ziph, none have produced large numbers of *lmlk* handles with their respective GN, as would be expected if they were store cities for those districts.

The second theory, which defines the four GNs as defensive zones, was formulated by Y. Yadin.[104] Yadin derives the fourfold division of Judah from the four geographical zones listed in Josh 15:20–62: the Negeb; the Hill Country; the Shephelah; and the Wilderness. He maintains that the defensive zones, each of which encompassed one or more administrative district, served as "fences" for the store cities within. To make his structure workable, Yadin identifies *Mmšt* as the Negeb site of Khirbet al-Gharra (Tel 'Ira), arriving at the name ממשת from that of nearby Tel Masos.[105] Besides the obvious difficulty of associating *Mmšt*

---

supports Ginsberg's argument. Recently, with the discovery of eighth century building remains at Ramat Raḥel, which may be attributed to a palace of Hezekiah, Barkay suggests that Ramat Raḥel rather than Jerusalem should be identified as ממשת ("Ramat Raḥel" in *NEAEHL*, 1267).

101. C. Clermont-Ganneau, "Jarres israëlites marquées à l'estampille des rois de Juda," *Recueil d'archeologie orientale* 4 (1900): 1–24; Albright, "The Administrative Division of Israel and Judah," 44–54; Aharoni, *Land of the Bible*, 398–399.

102. That the term למלך can signify payments of taxes made "to the crown" is discernable from an Ammonite ostracon (no. 4) listing payments of produce, animals, and silver to various individuals including the king (W.E. Aufrecht, *A Corpus of Ammonite Inscriptions* [Lewiston: Edwin Mellen Press, 1989], 80–81).

103. See map no. 28 (Aharoni, *Land of the Bible*). Note that Aharoni identifies Socoh as the Shephelah site.

104. Y. Yadin, "The Fourfold Division of Judah," *BASOR* 163 (1961): 6–12.

105. Another Negeb site previously identified as *Mmšt* is Mamshit-Mampsis (Kurnub), a Nabatean site that has no Iron Age occupation (R. Cohen and A. Negev, "Negev" in *NEAEHL*, 1134, 1140).

with Tel 'Ira, a critical barrier to this interpretation is that no substantial finds of *lmlk* handles exist from either the Negeb or Wilderness regions, a problem Yadin himself recognized.

The third theory, identifying the GNs with royal estates, was originally made by K. Galling.[106] It was adopted by O. Tufnell, who suggested that the crown lands in question were vineyards.[107] Tufnell's conclusion was reiterated by several scholars, including F.M. Cross, E. Stern, and A. Rainey.[108] Rainey's lengthy discussion on the topic can be summarized as follows. The four GNs appearing on *lmlk*-impressed handles correspond to Hezekiah's wineries in the Hill Country, the same geographical region designated by the Chronicler for the vineyards of Uzziah (2 Chr 26:10). Wine from those vineyards supplied most of Judah in an emergency situation. The Negeb sites, which show a scarcity of *lmlk* handles, had lesser needs that were furnished by a different source, the produce of private holdings in the form of taxes.[109]

In favor of Rainey's theory is the argument that wine has a history of being labeled with its vintage district, thereby explaining the four GNs.[110] The designation יין חלבון, "wine of Helbon" (Ezek 27:18), seems to be an example of wine known by its provenience. A weakness in this reconstruction is the lack of evidence from biblical or extra-biblical sources that Israelite monarchs, or those of other Near Eastern states, supplied garrisons with produce from their own estates. Usually the royal constituency and the king's troops were provisioned with the produce of private lands, as implied by Samuel's warning about the manner of the king (1 Sam 8:11–17). However, if the *lmlk* project was not designed exclusively for wartime, as can be argued, then this theory remains viable (see below).

Personal Name Seal Impressions

A total of 266 (184 provenienced) seal impressions bearing PNs, commonly

---

106. K. Galling, "Krügstempel" in *Biblisches Reallexikon* (Tubingen, 1937), 339.

107. O. Tufnell, "Tel En-Naṣbeh," *PEQ* 80 (1948): 149.

108. Cross, "Judean Stamps," 20–21; E. Stern, "Israel at the Close of the Period of the Monarchy: An Archaeological Survey," *BA* 38 (1975): 51–52; Rainey, "Wine from the Royal Vineyards," 57–62. Curiously, none of these scholars seem to be aware of Tufnell's earlier suggestion.

109. Rainey, "Wine from the Royal Vineyards," 59–61. Rainey maintains that Ziph refers to the site by that name in the Hill Country (Josh 15:55), as opposed to Ziph in the Negeb. Similarly, he locates Socoh in the southern Hill Country (Josh 15:48), rather than in the Shephelah as is commonly done. Rainey accepts the identification of *Mmšt* as Jerusalem and her surroundings.

110. Cross, "Judean Stamps," 21.

called "private seals," are extant on *lmlk* type handles.[111] At least 36 individuals (29 on provenienced handles) are represented on the 266 stamped handles. The seals of a number of persons have surfaced on handles from several different sites. Often seal impressions with the same PN were stamped with different seals, indicating either that one individual owned multiple seals or that the same PN was shared by two or more persons.[112] Among the three-dozen or so PNs appearing on the handles, only one contains a title: לאליקם נער יוכן, "belonging to *'lyqm* the *n'r* of *ywkn*."[113] Another stamp bearing a title that may be part of this group reads: לשבניהו בן המלך "belonging to *šbnyhw* son of the king." That title, however, occurs only once, on an unprovenienced handle resembling the *lmlk* type but which cannot be positively identified as belonging to a *lmlk* jar.[114]

Early on it was recognized that the handles bearing seal impressions with PNs should be associated with the *lmlk* jars. Not only are the handles of the same typological class as the *lmlk*-stamped handles, but their find-spots are usually amidst handles stamped with *lmlk* seals. That they actually belong to the same storage jars was confirmed when seal impressions with PNs were discovered on complete *lmlk* vessels.[115] On one handle from Ramat Raḥel, a stamp bearing a PN appears side by side with the *lmlk* seal impression.[116]

The distribution of seal impressions with PNs is widespread. They are attested at 15 of the 17 sites that have produced 10 or more *lmlk* handles and at eight other sites where lesser amounts of handles were found. The archaeological sample shows an overall ratio of about 1:7 (266:1716) between seal impressions

111. Vaughn, "The Chronicler's Account of Hezekiah," 219.

112. Vaughn, "The Chronicler's Account of Hezekiah," 131–133. Vaughn interprets the data as indicating that seven persons owned two seals, three owned three seals, one owned four seals, and another owned five seals (p. 162).

113. Albright, *The Excavation of Tell Beit Mirsim I*, 78, pl. 40:5; *The Excavation of Tell Beit Mirsim III*, 66–67, figs 5–6; Grant and Wright, *Ain Shems Excavations*, V, 80, fig. 10a:2; Aharoni, *Excavations at Ramat Raḥel: Seasons 1961 and 1962*, 33, fig. 37:6, pl. 40:4. The two handles from Tell Beit Mirsim (nos. 623 & 860) belong to two separate storage jars.

114. Barkay and Vaughn include this handle in the *lmlk* collection (Barkay, "A Bulla of Ishmael, the King's Son," 111 n. 4; Vaughn, "The Chronicler's Account of Hezekiah," 168–169). Avigad, who originally published the handle, did not associate it with *lmlk* types ("Titles and Symbols on Hebrew Seals," 304–305). The handle has not been tested for matching chemical composition to the *lmlk* jars, and even if the handle matched chemically, that would not certify that it belonged to a *lmlk* jar, since many jars of this type are not of the *lmlk* group.

115. D. Diringer, "The Royal Jar-Handle Stamps of Ancient Judah," *BA* 12 (1949): 71, fig. 2.

116. The handle bears the stamps למלך חברן and נרא שבנא (Aharoni, *Ramat Raḥel, Seasons 1959 and 1960*, 16–17, fig. 14:2 pl. 6:2). For an unprovenienced handle of this type, see Deutsch and Heltzer, *Forty*, 33–34.

with PNs and *lmlk* stamps.[117] These data, in addition to evidence from several reconstructed jars stamped with only *lmlk* seals, indicate that not all *lmlk* jars were impressed with a personal seal. Although the actual percentage of jars stamped with both a *lmlk* seal and a personal seal is unknown, the extant finds suggest that only a fraction of the jars bore stamps with PNs.[118]

Functional Implications

Issues pertaining to the function(s) of the *lmlk* jars, the significance of the four GNs on the *lmlk* seals, and the relationship of the personal seal impressions to the *lmlk* operation continue to be hotly debated. Certain early theories postulating a connection between the *lmlk* phenomenon and Josiah's reforms were laid to rest following the dating of the jars to the reign of Hezekiah.[119] However, the underlying interpretations behind some of those theories are applicable to the time period of Hezekiah as well and deserve reevaluation. In addition, alternate theories for explaining the *Sitz-im-Leben* of these jars need to be examined.

Initially, it is worthwhile to note two points of accord on the matter. First, based on the use of a symbol in conjunction with the designation *lmlk*, the widespread distribution of a plethora of jars and the concentration of finds in public buildings, it is generally agreed that the *lmlk* phenomenon represents a government-sponsored operation. Second, the shape of the Type 484 jars, especially their narrow mouth, indicates that they stored liquids. Wine and/or olive oil are the most likely products. Beyond these points of agreement, most explanations remain controversial.

The *LMLK* Stamp as a Guarantee of Volume

One important concern deals with the question of the uniformity of the vessels. More than 25 years ago, F.M. Cross suggested that the *lmlk* stamp guaranteed a uniform volume for the jars. Cross saw this phenomenon as the result of a

---

117. The same ratio of 1:7 is attained if only provenienced handles are considered.

118. Ussishkin, "Excavations at Tel Lachish (1973–1977)," 76–80; "Excavations at Tel Lachish 1978–1983," 160–163. Three of the ten restored jars from Lachish bear impressions of personal seals. Lachish, which produced the largest corpus of these handles from a single site (76), shows a ratio of 1:5 between handles impressed with personal seals and *lmlk* stamped handles. Presently, stamps with PNs are only found on jars showing the two-winged solar disc *lmlk* symbol. However, since the percentage of personal seal impressions is lowest at sites producing the highest percentage of solar disc *lmlk* stamps, no correlation can be drawn between the emblem on *lmlk* seals and the occurrence of personal stamps.

119. Diringer, "The Royal Jar-Handle Stamps of Ancient Judah," 75–76; Cross, "Judean Stamps," 20–22.

regulation standardizing weights and measures established by Josiah as part of his reforms. Cross cited as evidence the large emerging corpus of marked stone weights uncovered from seventh-century strata.[120] However, following the reconstruction of ten jars from Lachish, it was demonstrated that the capacities of the jars varied markedly (39.75–51.8 liters).[121] Cross's theory was generally abandoned. Recently I. Eph'al and J. Naveh proposed that although a standard volume cannot be assigned to the *lmlk* containers, it may be applicable to their contents, as the amount poured into jars can be controlled by using a standard measuring vessel.[122] This explanation has merit since it recognizes the difficulty in manufacturing large quantities of ceramic vessels of equal capacity but notes the relative ease in regulating the filling of the jars. Nevertheless, the solution is problematic. One difficulty is that it fails to account for the absence of a unit amount marked alongside the designation *lmlk*. In other cases where the term *lmlk* functions as a standard for weight or measure, a unit amount is specified. For example, the stone weights engraved with the royal shekel symbol or the word למלך bear numerical designations.[123] The expression בת למלך, incised on a jar from Lachish resembling the *lmlk* jars, indicates a *bat* measure (21–23 liters).[124] The expression חצי למלך, incised on a small jug from Beer-Sheba, signifies ½ an *'issaron/omer* measure (1.2 liters).[125] The two jar inscriptions from Shiqmona (4th century) are marked, 25 למלך.[126] A way out of this impasse is to assume that the unit amount contained in a *lmlk* jar, about two *bat*, was common

120. Cross, "Judean Stamps," 22.

121. Tufnell, *Lachish III*, 108–109, 341; Ussishkin, "Excavations at Tel Lachish (1973–1977)," 76–80; "Excavations at Tel Lachish 1978–1983," 162–163.

122. I. Eph'al and J. Naveh, "The Jar of the Gate," *BASOR* 289 (1993): 62.

123. See Systems of Accounting below.

124. Tufnell, *Lachish III*, 356–357, pl. 49:1. The inscription was incised before firing. For a discussion of the bath measure, see O.R. Sellers, "Weights and Measures" in *IDB* 5, 834; E. Stern, "Weights and Measures" in *EM* 4, 854.

125. Y. Aharoni, "Excavations at Tel Beer-Sheba: Preliminary Report of the Fifth and Sixth Seasons, 1973–1974," *TA* 2 (1975): 160–162, fig. 7 pl. 33:1. Deutsch and Heltzer recently published an unprovenienced type 484 jar incised after firing with the inscription למלך שמן שפר, "for the king high quality oil X units" (*Windows to the Past*, 65–67). They read the amount, depicted by two horizontally slanted lines, as 20 (Aramaic system) and based on the capacity of the jar calculate that the units must signify *'issaron* measures (1.2 liters each). It is highly unlikely, though, that an Aramaic numeral was used on a Judahite jar of the 8th century, rather the two lines may actually represent the hieratic numeral 2. Single digits 1–4 are usually written vertically, but on occasion they appear with horizonal stances (i.e. Arad nos. 3, 33, 60). The two units on the jar would then signify 2 *bat* measures, the normal capacity of a *lmlk* type jar.

126. F.M. Cross, "Jar Inscriptions from Shiqmona," *IEJ* 18 (1968): 232.

knowledge.[127] The latter solution is workable except in the case of *lmlk* jars with a capacity of less than 42 liters, the minimum amount considered to equal two *bat.* One such vessel, Storage Jar IV from Lachish, has a capacity of only 39.75 liters.[128]

The Significance of PN Seal Impressions on *LMLK* Jars

Another feature of the *lmlk* jars whose purpose is difficult to explain is the impression on some jars of an additional seal bearing a PN. The identity of those seal owners has precipitated much discussion. Originally Diringer proposed that they were potters, a theory he deduced from the recurrence of certain names on different seals.[129] Currently, however, in light of a far larger corpus of PNs, proof of a single production center and a general lack of potters' stamps on vessels, many scholars have opted to identify these persons as government officials involved in some aspect of the *lmlk* phenomenon.[130] Vaughn's recent analysis, showing that often great care was taken to assure the legibility of the stamp, strengthens this theory, since the identity of potters would not be essential.[131] In addition, if multiple seals bearing the same PNs are indicative of multiple seal ownership, then that phenomenon too is more suggestive of government officials than potters. Still, it is puzzling that only one of these officials included a title on his seal.

Beyond the knowledge that the personal seals were impressed on the *lmlk* jars at their production site and the supposition that they belonged to royal

127. Already 50 years ago Albright suggested that the volume of the *lmlk* jars was understood to be two royal bath (*The Excavation of Tell Beit Mirsim III*, 58 n. 7).

128. Ussishkin, "Excavations at Tel Lachish 1978–1983," 161. It can be argued that this jar is an anomaly. At present, however, too few complete vessels exist to assume an exception.

129. Diringer, "On Ancient Hebrew Inscriptions Discovered at Tell ed-Duweir (Lachish) II," 89–91.

130. Aharoni, *Land of the Bible*, 399; Y. Garfinkel, "A Hierarchic Pattern in the 'Private Seal Impressions' on the *lmlk* Jars," *EI* 18 (1985): 108–115 (Hebrew); G. Barkay, "A Group of Stamped Handles from Judah," *EI* 23 (1992): 122–126 (Hebrew). In his article, Garfinkel attempts to construct a three-tiered hierarchy consisting of state-wide, regional, and local officials, each category based on the number of sites that produced impressions of any one official and the distances between those sites. His theory, however, did not stand the test of additional data, which shifted many officials from local or regional status to state-wide ranking (Barkay, p. 125; Vaughn, "The Chronicler's Account of Hezekiah," 209–213).

131. Vaughn, "The Chronicler's Account of Hezekiah," 149–156; cf. Ussishkin, "Excavations at Tel Lachish (1973–1977)," 80. Vaughn shows that in some cases extra clay was applied to handles before they were stamped. He concludes that these handles had already semi-hardened and in order for the impression to be legible a piece of soft clay was added before stamping.

officials, little has been said about the roles that these individuals played, if any, in the *lmlk* operation. One important clue that seems to have been ignored previously is that not all *lmlk*-stamped jars also bear a personal seal impression. In fact, as mentioned above, the archaeological sample indicates a ratio of about 1:7 of stamps with PNs to *lmlk* stamps. Of the ten complete *lmlk* jars from Lachish, seven show *lmlk* stamps but no personal stamps.[132] One of the three jars stamped with a personal seal has two such impressed handles and two other handles stamped with a *lmlk* seal. The two remaining jars each bear one stamp with a PN and one or two *lmlk* stamps.[133] Even if it is assumed that the average jar bore more than one *lmlk* seal impression but only one personal stamp, the percentage of seal impressions with PNs in a random sample should be greater than the data at hand.

If persons whose names appear on the personal stamps were officials directly involved with the *lmlk* operation, as in a capacity of shipping and handling or as stewards of royal estates, then one would expect that their seals would be consistently impressed on jars for administrative purposes.[134] Since this is not the case, perhaps an alternate explanation should be sought. One possibility, that rests on the adoption of the theory that the four GNs represent royal estates, is that the seals bearing PNs belonged to officials or other royal functionaries who were recipients of land grants from the crown. These land grant recipients served the king in some capacity but were not necessarily connected to the *lmlk* operation. The *lmlk* store-jars, which seem to have been produced and stamped in a central location, would have been shipped empty to royal estates in the regions marked by the GNs. Those jars also stamped with personal seals were delivered to the sectors of estates that had been parceled to the king's servants. The personal seals thus distinguished those jars from the others bound for crown lands administered by the royal family. After the containers were filled, ownership of the produce could also be determined. Since royal grants were temporary awards to dignitaries serving at court, the land in essence still belonged to the crown, hence the *lmlk* stamp.[135]

132. Admittedly, Storage Jar VIII is missing one handle, which could add another jar to the three showing stamps with PNs (Ussishkin, "Excavations at Tel Lachish 1978–1983," 161).

133. Ussishkin, "Excavations at Tel Lachish (1973–1977)," 76–77; "Excavations at Tel Lachish 1978–1983," 161–162.

134. We would expect the personal seal of an official to appear on every jar unless it is assumed that the jars were shipped in groups consisting of several containers and that only one required the seal of an administrator.

135. The ideology behind this practice is reflected in Ezekiel 46:17, where the prophet stipulates that a gift of property to a servant of the king reverts back to the royal family in the year of release.

This new theory also partially accounts for the general lack of titles on the personal seals, as no pressing need exists for displaying a particular office on the store-jars. However, the name of the official, indicating that the contents derive from that individual's holdings, has important ramifications, such as crediting the right official with income or payment of taxes.[136] The exceptional title, נער, on four seal impressions of אליקם, may identify the steward of an official named יוכן, perhaps Conaniah the Levite (2 Chr 31:13), who administered the land grant of his superior.[137]

Interestingly, though few handles bearing personal seal impressions can be matched to *lmlk*-stamped handles from the same jar, in isolated exceptions where such matches are possible and a particular PN surfaces more than once, that PN appears with the same GN.[138] Conceivably, the appearance of a person's name on jars showing one of the four GNs specifies the location of his

---

136. The question of whether royal land grants in Israel were subject to taxation is difficult to assess due to a lack of proof one way or another. Sources from Mesopotamia indicate that in the Neo-Assyrian period royal grants were commonly exempt from *šibšu*, "tax payment" (J.N. Postgate, *Taxation and Conscription in the Assyrian Empire* [Rome: Biblical Institute Press, 1974], 238; M. Ellis, *Agriculture and the State in Ancient Mesopotamia* [Philadelphia: University Museum, 1976], 138–144). However, evidence that such holdings could be liable to taxes exists as well. For example, ND 413 shows that this type of land belonging to the governor of Kalhu was levied ŠE *nusāḫū*, "corn taxes" (in Postgate, pp. 38, 182, 186). Also, C. Edens notes that in the Kassite period land grants did not always include tax exemption. When the king conferred that added benefit, he did so in times of disintegration of the central authority in the hope of regenerating ties of obligation ("On the Complexity of Complex Societies: Structure, Power, and Legitimation in Kassite Babylonia" in G. Stern and M. Rothman eds. *Chiefdoms and Early States in the Near East: The Organizational Dynamics of Complexity* [Madison: Prehistory Press, 1994], 213, 219).

137. See Chapter 5-B. In the discussion on the roles of a נער it was shown that he could serve a superior of private or official standing and that several persons bearing this title also owned seals. The Bible provides examples of נערים who were in charge of large estates and their produce (e.g. Boaz's נער [Ruth 2:5–6]; Saul's נער Ziba [2 Sam 9:9–12]). Probably one of the obligations of these נערים was to oversee the packaging and shipping of the produce of the estate, for which they would have utilized their seals. Apparently אליקם used his own seal to stamp the store-jars.

138. For example, the following PNs have been identified as belonging to jars with *lmlk* stamps bearing these GNs:
נרא שבנא / למלך חברן – PN and GN impressed on the same handle: (1) Ramat Raḥel (Aharoni, *Ramat Raḥel, Seasons 1959 and 1960*, 16–17); (2) unprovenienced handle (seals distinct from above; Deutsch and Heltzer, *Forty*, 33–34).
משלם אחמלך / למלך שוכה – PN and GN found on separate handles: 2 jars from Lachish (jar no. 10457; jar from room 1089; Ussishkin, "Royal Judean Storage Jars and Private Seal Impressions, 1–6).
אליקם נער יוכן / למלך חברן – PN and GN found on separate handles: 2 jars from Tell Beit Mirsim

royal land grant.[139] Obviously, several officials could have received small tracts of land from the same large royal estate, as evidenced by different "l-men" on the Samaria Ostraca who received goods from estates with the same GNs.

The Jars as a Wartime Measure?

Probably the most critical area of contention concerns the primary objective of the *lmlk* project. Commonly scholars attribute the entire operation to Hezekiah's siege preparations in light of an anticipated Assyrian campaign against Judah. They understand the presence of the jars at most eighth-century sites as an indication that supplies, in this case wine and/or oil, were distributed throughout the kingdom in readiness for war. The dearth of jars at Negeb sites is usually explained strategically, as that region was not in the route of an Assyrian march and as a sparsely populated area would not bear the brunt of an attack.[140]

But the *lmlk* phenomenon need not be viewed solely as an emergency pre-war measure. Rather it seems to reflect an economic maneuver that was part of Hezekiah's reorganization following his revolt against Assyria and perhaps even earlier in preparation for independence.[141] Through a careful analysis of the distribution of the *lmlk* jars and the monumental architecture at find-sites, Vaughn shows that the jars were not only routed to garrison centers but also made their way to unfortified settlements and farmsteads. If the jars were solely earmarked for troop provision just prior to the Assyrian attack, then their distribution would expectedly be limited to fortified sites.[142] Vaughn sees the

---

(handles nos. 580 and 623; handles nos. 860 and 867 [match based on size, shape and color of clay]; Ussishkin, 6–11).

139. Even if future research shows that a certain PN is associated with more than one GN, it would not invalidate the theory. As seen from the texts of the Samaria ostraca, officials can acquire a number of grants from royal estates in different locations.

140. Rainey, "Wine from the Royal Vineyards," 57–58; N. Na'aman, "Hezekiah's Fortified Cities and the *LMLK* Stamps," *BASOR* 261 (1986): 11, 17; Mazar, *Archaeology of the Land of the Bible*, 457–458; B. Halpern, "Jerusalem and the Lineages in the Seventh Century BCE: Kingship and the Rise of Individual Moral Liability," in B. Halpern and D. Hobson eds. *Law and Ideology in Monarchic Israel* (Sheffield: JSOT Press, 1991), 23–25. On the issue of Negeb sites, cf. Na'aman (pp. 13–14) who claims that Beer-sheba and other sites already fell to Sargon II prior to Sennacherib's campaign.

141. I originally made this suggestion in an unpublished seminar paper in 1992, "Judah, from the Fall of Samaria to the Eve of the Babylonian Conquest: A Preliminary Evaluation of the Archaeological Data." A proposal on these same lines, but one more fully developed, is advanced by Vaughn in his dissertation ("The Chronicler's Account of Hezekiah," 180–209). Apparently we arrived at similar conclusions independently.

142. Vaughn, "The Chronicler's Account of Hezekiah," 187–194. In support of his the-

lmlk jars as one sign of Hezekiah's general economic buildup. He suggests that the wine and possibly oil laden jars were traded or deployed to government employees and troops kingdom-wide from certain key cities such as Jerusalem, Ramat Raḥel, Lachish, and Gibeon.[143]

Concentrations of *lmlk* jars at administrative centers that were seats of royalty and high officials indicate that at least a portion of the commodities was allocated for the bureaucrats of the kingdom. Simultaneously, those important centers would have housed a contingency of military personnel who required provisioning even in peacetime. Discoveries of *lmlk* handles in non-public buildings at Lachish suggests that they may have been distributed to private individuals as well. Smaller urban centers and even rural settlements apparently received allocations from key store-cities to satisfy their needs. The distribution of the jars may also reflect trade. Trade is a fundamental component of a flourishing economy and the wine and possibly oil stored in the *lmlk* jars represent products in constant demand.[144] How many of the filled jars were actually

ory Vaughn also notes that a number of sites not destroyed by Sennacherib produced large amounts of *lmlk* handles (pp. 194–202). That argument, however, is unconvincing since Hezekiah may not have been able to accurately predict all the sites vulnerable to Assyrian attack.

143. Vaughn, "The Chronicler's Account of Hezekiah," 202–208.

144. In reality, the close to two thousand handles from *lmlk* jars (1716+266-2[with both stamps]=1980) do not represent an enormous number of store-vessels, especially for provisioning military personnel in wartime. Each jar on the average holds 45 liters, probably no more than a one or two day supply of wine for 90 persons. Unfortunately, we have no idea what percentage of *lmlk* handles have survived and therefore cannot speculate as to the actual amount in circulation toward the end of the eighth century. No industrial centers for wine or oil production have been discovered to date that can be linked to the *lmlk* project. In other cases, such as the manufacture of wine at Gibeon or oil at Ekron, actual installations and storage facilities uncovered at those sites have helped to estimate output. For example, at Ekron (Tel Miqne), it is estimated, based on the size and installations of the industrial complex, that the minimal annual yield of olive oil during the city's peek was 1000 tons, 1.1 million liters. Such a large-scale operation, which reflects extensive commerce and a powerful political organization, is attributed to the seventh-century occupation of the city by Assyria (D. Eitam and A. Shomroni, "Research of the Oil Industry During the Iron Age at Tel Miqne: A Preliminary Report" in *Olive Oil in Antiquity* [Haifa: Haifa University Press, 1987], 48–49). Notably, the oil store-jars at Ekron show a capacity of 23 liters, indicating that they held about one *bat* or half the liquid of a *lmlk* jar (p. 54 n.29). At Gibeon, the 63 rock-cut cellars where jars of wine were apparently stored could accommodate at one time vessels holding in excess of 25,000 gallons, approx. 100,000 liters (J.B. Pritchard, *Winery, Defenses, and Soundings at Gibeon* [Philadelphia: University Museum, 1964], 1–27). Interestingly, a complete storage jar found in a cellar shows a capacity of 9.75 gallons or 37 liters (p. 25; fig. 32:8), about 16%-18% less than the restored *lmlk* jars (with one exception). This differential is identical to the mass deviation between the royal shekel and the *neṣef* (equal in mass to the

sold on the open market or traded, as suggested by Vaughn, is not discernable. But it certainly need not be assumed that the *lmlk* project was initiated by the crown expressly for an emergency situation. When war did become imminent, the operation switched gears and functioned toward that end. This type of system, which reflects the workings of a highly centralized government organization, probably was employed to distribute other supplies as well.

The Novelty of the LMLK *Phenomenon*

The above interpretation expands on a previously narrow understanding of the *lmlk* phenomenon, but still does not address issues such as the uniqueness of the *lmlk* operation. While government stockpiling of provisions in store chambers and trade has a long history, one that can be documented for several kings beginning in the 10th century,[145] the appearance of seal impressions of the *lmlk* type on store jars is new. Comparable unstamped store jars predate the late eighth century, and it can be assumed that those jars functioned similarly.[146] Thus, although the *lmlk* enterprise itself may not necessarily be innovative, its novelty lies in the use of royal seals and in the scope of the operation.[147] The latter phenomenon, the widespread distribution of the jars, can be attributed to two factors: a highly organized central government and a surge in population due to an influx of northerners and an enlarged kingdom territorially.[148] On the other hand, the significance of the seals may be multi-faceted. Initially it must be noted that in the eighth century, stamp seals were in vogue in Israel and

sanctuary shekel). Perhaps it suggests that the jars from Gibeon, which seem to reflect private enterprises, held the equivalent of two non-royal *bat* measures while the *lmlk* jars generally were made to hold two royal *bat* measures.

145. In addition to Hezekiah (32:28), the building of store facilities is recorded in the Bible for Solomon (1 Kgs 9:19 = 2 Chr 8:4, 6), Baasha (2 Chr 16:4) and Jehoshaphat (17:12).

146. Vaughn lists a number of ninth or early eighth-century storage jars that are either prototype forms or actual *lmlk* types ("The Chronicler's Account of Hezekiah," pp. 184–185). These originate from Lachish Stratum IV (S. Gitin, *Gezer III: A Ceramic Typology of the Late Iron II, Persian and Hellenistic Periods at Tell Gezer* (Jerusalem: Hebrew Union College, 1990), 123; Aharoni, *Lachish V*, pl. 44:10); Gezer Stratum VIA (Gitin, *Gezer III*, 48, pls. 15:11–12, 14–15; 16:1–2); Arad Strata X and IX (Z. Herzog et al., "The Israelite Fortress at Arad," *BASOR* 254 [1984]: 12, figs. 13:1; 19:1).

147. The Chronicler emphasizes the massive quantities of Hezekiah's supplies and his great wealth (2 Chr 31:5–11; 32:27–29). Although in one case (31:5–11) the piles of produce collected by Hezekiah are designated as Temple tithes, that categorization may actually be a reflection of the Chronicler's own time and his positive theological evaluation of Hezekiah's deeds.

148. On demographic issues, see Broshi, "The Expansion of Jerusalem in the Reigns of Hezekiah and Manasseh," 21–26; Broshi and Finkelstein, "The Population of Palestine in Iron Age II," 47–60.

Judah for private use as well. Still, it seems safe to assume that the data contained on the *lmlk* seals transcend a mere need to differentiate royal jars from those belonging to private individuals. One reason for utilizing royal emblems can be sought in the political climate of the time. The use of state symbols on government property precisely during Hezekiah's reign may manifest Judah's newly acquired status as an independent state. Interestingly, a similar phenomenon in the form of a rosette stamp is evident on late seventh-century store jars, probably dating to Josiah and also coinciding with a period of renewed independence.[149]

Conclusions

Based on the evaluation of the data, it is evident that the *lmlk* project was a kingdom-wide government-controlled operation in the reign of Hezekiah. Although problems pertaining to several issues of the *lmlk* phenomenon still cannot be solved satisfactorily, a number of tentative reconstructions have emerged. First, the question was raised whether the operation should be viewed solely as a wartime measure. While the efficacy of the project as a pre-war and wartime enterprise is apparent, evidence exists that it was part of a greater administrative network for trade, for the accrual of revenue for the crown and its officials, and for the distribution of goods. On certain specific issues, for example, the function of the *lmlk* stamps, the meaning of the four GNs and the purpose of the personal seal impressions, a few explanations are forthcoming. In addition to identifying the jars as royal property, the *lmlk* seals may have served as symbols of renewed independence and as indicators for the type or grade of the commodity stored in the jars. Probably the four GNs correspond to four agricultural regions of royal estates. The personal seal impressions on some of the jars, which seem to belong to officials, may designate government personnel who were awarded grants of crown land in the regions specified by the GNs on the corresponding *lmlk* stamps. Although not all these officials were necessarily involved directly with the *lmlk* project, some probably were. In the end, the accuracy of these theories, both old and new, remains to be tested by future discoveries.

C. Rosette Seal Impressions

Like the *lmlk* jars, jars stamped with rosette seals represent a government sponsored operation; comparable to the *lmlk* insignia, the rosette design seems to be a state symbol. Variations of the rosette were impressed on containers marked as royal property for distribution state-wide.

149. See Rosette Impressions below.

Scholarship on the rosette seal impressions is scant compared to that dealing with the *lmlk* stamps. Primarily, the lack of text and the simple design of the rosette seals render the subject matter less conducive to debate. In addition, the corpus of handles bearing rosette stamps is far smaller, their distribution more limited, and until recently, issues of dating appeared less controversial. Generally the handles bearing rosette designs are mentioned in conjunction with other finds in site excavation reports or in connection with the *lmlk* impressions. A brief evaluation of the rosette stamped handles is found in an article by N. Na'aman on the size of Josiah's kingdom.[150] A more detailed analysis of the corpus as a whole has been published only recently by J. Cahill.[151]

Corpus and Typology

Close to 250 jar handles bearing rosette seal impressions have been recovered to date. The rosette seal impression is usually located at the top of handles belonging to storage jars that are derivatives of Type 484 of the eighth century, stamped with *lmlk* seals. In keeping with the ceramic typology of the late seventh century, these vessels are taller and narrower than the eighth-century precursors.[152] Six complete or nearly complete jars show capacities ranging between 31.7 and 42 liters, approximately 25% less than the *lmlk* jars. One exceptional handle, stamped at its base, belongs to a different vessel, a large decanter.[153]

In contrast to the *lmlk* seal impressions, the rosette designs are not accompanied by text, but consist solely of a single flower motif. Notably, the rosettes are not identical, diverging in number of petals and style. Five stylistic classes and a sixth category of unclassifiable seals have been distinguished. Each class has been further divided into types and subtypes.[154] Apparently uniformity was not essential as long as a basic rosette motif was maintained. Based on the extant seal impressions, a minimum of 29 different seals are identifiable.[155] As is the

150. Na'aman, "The Kingdom of Judah Under Josiah," 31–33.

151. J. Cahill, "Rosette Stamp Seal Impressions from Ancient Judah," *IEJ* 45 (1995): 230–252.

152. A store-jar with two rosette seal impressions is pictured in Aharoni, *Lachish V*, pl. 35:5.

153. Cahill, "Rosette Stamp Seal Impressions," 241–244.

154. Cahill distinguishes six different classes (fancy, plain, crude, schematic, intaglio, and undetermined), types for each class (petal shape and framing), and subtypes (number of petals). She also outlines possibilities for relative dating of the various classes ("Rosette Stamp Seal Impressions," 231–240).

155. Cahill notes that the number 29 could change if different features of individual rosettes were measured ("Rosette Stamp Seal Impressions," 241 n. 5).

case with the *lmlk* stamped handles, the seals themselves, with one possible exception, have yet to surface.[156]

Chronology and Distribution

Of the nearly 250 handles, approximately 50% lack provenience or archaeological context. The remaining half are divided between those originating in chronologically mixed assemblages, such as dumps and fills (37%), and those found well stratified among homogeneous collections of artifacts (13%).[157] The latter group, consisting of 33 handles, comes from the following sites: Timnah, Lachish, Gibeah, Jerusalem, Ramat Raḥel, En-Gedi, Tel 'Ira, and Tel Malḥata. Based on ceramic typology and evidence of destruction, the stratigraphy of these 33 handles is dated to the latest occupation level of the Iron Age IIC, between the latter half of the seventh century and the Babylonian destruction of 586 BCE.[158]

One of the most significant indicators for analyzing the rosette-impressed handles is their distribution. The handles of known provenience come from 23 sites located in four geographical regions: the Shephelah,[159] the Judean Hills,[160] the Judean Desert,[161] and the northern Negeb.[162] Most of the handles, however, originate from Jerusalem (59) and Ramat Raḥel (42), indicating that the jars bearing the rosette impressions were distributed mainly in the region of the capital. Notably, the site that produced the third largest amount of handles is Lachish (23), the Shephelah administrative center rebuilt in the latter half of the seventh century.[163]

---

156. Cahill notes that a seal discovered in Tomb 106 at Lachish (Tufnell, *Lachish III*, 372, pl. 45:137) may have been used for stamping Type I.A.8 ("Rosette Stamp Seal Impressions," 240, n. 4).

157. Cahill, "Rosette Stamp Seal Impressions," 244–245.

158. For example, rosette handles were discovered in the following late seventh/early sixth-century strata: Lachish II (Aharoni, *Lachish V*, 18); Timnah II (Kelm and Mazar, "Three Seasons of Excavations at Tel Batash – Biblical Timnah," 30); Ramat Raḥel VA (Aharoni, *Excavations at Ramat Raḥel, Seasons 1961 and 1962*, 35, 63); and Ein Gedi V (A. Mazar et al, "En Gedi: The First and Second Seasons of Excavations, 1961–1962," *'Atiqot* 5 [1966]: 33–34, 38).

159. Shephelah sites include, from north to south: Gezer; Tel Timnah; Ekron; Azekah; Socoh; Tel el-Beidha; Tel Burna; Tel Erani; and Lachish.

160. Judean Hills sites consist of: Mizpah; Gibeon; Gibeah; Jerusalem; Manahat; ar-Ras; Ramat Raḥel; site #15–12/02/5; Nebi Daniel; and Beth Zur.

161. En-Gedi is the only Judean Desert site.

162. Sites in the northeastern Negeb include: Arad; Tel 'Ira; and Tel Malḥata.

163. For data on distribution of rosette-stamped handles, see Na'aman, "The Kingdom of Judah Under Josiah," 31. Handles from other sites number only in the single digits. Interestingly, the greatest concentration of *lmlk* handles (2/3 of the more than 1300

The distribution of the handles reveals primarily Judean territory, albeit in a smaller geographical area with fewer sites than are represented by the *lmlk*-stamped handles.[164] Interestingly, rosette seal impressions are present at potentially non-Israelite border sites such as Gezer, Timnah, Ekron, and Tel Erani.[165] This phenomenon, also observable for the *lmlk* handles, raises questions concerning the political status of certain sites during specific periods. In the case of the *lmlk* handles, it is commonly assumed that the presence of Judean pottery types at those sites reflects Hezekiah's control over the region (2 Kgs 18:8), although trade as a factor cannot be discounted.[166]

The chronological circumstances surrounding the rosette seal impressions are far more complicated because fewer historical data are available. Two theories on the topic each assign the introduction of the seal-impressed handles to a different king, Josiah or Jehoiakim. Na'aman associates the handles with the reign of Josiah (639–609 BCE).[167] His identification is based primarily on the distribution of findspots and their close correspondence to the town lists for the southern tribes in Joshua 15, 18, and 19. The association of the towns in these lists with the reign of Josiah was originally proposed by A. Alt. Alt argued that certain towns in Benjamin, such as Bethel, Ophrah, and Jericho, were part of the kingdom of Israel and would have transferred to Judah only after the Assyrian conquest and subsequent demise of Assyria.[168] Na'aman, building on Alt's theory, points out that rosette-impressed handles originate from many sites

---

provenienced handles) originates from these same three sites, although the largest amount comes from Lachish (see chart in Vaughn, "The Chronicler's Account of Hezekiah," 219).

164. See Distribution Map.

165. Gezer was under Assyrian rule from the time of Tiglath-pileser III's conquest in 732 BCE; Timnah, Ekron, and Tel Erani were Philistine towns.

166. Kelm and Mazar, "Three Seasons of Excavations at Tel Batash – Biblical Timnah," 29–30; Gitin, "Tel Miqne-Ekron," 26; T. Dothan and S. Gitin, "Miqne, Tel (Ekron)" in *NEAEHL*, 1056; A. Mazar, "The Northern Shephelah in the Iron Age: Some Issues in Biblical History and Archaeology" in M.D. Coogan, J.C. Exum and L.E. Stager eds. *Scripture and Other Artifacts: Essays on the Bible and Archaeology in Honor of Philip J. King* (Louisville: Westminster John Knox Press, 1994), 256–260.

167. Na'aman, "The Kingdom of Judah Under Josiah," 31–33.

168. *KS II*, 281–282. Notably, however, attempts to date the Joshua town lists have produced several distinct theories that champion the reigns of different kings: Jehoshaphat (F.M. Cross and G.E. Wright, "The Boundary and Province Lists of the Kingdom of Judah," *JBL* 75 [1956]: 224–225); Uzziah (Y. Aharoni, "The Province List of Judah," *VT* 9 [1959]: 246); Abijah (for Benjamin) and Hezekiah (for Judah; Z. Kallai, *The Northern Boundary of Judah* [Jerusalem: Y.L. Magnes, 1960], 24–26, 33–34). These conclusions reflect the complex nature of the task, which encompasses factors such as sources and the completeness of individual lists, not to mention the biblical writer's assumption that the lists refer to tribal allotments.

listed in the town registers.[169] In connection with the border sites, he maintains that handles from Gezer and Timnah reflect economic interconnections between those places and Judean towns of the Shephelah.[170] It is also possible that after the Assyrian withdrawal from Palestine some of these sites, in particular Timnah, fell under Josiah's sphere of influence.[171] At present, the extent of Judean control, whether purely economic or political, cannot be determined.

In her recent study, Cahill suggests that the rosette impressions fit more logically into the period of Jehoiakim's reign (608–598/7 BCE) than Josiah's. She reasons that since handles have not appeared at northern Judean sites such as Bethel, Ophrah, and Jericho, traditionally counted within Josiah's domain, they must have been introduced subsequent to Judah's loss of that territory following Josiah's defeat at Megiddo. Cahill links the handles to Jehoiakim's preparations for an anticipated Babylonian campaign following Egypt's defeat at Carchemish in 605 BCE. Commenting on the border sites, she notes that the handles are evidence of Jehoiakim's economic support of his Philistine neighbors' war efforts against the Babylonians.[172]

The discovery of rosette-stamped handles at sites with secure destruction dates provides a *terminus ad quem*. For example, Tel Batash, which produced six handles and suffered an early destruction, ca. 603 BCE, proves that the rosette impressions were already in use before the end of the seventh century. In contrast, it is extremely difficult to pinpoint the introduction of these handles to the reign of any one king. To do so on the basis of the absence of handles at a particular site seems tenuous, especially in light of the large percentage of unprovenienced handles and the presence at some sites of only one or two isolated finds.[173] Furthermore, as already discussed in connection with the *lmlk* seal impressions, the distribution of goods represented by these jars should

---

169. Na'aman, "The Kingdom of Judah Under Josiah," 31–33.

170. Na'aman, "The Kingdom of Judah Under Josiah," 33. When Na'aman wrote his article, handles from Ekron and Tel Erani had not yet been found. It should be noted that Na'aman does not support theories that Josiah expanded westward. Rather, he considers that territory, including the fort of Meṣad Ḥashavyahu, to be within the sphere of Egyptian influence. He assumes that those towns listed in the book of Joshua were later additions and do not reflect Josiah's realm (pp. 44–51).

171. Kelm and Mazar, "Three Seasons of Excavations at Tel Batash – Biblical Timnah," 31; Mazar, "The Northern Shephelah in the Iron Age," 260–263; cf. Gitin, who thinks that Philistia in general was under the Egyptian sphere of influence from ca. 630–603 ("Tel Miqne-Ekron," 46).

172. Cahill, "Rosette Stamp Seal Impressions," 247–248.

173. See distribution data: Na'aman, "The Kingdom of Judah Under Josiah," 31; Cahill ("Rosette Stamp Seal Impressions," 246; J.R. Zorn, "Two Rosette Stamp Impressions from Tell en-Nasbeh," *BASOR* 293 (1994): 81–82.

not be viewed as limited to wartime use. Instead, the jars stamped with rosette seals, like the *lmlk* precursors, should be seen within a greater organizational context.

Symbolism and Functional Implications

Before attempting to define possible functions for the rosette-stamped jars, it seems appropriate to examine the rosette motif and its purpose on the vessels. On one hand, the rosette motif is a cross-cultural symbol whose usage need not be attributed to borrowing. On the other hand, its prevalence in Mesopotamian iconography and in the art of Israel's neighbors in general suggests that its adoption in Judah is the result of foreign inspiration.[174] The rosette, originally a symbol of Inanna (later Ishtar), was employed by Assyrian kings as a mark of royalty. Rosettes decorate bracelets, armlets and diadems pictured on several Assyrian kings (e.g. Ashurnasirpal II, Sargon II and Ashurbanipal).[175] Seemingly, the rosette held similar significance for Hittite rulers, as indicated by its frequent appearance in Hittite art in combination with the Egyptian ankh or the Mesopotamian winged sun disc, other symbols adopted by royalty.[176]

In Judah, the rosette motif is found on items other than stamped handles dated to the seventh century. For example, the base of a jug from Gibeon bears a rosette that was incised after firing.[177] A circular plaque found in a tomb at Lachish is inscribed with two hieroglyphs, *nfr mꜣ ʿt*, "beautiful of truth," on the obverse and a rosette on the reverse.[178] Rosettes appear on a number of

174. E.D. Van Buren, "The Rosette in Mesopotamian Art," *ZA* 45 (1939): 99. The rosette is common in Egyptian iconography as well. For example, flower molds from Akhenaten's palace at el-Amarna show rosette designs among other flowers and plants (F. Petrie, *Tell El Amarna* [London: Methuen, 1894], pl. 18). Contrast O. Keel and C. Uehlinger, who trace the use of the rosette design in Israel to local origin (*Gods, Goddesses and Images of God in Ancient Israel* [trans. T. Trapp; Minneapolis: Fortress Press, 1998], 354).

175. Van Buren, "The Rosette in Mesopotamian Art," 99–107; R.K. Maxwell-Hyslop, *Western Asiatic Jewelry c. 3000–62 B.C.* (London: Methuen, 1971), 218, 247–253, figs. 121, 139, 142–143, 145–148, 156. The rosette already appears in Sumerian art. Later, in the second and first millennia, it was adapted into the form of an eight-pointed star. Both are symbols of Inanna/Ishtar. Rosettes are commonly found on ritual objects, sometimes in combination with lotus flowers and palmettes. Rosettes decorate game boards and the sound-box of a lyre from the cemetery at Ur (L. Woolley, *Ur Excavations: The Royal Cemetery*, II [London-Philadelphia: British Museum and Museum of the University of Pennsylvania, 1934], pls. 95–98, 104, 115).

176. K. Bittel and H.G. Güterbock, *Boğazköy, Neue Untersuchungen in der hethitischen Hauptstadt* (Berlin: W. de Gruyter, 1935), 74, 79, pl. 26:1, 3–5, 7–9, 11.

177. J.B. Pritchard, *The Water System of Gibeon* (Philadelphia: University Museum, 1961), pl. 46:258.

178. Tufnell, *Lachish III*, 372, pl. 45:137.

unprovenienced seals and a weight.[179] The utilization of the rosette as a mark of royalty in Assyria in periods contemporary to the Divided Monarchy lends support to the theory that in Judah it could have symbolized kingship as well.[180] Based on that premise and the statewide distribution of rosette-stamped handles, it is generally assumed that jars bearing this design were the property of the central government. As such, their function may have been analogous to that of the *lmlk*-stamped vessels.

Recent studies have shown that the kingdom of Josiah was substantially smaller than that of Hezekiah.[181] Nevertheless, certain circumstances in the reigns of these kings are strikingly similar and strengthen the contention that the rosette impressions were introduced by Josiah. Both Hezekiah and Josiah came to the throne while Judah was an Assyrian vassal and both kings took advantage of periods of Assyrian weakness and eventual collapse to reestablish autonomy and to expand their kingdoms territorially.[182] No doubt these resur-

---

179. Sass, "The Pre-Exilic Hebrew Seals," 211, nos. 66, 67. A rosette decorates the soundbox of a 12-string lyre on the well known seal engraved למעדנה בת המלך, "belonging to *M'dnh* the daughter of the king" (N. Avigad, "The King's Daughter and the Lyre," *IEJ* 28 (1978): 146–151). The authenticity of that seal has been called into question (*WSS*, no. 30). A rosette is incised on the base of a dome shaped stone בקע weight (G. Barkay, "A Group of Iron Age Scale Weights," *IEJ* 28 [1978]: 212–213).

180. Albright, cited in I. Mendelsohn, "Guilds in Ancient Palestine," *BASOR* 80 (1940): 21 n. 51; Barkay, "A Group of Iron Age Scale Weights," 212–213; Mazar, *Archaeology of the Land of the Bible*, 458; Cahill, "Rosette Stamp Seal Impressions," 250–252; cf. Mendelsohn, Cross and Welten who interpret the rosette as the mark of a potter's guild ("Guilds," 20–21; "Judean Stamps," 22; *Königs-Stempel*, 32–33).

Among unprovenienced artifacts, two Ammonite sculptured heads dated to the 9th–7th centuries, one of a male and one of a female, wear diadems decorated with rosettes. It has been suggested that the two heads portray a royal pair (T. Ornan, "The Dayan Collection," *Israel Museum Journal* 2 [1983]: 14–16).

181. For regional and site evaluations, see most recently Vaughn, "The Chronicler's Account of Hezekiah," 38–112. I. Finkelstein estimates the total built-up areas of late eighth-century Judahite sites to be about 470 hectares, as compared to 255 hectares for the late seventh-century. Based on these estimates, the population of Judah at the end of the monarchic period would have been only a little more than 50% of the population of the late eighth century, a ratio of ca. 65,000:120,000 ("The Archaeology of the Days of Manasseh," 176).

182. Hezekiah's father Ahaz was a vassal of Assyria (2 Kgs 16:7–8); Hezekiah broke that obligation (18:7), probably after the death of Sargon II in 705 BCE (Cogan and Tadmor, *II Kings*, 219–222). His territorial expansion into Philistia is reported in 2 Kgs 18:8 and confirmed by accounts in Sennacherib's annals of his third campaign (Padi king of Ekron is mentioned as Hezekiah's prisoner). Following Sennacherib's successful campaign in Judah, Hezekiah and his successor Manasseh were once again Assyrian vassals. In the case of Josiah, the biblical writer does not explicitly state that this king freed Judah from Assyrian

gences of independence and extension of national territory involved administrative reforms, including economic projects sponsored by the central government.[183] As discussed in connection to the *lmlk* seal impressions, the nationwide distribution of those store-jars reflects this type of organization. The rosette stamps, found on handles of similar storage vessels, may mirror a comparable system, albeit on a smaller scale in a much reduced kingdom.

Conclusions

Like the royal insignia of the *lmlk* jars, the rosette seems to symbolize kingship. Curiously, the only two occurrences of assemblages of vessels impressed with royal seals appear in periods of recent liberation. Perhaps in addition to serving as identification markings, the rosette stamps celebrated Judah's new status as an independent state. Admittedly though, the general lack of written data in association with the rosette seal impressions makes it difficult to reach any secure conclusions regarding their function(s).

D. Arad and Other Judean Inscriptions

Arad: Corpus and Chronology

Probably the most valuable corpus of epigraphic material for elucidating aspects of Judahite administration was uncovered at the tiny Negeb fortress of Arad. Of all the collections of Hebrew inscriptions known to date from a single site, the Arad material spans the widest time period from the earliest occupation of the site in the 11th century until the fall of the Judean monarchy. As such, this group of inscriptions provides a nearly continuous, albeit fragmentary, pic-

---

hegemony. However, Josiah's chance would have come around 627 BCE, after the death of Ashurbanipal (Cogan and Tadmor, p. 293); data on his territorial expansion (2 Kgs 23:15, 19; 2 Chr 34:6) are found amidst descriptions of cult reforms. Even if exaggerated, these records do suggest that minimally, Josiah annexed certain sites in Israel north of Jerusalem.

183. It may not be coincidental that both Hezekiah and Josiah instituted reforms encompassing centralization of worship. That type of centralization, which limited the place of sacrifice to Jerusalem and thereby increased the influx of products to the capital, seems to go hand in hand with centralization of political and economic power. On the political and economic ramifications of centralized worship, see among others: H.H. Rowley, "Hezekiah's Reform and Rebellion," *BJRL* 44 (1961): 425–430; M. Weinfeld, "Cult Centralization in Israel in Light of a Neo-Babylonian Analogy," *JNES* 23 (1964): 205–206 (contrast M. Cogan, *Imperialism and Religion: Assyria, Judah, and Israel in the Eighth and Seventh Centuries* [Missoula: Scholars Press, 1974], 33 n. 67); W.E. Claburn, "The Fiscal Basis of Josiah's Reform," *JBL* 92 (1973): 15–17 (contrast Tigay, *Deuteronomy*, 461); L. Tatum, "King Manasseh and the Royal Fortress at Horvat 'Usa," *BA* 54 (1991): 138, 141.

ture of record keeping from a small administrative center.[184] Although a comprehensive and detailed discussion of the texts is available in Aharoni's volume *Arad Inscriptions* (1981),[185] it seems worthwhile to review the data and evaluate their significance for the study of Israelite officialdom.

The corpus of Hebrew inscriptions from Arad consists of 91 ink-inscribed ostraca and vessels, 16 incised ostraca and vessels, ten *lmlk*-stamped handles, one personal seal-impressed *lmlk* handle, five personal seals, and 13 incised stone weights.[186] Aharoni dates these inscriptions, with one exception, to the six strata (XI-VI) identified by him as the citadel of Israelite Arad in the monarchic period. The exceptional ostracon was found in the earliest stratum (XII), that of the premonarchic enclosed settlement.[187] Of the 136 inscribed items, the largest percentage is dated by the excavators, either stratigraphically or paleographically, to the end of the monarchic period, the latter half of the seventh through the early sixth century (Strata VII-VI). Approximately two dozen inscriptions are dated stratigraphically or paleographically to Stratum VIII, the latter half of the eighth century. The remaining inscriptions, either recovered from earlier strata (Strata XI-IX) or dated paleographically to those strata, number about 20. Those strata are dated to the tenth, ninth, and mid-eighth centuries, respectively. A single ostracon discovered in Stratum XII is dated to the 11th century.

The original stratigraphic analysis of Arad has been called into question by a number of scholars. Most seriously affected by a reexamination of the ceramic remains are Strata X–VIII. Based on the uniformity of the pottery assemblages and their similarities to pottery from Lachish Stratum III, several scholars believe that the three levels belong to a single building phase, dated to the eighth century.[188] Opinions concerning Stratum XI are divided between a tenth and

184. The fortress at Arad is only 50 meters square (Y. Aharoni, "Arad: Its Inscriptions and Temple," *BA* 31 [1968]: 5).

185. Z. Herzog recently reevaluated and updated the Arad material: *Arad*, R. Amiran et al, *Ancient Arad – An Early Bronze Age on the Desert Fringe*; Z. Herzog, *The Arad Fortresses* (Tel Aviv: Hakibbutz Hameuchad, 1997 [Hebrew]).

186. Ink inscriptions (Aharoni, *Arad Inscriptions*, 12–104; Rainey, "Three Additional Texts" in *Arad Inscriptions*, 122–123); incised inscriptions (Aharoni, pp. 105–118); seals (pp. 119–121); weights and *lmlk* handles (M. Aharoni "Inscribed Weights and Royal Seals" in *Arad Inscriptions*, 126–127); personal seal-impressed handle, לשלם אחא (Vaughn, "The Chronicler's Account of Hezekiah," 143–144).

187. See Herzog for a detailed description of the premonarchic enclosed settlement of Arad and others in the region (*The Arad Fortresses*, 141–154).

188. M. Aharoni, "The Pottery of Strata 12–11 of the Iron Age Citadel at Arad," *EI* 15 (1981): 181–204 (Hebrew); "On the Israelite Fortress at Arad," *BASOR* 258 (1985): 73; O. Zimhoni, "The Iron Age Pottery of Tel 'Eton and Its Relation to the Lachish, Tell Beit

ninth century date. The date of Stratum XII is generally lowered to the tenth century.[189] In a recent updated publication reevaluating the Arad material, Z. Herzog reviewed these chronological issues. Based on his findings he dates Stratum XII to the 11th century, Stratum XI to the 10th century, Stratum X to the 9th century, and Strata IX and VIII to the 8th century.[190]

Implications for Israelite Administration

The Arad texts fall into two main categories: letters containing various instructions addressed to officers at Arad and records listing the names of individuals and/or commodities. Most of the letters belong to Stratum VI (end of 7th/early 6th century). Those found *in situ* were discovered in one of the casemate rooms in the south wall, a storechamber, together with broken ceramic vessels.[191] One exception originates from an adjacent room.[192] The only letter from an earlier period, Stratum VIII (late 8th c.), was found in a room at the center of the fortress that seems to have been used for perfume production.[193] This group of inscriptions provides detailed information, albeit fragmentary, on the administration of Arad and the surrounding region.

Initially it is observable that the letters are addressed to particular individuals. The single surviving letter from Stratum VIII preserving a heading (no. 40) is addressed to an officer named מלכיהו. From Stratum VI, all the letters that preserve a heading (nos. 1–12, 14–16, 18, 21, 24) are addressed to אלישב (בן אשיהו), with one exception (no. 21).[194] Thus it seems that in one period, letters are regularly directed to the same person, probably the commander who acted as head administrator of the fort.

The contents of the letters indicate that the commanders of Arad oversaw both military and civil matters, though the latter cannot be proven with certainty.

Mirsim and Arad Assemblages," *TA* 12 (1985): 85–88; A. Mazar and E. Netzer, "On the Israelite Fortress at Arad," *BASOR* 263 (1986): 87–90; D. Ussishkin, "The Date of the Judaean Shrine at Arad," *IEJ* 38 (1988): 150–151.

189. Aharoni, "The Pottery of Strata 12–11 of the Iron Age Citadel at Arad," 202; Zimhoni, "The Iron Age Pottery of Tel 'Eton," 87–88; Mazar and Netzer, "On the Israelite Fortress at Arad," 89.

190. Herzog, *The Arad Fortresses*, 136.

191. Ostraca nos. 1–18 (Aharoni, *Arad Inscriptions*, 11).

192. Ostracon no. 21 (Aharoni, *Arad Inscriptions*, 42).

193. Aharoni, *Arad Inscriptions*, 71. Perfume production is indicated by the compartments and installations found in this room.

194. The letters are addressed simply to אלישב. His patronym is known from his seals and from an ostracon (no. 17). The latter is addressed to נחם, who apparently brought his written orders to requisition oil from אלישב בן אשיהו from outside Arad but deposited the document at Arad.

Orders addressed to אלישב call for the provisioning of military units and other groups or individuals not identifiable as military, the deployment of troops, and the transport of commodities to neighboring settlements.[195] The many directives dealing with disbursements of staple supplies from Arad, namely flour, wine, and oil (cf. 2 Chr 32:28), demonstrate that a key responsibility of the fort commander was his charge over the central storehouse.[196] Notably, the sites mentioned as destinations for the commodities and troops all seem to be located in the Negeb: for example, Ziph, Ramat-Negeb (Horvat 'Uzza or Tel 'Ira), Kinah (Horvat Tov), and Beer-Sheba.[197] Evidently Arad was the administrative center for a network of Negeb fortresses in the seventh and early sixth centuries.

The status of the commander of Arad and other officials in the region is eluci-

---

195. One group that is provisioned at Arad and transports commodities to other forts is the כתים (*ktym*; see ostraca nos. 1–2, 4–5, 7–8, 10–11, 14). Generally the Kittim are identified as Greeks, although A. Rainey suggests that they were Phoenicians from Cyprus (Herzog et al., "The Israelite Fortress at Arad," 31). The group's Aegean origin is inferred from biblical references (Gen 10:4; Num 24:24; Isa 23:1; Jer 2:10; Ezek 27:6). Several sites in Israel have produced East Greek pottery usually associated with the Kittim. The greatest proportion of this pottery was found at Meṣad Ḥashavyahu, but lesser amounts continue to be uncovered at a number of inland sites (e.g. Tel Miqne, Tel Batash, Tell Malḥata; see Waldbaum, "Early Greek Contacts with the Southern Levant, ca. 1000–600 B.C.," 55). The roles of the Kittim at Arad and at other Israelite settlements continue to be debated. Several theories exist on the matter. Naveh argues that before the reign of Josiah Meṣad Ḥashavyahu was occupied by Greek mercenaries in the service of the Egyptian Pharaoh Psamtik I. Later Josiah conquered the fortress and it fell under Judahite rule ("The Excavations at Meṣad Ḥashavyahu: Preliminary Report," 98–99). Aharoni and Reich, among others, believe that the Kittim stationed at Meṣad Ḥashavyahu were in the service of Josiah and that they appear in the Arad letters as mercenaries of the Judean king (*Arad Inscriptions*, 12–13, 144–145; "A Third Season of Excavations at Meṣad Ḥashavyahu," 228–232). In contrast to Naveh, Aharoni, and Reich, Na'aman posits that Meṣad Ḥashavyahu as well as Arad were under Egyptian control during Josiah's reign and that the Kittim were mercenaries in the service of the Pharaoh ("The Kingdom of Judah Under Josiah," 44–48). Recently, in view of the growing corpus of Greek pottery at Israelite coastal and inland sites, Waldbaum has suggested that the Kittim were Greek traders. She notes that Meṣad Ḥashavyahu could have functioned as a trade colony in addition to a military garrison ("Early Greek Contacts," 60–61). Although the main function of the Kittim, whether they were mercenaries, traders or both, cannot presently be resolved, there is insufficient evidence to prove Na'aman's theory that Arad and Meṣad Ḥashavyahu were under Egyptian hegemony during the reign of Josiah. The Hebrew inscriptions and general lack of Egyptian artifacts at both sites rather support Judahite occupation.

196. Aharoni, *Arad Inscriptions*, 142–148. After the destruction of Beer-Sheba at the end of the eighth century, it seems that Arad became the most important Negeb center.

197. Aharoni identifies Ramat-Negeb with Horvat 'Uza (*Arad Inscriptions*, 146–147), while Rainey and Lemaire identify it with Tel 'Ira ("Ramat-negeb, Ramoth-negeb," *EM* 7, 298–299; *IH*, 189–190).

dated somewhat in these letters. As noted, all the letters dealing with administrative matters from Stratum VI, except one, are addressed to Eliashib. The exceptional letter, no. 21, is addressed to גדליהו בן אליאר, apparently another officer stationed at the fort but probably one of lesser rank.[198] From Stratum VIII a letter (no. 40) containing important military information is addressed to Malkiyahu, most likely the fort commander in the late eighth century.[199] One letter (no. 24) reveals the identity of the commander of the neighboring fort of Ramat Negeb, אלישע בן ירמיהו. Noticeably, none of these letters designates the specific title held by the officers, nor do three seals belonging to Eliashib, found in a small room in the storehouse of the southern wall, include a title.[200] It can probably be assumed from their military and civil duties that each was a שר of some kind. Perhaps Eliashib and Malkiyahu were called שר העיר or simply השר, as was the addressee of the letter from Meṣad Ḥashavyahu.[201] A somewhat comparative example of municipal administrators handling military and civil matters is attested in Assyria in reference to the *bēl āli*, "lord of the city."[202] In letters from the reign of Sargon II, the *bēl āli* is presented as a civil official who is charged with policing duties and the recruiting of troops from his city.[203]

Whatever title Eliashib bore, it is evident from the correspondence that he was in direct contact with the central authority in Jerusalem. One letter indicates that his orders originated from the king (no. 24); another is a message from the king written in the first person (no. 88).[204] Additional information can be

---

198. The partially preserved contents of letter no. 21 reveal a military matter having to do with Edom but they do not indicate that Gedalyahu held authority over the distribution of supplies or the deployment of troops as did Eliashib.

199. The letter was written by persons of lower rank than Malkiyahu as evidenced by the designation בן, "son," used to identify the senders in the heading. Its contents indicate that Malkiyahu was a senior administrator of Arad.

200. Aharoni, *Arad Inscriptions*, 119–120. Two additional seals from Arad that apparently belonged to other officials at the fort bear PNs not identifiable with any persons mentioned in the texts (pp. 120–121).

201. A fragmentary letter, no. 26, mentions, מן אדני שר, "from my lord *śr*...," but does not indicate who the שר is or his specific title. On the שר of Meṣad Ḥashavyahu, see Chapter 4-I.

202. See Chapter 4-I.

203. *TCL* 9 67, *ABL* 590, 342; Parpola, *The Correspondence of Sargon II*, Part II, nos. 100, 103, 217, 79–81, 154–155.

204. This personal note from the king, possibly Jehoahaz (Aharoni, *Arad Inscriptions*, 103–104), raises questions pertaining to the identity of Eliashib. Albright (*ANET*, 569 n. 17) speculated that Eliashib was a son of King Josiah, אשיהו being an abbreviated form of יאשיהו (cf. כניהו and יכוניה, Jer 22:24; 27:20). Although Albright's theory cannot be verified, it is supported in part by practices noted in the Bible. For example, King Jehoshaphat appointed those sons not bound for the throne as administrators of urban centers throughout Judah (2 Chr 21:3; see Chapter 3–A). Recently an unprovenienced ostracon came to light recording

gleaned about other senders as well. That a number of letters were written by persons of equal or lesser status is observable from the formulas employed in the greeting. For example, the greeting אחך, "your brother" (nos. 15 & 16) indicates an officer of equal rank. In contrast, the greetings, אל אדני, "to my lord" (no. 18) and בנך, "your son(s)" (nos. 21 & 40), signify writers of lower rank.[205] While it is indeterminable whether the commander of Arad held a higher status than other Negeb fortress commanders, this is a likely scenario for the seventh century, a time when the commander of Arad was charged over other sites (e.g. Beer-Sheba, ostracon no. 3).

In addition to the letters, other types of texts from Arad provide bits of information pertaining to economic administrative matters. Several inscriptions contain rosters of PNs and symbols or names of commodities. Usually each PN is followed by an amount of a particular commodity, though sometimes the commodity itself is not indicated (e.g. nos. 22, 29, 31, 36, 38, 41, 49, 60, 67, 72, 76). The archaeological context of those ostraca is either a room in or near the city wall or a building adjacent to the Arad sanctuary. Evidently, the registers represent allocations of supplies stored at Arad or incoming revenue, including contributions for the sanctuary.[206] In one case (no. 25), the commodity, recorded in (Egyptian) *ḥḳ3t* measures of barley, is logged beside three GNs: Upper ʿAnim, Lower ʿAnim, and Maʿon. This record may signify taxes dispatched from those southern hill towns to the Negeb administrative center at Arad,[207] or it may represent goods sent in trade. Two ostraca bearing symbols and numerals (nos. 33 & 34) appear to be inventory lists of commodities from the storehouses at Arad. One ostracon (no. 33) was discovered in the storehouse of Stratum VII and the other (no. 34) in the same room as Eliashib's seals.[208]

Other Administrative Texts from Judah

In contrast to the epigraphic material from Arad, other administrative texts

an obligatory contribution of three shekels to the temple of YHWH as ordered by a king named אשיהו. One of three proposed candidates is King Josiah (Bordreuil et al., "King's Command and Widow's Plea," 3–4).

205. Cf. the opening formula in the Lachish letters, nos. 2–6, 8–9 and the letter from Meṣad Ḥashavyahu.

206. No. 49, a broken bowl discovered in a room next to the shrine, is inscribed with more than a dozen names followed by numerals; several of the PNs are known from Levitical families mentioned in the Bible (e.g. Korah). Other bowls are marked as sanctuary gifts with the word קדש, "holy," or abbreviations thereof, קש (nos. 104, 102, 103). Aharoni, *Arad Inscriptions*, 80–82, 115–118, 148–149.

207. Aharoni, *Arad Inscriptions*, 50–51, 143.

208. Aharoni, *Arad Inscriptions*, 61–62. The symbols for the commodities and numerals on these as well as on other ostraca are discussed below.

from Judah derive from isolated or smaller group finds. The archive of ostraca found in the gatehouse at Lachish deals primarily with military matters pertaining to the last days of the Judahite monarchy. Several letters are addressed to the commander of Lachish, יאוש. A few inscriptions, however, are concerned with administrative issues. These, in addition to a number of ostraca from Beer-Sheba and Jerusalem and a papyrus from Murabba'at, are noteworthy.[209]

Among the Lachish ostraca (Stratum II), one letter (no. 9) lacking an addressee but presumed to be the commander יאוש,[210] contains a requisition for provisions of bread and wine. Its contents are comparable to those of several Arad letters suggesting that the commander of Lachish also supervised the disbursement of provisions. It is unclear, however, whether the recipients of the provisions were all military personnel or included civilians. The texts of two other Lachish ostraca (nos. 19 and 22) consist of a list of PNs and numerals or symbols of commodities. Ostracon no. 22, discovered in a storeroom containing several shekel weights and a juglet filled with 17 bullae, probably represents a record of the distribution of commodities stored in the archive.[211]

From the site of Beer-Sheba (Stratum II, late 8th c.), two fragmentary ostraca found in the store chambers bear PNs and amounts of unknown commodities. Apparently they represent receipts for provisions.[212] Three ostraca listing amounts of oil and grain were uncovered from the Ophel in Jerusalem (late 8th c.). The term מנו, "counted," on ostracon no. 3, indicates that at least some of

---

209. In addition, several unprovenienced bullae showing year dates and GNs (Lachish, Eltolad, Nezib, Arboth?) seem to be dockets that accompanied taxes from those towns to the king (N. Avigad, "Two Hebrew 'Fiscal' Bullae," *IEJ* 40 [1990]: 262–265; *WSS*, nos. 421 `422; Deutsch, *Messages from the Past*, 137–143 [no. 99 contains the word מכס, "tax"]). Allegedly, a bulla bearing the name אחיקם בן שפן (*WSS*, no. 431), possibly identifiable as the Judahite official Ahikam son of Shaphan (2 Kgs 22:12–14; Jer 26:24), was found together at an undisclosed site with the fiscal bulla marked Eltolad. Had these bullae not been illicitly acquired, but instead discovered *in situ*, contextual information could have provided important data about the system of taxation in Judah in the late seventh century.

Another four unprovenienced ostraca dated paleographically to the late seventh and early sixth centuries, supposedly originating from the region of the Judean Hills, show rosters of PNs and/or amounts of commodities and silver (Deutsch and Heltzer, *New Epigraphic Evidence*, 81–103). However, since the ostraca lack all contextual evidence, it cannot even be determined whether they originate from private or public installations. In keeping with the methodology adopted in this study (see Chapter 2–C), any potential significance of this unprovenienced material for understanding Israelite administration cannot be considered.

210. The designation אדני found in the greeting is common in other letters addressed to יאוש the commander of Lachish (e.g. nos. 2, 3, 6).

211. Aharoni, *Lachish V*, 19–24.

212. Y. Aharoni, *Beer-sheba I: Excavations at Tel Beer-sheba 1969–1971 Seasons* (Tel Aviv, 1973), 71–73, pl. 34:1–2; cf. Lemaire, *IH*, 271–273.

these receipts record allocations of commodities.[213] Although the ostraca from the Ophel lack a clear archaeological context, the large amounts of commodities recorded in the texts indicate government rather than private transactions.[214] A rare fragment of preserved papyrus from Murabba'at (late 8th/early 7th cent.) contains a list of four names, each followed by a symbol, possibly for the seah measure, plus a numeral.[215] While the context of this register is unknown, the content implies a delivery of grain. In this case, however, the smaller amounts could indicate a private enterprise.

Conclusions

The Hebrew epigraphic material presented above provides additional bits of data on the topic of Israelite officialdom and administration. As noted, the Arad inscriptions in particular afford an almost continuous, albeit fragmentary, picture of the organization of a government outpost over several centuries, from the period of the United Monarchy until the fall of Judah. Importantly, it seems that the commander of Arad was in control of both military and civil affairs at the fort. Although far removed from the seat of government in Jerusalem, he was in contact with and received orders from that central authority. Comparable information comes from documents from Lachish, a far larger and more important city in Judah. It should be emphasized, however, that any understanding of the municipal administration and its connection to the central authority based on this fragmentary and selective material is tentative and open to reinterpretation.

Of note is the dearth of titles in the Arad and other inscriptions. This phenomenon probably suggests that many more individuals whose PNs are attested on seals, bullae, ostraca, and pottery vessels could be included in the category "officials." Possibly, the need for titles was minimal in cases where municipal officials were well known, and no others bearing identical PNs existed in the same generation. Furthermore, the aforementioned inscriptions are important for the glimpses they provide into the accounting system operative in Israel throughout the monarchic period. That topic is detailed separately in the final section of this chapter.

---

213. A. Lemaire, "Les ostraca paléo-hébreux des fouilles de l'Ophel," *Levant* 10 (1978): 158–61, nos. 3–5.

214. For example, ostracon no. 2 notes 57 units (jars) of oil; ostracon no. 3 records 200 of an unspecified commodity, perhaps bread.

215. P. Benoit, J. Milik, R. de Vaux, *Les grottes de Murabba'at* (Oxford: Clarendon Press, 1961), 96–97, pl. 22.

B. Systems of Accounting: Hieratic Numerals and Other Symbols

Evidence of foreign influence in the administrative organization of the Israelite monarchies is often elusive because some components of government were common in the region, rather than peculiar to any one state. Therefore, Hebrew titles of officials, even if etymologically or semantically related to Egyptian, Akkadian, or Ugaritic terms, do not necessarily reflect modelling or borrowing from those cultures. Transliterations of foreign titles, a clearer indication of non-Israelite origins, are generally absent from the corpus of Israelite monarchic official titles.[216] This phenomenon is not surprising since a sovereign state with a distinct language would be expected to translate known imported terms.

In contrast to Hebrew official titles, certain indisputable foreign elements are attested in the form of Egyptian hieratic numerals and symbols for weights, measures, and commodities used in Hebrew inscriptions of the monarchic period. The extant material can be divided into three main categories: (1) administrative documents, sometimes dated, bearing inventories of provisions or records of payments; (2) scribal exercises; (3) stone weights inscribed with whole and fractional shekel values. Although it has been long-recognized that the Israelite system of accounting has Egyptian origins, its peculiarities and abnormal utilization of Egyptian characters have not been delineated. In addition, the historical time-frame of the adoption and adaptation of this Egyptian system requires further discussion. The important connection between accounting methods and the topic of administration warrants an examination of that kind in this study. Furthermore, the "Israelitization" of an originally foreign system is revealing for understanding other aspects of Israelite officialdom.

Corpus of Inscriptions

Ostraca bearing hieratic symbols, primarily numerals of whole and fractional values, originate from sites scattered throughout Israel. Larger group finds belong to the archives of Samaria, Arad, and Lachish;[217] small collections come from Yavneh-yam, the Ophel in Jerusalem, Tell Jemmeh, Beer-Sheba,

216. For the exceptional cases, סריס and possibly סכן, see Chapter 5-A & D. A later loan-word appearing in Hebrew is ציר, Akkadian *ṣīru* (NA, NB), "messenger, ambassador" (Isa 18:2; 57:9; Jer 49:14; Ob 1:1; Prov 13:17; 25:13; *CAD* Ṣ, 213; Tadmor, "Was the Biblical *sārîs* a Eunuch?" 323–324; P. Machinist, "The Image of Assyria in First Isaiah," *JAOS* 103 [1983]: 730 n. 65). That term, however, is only used as a designation for a foreign government official.

217. Reisner, *Harvard Excavations at Samaria*, 233–243; Aharoni, *Arad Inscriptions*, nos. 1–12, 14, 16–18, 22, 24–25, 29–34, 36, 38, 41–42, 46–49, 60–62, 65, 67, 72, 76, 79, 81, 83, 87, 112; Tur-Sinai, *Lachish Letters*, nos. 1, 9, 19–22.

Qadesh-Barnea, and Tell Qasile.[218] A papyrus fragment from Murabba'at also bears hieratic signs.[219]

Most of these inscriptions date to Iron Age IIB-C (late 9th–early 6th centuries), although a few isolated texts are earlier (11/10th century). The inscriptions from Arad, which comprise data from different periods, span the nearly continuous occupation of the site from the 11th century to the early 6th century.[220] Notably, of the 45 Arad ostraca bearing hieratic symbols, more than half date to the late 7th or early 6th centuries. Another third date to the 9th–8th centuries. Three ostraca currently dated to Iron IIA and Iron IB (10th and 11th century) are among the earliest archaeological attestations of record-keeping in Israel.[221] Other groups of ostraca date to a single period: the archive from Samaria probably dates to the mid-8th century;[222] the ostraca from Beer-Sheba date to the end of the 8th century;[223] the ostraca from the Ophel in Jerusalem are dated to the late 8th or 7th century paleographically, since their stratigraphy is unclear;[224] the ostraca from Tell Qasile and Yavneh-yam and the Murabba'at papyrus are all dated to the latter half of the 7th century;[225] the ostraca from Tell

---

218. Naveh, "Hebrew Inscriptions from Meṣad Ḥashavyahu," nos. 4 & 5 pls. 5:E, 6:A; Lemaire, "Les ostraca paléo-hébreux des fouilles de l'Ophel," nos. 2–4, pls. 23:B-E; J. Naveh, "Writing and Scripts in Seventh-Century B.C.E. Philistia: The New Evidence from Tell Jemmeh," *IEJ* 35 (1985): nos. 2, 3, pls. 3:B, 2:C; Aharoni, *Beer-Sheba I,* 71–73, pl. 34; R. Cohen, "Excavations at Kadesh-Barnea 1976–1978," *BA* 44 (1981): 105–107; A. Lemaire and P. Vernus, "Les ostraca paléo-hébreux de Qadesh-Barnea," *Or* 49 (1980): nos. 3, 4, pls. 72, 73; "L'ostracon paléo-hébreu n 6 de Tell Qudeirat (Qadesh-Barnea)," in M. Görg ed. *Ägypten und altes Testament* (Wiesbaden: O. Harrassowitz, 1983), no. 6, pl. 6; B. Maisler, "The Excavations at Tell Qasile," *IEJ* 1 (1951): no. 2, pl. 38:A. Hieratic numerals inscribed on unprovenienced ostraca, supposedly uncovered in the Judean hills (Deutsch and Heltzer, *New Epigraphic Evidence,* 81–102), will not be incorporated into the data (see Chapter 2–C).

219. Benoit, Milik, and de Vaux, *Les grottes de Murabba'at,* no. 17, pl. 28. Three unprovenienced bullae, one marked Eltolad, the second Lachish, and the third Nezib, contain year dates in hieratic numerals (Avigad, "Two Hebrew 'Fiscal' Bullae," no. 1, pl. 28:A & B; *WSS,* nos. 42Γ 422; Deutsch, *Messages from the Past,* 139–140).

220. Most of the Arad inscriptions are dated stratigraphically but a few, not found *in situ,* are dated paleographically. The stratigraphy at Arad is problematic; the earliest stratum, XII, was dated by Aharoni to the 12th/11th century. Others prefer a 11th/10th century date (Mazar and Netzer, "On the Israelite Fortress at Arad," 87–91). Herzog in his reevaluation of the stratigraphy arrived at a date within the 11th century (*The Arad Fortresses,* 141–145).

221. Nos. 76 and 79 date to the 10th century; no. 81 dates to the premonarchic settlement in the 11th century (Aharoni, *Arad Inscriptions,* 98–101).

222. See Chapter 6-A.

223. Aharoni, *Beer-Sheba I,* 71.

224. Lemaire, "Les ostraca paléo-hébreux des fouilles de l'Ophel," 159.

225. Maisler, "The Excavations at Tell Qasile," 210; Naveh, "Hebrew Inscriptions from

Jemme cannot be dated more precisely than the 7th century;[226] those from Kadesh Barnea antedate the destruction of the site's upper fortress in the late 7th or early 6th century;[227] and those from Lachish date primarily to the end of the Judahite monarchy in the early 6th century.[228]

Date Formulas

One function of hieratic numerals in Hebrew inscriptions is to record dates. This phenomenon was first observed on the hoard of ostraca discovered in a storehouse at Samaria, many of which bear regnal years. The year numbers, expressed both in words and symbols, apparently date receipts for goods delivered to the palace complex. About half of the decipherable dates on the ostraca read בשת התשעת, "in the ninth year," or בשת העשרת, "in the tenth year," the regnal year written with the Hebrew word for ninth or tenth. In contrast, the other half shows regnal year 15 in the form of two hieratic symbols: , with  denoting ten and  signifying five.[229] One set of symbols, in the date formula of ostracon no. 63, remains problematic. It consists of the hieratic sign for 10, followed by an enigmatic sign, depicted by Reisner as a "t," and two vertical lines indicating the value 2 ().[230] Two separate proposals suggest reading the "t" as a 5 or 4, thereby indicating regnal year 17 (10+5+2=17) or 16 (10+4+2=16).[231]

Meṣad Ḥashavyahu," 32; Cross, "Epigraphic Notes on Hebrew Documents of the Eighth–Sixth Centuries B.C.: II, 41.

226. Naveh, "Writing and Scripts in Seventh-Century B.C.E. Philistia," 14–15.

227. Cohen, "Excavations at Kadesh Barnea," 107; Lemaire-Vernus, "L'ostracon paléo-hébreu n 6..", 302.

228. Torczyner, *Lachish I*, 204; Tufnell, *Lachish III*, 338–339 (no. 19 is unstratified; no. 21 belongs to an earlier stratum).

229. G. Möller, *Hieratische Paleographie, die ägyptische Buchschrift in ihrer Entwicklung von der fünften Dynastie bis zur römischen Kaiserzeit*, II (Osnabruck: O. Zeller, 1965) nos. 623 618. Yadin theorized that the signs  and  symbolize four and five, respectively, and that the regnal year indicated on these Samaria ostraca is "nine" ("Ancient Judean Weights and the Date of the Samaria Ostraca," 9–25). Yadin's conclusions were based on the assumption that the signs on weights represented the numerical shekel value and that the numerals on Hebrew materials would resemble those on Aramaic documents. His theory was abandoned subsequently when Scott and Aharoni showed that the numerals on shekel weights are Egyptian hieratic, not Aramaic, and that they are not equivalent to the shekel amount, but rather to the Egyptian *qedet* weight, 20% less than the royal shekel (R.B.Y. Scott, "The Scale Weights from the Ophel, 1963–64," *PEQ* 97 [1965]: 135; Y. Aharoni, "The Use of Hieratic Numerals in Hebrew Ostraca and the Shekel Weights," *BASOR* 184 [1966]: 13–19). See below for the discussion on weights.

230. Reisner, *Harvard Excavations at Samaria*, 238, 243.

231. D. Diringer interprets the "t" as the number 5 (*Le inscrizioni*, 57–58); Benoit et al interpret this sign as the number 4 since it slightly resembles the numeral on the first line of a papyrus fragment from Murabba'at that lists persons and quantities of a commodity (*Les*

Both of these suggestions, however, are based on comparisons with Aramaic, Palmyrean, and Nabatean numerals utilized hundreds of years later. After examining this ostracon at length, I.T. Kaufman concludes in his dissertation that the signs represent the hieratic symbol for 10 followed by three vertical strokes (), thus indicating regnal year 13.[232]

In addition to the Samaria ostraca, dates are found on inscriptions nos. 7, 8, 17, 20, 32 from Arad (late 7th–early 6th centuries). The dates on the Arad ostraca are recorded by variant methods: as numerical symbols; as number names; or as a combination thereof. For example, in the date on ostracon no. 7, the month number is expressed by its name, one day number is denoted with a numeral, but the other is noted by name:

לעשרי ב  לחדש עד הששה לחדש
For the tenth (month), on the first of the month up to the sixth of the month

Ostracon no. 8 bears a date written entirely in number words:

מן השלשה עשר לחדש עד השמנה עשר לחדש
From the 13th of the month to the 18th of the month

On ostracon no. 20 the date is represented similarly to inscription no. 8:

בשלשת [ב/ל] ירח צח
In the third (year) [in the] month of a, OR
On the third (day) [of the] month a

Interestingly, provision amounts registered on these ostraca are consistently rendered with numerals.

In contrast to the above, in inscription no. 17 the day of the month, 24, is written in hieratic numerals, 20 and 4:

ב  לחדש On the 24th of the month

Ostracon no. 32 also shows the day of the month, eight, in hieratic numerals, five and three:[233]

---

grottes de Murabba'at, 98, pl. 22). The numeral on the Murabba'at papyrus, however, more closely resembles the hieratic number 6, not 4 (cf. Arad no. 34 l. 6).

232. Kaufman, "The Samaria Ostraca," 140. He notes that the cross-bar of the "t" appears to be a groove of the decoration of the sherd.

233. On three unprovenienced fiscal bullae, which seem to record the payment of annual taxes from the towns of Eltolad, Lachish, and Nezib to the king, year dates are depicted in the hieratic numerals, 26 (20 + 6), 13 (10 + 3) and 20 respectively:

ב 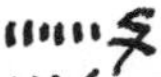 שנה In the 26th year
ב  שנה In the 13th year

לחדש  ב On the 8th of the month

Although the numerals in the aforementioned dates are undoubtedly Egyptian hieratic numerals, it must be noted that the Israelite system for recording date formulas deviates from the Egyptian method. Egyptian documents containing dates, from the Old Kingdom (27th century) onwards, use standard hieratic numerals to mark the year and month number but utilize special numerical symbols to depict the days of the month.[234] In some cases the distinction between the standard and special numerals is simply their stance: a normally vertical number is written horizontally and vice versa; in other cases the number is completely different. In the dates that appear on ostraca nos. 17 and 32 from Arad no differentiation exists between year and month numerals and those signifying days.

It is noteworthy that the authentic Egyptian method for recording dates appears to have been perpetuated in Canaan in the New Kingdom, either by Egyptian scribes or Canaanite scribes trained in the Egyptian system. A late 19th or 20th Dynasty (late 13th to mid 12th century) bowl from Lachish that registers a harvest tax, bears a complete Egyptian date formula:[235]

ḥ3t-sp 4 *3bd* 4 *(n) 3ẖt sww* 26
Year 4 month 4 (of the) inundation day 26

The signs for the year and month numbers are each written with four vertical lines, the usual marks for the number four, but the symbol for the day number, 26, follows the alternate numerical system designated for days of the month.[236] Notably, documents from Egypt contemporary with the Arad inscriptions confirm that the Egyptian method of numerical differentiation for days of the month was still operative in Egypt in the late seventh century. This is evident in records from the 45th and 47th year (619, 617 BCE) of Psammetichus I, in which day numbers are written with the special numerical symbols for days of

---

שנה  ב In the 20th year

(The difference in representation of the numeral 20 on the bulla from Nezib and Arad ostracon no. 17 from the bulla from Eltolad is probably due to paleographic variants, providing the latter is genuine.)

234. Compare the standard numerals (Möller, II nos. 614–624) with those used to represent the days in the month (Möller, II nos. 656–666). An exception beginning in the New Kingdom is the standard representation used for the first day of the month, a vertical line (Möller, no. 614).

235. Černý, "Report on Inscriptions," 133, pl. 44, no. 3.

236. The numeral 26 as the day of the month (Lachish bowl, inside) is depicted as 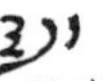 (Möller, II nos. 66Γ 666). Cf. the standard numeral 26 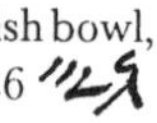 (Möller, II nos. 619 & 624).

the month.[237] It is unclear when or why this Egyptian method was lost in Israel. Apparently Israelite scribes employed hieratic numerals without adhering to specific patterns originally designed for their use.

Peculiar Depictions of Numerals

Other Israelite scribal aberrations are apparent in the stance of certain numerals and in the variant combinations of signs used to depict the same number. The latter phenomenon primarily affects the numbers six and eight, while the former deviation is most apparent in depictions of the numbers two, three, and four. Several renderings of the numbers two, three, and four from Israel consist of diagonal or horizontal strokes in place of the usual vertical lines found in Egyptian hieratic records.[238] Although these numbers are usually written with vertical or nearly vertical strokes in Hebrew inscriptions, diagonal and horizontal stances are clearly observable on ostraca nos. 3, 16, 33, 34, and 60 from Arad.[239] The stance becomes critical when it affects the reading of the number, as in ostracon no. 16, where the two diagonal lines could signify the number two or eight.[240]

Israelite peculiarities are further illustrated by the following alternate representations of the same number. The numeral six in Egyptian hieratic texts is represented by a single sign, $\mathcal{L}$; occasionally six vertical strokes written in two groups of three, *III III* , are used in its place.[241] In Hebrew inscriptions, the numeral six is attested in three forms: as a single sign, $\mathcal{L}$ or $\mathcal{E}$ (Arad nos. 25, 31, 34, 112; Kadesh Barnea nos. 6, 8), as six successive vertical strokes, *IIIIII* (Arad no. 46);[242] and as a combination of the sign for five plus a single vertical stroke, *I⅂* (Arad nos. 48, 60). Similarly, the numeral eight, consistently rendered in Egyptian hieratic by one symbol, $\rightleftharpoons$, from the time of the 12th Dynasty (ca. 1990 BCE),[243] appears in Hebrew inscriptions in three forms: as eight consecutive vertical strokes, *IIIIIIII* (Ophel no. 4); as the sign for five plus

---

237. Papyrus Turin nos. 247, 248 (written in abnormal hieratic) photos in H.C. Brügsch, *Grammaire démotique: contenants les principes generaux de la langue et de l'écriture populaires des anciens Égyptiens* (Berlin: F. Dummler, 1855), pls. I, II. In later periods as well, even in Ptolemaic and Roman times, this method for recording dates is evident from Egyptian demotic texts (W. Erichsen, *Demotisches Glossar* [Copenhagen: Munksgaard, 1954], 707–712).

238. Möller, II nos. 615–617.

239. The number 3 = *III* (Arad no. 3, ll. 2, 11); the number 3 = $\mathbf{\approx}$ (Arad no. 33, l. 2); the number 2 = $\mathbf{\mathcal{L}}$ (Arad no. 34, l. 15); the number 2 or 8 = $\mathbf{\sim}$ (Arad no. 16, l. 5); the number 4 = $\mathbf{\mathcal{Z}}$ (Arad no. 60, l. 1).

240. Aharoni reads the two diagonal strokes as the number 8 (*Arad Inscriptions*, 30–31).

241. Möller, II no. 619.

242. On the bulla from Eltolad, the number six is expressed by six vertical strokes as well.

243. Möller, II no. 621.

three vertical strokes, (Arad no. 32); and as a single sign of two horizontal lines identical to the Egyptian symbol (Arad nos. 16, 31; Ophel no. 3; Kadesh Barnea nos. 3, 6).[244] Seemingly, in Israel, scribal practices permitted flexibility in utilizing Egyptian numerals. Although the Israelite variations reflect a more fluid system, it is certainly functional, especially if one considers modern diversity for numerical representation (e.g. Roman numerals and Arabic numerals).

Other uniquely "Israelite" representations of hieratic numerals are noticeable on the ostraca from Kadesh Barnea. These, however, must be dealt with separately because the Kadesh Barnea ostraca probably represent school exercises and their peculiarities may be indicative of the scribes' inexperience.[245] The largest of the Kadesh Barnea ostraca, no. 6, contains six columns of writing that include numerals up to 10,000. Many are accompanied by symbols for units of weight and measure. Most curious is the symbol for the number 10,000, , a combination of the hieratic sign for 10 () and the Hebrew word for thousands, אלפם (10×1000=10,000).[246] In Egyptian hieratic the sign for 10,000 is .[247] Since the number 10,000 only appears on the Kadesh Barnea ostracon, it is impossible to ascertain whether it was regularly depicted in this Israelitized fashion of hybrid numeration or whether the novice scribe forgot the symbol for 10,000 and devised a clever substitute.[248] Additional un-Egyptian types on this ostracon include the numbers 70 and 6,000, identifiable from the sequential order of the numerals.[249] These too are unattested in other Hebrew inscriptions and thus the reason for the anomalies is uncertain.

244. The diagonal stance of the two strokes in Arad no. 16 (l. 5) can be interpreted as either the numeral two or eight.

245. Cohen, "Excavations at Kadesh Barnea," 106; Lemaire and Vernus, "L'ostracon paléo-hébreu n 6..," 325. In addition to the square-like depiction of the numerals and some odd shapes unattested in Egypt, the unrealistic lists of consecutive denominations of numerals (e.g. units of *gerah* in the hundreds [ostracon no. 3]) imply an exercise rather than a reference chart.

246. Column 3 line 12 and column 6 line 6.

247. Möller, II no. 650.

248. Note that in several fifth-century Aramaic papyri from Elephantine the numeral for thousands is expressed by a numeral for the multiples of 1000 followed by an abbreviation of the word אלף consisting of לפ, (e.g. A4.7 1.28 [Cowley no. 30] and C3,19 1.3 [Cowley no. 73]); the numeral for 10,000 appears as the sign , seemingly a combination of the signs 100, 10, and 10 (C2.1:27, 43 [Cowley Bisitun]). See B. Porten and I. Yardeni, *Textbook of Aramaic Documents,* 1, 3. This hybrid numeration in the Elephantine papyri apparently represents actual symbols (Aramaic), in contrast to the phenomenon on the Kadesh Barnea ostracon.

249. Compare the symbol for 70 on ostracon no. 6 (col. 5, l. 3) with Möller, II & III no. 629 and the symbol for 6,000 on ostracon no. 6 (col. 3, l. 8; col. 6, l. 2) with Möller, II & III no. 646.

Aramaic vs. Hieratic Numerals

In light of the preceding observations concerning Israelite deviations from the Egyptian system, it seems appropriate to reexamine previous readings of numerals on three ostraca, two from Tell Jemmeh and one from Tell Qasile. On the Tell Qasile ostracon, which registers a shekel amount of Ophir gold allocated for Beit Horon (no. 2), there appears a numerical sign composed of three horizontal lines, ≡. B. Mazar, and more recently, Naveh read this symbol as the number 30, based on the Phoenician and Aramaic system, where each horizontal bar represents a unit of 10.[250] The ostraca from Tell Jemmeh (nos. 2 & 3) bear names, numerals, and other signs. Both ostraca show a numeral rendered of two horizontal bars, =, and in no. 3 this numeral is preceded by a symbol resembling a "Z" and followed by a vertical line representing the numerical value 1.[251] Naveh interprets the numerals on these Philistine ostraca as belonging to the Phoenician and Aramaic system, although he notes that in Israel in the First Temple period the Egyptian hieratic system was normative. Naveh reads the numeral depicted by two horizontal bars, found on both ostraca, as the number 20, and on no. 3, where a vertical line follows, as a total value of 21.[252]

Both Mazar's and Naveh's understanding of the Tell Qasile and Tell Jemmeh numerals are based on comparisons with Phoenician and Aramaic examples. However, a careful examination of comparative pre-exilic data shows a variety of forms, none of which closely resembles the three unconnected broad horizontal bars on the Tell Qasile ostracon or the two unconnected horizontal bars on the Tell Jemme ostraca. Units of tens in pre-Persian Aramaic records are indicated by dots, short horizontal dashes, stacks of horizontal bars of various lengths connected by diagonal shafts (ligatures), or by combinations of symbol types.[253] In the fifth and fourth centuries, two units of 10 are regularly depicted

250. Maisler, "The Excavations at Tell Qasile," 209–210; Naveh, "Writing and Scripts in Seventh-Century B.C.E. Philistia," 15.

251. Naveh, "Writing and Scripts in Seventh-Century B.C.E. Philistia," figs. 2:2, 3, pls. 3:B, 2C.

252. Naveh, "Writing and Scripts in Seventh-Century B.C.E. Philistia," 15.

253. In the Panammu Aramaic inscription, dated to the reign of Tiglath-Pileser III, the number 70 appears as the word שבעי (accusative *status constructus* – i) followed by seven dots (*KAI*, 225). In an Aramaic inscription from Zinjirli, the number 30 is expressed by the word שלשן followed by three short horizontal dashes the size of the word-dividers in the inscription (M. Lidzbarski, *Handbuch der nordsemitischen Epigraphik* [Weimar: Emil Felber, 1898], pl. 24:3). On a bronze lion weight from Nineveh dated to the end of the 8th century, the sum 15 minas is represented three ways: by one short horizontal dash plus five vertical lines at least twice as long; by 15 vertical lines; by the words חמשת עשר (*CIS* II:1). On several 7th-century tablets from Ashur inscribed in Aramaic, units of tens are depicted by stacked

by two short horizontal or vertical bars connected by a ligature.[254] A single unit of ten is sometimes represented by a horizontal crescent-shaped line.

Naveh's interpretation of the Tell Jemme numerals is based on the assumption that scribes in Israel and Philistia strictly adhered to the Egyptian system, in which numerals between five and ten are denoted by a single symbol. Therefore, the two horizontal bars, which in hieratic denote the number eight, followed by the vertical bar signifying one, cannot be understood as signifying the number nine. However, as shown by several examples from the Arad ostraca, in Israel variant methods of combining numerals to express a certain number co-existed. Since the numerical values for six and eight were sometimes depicted by two or more symbols instead of one, as in Arad nos. 32, 48 and 60, it is possible that the numerical value for nine would be rendered similarly. In that case, the numbers on ostracon no. 3 from Tel Jemme should read: 8+1=9. The significance of thc "Z" shaped sign preceding the two numerals on this ostracon remains enigmatic.[255]

In addition to the mixed methods for depicting a single numeral in Israel, the unusual diagonal and horizontal stance of the numbers 2, 3, & 4 on certain Arad ostraca have been noted above. This variation in stance may suggest that the

---

horizontal bars, two for the number 20, three for 30, with a diagonal shaft connecting the bars from the top right to the bottom left. On one of the Ashur tablets, 50 is rendered by five short horizontal dashes comparable to those on the Zinjirli inscription (M. Lidzbarski, "Altaramäische Urkunden aus Assur," *WVDOG* 38 [1921]: 15–20, Pl. 2). A late 7th/early 6th-century Ammonite ostracon from Heshbon (no. 4) shows the number twenty as two short horizontal bars connected by a diagonal shaft; the number thirty consists of a twenty plus a separate horizontal bar, crescent-shaped (Cross, "Ammonite Ostraca from Heshbon," fig. 1, pl. 1:4. It should be noted that Aufrecht incorrectly identifies the Aramaic numerals on the Heshbon ostracon as "hieratic" [*A Corpus of Ammonite Inscriptions*, 215]). A 6th-century Aramaic tablet from Sefire records a shekel amount and date with a mixture of symbols. The number 20 is shaped like a rounded "Z," but the number 30 is comprised of a rounded "Z" plus a separate short horizontal dash (J. Starcky, "Une tablette araméenne de l'an 34 de Nabuchodonosor," *Syria* 37 [1960]: fig. 1). The diagonal shafts in these examples appear to be ligatures connecting the horizontal strokes. This ligature form also appears in numerals of the Persian period (Aharoni, *Beer-Sheba I*, pl. 35:3, note the numeral 20).

254. For example, 5th-century Aramaic papyri from Saqqara (*CIS* 2, nos. 145, 146); 4th-century Phoenician inscriptions from Kition (*CIS* 1, nos. 11, 13); 4th-century Phoenician seals (J. Greenfield, "A Group of Phoenician City Seals," *IEJ* 35 [1985]: fig. 1); 4th-century Aramaic ostraca (J. Naveh, "The Aramaic Ostraca from Tel Arad" in *Arad Inscriptions*, nos. 7, 9, 10).

255. Naveh's suggestion that the "Z" represents a letter, perhaps a *yod* missing the center horizontal cross-bar, is possible ("Writing and Scripts in Seventh Century B.C.E. Philistia," 15). Another option is the letter *zayin*. In the Deir 'Alla inscriptions the *zayin* is shaped like a "Z" (J. Hoftijzer and G. van der Kooij, *Aramaic Texts from Deir 'Alla* [Leiden: E.J. Brill, 1976], pl. 26).

numeral incised on ostracon no. 2 from Tell Qasile, rendered by three horizontal bars, belongs to the hieratic number system as well. If each bar signifies a single unit rather than 10, then the shekel value on the ostracon would be equal to three rather than 30, as previously proposed. However, since this alternate reading is based on a single parallel example (Arad no. 33), the possibility that the numeral on the Tel Qasile ostracon is actually an atypical Aramaic or Phoenician type cannot be completely discounted.

Symbols for Weights, Measures and Commodities

In addition to hieratic numerals, several Egyptian hieratic symbols for weights, measures, and commodities appear in Hebrew inscriptions. These are especially conspicuous since normally units of weights and measures used in Israel are expressed by names that are of Mesopotamian and Canaanite origin.[256] One sign found on six Arad ostraca (nos. 25, 33, 34, 60, 76, 112) seems to represent the small Egyptian symbol for a single quadruple *ḥḳ3t* (or *oipe*),  , although it is utilized differently than in the Egyptian system.[257]

256. Sellers, "Weights and Measures," 828–839; Stern, "Weights and Measures," 846–878. For example, capacity measures found in Hebrew inscriptions (Arad ostraca nos. 1-11, 18, 22, 31, 33, 41–42, 46, 61, 79, 83; Lachish ostracon no. 22; Qadesh Barnea ostracon no. 6; Murabba'at papyrus) include symbols, as opposed to names, for the following: סאה (*s'h*; Akkad. *sūtu*), בת (*bt*), איפה (*'yph*; Egyp. *ipt*), לתך (*ltk*; Ugar. *lth*), חמר (*ḥmr*; Akkad. *imēru*; Ugar. *ḥmr*), כר (*kr*; Akkad. *kurru*). The הין (*hyn*), an Egyptian liquid measure, is attested in the Bible (in the P source), but the capacity of the Israelite measure (3.5–4.0 liters) far exceeds that of the Egyptian *hnw* (.5 liters). The larger Israelite הין may be indicated in several Arad ostraca by the diagonal lines slanted to the left following the בת measure (e.g. nos. 1, 2, 4, 9; J. Naveh, "The Numbers of *Bat* in the Arad Ostraca," *IEJ* 45 [1995]: 52–54). Apparently, though, the Egyptian *hnw* was known in Israel. An alabaster jar found at Samaria bearing the cartouche of Osorkon II (874–850 BCE) is marked with the capacity of 81 *hnw* (Reisner, *Harvard Excavations at Samaria*, 247). The origin of the בת measure (Greek *βάτος*) is uncertain (M. Heltzer equates the בת with the Ugaritic and Phoenician *kd*. The term carries the general meaning "jar" but also specifies a standard unit of measure, ca. 22 liters ["Some Questions of the Ugaritic Metrology and its Parallels in Judah, Phoenicia, Mesopotamia and Greece," *UF* 21 (1989): 197–208]). Names of units of weights inscribed on stone and bronze weights include: נצף (*nṣp*; Ugar. *nṣp*), פים (*pym*; Akkad. *šinipu*), בקע (*bq'*), גרה (*grh*; Akkad. *girû*) and the symbol for שקל (*šql*; Akkad. *šiklu*). Shekel symbols, ש or , are also found on ostraca (Arad nos. 16, 65, 81; Yavneh-Yam nos. 4, 6; Tel Qasile; Qadesh Barnea no. 6), as is the term גרה (Kadesh-Barnea no. 3). None of these weight-names seems to be of Egyptian origin. The origin of the בקע is uncertain; its name indicates a "fraction," from the verb to break. Additional weight-names attested in the Bible include the מנה (*mnh*; Akkad. *manû*) and ככר (*kkr*), "talent" (Ugar. *kkr*).

257. Möller, II no. 695; Gardiner, *Egyptian Grammar*, 198–199; Helck, "Masse und Gewichte," *Lexikon* 3, 1201. The Egyptian *ḥḳ3t* is a measure for grain approximately equivalent to 4.5 liters.

In Egypt, beginning in the 18th Dynasty (ca. 1540 BCE), units of grain were expressed in *ẖ3r*, "sack," measurements (1 *ẖ3r* = 4 quadruple *ḥḳ3t*). A record registering amounts of grain would include the regular symbol for the quadruple *ḥḳ3t*, , followed by the sign *ẖ3r*, , and numerals.[258] The total quadruple *ḥḳ3t* measures would be equal to a multiple of four of the numerals. Any partial *ẖ3r* (¼, ½ or ¾) was indicated by one, two, or three of the small dot-like symbols for a single quadruple *ḥḳ3t*.[259] Sometimes fractional quadruple *ḥḳ3t* amounts also appear.[260] In Hebrew sources, where the *ẖ3r* measure and the full symbol for *ḥḳ3t* are unattested, the small symbol for a single quadruple *ḥḳ3t* seems to have been employed to express the *ḥḳ3t* standard of measure.[261] The quantity of *ḥḳ3t* units is calculated by multiplying the first numeral following the *ḥḳ3t* symbol by ten and adding subsequent numbers to that value. If a numeral precedes the *ḥḳ3t* sign, as in ostracon no. 76, the value is equal to a multiple of 100.[262] Notably, this *ḥḳ3t* measure already appears in use in Israel as early as the 10th century (no. 76). In the case of the *ḥḳ3t* measuring system, as in date formulas, it is unclear when or why the Egyptian method underwent changes in the process of local adaptation.

Another common Egyptian symbol with a long tradition in Canaan is the sign for grain, . It is found in hieratic inscriptions on bowls from Tel Sera' and Lachish dated to the late 19th or 20th Dynasty.[263] Both inscriptions register quantities of grain, on the Lachish bowl specified *swt*, "reed plant," presumably wheat. It is assumed that the grain represents harvest tax offerings to Egyptian temples in Canaan. One candidate for such an Egyptian temple is the Acropolis Temple at Lachish, dated to the 12th century (level VI) and showing an Egyptian building plan.[264] Noticeably, the sign for grain on these bowls is almost

---

258. Möller, II nos. 470 & 471.

259. Numerous examples appear in Papyrus Louvre 3226.

260. Möller, II nos. 708–713.

261. Pre-Israelite inscriptions from Canaan show the full quadruple *ḥḳ3t* and *ẖ3r* signs (see bowls nos. 1, 3 from Tel Sera' [Goldwasser, "Hieratic Inscriptions from Tel Sera' in Southern Canaan," pls. 4, 6]).

262. Gardiner, *Egyptian Grammar*, 198. This calculation presumes that the Egyptian method of figuring multiple *ḥḳ3t* measures was applied in Israel.

263. The Tel Sera' inscription (bowl no. 1) is dated to the 22nd regnal year, probably of Rameses III (Goldwasser, "Hieratic Inscriptions from Tel Sera'," 77–90, pl. 4. Bowl no. 3 from Lachish is dated by Černý to the late 19th or 20th Dynasty (*Lachish IV*, 133, pl. 44).

264. D. Ussishkin, "Lachish" in *NEAEHL*, 901–904. Cf. Papyrus Harris (34a, 53a, 71b) from the reign of Rameses III, which registers grain offerings from Syria-Palestine to Egyptian temples in Egypt (J. Wilson, *ANET*, 261; P. Grandet, *Papyrus Harris. Institut franais d'archéologie orientale* 109/1 (1994): 270, 295, 328).

identical to a symbol repeated several times on Arad ostraca nos. 25 and 34, probably a reference to supplies of grain stored at Arad.[265]

Other, more enigmatic hieratic symbols on ostracon no. 34 from Arad may represent additional commodities listed in the inventory.[266] One sign, , which appears four times, could signify a hieratic symbol for a vessel.[267] This explanation is especially plausible if another problematic symbol, , which precedes the vessel sign three times, can be interpreted as a hieratic form of *irp*, "wine."[268] In that case, the commodity in question would be a container of wine. Another sign, 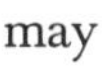, which resembles the hieratic symbol for *swt*, may refer to wheat, the grain recorded on the Lachish bowl.[269] Additional symbols on this ostracon are too uncertain to decipher.[270] They may represent local variations of hieratic signs or independent Israelite developments.

Symbols on Weights

Numerous weights of various whole and fractional shekel values, carved predominately of stone, are attested from different regions in Israel. The provenienced pieces originate primarily from sites in Judah. Included are sites

265. The sign is notated "f" by Aharoni (p. 62). Cf. S. Yeivin, who interprets this symbol as a ligature of *šmʿ*, signifying Upper-Egyptian barley ("A Hieratic Ostracon from Tel Arad," *IEJ* 16 [1966]: 154). Notably, the grain symbol on a late Egyptian document (7th century) differs from the Arad types (J. Černý, "The Abnormal Hieratic Tablet Leiden I 431" in *Studies Presented to F.L.L. Griffith* [London: Oxford University Press, 1932], pls. 2, 3).

266. Cf. Yeivin, "A Hieratic Ostracon from Tel Arad," 153–154. Aharoni proposes that the inventory of supplies on this ostracon was written by an Egyptian scribe at a time Arad was in Egyptian hands, probably after the death of Josiah (*Arad Inscriptions*, 64). Aharoni bases his assumption on the fact that the ostracon is inscribed entirely in hieratic characters. It is equally possible, however, that the list simply represents an Israelite invoice of commodities at Arad written in a hieratic short-hand style. Other records from Israel, such as the Kadesh Barnea ostraca, also show hieratic numbers and symbols. At any rate, the inscription on ostracon no. 34 is the work of a scribe well trained in hieratic.

267. Möller, II no. 496 or 503. Yeivin interprets the symbol as Möller no. 506 ("A Hieratic Ostracon from Tel Arad," 157), but the two show little resemblance to each other.

268. Following a suggestion by S. Groll (cited in, *Arad Inscriptions*, 64 n. 10).

269. Aharoni, *Arad Inscriptions*, 64; Möller, II nos. 289/290.

270. Cf. Aharoni, *Arad Inscriptions*, 62–64.

in the Shephelah,[271] the Judean hills,[272] the Judean desert,[273] and the Negeb.[274] A number of weights also come from sites on the coastal plain[275] and from northern Israel.[276] Unfortunately, many weights cannot be dated accurately, even though their provenience is known, because their stratification is uncertain. Those that are stratified, all from Judean sites, date predominately to the

271. For example, Gezer (R.A.S. Macalister, *The Excavation of Gezer II* (London: J. Murray, 1912), 283–287); Lachish (Tufnell, *Lachish III*, 354–355, pl. 51; Aharoni, *Lachish V*, pl. 17); Azekah (F.J. Bliss and R.A.S. Macalister, *Excavations in Palestine 1898–1900* [London: Palestine Exploration Fund, 1902], 145–146); Beth-shemesh (E. Grant, *Ain Shems Excavations III* [Haverford: Haverford College, 1934], 55); Ekron (Gitin, "Tel Miqne-Ekron," 51); and Khirbet el-Qom (W. Dever, "Iron Age Epigraphic Material from the Area of Khirbet el-Kom," *HUCA* 40/41 [1970]: 174–175).

272. For example, Jerusalem (Scott, "The Scale-Weights from Ophel, 1963–64," 128–139; Ramat Raḥel (Y. Aharoni, "Excavations at Ramat Raḥel, 1954," *IEJ* 6 [1954]: 137–138; *Excavations at Ramat Raḥel, Seasons 1961–1962*, 14); Gibeon (Pritchard, *Hebrew Inscriptions and Stamps from Gibeon*, fig. 12); Tell en-Naṣbeh (C.C. McCown, *Tell en-Naṣbeh I* [Berkeley: Palestine Institute of Pacific School of Religion and ASOR, 1947], 163–164, 259, 276; Scott, "The *N-Ṣ-F* Weights from Judah," *BASOR* 200 [1970]: 65); and Beth-Zur (Sellers, *Citadel of Beth-zur*, 60, fig. 53).

273. For example, Ein Gedi (A. Mazar, M. Dothan, I. Dunayevsky, *En-gedi the First and Second Seasons of Excavations, 1961–1962 'Atiqot* 5 [1966], pl. 26:2; R. Hestrin, *Inscriptions Reveal: Documents from the Time of the Bible, the Mishna and the Talmud* [Jerusalem: Israel Museum, 1973], no. 91).

274. For example, Tel Malḥata (G. Barkay, "Iron Age Gerah Weights," *EI* 15 [1981]: 291 [Hebrew]); Arad (Aharoni, *Arad Inscriptions*, 126); Tel Ira (I. Beit-Arieh, "Tel 'Ira – A Fortified City of the Kingdom of Judah," *Qadmoniot* 18 [1985]: 23 [Hebrew]); and Beer-Sheba (Aharoni, *Beer-sheba I*, 23–30, pl. 39).

275. For example, Tell Jemme (F. Petrie, *Gerar* [London: British School of Archaeology in Egypt, 1928], pl. 17); Tell Farah S. (R. Scott, "Shekel-Fraction Markings on Hebrew Weights," *BASOR* 173 [1964]: 58–59; Dever, "Iron Age Epigraphic Material," 184; Barkay, "Iron Age Gerah Weights," 290); Ashdod (M. Dothan, *Ashdod II-III, the Second and Third Seasons of Excavations 1963, 1965, 'Atiqot* 9–10 [1971], 40); Yavneh-yam (Naveh, "More Hebrew Inscriptions from Meṣad Ḥashavyahu," 31); and Nebi Rubin (N. Glueck, "A Seal Weight from Nebi Rubin," *BASOR* 153 (1959): 35–38).

276. For example, Bethel (W.F. Albright and J. Kelso, *The Excavation of Bethel (1934–1960), AASOR* 39 [Cambridge: Jane Dows Nies, 1968]: 87, pl. 44:6); Tell Farah N. (E. Puech, "Les poids" in A. Chambon ed., *Tell el-Far'ah I. L'âge du fer* [Paris: Édition recherche sur les civilisations, 1984], 81); Shechem (V. Kerkhof, "An Inscribed Stone Weight from Shechem," *BASOR* 184 (1966): 20–21); Megiddo (R. Lamon and G. Shipton, *Megiddo I: Seasons of 1925–34 Strata I-V* [Chicago: University of Chicago, 1939], pl. 104, no. 37); and Samaria (T. Chaplin, "An Ancient Hebrew Weight from Samaria," *PEFQS* 22 [1890]: 267; G. Barton, "Three Objects in the Collection of Mr. Herbert Clark, of Jerusalem," *JAOS* 27 [1906]: 400; these weights were not found in controlled excavations).

seventh and early sixth centuries, with a few exceptions from eighth-century occupation levels.[277]

A majority of the weights are inscribed with one or more of the following: hieratic numerals, the name for a unit of weight, a PN, or another symbol. The mass of the stone weight is most frequently indicated by a hieratic numeral(s) plus the sign ɤ, recognized as symbolic of the royal shekel. The significance of the looped sign as the mark of a royal weight standard is deduced from a bronze two-shekel weight (22.28 grams) from Gezer inscribed with two vertical strokes and the word למלך, "belonging to/of the king."[278]

Initially, the interpretation of the numerals on the weights was problematic because the hieratic numbers do not correspond to the shekel values. For example, weights marked with a hieratic 5, 10, 20, or 30 are equivalent, according to their weight, to 4, 8, 16, and 24 royal shekels, respectively.[279] As shown by R.B.Y. Scott and later confirmed by Y. Aharoni, the basic unit is the 8-shekel weight, which is equivalent to one Egyptian *deben*, approximately 91 grams (1 shekel = approx. 11.4 grams). One deben consists of 10 smaller units called *qedets*, each weighing about 9.1 grams.[280] The hieratic numerals on the weights are actually equivalent to the *qedet* mass. Thereby, a weight marked ᒣɤ, the shekel symbol plus a hieratic five, is equal to the mass of five *qedets* but only four royal shekels, a difference of 20%. Apparently the conversion from the Egyptian to the Israelite system was readily understood and practiced, as indicated by an inscription from Yavneh-yam: [נ]תצבעל ארבע כסף ᒣɤ שי שקל, "[N]tṣb'l

277. Three weights securely dated to the 8th century include: a *neṣef* and a four-shekel weight from Beer-Sheba Stratum 2 (Aharoni, *Beer-sheba I*, 23–30, pl. 39:1, 2); an eight-*gerah* weight from Lachish Stratum III (Tufnell, *Lachish III*, 349, pl. 114). Another three weights possibly come from 8th-century contexts: a two-shekel weight from Arad Stratum 8 (M. Aharoni, "Inscribed Weights and Royal Seals," 126); a two-shekel weight from Beth-Shemesh Stratum 2 (Grant, *Ain Shems III*, 55, pl. 5:4); a one-shekel weight from Tell Farah (N) Stratum 7 (Puech, "Les poids," 81).

278. Macalister, *The Excavation of Gezer II*, 285, fig. 433. Another bronze two-shekel weight (21.7 grams) is inscribed למלך plus a looped shekel sign and two vertical strokes. That weight, however, is unprovenienced and its authenticity is not confirmed (Deutsch and Heltzer, *Forty*, 66–67).

279. Yadin interpreted the symbol ᒣ as the numerical sign for 4 and the symbol ʌ as the numerical sign for 8 ("Ancient Judean Weights and the Date of the Samaria Ostraca," 21). Although his reading correctly identified the actual shekel value of the weights, he misunderstood the system of representation. Only in the case of weights marked one and two are the numbers and weights considered to be equal in value. Apparently the difference in weight was too small to be significant.

280. In the 18th Dynasty the *deben-qedet* system became standard in Egypt (Gardiner, *Egyptian Grammar*, 200; Scott, "The Scale-Weights from Ophel," 135; Aharoni, "The Use of Hieratic Numerals in Hebrew Ostraca and the Shekel Weights," 17–18).

weighed 4 (shekel) silver according to 4 royal shekel (hieratic five plus the shekel symbol) as a donation."[281]

An unresolved issue concerning the shekel weights is the origin of the looped shekel symbol. Numerous proposals have been put forth. Y. Yadin posits that the sign is an abstraction of the four-winged beetle depicted on the *lmlk* stamps.[282] Scott, who originally suggested that the sign symbolizes a צרור, "bag," used to carry small weight-stones, later changed his mind following Albright's theory that the symbol signifies the hieratic rope sign *šs*.[283] Building on Albright's theory, A. Lemaire and P. Vernus have attempted to elucidate the significance of the *šs* sign by identifying it as "Egyptian alabaster (calcite)," one meaning of *šs*. They note that alabaster may have been used as a standard of weights in Egypt, as evidenced occasionally by inscribed weights designating alabaster as the "stone of weight."[284] But as Lemaire and Vernus recognize, no clear relationship is visible between the use of alabaster as a standard for weights in Egypt and its notation next to the numerical value on Israelite weights. R. Kletter recently posited that the *šs* sign was not used for its Egyptian value but rather as a phonetic indicator for "š", similar to the ש sometimes used as an abbreviation for shekel.[285] While this proposal is feasible, the utilization of an Egyptian phonetic sign to designate an Israelite weight unit would seem confusing.

In addition to the problems noted in conjunction with the explanations proposed above, none touch the heart of the matter, the association of the looped shekel sign with "royal." D. Redford offers an alternate proposal in this regard. He reasons that since in Egyptian Ɣ, when used to signify "linen," is sometimes followed by the sign 𓇓, *nswt*, "king, royal," in the expression *šs-nswt*, "royal linen,"[286] a connection was incorrectly established in Israel between Ɣ and "royal."[287] However, when or under what circumstances this idea developed is enigmatic. Thus at present, no single theory adequately explicates the royal shekel symbol and the issue remains open.

The royal shekel discussed above seems to have been in use in Israel concur-

---

281. Naveh, "Hebrew Inscriptions from Meṣad Ḥashavyahu," pl. 6:a, c; cf. Aharoni who reads 33 instead of 4 shekels ("The Use of Hieratic Numerals in Hebrew Ostraca and the Shekel Weights," 19).

282. Yadin, "Ancient Judean Weights and the Date of the Samaria Ostraca," 13–15.

283. R. Scott, "The Shekel Sign on Stone Weights," *BASOR* 153 (1959): 32–35; "Shekel-Fraction Markings on Hebrew Weights," 56 n. 12.

284. A. Lemaire and P. Vernus, "L'origine égyptienne du signe Ɣ des poids inscrits de l'époque royale israelite," *Semitica* 28 (1978): 53–58. Notably, none of these weights are of alabaster.

285. R. Kletter, "The Inscribed Weights of the Kingdom of Judah," *TA* 18 (1991): 124.

286. Erman and Grapow, *Wörterbuch* 4, 542.

287. Redford, oral communication 4/96.

rently with another, smaller shekel. This lighter shekel is designated by the term נצף (*nṣp*), found engraved on a number of weights with a mass of about 17% less than the royal shekel. Evidently, two shekel standards existed simultaneously, that of the 20 *gerah* (גרה) נצף and that of the heavier 24 *gerah* royal shekel.[288] Although the term נצף is unattested in the Bible, this unit of weight is clearly equivalent to the שקל הקדש, "sanctuary shekel," of 20 *gerah* (Exod 30:13; Lev 27:25; Num 3:47; 18:16; Ezek 45:12). The larger, royal shekel is probably the standard of weight referred to in 2 Sam 14:26, מאתים שקלים באבן המלך, "200 shekels according to the royal weight."[289] Weights of shekel fractions are also at-

---

288. *Gerah* weights can be calculated based on the numbers engraved on small fractional shekel weights (1 *gerah* = ½ gram). The term *nṣp* appears in Ugaritic texts where it seems to denote half the heavy (approx. 17 grams) Mesopotamian shekel (RS 10066:1,4,5 in C. Virolleaud, "Les villes et les corporations du royaume d'Ugarit," *Syria* 21 [1940]: 133; *UT* 1017:6, 50, 219). In Arabic *nuṣf* means "half".

289. The existence of a dual standard of weights in Israel is contested by Kletter ("The Inscribed Weights of the Kingdom of Judah," 131–139) and Y. Ronen ("The Enigma of the Shekel Weights of the Judean Kingdom," *BA* 59 [1996]: 122–125). Kletter argues for a single uniform Israelite standard according to which the נצף represents ⅚ of a shekel, not an independent standard. He points to the absence of weights of multiple *neṣefs*. The latter concern is valid but disappears if Lemaire and Vernus ("L'ostracon paléo-hébreu n 6," 322) are correct in their explanation that the value of the hieratic numerals engraved on weights represents the *neṣef* mass (its mass is only 3% greater than the *qedet* mass, a normal discrepancy for ancient weights). The lighter Israelite נצף standard would then more closely parallel the Egyptian *qedet-deben* system. Furthermore, Kletter's contention depends on the assumption that the biblical 20 *gerah* sanctuary shekel represents an ideal system never used in Judah (p. 138), a forced and unproven theory.

Ronen, in contrast to Kletter, maintains that the two standards of weights reflect consecutive rather than concurrent systems. He posits that the smaller shekel standard, based on the Egyptian *deben/qedet* system, was replaced by the larger royal shekel around 700 BCE as a result of Assyrian influence. Ronen's theory, however, is not supported by evidence from eighth-century weights, which all show the heavier shekel mass of between 11.2 and 11.6 grams (e.g. a 4-shekel weight from Beer-Sheba weighs 46.65 grams; a 2-shekel weight from Arad weighs 22.56 grams; another from Beth-Shemesh weighs 22.42 grams; and a 1-shekel weight from Tel Farah N. weighs 11.79 grams [see note 277 for citations]).

An alternate theory, proposed by Eph'al and Naveh, posits on the basis of Mesopotamian evidence that three systems of weights and measures coexisted: 1. the local standard, marked "of the gate" or "sanctuary"; 2. the standard of the kingdom with the name "of the country" specified; 3. the imperial standard designated "royal" ("The Jar of the Gate," 62–63). It is possible, however, that the "kingdom" or "country" standard was one and the same as the "sanctuary" standard. After all, the *neṣef* mass was equal to the 20 *gerah* sanctuary shekel. A Neo-Assyrian reference to an Israelite "country" standard, *sūtu ša* KUR *ia-ú-di*, "*seah* of Judah" (*ADD* 148:2 [cited by Eph'al and Naveh, p. 63]), does not prove the existence of a third, distinct standard in Israel, as that reference may allude to either the "sanctuary" or "royal" standard. Furthermore, Eph'al's and Naveh's categorization of the stone weight

tested. Their masses are marked by Hebrew weight-names, Hebrew number-names, hieratic numerals denoting *gerah* values, and hieratic fraction symbols. Units of weights attested both in the archaeological record and in the Bible include the פים, two-thirds of a shekel (1 Sam 13:21) and the בקע, one-half of a shekel (Gen 24:22; Exod 38:26).[290] Unfortunately many of the fraction-shekel weights are of unknown provenience.[291]

Possible Periods of Transmission

The utilization of Egyptian hieratic numerals and other symbols in the land of Israel is clearly discernable from the material evidence. What is not easily adduced is the precise time-period or periods in which various aspects of the Egyptian system were introduced, adopted, and adapted by the Canaanites and later by the Israelites. Hieratic inscriptions from Canaanite occupation levels, especially at sites in southern Canaan such as Tell Sera' and Lachish, attest to the use of an Egyptian system of accounting in the latter part of the New Kingdom, the late 13th through mid-12th centuries. This is not surprising in light of historical documentation of Egyptian hegemony in the region throughout the Late Bronze Age and in the beginning of the Iron Age I.[292]

Even after the decline of Egyptian power in Canaan at the end of the Empire

from Deir 'Alla marked אבן שרעא, "weight of the gate," as belonging to a local standard is questionable. This stone, whose weight is not mentioned in their publication, weighs 3850 grams (the weight is published in G. van der Kooij and M. Ibrahim eds., *Picking Up the Threads... A Continuing Review of Excavations at Deir 'Alla Jordan* [Leiden: University of Leiden Archaeological Centre, 1989], 101 no. 97). The heavy mass makes it difficult to identify the weight as belonging to any one standard but the possibility that it represents the imperial standard certainly exists (it weighs between 300 and 350 royal shekels, the equivalent of 6 or 7 *minas*). In that light, the inscription "weight of the gate" could indicate that the weight was used at the city gate for commodities packaged in such large units. An equally heavy stone (4565 grams), though uninscribed, was discovered by Albright in the West Tower, a public building at Tell Beit Mirsim. Albright interprets the stone as a 400 shekel weight, or 8 *minas* (*Excavation of Tell Beit Mirsim, III,* 76, pl. 57 d:1).

290. Scott, "Shekel-Fraction Markings on Hebrew Weights," 53–64. Note that the בקע mentioned in Exod 38:6 is the lighter 10 *gerah* weight; artifacts marked בקע weigh 12 gerah (pp. 57–58).

291. A. Spaer lists a number of unprovenienced *gerah* weights ("A Group of Iron Age Stone Weights," *IEJ* 32 [1982]: 251). One unprovenienced stone weight (5.9 grams) is inscribed with the term בקע on its top and with the hieratic sign for 2/3 (Möller, II no. 667), probably of a *qedet,* on its base (I. Kaufman, "New Evidence for Hieratic Numerals on Hebrew Weight," *BASOR* 188 (1967): 41; cf. Scott, "Shekel-Fraction Markings on Hebrew Weights," 57–58).

292. Some of the best archaeological evidence of Egyptian administrative activities in Canaan come from the site of Beth-Shean Strata IX–VI (A. Mazar, "Beth-Shean" in *NEAEHL,* 216–222).

Period, it is highly likely that hieratic numerals and other Egyptian symbols remained in use in the local Canaanite administrations. After all, the Egyptian numerical system was efficient as a shorthand method of accounting, in contrast to writing out numerals with word names. O. Goldwasser posits that hieratic writing in general was perpetuated in the land of Israel in a provincial style. She theorizes that at the end of the New Kingdom, Egyptian scribes in Canaan and/or Canaanite scribes trained in Egyptian offered their skills to local administrators.[293] Although the Egyptian system of hieratic numerals could have been transmitted directly from Egypt to Israel during the period of the United Monarchy, there is no compelling reason to argue that it was abandoned in Canaan in the 11th century and reintroduced in the 10th century. Hebrew texts containing hieratic numerals and other symbols dated to the 10th-8th centuries, both from Israel and Judah, certainly indicate that this system was operative throughout the Israelite kingdoms. Even the stone weights inscribed with hieratic numerals, which date predominately to the seventh century, have eighth-century precursors that suggest an older system than previously assumed.

The scarcity of written material from Israel prior to the eighth century precludes accurate dating of the transmission of Egyptian hieratic numerals and other symbols. However, isolated earlier documents containing these signs, in addition to certain peculiar Egyptian symbols in Hebrew inscriptions, bespeak a long evolutionary process. The earliest ostracon from Arad bearing numerals (no. 81) comes from Stratum XII (11th century), the first occupation level of the town. Although the symbols for the numerals on this ostracon, |||, "three," and |, "one," are not peculiar to any one system of numerical representation, they can be interpreted as hieratic. More solid evidence for early use of Egyptian hieratic is secured from Arad ostracon no. 76 (10th century), which seems to record allocations of quantities of *ḥḳꜣt* units, perhaps wheat or other grains. As noted, it is significant that the *ḥḳꜣt* standard in Israel, already at this time (probably in the reign of Solomon), differs from the use of its Egyptian counterpart.

Another time indicator for the transmission of this Egyptian system may be the New Kingdom shapes of certain numerals in Hebrew inscriptions. Aharoni notes the distinct form of the hieratic numeral six on Arad ostraca nos. 25, 31 and 112 and suggests that it resembles early 18th Dynasty examples.[294] This is also observable for the number 50 found on an ostracon from Lachish (no. 19) and another from the Ophel in Jerusalem (no. 2).[295] These isolated examples,

293. O. Goldwasser, "An Egyptian Scribe from Lachish and the Hieratic Tradition of the Hebrew Kingdoms," *TA* 18 (1991): 251–252.

294. Aharoni, *Arad Inscriptions*, 50. See Möller, II no. 619 for Thutmose III.

295. Möller, II no. 627.

however, do not provide adequate data for dating the adoption of hieratic numerals in Israel/Canaan, even though Israelite forms may very well have evolved from earlier Egyptian models. At the same time, the numerals in Hebrew inscriptions clearly cannot be identified as characteristically late Egyptian types.[296]

In sum, as demonstrated above, Israelite depictions of Egyptian hieratic numerals and other symbols show deviations from the Egyptian system of representation. This is recognizable in the method of writing date-formulas, in alternate means of expressing the same numeral, in certain peculiar numerical symbols, and in the use of the *ḥḳꜣt* measure. The evidence implies that an originally Egyptian system was adopted early on in Israel, probably from indigenous scribes in Canaan, but that it subsequently underwent independent development at the hands of Israelite scribes during the monarchic period. If this reconstruction is accurate, then we may venture to say that conscious borrowing of a foreign phenomenon never actually took place. Instead, Israelite bureaucrats beginning in the early monarchy and perhaps even before simply made use of a familiar, local system of accounting for their own administrative needs.

296. Lemaire and Vernus suggest that the hieratic numeral 10, as well as others on the Kadesh-Barnea ostraca, are late Egyptian forms ("L'ostracon paléo-hébreu no. 6," 343–345). However, as discussed above, in the case of these ostraca it must be taken into account that the writing represents an inexperienced hand. In addition, it should be noted that this so called "late" form of the numeral 10 also appears in late 19th Dynasty documents (Moller, II no. 623 for Mernephtah and Seti II [13th century]). Furthermore, a late Egyptian text (7th century) containing the numeral 10 shows forms that resemble earlier types, not the more unusual ones of the Kadesh-Barnea inscription. Notably in that Egyptian document the numeral 20 matches the Kadesh-Barnea 10 (Černý, "The Abnormal Hieratic Tablet Leiden I 431," pls. 2, 3).

7
Conclusions

Royal Functionaries and the State-Organization

A key objective of this study was to refine current definitions of titles of royal functionaries and their roles in the monarchic state-organization and to create a tentative reconstruction of the government structure. Central to this reconstruction is an understanding of the composition of the bureaucracy, its hierarchal organization, and the interrelationships between its members. The following summary observations are built on a combination of factors: a reevaluation of comparative data, especially Egyptian sources; a reexamination of the biblical evidence; utilization of recent epigraphic and other archaeological discoveries; and, not insignificantly, on previous research.

A few remarks are warranted in connection with the classification of the titles themselves. In Israel and Judah, as in other ancient Near Eastern states, not all titles were descriptive of specific positions. While the corpus of Hebrew titles differs dramatically from the Egyptian in that honorific epithets are rarely attested for Israelite functionaries, four designations apparently are rank-related: בן המלך, עבד המלך, זקנים, ילדים (Chapter 3 A–D). These titles, attached to individuals or groups, denote status, either ascribed by virtue of genealogy or acquired through membership in a special court circle. They are characteristic of the particular office-holder who bore them, but not of any one particular office. Most titles, however, are related to specific positions or are generic terms applicable to a number of jobs. Of those, eleven titles are related functionally to certain posts in the state-organization that carry independent status not dependent on the personal status of office-holders: אשר על הבית, ספר, מזכיר, רע(ה) המלך, משנה המלך, יועץ המלך, אשר על המס, נצב, שר העיר, שפט, שער (Chapter 4 A–K). Four other designations are more general, referring to a variety of distinct functionaries or seemingly in one case, the סריס, to a trait common among title-bearers but not directly related to status: סכן, נער, שטר, סריס (Chapter 5 A–D).

בן המלך

One status-related title, בן המלך, was reserved for members of the royal family, a son of a king or a son of a prince. This title is included in the present study because Israelite princes apparently served in the state-administration at the royal court and in municipal government. Seal-impressions bearing the title בן המלך are somewhat indicative of the administrative functions.[1] Probably, the proportion of royalty represented in official positions was greater than implied by the limited data, and a number of office-holders carrying other titles may in fact have been princes. Any notions, however, that the title בן המלך was held by non-royal, low-ranking officials should be dismissed. Not a single case exists of a בן המלך or בת המלך who can be identified as a commoner, while there is ample evidence to the contrary. The Egyptian title *s3 nswt*, "son of the king," which was sometimes borne by Egyptian officials of non-royal descent, cannot be used as a model for defining the Hebrew title because the evolution of the usage of the Egyptian title is unparalleled in Israel.

עבד המלך

The best example of an honorific epithet conferred on certain Israelite officials, and the one most widely attested, is עבד המלך. Previously the usage of this designation as a title received little attention, possibly because it cannot be associated with any particular office. A variety of prominent persons, some high-ranking officials, who had a special close relationship to the king, bore this title while concurrently holding other, function-related titles. Conceivably, the label עבד המלך or the alternate form עבד RN, which is attested on seals as well, marked the title-bearer as a minister authorized to seal documents in the king's name—a royal seal-bearer. Seals from Mesopotamia incised ARAD-*zu* may be parallels to the עבד המלך seals.

זקנים, ילדים

Two other status-related titles are זקנים and ילדים, the latter appearing only in conjunction with the former. The designation זקנים shows two usages: it can denote the traditional clan elders or signify senior ranking within the bureaucracy of the central government. As clan elders the זקנים of the monarchic period represented for the most part non-government local leadership, while senior royal functionaries called זקנים served the king at court as state appointees. Although the exact offices held by senior officials entitled זקנים are never specified, this sense of the term is evident from 2 Samuel 12 and 1 Kings 12. In contrast,

1. The predominance of unprovenienced, unauthenticated seals and bullae precludes the full utilization of that evidence.

the ילדים who appear in 1 Kings 12 as a group opposite Solomon's elder ministers, the זקנים, are junior officials recently appointed by the new king Rehoboam. Their title ילדים seems to be a technical term signifying membership in a special court circle comparable to that of the *ẖrdw n k3p* in Egypt. As contemporaries of the king who were raised with him, they apparently belonged to a palace household institution that schooled the offspring of court families, some of whom later rose to positions of power. Ample evidence that several generations of certain families held key government offices testifies to the practice. While in the period of the United Monarchy these office-holders were often royal relatives, no parallel data exist that prominent court families during the Divided Kingdom, either in Israel or Judah, were of royal blood, although the possibility cannot be discounted.

אשר על הבית

The bureaucratic organization of united Israel and later of the states of Israel and Judah was comprised of major and minor functionaries. Significantly, though, unlike in the monarchies of Egypt, Mesopotamia, and even Ugarit, no vizier-like Israelite minister seems to have functioned at any time. Generally, delineating a hierarchy within the civil administration is problematic due to a lack of explicit evidence either in the biblical or epigraphic material. Despite the lacuna, fragmentary data point to the position of אשר על הבית as the highest office. Importantly, this minister is always attested in biblical accounts in connection with the king or a capital city. His jurisdiction as royal house minister encompassed at least the palace complex but may have extended to royal property state-wide. Probably subordinate officials managed the king's estate outside the capital, especially during the Divided Monarchy when the activities of אשר על הבית title-bearers appear to have been centered in the capitals of Samaria and Jerusalem and included a range of responsibilities. In Judah in particular, the realm of the אשר על הבית incorporated diplomatic missions, such as leading the delegation to the Assyrians in 701 BCE. Notably, the title אשר על הבית is absent in Chronicles and seems to be replaced by the expression נגיד הבית. Quite possibly, in the post-exilic era the title נגיד הבית, usually associated with Temple overseers even in pre-exilic Judah, was utilized by the Chronicler to also designate the royal house minister, a monarchic civil official whose office no longer existed.

ספר

A second top-level royal official was the ספר. The court scribe(s) must be differentiated from other scribes attested in the biblical and epigraphic material who operated in the Temple, military, and municipal administrations. Probably the royal court scribe, already mentioned in the earliest lists from the reign of David, was the most indispensable civil servant, since he handled the royal correspondence and carried out basic accounting tasks essential to every administrative organization. A glimpse into this type of record-keeping is provided by the Samaria ostraca. These ostraca apparently contain accounts of provisions designated for officials at the royal court, though they may have been written by court scribes of lesser status than the ספר המלך. Information about scribes from eighth- and seventh-century Judah reveals that at least during the late monarchy this minister exercised some control over the Temple treasury and worked in concert with cult personnel. The scribe's proximity to the king and other top ministers as well as his involvement in important diplomatic ventures, such as his mission to the Assyrians together with the royal house minister and the herald, indicate his prestigious rank at court.

מזכיר

A third high-level royal official was the מזכיר. Although some uncertainties remain about his position, overall the evidence points to the office of herald, not "recorder" as is often surmised. The usage of the *hiphil* stem of זכר in pre-exilic biblical texts generally exhibits a *verbum-dicendi* sense and only in post-exilic literature is the term definitively associated with annals, ספר הזכרנות. Importantly, the position of court herald is attested in Mesopotamia, Ugarit, and Egypt suggesting that it probably existed in the Israelite bureaucracies as well, and the מזכיר is the most likely candidate. The title מזכיר, like that of ספר, already appears in the Davidic lists of officials. Only a few hints concerning the roles of this minister are revealed, though, and those derive from two narratives of events in Judah where the מזכיר appears to function in a military diplomatic capacity and maybe secondarily as a financial officer. Notably, the מזכיר consistently appears side by side with the ספר, in lists either preceding or following him and in records of specific events. Apparently these two officials worked closely together, the scribe functioning primarily as recorder and the herald as spokesperson for the king.

רעה, משנה, יועץ למלך

Three other officials who apparently comprised the king's suite, serving in close proximity to the monarch and the royal family, were the רע(ה) המלך, משנה ל/המלך and יועץ למלך. The first two titles, literally, "companion" of the king and "second" to the king, do not seem to be honorary epithets applicable to various courtiers, despite their non-function-specific nature. In the case of the "companion," the title is found exclusively for the reigns of David and Solomon.[2] Depictions of

2. A form of the title in 1 Kgs 16:11 does not seem to refer to the functionary.

one office-holder intimate that the רע(ה) functioned as a confidant and counselor of the king. Officials entitled "second" to the king, attested sporadically in different periods, also appear to be special trusted courtiers, perhaps serving as the king's personal escort. The third title, advisor to the king, is role-specific. Individual named office-holders bearing this title, however, are recorded solely in connection with David's reign. Under subsequent kings, groups of different functionaries are referred to occasionally in their capacity as royal advisors, implying but not certifying that the title יועץ no longer signified a distinct position.

אשר על המס, נצבים

A prominent official of the central government, but one whose responsibilities were oriented more state-wide than centered in the palace complex, was the אשר על המס. The title itself is attested in the Bible only for the United Monarchy and the period immediately following the division of the kingdom. Nevertheless, evidence from the Kingdom of Judah indicating that the practice of forced labor continued there until the exile, suggests that the office of the אשר על המס spanned the entire monarchic period. For the reign of Solomon, there is information on officials subordinate to this minister. Jeroboam served as supervisor of the corvée for the region of Ephraim and Manasseh. The twelve נצבים charged over general taxation of the individual districts may also have answered to the chief minister over the corvée. The שרי הנצבים, interpreted as officers under the נצבים who oversaw local labor gangs, probably belong to this government department as well. This hierarchy of officials, which reflects a complex system of organized forced labor, may have been unique to the period of Solomon when northern Israelites in particular were subjected to that form of levy.

The direct superior of the נצבים was the (אשר) על הנצבים, who was stationed at court. This office, attested once in the Solomonic list of appointees, probably entailed the overall supervision of the district prefects and may have included the position of prefect of Judah. Since the district prefects were responsible for provisioning the palace household twelve months a year on a rotating system, the superior at the palace would have coordinated the system and guaranteed its efficacy. After the division of the kingdom some of the duties of the על הנצבים, such as overseeing incoming supplies for the palace household, could have been absorbed by the office of the אשר על הבית.

סריס, סכן, נער/נערה

In addition to the high-level ministers of state and special confidants who surrounded the king, a variety of household functionaries whose duties were less administrative served in the palace complex. One class of courtiers known by the designation סריס functioned primarily as palace attendants for different members of the royal family. Seemingly, these title-bearers were characterized by a common trait—they were foreigners, possibly eunuchs, imported from Syria and/or Mesopotamia for the purpose of serving in the inner-palace. The non-Hebrew term סריס coupled by prohibitions against castration in Israelite law lends support, albeit not proof, to that interpretation.

Another type of palace attendant was the סכנת, a female servant known from the reign of David who was assigned to the king to minister to his personal needs day and night. The meaning of the male equivalent of the title, סכן, which occurs once in Isaiah in reference to Shebnah the royal house minister, remains enigmatic because of the nature of the prophetic message and the fact that non-Hebrew West Semitic usages of the root *skn* encompass a wide range of offices of varying status.

Attendants designated נער/נערה were more common, although that term too encompassed a variety of positions, from that of a lowly handmaid, to a squire or guard in attendance of a royal personage, to the prestigious post of steward of a royal estate. The latter actually depicts an administrative position, as is apparent from the examples of Ziba the steward of Saul's estate and אליקים נער יוכן who was directly involved with the *lmlk* jar enterprise.

שר העיר

Municipal administrators were also part of the state-organization. The highest city official was the שר העיר or אשר על העיר, the governor, whose jurisdiction seems to have extended to the regions surrounding the city. Notably the term פלך, a geo-political designation for a city and its environs found in Nehemiah, which is not attested in association with this monarchic official or in reference to Solomon's district prefects, reflects post-exilic usage. The title שר העיר or אשר על העיר is attached to the governors of Shechem (pre-monarchic), Samaria, and Jerusalem, but lesser urban centers seem to have been governed by this class of official as well. In the letter from Meṣad Ḥashavyahu an abbreviated form of these titles, השר, appears to designate the highest officer of the small fortress. Often the titles of officials charged over urban centers are lacking, for example that of Eliashib at Arad and those of Jehoshaphat's sons at various Judean fortified towns, but it may be inferred that they fit one of the three attested forms. In cases where these governors were members of the royal family, they were obviously commissioned by the crown, but it is uncertain whether all such officials were directly appointed by the king. Apparently the governors of capital cities performed duties jointly with officials of the central government on matters pertaining to the crown, such as the incarceration of dissidents and the regulation of Temple funds. That these governors in particular were influential officials is evident from the account of the revolt of Jehu in which the usurper demanded the allegiance of the אשר על העיר in addition to the loyalty of royal ministers and courtiers.

שער, שפט, שטר

Other officials who functioned primarily at the municipal level were the שפטים, שערים, and שטרים. The שערים, gatekeepers, who are attested for capitals and other fortified centers, were stationed at city gates as guards and messengers. Post-exilic sources record a hierarchy of Temple gatekeepers, possibly a reflex of an operative system for city and palace gatekeepers as well. Assumingly the latter would have served in the palace organization just as Temple gatekeepers functioned within the Temple administration.

Records from the reigns of David and Jehoshaphat indicate that at least some of the שפטים of the monarchic period were judges appointed by the king. These judges did not necessarily replace the elders in their judicial roles entirely. Instead, they frequently cooperated with them in the legal process. The Chronicler's account that a high court in Jerusalem composed of lay judges and priests dealt with difficult cases is credible, as such an entity could be scrutinized under the watchful eye of the monarchy. Officers designated by the generic title שטרים apparently functioned with judges on some level of the judiciary, conceivably as record-keepers, if the original meaning of the root *šṭr* is maintained. However, the varying status of title-bearers, gleaned from contexts in which they appear, suggests that the title שטר covered a wider range of officers, both civil and military.

Epigraphic Evidence

For the Kingdom of Judah, administrative records from cities and towns removed from the seat of government in Jerusalem, such as Lachish, Beer-Sheba, Arad, and Meṣad Ḥashavyahu, illustrate the network that connected the central authority to the local administrators. The archive of ostraca from Arad, for example, which spans the monarchic period, provides detailed information, albeit fragmentary, on the administration of Arad and the surrounding region. Although officials at the fort are not identified by titles, the letters do indicate that the chief administrator, Eliashib, probably the שר of Arad, was in contact with and received orders from the highest authority, the king.

The highly centralized government of Judah is further illuminated by the *lmlk* and rosette seal-impressions. The kingdom-wide *lmlk* operation in the reign of Hezekiah reflects the intricate network established by the crown for the distribution of goods. A similar national system, albeit on a smaller scale, is indicated by the rosette-impressed handles, probably attributable to Josiah. The *lmlk* and rosette symbols impressed on these jars may not only have served to identify the containers and their content as crown property, but signified renewed national independence. In addition, the personal seal-impressions on a percentage of *lmlk* handles seem to imply that certain Judean royal functionaries were the recipients of land grants from the king, as appears to be the case for officials in Israel recorded on the Samaria ostraca. This practice, mentioned in the Bible by the prophet Ezekiel (46:17), reflects a system of compensation for state administrators during their tenure in office.

The Appearance and Disappearance of Titles

As a corollary to the above observations, a few comments are called for concerning institutions initiated in certain periods and distinctions that may have existed between the bureaucracies of united Israel under David and Solomon and the two states of Israel and Judah that emerged subsequently. Apparently the title אשר על הבית originated in the reign of Solomon, although ministers charged over royal holdings who represented multiple offices of lesser authority operated previously in David's reign. Certain other titles of royal functionaries, such as על הנצבים, נצבים, and רע(ה) המלך, are attested only for the period of the United Monarchy. In the case of the overseer of the prefects and the individual district prefects, it can be assumed that since these offices were created by Solomon primarily to administer the territory of Israel outside Judah, they either disappeared in the diminished state of Judah or were absorbed by other posts after the division of the kingdom. In contrast, the absence of the title "companion" of the king from records of the Divided Monarchy may simply be accidental, the result of a general lack of comprehensive official lists for that period. A similar explanation undoubtedly accounts for the absence of the titles "scribe" and "herald" from the corpus of north Israelite officials, since these offices are integral components of the state-organization and most certainly existed. An interesting distinction between Israel and Judah is the lack of evidence for a system of corvée in the Northern kingdom. This is not surprising in light of the grievances expressed by northerners on that issue just prior to their secession. Additional differentiating features between the administrative organizations of Israel and Judah or between different periods in their history cannot be adduced based on the scant biblical data and inscriptional material.

Foreign Influence on the Israelite Bureaucracy

An important goal of this study was to reevaluate theories postulating that Israelite officialdom and administrative practices were modeled after foreign prototypes, whether Egyptian, Syro-Palestinian or Mesopotamian. Evidence gleaned from reexamining the various official titles and from analyzing the use of Egyptian hieratic numerals and other symbols by Israelite scribes facilitates assessing the impact of foreign influence on the Israelite state organizations.

Initially, it is observable that data attesting to direct contact between pre-monarchic through early monarchic Israel (11–10th century) and the empires of Egypt and Mesopotamia are generally absent. Not until the reign of Solomon at the earliest is there any evidence of interrelationships between the rulers and administrators of these states. That is not to say that contact prior to Solomon was non-existent, but simply that the written record is silent. Since the kingdom of Ugarit had been destroyed more than a century earlier, direct borrowing via that avenue cannot be considered at all; those states that did communicate with Israel in the early monarchic period, such as Phoenicia and Philistia, did not leave records detailing their government organization. Consequently, the extent of their influence on the Israelite structure, if any, is presently unknowable.[3]

In light of the scarcity of pertinent sources on interconnections between Israel and her neighbors at the inception of the monarchy, proof that titles of Israelite royal functionaries were of non-Israelite origin is limited to examples of Hebrew transliterations or loan translations of foreign terms. The former phenomenon is rare, in fact, it can be ascribed definitively solely to the title סריס (= *ša rēši*), a general designation for a special type of palace attendant, possibly a eunuch, who may have been imported to serve at the Israelite royal courts. Another generic title, סכן/סכנת, which is etymologically equivalent to Ugaritic/Phoenician/Aramaic *skn/sknt*, apparently was known in Israel but not adopted as the regular title for key court functionaries analogous to the foreign title-bearers. Notably, Phoenician and Aramaic examples of *skn* in first millennium sources demonstrate that the title *could* have served as a prototype for the contemporaneous Israelite monarchies; curiously it did not.

Potential calques or loan translations of foreign titles reveal little evidence of clear-cut borrowing. For example, the existence of titles in Ugaritic and Akkadian parallel to אשר על הבית challenge theories that the Hebrew title was calqued

3. On the other hand, Israelite influence on Moab, Ammon and Edom, especially during the 10–9th century, when the Transjordanian "states" seem to have been vassals of Israel and Judah, may account for certain parallel Moabite, Ammonite, and Edomite official titles (For Moab see 2 Sam 8:2; 2 Kgs 1:1; 3:4–5; W.F. Albright, *ANET*, 320-321; for Ammon see 2 Sam 12:26–31; for Edom see 2 Sam 8:14; 2 Kgs 8:20–22). For a discussion on secondary state formation in Moab and Edom, see E. Knauf, "The Cultural Impact of Secondary State Formation: The Cases of the Edomites and Moabites" in P. Bienkowski ed. *Early Edom and Moab: The Beginning of the Iron Age in Southern Jordan* (Sheffield: J.R. Collis, 1992), 47–54.

after the Egyptian *mr pr wr*. Furthermore, the Semitic equivalents from states in Syria-Palestine and Mesopotamia seem to reflect a linguistic connection, as is apparent from the morphologically parallel אשר על and *ša mḫḫui*. In the case of the title רע(ו)ה המלך, which may be a loose translation of the Egyptian *rḫ nswt*, the attestation of *ruḫi šarri* in an Amarna letter and מרעהו in a biblical reference to a Canaanite official may signal the transmission of an originally Egyptian title via Canaanite intermediaries. On the other hand, the existence of the seemingly equivalent designation *ibru* for a functionary of Nebuchadnezzar I raises the possibility of a merely typological similarity.

Typological similarities independent of historical connections appear to explain the parallel offices of a number of royal ministers (see Table B). A case in point is the office of the herald, for which semantic distinctions in Akkadian, Ugaritic, Egyptian, and Hebrew titles intimate independent development. The sheer necessity of the office could account for its origin. That phenomenon is even more apparent in the case of the scribe, whose skills would have been vital for the operation of any state.[4] Therefore, resemblances between the appellations of David's scribe and a number of foreign PNs or the Egyptian title for scribe are not sufficient proof that the office itself was borrowed.

Notably, a number of Israelite official titles have Moabite, Ammonite and Edomite analogues (see Table B). Despite the unfortunate dearth of provenienced Transjordanian inscriptional material, the titles עבד המלך and מזכיר appear on seals and seal impressions derived from controlled archaeological excavations. The designation עבד המלך and its equivalents are too widespread to speculate about Israelite influence on the Transjordanian states. However, the attestation (on a Moabite seal) of the term מזכיר, which to date is unique in extra-biblical sources, may indicate that the Moabite title was borrowed from Israel, perhaps when Moab was a vassal of Israel.

Similar to potential Israelite influence on the bureaucracies of neighboring Transjordanian states, some foreign inspiration is evident in certain Israelite administrative features. These may have been adopted during the empire-building phase of Solomon's reign. For example, the title ילדים, which is associated with a large palace household institution, probably was transmitted either via a direct historical link with Egypt or indirectly via Canaan; the latter is more plausible. The most obvious system antedating any Israelite state is the corvée system, which shows a long continuous tradition in Syria/Palestine. Although the title אשר על המס has no equivalent in Akkadian documents, the expression *massu* is attested in connection with corvée laborers in Alalakh and Canaan.

4. Redford's observations 25 years ago already spoke to this issue ("Studies in Relations between Palestine and Egypt," 141–144).

In contrast to the above, another feature of Solomon's administrative organization, the twelve-district division headed by the נצבים, actually seems to reflect an Israelite innovation established for efficient governing of a complex system. While taxation systems of some kind or another based on twelve monthly divisions were not unique to Israel, this type of organization instituted for the purpose of national administration appears to be limited to Israel. An analogous system that operated on the local level in Egypt during the reign of Shishak apparently postdates Solomon's structure.

Other signs of independent development in the realm of Israelite administration are best illustrated by the usage of hieratic numerals and other symbols. Although indisputably of foreign origin, these Egyptian glyphs found in Hebrew inscriptions spanning the monarchic period in Israel and Judah show unmistakable deviations from their Egyptian counterparts. Distinctions in shape, alternate methods of expressing the same symbol, peculiar symbols, and most importantly aberrant uses of conservative Egyptian patterns for writing dates and measures demonstrate the "Israelitization" of a once foreign system. Comparable Egyptian inscriptions from Late Bronze Age Canaan closely resembling the native Egyptian representations suggest that this evolution took place in Israel over time at the hands of Israelite scribes who initially were trained locally by indigenous Canaanites. The development of an "Israelite" hieratic system for accounting purposes implies that conscious borrowing of a foreign phenomenon never actually took place. Instead, a local system of record-keeping was adopted and adapted for an increasingly complex organization. Some of the phenomena discernible in connection with the process of the adoption and evolution of the hieratic system in Israel seem applicable in understanding certain titles and roles of monarchic officials. For example, some titles that were prevalent in the Canaanite city-states were assimilated at the time of the formation of the Israelite state but subsequently evolved into positions compatible with a larger kingdom.

In sum, the picture that emerges from the evidence at hand reveals the following. The low frequency of unquestionably foreign terms and features in the Israelite state-organization precludes tracing it to any single foreign prototype or even a combination of prototypes. Therefore, notions that the Israelite bureaucracy as a whole was modeled after one of a pre-existing state should be revised. Evidence pointing to foreign inspiration, whether Egyptian, Canaanite or Mesopotamian, must be viewed in its proper perspective. Egyptian influence, which is exemplified by the hieratic numerals and other symbols in Hebrew administrative documents and probably in the resemblance of certain titles, can be attributed primarily to indirect transmission mediated via local Canaanite institutions. Even parallels that apparently derive from Canaanite institutions show distinctive features in the Israelite system, thereby suggesting that local administrative components were modified to accommodate the more complex operation of a territorial state. Similar Mesopotamian and Israelite titles are usually too widespread regionally to identify a point of origin, or they seem to be the natural consequence of a common language family. Occasionally, however, comparable practices that are aspects of pre-established institutions (i.e. secondary roles of the אשר על הבית and the מזכיר) can be traced to the later monarchic period, when active diplomatic contact existed between Israel and Judah and Egypt, Assyria and Babylon. Ideas as well as goods would have been traded at that time.

The significance of these conclusions extends beyond the definition of individual Israelite official titles. This investigation has raised a number of fundamental questions necessary for the understanding of the administrative organization of the Israelite states. In reference to the corpus of Hebrew titles, it has been shown that while honorific epithets were rare, certain titles were rank rather than function-related. Two of those, זקנים and ילדים, are multi-vocal and must be interpreted accordingly. Another issue addressed is the *Sitz-im-Leben* for the personal seal impressions appearing on a percentage of *lmlk* handles. The possibility that they reflect land grants, a system of compensation for service to the crown, fits hints in the biblical text pertaining to royal policy and evidence gleaned from the Samaria ostraca. Finally, this study has challenged prior theories that the Israelite system depended heavily on foreign models. Among methods introduced for the evaluation of foreign influence is the detailed analysis of Israelite utilization of Egyptian hieratic numerals and other symbols. One topic that remains open and lends itself to future research is the role of cult personnel in the state-organization of the Israelite monarchies.

Table A

1. A Chronological Index of PNs and Titles of Functionaries in the Bible and in Provenienced Epigraphic Records

King's Reign	Official's Name	Position	Reference
1 SAUL	Abner son of Ner (Saul's uncle)[1]	army commander	1 Sam 14:50–51 1 Chr 8:33
2	Doeg the Edomite	אביר הרעים "strongman"[2]	1 Sam 21:8
3	Ahijah son of Ahitub son of Phinehas son of Eli	priest	1 Sam 14:3
4	David son of Jesse	arms bearer, chief of thousands	1 Sam 16:21; 18:13
5 ISH-BOSHETH (Eshbaal)	Abner son of Ner (#1)	army commander	2 Sam 2:8
6	Baanah son of Rimon	company commander	2 Sam 4:2
7	Rechab son of Rimmon	company commander	2 Sam 4:2
8 DAVID	Joab son of Zeruiah (David's nephew, 1 Chr 2:16)	army commander	2 Sam 8:16
9	Jehoshaphat son of Ahilud	herald	2 Sam 8:16

1. According to 1 Sam 9:1 Ner is Saul's first cousin. However, based on 1 Sam 14:50–51 and 1 Chr 8:33 it is more likely that Abiel was the grandfather of Kish rather than his father.

2. A possible analogous Assyrian title is *rab rā'î*, "chief of the shepherds," held by a court official of the crown prince who is listed together with various types of guards, including body guards (*ADD* 857 in Fales and Postgate, *Imperial Administrative Records,* Part I, no. 5:36r).

King's Reign	Official's Name	Position	Reference
10	Seraiah/Sheya/Shavsha	scribe	2 Sam 8:17; 20:25; 1 Chr 18:16
11	Adoram son of Abda	chief of the corvée	2 Sam 20:24
12	Amasa son of Abigail (David's nephew, 1 Chr 2:16-17)	army officer	2 Sam 17:25
13	Abishai son of Zeruiah (David's nephew, 1 Chr 2:16)	army officer, commander of 3 (or 30)	2 Sam 23:18-19
14	Jonathan (David's uncle)[3]	advisor, scribe	1 Chr 27:32
15	Benaiah son of Jehoiada	commander of the Cherethites and Pelethites, commander of 30	2 Sam 8:18; 1 Chr 27:6
16	Hushai the Archite	"companion" of the king	1 Chr 27:33
17	Ahitophel the Gilonite[4]	advisor	2 Sam 15:12
18	Jonadab son of Shimah (David's nephew)	"courtier"	2 Sam 13:32
19	Jehiel son of Hachmoni	עם בני המלך, "tutor(?) of the princes"	1 Chr 27:32
20	Jashobeam son of Hachmoni	chief officer of David's warriors	1 Chr 11:11
21	Azmaveth son of Adiel	על אצרות המלך "steward over royal treasuries"	1 Chr 27:25
22	Jonathan son of Uzziah	על האצרות בשדה בערים בכרמים ובמגדלות, "steward over provincial treasuries"	1 Chr 27:25

3. Possibly Jonathan was David's nephew (2 Sam 21:21).
4. Ahitophel was the father of Eliam, one of David's 30 warriors (2 Sam 23:34).

King's Reign	Official's Name	Position	Reference
23	Ezri son of Chelub	steward over agricultural laborers	1 Chr 27:26
24	Shimei the Ramathite	steward over vineyards	1 Chr 27:27
25	Zabdi the Shiphmite	steward over wine production	1 Chr 27:27
26	Baal-hanan the Gederite	steward over olive and sycamore orchards	1 Chr 27:28
27	Joash	steward over oil-stores	1 Chr 27:28
28	Shirtai the Sharonite	steward over cattle (Sharon)	1 Chr 27:29
29	Shaphat son of Adlai	steward over cattle (in the valleys)	1 Chr 27:29
30	Obil the Ishmaelite	steward over camels	1 Chr 27:30
31	Jehdeiah the Meronothite	steward over she-asses	1 Chr 27:30
32	Jaziz the Hagrite	steward over flocks	1 Chr 27:31
33	Eliezer son of Zichri	clan chief officer (Reuben)	1 Chr 27:16
34	Shephatiah son of Maaca	clan chief officer (Simeon)	1 Chr 27:16
35	Hashabiah son of Kemuel	clan chief officer (Levi)	1 Chr 27:17
36	Elihu son of Jesse (David's brother)	clan chief officer (Judah)	1 Chr 27:18
37	Omri son of Michael	clan chief officer (Issachar)	1 Chr 27:18
38	Ishmaiah son of Obadiah	clan chief officer (Zebulun)	1 Chr 27:19
39	Jerimoth son of Azriel	clan chief officer (Naphtali)	1 Chr 27:19
40	Hoshea son of Azaziah	clan chief officer (Ephraim)	1 Chr 27:20

King's Reign	Official's Name	Position	Reference
41	Joel son of Pedaiah	clan chief officer (half of Manasseh)	1 Chr 27:20
42	Iddo son of Zechariah	clan chief officer (half of Manasseh in Gilead)	1 Chr 27:21
43	Jaasiel son of Abner	clan chief officer (Benjamin)	1 Chr 27:21
44	Azarel son of Jeroham	clan chief officer (Dan)	1 Chr 27:22
45	Jashobeam son of Zabdiel	1st division commander	1 Chr 27:2
46	Dodai the Ahohite	2nd division commander	1 Chr 27:4
47	Mikloth	chief officer of Dodai's division	1 Chr 27:4
48	Benaiah son of Jehoiada (#15)	3rd division commander	1 Chr 27:5
49	Ammizabad son of Benaiah	chief officer of Benaiah's division	1 Chr 27:6
50	Asahel son of Zeruiah (David's nephew)	4th divsion commander	1 Chr 27:7
51	Zebadiah son of Asahel (above)	chief officer of Asahel's division	1 Chr 27:7
52	Shamhut the Izrahite	5th division commander	1 Chr 27:8
53	Ira son of Ikkesh the Tekoite	6th division commander	1 Chr 27:9
54	Helez the Pelonite	7th division commander	1 Chr 27:10
55	Sibbecai the Hushathite	8th division commander	1 Chr 27:11
56	Abiezer the Anathothite	9th division commander	1 Chr 27:12
57	Mahrai the Netophathite	10th division commander	1 Chr 27:13

King's Reign	Official's Name	Position	Reference
58	Benaiah the Pirathonite	11th division commander	1 Chr 27:14
59	Heldai the Netophathite	12th division commander[5]	1 Chr 27:15
60	Naharai the Beerothite	Joab's arms bearer	2 Sam 23:37
61	Zadok son of Ahitub	priest	2 Sam 8:17; 20:25
62	Abiathar son of Ahimelech	priest	1 Sam 30:7; 2 Sam 20:25
63	Ira the Jairite	priest	2 Sam 20:26
64	Uriel	chief of sons of Kohath (Levite clan)	1 Chr 15:5
65	Asaiah	chief of sons of Merari (Levite clan)	1 Chr 15:6
66	Joel	chief of sons of Gershom (Levite clan)	1 Chr 15:7
67	Shemaiah	chief of sons of Elizaphan (Levite clan)	1 Chr 15:8
68	Eliel	chief of sons of Hebron (Levite clan)	1 Chr 15:9
69	Amminadab	chief of sons of Uzziel (Levite clan)	1 Chr 15:10
70	Chenaniah	Levite music director	1 Chr 15:22
71	Shemaiah son of Nathanel	scribe of Levites	1 Chr 24:6
72	Jehiel the Gershonite	officer of Temple treasuries	1 Chr 29:8
73	Shebuel the Gershonite	chief officer of Temple treasuries	1 Chr 26:24
74	Shelomith son of Zichri (and his brothers)	officers of treasuries of dedicated things	1 Chr 26:26

5. Of the 12 monthly officers six, Asahel, Ira, Helez, Abiezer, Mahrai and Benaiah the Pirathonite were members of David's warriors (2 Sam 23:24–39).

King's Reign	Official's Name	Position	Reference
75	Chenaniah the Izharite (and his sons)	Levite officials outside the sanctuary	1 Chr 26:29
76	Hashabiah the Hebronite (and his brother)	Levite officials west of the Jordan	1 Chr 26:30
77	Jeriah the Hebronite (and his brothers)	Levite officials east of the Jordan	1 Chr 26:31-32
78 SOLOMON	Benaiah son of Jehoiada (#15)	army commander	1 Kgs 4:4
79	Jehoshaphat son of Ahilud (#9)	herald	1 Kgs 4:3
80	Elihoreph son of Shisha[6]	scribe	1 Kgs 4:3
81	Ahijah son of Shisha	scribe	1 Kgs 4:3
82	Zabud son of Nathan the priest	"companion" of the king	1 Kgs 4:5
83	Azariah son of Nathan	overseer of the prefects	1 Kgs 4:5
84	Ahishar	royal house minister	1 Kgs 4:6
85	Adoram (Adoniram) son of Abda (#11)	chief of the corvée	1 Kgs 4:6
86	Azariah son of Ahimaaz son of Zadok the priest	priest	1 Kgs 4:2; 1 Chr 5:35
87	Ben-hur	district prefect – Ephraim hill country	1 Kgs 4:8
88	Ben-deker	district prefect – Makaz, Shaalbim, Beth-shemesh, Elon-beth-hanan	1 Kgs 4:9
89	Ben-hesed	district prefect – Arubboth, Socho, Hepher	1 Kgs 4:10

6. Shisha was David's scribe (#10 – Seraiah, Sheya, Shavsha).

King's Reign	Official's Name	Position	Reference
90	Ben-abinadab (Solomon's son- in-law)	district prefect – Naphath-dor	1 Kgs 4:11
91	Baana son of Ahilud[7]	district prefect – Taanach, Megiddo, Beth-shean	1 Kgs 4:12
92	Ben-geber	district prefect – Ramoth-gilead, Argob	1 Kgs 4:13
93	Ahinadab son of Iddo	district prefect – Mahanaim	1 Kgs 4:14
94	Ahimaaz (Solomon's son-in-law)	district prefect – Naphtali	1 Kgs 4:15
95	Baana son of Hushi[8]	district prefect – Asher and Bealoth	1 Kgs 4:16
96	Jehoshaphat son of Paruah	district prefect – Issachar	1 Kgs 4:17
97	Shimei son of Ela	district prefect – Benjamin	1 Kgs 4:18
98	Geber son of Uri[9]	district prefect – Gilead, country of Sihon and Og	1 Kgs 4:19
99	Hiram	Temple master craftsman	1 Kgs 7:13-14
100	Jeroboam son of Nebat	officer over the corvée for the House of Joseph	1 Kgs 11:26, 28
101	Zadok (son of Ahitub) (#61)	priest	1 Kgs 4:4
102	Abiathar (son of Ahimelech) (#62)	priest	1 Kgs 4:4

7. Probably the brother of Jehoshaphat son of Ahilud the herald.
8. Possibly the son of Hushai the Archite (#16).
9. Possibly the same person as Ben-geber (#92).

King's Reign	Official's Name	Position	Reference
103 REHOBOAM	Adoram son of Abda (#s 11 & 85)	chief of the corvée	1 Kgs 12:18
104 ELA	Omri	army commander	1 Kgs 16:16
105	Zimri	commander of half the chariotry	1 Kgs 16:9
106	Arza	royal house minister	1 Kgs 16:9
107 AHAB	Joash	son of the king	1 Kgs 22:26
108	Amon	governor, Samaria	1 Kgs 22:26
109	Obadiah	royal house minister	1 Kgs 18:3
110 JEHOSHAPHAT	Ben-hail	officer	2 Chr 17:7
111	Obadiah	officer	2 Chr 17:7
112	Zechariah	officer	2 Chr 17:7
113	Nethanel	officer	2 Chr 17:7
114	Michaiah	officer	2 Chr 17:7
115	Adnah	chief of thousand, Judah	2 Chr 17:14
116	Jehohanan	chief of thousand, Judah	2 Chr 17:15
117	Amasiah son of Zichri	chief of thousand, Judah	2 Chr 17:16
118	Eliada	chief of thousand, Benjamin	2 Chr 17:17

King's Reign	Official's Name	Position	Reference
119	Jehozabad	chief of thousand, Benjamin	2 Chr 17:18
120	Zebadiah son of Ishmael	chief officer, Judah	2 Chr 19:11
121	Amariah	chief priest	2 Chr 19:11
122 JEHORAM (Israel)	Bidkar	Jehu's שליש (3rd man on the chariot)[10]	2 Kgs 9:25
123 ATALIAH	Mattan	priest of Baal	2 Kgs 11:18
124 JOASH (Judah)	Azariah son of Jeroham	chief of hundred	2 Chr 23:1
125	Ishmael son of Jehohanan[11]	chief of hundred	2 Chr 23:1
126	Azariah son of Obed	chief of hundred	2 Chr 23:1
127	Maaseiah son of Adaiah	chief of hundred	2 Chr 23:1
128	Elishaphat son of Zichri[12]	chief of hundred	2 Chr 23:1
129	Jehoiada	priest (high ?)	2 Kgs 11-12
130	Jozacar son of Shimeath	עבד המלך, "servant" of the king	2 Kgs 12:22
131	Jehozabad son of Shomer	עבד המלך, "servant" of the king	2 Kgs 12:22

10. *EM* 6, 560.
11. Possibly the son of Jehohanan chief of thousands of Judah (#116).
12. Possibly the brother of Amasiah son of Zichri, chief of thousand in Judah (#117).

King's Reign	Official's Name	Position	Reference
132 AMAZIAH	Obed-edom	officer of Temple treasury	2 Chr 25:24
133 JEROBOAM (son of Joash)	Amaziah	priest of Bethel	Amos 7:10
134	שמע	עבד המלך, "servant" of the king	seal (לשמע עבד ירבעם)[13]
135	שמריו	"l-man" at Samaria[14]	Samaria ostraca[15] #s 1, 13-14, 21
136	גדיו	"l-man" at Samaria	#s 2, 4-7, 16- 18
137	אחמא	"l-man" at Samaria	#s 3, 36-39
138	בעלא	"l-man" at Samaria	# 3
139	אב/חנעם	"l-man" at Samaria	#s 8-11, 19
140	בעלזמר	"l-man" at Samaria	# 12
141	אשחר	"l-man" at Samaria	# 13
142	אשא אחמלך	"l-man" at Samaria	#s 22-29
143	חלץ גדיו	"l-man" at Samaria	#s 30, 33-35
144	חלץ אפצח	"l-man" at Samaria	#s 31, 90

13. Cook, "A Newly Discovered Hebrew Seal," 287–292; *WSS*, no. 2.
14. For a discussion of the "l-men" and the dating of the Samaria Ostraca see Chapter 5–A.
15. *HDAE* 3, 5–11.

King's Reign	Official's Name	Position	Reference
145	חלץ אחמא	"l-man" at Samaria	# 32
146	ידעיו אחמלך	"l-man" at Samaria	#s 42, 48
147	חנן בערא	"l-man" at Samaria	#s 43, 45-47
148	גמר	"l-man" at Samaria	# 50
149	אביו	"l-man" at Samaria	# 52
150	נמשי	"l-man" at Samaria	# 56
151	בדיו	"l-man" at Samaria	# 58
152 AZARIAH (Uzziah)	Jotham	son of the king, על הבית, שפט[16]	2 Kgs 15:5
153	Jeiel	army scribe	2 Chr 26:11
154	Maaseiah	שוטר, "officer"	2 Chr 26:11
155	Hananiah	officer	2 Chr 26:11
156	Azariah	chief priest	2 Chr 26:20
157 PEKAHIAH	Pekah son of Remaliah	שליש (3rd man on chariot)	2 Kgs 15:25
158 AHAZ	Maaseiah	son of the king	2 Chr 28:7
159	Azrikam	נגיד הבית, "minister over the royal house"	2 Chr 28:7

16. For Jotham's roles see Chapter 3-A.

King's Reign	Official's Name	Position	Reference
160	Elkanah	משנה המלך, "'second' to the king"	2 Chr 28:7
161	Uriah	priest	2 Kgs 16:10
162 HEZEKIAH	Shebna	royal house minister	Isa 22:15
163	Eliakim son of Hilkiah	royal house minister	2 Kgs 18:18; Isa 22:20
164	Shebna	scribe	2 Kgs 18:18
165	Joah son of Asaph	herald	2 Kgs 18:18
166	Azariah	high priest	2 Chr 31:10
167	Conaniah the Levite	official over store-chambers	2 Chr 31:12
168	Shimei (Conaniah's brother)	Conaniah's assistant	2 Chr 31:12
169	Kore son of Imlah the Levite	east gate-keeper, official over freewill offerings	2 Chr 31:14
170	מלכיהו	commander of Arad Stratum 8	Arad ostracon #40[17]
171	גמריהו	officer of a fort near Arad	Arad ostracon #40
172	נחמיהו	officer of a fort near Arad	Arad ostracon #40
173	אליקם	נער, "steward," of יוכן	PN + title seal-stamp on *lmlk* jar handle[18]

17. *HDAE* 3, 13–14.
18. For references and discussion, see Chapter 5–B.

King's Reign	Official's Name	Position	Reference
174	נרא שבנא	official	PN stamp on *lmlk* jar handle[19]
175	צפן עזריהו	official	PN stamp on *lmlk* jar handle
176	יהוחיל שחר	official	PN stamp on *lmlk* jar handle
177	מנחם יובנה	official	PN stamp on *lmlk* jar handle
178	נחם עבדי	official	PN stamp on *lmlk* jar handle
179	אחזיהו תנחם	official	PN stamp on *lmlk* jar handle
180	הושע צפן	official	PN stamp on *lmlk* jar handle
181	חשי אלשמע	official	PN stamp on *lmlk* jar handle
182	נחם הצליהו	official	PN stamp on *lmlk* jar handle

19. This list represents the minimum number of PNs on provenienced handles. Variations of some of these names may actually indicate additional persons (see Chapter 2, Prosopography). Seven additional names appear only on unprovenienced handles: אחמלך עמדיהו, אלזכר עזרם, געי אחא, חרי חגי, ידעיה, ערב נבי, עזר שבנא, אלעזר. All PNs stamped on *lmlk* handles are listed in Vaughn, "The Chronicler's Account of Hezekiah," 277–289.

King's Reign	Official's Name	Position	Reference
183	סמך צפניהו	official	PN stamp on *lmlk* jar handle
184	שבניהו עזריהו	official	PN stamp on *lmlk* jar handle
185	שוכי שבנא	official	PN stamp on *lmlk* jar handle
186	בנאי יהוכל	official	PN stamp on *lmlk* jar handle
187	כסלא זכא	official	PN stamp on *lmlk* jar handle
188	שלם אחא	official	PN stamp on *lmlk* jar handle
189	תנחם נגב	official	PN stamp on *lmlk* jar handle
190	שבנא שחר	official	PN stamp on *lmlk* jar handle
191	בכי שלם	official	PN stamp on *lmlk* jar handle
192	הושעם חגי	official	PN stamp on *lmlk* jar handle
193	חסדא ירמיהו	official	PN stamp on *lmlk* jar handle

King's Reign	Official's Name	Position	Reference
194	כרמי יפיהו	official	PN stamp on *lmlk* jar handle
195	משלם אחמלך	official	PN stamp on *lmlk* jar handle
196	משלם אלנתן	official	PN stamp on *lmlk* jar handle
197	עזר חגי	official	PN stamp on *lmlk* jar handle
198	צדק סמך	official	PN stamp on *lmlk* jar handle
199	צפן אבמעץ	official	PN stamp on *lmlk* jar handle
200	תנחם מגן	official	PN stamp on *lmlk* jar handle
201	עבדי	official	PN stamp on *lmlk* jar handle
202 JOSIAH	Shaphan son of Azaliah son of Meshullam	scribe	2 Kgs 22:3; 2 Chr 34:8
203	Maaseiah	governor of the city (Jerusalem)	2 Chr 34:8
204	Joah son of Joahaz	herald	2 Chr 34:8
205	Asaiah	official	2 Kgs 22:12

King's Reign	Official's Name	Position	Reference
206	Ahikam son of Shaphan[20]	עבד המלך, "servant" of the king	2 Kgs 22:12
207	Achbor son of Michaiah	official	2 Kgs 22:12
208	Shallum son of Tikvah son of Harhas	keeper of wardrobe	2 Kgs 22:14
209	Joshua	governor of the city (Jerusalem)	2 Kgs 23:8
210	Nathan-melech	סריס (palace attendant, eunuch)	2 Kgs 23:11
211	Hilkiah	high priest	2 Kgs 22:4
212	Jahath the Merarite	Levite overseer of Temple repairs	2 Chr 34:12
213	Obadiah the Merarite	Levite overseer of Temple repairs	2 Chr 34:12
214	Zechariah the Kohathite	chief Temple officer	2 Chr 34:12
215	Meshullam the Kohathite	chief Temple officer	2 Chr 34:12
216	Zechariah	נגיד בית יהוה Levite Temple overseer	2 Chr 35:8
217	Jehiel	נגיד בית יהוה Levite Temple overseer	2 Chr 35:8
218	Conaniah	Levite officer	2 Chr 35:9
219	Shemaiah	Levite officer	2 Chr 35:9
220	Nethanel	Levite officer	2 Chr 35:9
221	Hashabiah	Levite officer	2 Chr 35:9
222	Jeiel	Levite officer	2 Chr 35:9

20. Son of Shaphan the scribe (#202).

King's Reign	Official's Name	Position	Reference
223	Jozabad	Levite officer	2 Chr 35:9
224	אלישב בן אשיהו	commander of Arad Stratum 7	3 seals (לאלישב בן אשיהו)[21]
225	ברכיהו בן ...הו בן שלמיהו	officer at Arad	seal (לברכיהו בן ...הו בן שלמיהו)[22]
226	השעיהו בן שבי	officer at Meṣad Ḥashavyahu	letter on ostracon[23]
227 JEHOIAKIM	Jerahmeel	son of the king	Jer 36:26
228	Elnathan son of Archbor[24]	army officer	Jer 26:22
229	Gemariah son of Shaphan[25]	scribe	Jer 36:10; bulla (לגמריהו בן שפן)[26]
230	Elishama	scribe	Jer 36:12
231	Maaseiah son of Shallum	guard of Temple threshold	Jer 35:4
232	Micaiah son of Gemariah son of Shaphan[27]	palace official	Jer 36:11
233	Delaiah son of Shemiah	palace official	Jer 36:12

21. Aharoni, *Arad Inscriptions*, 119; *WSS*, nos. 70- 72.
22. Aharoni, *Arad Inscriptions*, 120; *WSS*, no. 111.
23. *HDAE* 3, 25.
24. Son of Achbor the official under Josiah (#207).
25. Son of Shaphan the scribe (#202).
26. Shiloh, "A Group of Hebrew Bullae from the City of David," 26 no. 2; *WSS*, no. 470.
27. Son of Gemariah the scribe (#229).

King's Reign	Official's Name	Position	Reference
234	Zedekiah son of Hananiah	palace official	Jer 36:12
235	Jehudi son of Nethaniah son of Shelemiah son of Cushi	palace official (messenger)	Jer 36:14
236	Seraiah son of Azriel	palace guard	Jer 36:26
237	Shelemiah son of Abdeel	palace guard	Jer 36:26
238	Baruch son of Neriah son of Mahseiah	Jeremiah's scribe	Jer 32:12; 36:4
239	Azariah son of Hilkiah	priest	1 Chr 5:39; bulla (לעזריהו בן חלקיהו)[28]
240	אלישב בן אשיהו (#226)	Arad commander Stratum 6	Arad ostraca[29] #s 1–12, 14, 16–18
241	גדליהו בן אליאר	officer, Arad	Arad ostracon #21
242	אלישע בן ירמיהו	officer, Ramat Negev	Arad ostracon #24
243	חנניהו	officer (commander)	Arad ostracon #s 3, 16
244	שמיה בן משלם	נער אלנתן, "steward" or "squire"[30]	Arad ostracon #110
245	מכי	נער גדליה[31]	Arad ostracon #110

28. Shiloh, "A Group of Hebrew Bullae from the City of David," 29 no. 27; *WSS*, no. 596. Possibly the seal-owner was the biblical Azariah. The seal shows hypocoristic forms of the names.

29. *HDAE* 3, 26–31.

30. Possibly the נער of Elnathan son of Achbor, the army officer (#228).

31. Possibly the נער of Gedaliah son of Pashhur (#255) or Gedaliah son of Ahikam (#276), both officials in Jerusalem.

King's Reign	Official's Name	Position	Reference
246	נחם	official	Arad ostracon #17
247	מלכיהו בן קרבאור	official	Arad ostracon #24
248	שמריהו	official	Arad ostracon #18
249 ZEDEKIAH	Malchiah	son of the king	Jer 38:6
250	Jonathan	scribe	Jer 37:15
251	Irijah son of Shelemiah son of Hananiah	guard officer	Jer 37:13
252	Elasah son of Shaphan[32]	official (envoy to Babylon)	Jer 29:3
253	Gemariah son of Hilkiah[33]	official (envoy to Babylon)	Jer 29:3
254	Shephatiah son of Mattan	official	Jer 38:1
255	Gedaliah son of Pashhur	official	Jer 38:1
256	Jucal son of Shelemiah	official	Jer 38:1
257	Pashhur son of Malchiah[34]	official	Jer 38:1
258	Seraiah son of Neriah son of Mahseiah[35]	שר מנוחה "quartermaster"	Jer 51:59
259	Jaazniah son of Shaphan[36]	official	Ezek 8:11

32. Probably the son of Shaphan the scribe (#202).
33. Possibly the son of Hilkiah the high priest (#211).
34. Possibly the father of Gedaliah (#255) of a priestly family (1 Chr 9:12).
35. Brother of Baruch the scribe (#238).
36. Probably another son of Shaphan the scribe (#202).

King's Reign	Official's Name	Position	Reference
260	Jaazniah son of Azzur	officer	Ezek 11:1
261	Pelatiah son of Beniah	officer	Ezek 11:1
262	Ishmael son of Nethaniah son of Elishama	officer of royal descent	2 Kgs 25:25
263	Johanan son of Kareah	army officer	2 Kgs 25:23; Jer 40:8
264	Jonathan son of Kareah	army officer	Jer 40:8
265	Seraiah son of Tanhumeth	army officer	2 Kgs 25:23; Jer 40:8
266	Jaazaniah son of the Maachite	army officer	2 Kgs 25:23; Jer 40:8; seal (ליאזניהו עבד המלך)[37]
267	Azariah son of Hoshaiah	official	Jer 43:2
268	Seraiah son of Azariah	high priest	2 Kgs 25:18; 1 Chr 5:40
269	Zephaniah son of Maaseiah	deputy priest	2 Kgs 25:18; Jer 21:1
270	Jehozadak son of Seraiah	priest	1 Chr 5:40-41
271	יאוש	commander of Lachish	Lachish ostraca #s 2, 3[38]

37. Bade, "The Seal of Jaazaniah," 150–151; *WSS*, no. 8. The provenience of the seal, Tel Naṣbeh (Mizpah), raises the possibility that it belonged to the biblical Jaazaniah.

38. *HDAE* 3, 31–32.

39. Possibly the son of Elnathan son of Achbor (#228).

King's Reign	Official's Name	Position	Reference
272	כניהו בן אלנתן[39]	army commander	Lachish ostracon #3
273	טביהו	עבד המלך	Lachish ostracon #3
274	הודיהו בן אחיהו	army officer	Lachish ostracon #3
275	הושיהו	officer	Lachish ostracon #3
276	Gedaliah son of Ahikam son of Shaphan[40]	governor of Judah under Babylon	2 Kgs 25:22
277	גדליהו	royal house minister	bulla (לגדליהו אשר על הבית)[41]
278	גאליהו	son of the king	bulla (לגאליהו בן המלך)[42]
279	טבשלם בן זכר	physician	bulla ([לטבשלם] בן זכר הרפא)[43]
280	שבניהו	son of the king	bulla(לשבניהו[בן]המלך)[44]

40. Grandson of Shaphan the scribe (#202) and son of Ahikam the king's officer (#206).
41. Tufnell, *Lachish III*, 348 no. 173; *WSS*, no. 405. Possibly the son of Ahikam (#206) or the son of Pashhur (#257).
42. Sellers, *Citadel of Beth-Zur*, 60–61; *WSS*, no. 412.
43. Shiloh, "A Group of Hebrew Bullae from the City of David," 29 no. 4; *WSS*, no. 420.
44. Aharoni, *Lachish V*, 21 no. 5; *WSS*, no. 416.

Table A

2. An Inventory of Titles with or without PNs on Published Unprovenienced Epigraphic Material

Estimated Date	**PN + Title**	**Position**	**Reference***
1 1st half 8th c.	למקניו עבד יהוה (seal)	"servant of YHWH" – cult official	*WSS*, no. 27
2 mid 8th c.	לאביו עבד עזיו (seal)	"servant" (of the king)	*WSS*, no. 4
3 mid 8th c.	לשבניו עבד עזיו (seal)	"servant" (of the king)	*WSS*, no. 3
4 mid 8th c.	לזכריהו כהן דאר (seal)	priest	*WSS*, no. 29
5 mid 8th c.	לחלציהו בן המלך (seal)	son of the king	*Windows*, no. 101
6 mid 8th c.	לאחז יהותם מלך יהדה (bulla)	king of Judah	*Messages*, no. 1
7 3rd quarter 8th c.	לעבדי עבד הושע (seal)	"servant" (of the king)	Lemaire, "Name of Israel's Last King," 48
8 3rd quarter 8th c.	לחזקיהו אחז מלך יהדה (bulla)	king of Judah	Cross, "King Hezekiah's Seal," 42–45
9 3rd quarter 8th c.	לאשנא עבד אחז (seal)	"servant" (of the king)	*WSS*, no. 5
10 late 8th c.	גדיהו בן המלך (seal)	son of the king	*WSS*, no. 12
11 late 8th c.	לשבניהו בן המלך (stamped jar handle)	son of the king	*WSS*, no. 662
12 late 8th c.	לאליקם עבד המלך (seal)	"servant" of the king	*WSS*, no. 6

* For convenience, where possible, seals are referenced to Avigad and Sass, *Corpus of West Semitic Stamp Seals* (earlier publications are listed therein). All others, unless noted, were published by Deutsch, or Deutsch and Heltzer.

Estimated Date	PN + Title	Position	Reference
13 late 8th c.	ליהוזרח בן חלקיהו עבד חזקיהו (2 bullae)	“servant” (of the king)	*WSS*, no. 407 *Messages*, no. 2
14 late 8th c.	לעזריהו בן יהואח עבד חזקיהו (bulla)	“servant” (of the king)	*Messages*, no. 3
15 late 8th c.	עבד חזקיהו... (bulla)	“servant” (of the king)	*Messages*, no. 4
16 8th–7th c.	לשמע עבד המלך (seal)	“servant” of the king	*WSS*, no. 10
17 late 8th/7th c.	לעבדיהו עבד המלך (seal)	“servant” of the king	*WSS*, no. 9
18 early 7th c.	למנשה בן המלך (seal)	son of the king	*WSS*, no. 16
19 early 7th c.	לאלשמע בן המלך (seal)	son of the king	*WSS*, no. 11
20 mid 7th c.	שר הער (2 bullae)	governor of the city	*WSS*, no. 402
21 mid 7th c.	למאש בן מנח הספר (seal)	scribe	*WSS*, no. 22
22 mid 7th c.	לבניהו נער חגי (seal)	steward or squire	*WSS*, no. 24
23 mid 7th c.	למלכיהו נער שפט (seal)	steward or squire	*WSS*, no. 25
24 7th c.	לידו אשר על הבית (seal)	royal house minister	*WSS*, no. 1
25 7th c.	לפלאיהו אשר על המס (seal)	minister over the corvée	*WSS*, no. 20
26 7th c.	לנתביהו נער מתן (seal)	steward or squire	*WSS*, no. 26
27 7th c.	לאדנמלך נער פרעש (seal)	steward or squire	*Forty*, no. 22
28 7th c.	לעזריהו שער המסגר (bulla)	gatekeeper of the “prison”	*WSS*, no. 418
29 7th c.	למעדנה בת המלך (seal)	daughter of the king	*WSS*, no. 30

Estimated Date	PN + Title	Position	Reference
30 7th c.	לחנן בן חלקיהו הכהן (seal-ring)	priest	*WSS*, no. 28
31 late 7th c.	לנתנמלך עבד המלך (bulla)	"servant" of the king	*Messages*, no. 9
32 late 7th c.	גאליהו עבד המלך (seal)	"servant" of the king	*WSS*, no. 7
33 late 7th c.	לגאליהו בן המלך (bulla)	son of the king	*WSS*, no. 412
34 late 7th c.	לאדניהו אשר על הבית (4 bullae)	royal house minister	*WSS*, nos. 403, 404 *Messages*, no. 5
35 late 7th/early 6th c.	לירחמאל בן המלך (bulla)	son of the king	*WSS*, no. 414
36 late 7th/early 6th c.	ליהואחז בן המלך (seal)	son of the king	*WSS*, no. 13
37 late 7th/early 6th c.	לישמעאל בן המלך (bulla)	son of the king	Barkay, "A Bulla of Ishmael," 110
38 late 7th/early 6th c.	לפדיהו בן המלך (seal)	son of the king	*WSS* , no. 19
39 late 7th/early 6th c.	לנריהו בן המלך (2 seals & bulla)	son of the king	*WSS* , nos. 17, 18, 415
40 late 7th/early 6th c.	לגדליהו עבד המלך (bulla)	"servant" of the king	*Messages* no. 8
41 late 7th/early 6th c.	לגדליהו עבד המלך (bulla)	"servant" of the king	*WSS*, no. 409
42 late 7th/early 6th c.	לאלשמע עבד המלך (bulla)	"servant" of the king	*WSS*, no. 408
43 late 7th/early 6th c.	לשמעיהו עבד המלך (bulla)	"servant" of the king	*Forty*, 39
44 late 7th/early 6th c.	למבטחיהו עבד המלך (bulla)	"servant" of the king	*WSS*, no. 410
45 late 7th/early 6th c.	למבטחיהו אשר על הבית (bulla)	royal house minister	*Messages*, no. 6
46 late 7th/early 6th c.	לעשיהו עבד המלך (seal)	"servant" of the king	*Forty*, no. 21

Estimated Date	PN + Title	Position	Reference
47 late 7th/early 6th c.	לנתן אשר על הבית (bulla)	royal house minister	*WSS*, no. 406
48 late 7th/early 6th c.	לברכיהו בן נריהו הספר (2 bullae)	scribe	*WSS*, no. 417
49 undated	נער עשיהו בן נמשר (ostracon)	steward or squire	*New Epigraphic Evidence*, no. 79
50 undated	למלכיהו בן המלך (seal)	son of the king	*WSS*, no. 15
51 undated	ליראיהו בן המלך (seal)	son of the king	*WSS*, no. 14
52 undated	לגאליהו בן עדיהו הספר (seal)	scribe	*WSS*, no. 21
53 undated	לשלם בן אדניה הספר (seal)	scribe	*WSS*, no. 23
54 undated	לאביהו עבד המלך (bulla)	"servant" of the king	*Messages*, no. 7
55 undated	לעזריהו עבד המלך (bulla)	"servant" of the king	*Messages*, no. 10
56 undated	לטבשלם שר הער (bulla)	governor of the city	*Messages*, no. 11
57 undated	לפקדיהו שר הער (bulla)	governor of the city	*Messages*, no. 12
58 undated	שר הער (bulla)	governor of the city	*Messages*, no. 13
59 undated	לנויה בת המלך (bulla)	daughter of the king	*Messages*, no. 14
60 undated	לעזר... עבד המלך (bulla)	"servant" of the king	*WSS*, no. 411

Table B

Hebrew Titles in the Biblical and Epigraphic Records and Their Foreign Analogues

(The degree of similarity between the Hebrew titles and their foreign analogues varies)

Bible	**Hebrew Inscriptions**	**Foreign Analogues**
בן המלך	בן המלך	בן המלך* (Moabite) *mār šarri* (Akkadian) *s3 nswt* (Egyptian)
עבד המלך עבד RN	עבד המלך עבד RN	עבד המלך (Edomite) *ʿbd mlk* (Ugaritic) *(w)arad šarri* (Akkadian) *b3k nswt* (Egyptian) עבד RN (Ammonite)
זקנים	– – –	*šībūtu* (Akkadian) *smsw* (Egyptian)
ילדים	– – –	*ẖrdw n k3p* (Egyptian)
אשר על הבית	אשר על הבית	*ʿl bt* (Ugaritic) *ša muḫḫi ekalli, rab ekalli* (Akkadian) *mr pr wr* (Egyptian)
(ה)ספר ספר המלך	(ה)ספר	(ה)ספר* (Moabite, Ammonite) ספר(א) (Aramaic) *spr* (Ugaritic) *ṭupšar šarri* (Akkadian) *sš šʿt nswt n pr-ʿ3* (Egyptian)
(ה)מזכיר	– – –	המזכר (Moabite); *yṣḥ* (Ugaritic) *nāgiru* (Akkadian); *wḥmw* (Egyptian)
רע(ה) המלך	– – –	*ibir bēlišu* (Akkadian) *rḫ-nswt* (Egyptian)
משנה המלך	– – –	*šanû mār šarri* (Akkadian)
יועץ למלך	– – –	*mālik šarri* (Akkadian)
אשר על המס	אשר על המס*	– – –
נצב, על הנצבים	– – –	– – –
שר העיר אשר על העיר	שר הער* שרער השר	*rb qrt, skn qrt* (Ugaritic) *ḫazannu, bēl āli, rab āli, ša muḫḫi āli* (Akkadian) *ḥ3ty-ʿ, sr* (Egyptian)

* Only on unprovenienced inscriptions

Bible	Hebrew Inscriptions	Foreign Analogues
שפט	– – –	*dayyānu* (Akkadian) *sḏmw* (Egyptian)
שער	שער המסגר*	*ṯǵr* (Ugaritic) LÚ *atû*, LÚ *pētû, mār abulli* (Akkadian) *iry-ʿȝ* (Egyptian)
סכן/סכנת	– – –	סכן (Phoenician, Aramaic) *skn/sknt* (Ugaritic) *šaknu* (Akkadian)
נער/נערה	נער	נער* (Ammonite) *nʿr/nʿrt* (Ugaritic) *ṣuḫāru/ṣuḫārtu* (Akkadian)
שטר	– – –	– – –
סריס	– – –	סרס RN (Aramaic) *ša rēši* (Akkadian)

Table C

Geneaologies of Families at Court*

1.

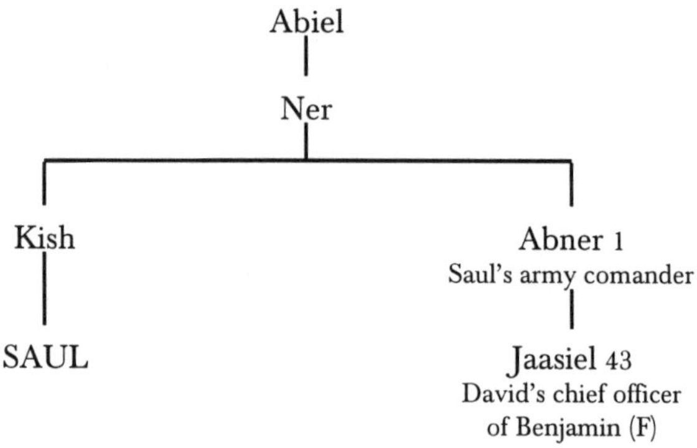

2.

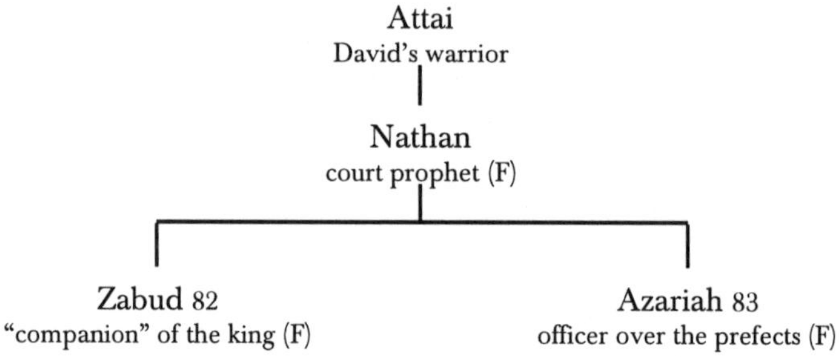

* Numbers in Table C correspond to the numbers in Table A–1. Biblical citations are noted in Table A–1. Persons without numbers are mentioned in the biblical citations of family members with numbers.

(F) indicates possible filiation.

3.

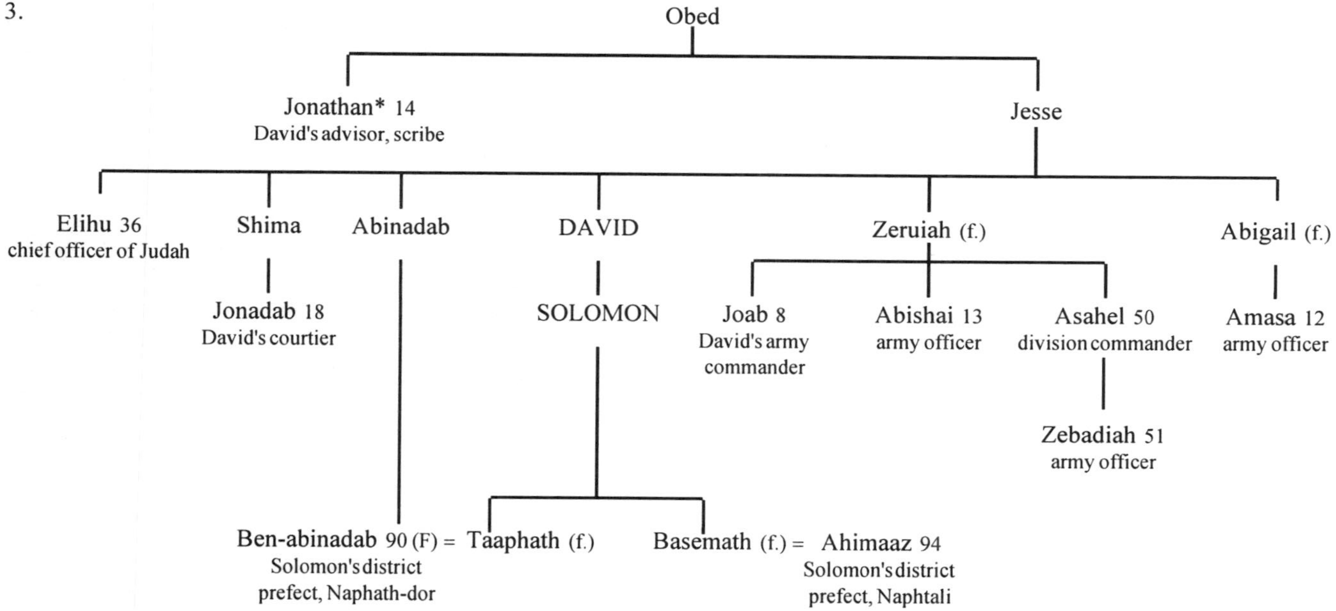

* Or the son of David's maternal grandfather.

4.

Seraiah (Shisha) 10
David's Scribe

Elihoreph 80
Solomon's scribe

Ahijah 81
Solomon's scribe

5.

Ahilud

Baana 91 (F)
Solomon's district prefect
Taanach, Megiddo, Beth-Shean

Jehoshaphat 9, 79
David's and Solomon's *mazkir*

6.

Zichri

Amasiah 117
Jehoshaphat's chief of thousands
Judah

Elishaphat 128 (F)
Joash's chief of hundreds

7.

Meshullam

Azaliah

Shaphan 202
Josiah's scribe

Jaazniah 259
Zedekiah's Official

Elasah 252
Zedekiah's Official

Gemariah 229
Jehoiakim's Scribe

Micaiah 232
Jehoiakims' official

Ahikam 206
Josiah's official

Gedaliah 276
governor of Judah

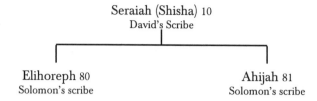

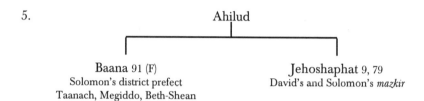

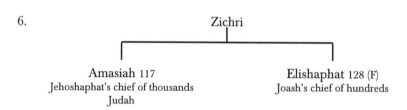

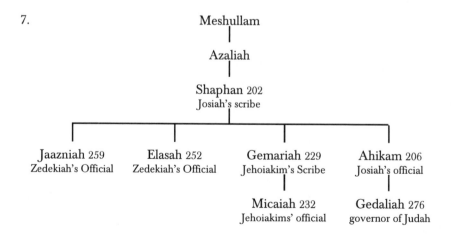

8\.

Achbor 207
Josiah's official

- Elnathan 228
  Jehoiakim's envoy to Egypt
  - JEHOIAKIM = Nechusta (f.) (F)
    - JEHOIACHIN
  - Coniahu 272 (F)
    Zedekiah's army commander

9\.

Mahseiah

- Neriah
  - Baruch 238
    Jeremiah's scribe
  - Seraiah 258
    Zedekiah's quartermaster

10\.

Hilkiah 211
Josiah's high priest

- Azariah 239
  Jehoiakim's high priest
  - Seraiah 268
    Zedekiah's high priest
    - Jehozadak 270
      Zedekiah's priest
- Gemariah 253
  Zedekiah's official

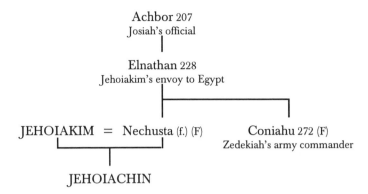

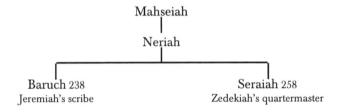

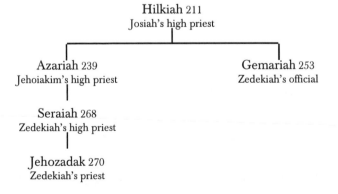

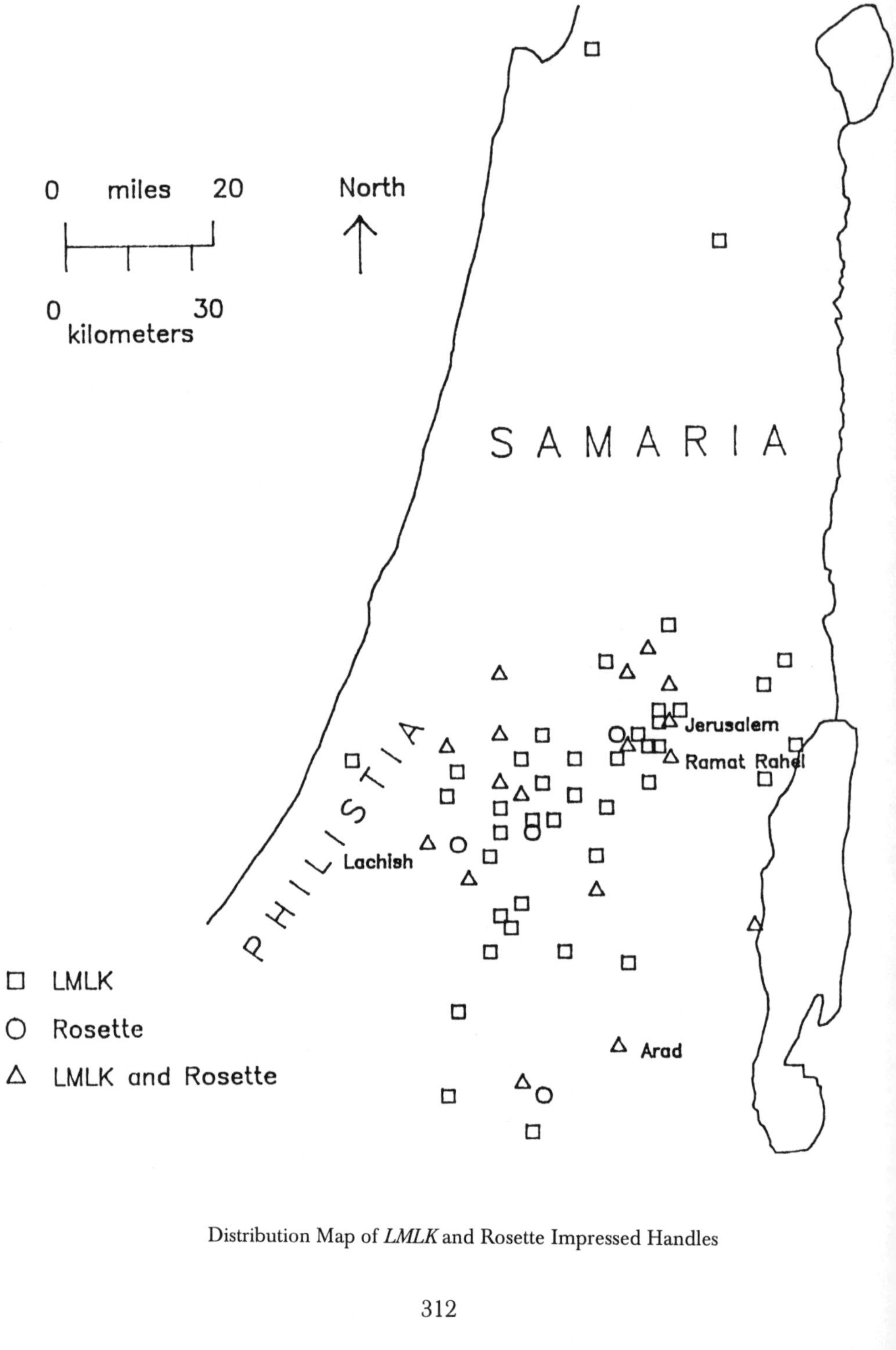

Distribution Map of *LMLK* and Rosette Impressed Handles

Bibliography

Abu Taleb, Mahmud. "The Seal of *plṭy bn m'š* the *mazkir*." *ZDPV* 101 (1985): 21–29.

Aharoni, Miriam. "The Pottery of Strata 12–11 of the Iron Age Citadel at Arad." *EI* 15 (1981), 181–204 (Hebrew).

——. "Inscribed Weights and Royal Seals." In *Arad Inscriptions*, Y. Aharoni, 126–127. Jerusalem: Israel Exploration Society, 1981.

——. "On the Israelite Fortress at Arad." *BASOR* 258 (1985): 73.

——. "Arad: The Israelite Citadels." In *NEAEHL*, 82–97.

Aharoni, Yohanan and Ruth Amiran. "A New Scheme for the Sub-Division of the Iron Age in Palestine." *IEJ* 8 (1958): 171–184.

Aharoni, Yohanan. "Excavations at Ramat Raḥel, 1954." *IEJ* 6 (1956): 137–157.

——. "The Province-List of Judah." *VT* 9 (1959): 225–246.

——. *Excavations at Ramat Raḥel, Seasons 1959 and 1960.* Rome: Centro di Studi Semitici, 1962.

——. *Excavations at Ramat Raḥel, Seasons 1961–1962.* Rome: Centro di Studi Semitici, 1964.

——. "The Use of Hieratic Numerals in Hebrew Ostraca and the Shekel Weights." *BASOR* 184 (1966): 13–19.

——. "Arad: Its Inscriptions and Temple." *BA* 31 (1968): 2–32.

——. *Beer-sheba I: Excavations at Tel Beer-sheba 1969–1971 Seasons.* Tel-Aviv: Tel-Aviv University Institute of Archaeology, 1973.

——. "Excavations at Tel Beer-Sheba: Preliminary Report of the Fifth and Sixth Seasons, 1973–1974." *TA* 2 (1975): 146–168.

——. *Lachish V: Investigations at Lachish – The Sanctuary and the Residency.* Tel-Aviv: Tel-Aviv University Institute of Archaeology, 1975.

——. *The Land of the Bible: A Historical Geography.* Philadelphia: Westminster Press, 1979.

——. *Arad Inscriptions.* Jerusalem: Israel Exploration Society, 1981.

——. "*nṣyb, nṣybym, nṣb, nṣbym.*" In *EM* 5, 914 (Hebrew).

Ahituv, S. "Pashhur." *IEJ* 20 (1970): 95–96.

Ahlström, Gösta W. *Royal Administration and National Religion in Ancient Palestine.* Leiden: E.J. Brill, 1982.

——. *The History of Ancient Palestine from the Palaeolithic Period to Alexander's Conquest.* Sheffield: JSOT Press, 1993.

——. "The Seal of Shema." *SJOT* 7 (1993): 208–215.

Albright, William F. "The Date and Personality of the Chronicler." *JBL* 40 (1921): 104–124.

——. "The Administrative Divisions of Israel and Judah." *JPOS* 5 (1925): 17–54.

——. "Mitannian *maryannu* 'chariot-warrior', and the Canaanite and Egyptian Equivalents." *AfO* 6 (1930–1931): 217–221.

——. "The Seal of Eliakim and the Latest Preexilic History of Judah, with Some Observations on Ezekiel." *JBL* 51 (1932): 77–106.

——. *The Excavation of Tell Beit Mirsim I: The Pottery of the First Three Campaigns.* *AASOR* 12; New Haven: Yale University Press, 1932.

——. *The Excavation of Tell Beit Mirsim III: The Iron Age.* *AASOR* 21–22; New Haven: Jane Dows Nies, 1943.

——. "Cuneiform Material for Egyptian Prosopography." *JNES* 5 (1946): 7–25.

——. "The Judicial Reform of Jehoshaphat." In *A. Marx Jubilee Volume,* ed. S. Lieberman, 61–82.New York: JTS, 1950.

——. *Archaeology and the Religion of Israel.* Baltimore: Johns Hopkins University Press, 1953.

——. *From Stone Age to Christianity, Monotheism and the Historical Process.* Baltimore: Johns Hopkins University Press, 1957.

——. "Beit Mirsim, Tell." In *NEAEHL*, 177–180.

Albright, William F. and James L. Kelso. *The Excavation of Bethel (1934–1960).* *AASOR* 39; Cambridge: Jane Dows Nies, 1968.

Allam, S. "Egyptian Law Courts in Pharaonic and Hellenistic Times." *JEA* 77 (1991): 109–128.

Alt, Albrecht. "Hohe Beamte in Ugarit." *Studia Orientalia* 19 (1954): 1–11.

Artzi, P. "*Sablum* = סבל." *BIES* 18 (1954): 66–70 (Hebrew).

Ash, Paul S. "Solomon's? District? List." *JSOT* 67 (1995): 67–86.

——. "The Relationship Between Egypt and Palestine During the Time of David and Solomon: A Reexamination of the Evidence." Ph.D. Dissertation Emory University, 1998.

Aubet, Maria E. *The Phoenicians and the West: Politics, Colonies and Trade.* Cambridge: Cambridge University Press, 1993.

Aufrecht, Walter E. *A Corpus of Ammonite Inscriptions.* Lewiston: Edwin Mellen Press, 1989.

Avigad, Nahman. "The Epitaph of a Royal Steward from Siloam Village." *IEJ* 3 (1953): 137–152.

——. "The Jotham Seal from Elath." *BASOR* 163 (1961): 18–22.

——. "A Seal of Manasseh Son of the King." *IEJ* 13 (1963): 133–136.

——. "A Sculptured Stone Weight with Hebrew Inscription." *Qadmoniot* 2/2 (1969): 60–61 (Hebrew).

——. "A Group of Hebrew Seals." *EI* 9 (1969): 1–9 (Hebrew).

——. "Ammonite and Moabite Seals." In *NEATC*, 284–295.

——. "Hebrew Epigraphic Sources." In *WHJP* 4/1, 20–43.

——. "Two Hebrew Inscriptions on Wine Jars." *IEJ* 22 (1972): 1–9.

——. "New Light on the *Na'ar* Seals." In *Magnalia Dei, the Mighty Acts of God. Essays on the Bible and Archaeology in Memory of G.E. Wright*, eds. F.M. Cross, W.E. Lemke and P.D. Miller, 294–300. Garden City: Doubleday, 1976.

——. "Baruch the Scribe and Jerahme'el the King's Son." *IEJ* 28 (1978): 52–56.

——. "The King's Daughter and the Lyre." *IEJ* 28 (1978): 146–151.

——. "The Seal of Seriah, Son of Neriah." *EI* 14 (1978): 86–87 (Hebrew).

——. "A Group of Seals from the Hecht Collection." In *Festschrift Reuben R. Hecht*, 119–126. Jerusalem: Koren, 1979.

——. "The Chief of the Corvée." *IEJ* 30 (1980): 170–173.

——. "Titles and Symbols on Hebrew Seals." *EI* 15 (1981): 303–305 (Hebrew).

——. *Hebrew Bullae from the Time of Jeremiah: Remnants of a Burnt Archive*. Jerusalem: Israel Exploration Society, 1986.

——. "Hebrew Seals and Sealings and Their Significance for Biblical Research." *VTS* 40 (1986): 7–16.

——. "Three Ancient Seals." *BA* 49 (1986): 51–53.

——. "On the Identification of Persons Mentioned in Hebrew Epigraphic Sources." *EI* 19 (1987): 235–237 (Hebrew).

——. "The Contribution of Hebrew Seals to an Understanding of Israelite Religion and Society." In *Ancient Israelite Religion. Essays in Honor of F.M. Cross*, eds. P.D. Miller, P.K. McCarter and P.D. Hanson, 195–208. Philadelphia: Fortress Press, 1987.

——. "The Seals of Neriahu the Prince." In *Exile and Diaspora. Studies in the History of the Jewish People Presented to Professor Haim Beinhart on the Occasion of His Seventieth Birthday*, eds. A. Mirsky, A. Grossman and Y. Kaplan, 40–44. Jerusalem: Ben Zvi Institute of Yad Izhak, 1988 (Hebrew).

——. "Two Hebrew 'Fiscal' Bullae." *IEJ* 40 (1990): 262–266.

——. "A New Seal of a 'Son of the King'." *Michmanim* 6 (1992): 27*–31*.

Avishur Y. and M. Heltzer. *Studies on the Royal Administration in Ancient Israel in Light of Epigraphic Sources*. Jerusalem: Acadamon, 1996 (Hebrew).

Badè, William F. "The Seal of Jaazaniah." *ZAW* 51 (1933): 150–156.

Barkay, Gabriel. "A Second Bulla of the 'Governor of the City'." *Qadmoniot* 10 (1977/78): 69–71 (Hebrew).

——. "A Group of Iron Age Scale Weights." *IEJ* 28 (1978): 209–217.

——. "Iron Age Gerah Weights." *EI* 15 (1981): 288–296 (Hebrew).

——. "Northern and Western Jerusalem in the End of the Iron Age." Ph.D. Dissertation, Tel Aviv University, 1985.

——. “A Group of Stamped Handles from Judah.” *EI* 23 (1992): 113–128 (Hebrew).

——. “A Bulla of Ishmael, the King’s Son.” *BASOR* 290–291 (1993): 109–114.

Barton, George. “Three Objects in the Collection of Mr. Herbert Clark, of Jerusalem.” *JAOS* 27 (1906): 400–401.

Beek, G.W. van and A. Jemme. “An Inscribed South Arabian Clay Stamp from Bethel.” *BASOR* 151 (1958): 9–16.

——. “The Authenticity of the Bethel Stamp Seal.” *BASOR* 199 (1970): 59–65.

Begrich, Joachim. “Sōfēr und Mazkīr. Ein Beitrag zur inneren Geschichte des davidisch-salomonischen Grossreiches und des Königsreiches Juda.” *ZAW* 58 (1940–1941): 1–29.

Beit-Arieh, Itzhaq. “Tel ‘Ira – A Fortified City of the Kingdom of Judah.” *Qadmoniot* 18 (1985): 17–25 (Hebrew).

Benoit, P., J. Milik and R. de Vaux. *Les grottes de Murabba‘ât. Discoveries in the Judaean Desert* II. Oxford: Clarendon Press, 1961.

Beswick, S. “The Ancient Hebrew Inscription in the Pool of Siloam, V.” *PEFQS* 13 (1881): 293–296.

Biram, Arthur. “*Mas ‘obed.*” *Tarbiz* 23 (1952): 137–142 (Hebrew).

Biran, Avraham. *Biblical Dan.* Jerusalem: Israel Exploration Society; Hebrew Union College, 1994.

Biran, Avraham and Joseph Naveh. “An Aramaic Stele Fragment from Tell Dan.” *IEJ* 43 (1993): 81–98.

——. “The Tell Dan Inscription: A New Fragment.” *IEJ* 45 (1995): 1–18.

Birnbaum, S.A. “The Dates of the Gezer Tablet and the Samaria Ostraca.” *PEQ* 74 (1942): 104–108.

Bittel, Kurt and Hans G. Güterbock. *Bógazköy, neue Untersuchungen in der hethitischen Hauptstadt.* Berlin: W. de Gruyter, 1935.

Blackman, Aylward M. *Middle Egyptian Stories. Biblioteca Aegyptica* 2; Brussels: Édition de la foundation égyptologique, 1932.

Blau, Ernst O. “Bibliographische Anzeigen.” *ZDMG* 12 (1858): 723–728.

Blenkinsopp, Joseph. *Ezra-Nehemiah: A Commentary.* Philadelphia: Westminster Press, 1988.

Bliss, Frederick J. and Robert A.S. Macalister. *Excavations in Palestine 1898–1900.* London: Palestine Exploration Fund, 1902.

Boecker, Hans J. “Erwägungen zum Amt des Mazkir.” *TZ* 17 (1961): 212–216.

Boer, P.A.H. “The Counsellor.” *VTS* 3 (1955): 2–71.

Boorn, G.P.F. van den. *Duties of the Vizier: Civil Administration in the Early New Kingdom.* London: Kegan Paul International, 1988.

Bordreuil, Pierre and Felice Israel. “À propos de la carrière d’Elyaqim: du page au majordome.” *Semitica* 41/42 (1991–1992): 81–87.

Bordreuil, Pierre et al. "King's Command and Widow's Plea: Two New Hebrew Ostraca of the Biblical Period," *Near Eastern Archaeology* 61 (1998): 2–13.

Borger, Riekele. *Die Inschriften Asarhaddons Königs von Assyrien. AfO* Beiheft 9; Graz, 1956.

Breasted, James H. *Ancient Records of Egypt*, 1–5. Chicago: University of Chicago Press, 1906.

Brettler, Mark. *The Creation of History in Ancient Israel.* London: Routledge, 1995.

Bright, John. *The Anchor Bible, Jeremiah.* New York: Doubleday, 1965.

Brin, Gershon. "The Title בן (ה)מלך and its Parallels." *AION* 29 (1969): 433–465.

Briquel-Chatonnet, Francoise. *Les relations entre les cités phénicienne et les royaumes d'Israël et de Juda.* Leuven: Peeters, 1992.

Broshi, Magen. "The Expansion of Jerusalem in the Reigns of Hezekiah and Manasseh." *IEJ* 24 (1974): 21–26.

Broshi, Magen and Israel Finkelstein. "The Population of Palestine in Iron Age II." *BASOR* 287 (1992): 47–60.

Brownlee, William. "Philistine Manuscripts from Palestine? – A Supplementary Note." *Kadmos* 10 (1971): 173.

Brownlee, William and George Mendenhall. "An announcement published by the Department of Antiquities of Jordan and the Archaeologists Dr. William Brownlee and Dr. George Mendenhall regarding the decipherment of Carian Leather Manuscripts found in 1966 in the Hebron Area, the Hashemite Kingdom of Jordan." *ADAJ* 15 (1970): 39–40.

Brownlee, William, George Mendenhall and Y. Oweis. "Philistine Manuscripts from Palestine?" *Kadmos* 10 (1971): 102–104.

Brügsch, Heinrich C. *Grammaire démotique: contenants les principes generaux de la langue et de l'écriture populaires des ancients Égyptiens.* Berlin: F. Dummler, 1855.

Cahill, Jane. "Rosette Stamp Seal Impressions from Ancient Judah." *IEJ* 45 (1995): 230–252.

Calice, Franz. *Grundlagen der ägyptisch-semitischen Wortvergleichung.* Vienna: Orientalischen Instituts der Universität, 1936.

Caminos, Ricardo A. *The Chronicle of Prince Osorkon. AnOr* 37; Rome: Pontifical Biblical Institute,1958.

Caquot, A. "Préfets." In *Dictionnaire de la bible: Supplément*, 8, eds. L. Pirot and A. Robert, 273–286. Paris: Letouzey Ané, 1972.

Černý, Jaroslav. "The Abnormal Hieratic Tablet Leiden I 431." In *Studies Presented to L.L. Griffith*, 46–56. London: Oxford University Press, 1932.

——. "Egyptian Hieratic." In *Lachish IV: The Bronze Age*, O. Tufnell, 132–133. London: Oxford University Press, 1958.

——. "Egypt from the Death of Ramesses III to the End of the Twenty-First Dynasty." *CAH* II/2, 606–657.

——. *A Community of Workmen at Thebes in the Ramesside Period.* Cairo: French Institute of Oriental Archaeology, 1973.

Chaplin, Thomas C. "An Ancient Hebrew Weight from Samaria." *PEFQS* 22 (1890): 267.

Claburn, W. Eugene. "The Fiscal Basis of Josiah's Reform." *JBL* 92 (1973): 1–22.

Clermont-Ganneau, Charles. "The Shapira Collection." *PEFQS* 6 (1874): 114–118.

——. "Le sceau de Obadyahu, functionnaire royal israëlite." *RAO* 1 (1888): 33–36.

——. "Jarres israëlites marqées à l'estampille des rois de Juda." *RAO* 4 (1900): 1–24.

Cody, Aelred. "Le titre égyptien et le nom propre du scribe de David." *RB* 72 (1965): 381–393.

Cogan, Mordechai (Morton). *Imperialism and Religion: Assyria, Judah, and Israel in the Eighth and Seventh Centuries.* Missoula: Scholars Press, 1974.

Cogan, Mordechai and Hayim Tadmor. *The Anchor Bible, II Kings.* New York: Doubleday, 1988.

Cohen, Ronald and Elman R. Service eds. *Origins of the State: The Anthropology of Political Evolution.* Philadelphia: Institute for the Study of Human Issues, 1978.

Cohen, Rudolph. "Excavations at Kadesh-Barnea 1976–1978." *BA* 44 (1981): 93–107.

——. "Kadesh-Barnea: The Israelite Fortress." In *NEAEHL*, 843–847.

——. "Negev." In *NEAEHL*, 1123–1133.

Collins, John. *Daniel: A Commentary on the Book of Daniel.* Minneapolis: Fortress Press, 1993.

Conder, C.L. "The Hebrew Inscription in the Pool of Siloam, II-III." *PEFQS* (1881): 285–292.

Cook, S.A. "A Newly Discovered Hebrew Seal." *PEFQS* 36 (1904): 287–291.

Cooke, G.A. *A Text-Book of North Semitic Inscriptions.* Oxford: Clarendon Press, 1903.

Cowley, Arthur E. *Aramaic Papyri of the Fifth Century* B.C. Asnabrück: Otto Zeller, 1967 (1923 reprint).

Craddock, Paul and Sheridan Bowman. "The Scientific Detection of Fakes and Forgeries." In *Fake? The Art of Deception*, ed. M. Jones, 275–290. London: British Museum, 1990.

Cross, Frank M. and G. Ernest. Wright. "The Boundary and Province List of the Kingdom of Judah." *JBL* 75 (1956): 202–226.

Cross, Frank M. "Epigraphic Notes on the Hebrew Documents of the Eighth–Sixth Centuries B.C.: I. A New Reading of a Place Name in the Samaria Ostraca." *BASOR* 163 (1961): 12–14; "II. The Murabba'at Papyrus and the Letter Found Near Yabneh-Yam." *BASOR* 165 (1962): 34–46; "III. The Inscribed Jar Handles from Gibeon." *BASOR* 168 (1962): 18–23.

——. "Jar Inscriptions from Shiqmona." *IEJ* 18 (1968): 226–233.

——. "Judean Stamps." *EI* 9 (1969): 20*–27*.

——. *Canaanite Myth and Hebrew Epic: Essays in the History of the Religion of Israel.* Cambridge: Harvard, 1973.

——. "Ammonite Ostraca from Heshbon: Heshbon Ostraca IV-VIII." *AUSS* 13 (1975): 1–20.

——. "The Contribution of the Qumran Discoveries to the Study of the Biblical Text." In *Qumran and the History of the Biblical Text*, eds. F.M. Cross and S. Talmon, 278–292. Cambridge: Harvard University Press, 1975.

——. "Alphabets and Pots: Reflections on Typological Methods in the Dating of Human Artifacts." *Maarav* 3/2 (1982): 121–136.

——. "The Seal of Miqneyaw, Servant of Yaweh." In *Ancient Seals and the Bible*, eds. L. Gorelick and E. Williams-Forte, 55–63. Malibu: Undena, 1983.

——. "A Literate Soldier: Lachish Letter III." In *Biblical and Related Studies Presented to Samuel Iwry*, eds. A. Kort and S. Morschauser, 41–47. Winona Lake: Eisenbraun, 1985.

——. "King Hezekiah's Seal Bears Phoenician Imagery," *BAR* 25 (1999): 42–45, 60.

Crowfoot, John W., Kathleen M. Kenyon and E.L. Sukenik. *Samaria–Sebaste I. The Buildings at Samaria.* London: Palestine Exploration Fund, 1942.

Crown, A.D. "The Fate of the Shapira Scroll." *RdQ* 27 (1970): 421–423.

Curtis, Edward L. *A Critical and Exegetical Commentary on the Books of Chronicles.* New York: Charles Scribner's Sons, 1910.

Dandamayev, M.A. "The Neo-Babylonian Elders." In *Societies and Languages of the Ancient Near East. Studies in Honour of I.M. Diakonoff*, 38–41. Westminster: Aris and Phillips, 1982.

Davies, Phillip R. *In Search of Ancient Israel.* Sheffield: JSOT, 1992.

Demsky, Aaron. "'Dark Wine' from Judah." *IEJ* 22 (1972): 233–234.

——. "A Note on 'Smoked Wine'." *TA* 6 (1979): 163.

——. "Pelekh in Nehemiah." *IEJ* 33 (1983): 242–244.

Deutsch, Robert. "Seal of Ba'alis Surfaces: Ammonite King Plotted Murder of Judahite Governor," *BAR* 25 (1999): 46–49, 66.

——. "First Impression: What We Learn from King Ahaz's Seal," *BAR* 24 (1998): 54–56, 62.

——. *Messages from the Past: Hebrew Bullae from the Time of Isaiah Through the Destruction of the First Temple.* Tel Aviv, 1997 (Hebrew).

Deutsch, Robert and Michael Heltzer. *Forty New Ancient West Semitic Inscriptions.* Tel Aviv–Jaffa: Archaeological Center, 1994.

——. *New Epigraphic Evidence from the Biblical Period.* Tel Aviv–Jaffa: Archaeological Center, 1995.

——. *Windows to the Past.* Tel Aviv–Jaffa, 1997.

Dever, William. "Iron Age Epigraphic Material from the Area of Khirbet el-Kôm." *HUCA* 40/41 (1969/1970): 139–204.

——. "From Tribe to Nation: State Formation Processes in Ancient Israel." In *Nuove fondazioninel Vicino Oriente Antico: Realtà e ideologia*, ed. S. Mazzoni, 213–229. Pisa: University of Pisa, 1994.

——. "Archaeology and the 'Age of Solomon': A Case-Study in Archaeology and Historiography." In *Solomon*, 217–251.

Diringer, David. *Le inscrizioni antico-ebraiche palestinesi.* Florence: Felice le Monnier, 1934.

——. "On Ancient Hebrew Inscriptions Discovered at Tell ed-Duweir (Lachish) II." *PEQ* 73 (1941): 89–109.

——. "The Royal Jar-Handle Stamps of Ancient Judah." *BA* 12 (1949): 70–86.

Donner, Herbert. "Der 'Freund des Königs'." *ZAW* 73 (1961): 269–277.

Dossin, Georges. "L'inscription de fondation de Iadun-Lim roi de Mari." *Syria* 32 (1955): 1–28.

Dothan, Moshe. *Ashdod II-III, the Second and Third Seasons of Excavations 1963, 1965.*" *'Atiqot* 9–10; Jerusalem: Israel Antiquities Authority, 1971.

Dothan, Trude and Seymour Gitin. "Miqne, Tel (Ekron)." In *NEAEHL*, 1051–1059.

Dougherty, Raymond P. "Cuneiform Parallels to Solomon's Provisioning System." *AASOR* 5 (1923–1924): 23–65.

——. "Writing Upon Parchment and Papyrus Among the Babylonians and Assyrians." *JAOS* 48 (1928): 109–135.

Doxey, Denise M. *Egyptian Non-Royal Epithets in the Middle Kingdom.* Leiden: Brill, 1998.

Edens, Christopher. "On the Complexity of Complex Societies: Structure, Power, and Legitimation in Kassite Babylonia." In *Chiefdoms and Early States in the Near East: The Organizational Dynamics of Complexity*, eds. G. Stern and M. Rothman, 209–223. Madison: Prehistory Press, 1994.

Edgerton, William F. "The Strikes in Ramses III's Twenty-Ninth Year." *JNES* 10 (1951): 137–145.

Ehrlich, Carl S. "'How the Mighty Are Fallen': The Philistines in Their Tenth Century Context." In *Solomon*, 179–201.

Eiser, G. and J. Lewy. *Die altassyrischen Rechtsurkunden von Kültepe. MVAG* 35; Leipzig: J.C. Hinrich, 1931.

Eising, H. "זכר." In *Theologisches Wörterbuch zum alten Testament* 2, eds. G.J. Botherweck and H. Ringgren, 584–585. Stuttgart: W. Kohlhammer, 1975.

Eitam, David and Amir Shomroni. "Research of the Oil Industry During the Iron Age at Tel Miqne: A Preliminary Report." In *Olive Oil in Antiquity*, 37–56. Haifa: Haifa University Press, 1987.

Ellis, Maria. *Agriculture and the State in Ancient Mesopotamia: An Introduction to Problems of Land Tenure.* Philadelphia: University Museum, 1976.

Eph'al, Israel and Joseph Naveh. "The Jar at the Gate." *BASOR* 289 (1993): 59–65.

Erichsen, Wolja. *Demotisches Glossar.* Copenhagen: Munksgaard, 1954.

Erman, Adolf and Hermann Grapow. *Wörterbuch der ägyptischen Sprache*, 1–7. Leipzig: J.C. Hinrichs, 1926–1963.

Evans, C.D. "Judah's Foreign Policy from Hezekiah to Josiah." In *Scripture in Context: Essays on the Comparative Method*, eds. C.D. Evans, W.W. Hallo and J.B. White, 157–178. Pittsburgh: Pickwick Press, 1980.

Evans, D. Geoffrey. "Rehoboam's Advisors at Shechem, and Political Institutions in Israel and Sumer." *JNES* 25 (1966): 273–279.

Eyre, Christopher. "Work and the Organization of Work in the New Kingdom." In *Labor in the Ancient Near East,* ed. M. Powell, 167–221. New Haven: American Oriental Society, 1987.

Fales, F.M. and J.N. Postgate. *Imperial Administrative Records, Part I, Palace and Temple Administration.* Helsinki: Helsinki University Press, 1992.

Falkenstein, A. "Zu 'Gilgameš und Agga'." *AfO* 21 (1966): 47–50.

Faulkner, Raymond O. *A Concise Dictionary of Middle Egyptian.* Oxford: Griffith Institute, 1991.

Feucht, Erika. "The ḪRDW N K3P Reconsidered." In *Pharaonic Egypt: The Bible and Christianity*, ed. S.I. Groll, 38–47. Jerusalem: Magnes Press, 1985.

Finkelstein, Israel. "The Emergence of the Monarchy in Israel, the Environmental and Socio-Economic Aspects." *JSOT* 44 (1989): 43–74.

——. "The Archaeology of the Days of Manasseh." In *Scripture*, 169–187.

Flanagan, James W. "Chiefs in Israel." *JSOT* 20 (1981): 47–73.

Fox, Nili. "Royal Officials and Court Families: A New Look at the ילדים (*yĕlādîm*) in 1 Kings 12," *BA* 59 (1996): 225–232.

Franke, Judith A. "Presentation Seals of the Ur III/Isin-Larsa Period." In *Seals and Sealing in the Ancient Near East*, eds. M. Gibson and R. Biggs, 61–66. Malibu: Undena, 1977.

Frick, Frank S. *The Formation of the State in Ancient Israel: A Survey of Models and Theories.* Sheffield: Almond, 1985.

Fulco, W.J. "A Seal from Umm el Qanafid, Jordan; *g'lyhw 'bd hmlk.*" *Or* 49 (1979): 107–108.

Galling, Kurt. "Krügstempel." In *Biblisches Reallexikon*, 337–340. Tübingen: J.C.B. Mohr, 1937.

Garbini, Giovanni. "I sigilli del Regno di Israele." *OrAn* 21 (1982): 163–175.

Gardiner, Alan. *Egyptian Hieratic Texts.* Leipzig: J.C. Hinrichs, 1911.

——. "The Autobiography of Rekhmerē'." *ZAS* 60 (1925): 62–76.

——. *Late Egyptian Stories. Bibliotheca Aegyptica* 1; Brussels: Édition de la fondation égyptologique, 1931.

——. *Onomastica* I–II. Oxford: Oxford University Press, 1947.

——. *Egyptian Grammar.* Oxford: Oxford University Press, 1957.

Garelli, Paul. "Remarques sur l'administration de l'empire assyrien." *RA* 68 (1974): 129–140.

Garfinkel, Yosef. "A Hierarchic Pattern in the 'Private Seal Impressions' on the *lmlk* Jars." *EI* 18 (1985): 108–115 (Hebrew).

Gelb, Ignace J. *Glossary of Old Akkadian.* Chicago: University of Chicago Press, 1957.

Ginsberg, H.L. "MMŠT and MṢH." *BASOR* 109 (1948): 20–22.

——. "Gleanings in First Isaiah." In *M.M. Kaplan Jubilee Volume*, 245–262. New York: JTS, 1953.

Gitin, Seymour. *Gezer III: A Ceramic Typology of the Late Iron II, Persian and Hellenistic Periods at Tell Gezer.* Jerusalem: Hebrew Union College, 1990.

Gitin, Seymour, Trude Dothan and Joseph Naveh. "A Royal Dedicatory Inscription from Ekron," *IEJ* 47 (1997): 1–16.

Glanville, S.R.K. "Records of a Royal Dockyard of the Time of Thutmosis III." *ZAS* 66 (1930): 105–120; *ZAS* 68 (1932): 7–41.

Glueck, Nelson. "The Third Season of Excavation at Tell el-Kheleifeh," *BASOR* 79 [1940]: 13–15.

——. "A Seal Weight from Nebi Rubin." *BASOR* 153 (1959): 35–38.

——. "Tell el-Kheleifeh Inscriptions." In H. Goedicke ed. *Near Eastern Studies in Honor of William Foxwell Albright*, 225–242. Baltimore: Johns Hopkins Press, 1971.

Glueck, Nelson and Gary D. Pratico. "Kheleifeh, Tell el." In *NEAEHL*, 867–870.

Goedicke, Hans. *The Report of Wenamun.* Baltimore: Johns Hopkins University Press, 1975.

Goetze, Albrecht. "The Sibilants of Old Babylonian." *RA* 52 (1958): 137–149.

——. "Old Babylonian Documents from Sippar in the Collection of the Catholic University of America." *JCS* 11 (1951): 15–41.

Goetze, A. and S. Levy. "Fragment of the Gilgamesh Epic from Megiddo." *'Atiqot* 2 (1959): 121–128.

Goldstein, Jonathan A. *The Anchor Bible, I Maccabees.* Garden City: Doubleday, 1976.

Goldwasser, Orly. "Hieratic Inscriptions from Tel Sera' in Southern Canaan." *TA* 11 (1984): 77–93.

——. "An Egyptian Scribe from Lachish and the Hieratic Tradition of the Hebrew Kingdoms." *TA* 18 (1991): 248–253.

Good, Robert M. "The Israelite Royal Steward in the Light of Ugaritic *'l bt.*" *RB* 96 (1979): 580–582.

——. "The Ugaritic Steward." *ZAW* 95 (1983): 110–111.

Gorelick, Leonard and A. John Gwinnett. "Ancient Seals and Modern Science: Using the Scanning Electron Microscope as an Aid in the Study of Ancient Seals." *Expedition* 20 (1978): 38–47.

Görg, Manfred. "Zum Titel *BN HMLK* ('Königssohn')." *BN* 29 (1985): 7–11.

Graham, M. Patrick. *The Utilization of 1 and 2 Chronicles in the Reconstruction of Israelite History in the Nineteenth Century.* Atlanta: Scholars Press, 1990.

Grandet, Pierre. *Papyrus Harris. Institut français d'archéologie orientale* 109/1–2; Le Claire, 1994.

Grant, Elihu. *Ain Shems Excavations,* III. Haverford: Haverford College, 1934.

Grant, Elihu and G. Ernest Wright, *Ains Shems Excavations* V. Haverford: Haverford College, 1939.

Gray, J.B. *Isaiah,* 1. New York: Charles Scribner's Sons, 1912.

Gray, John. *I and II Kings: A Commentary.* Philadelphia: Westminster Press, 1963.

Grayson, A. Kirk. *Assyrian Rulers of the Early First Millennium BC I (1114–859 BC).* Toronto: University of Toronto Press, 1991.

——. "Eunuchs in Power: Their Role in the Assyrian Bureaucracy." In *Von alten Orient zum alten Testament,* eds. M. Dietrich and O. Loretz, 85–173. Neukirchen-Vluyn: Neukirchener, 1995.

Green, Alberto R. "Israelite Influence at Shishak's Court?" *BASOR* 233 (1979): 59–62.

Greenfield, Jonas C. "Studies in Aramaic Lexicography, I." *JAOS* 82 (1962): 290–299.

——. "A Group of Phoenician City Seals." *IEJ* 35 (1985): 129–134.

Griffith, F.L. "The Jar Inscriptions." In *Tell El Amarna,* ed. W.M.F. Petrie, 32–34. Warminster: Aris & Phillips, 1974.

Gurney, O.R. *The Hittites.* Baltimore: Penguin Books, 1964.

Habachi, Labib. "Königssohn von Kusch." In *Lexikon* 3, 630–640.

Hallo, William. "A Sumerian Amphictyony." *JCS* 14 (1960): 88–114.

——. "Biblical History in its Near Eastern Setting: The Contextual Approach." In *Scripture in Context: Essays on the Comparative Method*, eds. C.D. Evans, W.W. Hallo and J.B. White, 1–26. Pittsburgh: Pickwick Press, 1980.

——. "Compare and Contrast: The Contextual Approach to Biblical Literature." In *The Bible in the Light of Cuneiform Literature: Scripture in Context III*, eds. W.W. Hallo, M. Jones and G. Mattingly, 1–30. Lewiston: E. Mellen Press, 1990.

Hallo, William and Hayim Tadmor. "A Lawsuit from Hazor." *IEJ* 27 (1977): 1–11.

Halpern, Baruch. *The First Historians: The Hebrew Bible and History*. San Francisco: Harper and Row, 1988.

——. "Jerusalem and the Lineages in the Seventh Century BCE: Kingship and the Rise of Individual Moral Liability." In *Law and Ideology in Monarchic Israel*, eds. B. Halpern and D. Hobson, 11–107. Sheffield: JSOT Press, 1991.

——. "Erasing History: The Minimalist Assault on Ancient Israel." *Bible Review* 11/6 (1995): 26–35, 47.

Hammond, N.G.L. *The Macedonian State: Origins, Institutions, and History*. Oxford: Clarendon Press,1982.

Hammond, N.G.L. and G. Griffith. *A History of Macedonia* II. Oxford: Clarendon Press, 1979.

Haran, Menachem. "On the Diffusion of Literacy and Schools in Ancient Israel." *VTS* 40 (1986), 81–95.

Harris, Rivka. "Notes on the Nomenclature of Old Babylonian Sippar." *JCS* 24 (1972): 102–104.

Hartman, Louis F. and Alexander A. DiLella. *The Anchor Bible. The Book of Daniel.* Garden City: Doubleday, 1978.

Hayes, John H. and Stuart A. Irvine. *Isaiah the Eighth Century Prophet: His Times and His Preaching.* Nashville: Abington Press, 1987.

Hayes, William C. "Inscriptions from the Palace of Amenhotep III." *JNES* 10 (1951): 35–56, 82–111.

Heaton, E.W. *Solomon's New Men.* New York: Pica Press, 1974.

Helck, Wolfgang. *Der Einfluss der Militärführer in der 18. ägyptischen Dynastie.* Leipzig: J.C. Hinrichs, 1939.

——. *Zur Verwaltung des mittleren und neuen Reichs.* Leiden: E.J. Brill, 1958.

——. *Die Beziehungen Ägyptens zu Vorderasien im 3. und 2. Jahrtausend v. Chr.* Wiesbaden: O. Harrassowitz, 1971.

——. "Beamtentum." In *Lexikon* 1, 672–675.

——. "Bürgermeister." In *Lexikon* 1, 875–880.

——. "Domänenvorsteher." In *Lexikon* 1, 1120.

——. "Masse und Gewichte." In *Lexikon* 3, 1199–1209.

——. "Palastverwaltung." In *Lexikon* 4, 647–651.

——. "Richtertitel." In *Lexikon* 5, 255–256.

——. "Türhüter." In *Lexikon* 6, 787–789.

Held, Moshe. "The Root ZBL/SBL in Akkadian, Ugaritic and Biblical Hebrew." *JAOS* 88 (1968): 90–96.

Heltzer, Michael. *The Rural Community in Ancient Ugarit.* Wiesbaden: Dr. Ludwig Reichart, 1976.

——. *The Internal Organization of the Kingdom of Ugarit.* Wiesbaden: Dr. Ludwig Reichert, 1982.

——. "Some Questions of the Ugaritic Metrology and its Parallels in Judah, Phoenicia, Mesopotamia and Greece." *UF* 21 (1989): 195–208.

Henshaw, Richard A. "The Office of *šaknu* in Neo-Assyrian Times." *JAOS* 87 (1967): 517–525.

Herr, Larry G. *The Scripts of Ancient Northwest Semitic Seals.* Missoula: Scholar Press, 1978.

——. "Paleography and the Identification of Seal Owners." *BASOR* 239 (1980): 67–70.

Hertzberg, Hans W. *I and II Samuel.* Philadelphia: Westminster Press, 1964.

Herzog, Ze'ev. "Israelite City Planning." *Expedition* 20/4 (1978): 38–43.

——. *The Arad Fortresses.* In R. Amiran, O. Ilan and M. Sebanne, *Arad: Ancient Arad - An Early Bronze Age on the Desert Fringe.* Tel Aviv: Hakibbutz Hameuchad; IES; IAA, 1997 (Hebrew).

—— et al. "The Israelite Fortress at Arad." *BASOR* 254 (1984): 1–34.

Hestrin, Ruth. *Inscriptions Reveal: Documents from the Time of the Bible, the Mishna and the Talmud.* Jerusalem: Israel Museum, 1973.

Hinke, William. *A New Boundary Stone of Nebuchadrezzar I from Nippur.* Philadelphia: University Museum, 1907.

Hoch, James E. *Semitic Words in Egyptian Texts of the New Kingdom and Third Intermediate Period.* Princeton: Princeton University Press, 1994.

Hoffmeier, James K. *Israel in Egypt: The Evidence for the Authenticity of the Exodus Tradition.* New York: Oxford University Press, 1997.

Hoffner, Harry H. "The Laws of the Hittites." Ph.D. Dissertation, Brandeis University, 1963.

Hoftijzer, J. Jacob and G. van der Kooij. *Aramaic Texts from Deir 'Alla.* Leiden: E.J. Brill, 1976.

Holladay, John S. "Of Sherds and Strata." In *Magnalia Dei, the Mighty Acts of God. Essays on the Bible and Archaeology in Memory of G.E. Wright*, eds. F.M. Cross, W.E. Lemke and P.D. Miller, 253–93. Garden City: Doubleday, 1976.

——. "The Kingdoms of Israel and Judah: Political and Economic Centralization in the Iron IIA-B (ca. 1000–750 BCE)." In *The Archaeology of Society in the Holy Land*, ed. T. Levy. 368–398. New York: Facts on File, 1995.
Holladay, William L. *Jeremiah, A Commentary on the Book of Jeremiah* 1–2. Philadelphia: Fortress Press, 1986; 1989.
Holloway, Steven W. "Assyria and Babylonia in the Tenth Century BCE." In *Solomon*, 202–216.
Hooke, S.H. "A Scarab and Sealing from Tell Duweir." *PEQ* 67 (1935): 195–197.
Hornblower, Simon and Anthony J.S. Spawforth. "Prosopography." In *The Oxford Classical Dictionary* 3rd ed. New York: Oxford University Press, 1996.
Hubner, Ulrich. "Fälschungen ammonitischer Siegel." *UF* 21 (1989): 217–226.
Huizinga, Johan. "A Definition of the Concept of History." In *Philosophy and History: Essays Presented to Ernst Cassirer*, eds. R. Klibansky and H.J. Paton, 1–10. New York: Harper & Row, 1963.
Hurowitz, Victor A. "Another Fiscal Practice in the Ancient Near East: 2 Kings 12:5–17 and a Letter to Esarhaddon (*LAS* 277)." *JNES* 45 (1986): 289–294.
——. *Divine Service and Its Rewards: Ideology and Poetics in the Hinke Kudurru.* Beer-Sheva: Ben-Gurion University of the Negev Press, 1997.
Immerwahr, Henry R. *Attic Script: A Survey.* Oxford: Clarendon Press, 1990.
Japhet, Sara. "The Historical Reliability of Chronicles: The History of the Problem and its Place in Biblical Research." *JSOT* 33 (1985): 83–107.
——. *I & II Chronicles, A Commentary.* Louisville: Westminster/John Knox Press, 1993.
Kadish, G.E. "Eunuchs in Ancient Egypt?" In *Studies in Honor of John A. Wilson*, 55–62. Chicago, University of Chicago Press, 1969.
Kaiser, Otto. *Isaiah 13–39: A Commentary.* Philadelphia: Westminster Press, 1974.
Kallai-Kleinmann, Z. "The Town Lists of Judah, Simeon, Benjamin and Dan." *VT* 8 (1958): 134–160.
——. *The Northern Boundary of Judah.* Jerusalem: Y.L. Magnes, 1960 (Hebrew).
——. "Note on the Town Lists." *VT* 11 (1961): 223–227.
Katzenstein, H. Jacob. "The Royal Steward." *IEJ* 10 (1960): 149–154.
——. *The History of Tyre: From the Beginning of the Second Millenium B.C.E. until the Fall of the Neo-Babylonian Empire in 538 B.C.E.* Jerusalem: Schocken Institute, 1973.
Kaufman, Ivan T. "The Samaria Ostraca: A Study in Ancient Hebrew Paleography." Ph.D. Dissertation, Harvard University, 1966.
——. New Evidence for Hieratic Numerals on Hebrew Weights." *BASOR* 188 (1967): 39–41.

——. "The Samaria Ostraca: An Early Witness to Hebrew Writing." *BA* 45 (1982): 229–239.

Kaufman, Stephen. "The Pitfalls of Typology: On the Early History of the Alphabet." *HUCA* 57 (1986): 1–14.

Keel, Othamar and Christoph Uehlinger. *Gods, Goddesses and Images of God in Ancient Israel* (trans.T. Trapp). Minneapolis: Fortress Press, 1998.

Kelm, George L. and Amihai Mazar. "Three Seasons of Excavations at Tell Batash." *BASOR* 248 (1982): 1–36.

Kelso, James L. "A Reply to Yadin's Article on the Finding of the Bethel Seal." *BASOR* 199 (1970): 65.

Kenyon, Kathleen M. "The Date of the Destruction of Iron Age Beer-Sheba." *PEQ* 108 (1976): 63–64.

Kerkhof, Vera I. "An Inscribed Stone Weight from Shechem." *BASOR* 184 (1966): 20–21.

Kilmer, Anne D. "The First Tablet of MALKU=ŠARRU Together with Its Explicit Version." *JAOS* 83 (1963): 421–446.

Kinnier-Wilson, J.V. *The Nimrud Wine Lists.* London: British School of Archaeology in Iraq, 1972.

Kissane, Edward J. *The Book of Isaiah*, 1. Dublin: Brown and Nolan, 1941.

Kitchen, Kenneth A. *Ramesside Inscriptions* 6. Oxford: B.H. Blackwell, 1969.

——. *The Third Intermediate Period in Egypt (1100–650 B.C.).* Warminster: Aris and Phillips, 1973.

——. "From the Brickfields of Egypt." *Tyndale Bulletin* 27 (1976): 137–147.

——. "Egypt and Israel During the First Millenium B.C.." *VTS* 40 (1986): 107–123.

——. "Egypt and East Africa." In *Solomon*, 106–125.

Klauber, Ernst G. *Assyrisches Beamtentum nach den Briefen aus der Sargonidenzeit.* Leipzig: J.C. Hinrichs, 1910.

Klein, Ralph W. "Abijah's Campaign Against the North (2 Chr. 13) – What Were the Chronicler's Sources?" *ZAW* 95 (1983): 210–217.

Kletter, Raz. "The Inscribed Weights of the Kingdom of Judah." *TA* 18 (1991): 121–163.

Knauf, Ernst A. "The Cultural Impact of Secondary State Formation: The Cases of the Edomites and Moabites." In *Early Edom and Moab: The Beginning of the Iron Age in Southern Jordan*, ed. P. Bienkowski, 47–54. Sheffield: J.R. Collis, 1992.

Knoppers, Gary N. "The Vanishing Solomon: The Disappearance of the United Monarchy from Recent Histories of Ancient Israel." *JBL* 116 (1997): 19–44.

Knudtzon, J.A. *Die El-Amarna-Tafeln, mit Einleitung und Erläuterungen*, 1–2. Aalen: O. Zeller, 1915.

Köhler, Ludwig. *Hebrew Man.* (Trans. P. Ackroyd) London: SCM Press, 1956.

Kooij, G. van de, and M. Ibrahim eds. *Picking Up the Threads...A Continuing Review of Excavations at Deir 'Alla Jordan.* Leiden: University of Leiden Archaeological Centre, 1989.

Kümmel, Hans M. "Ugaritica Hethitica." *UF* 1 (1969): 159–165.

——. *Familie, Beruf und Amt im spätbabylonischen Uruk.* Berlin: Gebr. Mann Verlag, 1979.

Kwasman, Theodore and Simo Parpola. *Legal Transactions of the Royal Court of Nineveh, Part I: Tiglath-Pileser III through Esarhaddon.* Helsinki: Helsinki University Press, 1991.

Lacheman, Ernest R. "Nuziana II." *RA* 36 (1939): 114–219.

Lambert, W.G. "Three Unpublished Fragments of the Tikulti-Ninurta Epic." *AfO* 18 (1957–1958): 38–51.

Lamon, Robert S. and Geoffrey M. Shipton. *Megiddo I: Seasons of 1925–34 Strata I-V.* Chicago: University of Chicago, 1939.

Landsberger, Benno and Hayim Tadmor. "Fragments of Clay Liver Models from Hazor." *IEJ* 14 (1964): 201–218.

Lanfranchi, Giovanni B. and Simo Parpola. *The Correspondence of Sargon II, Part II, Letters from the Northern and Northeastern Provinces.* Helsinki: Helsinki University Press, 1990.

Langdon, St. "Inscriptions on Cassite Seals." *RA* 16 (1919): 69–95.

Lapp, Paul. "Late Royal Seals from Judah." *BASOR* 158 (1960): 11–22.

Layton, Scott C. "The Steward in Ancient Israel: A Study of Hebrew (*'ăšer*) *'l-habbayit* in Its Near Eastern Setting." *JBL* 109 (1990): 633–649.

Leichty, Erle. "A Remarkable Forger." *Expedition* 20 (1970): 17–21.

Lemaire, André. "L'ostracon de Meṣad Ḥashavyahu (Yavneh-Yam) replacé dans son contexte." *Semitica* 21 (1971): 57–79.

——. "Les ostraca paléo-hébreaux des fouilles de l'Ophel." *Levant* 10 (1978): 158–161.

——. "Note sur le titre *bn hmlk* dans l'ancien Israël." *Semitica* 29 (1979): 59–65.

——. "Classification des estampilles royales judéenes." *EI* 15 (1981): 54*–60*.

——. "Les critères non-iconographiques de la classification des sceaux nord-ouest sémitiques inscrits." In *SINSIS*, 1–26.

——. "Name of Israel's King Surfaces in a Private Collection." *BAR* 21/6 (1995): 48–52.

Lemaire, André and Pascal Vernus. "Les ostraca paléo-hébreux de Qadesh-Barnéa." *Or* 49/4 (1980): 341–345.

——. "L'ostracon paléo-hébreau n 6 de Tell Qudeirat (Kadesh-Barnéa)." In *Fontes Atque Pontes: Eine Festgabe für Hellmut Brunner*, ed M. Görg, 302–326. Wiesbaden: O. Harrassowitz, 1983.

——. "L'origine égyptienne du signe ɤ des poids inscrits de l'époque royale israélite." *Semitica* 28 (1978): 53–58.

Lemche, Niels P. "Did Biran Kill David? The Bible in the Light of Archaeology." *JSOT* 64 (1994): 3–22.

Leslau, Wolf. "Semitic and Egyptian Comparisons." *JNES* 21 (1962): 44–49.

Lewy, Julius. "The Problems Inherent in Section 70 of the Bisutun Inscription." *HUCA* 25 (1954): 169–208.

Lidzbarski, Mark. *Handbuch der nordsemitischen Epigraphik.* Weimar: Emil Felber, 1898.

——. "Altaramäische Urkunden aus Assur." *WVDOG* 38 (1921): 15–20.

Lie, Arthur G. *The Inscriptions of Sargon II, King of Assyria.* Paris: P. Geuthner, 1929.

Lipiski, E. "Le récit de 1 Rois XII 1–19 à la lumière de l'ancien usage de hébreu et de nouveaux textes de Mari." *VT* 24 (1974): 430–437.

——. "Royal and State Scribes in Ancient Jerusalem." *VTS* 40 (1986): 157–164.

Liver, J. "The Book of the Acts of Solomon." *Biblica* 48 (1967): 75–101.

Livingston, Alasdair. *Court Poetry and Literary Miscellanea.* Helsinki: Helsinki University Press, 1989.

Long, Burke O. *1 Kings, with an Introduction to Historical Literature.* Grand Rapids: W.B. Eerdmans, 1984.

Longpérier, Henri A. de. "Cachet de Sébénias fils d'Osias." *CRAIBL* 6 (1863): 288–289.

Loretz, Oswald. "Ugaritisch *skn–sknt* und hebräisch *skn–sknt.*" *ZAW* 94 (1982): 123–127.

Luckenbill, Daniel D. *The Annals of Sennacherib.* Chicago: University of Chicago Press, 1924.

Lundbom, J.R. "Baruch, Seriah, and Expanded Colophons in the Book of Jeremiah." *JSOT* 36 (1986): 89–114.

Lurje, I.M. *Studien zum altägyptischen Recht, Forschungen zum römischen Recht* 30. Weimar: Hermann Bohlaus, 1971.

Macalister, Robert A.S. *The Excavation of Gezer*, II. London: J. Murray, 1912.

MacDonald, John. "The Status and Role of the Na'ar in Israelite Society." *JNES* 35 (1976): 147–170.

——. "The Role and Status of the *ṣuḫāru* in the Mari Correspondence." *JAOS* 96 (1976): 57–68.

Machinist, Peter. "The Epic of Tikulti-Ninurta I: A Study in Middle Assyrian Literature." Ph.D. Dissertation, Yale University, 1978.

——. "The Image of Assyria in First Isaiah." *JAOS* 103 (1983): 719–737.
Macholz, von Georg C. "Zu Geschichte der Justizorganisation in Juda." *ZAW* 84 (1972): 314–340.
Malamat, Abraham. "Kingship and Council in Israel and in Sumer." *JNES* 22 (1963): 247–253.
——. "Hazor 'The Head of All Those Kingdoms'." *JBL* 79 (1960): 12–19.
Malul, Meir. *The Comparative Method in Ancient Near Eastern and Biblical Legal Studies.* Neukirchen-Vluyn: Neukirchener, 1990.
Margalit, Baruch. "K–R–T Studies." *UF* 27 (1995): 215–315.
Mariette, Auguste. *Karnak.* Leipzig: J.C. Hinrichs, 1875.
Marquart, J. Josef. *Fundamente israelitischer und jüdischer Geschichte.* Göttingen: Dieterich, 1896.
Martin, Geoffrey T. *Egyptian Administrative and Private-Name Seals.* Oxford: Griffith Institute, 1971.
Maspero, Gaston C.C. *Une enquête judiciare à Thebes au temps de la XX*[e] dynastie. Paris: Imprimerie nationale, 1871.
Matthiae, Paolo. *Ebla: An Empire Rediscovered.* London: Hodder and Stoughton, 1980.
Maxwell-Hyslop, K.R. *Western Asiatic Jewelry c. 3000–62 B.C.* London: Methuen, 1971.
Mazar, Amihai. *The Archaeology of the Land of the Bible, 10,000–586 B.C.E.* New York: Doubleday, 1990.
——. "The Northern Shephelah in the Iron Age: Some Issues in Biblical History and Archaeology." In *Scripture*, 247–267.
——. "Beth-Shean." In *NEAEHL*, 216–222.
Mazar, Amihai, Moshe Dothan and I. Dunayevsky. "En Gedi: The First and Second Seasons of Excavations, 1961–1962." *'Atiqot* 5; Jerusalem: Israel Antiquities Authority, 1966.
Mazar, Amihai, David Amit and Zvi Ilan. "The 'Border Road' between Michmash and Jericho and Excavations at Horvat Shilah." *EI* 17 (1984): 236–250 (Hebrew).
Mazar, Amihai and Ehud Netzer. "On the Israelite Fortress at Arad." *BASOR* 263 (1986): 87–90.
Mazar (Maisler), Benjamin. "King David's Scribe and the High Officialdom of the United Monarchy of Israel." In *The Early Biblical Period*, eds. S. Ahituv and B. Levine, 134–135. Jerusalem: Israel Exploration Society, 1986.
——. "The Historical Background of the Samaria Ostraca." *JPOS* 21 (1948): 117–133.
——. "The Excavations at Tel Qasile: Preliminary Report." *IEJ* 1 (1950–1951): 194–218.

——. "Adoram." In *EM* 1, 116–117 (Hebrew).

Mazori, Dalya. "A. Yitzhak, the Sculptor from Afula, Laughs at the Experts." *Ma'ariv* July 11, 1975 (Hebrew).

McCarter, P. Kyle. *The Anchor Bible, I Samuel.* Garden City: Doubleday, 1980.

——. *The Anchor Bible, II Samuel.* Garden City: Doubleday, 1984.

McClellan, Thomas L. "Quantitative Studies in the Iron Age Pottery of Palestine." Ph.D. Dissertation, University of Pennsylvania, 1975.

McCown, Chester C. *Tell en-Naṣbeh* I. Berkeley: Palestine Institute of Pacific School of Religion and ASOR, 1947.

McKenzie, John L. "The Elders in the Old Testament." *AnBib* 10 (1959): 388–406.

McKenzie, Steven L. *The Chronicler's Use of the Deuteronomistic History.* Atlanta: Scholars Press,1984.

Mendelsohn, I. "Guilds in Ancient Palestine." *BASOR* 80 (1940): 17–21.

——. "State Slavery in Ancient Palestine." *BASOR* 85 (1942): 14–17.

——. "Samuel's Denunciation of Kingship in the Light of Akkadian Documents from Ugarit." *BASOR* 143 (1956): 17–22.

——. "On Corvée Labor in Ancient Canaan and Israel." *BASOR* 167 (1962): 31–35.

Mendenhall, George. "The 'Philistine' Documents from the Hebron Area." *ADAJ* 16 (1971): 99–102.

Meshel, Ze'ev. *Kuntillet 'Ajrud – A Religious Center from the Time of the Judaean Monarchy on the Border of Sinai.* Israel Museum Catalogue 175; Jerusalem, 1978.

Mettinger, Tryggve N.D. *Solomonic State Officials: A Study of the Civil Government Officials of the Israelite Monarchy.* Lund: CWK Gleerups Forlag, 1971.

Meulenaere, H. de, M.L. Bierbrier and J. Quaegebeur. "Notes de prosopographie thébaine." *CdE* 114 (1982): 201–230.

Millard, A.R. "The Assyrian Royal Seal Type Again." *Iraq* 27 (1965): 12–16.

——. "The Assyrian Royal Seal: An Addendum." *Iraq* 40 (1978): 70.

Miller, J. Maxwell. "Separating the Solomon of History from the Solomon of Legend." In *Solomon,* 1–24.

Möller, Georg. *Hieratische Paleographie, die ägyptische Buchschrift in ihrer Entwicklung von der fünften Dynastie bis zur römischen Kaiserzeit.* Osnabruck: O. Zeller, 1965.

Momsen, H., L. Perlman and J. Yellin. "The Provenience of the *lmlk* Jars." *IEJ* 34 (1984): 89–113.

Montet, Pierre. "La nécropole des rois tanites." *Kêmi* 9 (1942): 1–96.

Montgomery, James. *A Critical and Exegetical Commentary on the Book of Daniel.* New York: Charles Scribner's Sons, 1927.

——. "Archival Data in the Books of Kings." *JBL* 53 (1934): 46–52.
Moore, George F. *A Critical and Exegetical Commentary on Judges.* Edinbrugh: T. & T. Clark, 1895.
Moran, William. "The Hebrew Language in Its Northwest Semitic Background." In *The Bible and the Ancient Near East. Essays in Honor of William Foxwell Albright*, ed G.E. Wright, 56–72. London: Routledge and Kegan Paul, 1961.
——. "The Syrian Scribe of the Jerusalem Amarna Letters." In *Unity and Diversity: Essays in the History, Literature and Religion of the Ancient Near East*, eds. H. Goedicke and J. Roberts, 146–166. Baltimore: Johns Hopkins University Press, 1975.
——. *The Amarna Letters.* Baltimore: Johns Hopkins University Press, 1992.
Muilenburg, James. "Baruch the Scribe." In *Proclamation and Presence*, eds. J. Durham and J. Porter, 215–238. Macon: Mercer University Press, 1983.
Mulder, Martin J. "Versuch zur Deutung von *sokènèt* in Kön. I 2,4." *VT* 22 (1972): 43–54.
Myers, Jacob M. *The Anchor Bible, I Chronicles.* Garden City: Doubleday, 1965.
Mykytiuk, Lawrence J. "Identifying Biblical Persons in Hebrew Inscriptions and Two Stelae from Before the Persian Era." Ph.D. Dissertation University of Wisconsin–Madison, 1998.
Na'aman, Nadav. "Hezekiah's Fortified Cities and the *LMLK* Stamps." *BASOR* 261 (1986): 5–21.
——. "The Kingdom of Judah Under Josiah." *TA* 18 (1991): 3–71.
Naveh, Joseph. "A Hebrew Letter from the Seventh Century B.C." *IEJ* 10 (1960): 129–139.
——. "More Hebrew Inscriptions from Meṣad Ḥashavyahu. *IEJ* 12 (1962): 27–32.
——. "The Excavations at Meṣad Ḥashavyahu: Preliminary Report." *IEJ* 12 (1962): 97–99.
——. "Aramaica Dubiosa." *JNES* 27 (1968): 319–325.
——. "A Paleographic Note on the Distribution of the Hebrew Script." *HTR* 61 (1968): 68–74.
——. "The Scripts in Palestine and Transjordan in the Iron Age." In *NEATC*, 277–283.
——. Review, L. Herr, *Scripts of Ancient Northwest Semitic Seals. BASOR* 239 (1980): 75–76.
——. "The Aramaic Ostraca from Tel Arad." In *Arad Inscriptions*, 153–176.
——. *Early History of the Alphabet: An Introduction to West Semitic Epigraphy and Paleography.* Jerusalem: Magnes Press, 1982.
——. "Some Recently Forged Inscriptions." *BASOR* 247 (1982): 53–58.

——. "Clumsy Forger Fools the Scholars - But Only for a Time." *BAR* 10/3 (1984): 66–72.

——. "Writing and Scripts in Seventh-Century B.C.E. Philistia: The New Evidence from Tell Jemmeh." *IEJ* 35 (1985): 8–21.

——. "The Numbers of *Bat* in the Arad Ostraca." *IEJ* 45 (1995): 52–54.

Naveh, Joseph and Hayim Tadmor. "Some Doubtful Aramaic Seals." *AION* 18 (1968): 448–452.

Neufeld, E. *The Hittite Laws.* London: Luzac, 1951.

Niemann, Hermann M. "The Socio-Political Shadow Cast by the Biblical Solomon." In *Solomon*, 252–299.

North, Robert. "Does Archaeology Prove Chronicles' Sources?" In *A Light unto My Path*, eds. H. Bream, R. Heim and C. Moore, 375–401. Philadelphia: Temple University Press, 1974.

Noth, Martin. "Das Krongut der Israel. Könige und seine Verwaltung." *ZDPV* 50 (1927): 211–244.

——. *The Deuteronomistic History.* Sheffield: JSOT, 1981 (trans. of 1943 German).

——. *Könige.* Neukitchen-Vluyn: Neukirchener, 1968.

Oates, David. "Fort Shalmaneser: An Interim Report." *Iraq* 21 (1959): 98–129.

O'Connor, David. "New Kingdom and Third Intermediate Period, 1552–664 BC." In *Ancient Egypt, A Social History*, eds. B.G. Trigger, D. O'Connor and A.B. Lloyd, 226–242. Cambridge: Cambridge University Press, 1983.

Oppenheim, A. Leo. "Idiomatic Accadian." *JAOS* 61 (1941): 251–271.

——. "The Archives of the Palace of Mari II: A Review Article." *JNES* 13 (1954): 141–148.

——. "A Note on the Scribes in Mesopotamia." In *Studies in Honor of Benno Landsberger*, eds. H. Güterbock and T. Jacobsen, 253–256. Chicago: University of Chicago Press, 1965.

——. "A Note on *ša rēši.*" *JANES* 5 (1973): 325–334.

Ornan, Tallay. "The Dayan Collection." *Israel Museum Journal* 2 (1983): 5–18.

Ottosson, Magnus. *Gilead: History and Tradition.* Lund: Gleerup, 1969.

Owen, David I. "An Akkadian Letter from Ugarit at Tel Aphek." *TA* 8 (1981): 1–17.

Pack, Melvin D. "The Administrative Structure of the Palace at Mari." Ph.D. Dissertation, University of Pennsylvania, 1981.

Pardee, Dennis. "The Judicial Plea from Meṣad Ḥashavyahu (Yavneh-Yam): A New Philological Study." *Maarav* 1 (1978): 33–66.

Parker, Barbara. "Economic Tablets from the Temple of Mamu at Balawat." *Iraq* 25 (1963): 86–103.

Parpola, Simo. *The Correspondence of Sargon II, Part I, Letters from Assyria and the West.* Helsinki: Helsinki University Press, 1987.

Paul, S.M. "Classifications of Wine in Mesopotamian and Rabbinic Sources." *IEJ* 25 (1975): 42–44.

Peckham, Brian. "Phoenicia, History of." In *ABD* 5, 349–357.

Pederson, Johannes. *Israel: Its Life and Culture.* London: Oxford University Press, 1946.

Péčırková, Jana. "The Administrative Organization of the Neo-Assyrian Empire." *ArOr* 45 (1977): 211–228.

Peet, Thomas E. *The Great Tomb-Robberies of the Twentieth Egyptian Dynasty.* Oxford: Clarendon Press, 1930.

Petrie, W.M. Flinders. *Tell El Amarna.* London: Methuen, 1894.

——. *Gerar.* London: British School of Archaeology in Egypt, 1928.

Pettinato, Giovanni. *The Archives of Ebla: An Empire Inscribed in Clay.* Garden City: Doubleday,1981.

Pfluger, Kurt. "The Edict of King Haremhab." *JNES* 5 (1946): 260–276.

Pike, Dana M. "Israelite Theophoric Personal Names in the Bible and Their Implications for Religious History." Ph.D. Dissertation, University of Pennsylvania, 1990.

Ploeg, J. van der. "Les šoṭerim d'Israël." *OTS* 10 (1954): 185–196.

Porten, Bezalel and Ida Yardeni. *Textbook of Aramaic Documents from Ancient Egypt* 1–3. Jerusalem: Hebrew University, 1986–1993.

Postgate, J.N. "More 'Assyrian Deeds and Documents'." *Iraq* 32 (1970): 129–164.

——. *Taxation and Conscription in the Assyrian Empire.* Rome: Biblical Institute Press, 1974.

——. "The Place of the *šaknu* in Assyrian Government." *AnSt* 30 (1980): 67–76.

Pritchard, James B. *Hebrew Inscriptions and Stamps from Gibeon.* Philadelphia: University Museum,1959.

——. *The Water System of Gibeon.* Philadelphia: University Museum, 1961.

——. *Winery, Defenses, and Soundings at Gibeon.* Philadelphia: University Museum, 1964.

——. "Gibeon." In *NEAEHL*, 511–514.

Puech, E. "Les poids." In *Tell el-Far'ah I. L'âge du fer,* ed. A. Chambon, 79–84. Paris: Éditions recherche sur les civilisations, 1984.

Quirke, Stephen. "The Regular Titles of the Late Middle Kingdom." *RdE* 37 (1986): 107–130.

——. *The Administration of Egypt in the Late Middle Kingdom.* Kent: New Malden, 1990.

Rainey, Anson F. "Administration in Ugarit and the Samaria Ostraca." *IEJ* 12 (1962): 62–63.

——. "The Social Stratification of Ugarit." Ph.D. Dissertation, Brandeis University, 1962.

——. "The Military Personnel of Ugarit." *JNES* 24 (1965): 17–27.

——. "The Scribe at Ugarit." *Proceedings of the Israel Academy of Sciences and Humanities* 3 (1965): 126–147.

——. "LÚ MAŠKIM at Ugarit." *Or* 35 (1966): 426–428.

——. "The Samaria Ostraca in the Light of Fresh Evidence." *PEQ* 99 (1967): 32–41.

——. "Compulsory Labour Gangs in Ancient Israel." *IEJ* 20 (1970): 191–202.

——. *El Amarna Tablets 359–379.* Neukirchen-Vluyn: Neukirchener, 1970.

——. "Semantic Parallels to the Samaria Ostraca." *PEQ* 102 (1970): 45–51.

——. "Observations on Ugaritic Grammar." *UF* 3 ((1971): 151–172.

——. "Ramat-negeb, Ramoth-negeb." In *EM* 7, 298–299 (Hebrew).

——. "The World of Sinuhe." *IOS* 2 (1972): 369–408.

——. "More Gleanings from Ugarit." *IOS* 5 (1975): 18–31.

——. "The Fate of Lachish During the Campaigns of Sennacherib and Nebuchadrezzar." In *Lachish V*, ed. Y. Aharoni, 47–60. Tel Aviv: Tel Aviv University Institute of Archaeology, 1975.

——. "The Prince and the Pauper." *UF* 7 (1975): 427–432.

——. "The *Sitz im Leben* of the Samaria Ostraca." *TA* 6 (1979): 91–94.

——. "Three Additional Texts." In *Arad Inscriptions*, 122–123. Jerusalem: Israel Exploration Society, 1981.

——. "Wine from the Royal Vineyards." *BASOR* 245 (1982): 57–62.

——. "Toward A Precise Date for the Samaria Ostraca." *BASOR* 272 (1988): 69–74.

Redford, Donald B. *A Study of the Biblical Story of Joseph (Genesis 37–50). VTS* 20; Leiden: E.J. Brill, 1970.

——. "Studies in Relations Between Palestine and Egypt During the First Millenium B.C." In *Studies on the Ancient Palestinian World*, eds. J.W. Wevers and D.B. Redford, 141–156. Toronto: University of Toronto, 1972.

——. *Akhenaten Temple Project III.* Toronto: University of Toronto, 1988.

——. *Egypt, Canaan, and Israel in Ancient Times.* Princeton: Princeton University, 1992.

Redford, Susan and Donald. *The Akhenaten Temple Project 4: The Tomb of Re'a (TT201).* Toronto: University of Toronto, 1994.

Reich, Ronny. "A Third Season of Excavations at Meṣad Ḥashavyahu." *EI* 20 (1989): 228–232 (Hebrew).

Reisner, George A. et al. *Harvard Excavations at Samaria 1908–1910, I.* Cambridge: Harvard University Press, 1924.

Renger, Johannes. "Zur Wurzel MLK in akkadischen Texten aus Syrien und Palästina." In *Eblaite Personal Names and Semitic Name-Giving*, ed. R. Archi, 165–172. Rome: Italian Archaeological Mission in Syria, 1988.

Reventlow, Henning Graf. "Das Amt des Mazkir." *TZ* 15 (1959): 161–175.

Reviv, Hanoch. *The Elders in Ancient Israel: A Study of a Biblical Institution.* Jerusalem: Magnes Press, 1989.

——. *The Society in the Kingdoms of Israel and Judah.* Jerusalem: Bialik Institute, 1993 (Hebrew).

Robinson, Edward. *Biblical Research in Palestine and Adjacent Regions: A Journal of Travels in the Years 1838 & 1852*, I. London: Murray, 1867.

Rofé, Alexander. "The Acts of Nahash According to 4QSam[a]." *IEJ* 32 (1982): 129–133.

——. "Notes on Biblical Historiography and Historical Thought." (Unpublished paper, 1999)

Ronen, Yigal. "The Enigma of the Shekel Weights of the Judean Kingdom." *BA* 59 (1996): 122–125.

Rosen, Baruch. "Wine and Oil Allocations in the Samaria Ostraca." *TA* 13 (1986): 39–45.

Roth, Martha T. *Law Collections from Mesopotamia and Asia Minor.* Atlanta: Scholars Press, 1995.

Rowley, H.H. "Hezekiah's Reform and Rebellion." *BJRL* 44 (1961): 395–431.

Rozenberg, Martin C. "The Stem *špṭ*: An Investigation of Biblical and Extra-Biblical Sources." Ph.D. Dissertation, University of Pennsylvania, 1963.

Rudolph, Wilhelm. *Chronikbücher.* Tübingen: J.C.B. Mohr, 1955.

Rüterswörden, Udo. *Die Beamten der israelitischen Königszeit: Eine Studie zu śr und vergleichbaren Begriffen.* Stuttgart: Kohlhammer, 1985.

Sachs, A.J. "The Late Assyrian Royal Seal Type." *Iraq* 15 (1953): 167–170.

Safren, J. "New Evidence for the Title of the Provincial Governor of Mari." *HUCA* 50 (1979): 1–15.

Saggs, H.W.F. "The Nimrud Letters, 1952 Part II." *Iraq* 17 (1955): 126–154.

——. "The Nimrud Letters, 1952 - Part IV; The Urartian Frontier." *Iraq* 20 (1958): 182–212.

——. *Babylonians.* London: British Museum, 1995.

Sandison, A.T. "Eunuchen." In *Lexikon* 2, 46–47.

Sarna, Nahum. *The JPS Torah Commentary, Exodus.* Philadelphia: Jewish Publication Society, 1991.

Sass, Benjamin. "The Pre-Exilic Hebrew Seals: Iconism vs. Aniconism." In *SINSIS*, 194–256.

Sassmannshausen, Leonard. "Funktion und Stellung der Herolde (NIMGIR/*nāgiru*) im alten Orient." *Baghdader Mitteilungen* 26 (1995): 85–194.

Sasson, Victor. "An Unrecognized Juridical Term in the Yabneh-Yam Lawsuit and in an Unnoticed Biblical Parallel." *BASOR* 232 (1978): 57–62.

Sauneron, Serge. "La justice à la porte des temples." *BIFAO* 54 (1954): 117–127.

Sayce, A.H. "The Ancient Hebrew Inscription in the Pool of Siloam, I." *PEFQS* 13 (1881): 282-285.

——. "Hebrew Inscriptions of the Pre-Exilic Period." *The Academy* (August 2, 1890): 94.

Schmitz, B. *Untersuchungen zum Titel s3-njśwt "Königssohn"*. GMBH; Bonn: Habelt, 1976.

Schneider, Tsvi. "Azaryahu son of Ḥilkiahu (High Priest?) on a City of David Bulla." *IEJ* 38 (1988): 139–141.

Schottroff, W. *'Gedenken und Gedächtnis' im alten Orient und im alten Testament.* Neukirchen-Vluyn: Neukirchener, 1964.

Schuler, Einar von. *Hethitische Dienstanweisungen für höhere Hof- und Staatsbeamte. AfO Beiheft* 10; Graz, 1957.

Schulman, A.R. *Military Rank, Title, and Organization in the Egyptian New Kingdom.* Berlin: B. Hessling, 1964.

Scott, R.B.Y. "The Shekel Sign on Stone Weights." *BASOR* 153 (1959): 32–35.

——. "Shekel Fraction Markings on Hebrew Weights." *BASOR* 173 (1964): 53–64.

——. "The Scale Weights from the Ophel, 1963–64." *PEQ* 97 (1965): 128–139.

——. "The *N-Ṣ-F* Weights from Judah." *BASOR* 200 (1970): 62–66.

Segert, Stanislav. *A Basic Grammar of the Ugaritic Language.* Berkeley: University of California, 1984.

Seipel, Wilfried. "Harimzögling." In *Lexikon* 2, 991–992.

Sekine, Masao. "Beobachtungen zu der Josianischen Reform." *VT* 22 (1972): 361–368.

Sellers, O.G. *The Citadel of Beth-Zur.* Philadelphia: Westminster Press, 1933.

Sellers, O.R. "Weights and Measures." In *IDB* 5, 828–839.

Selms, A. van. "The Origin of the Title 'the King's Friend'." *JNES* 16 (1957): 118–123.

Service, E.R. *Origins of the State and Civilization.* New York: Norton, 1975.

Shanks, Hershel. "Jeremiah's Scribe and Confident Speaks from a Hoard of Clay Bullae." *BAR* 13/5 (1987): 58–65.

——. (moderator) "Face to Face: Biblical Minimalists Meet Their Challengers." *BAR* 23/4 (1997): 26–42, 66.

Shea, William H. "The Date and the Significance of the Samaria Ostraca." *IEJ* 27 (1977): 16–27.

——. "Israelite Chronology and the Samaria Ostraca." *ZDPV* 101 (1985): 9–20.
Shiloh, Yigal. *Excavations at the City of David I.* Jerusalem: Institute of Archaeology, 1984.
——. "A Group of Hebrew Bullae from the City of David." *IEJ* 36 (1986): 16–38.
——. "Judah and Jerusalem in the Eighth-Sixth Centuries B.C.E." In *Recent Excavations in Israel: Studies in Iron Age Archaeology*, eds. S. Gitin and W. Dever, 97–105. *AASOR* 49; Winona Lake: Eisenbrauns, 1989.
Shoham, Yair. "A Group of Hebrew Bullae from Yigal Shiloh's Excavations in the City of David." In *Ancient Jerusalem Revealed*, ed. H. Geva, 55–61. Jerusalem: Israel Exploration Society, 1994.
Silberman, Neil A. *Digging for God and Country: Exploration, Archaeology, and the Secret Struggle for the Holy Land 1799–1917.* New York: Knopf, 1982.
Singer, Itamar. "Takuḫlinu and Ḫaya: Two Governors in the Ugarit Letter from Tel Aphek." *TA* 10 (1983): 13–25.
Smelik, Klaus A.D. "The Literary Structure of the Yavneh-Yam Ostracon." *IEJ* 42 (1992): 55–61.
Smith, H.S. *The Fortress of Buhen: The Inscriptions.* London: Egypt Exploration Society, 1976.
Soggin, J. Alberto. *Introduction to the Old Testament: From Its Origins to the Closing of the Alexandrian Canon.* Louisville: Westminster/John Knox Press, 1989.
Spaer, Arnold. "A Group of Iron Age Stone Weights." *IEJ* 32 (1982): 251.
Spafford-Vester, Bertha. *Our Jerusalem.* Garden City: Doubleday, 1950.
Speiser, Ephraim A. "The Manner of the King." In *WHJP* 3, 280–287.
Stager, Larry. "The Archaeology of the Family in Ancient Israel." *BASOR* 260 (1985): 1–35.
Stähli, Hans P. *Knabe, Jüngling, Knecht: Untersuchung zum Begriff* נער *im alten Testament.* Frankfort: Peter Lang, 1978.
Starcky, J. "Une tablette araméenne de l'an 34 de Nabuchodonosor." *Syria* 37 (1960): 99–115.
Starkey, J.L. "Excavations at Tell ed-Duweir." *PEQ* 69 (1937): 228–241.
Steinkeller, P. "The Foresters of Umma: Toward a Definition of Ur III Labor." In *Labor in the Ancient Near East,* ed. M. Powell, 73–115. New Haven: American Oriental Society, 1987.
——. "The Administration and Economic Organization of the Ur III State: The Core and the Periphery." In *The Organization of Power: Aspects of Bureaucracy in the Ancient Near East*, eds. M. Gibson and R. Biggs, 19–41. Chicago: Oriental Institute of the University of Chicago, 1987.
Stern, Ephraim. "Israel at the Close of the Period of the Monarchy: An Archaeological Survey." *BA* 38 (1975): 26–54.
——. "Weights and Measures." In *EM* 4, 846–878 (Hebrew).

Streck, Maximilian. *Assurbanipal und die letzten assyrischen Könige bis zum Untergang*, II. Leipzig: J.C. Hinrichs, 1916.

Strugnell, John. "'Amen, I Say Unto You' in the Sayings of Jesus and in Early Christian Literature." *HTR* 67 (1974): 177–181.

Sulley, H. "The Ancient Hebrew Inscription in the Pool of Siloam, VI." *PEFQS* 13 (1881): 296–297.

Suzuki, Y. "A Hebrew Ostracon from Meṣad Ḥashavyahu: A Form-Critical Reinvestigation." *Annual of the Japanese Biblical Institute* 8 (1982): 33–36.

Tadmor, Hayim. "'The People' and the Kingship in Ancient Israel: The Role of Political Institutions in the Biblical Period." In *Jewish Society Through the Ages: The Role of Political Institutions in the Biblical Period*, eds. H. Ben-Sasson and S. Ettinger, 46–68. New York: Schocken Books, 1971.

——. "Rab-saris and Rab-shakeh in 2 Kings 18." In *The Word of the Lord Shall Go Forth. Essays in Honor of D.N. Freedman*, eds. C.L. Meyers and M. O'Connor, 279–285. Winona Lake: Eisenbrauns, 1983.

——. "Was the Biblical *sārîs* a Eunuch?" In *Solving Riddles and Untying Knots*, eds. Z. Zevit, S.Gitin and M. Sokoloff, 317–325. Winona Lake: Eisenbrauns, 1995.

Talmon, Shemaryahu. "*Amen* as an Introductory Oath Formula." *Textus* 7 (1969): 124–129.

——. "The 'Comparative Method' in Biblical Interpretation - Principles and Problems." *VTS* 29 (1977): 320–356.

Tatum, Lynn. "King Manasseh and the Royal Fortress at Horvat 'Usa." *BA* 54 (1991): 136–145.

Taylor, I. "The Ancient Hebrew Inscription in the Pool of Siloam, IV." *PEFQS* 13 (1881): 292–292.

Thiel, Winfried. "Zur gesellschaftlichen Stellung des MŪDŪ in Ugarit." *UF* 12 (1980): 349–356.

Thompson, Thomas L. *Early History of the Israelite People from the Written and Archaeological Sources*. Leiden: E.J. Brill, 1992.

Thureau-Dagin, F. "Nouvelles lettres d'El-Amarna." *RA* 19 (1922): 91–108.

Tigay, Jeffrey H. *You Shall Have No Other Gods: Israelite Religion in the Light of Hebrew Inscriptions*. Atlanta: Scholars Press, 1986.

——. "On Evaluating Claims of Literary Borrowing." In *The Tablet and the Scroll, Near Eastern Studies in Honor of William Hallo*, eds. M.E. Cohen, D.C. Snell and D.B. Weisberg, 250–255. Bathesda: CDL Press, 1993.

——. *The JPS Torah Commentary, Deuteronomy*. Philadelphia: Jewish Publication Society, 1996.

Torczyner (Tur-Sinai), Harry. *Lachish I: The Lachish Letters*. London: Oxford University Press, 1938.

——. *The Lachish Ostraca.* Jerusalem: Bialik Institute, 1987 (Hebrew).

Torrey, Charles C. "A Hebrew Seal from the Reign of Ahaz." *BASOR* 79 (1940): 27–28.

Tov, Emanuel. *The Text-Critical Use of the Septuagint.* Minneapolis: Fortress Press, 1992.

Tsevat, Matitiahu. "Some Biblical Notes." *HUCA* 24 (1952–1953): 107–114.

Tufnell, Olga. "Tel En-Nasbeh." *PEQ* 80 (1948): 145–150.

——. *Lachish III: The Iron Age.* London: Oxford University Press, 1953.

Tushingham, A.D. "A Royal Israelite Seal (?) and the Royal Jar Handle Stamps (part one)." *BASOR* 200 (1970): 71–78; (part two) *BASOR* 201 (1971): 23–35.

——. "New Evidence Bearing on the Two-Winged LMLK Stamp." *BASOR* 287 (1992): 61–64.

Uehlinger, Christoph. "Northwest Semitic Inscribed Seals, Iconography and Syro-Palestinian Religions of Iron Age II: Some Afterthoughts and Conclusions." In *SINSIS,* 257–288.

Ussishkin, David. "Royal Judean Storage Jars and Private Seal Impressions." *BASOR* 223 (1976): 1–13.

——. "The Destruction of Lachish by Sennacherib and the Dating of the Royal Judean Storage Jars." *TA* 4 (1977): 28–60.

——. "Excavations at Tel Lachish – 1973–1977." *TA* 5 (1978): 1–97.

——. "Excavations at Tel Lachish 1978–1983: Second Preliminary Report." *TA* 10 (1983): 97–185.

——. "The Date of the Judaean Shrine at Arad." *IEJ* 38 (1988): 42–157.

——. "Lachish." In *NEAEHL,* 897–911.

——. "Gate 1567 at Megiddo and the Seal of Shema, Servant of Jeroboam." In *Scripture,* 410–428.

Van Buren, E. Douglas. "The Rosette in Mesopotamian Art." *ZA* 45 (1939): 99–107.

Vargyas, P. "Le MŪDŪ à Ugarit. Ami du roi?" *UF* 13 (1981): 165–179.

Vaughn, Andrew. "The Chronicler's Account of Hezekiah: The Relationship of Historical Data to a Theological Interpretation of 2 Chronicles 29–32." Ph.D. Dissertation, Princeton Theological Seminary, 1996.

Vaux, Roland de. "Le sceau de Godolias, maitre du palais." *RB* 45 (1936): 96–102.

——. "Titres et funcionnaires égyptiens à la cour de David et de Salomon." *RB* 48 (1939): 394–405.

——. *Ancient Israel: Social Institutions* 1. New York: McGraw-Hill, 1961.

Virolleaud, C. "Les villes et les corporations du royaume d'Ugarit." *Syria* 21 (1940): 123–151.

Waldbaum, Jane C. "Early Greek Contacts with the Southern Levant, ca. 1000–600 B.C.: The Eastern Perspective." *BASOR* 293 (1994): 53–66.

Walther, Arnold. *Das altbabylonische Gerichtswesen.* Leipzig: J.C. Hinrichs, 1917.

Ward, William A. "The Egyptian Office of Joseph." *JSS* 5 (1960): 144–150.

——. "Some Effects of Varying Phonetic Conditions on Semitic Loan Words in Egyptian." *JAOS* 80 (1960): 322–327.

——. "Comparative Studies in Egyptian and Ugaritic." *JNES* 20 (1961): 31–40.

——. *Index of Egyptian Administrative and Religious Titles of the Middle Kingdom.* Beirut: American University of Beirut, 1982.

Ward, William A. and Martha S. Joukowsky eds. *The Crisis Years: The 12th Century B.C.* Dubuque: Kendall/Hunt, 1992.

Waterman, Leroy. *Royal Correspondence of the Assyrian Empire.* Ann Arbor: University of Michigan Press, 1930.

Weidner, Ernest. "Hof- und Harems-Erlasse assyrischer Könige aus dem 2. Jahrtausend v. Chr." *AfO* 17 (1954–1956): 257–293.

Weinfeld, Moshe. "Cult Centralization in Israel in Light of a Neo-Babylonian Analogy." *JNES* 23 (1964): 202–212.

——. "Judge and Officer in Ancient Israel." *IOS* 7 (1977): 65–88.

Wellhausen, Julius. *Prolegomena to the History of Israel* (trans. J.S. Black and A. Menzies). New York: Meridian Books, 1957.

Welten, Peter. *Die Königs-Stempel. Ein Beitrag zur Militärpolitik Judas unter Hiskia und Josia.* Wiesbaden: Harrassowitz, 1969.

——. *Geschichte und Geschichtsdarstellung in den Chronikbücher.* Neukirchen-Vluyn:Neukirchener, 1973.

Wenning, Robert. "Meṣad Ḥašavyāhū: Ein Stützpunkt des Jojakim?" In *Vom Sinai zum Horeb: Stationen alttestamentlicher Glaubensgeschichte.* F.L. Hossfeld ed., 169–196. Würzburg: Echter, 1989.

Wette, W.M.L. de. *Beiträge zur Einleitung in das alte Testament.* Darmstadt: Wissenschaftliche Buchgesellschaft, 1971 (reprint of Halle, 1806).

Whitelam, Keith W. *The Just King: Monarchical Judicial Authority in Ancient Israel.* Sheffield: University of Sheffield, 1979.

Wildberger, H. *Jesaja.* Neukirchen-Vluyn: Neukirchener, 1978.

Williams, R.J. "A People Came Out of Egypt." *VTS* 28 (1975): 231–252.

Williamson, H.G.M. "The Death of Josiah and the Continuing Development of the Deuteronomic History." *VT* 32 (1982): 242–248.

Willis, Timothy M. "Yahweh's Elders (Isa 24,23): Senior Officials of the Divine Court." *ZAW* 103 (1991): 375–385.

Wilson, Robert. "Israel's Judicial System in the Preexilic Period." *JQR* 74 (1983): 229–248.

Winckler, Hugo. "Bemerkungen zur Chronik als Geschichtsquelle." In *Alttestamentliche Untersuchungen.* Leipzig: J.C. Hinrichs, 1892.

Winter, Irene. "Legitimation of Authority Through Image and Legend: Seals Belonging to Officials in the Administrative Bureaucracy of the Ur III State." In *The Organization of Power: Aspects of Bureaucracy in the Ancient Near East*, eds. M. Gibson and R. Biggs, 69–116. Chicago: Oriental Institute of the University of Chicago, 1987.

Wiseman, David J. "The Nimrud Tablets." *Iraq* 14 (1952): 61–71.

——. *The Alalakh Tablets.* London: British Institute of Archaeology at Ankara, 1953.

——. "Supplementary Copies of Alalakh Tablets." *JCS* 8 (1954): 1–30.

——. "Ration Lists from Alalakh VII." *JCS* 13 (1959): 19–33.

Woolley, C. Leonard. *Ur Excavations: The Royal Cemetery*, II. London and Philadelphia: British Museum and Museum of the University of Pennsylvania, 1934.

Wright, G. Ernest. "The Provinces of Solomon." *EI* 8 (1967): 58*–68*.

——. Review of O. Tufnell, *Lachish III. JNES* 14 (1955): 188–189; *VT* 5 (1955): 100–104.

Wyatt, Nicolas. "Atonement Theology in Ugarit and Israel." *UF* 8 (1976): 415–430.

Yadin, Yigael. "Recipients or Owners: A Note on the Samaria Ostraca." *IEJ* 9 (1959): 184–187.

——. "Ancient Judean Weights and the Date of the Samaria Ostraca." *SH* 8 (1960): 1–25.

——. "The Fourfold Division of Judah." *BASOR* 163 (1961): 6–12.

——. "An Inscribed South-Arabian Clay Stamp from Bethel?" *BASOR* 196 (1969): 37–45.

——. "Symbols of Deities at Zinjirli, Carthage and Hazor." In *NEATC*, 199–216.

——. "Beer-Sheba: The High Place Destroyed by King Josiah." *BASOR* 222 (1976): 5–17.

Yeivin, Shmuel. "The Date of the Seal 'Belonging to Shema [the] Servant [of] Jeroboam'." *JNES* 19 (1960): 205–212.

——. "The Judicial Petition From Mezad Hashavyahu." *BibOr* 19 (1962): 3–10.

——. "Rehoboam and Jeroboam." In *Sefer Korngrin – Festschrift Korngrin*, eds. A. Vaiser and B.T. Lurya, 73–97. Tel-Aviv: ha-Hevrah le-heker ha-Mikra be-Yisrael, 1964 (Hebrew).

——. "A Hieratic Ostracon from Tel Arad." *IEJ* 16 (1966): 154–159.

——. "*Pequdut*" (Officialdom). In *EM* 6, 540–575 (Hebrew).

——. "Administration." In *WHJP* 4/2, 147–171.

Younker, Randall W. "Israel, Judah, and Ammon and the Motifs on the Baalis Seal from Tell el-'Umeiri." *BA* 48 (1985): 173–180.

Zaccagnini, Carlo. "Notes on the Pazarcik Stela." *SAAB* 7 (1993): 53–72.

Zettler, Richard. "The Sargonic Royal Seal: A Consideration of Sealing in Mesopotamia." In *Seals and Sealing in the Ancient Near East*, eds. M. Gibson and R. Biggs, 33–39. Malibu: Undena, 1977.

Zimhoni, O. "The Iron Age Pottery of Tel 'Eton and Its Relation to the Lachish, Tell Beit Mirsim and Arad Assemblages." *TA* 12 (1985): 85–88.

Zivie, Alain. *Découverte à Saqqarah: Le vizier oublié.* Paris: Seuil, 1990.

Zorn, Jeffrey R. "Two Rosette Stamp Impressions from Tell en-Naṣbeh." *BASOR* 293 (1994): 81–82.

Index of Biblical Sources Cited

Genesis
10:4 245*
12:15 147*
16:5 165
19:4 183
21:12 183
21:22 162
22:3 184*
24:2 67*
24:16 183
24:22 266
24:34 54
24:61 185*
26:26 121, 163
31:28 44
34:3 183
37:2 183
37:36 162, 199
39:1 199
39:4 82, 92
39:20 83
39:21 150, 162
40:2 150, 162
40:14 112
40:2 199
40:7 199
41:9 112, 113
41:40 82, 92, 129*
41:42 59
41:43 129
41:46 64
43:19 82
45:8 91*, 92
47:14–26 92
49:15 137*
50:7 54, 67*

Exodus
1:11 137*
2:5 184
2:6 183
2:14 164*
5:10–19 194
17:14 112*
18:21–22 162*, 166, 172
20:10 165*
20:24 112
21:2–11 54
21:18 122
22:27 46
23:13 112
24:5 185*
28:12 112*
30:13 265
32:13 54
33:11 185*
38:6 266*
38:26 266

Leviticus
22:24 200
25:55 55
27:25 265

Numbers
3:47 265
5:15 112, 112*, 113
5:21–22 109*
11:16 194
18:16 265
22:4 70
22:7 63*
22:18 54
22:22 184*
24:24 245*
35:24 165

Deuteronomy
1:15-17 165, 166, 172 193, 194
5:14 165*
6:9 166*
11:20 166*
12:12 165*
12:15, 17 165*
13:7 122
14:28–29 165*
15:7 165*
15:12–18 54
16:14 165*
16:18 68*, 165, 165*, 193, 194, 195*
16:5–6 165*
16:19–20 165
17:6–13 67*
17:9 165, 166
17:12 165
19:17–18 165
20 193*
20:5 83
20:5–9 194
20:11 138*
21:2 165, 168
21:19 166
22:13–22 184
22:15-16 183, 184
22:15–21 63, 166
22:23–29 183, 184
23:2 200
25:2 165, 166, 169
25:7–9 63, 166
26:12 165*
28:50 74
29:9 193, 194
31:28 193, 194
34:5 54

Joshua
3:2–4 194
6:21 183
6:23 185*
7:20 109*
8:33 194
15 145
15:20–62 224
15:48 225*
15:55 225*
16:10 138*
17:13 138*
23:2 165, 194
23:7 112
24:1 165, 194
24:29 54

Judges
1:28 138*
1:30 138*
1:33 138*
1:35 138*
2:16–19 164
3:15 164*
4:4 164*
4:2, 7 163
5:14 99*
6:8 164*
8:3 161*
8:5–16 70*
8:18 43
9:2 156
9:28 150
9:30 150
9:54 185*
11:8 164*
11:12 20*
11:27 165
11:37–38 122
13:8 183
19:19 185*
21:12 183

1 Samuel
1:24 183
2:13 185*
2:15 185*
2:35 83
4–8 5, 13
4:18 112
7:16 164
8 167
8:1–3 49*, 164
8:1–5 5
8:2 129
8:4–5 13
8:11–17 140, 225
8:14 212
8:15 56, 197*
9:1 281*
9:27 184*
10:5 5*, 142
11 5
11:3 63*
12:13 68*
13:3 143
13:21 266
14 49
14:1 185*
14:3 281
14:47 7
14:50–51 281, 281*
15 5
15:28 122
16:11 183
16:15 54
16:21 64, 281
17:13 129
17:33 183
18:13 281
21:3 185*
21:8 53, 281
21:12 54
22:7 212
22:9 142*
23:11 156
23:17 128
24:13 165
24:16 165
25:5 185*
25:8–9 185*
25:42 185*
26:8 119
29:3 53, 150
30:7 285
30:17 185*

2 Samuel
1:15 185*
1:26 132*
2:8 150, 281
2:12 54
2:14 185*
2:16 122
2:17 54
3:1 83
3:3 129, 132*
3:18 54
4:2 281
4:12 185*
5:3 64
5:11 8, 80, 83
7 38
8 7
8:2 55, 277*
8:6 55, 143, 146
8:7 54
8:14 55, 143, 146, 277*
8:15–18 16
8:16 49, 110, 113*, 117, 146, 281
8:16–18 132*
8:17 97, 98, 101, 282, 285
8:18 39*, 49, 123*, 282
9:2 54
9:7–10 212

9:9 185
9:9–11 185
9:9–12 231*
9:11 43
12 67, 72, 270
12:1–6 48
12:17 67
12:18 67
12:26–31 277*
13:3 122
13:4 43
13:17 184, 184*
13:18 43
13:23–36 43
13:28–29 184
13:32 183, 282
14:1–11 48
14:21 184, 183
14:26 265
14:27 184
14:30 54
15:1 46
15:1–6 49
15:2–6 65
15:3–4 167
15:4 165
15:12 132, 134, 282
15:27 146
15:37 121, 122, 146
15–17 121, 122
16:1–4 185
16:10 20*
16:15–17:14 134
16:16-17 121, 122
17:4 65
17:25 49, 68*, 282
18 173, 174, 174*
18:12 43
18:15 185*
18:20 43
18:24 173
18:26 173, 174
18:29 53, 184
19:9 174*
19:11 132*
19:18 185
19:23 20*
19:29 53
20:23–24 137
20:23–26 16
20:24 77, 110, 113*, 117, 136, 282
20:25 97, 101*, 133*, 134*, 282, 285
20:26 285
21:12 156
21:21 134*, 282*
23:18 49
23:18–19 282
23:24–39 285*
23:34 282*
23:37 285
24:2 162*

1 Kings
1:2 64, 86, 178
1:4 86, 178
1:5 46
1:9–25 43
1:19 55
1:42 97*
2:26 189*
3:1 16, 78
3:7 183
3:16–28 16
4 2, 76, 83, 121, 144
4:1–19 16
4:2 286
4:2–6 162
4:3 76, 97, 98, 101, 105, 110, 113*, 117, 146, 286
4:4 286, 287
4:5 38, 76, 121, 122, 142, 145, 146, 286
4:6 77, 81, 84, 136, 136*, 137, 286
4:7 139, 144, 145
4:7–19 142
4:8 286
4:8–19a 145
4:9 286
4:10 286
4:11 49, 146, 287
4:12 146, 287
4:13 145, 287
4:14 287
4:15 49, 146, 287
4:16 287
4:17 287
4:18 287
4:19 143, 287
4:19a 145, 145*
4:19b 143*, 145
5–9 8, 80
5:2 148*
5:7 144
5:27–28 138*
5:27–30 137*
5:28 136
5:30 139*, 142, 146, 146*, 162*
6:1 83
7:13–14 287
8:1 63*, 64, 65*
8:3 65*
9:15 137*, 138*
9:19 234*
9:20–22 138*
9:22 56
9:23 139, 142, 143*, 146, 147*
9:27 54
10:1–13 16
10:28–29 78
11:4–10 214*
11:26, 28 184*, 287
11:28 136, 137*, 184*, 287

11:40 149
11:41 15, 104
11:42 136*
12 64, 65, 66, 67, 72, 75, 80, 270, 271
12:6 64, 133, 133*, 178*
12:6–11 64
12:8 64, 72, 77, 133, 133*, 178*
12:10 72
12:14 72
12:18 77, 136, 139, 288
12:28 132
14:18 54
14:19 15
14:21 74
14:29 15
15:13 214*
15:17–24 143*
15:22 139
16:9 55, 81, 89, 150, 162*, 288
16:11 121, 123, 123*, 272*
16:16 288
16:23–28 17*
16:31–33 214*
16:32 83
17:1 64
17:18 20*, 112, 113
18:3 81, 288
18:5–6 89
18:34 119
20:7 65, 66
20:8 66
20:14–15 143*
20:14–19 185*
20:17 143*
20:19 143*
21 212*
21:8–11 63
21:9–14 46
22:9 197
22:10 165
22:17–28 151
22:26-27 43, 45, 150, 151, 157, 288
22:30 20
22:34–37 20
22:48 142, 143, 143*, 146

2 Kings
1:1 17*, 277*
1:2 214*
2:46h 84, 105*
3:4–5 17*, 277*
3:13 20*
4:6 84
4:12 185*
5:6 53
6:8 133, 133*
6:21 91*
7:1 165
7:10–11 173, 174
8:6 197
8:20–22 277*
9–10 17*
9:7 55
9:25 289
9:32 197
9:34 43
9:36 54
10:1 161*
10:1–5 67, 88
10:5 56, 81, 83, 150, 151, 156
10:6–13 43
10:11 123, 123*
11:2 43
11:4 43
11:12 43
11:14 85*
11:18 289
12 102*
12:11 97, 98
12:11–13 102
12:21 55
12:22 289
13:14 91*
14:5 56
14:25 54
15:5 43, 49, 81, 85, 291
15:17–31 17*
15:25 56*, 291
16:1–17:4 17*
16:7–8 241*
16:10 292
17:3 55
18 88*
18–21:18 17*
18:7 241*
18:8 220*, 238, 241*
18:17 89*, 163, 201*
18:17–35 94*
18:18 40, 58*, 81, 83, 89, 94, 97, 98, 101, 110, 113*, 118, 187, 292
18:26 101
18:37 97, 98, 101, 110
19:2 66*, 83, 89, 94, 97, 98, 101, 119
19:6 184
20:8 66*
20:18 199
20:20 17*, 19, 19*
20:21 50
21:2–7 214*
21:23 54, 55
21:24 85*
22:3 38, 77, 97, 98, 295
22:3–4 151*
22:3–6 103
22:4 76, 296
22:8–10 97, 98
22:12 53, 58*, 76, 97, 98, 102*, 295, 296

22:12–14 248*
22:14 102*, 296
23:2 104*
23:4 129
23:8 150, 296
23:11 198, 296
23:15 242*
23:19 242*
23:30 50, 85*
23:34 188
24:1 55
24:8 39, 186*
24:8–17 17*
24:12 150, 198
24:14 150
24:15 198
25:8 53, 163
25:18 76, 100*, 129, 300
25:19 97, 97*, 98, 103, 105*, 198
25:22 37, 38, 76, 77, 82, 102*, 186*, 301
25:23 58, 68*, 100*, 300
25:25 50, 300
25:27–30 17*

Isaiah
1:23 162
1:26 164*
2:4 165
12:4 112
16:5 165
18:2 250*
19:17 112
20:3 54
21–24 87, 175*, 180*
22:9–11 19*
22:15 40, 58*, 81, 86, 178, 179, 292
22:15–25 82
22:20 54, 292
22:22 87
23:1 245*
24:23 65*
33:22 164*
36:3 81, 97, 98, 101, 110, 113*, 118
36:22 97, 98, 101, 110, 118
37:2 97, 98, 101
38:9 104*
39:7 199
40:23 164*
42:1 54
43:26 112, 113
49:1 112
56:3 198*
56:5 198*
56:6 55
57:9 250*
66:3 112*

Jeremiah
2:10 245*
4:16 112, 114
6:21 122
11:5 109*
20:1 95*
21:1 300
22:13 139
22:24 188*, 246*
22:28 188*
24:1 188*
25:9 54
26:10 162
26:10–16 166*
26:10–19 168
26:22 39, 76, 102*, 297
26:24 102*, 248*
27:20 188*, 246*
29:2 198
29:3 76, 299
32:10 104*
32:12 38, 77, 298
34:19 161*, 198
35:4 297
36 99*
36:4 76, 298
36:8–19 77*
36:10 37, 97, 98, 297
36:10–12 76
36:10–20 105
36:11 38, 77, 297
36:12 39, 97, 98, 102*, 186*, 297, 298
36:20–21 97, 98
36:21 104*
36:26 37, 43, 45, 50, 97, 100*, 297, 298
36:32 97
37:1 188*
37:13 299
37:15 97, 98, 299
37:20 97, 98
38:1 37, 82, 186*, 299
38:6 43, 45, 299
38:7 198
39:3 163*
39:13 163*
40:5 186*
40:8 300
40:14 221*
41:1 50
41:10 43
41:16 198
43:2 300
43:6 43
49:14 250*
51:59 37, 38, 76, 77, 299
52:24 100*, 129
52:25 97*, 98, 99*, 103, 105*, 198

Ezekiel
1:2 188*
8:1 63*

8:11 76, 299
11:1 300
11:2 132*
21:28–29 112, 113
22:27 150, 162
27:6 245*
27:18 225
29:16 112, 113
45:12 265
46:17 212, 230*, 276

Hoseah
5:10 162
7:7 164

Amos
2:3 164*
6:10 112, 134*
7:10 290
7:17 189*

Obadiah
1:1 250*

Jonah
1:6 163*

Micah
4:3 165
4:9 132*
7:3 164

Zephaniah
1:8 43, 45
3:3 164

Haggai
2:23 54

Malachi
3:16 112

Psalms
2:10 164
148:11 164
45:14 43
45:15 122
72:1 43
81:7 137*
87:4 112

Proverbs
13:17 250*
17:9 119
19:14 83
20:28 1
25:13 250*

Job
1:8 54
3:14 132*
12:17 132*
29:4 105*
29:22 119
38:33 192*

Songs of Songs
8:6 52*

Ruth
2:5–6 142*, 184*, 185, 231*
2:8–9 185
2:21 185
2:23 185
4:1–12 63, 165
4:12 184*
4:17 44

Lamentations
1:2 122

Esther
1:10 199
1:12 199
1:15 199
1:18 147*
2:2-4 183, 184, 184*
2:14 199
2:21 199
2:3, 15 199
3:10 59
3:12 97, 99, 102
3:13 183
4:4 184
4:5 199
4:6 184
6:1 112
6:2 199
6:3 184*
6:14 199
7:9 199
8:2 59
8:9 97, 99, 102
10:3 128, 129*

Daniel
1:4 73, 73*
1:10 73
1:13 73
1:15 73
1:17 73
2:12 73
10:20–21 159

Ezra
4:15 112
7:14–15 133
7:28 132
7:6, 11 97
8:25 132
10:14 165

Nehemiah
3 140*
3:9–19 152
3:19 152*
5:12–13 109*
7:24 105*
7:72 173*
8:1 97
8:4 97
8:9 97
8:13 97
11:9 129
11:17 129
11:19 173*
13:5 173*
13:13 97

1 Chronicles
2:16-17 281, 282
2:51 105*
2:55 97
3:16–17 188*
3:17–19 50
4:5–6 182*
5:12 129
5:35 286
5:39 298
5:39–41 76
5:40–41 300
8:33 281, 281*
9:11 37
9:12 299
9:26 175
11:11 40*, 282
11:16 142
11:22–25 134*
13:1 133, 133*
15:5 285
15:6 285
15:7 285
15:8 285
15:9 285
15:10 285
15:17 68*
15:18 129
15:22 285
16:5 129
18:13 143
18:15 110, 117
18:15–17 132*
18:16 97, 98, 134*, 282
18:17 49*
23:3–5 167, 172, 173*, 193
24:6 97, 98, 102, 285
26:14 132*
26:18 198*
26:24 285
26:26 285
26:29 167, 172, 193, 194, 286
26:30-32 286
27:1 194
27:2 40*, 284
27:4 284
27:5 284
27:6 282, 284
27:7 284
27:8 284
27:9 284
27:10 284
27:11 284
27:12 284
27:13 284
27:14 39*, 285
27:15 285
27:16 283
27:17 283
27:18 283
27:19 283
27:20 283, 284
27:21 284
27:22 284
27:25 39*, 282
27:25–31 90, 95*
27:26 283
27:27 283
27:28 283
27:29 283
27:30 283
27:31 100*, 283
27:32 39*, 43, 97, 133, 133*, 282
27:32–34 132, 133
27:33 121, 122, 282
27:34 134
28:1 197
29:8 285
29:24 43

2 Chronicles
1:2 164*
2:1 139*
8:4 234*
8:6 234*
8:7–9 138*
8:9 56*
8:10 139, 142, 143*, 146
9:10 54
10 64, 72
10:6, 8 133, 133*
10:8 72
10:14 72
10:18 136
11:22 49*
11:23 49, 52*
12:10 162*
13:6 53
16 143*
16:4 234*
16:6 139*
17:2 68*, 143, 168*
17:7 288
17:7–9 168*
17:7–19 68*
17:12 168*, 234*
17:14 288
17:15 288
17:16 288

17:17 288
17:18 289
18:8 197
18:25 43, 150, 151, 157
19 67, 193*
19:5 165*
19:5–6 165
19:5–8 167
19:8 68, 166, 172
19:11 168*, 193, 289
20:21 133, 133*
21:2–3 68*, 168*
21:3 246*
21:4 161*
22:3–4 132
22:15 86
22:18 86
23:1 289
23:3 43
23:11 43
24:11 97, 98
24:20 97*
25:16 132
25:17 133
25:24 290
26:10 19, 225
26:11 97, 98, 103, 105*, 192, 193*, 194, 291
26:20 291
26:21 49, 81, 85
27:4 19
28:7 43, 45, 81, 83, 95, 128, 129, 129*, 130, 291, 292
29:11 64
29:20 150, 152
30:1–9 222
30:2 133
31:2 68*
31:5–11 188, 234*
31:10 292
31:12 129, 188, 292
31:13 231
31:14 292
32:3 133, 133*
32:3–4 19*
32:16 54
32:27–29 234*, 245
32:30 19, 90*
32:31 161*
33:1–20 21
33:11–12 21
33:13–14 21
34:3 183
34:6 242*
34:8 110, 119, 150, 151, 157, 295
34:8–13 119
34:12 296
34:13 97, 193, 193*
34:15 97, 98
34:18 97, 98
34:20 53, 97, 98
35:8 296
35:9 150, 162*, 296, 297
35:20–24 20
35:23–24 131
35:24 129
36:14 150, 162*

1 Maccabees
2:18 124*
13:36 124*
14:39 124*

2 Maccabees
8:9 124*

General Index

Abu Taleb, M. 111*
advisor 122, 124, 128, 132–135, 160, 273, 282
Ahab 17, 20, 43, 65–67, 81, 83, 89, 123, 132, 143*, 150, 151, 197, 198, 206*, 288
Aharoni, M. 243*
Aharoni, Y. 26* 51*, 52* 143*, 144*, 145*, 147, 186*, 205*, 206*, 207*, 217, 218*, 223*, 224, 226*, 228*, 229*, 231*, 234*, 236*, 237*, 238*, 243, 243*, 244*, 245*, 246*, 247*, 248*, 250*, 251*, 252*, 255*, 258*, 261*, 262*, 263, 264*, 267, 297, 301
Ahaziah 17*, 43, 132
Ahituv, S. 10*, 100*, 213*
Ahlström, G. 4*, 7*, 57*, 187*, 193*
Albright, W.F. 9*, 10*, 17*, 19, 52*, 67*, 68*, 70*, 86*, 98*, 101*, 126*, 141*, 144*, 145*, 168*, 186*, 187*, 189*, 206*, 208*, 209, 218, 224, 226*, 229*, 241*, 246*, 262*, 264, 266*, 277*
Allam, S. 108*, 161*, 172*, 193*
Alt, A. 144*, 145*, 180, 238
Amalek 112*
Amalekites 5
Amarna letters 11*, 61, 75*, 78, 79*, 103*, 106*, 125*, 126*, 135*, 155, 179*, 181*
Amarna 11*, 61, 69, 70*, 75*, 78, 79, 101, 103*, 106*, 125, 126*, 128, 135, 141, 142*, 155, 179*, 181*, 214*, 240*, 278
Amaziah 56, 132, 133, 189*, 290
Amiran, R. 218*, 243*
Ammon 133, 146*, 221*, 277*
Ammonite 24, 27*, 28*, 32, 34*, 57, 58, 98*, 111*, 205*, 209*, 221*, 224*, 241*, 258*, 277*, 278
Ammonites 5, 221*
Amon 45, 54, 55, 85*, 150, 151, 157, 288
Arad 19*, 40*, 52*, 60, 61, 88, 153*, 154*, 158, 186, 207, 215*, 219, 223, 228*, 234*, 237*, 242–246*, 247, 248, 249, 250, 251, 253, 254, 255, 256, 258, 259, 261, 262*, 263*, 265*, 267, 270, 274, 275, 292, 297–299
Aramaic 2, 17*, 27*, 32, 35, 36, 59*, 87*, 100, 106, 112, 118, 123*, 134*, 143*, 154, 159, 178, 179, 181, 192*, 201, 207*, 228*, 252*, 253, 256*, 257, 258*, 259, 277
Arameans 6, 66, 151, 174
Artzi, P. 140*
Asa 53, 113, 120, 139, 143, 171, 175*, 178, 183*, 199, 235
Ash, P. 6*, 78, 102, 145*
Ashurbanipal 59*, 240, 242*
Ashurnasirpal 240
Assur-bel-kala 6
Assyria 6, 11, 46, 89, 94*, 115*, 118*, 121, 131, 133, 155*, 176, 232, 233*, 238, 241, 242*, 246, 250*, 280
Attic, Attic inscriptions 34, 35*
Aubet, M. 8*, 80*, 181*
Aufrecht, W. 224*, 258*
Avigad, N. 24*, 26, 28*, 29, 36, 37, 39, 40*, 44, 45*, 50*, 51*, 82*, 85*, 86*, 98*, 138*, 139*, 153*, 173*, 189*, 223*, 226*, 241*, 248*, 251*, 302
Avishur, Y. 3, 4, 24*, 44, 45*, 57*, 85*, 86*, 98*, 165*, 179*, 193*

Babylon 6, 11, 21, 22, 53, 54, 55, 69, 70, 73, 105*, 127, 161*, 198, 199, 280, 299, 301

Babylonian Chronicle 17
Bade, W. 57*, 58*, 300
Barkay, G. 44, 50*, 51*, 153*, 223*, 224*, 226*, 229*, 241*, 262*, 304
Barton, G. 262*
Beek, G.W. 27*
Beer-sheba 49*, 151*, 152*, 164, 217*, 218*, 220, 228, 232*, 245, 247, 248, 250, 251, 258*, 262*, 263*, 265*, 275
Begrich, J. 10*, 105*, 111*, 117, 118, 119*, 163*
Beit-Arieh, I. 262*
Benoit, P. 249*, 251*, 252*
Beswick, S. 25*
Beth Shemesh 186, 219
Beth Zur 44, 51, 237*
Biram, A. 138*
Biran, A. 17*, 18*, 174*
Birnbaum, S.A. 205*
Bittel, K. 240*
Blackman, A. 130*
Blau, E. 58*
Blenkinsopp, J. 152*
Bliss, F. 262*
Boecker, H. 114*
Boer, P. 133
Boorn, G. 91*, 157*, 161*
Bordreuil, P. 31*, 52*, 58*, 187, 247*
Borger, R. 22*, 179*
Bowman, S. 30*
Breasted, J. 108*, 117*, 161*
Brettler, M. 21
Bright, J. 140*, 163*
Brin, G. 44, 45, 46
Briquel-Chatonnet, F. 8*, 80*
Broshi, M. 137*, 146*, 222*, 234*
Brownlee, W. 28
Brügsch, H. 255*
bulla, bullae 4, 23, 24, 26, 27*, 28, 29, 30, 31, 31*, 33, 36, 37, 40, 41, 41*, 42, 44, 45*, 49, 50, 50*, 51, 52, 53, 57, 58*, 59, 59*, 82, 82*, 88, 98, 98*, 153, 153*, 173*, 201, 215*, 221*, 226*, 248, 248*, 249, 251*, 253*, 254*, 255*, 270*, 297, 298, 301, 302, 303, 304, 305
Byblos 6, 7

Cahill, J. 236, 237*, 239, 241*
Calice, F. 159*
Caminos, R. 47*, 149*
Caquot, A. 144*
Černý, J. 6*, 79*, 108*, 148*, 176*, 177*, 254*, 260*, 261*, 268*
Chaplin, T. 262*
City of David 19*, 21, 33, 37*, 40, 41*, 98, 215*, 219, 297, 298, 301
Claburn, W.E. 242*
Clermont-Ganneau, C. 25, 44, 224
Cody, A. 100*
Cogan, M. 84*, 85*, 88*, 89*, 94*, 102*, 111, 174*, 197*, 198*, 241*, 242*
Cohen, R. 4*, 10*, 20*, 224*, 251*, 252*, 256*
Collins, J. 73*
Conder, C.L. 19*, 25*
Cook, S.A. 57*, 290
Cooke, G.A. 181*
corvée 53, 55, 56, 64, 115, 117, 133, 136, 137, 138, 139, 140, 141, 142, 146, 147, 148*, 149, 154, 194*, 273, 276, 278, 282, 286, 287, 288, 303
Cowley, A. 256*
Craddock, P. 30*
Cross, F.M. 1, 15*, 20*, 27*, 28, 31*, 32*, 33, 50*, 54*, 59*, 96, 98*, 144*, 150, 189*, 205*, 206*, 207*, 208*, 209, 210, 218*, 225, 227, 228, 238*, 240, 241*, 252*, 253*, 258*, 302
Crowfoot, J. 205*, 221*
Crown, A.D. 25*
cursive style 33
Curtis, E. 134*

Dandamayev, M.A. 70*

David 4*, 5, 6*, 7, 8, 9, 10*, 13, 16, 17, 18*, 19*, 21, 33, 37*, 38, 39, 40, 41*, 43, 46, 48, 49, 53, 54, 55, 64, 65, 67, 72, 76, 77, 80, 86, 87, 90, 95*, 97, 98, 99*, 100, 101*, 102, 104*, 105, 110, 117, 121, 122, 123*, 128, 129, 131–134, 136, 137, 141*, 142, 144*, 146, 167, 173, 174, 175*, 178, 180*, 183, 184*, 185, 197, 212, 215*, 219, 271–276, 278, 281–286, 297, 298, 301
Davies, P. 15*
Dead Sea Scrolls 19, 25*
Demsky, A. 152*, 223*
Deuteronomist 22, 49, 56, 66, 84
Deutsch, R. 26, 27*, 31*, 37*, 44*, 57*, 58*, 59*, 63*, 82*, 98*, 153*, 173*, 186*, 226*, 228*, 231*, 248*, 251*, 263*, 302
Dever, W. 4*, 16*, 138*, 219*, 262*
DiLella, A. 73*
Diringer, D. 27, 153*, 217, 226*, 227*, 229, 252*
Divided Monarchy 49, 83, 90, 95*, 104, 111, 166*, 188, 241, 271, 276
Donner, H. 79*, 124*
Dossin, G. 169*
Dothan, M. 262*
Dothan, T. 158*, 238*
Dougherty,R. 100*, 106*, 147, 148
Doxey, D. 62*, 160*, 161*
Dunayevsky, I. 262*

Edens, C. 231*
Edgerton, W. 108*
Edom 55, 142, 143, 146*, 246*, 277*, 290
Edomite 24, 32, 57, 86*, 132, 142*, 277*, 278, 281
Ehrlich, C. 7*
Eiser, G.169*
Eising, H. 112
Eitam, D. 233*
Elah, 55, 81, 89
elders 13, 63–74, 81, 83, 88, 89, 135, 151, 156, 161, 162*, 165–169, 170*, 171, 172, 176, 194, 270, 275
Ellis, M. 231*
Eph'al, I. 228, 265*
epigraphic material 1, 4, 9, 23, 32, 36, 53, 88*, 90, 97, 108, 165*, 183, 187, 242, 247, 249, 262*, 271, 302
Erichsen, W. 255*
Erman, A. 62*, 71*, 75*, 91*, 100*, 116*, 119*, 160*, 189*, 202*, 264*
Esarhaddon, 22*, 46*, 103*, 127
eunuch 89*, 115*, 196*, 197*, 198, 199, 200*, 201–203, 250*, 277, 296
Evans, C. 22*
Evans, D. 10*, 65*, 74*
Eyre, C. 137*

Fales, F.M. 176*, 281
Falkenstein, A. 74*
Faulkner, R. 71*, 75*, 92*, 100*, 107*, 116*, 119*, 124*, 130*, 156*, 160*, 176*, 202*
Feucht, E. 75*, 76*
Finkelstein, I. 4*, 22*, 137*, 146*, 234*, 241*
Flanagan, J. 4*
forgery 24*, 25, 27, 28, 50
Fox, N. 72*
Franke, J. 61*
Frick, F. 4*, 13*
Fulco, W..J. 58*

Galling, K. 225
Garbini, G. 27
Gardiner, A. 71*, 80*, 91*, 92*, 106*, 107*, 116*, 120*, 125*, 130*, 156*, 157*, 176*, 202*, 259*, 260*, 263*
Garelli, P. 196*, 202*
Garfinkel, Y. 229*
gatekeeper 79, 172, 173, 174, 175, 176, 180, 292, 303

Gelb, I. 159*
Ginsberg, H.L. 87*, 88*, 223*, 224*
Gitin, S. 158*, 159*, 196*, 219*, 234*, 238*, 239*, 262*
Glanville, S. 192*
Glueck, N. 85*, 86*
Goedicke, H. 71, 79*, 86*
Goetze, A. 11*, 69*, 159*, 171*, 176*
Goldstein, J. 124*
Goldwasser, O. 79*, 148*, 260*, 267
Good, R. 42, 95*, 103*
Gorelick, L. 30, 55*
Görg, M. 44*, 251*
governor 11*, 47, 50, 56, 77, 82, 83, 88, 99, 115, 119, 124*, 127, 135, 140, 150, 151, 153, 154, 157, 161, 169*, 171, 181, 201, 231*, 274, 288, 295, 296, 301, 303, 305
Graham, M.P. 18
Grandet, P. 260*
Grant, E. 186*, 226*, 262*, 263*
Grapow, H. 62*, 71*, 75*, 91*, 100*, 116*, 119*, 160*, 189*, 202*, 264*
Gray, J. 15*, 16*, 56*, 74*, 86*, 123*, 128*, 137*, 139*, 142*, 143*, 144*, 145*, 146*, 147*, 178*, 184*
Gray, J.B. 86*
Grayson, A.K. 6*, 196*, 201, 202*
Green, A. 149
Greenfield, J. 59*, 258*
Griffith, F.L. 214*
Griffith, G. 73*
Gurney, O.R. 69*
Güterbock, H. 79*, 240*
Gwinnett, A.J 30

Habachi, L. 47*
Hallo, W. 10, 11*, 147
Halpern, B. 15*, 232*
Hammond, N.G.L. 73*
Haran, M. 104*
Hartman, L. 73*
Harris, R. 39, 41, 260*
Hayes, J. 86*
Hayes, W. 214*
Heaton, E.W. 2, 103*
Helck, W. 71*, 75*, 76*, 92, 106*, 107*, 116*, 124*, 125*, 157*, 160*, 161*, 171*, 177*, 202*, 259*
Held, M. 140*
Heltzer, M. 3, 4, 24*, 26, 37*, 44, 45*, 57*, 58*, 63*, 85*, 86*, 98*, 106*, 114*, 124*, 154*, 155*, 165*, 171*, 173*, 175*, 179*, 180, 181*, 186*, 193*, 196*, 201*, 211*, 226*, 228*, 231*, 248*, 251*, 259*, 263*, 302
Henshaw, R. 182*
herald 3, 68, 83, 89, 102, 104, 110, 114, 116, 117, 118, 119, 120, 121, 137, 151, 201, 272, 278, 281, 286, 287, 292, 295
Herr, L. 27, 28*, 32*, 34*
Hertzberg, H. 142*
Herzog, Z. 219*, 234*, 243*, 244, 245*, 251*
Hestrin, R. 262*
Hezekiah 17, 19, 21, 22*, 27*, 31*, 34*, 36*, 40, 41*, 50, 51*, 54, 59*, 76, 81, 83, 89, 94, 98, 101, 104*, 110, 118, 121, 133, 150, 152, 168*, 187, 188, 199, 201*, 216*, 217*, 218, 219*, 220, 222, 224, 225, 226*, 227, 229*, 232, 233, 234*, 235, 238, 241, 242*, 243*, 275, 292, 293, 302
hieratic 79*, 101*, 106*, 148*, 205*, 206, 207*, 228*, 250, 251, 252, 253, 254, 255, 256, 257, 258, 259, 260, 261, 263, 264, 265*, 266, 267, 268, 277, 279, 280
Hinke, W. 127*, 128*
Hoch, J. 160*, 192*, 196*
Hoffmeier, J. 76*, 92*
Hoffner, H. 69*
Hoftijzer, 258*
Holladay, J.S. 4*, 16*, 218*
Holladay, W.L. 40*

Holloway, S. 6*, 7*
Hooke, S.H 82*
Hornblower, S. 36*
Hubner, U. 27, 28*
Huizinga, J. 21
Hurowitz, V. 103*, 128*

Ibrahim, M. 266*
Immerwahr, H. 34, 35
Irvine, S. 86*
Israel, F. 58*, 187

Japhet, S. 18, 22*, 49*, 67*, 90*, 97*, 102*, 111, 129*, 132*, 133*, 134*, 139*, 147*, 152*, 165*, 167*, 173*, 193*, 197*
jar handles 4, 32*, 186, 187, 214*, 216, 218, 236
Jehoahaz 50, 85*, 174*, 197*, 206, 246*
Jehoash 98, 206, 207, 209
Jehoiachin 17, 36*, 39, 50, 186*, 187*, 188*, 197, 198
Jehoiakim 38, 39, 50, 55, 76, 77, 98, 104*, 105, 139, 238, 239, 297
Jehoram 17, 56, 197, 289
Jehoshaphat 19*, 64, 67, 68, 110, 117, 133, 142, 143, 146, 158, 167, 168, 171, 172, 234*, 238*, 246*, 274, 275, 281, 286, 287, 288
Jehu 17, 56, 66, 81, 83, 88, 123, 150, 151, 158, 197, 275, 289
Jeroboam I 57*
Jeroboam II 57, 206
Jonathan 39*, 49, 53, 90, 97, 98, 99*, 102, 113, 128, 129, 131, 132, 133, 134, 143, 212, 282, 299, 300
Joseph 59, 76*, 82, 91, 92, 129, 131, 137, 162*, 183, 197*, 199, 287
Josiah 20, 38, 50, 52*, 53, 58*, 76, 77, 85*, 98, 102, 103, 104*, 110, 119, 121, 129, 131, 150, 151, 153*, 168*, 183, 197, 218, 222, 227, 228, 235, 236, 237*, 238, 239, 241, 242*, 245*, 246*, 247*, 261*, 276, 295, 297
Jotham 19*, 36*, 43, 49, 81, 84, 85, 86*, 91, 291
Joukowsky, M. 7*
judge, judges 49*, 64, 68, 69*, 71*, 99*, 109, 154, 156, 164, 165, 166, 167, 168, 169, 170, 171, 172, 193, 194, 195, 275

Kadesh Barnea 252, 255, 256, 261*
Kadish, G.E. 199*, 202*
Kaiser, O. 86*
Kallai-Kleinmann, Z. 144*
Katzenstein, H.J. 8*, 80*, 83*, 85*, 89*, 90*
Kaufman, I. 266*
Kaufman, S. 36*
Keel, O. 240*
Kelm, G. 219*, 220*, 237*, 238*, 239*
Kelso, J. 27*, 262*
Kenyon, M. 205*, 218*, 221*
Kerkhof, V. 262*
Kilmer, A. 159*
Kinnier-Wilson, J.V. 89*, 93, 93*, 94, 94*, 107*, 115*, 116*, 118*, 131*, 155*, 156*, 170*, 176*, 196*, 201*
Kissane, E. 86*
Kitchen, K. 5*, 74*, 78, 101*, 120*, 124*, 195*
kittim 245*
Klauber, E. 115*
Klein, R. 21*
Kletter, R. 264, 265*
Knauf, E. 277*
Knoppers, G. 15*
Knudtzon, J.A. 70*, 79*, 101*, 126*
Köhler, L. 166
Kooij, G. van der 258*, 266*
Kümmel, H. 106*, 179*
Kuntillet 'Ajrud 153
Kwasman, T. 46*, 156*, 176*

Lacheman, E. 156*
Lachish 17, 19*, 26*, 33, 44, 51, 57, 79*, 82, 88, 89, 98, 99, 148*, 153*, 174, 186*, 217*, 218, 219, 220, 223, 227*, 228, 229, 230, 231*, 233, 234*, 236*, 237, 238*, 240, 243, 247*, 248, 249, 250, 251*, 252, 253*, 254, 259*, 260, 261, 262*, 263*, 266, 267, 275, 300, 301
Lambert, W.G. 127*
Lamon, R. 262*
Landsberger, B. 11*, 79*
Lanfranchi, G. 155*, 156*
Langdon, St. 60*
lapidary style 33
Lapp, P. 217, 218*
Layton, S. 84, 85*, 86*, 88*, 89*, 90*, 91*, 175*, 179*, 180*
Leichty, E. 28*
Lemaire, A. 24*, 27*, 44, 45*, 57*, 58*, 109*, 206*, 208*, 210*, 213*, 215*, 217, 218*, 222*, 245*, 248*, 249*, 251*, 252*, 256*, 264, 265*, 268*, 302
Lemche, N. 18*
Leslau, W. 160*
Levy, S. 3, 4*, 11*, 137*, 138*, 148, 273
Lewy, J. 106*, 169*
Libyans 5, 78
Lidzbarski, M. 257*, 258*
Lie, A. 16, 66, 115*
Lipinski, E. 73*, 74*, 100*, 104*
Liver, J. 11*, 16*, 74*
Livingston, A. 135*
lmlk handles 33, 40, 41, 42, 88*, 187*, 188, 215*, 216, 217*, 220, 221, 224, 225, 226, 233, 237*, 238, 243*, 276, 280, 293
Long, B. 2, 25, 38, 63, 74*, 84, 119, 141, 234, 236, 250, 257*, 260, 267, 278
Longpérier, H. 58*
Loretz, O. 95*, 179*, 196*
Luckenbill, D.D. 116*
Lundbom, J.R. 104*
Lurje, I.M. 75*

Macalister, R. 262*, 263*
MacDonald, J. 183*, 184*, 185*, 190
Machinist, P. 127*, 250*
Macholz, G. von 167*, 168*
Malamat, A. 11*, 65*, 74*
Malul, M. 9*, 10
Manasseh 17, 21, 22, 45*, 50, 139, 150, 164, 222, 234*, 241*, 242*, 273, 284
Margalit, B. 114*
Mari 11*, 69, 74, 107, 113*, 126, 140, 141, 169*, 185*, 190, 191
Mariette, A. 189*, 190*
Marquart, J. 100*
Martin, G. 60*, 76*, 160*
Maspero, G. 161*
Matthiae, P. 159*
Maxwell-Hyslop, K.R. 240*
Mazar, A. 219*, 237*, 238*, 244*, 262*, 266*
Mazar, B. 10*, 27*, 100*, 105*, 136*, 206*, 209, 257
Mazori, D. 29*
McCarter, P.K. 15*, 50*, 113*, 142*, 174*, 197*
McClellan, T. 152*
McCown, C. 262*
McKenzie, J. 63*
McKenzie, S. 20*
Menahem 206*, 207*
Mendelsohn, I. 138*, 140*, 212*, 241*
Mendenhall, G. 28
Mephibosheth 53, 54, 185, 212
Meṣad Ḥashavyahu 108, 109*, 110, 114*, 140, 153, 154, 157, 166*, 194*, 239*, 245*, 246, 251*, 252*, 262*, 264*, 274, 275, 297
Mesha stele 17, 25

Meshel, Z. 153*
Mettinger, T. 2, 3, 4, 78*, 83*, 84, 86*, 88*, 89*, 90, 91, 92, 96, 97*, 99, 100*, 101*, 104*, 105*, 107*, 111, 112*, 113*, 114, 119*, 122, 124*, 125*, 126*, 136*, 137*, 138*, 143*, 144*, 145*, 149*, 163*, 179*
Meulenaere, H. 172*
Middle Assyrian 6, 115, 170, 200*, 201
Milik, J. 249*, 251*
Millard, A.R. 59*
Moab 17, 54, 55, 63*, 70, 133, 146*, 277*, 278
Moabite 24, 25, 28*, 32, 44*, 98*, 111, 114, 121, 277*, 278
Möller, G. 252*, 254*, 255*, 256*, 259*, 260*, 261*, 266*, 267*
Mommsen, H. 30*, 217*
Montet, P. 52*
Montgomery, J. 15*, 16*, 73*, 105*, 137*, 139*, 143*, 145*
Moore, G. 21*, 99*
Moran, W. 70*, 79*, 125*, 126*, 135*, 141*
Muilenburg, J. 77*, 99*
Mulder, M. 179*
Myers, J. 97*
Mykytiuk, L. 36*, 37, 38*, 58*

Na'aman, N. 232*, 236, 237*, 238, 239*, 245*
Naveh, J. 17*, 27, 28, 29*, 32*, 33, 34*, 35, 36*, 86*, 108*, 109*, 153*, 157*, 158*, 228, 245*, 251*, 252*, 257, 258, 259*, 262*, 264*, 265*
Necho II 106
Neo-Assyrian 46, 59*, 93, 94*, 107, 115, 118, 155, 156, 164*, 170, 175, 176, 182*, 201*, 231*, 265*
Netzer, E. 244*, 251*
Neufeld, E. 69*
neutron activation analysis 30
New Kingdom 5, 7*, 11*, 48, 62, 71, 75, 78, 91*, 107*, 116, 118, 120, 148, 157, 160, 161, 163, 176, 190*, 193, 202, 254, 266, 267
Niemann, H. 16*
Nineveh 17, 22*, 46, 156*, 176, 219, 257*
Nippur 7*, 70, 127*, 147
North, R. 21*, 58, 64, 67, 136, 137*, 139, 145*, 181*, 219, 220, 222, 223, 237*, 242*, 276
Noth, M. 15*, 16*, 65*, 73*, 84*, 139*, 143*, 144*, 147*, 208*, 209
numerals 101*, 206, 207, 247, 248, 250, 251*, 252, 253, 254, 255, 256, 257, 258, 259, 260, 263, 264*, 265*, 266, 267, 268, 277, 279, 280

Oates, D. 94*
O'Connor, D. 5*, 6*, 48*, 89*
officer, officers 48, 49, 53, 55, 56, 58, 62, 67*, 68*, 69, 73*, 75, 77, 81–84, 89, 90, 99, 102, 108–110, 115, 117, 118, 122, 123, 123*, 133, 136, 137, 139*, 140, 142, 143, 143*, 146–150, 152*, 154, 157, 158, 161–168*, 170, 171*, 173, 174, 182, 193*–195, 197–201, 208, 209, 212*, 244, 246, 247, 272–275, 282–285, 287–292, 296–301
Old Assyrian 169
Old Babylonian 39*, 69, 115, 159*, 169, 170, 176, 193*
Old Kingdom 47, 160*, 254
Oppenheim, A.L. 17*, 22*, 59*, 64*, 79*, 103*, 126*, 196*, 202*
Ornan, T. 241*
ostracon, ostraca 4, 17, 18, 23, 24, 26*, 29, 31–33, 35, 36, 40*, 52*, 57, 88, 98, 98*, 99, 108–110*, 153, 153*, 154, 157, 186, 194*, 204–216, 223, 224*, 232, 243–268*, 272, 275, 276, 280, 290, 292, 297–301, 305

Ottosson, M. 145*
overseer 55, 76, 91*, 99, 106, 108, 117, 124*, 134*, 141, 143, 144, 145, 146, 149, 150, 154, 155, 157, 184*, 185, 188, 190, 202, 276, 286, 296
over the house 81, 82, 85, 87, 92
Oweis, Y. 28*
Owen, D. 11*

Pack, M. 189, 190*
palace attendants 56, 196, 200, 202, 274, 277, 296
paleographical dating 34, 35, 36
Pardee, D. 109*
Parker, B. 170*
Parpola, S. 46*, 155*, 156*, 176*, 246*
patronym 37, 38, 38* 39, 40, 41, 42, 46, 50, 52*, 77, 97, 136*, 139*, 144*, 165*, 186*, 188, 206*, 215*, 244*
Paul, S. 6*, 91*, 141*, 223*
Peckham, B. 8*
Pederson, J. 63*
Pečírková, J. 93*, 94*, 107*, 118*
Peet, T. 120*
Pekah 17, 56*, 83, 129, 131, 206*, 291
Perlman, L. 30*, 217*
personal attendant 83, 86, 89*, 124, 128, 178, 179, 190, 198, 202
Petrie, W.M.F. 214*, 240*, 262*
Pettinato, G. 159*
Pfluger, K. 68*, 171*
Philistines 5, 7, 163
Phoenicians 7, 8*, 80*, 181*, 221, 245*
Pike, D. 105*, 136*
Ploeg, J. van der 195
Porten, B. 134*, 256*
Postgate, J.N. 170*, 176*, 182*, 231*, 281
Pritchard, J. 210*, 223*, 233*, 240*, 262*
prosopography 36, 70*, 77*, 101*, 126*, 293
Psammetichus, 254
Psamtik, 245*
Puech, E. 262*, 263*

Quirke, S. 60*, 71*, 75*, 125*, 202*

Rainey, A. 44, 45, 46, 104*, 106*, 137*, 141*, 175*, 179*, 180, 186*, 189*, 206*, 207*–212, 217*, 218*, 225, 232*, 243*, 245*
Ramat Raḥel 186*, 219, 223, 224*, 226, 231*, 233, 237, 262*
Rameses III 5, 7, 108, 260*
Rameses VI 5
Rameses IX 108*, 120, 161
recorder 104*, 272
Redford, D. 5*, 7*, 11*, 75*, 78*, 79*, 87*, 91*, 116*, 120*, 126, 148, 162*, 199*, 264, 278*
Redford, S. 116*, 120*
Rehoboam 49, 52*, 64, 65, 66, 72, 73, 74, 76, 77, 80, 104*, 133, 136, 139*, 178*, 271, 288
Reich, R. 245*
Reisner, G.A. 196*, 204, 205*, 206*, 213*, 250*, 252, 259*
Renger, J. 135
Reventlow, H. Graf 113, 113*
Reviv, H. 63*, 65*, 66*, 67*, 68, 69*, 70*, 73*, 85*, 166
Robinson, E. 19*
Rofé A. 194*
Ronen, Y. 265*
Rosen, B. 213, 214
rosette 30*, 235, 236, 237, 238, 239, 240, 241, 242, 275, 276
rosette seals, 235, 236
Roth, M. 170*, 176*
Rowley, H.H. 242*
Rozenberg, M. 164*, 167*, 169*, 171*
Rudolph, W. 97*
Rüterswörden, U. 2, 3, 4, 55*, 84, 85*, 86*, 89*, 90*, 103*, 119*, 123*–126*, 128, 134*, 146*, 154*, 158, 160*,

162*, 166, 179*, 180, 189*, 195*

Sachs, A.J. 59*
Safren, J. 169*
Saggs, H.W.F. 6*, 89*, 176*
Samaria 17, 32*, 45, 52*, 56, 65, 66, 72, 81, 88, 89, 150, 151, 157, 174, 197, 204–216, 219*, 221*, 223, 232, 250–253, 259*, 262*, 263*, 264*, 271, 272, 274, 276, 280, 288, 290, 291
Samuel 5, 13–15*, 18, 20, 22, 23, 49*, 98*, 113*, 122, 128, 140, 142*, 164, 174*, 183, 195, 197*, 211, 212, 225, 270
Sandison, A.T. 199*, 202*
Sargon II 17, 89*, 115*, 155*, 156*, 201, 220*, 232*, 240, 241*, 246
Sarna, N. 195*
Sass, B. 24*, 26, 29, 30*, 31*, 57*, 58*, 221*, 222*, 241*, 302
Sassmannshausen, L. 115*, 116
Sasson, V. 65*, 109
Saul 4*, 5, 38, 49, 53, 54, 129, 131, 134*, 142*, 183, 184*, 185, 212, 231*, 274, 281
Sauneron, S. 71*
Sayce, A.H. 19*, 25*, 50*
scanning electron microscope 30
scarab beetle 217, 221
Schmitz, B. 47*, 48*
Schneider, T. 37*
Schottroff, W. 111*, 113*
Schuler, E. von 69*, 171*
Schulman, A.R. 107*, 190*
Scott, R.B.Y. 252*, 262*, 263, 264, 266*
scribe 26*, 33, 37, 38, 40, 45, 50*, 60*, 61, 70, 76, 77, 79*, 83, 88*, 89, 92, 94, 96–110, 113, 114*, 117–120, 133, 134*, 137*, 151, 156, 170, 172, 176, 193, 194, 256, 261*, 267*, 271, 272, 278, 282, 285, 286, 291, 292, 295, 296, 297–299, 301, 303, 305
seals 4, 18, 23–36, 38*, 40*, 41, 42, 44, 45*, 49, 50–53, 55*, 57–61, 63, 76, 82*, 88, 98*, 130, 160*, 165*, 173*, 186*–189*, 191, 204, 207, 210, 215*–218, 220–223, 226, 227, 229, 230, 231, 234–237, 240–244*, 246, 247, 249, 258*, 263*, 270, 278, 297, 302, 304
Sea Peoples 5, 7
Segert, S. 154*
Seipel, W. 75*
Sekine, M. 194*
Sellers, O.G. 262*, 301
Sellers, O.R. 51*, 228*, 259*
Selms, A. van 123*, 128*
Sennacherib 17, 89, 116, 118, 184, 201*, 218, 219, 220, 232*, 233*, 241*
servant of the king 53, 57, 230*
Service, E. 4*, 55, 64, 79, 86, 103, 124*, 125*, 126*, 128*, 134, 137*, 147*, 152*, 181, 184, 186, 189*, 190, 191, 194, 197, 202, 211, 245*, 280
Shanks, H. 26*, 27*, 32*
Shea, W. 206*, 207*, 208*, 209
Sheba, Queen of 16
Shiloh, Y. 37*, 40*, 41, 98, 219*, 297, 298, 301
Shipton, G. 262*
Shishak 148, 149, 279
Shoham, Y. 40*
Shomroni, A. 233*
Silberman, N. 25*
Siloam Tunnel inscription 19*, 25, 33, 153*
Singer, I. 181*
Sippar 39, 41, 70, 176*
Smelik, K. 109*
Smendes, 6, 48*
Smith, H.S. 157*, 161
Soggin, J.A. 16*
solar disc 217, 218, 220, 221, 223, 227*
Solomon 2, 5–8, 10, 15*, 16, 21, 38, 43, 49, 53–56, 64–66, 72, 73, 76–78,

80, 90, 98, 103*–105, 110, 122, 123, 136–139, 142–149, 152, 178*, 183, 184*, 197, 234*, 267, 271–274, 276–279, 286, 287
son of the king 43, 45*, 47, 49, 50*, 131, 226, 288, 291, 297, 299, 301–305
Spaer, A. 266*
Spafford, B. 19*
Spawforth, A. 36*
Speiser, E. 169*
Stager, L. 22*, 57*, 183*, 184*, 186*, 238*
Stähli, H. 183, 184*, 190
stamp seals 24*, 26, 27, 59*, 234, 302
Starkey, J. 218
Steinkeller, P. 137*, 147*
Stern, E. 225, 228*, 231*, 259*
Streck, M. 59*
Strugnell, J. 109*
Sukenik, E.L. 205*, 221*
Sulley, H. 25*
Suzuki, Y. 154

Tadmor, H. 11*, 27*, 65*, 73*, 74*, 84*, 85*, 88*, 89*, 94*, 102*, 111, 115*, 174*, 196*–200*, 202*, 241*, 242*, 250*
Talmon, S. 10, 20*, 109*
Tatum, L. 242*
Taylor, I. 25*
Tel Fakhariyah bilingual inscription 36
Tel Sera‘ 79*, 148*, 260
Tell Batash 219*, 220*
Tell Beit Mirsim 19*, 26, 186, 218*, 226*, 229*, 231*, 266*
Tell Dan 17, 174*
Tell Jemmeh 250, 251*, 257
Tell Qasile 27*, 251, 257, 259
thermoluminescence 30
Thiel, W. 124*
Thompson, T. 15*, 18*
Thureau-Dagin, F. 141*
Tigay, J. 10, 29*, 67*, 105*, 165*, 194*, 213*, 214*, 215*, 242*
Tiglath-pileser I 6
Tjekker 7
Torczyner, H. 57*, 98*, 252*
Tur-Sinai, 98*, 250*
Torrey, C. 58*
Tov, E. 84*, 245
Tsevat, M. 99*
Tufnell, O. 79*, 82*, 217, 218, 219, 220, 225, 228*, 237*, 240*, 252*, 262*, 263*, 301
Tushingham, A.D. 220, 221, 222
Tyre 7, 8, 54, 80, 127, 181

Uehlinger, C. 24*, 30*, 31*, 52*, 222*, 240*
Ugarit 7, 11*, 62, 68, 69, 70, 95, 104*, 106*, 114, 121, 123*, 124*, 135, 144*, 154*, 155, 158, 159*, 171, 175, 179, 180, 181*, 189*, 191, 201, 211, 212*, 213, 265*, 271, 272, 277
United Monarchy 3, 10*, 15*, 16, 38, 49, 77, 84, 91, 94, 100*, 101, 104, 105, 111, 112*, 128, 141, 146*, 163*, 249, 267, 271, 273, 276
unprovenienced material 23, 24, 26, 32, 42, 248*
Uruk 70, 103*, 106*
Ussishkin, D. 51*, 57*, 98*, 187*, 217*, 218, 219, 220*, 223*, 227*, 228*, 229*, 230*, 231*, 232*, 244*, 260*
Uzziah 19*, 39*, 58*, 90, 98, 103, 194, 225, 238*, 282, 291

Van Buren, E.D. 240*
Vargyas, P. 124*
Vaughn, A. 33, 34, 36*, 40*, 41, 51*, 216, 217*, 219, 220*, 226*, 229, 232, 233*, 234, 238*, 241*, 243*, 293
Vaux, R. de 2, 10*, 37*, 44, 82*, 90, 91, 92, 94*, 100*, 105*, 111*, 119*, 124*, 126*, 128*, 145*, 249*, 251*

Vernus, P. 251*, 252*, 256*, 264, 265*, 268*
Virolleaud, C. 62*, 265*

Waldbaum, J. 154*, 245*
Walther, A. 169*, 193*
Ward, W. 7*, 19*, 62, 79*, 91*, 130*, 159*, 161*
Waterman, L. 164*
Weidner, E. 115*, 201*
weights 23, 26*, 51, 206*, 228, 241*, 243, 248, 250, 252*, 259, 261, 262, 263, 264, 265, 266, 267
 deben 263, 265*
 gerah 256*, 262*, 263*, 265, 266
 neṣef 233*, 263*, 265*
 pym 259*
 qedet 252*, 263, 265*, 266*
 shekel 29, 228, 233*, 234*, 248, 250, 252*, 257, 258*, 259, 261, 263, 264, 265, 266
Weinfeld, M. 67*, 68*, 164*, 165*, 166, 167*, 168*, 171*, 193, 242*
Wellhausen, J. 18, 19*
Welten, P. 20*, 217, 218, 220*, 222*, 241*
Wenamun, report of 5, 6, 7, 71*, 80
Wenning, R. 153*
Wette, M. de 18
Whitelam, K. 165*, 168*
Wildberger, H. 87*
Williams, R.J. 55*, 78*
Williamson, H.G.M. 20*
Willis, T. 65*, 67*
Wilson, R. 6*, 7*, 80*, 89*, 93, 94, 106*, 107*, 115*, 116*, 118*, 131*, 155*, 156*, 167*, 168*, 170*, 176*, 189*, 190*, 196*, 199*, 201*, 260*
Winckler, H. 19
Winter, I. 61
Wiseman, D. 69*, 107*, 130*, 141*, 156*
Woolley, C.L. 240*
Wright, G.E. 141*, 144*, 145, 186*, 189*, 218*, 226*, 238*
Wyatt, N. 159*

Yadin, Y. 27*, 151*, 206*, 207*, 208*, 209, 210, 212*, 215*, 221*, 224, 225, 252*, 263*, 264
Yardeni, I. 134*, 256*
Yellin, J. 30*, 217*
Yeivin, S. 2, 44, 45*, 48*, 57*, 58*, 74*, 109*, 112, 126*, 130*, 179*, 261*
Younger, R. 65, 66, 72, 80*

Zabud 38, 40, 76, 121, 122, 123, 146, 286
Zaccagnini, C. 135
Zedekiah 38, 43, 76, 77, 82, 98, 103, 197, 198, 298, 299
Zettler, R. 60, 60*, 61
Ziba 191, 212, 231*, 274
Zimhoni, O. 243*, 244*
Zimri 55, 89, 122, 123, 288
Zivie, A. 75*, 76*
Zorn, J. 239*

Index of Foreign Terms

Akkadian
abarakku rabû 89, 93, 94
abbūtū 68
amēl šanî 130
amīlū damqūti 69
amīlū ša bābišunu 68
arad šarri 60
ardu 60, 61, 62
atû 175, 176

bēl āli 155, 156, 246
bēl dumqi 126
bēl madgalti 69, 171
bīt šutummu 176

dayyānu 169, 170, 171
dayyānū šarrim 170

ekal mašarti 94

girû 259*

ḫazannu 61, 69, 70, 124*, 125, 141, 155, 156, 170, 176

ibru 126, 127, 128, 278
imēru 259*

kudurru 127, 128*, 135*
kurru 259*

madārū 74
mālik šarri 135
māliku(ū) 134
manû 259*
mār abulli 175, 176
mār šarri 46, 130
massu 140, 141, 278
mūdû 123, 124
mūdē šarri 124*
nāgir ekalli 115, 118*
nāgiru 114, 115, 118, 120*, 139*
nīš ekalli 93

pētiūte 176
pētû 175, 176

qēpūtu ša LUGAL 170
quppu 147, 148*

rab abulli 176
rab āli 155, 156, 176
rab atû 176
rab ekalli 93, 94, 115
rab pētiūte 176
rab ša rēši 115*, 201
rab šaqî 89*, 115, 118
rabianu 159*
rābiṣu 135, 179*, 180*, 181*, 193*
rabû 89, 93, 94, 135*, 154
rū'u 126
ruḫi 79, 125, 126, 278

sablu 140
sākinu 86, 179, 180*, 181, 182
sartennu 156, 170
si/epir 106
sukallu 106*, 170
sūkini/a 135
sūtu 259*, 265*

ša abulli 176
ša muḫḫi āli 93*, 155, 156, 158
ša muḫḫi bīti 93
ša muḫḫi ekalli 93, 94, 96*, 115
ša pān ekalli 93
ša rēš ekalli 201
ša rēš šarri 201

ša rēši 12*, 89*, 115*, 196, 201, 202*
šakānu 179
šakin ālim 154, 155
šakin ekallim 181
šaknu 179*, 181, 182
šalšu 156
šanannu 130
šangû 170
šanû 130, 156
šapāru 99
šāpiru 99
šāpiṭu 164*, 169
šarru 94*, 158, 159, 160, 163, 164*
šasû 115, 120*
šaṭāru(m) 192
šiklu 259*
šinipu 259*
šību 68, 69*
šībūt āli 69
šībūtu 68, 69
šipru 99
šisītu 115, 120*
šūt rēši 196, 201, 202

ṣuḫārtu 190, 191
ṣuḫāru 185*, 190, 191

ṭupšar āli 107, 156, 176
ṭupšar Amurri 107
ṭupšar bīt ili 107
ṭupšar ekalli 94, 107
ṭupšar šarri 101*, 103*, 106, 107
turtānu 89*, 115

úeú 79, 125, 126

Aramaic
מודד 123*, 124*
סכן 12*, 86, 87, 175*, 178, 179, 180*, 181, 182, 250*, 269, 273, 274, 277
סרס 201
האמנים 83

Egyptian
ꜥry.t 116

bꜣk 62
bꜣk nswt 62

hnw 259*

ḥꜣty-ꜥ 48, 156, 157
ḥḳꜣt 247, 259, 260, 267, 268
ḥry iry-ꜥꜣ 177
ḥry-pr 92
ḥry sš(w) 107

ḫry-ḥbt smsw 70

ẖꜣr 260
ẖrd n kꜣp 75, 76, 79, 202*
ẖrdw n kꜣp 75, 76, 77, 78, 80, 271

imy-ḫnt 125
imy-r ꜥẖnwty n kꜣp 202
ipt 259*
iry-ꜥꜣ 176, 177
iry-ꜥt n kꜣp 202
it-nṯr 91*, 172*

ḳnbt 161, 171, 172
ḳnbt ꜥꜣt 161, 171, 172

mr ḫꜣswt rsyt 47
mr pr wr 91, 92, 93, 278
mśtyr 192, 195

nswt 46–48, 53, 62, 79*, 91, 107, 116, 124, 125, 128, 264, 270, 278

pr-nswt 91

rḫ-nswt 124, 125, 128
rpꜥt 48
sꜣ nswt 46, 47, 48, 53, 270
sꜣ nswt n kš 47

s3 nswt tpy 47
s3b (iry) Nḫn 157
sḏ3wty bity 60*
sḏmw 167*, 171
sḫ3 119
sḫ š'.t 100
smr 124
smsw 70, 71, 72
smsw h3yt 70, 71
smsw ist 70
smsw n wsḫt 70
śnn 130
śnw 130, 131
śr 18, 150, 152, 154, 157, 158, 159, 160, 161, 162*, 163, 172*, 246*
śr n ḳnbt 161
śrw 160, 161
sš ḥwt-nṯr 107
sš mnf3t 107
sš nswt 107
sš nswt (n p3) ms' 107
sš š't 100, 107, 108
sš š't (n) nsw n pr-'3 108
sš š't n r Ḥk3 nt 107
sš smsw hwt-wrt 70

ṯ3ty 91
ṯsw n Bhny 157

w'w 79*, 126
wḥm tpy nswt n ḥm.f 116
wḥm-stny 117
wḥm.w 116, 118, 119, 120

Greek
ἀναμιμνήσκων 113

βασιλικοί παιδες 73
βατος 259

γραμματςύς 192, 193
γραμματοεισαγωγεῖς 193

διάδοχος 129*

εις̧αγωγες 193

ὑπομιμνήσκων 113
ὑπομνηματογράφος 112
ὑπομνήάτων 113

Hebrew
אמנים 83
אשר על הבית 18, 22, 81–96, 149, 178, 182, 187, 188, 209, 269, 271, 273, 276, 277, 280, 301, 303–305
אשר על המס 136–138, 139*, 140, 141, 269, 273, 278, 303

בן המלך 18, 28, 41*, 43–46, 48–53, 83, 84, 129, 151*, 187*, 226, 269, 270, 301–305
בנות המלך 43
בני המלך 43, 45, 282
בקע 241*, 259*, 266
בת המלך 28, 50, 52, 241*, 270, 303, 305

זקני הארץ 66
זקנים 63–68, 71–74, 83, 133, 165, 166*, 168*, 178*, 269–271, 280

ילדים 64–66, 72–77, 80, 133, 178*, 269–271, 278, 280
יועץ למלך 128, 132, 133, 134*, 136, 272
יועץ המלך 269

כהן משנה 129

מזכיר 104*, 110–114, 117–121, 146, 195*, 269, 272, 278, 280
משנה המלך 83, 128–131, 269, 292
משנה למלך 129
משנה על העיר 129

נגיד הבית 22, 45, 81, 83, 95, 129, 271, 291
נער 13*, 18, 36*, 41, 74, 182–191, 215*,

226, 231, 269, 273, 274, 292, 298, 303, 305
נערה 179, 182–184, 191, 273, 274
נערות 182, 184, 185, 191
נערים 182–186, 189, 191, 231*
נצב 141–145, 149, 269
נצבים 55, 139, 141–147, 149, 152, 162*, 273, 276, 279

סכן 12*, 86, 87, 175*, 178, 179, 180*, 181, 182, 250*, 269, 273, 274, 277
סכנת 86, 87, 178, 179*, 182, 274, 277
ספר 13*, 15, 28, 37, 94, 96–99, 101–104, 106–108, 112–114, 117, 118, 120, 194*, 269, 271, 272, 303, 305
ספר המלך 97, 98, 102, 104, 106, 107, 272
ספרים 96, 97*
ספר שר הצבא 97
סריס 12*, 163, 196–200, 201*, 202, 203, 250*, 269, 273, 274, 277, 296
סריסים 56, 196–203

עבד המלך 18, 27*, 51*, 53–57, 58*, 59, 60, 62, 63, 187, 267, 270, 278, 289, 290, 296, 301–305
עבד יהוה 54, 55, 59, 60, 63, 302
עבדי המלך 53, 67
עבדים 54–56, 62, 67*, 72, 132, 133, 146*, 185, 197*, 198
על אצרות בשדה 90
על אצרות המלך 90, 282
על בית המלך 81*, 85
על הנצבים 141, 142, 144, 149, 273, 276

פים 259*, 266
פקיד 95*, 150, 198

צרור 264

ראשי האבות לישראל 67
רב סריס 163, 201*
רע המלך 121, 124, 128
רעה המלך 121, 122, 125

שר העיר 150–157, 162*, 166*, 246, 269, 274
שר צבא 89, 162, 163
שרי הנצבים 139, 141, 142, 146, 147, 162*, 273
שרי העיר 150, 152
שטר 13*, 22, 103, 103*, 108*, 192–195, 269, 275, 291
שטרים 23*, 165, 167, 192–195, 196*, 275
שליש 56*, 130, 289, 291
שער 160*, 172–174, 177, 269, 275, 303
שפט 49, 84, 85*, 132*, 164, 165, 169, 171*, 172, 269, 275, 291, 303
שפטים 67, 164–167, 168*, 172, 195, 275
שר 89, 97, 108, 109, 140, 150–154, 156–164, 166*, 195, 200, 246, 269, 274, 275, 299, 303, 305
שרים 45, 66, 70*, 132, 133, 139*, 144, 147*, 161, 162, 166, 172, 197, 198
שקל 259*, 263, 265

Hittite
awariyaš išḫaš 69
auriyaš išḫaš 171

Ugaritic
bnš mlk 114, 154, 155, 175, 201

ḥmr 259*

yṣḥ(m) 114

kd 259*
kkr 259*

ltḥ 259*

md(m) 123*

nʿr 182, 183, 186, 189, 191, 226
nʿrm 189, 191
nʿrt 189
nṣp 265*

spr 96, 106

ʿbd 62
ʿbd mlk 62
ʿl bt 95

ṣwḥ 114, 120

rb 106, 154, 155, 163
rb qrt 154, 155
rb spr 106

ṯǵr(m) 175, 180*
ṯǵr hkl 175
ṯnn 130